Aaron Sexton
#19D

enVisionMATH®
Common Core

## Authors

**Randall I. Charles**
Professor Emeritus
Department of Mathematics
San Jose State University
San Jose, California

**Janet H. Caldwell**
Professor of Mathematics
Rowan University
Glassboro, New Jersey

**Mary Cavanagh**
Executive Director of Center for Practice,
Research, and Innovation in Mathematics
Education (PRIME)
Arizona State University
Mesa, Arizona

**Juanita Copley**
Professor Emerita, College of Education
University of Houston
Houston, Texas

**Warren Crown**
Professor Emeritus of Mathematics Education
Graduate School of Education
Rutgers University
New Brunswick, New Jersey

**Francis (Skip) Fennell**
L. Stanley Bowlsbey Professor of Education and
Graduate and Professional Studies
McDaniel College
Westminster, Maryland

**Stuart J. Murphy**
Visual Learning Specialist
Boston, Massachusetts

**Kay B. Sammons**
Coordinator of Elementary Mathematics
Howard County Public Schools
Ellicott City, Maryland

**Jane F. Schielack**
Professor of Mathematics
Associate Dean for Assessment and
Pre K-12 Education, College of Science
Texas A&M University
College Station, Texas

**William Tate**
Edward Mallinckrodt Distinguished University
Professor in Arts & Sciences
Washington University
St. Louis, Missouri

## Mathematicians

**David M. Bressoud**
DeWitt Wallace Professor of Mathematics
Macalester College
St. Paul, Minnesota

**Roger Howe**
Professor of Mathematics
Yale University
New Haven, Connecticut

**Gary Lippman**
Professor of Mathematics and Computer Science
California State University East Bay
Hayward, California

Glenview, Illinois • Boston, Massachusetts • Chandler, Arizona • Upper Saddle River, New Jersey

**Consulting Author**

**Grant Wiggins**
Researcher and Educational Consultant
Hopewell, New Jersey

**ELL Consultant**

**Jim Cummins**
Professor
The University of Toronto
Toronto, Canada

**Common Core State Standards Reviewers**

**Elizabeth Baker**
Mathematics Coordinator
Gilbert Public Schools
Gilbert, Arizona

**Amy Barber**
K-12 Math Coach
Peninsula School District ESC
Gig Harbor, Washington

**Laura Cua**
Teacher
Columbus City Schools
Columbus, Ohio

**Wafa Deeb-Westervelt**
Assistant Superintendent for
Curriculum, Instruction, and
Professional Development
Freeport Public Schools
Freeport, New York

**Lynn Gullette**
Title 1 Math Intervention
Mobile County Public Schools
Gilliard Elementary
Mobile, Alabama

Director of Mathematics
Birmingham City Schools
Birmingham, Alabama

**Kelly O'Rourke**
Elementary School Assistant Principal
Clark County School District
Las Vegas, Nevada

**Piper L. Riddle**
Evidence-Based Learning Specialist
Canyons School District
Sandy, Utah

**Debra L. Vitale**
Math Coach
Bristol Public Schools
Bristol, Connecticut

**Diane T. Wehby**
Math Support Teacher
Birmingham City Schools
Birmingham, Alabama

ISBN-13: 978-0-328-67261-5
ISBN-10: 0-328-67261-0

3 4 5 6 7 8 9 10 V064 15 14 13 12 11

# Grade 3 Topic Titles

## Common Core

### Standards for Mathematical Content

**Domain:** Number and Operations in Base Ten
**Topics:** 1, 2, and 3

**Domain:** Operations and Algebraic Thinking
**Topics:** 4, 5, 6, 7, and 8

**Domain:** Number and Operations—Fractions
**Topics:** 9 and 10

**Domain:** Geometry
**Topic:** 11

**Domain:** Measurement and Data
**Topics:** 12, 13, 14, 15, and 16

### Standards for Mathematical Practice

☑ Make sense of problems and persevere in solving them.

☑ Reason abstractly and quantitatively.

☑ Construct viable arguments and critique the reasoning of others.

☑ Model with mathematics.

☑ Use appropriate tools strategically.

☑ Attend to precision.

☑ Look for and make use of structure.

☑ Look for and express regularity in repeated reasoning.

## Domain: Number and Operations in Base Ten

Topic **1** Numeration

Topic **2** Number Sense: Addition and Subtraction

Topic **3** Using Place Value to Add and Subtract

## Domain: Operations and Algebraic Thinking

Topic **4** Meanings of Multiplication

Topic **5** Multiplication Facts: Use Patterns

Topic **6** Multiplication Facts: Use Known Facts

Topic **7** Meanings of Division

Topic **8** Division Facts

## Domain: Number and Operations—Fractions

Topic **9** Understanding Fractions

Topic **10** Fraction Comparison and Equivalence

## Domain: Geometry

Topic **11** Two-Dimensional Shapes and Their Attributes

## Domain: Measurement and Data

Topic **12** Time

Topic **13** Perimeter

Topic **14** Area

Topic **15** Liquid Volume and Mass

Topic **16** Data

# Grade 3 Contents

## Common Core

### Standards for Mathematical Practice

- ☑ Make sense of problems and persevere in solving them.
- ☑ Reason abstractly and quantitatively.
- ☑ Construct viable arguments and critique the reasoning of others.
- ☑ Model with mathematics.
- ☑ Use appropriate tools strategically.
- ☑ Attend to precision.
- ☑ Look for and make use of structure.
- ☑ Look for and express regularity in repeated reasoning.

### Grade 3 Domain Colors

● **Domain: Number and Operations in Base Ten**
**Topics:** 1, 2, and 3

● **Domain: Operations and Algebraic Thinking**
**Topics:** 4, 5, 6, 7, and 8

● **Domain: Number and Operations–Fractions**
**Topics:** 9 and 10

● **Domain: Geometry**
**Topic:** 11

● **Domain: Measurement and Data**
**Topics:** 12, 13, 14, 15, and 16

---

### Standards for Mathematical Content

**Domain**
Number and Operations in Base Ten

**Cluster**
• Use place value understanding and properties of operations to perform multi-digit arithmetic.

**Standards**
3.NBT.1, 3.NBT.2

## Topic 1 — Numeration

# Topic 2   Number Sense: Addition and Subtraction

## Standards for Mathematical Content

**Domain**

Number and Operations in Base Ten

**Clusters**

• Use place value understanding and properties of operations to perform multi-digit arithmetic.

• Solve problems involving the four operations, and identify and explain patterns in arithmetic.

**Standards**

3.NBT.1, 3.NBT.2, 3.OA.8, 3.OA.9

---

# Topic 3   Using Place Value to Add and Subtract

*(continued on next page)*

## Standards for Mathematical Content

**Domain**

Number and Operations in Base Ten

**Clusters**

• Use place value understanding and properties of operations to perform multi-digit arithmetic.

• Solve problems involving the four operations, and identify and explain patterns in arithmetic.

**Standards**

3.NBT.1, 3.NBT.2, 3.OA.8

**Standards for Mathematical Content**

**Domain**

Operations and Algebraic Thinking

**Clusters**

• Represent and solve problems involving multiplication and division.

• Understand properties of multiplication and the relationship between multiplication and division.

• Solve problems involving the four operations, and identify and explain patterns in arithmetic.

**Standards**

3.OA.1, 3.OA.3, 3.OA.5, 3.OA.9

**Standards for Mathematical Content**

**Domain**

Operations and Algebraic Thinking

**Clusters**

• Represent and solve problems using multiplication and division.

• Multiply and divide within 100.

• Solve problems involving the four operations, and identify and explain patterns in arithmetic.

• Use place value understanding and properties of operations to perform multi-digit arithmetic.

**Standards**

3.OA.3, 3.OA.7, 3.OA.8, 3.OA.9, 3.NBT.3

# Division Facts

## Standards for Mathematical Content

**Domain**

Operations and Alegbraic Thinking

**Clusters**

• Represent and solve problems involving multiplication and division.

• Understand properties of multiplication and the relationship between multiplication and division.

• Multiply and divide within 100.

• Solve problems involving the four operations, and identify and explain patterns in arithmetic.

**Standards**

3.OA.3, 3.OA.4, 3.OA.5, 3.OA.7, 3.OA.8

# Understanding Fractions

## Standards for Mathematical Content

**Domain**

Number and Operations–Fractions

**Clusters**

• Develop understanding of fractions as numbers.

• Represent and solve problems involving multiplication and division.

**Standards**

3.NF.1, 3.NF.2, 3.NF.2.a, 3.NF.2.b, 3.OA.3

# Fraction Comparison and Equivalence

# Two-Dimensional Shapes and Their Attributes

## Topic 12   Time

## Topic 13   Perimeter

# Area

**Standards for Mathematical Content**

**Domain**
Measurement and Data

**Clusters**
- Geometric measurement: understand concepts of area and relate area to multiplication and to addition.
- Geometric measurement: recognize perimeter as an attribute of plane figures and distinguish between linear and area measures.
- Reason with shapes and their attributes.

**Standards**
3.MD.5, 3.MD.5.a, 3.MD.5.b, 3.MD.6, 3.MD.7, 3.MD.7.a, 3.MD.7.b, 3.MD.7.c, 3.MD.7.d, 3.MD.8, 3.G.2

# Liquid Volume and Mass

**Standards for Mathematical Content**

**Domain**
Measurement and Data

**Cluster**
- Solve problems involving measurement and estimation of intervals of time, liquid volumes, and masses of objects.

**Standard**
3.MD.2

# Topic 16 Data

**Standards for
Mathematical Content**

**Domain**
Measurement and Data

**Cluster**
• Represent and interpret data.

**Standards**
3.MD.3, 3.MD.4

# Problem-Solving Handbook

Scott Foresman·Addison Wesley

# enVisionMATH®
## Common Core

# Problem-Solving Handbook

Use this Problem-Solving Handbook throughout the year to help you solve problems.

Pictures help me understand!

Explaining helps me understand!

Everybody can be a good problem solver!

There's almost always more than one way to solve a problem!

Don't give up!

# Problem-Solving Process

MATHEMATICAL PRACTICES

## Read and Understand

ⓒ Answer these questions to make sense of problems.

**❓ What am I trying to find?**
- Tell what the question is asking.

**❓ What do I know?**
- Tell the problem in my own words.
- Identify key facts and details.

## Plan and Solve

ⓒ Choose an appropriate tool.

**❓ What strategy or strategies should I try?**

**❓ Can I show the problem?**
- Try drawing a picture.
- Try making a list, table, or graph.
- Try acting it out or using objects.

**❓ How will I solve the problem?**

**❓ What is the answer?**
- Tell the answer in a complete sentence.

### Strategies
- Show What You Know
- Draw a Picture
- Make an Organized List
- Make a Table
- Make a Graph
- Act It Out/ Use Objects
- Look for a Pattern
- Try, Check, Revise
- Write an Equation
- Use Reasoning
- Work Backward
- Solve a Simpler Problem

## Look Back and Check

ⓒ Give precise answers.

**❓ Did I check my work?**
- Compare my work to the information in the problem.
- Be sure all calculations are correct.

**❓ Is my answer reasonable?**
- Estimate to see if my answer makes sense.
- Make sure the question was answered.

# Using Bar Diagrams

© Bar diagrams are tools that will help you understand and solve word problems. Bar diagrams show how the quantities in a problem are related.

**Problem 1**

The third-grade students are participating in an art fair. How many projects are from the Hilltop and Banneker schools?

**Projects for the Art Fair**

| School | Number of Projects |
|--------|-------------------|
| Banneker | 11 |
| Edison | 12 |
| Hilltop | 8 |
| Jefferson | 13 |

**Bar Diagram**

TOTAL: Total number of projects from the Banneker and Hilltop schools ⟶ **?**

| 11 | 8 |
|----|----|

PART: Number of projects from the Banneker school    PART: Number of projects from the Hilltop school

$11 + 8 =$ ▢

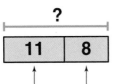 **Think** I can add to find the total.

**Problem 2**

The music club decided to buy 17 new CDs. In September, it purchased 8 CDs. How many more CDs will the club purchase?

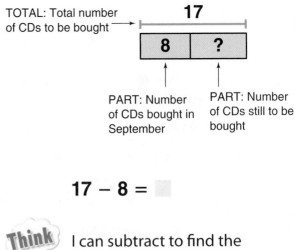

**Bar Diagram**

TOTAL: Total number of CDs to be bought ⟶ **17**

| 8 | ? |
|----|----|

PART: Number of CDs bought in September    PART: Number of CDs still to be bought

$17 - 8 =$ ▢

**Think** I can subtract to find the missing part.

**Pictures help me understand!**

**Don't trust key words!**

**Problem 3**

Tickets to a movie on Saturday afternoon cost only $5 each no matter what age you are. What is the cost of tickets for a family of four?

**Bar Diagram**

TOTAL: Total cost of the tickets → | ? |

| 5 | 5 | 5 | 5 |

↑
PART:
Cost of
each ticket

$$4 \times 5 = \blacksquare$$

**Think** I can multiply because the parts are equal.

**Problem 4**

Thirty students traveled in 3 vans to the zoo. The same number of students were in each van. How many students were in each van?

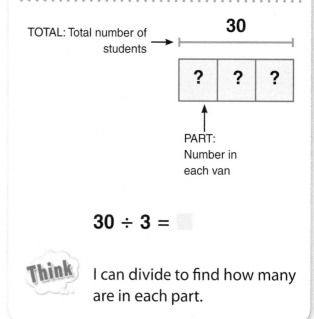

**Bar Diagram**

TOTAL: Total number of students → | 30 |

| ? | ? | ? |

↑
PART:
Number in
each van

$$30 \div 3 = \blacksquare$$

**Think** I can divide to find how many are in each part.

# Problem-Solving Strategies

© These are tools for understanding and solving problems.

| Strategy | Example | When I Use It |
|---|---|---|
| **Draw a Picture** | A garden that is 4 yards wide has a fence post at each end and one at each yard. How many fence posts are needed for the garden?<br><br>Four yards<br>1 yard 1 yard 1 yard 1 yard<br>Fence posts | Try drawing a picture when it helps you visualize the problem or when the relationships such as joining or separating are involved. |
| **Make a Table** | Emily runs 2 miles everyday. Jana runs 5 miles every other day. After 5 days, which runner has run farther?<br><br>| Day | 1 | 2 | 3 | 4 | 5 |<br>| Emily | 2 | 2 | 2 | 2 | 2 |<br>| Jana | 5 | | 5 | | 5 | | Try making a table when:<br>• there are 2 or more quantities,<br>• amounts change using a pattern. |
| **Look for a Pattern** | The card with 1 is red. The card with 2 is green. The card with 3 is blue. If this color pattern continues, what color is the card with 12?<br><br>1  2  3 | Look for a pattern when something repeats in a predictable way. |

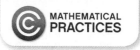

MATHEMATICAL PRACTICES

| Strategy | Example | When I Use It |
|---|---|---|
| **Make an Organized List** | How many ways can you make change for a quarter using dimes and nickels? | Make an organized list when asked to find combinations of two or more items. |
| | 1 quarter = <br><br>1 dime + 1 dime + 1 nickel<br><br>1 dime + 1 nickel + 1 nickel + 1 nickel<br><br>1 nickel + 1 nickel + 1 nickel + 1 nickel + 1 nickel | |
| **Try, Check, Revise** | Ashley spent $27, not including tax, on dog supplies. She bought two of one item and one of another item. What did she buy?<br><br>$8 + $8 + $15 = $31<br>$7 + $7 + $12 = $26<br>$6 + $6 + $15 = $27 | Use Try, Check, Revise when quantities are being combined to find a total, but you don't know which quantities.<br><br>**Dog Supplies Sale!**<br>Leash...............................$8<br>Collar...............................$6<br>Bowls ..............................$7<br>Medium Beds.....................$15<br>Toys .................................$12 |
| **Write an Equation** | Malik collects action figures. He had 27 of them, then he gave 3 to his brother. How many did he have left?<br><br>Find $27 - 3 = n$. | Write an equation when the story describes a situation that uses an operation or operations. |

# Even More Strategies

© These are more tools for understanding and solving problems.

| Strategy | Example | When I Use It |
|---|---|---|
| **Act It Out** | There are 26 students in the class. Four students can sit at each table. How many tables are needed for the class? | Think about acting out a problem when the numbers are small and there is action in the problem you can do. |
| **Use Reasoning** | One side of the large square is 8 inches. What is the perimeter of one of the small squares?<br><br>8 inches | Use reasoning when you can use known information to reason out unknown information. |
| **Work Backward** | There are bicycles and tricycles in the bike rack at the park. There are 8 wheels in the bike rack. If every child has only one bike, how many children are at the park?<br><br>3 wheels · 5 wheels<br>– ? ← –1 bicycle ← –1 tricycle<br>? children · 2 children · 1 child | Try working backward when:<br>• you know the end result of a series of steps,<br>• you want to know what happened at the beginning. |

| Strategy | Example | When I Use It |
|---|---|---|
| **Solve a Simpler Problem** | Each side of each triangle in the figure at the left is one centimeter. If there are 12 triangles in a row, what is the perimeter of the figure?<br><br>I can look at 1 triangle, then 2 triangles, then 3 triangles.<br><br>perimeter = 3 cm<br><br>perimeter = 4 cm<br><br>perimeter = 5 cm | Try solving a simpler problem when you can create a simpler case that is easier to solve. |
| **Make a Graph** | Taj asked his class what was their favorite outdoor activity. What two activities had about the same number of responses?<br><br>**Favorite Outdoor Activities**<br><br>*(bar graph: Number of Students vs. Activity — Bike riding = 6, Soccer = 10, Walking = 4, Swimming = 7)* | Make a graph when:<br>• data for a survey are given,<br>• the question can be answered by reading the graph. |

# Writing to Explain

© Good written explanations communicate your reasoning to others. Here is a good math explanation.

**Writing to Explain** Can you divide this rectangle into 4 equal parts? Is there more than one way to do it?

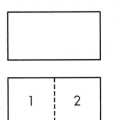

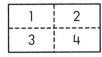

I can think about folding it. If I fold it over in one way I'll get 2 equal parts. If I fold it again, but the other way, I get 2 more equal parts.

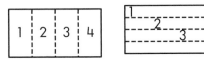

If I fold the rectangle twice in the same direction I get 4 different equal parts. So that is 3 ways to do it.

## Tips for Writing Good Math Explanations ...

A good explanation should be:
- correct
- simple
- complete
- easy to understand

Math explanations can use:
- words
- pictures
- numbers
- symbols

# Problem-Solving Recording Sheet

MATHEMATICAL PRACTICES

© This helps you organize your work and make sense of problems.

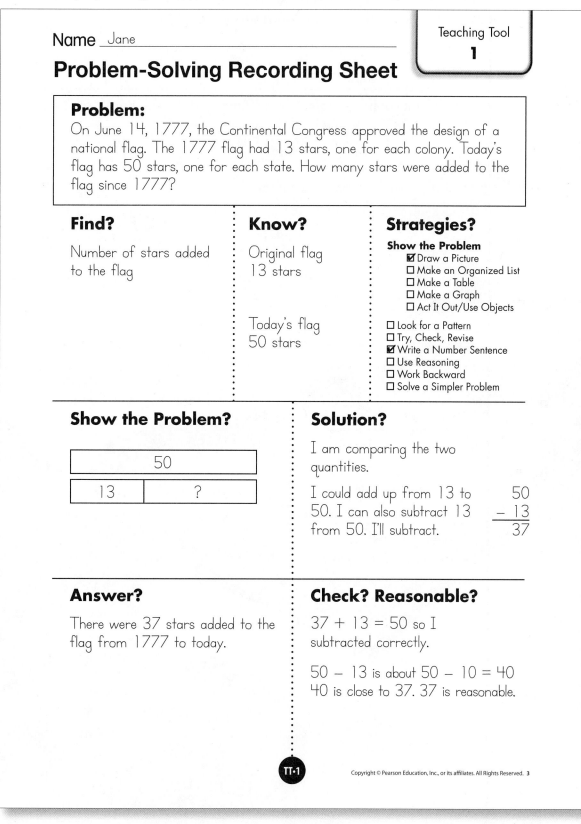

Name _Jane_

Teaching Tool
**1**

## Problem-Solving Recording Sheet

**Problem:**
On June 14, 1777, the Continental Congress approved the design of a national flag. The 1777 flag had 13 stars, one for each colony. Today's flag has 50 stars, one for each state. How many stars were added to the flag since 1777?

**Find?**

Number of stars added to the flag

**Know?**

Original flag
13 stars

Today's flag
50 stars

**Strategies?**

**Show the Problem**
- ☑ Draw a Picture
- ☐ Make an Organized List
- ☐ Make a Table
- ☐ Make a Graph
- ☐ Act It Out/Use Objects

- ☐ Look for a Pattern
- ☐ Try, Check, Revise
- ☑ Write a Number Sentence
- ☐ Use Reasoning
- ☐ Work Backward
- ☐ Solve a Simpler Problem

**Show the Problem?**

| 50 | |
|----|----|
| 13 | ? |

**Solution?**

I am comparing the two quantities.

I could add up from 13 to 50. I can also subtract 13 from 50. I'll subtract.

$$\begin{array}{r} 50 \\ -\ 13 \\ \hline 37 \end{array}$$

**Answer?**

There were 37 stars added to the flag from 1777 to today.

**Check? Reasonable?**

$37 + 13 = 50$ so I subtracted correctly.

$50 - 13$ is about $50 - 10 = 40$
40 is close to 37. 37 is reasonable.

TT·1

# Getting to Know Your Math Book

Before you start working on lessons, look through your textbook. Here are some questions to help you learn more about your book— and about the math you will learn this year.

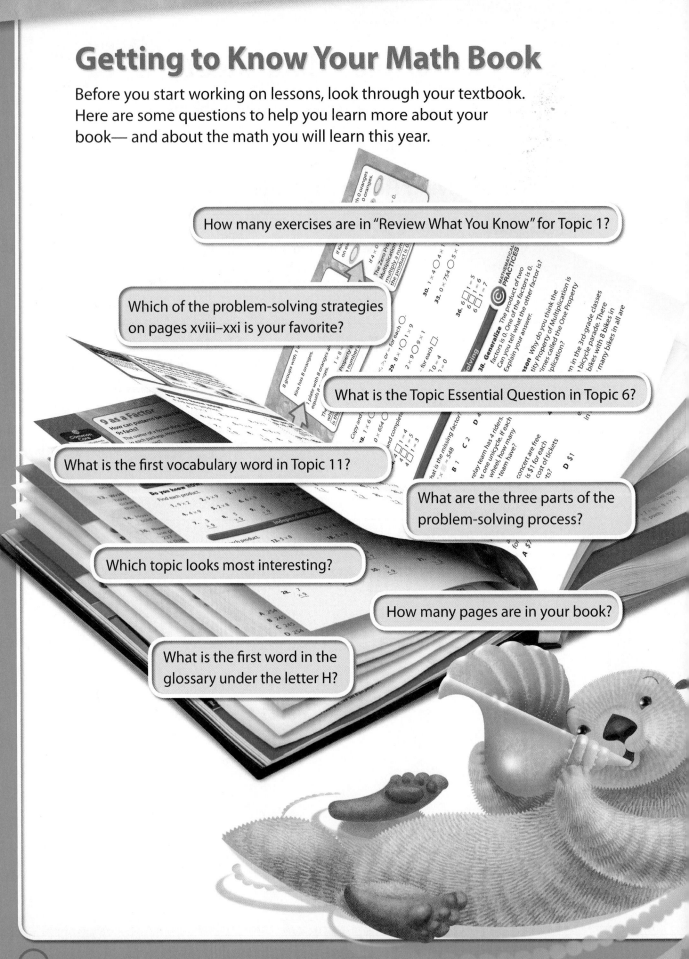

How many exercises are in "Review What You Know" for Topic 1?

Which of the problem-solving strategies on pages xviii–xxi is your favorite?

What is the Topic Essential Question in Topic 6?

What is the first vocabulary word in Topic 11?

What are the three parts of the problem-solving process?

Which topic looks most interesting?

How many pages are in your book?

What is the first word in the glossary under the letter H?

## Topic 1 Numeration

▼ How many grooves, or reeds, do some coins have around their edges? You will find out in Lesson 1-7.

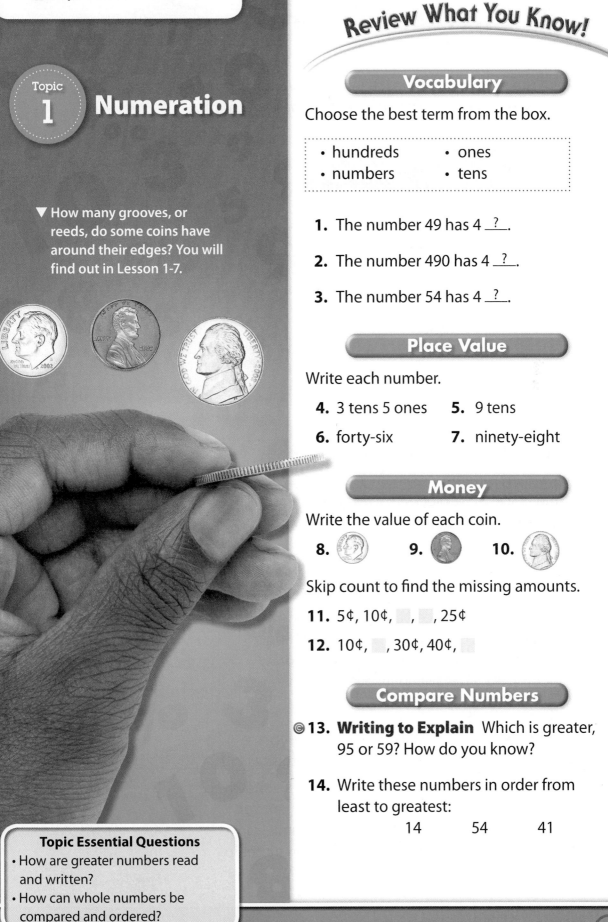

**Topic Essential Questions**
- How are greater numbers read and written?
- How can whole numbers be compared and ordered?

# Review What You Know!

## Vocabulary

Choose the best term from the box.

- hundreds
- ones
- numbers
- tens

**1.** The number 49 has 4 _?_.

**2.** The number 490 has 4 _?_.

**3.** The number 54 has 4 _?_.

## Place Value

Write each number.

**4.** 3 tens 5 ones

**5.** 9 tens

**6.** forty-six

**7.** ninety-eight

## Money

Write the value of each coin.

**8.** **9.** **10.**

Skip count to find the missing amounts.

**11.** 5¢, 10¢, ▢, ▢, 25¢

**12.** 10¢, ▢, 30¢, 40¢, ▢

## Compare Numbers

**13. Writing to Explain** Which is greater, 95 or 59? How do you know?

**14.** Write these numbers in order from least to greatest:

14      54      41

# Interactive Learning

Hands-On Minds-On

**Pose the problem.** Start each lesson by working together to solve problems. It will help you make sense of math.

## Applying Math Practices

- What am I asked to find?
- What else can I try?
- How are quantities related?
- How can I explain my work?
- How can I use math to model the problem?
- Can I use tools to help?
- Is my work precise?
- Why does this work?
- How can I generalize?

### Lesson 1-1

© **Use Tools** Solve using place-value blocks.

How many different ways can you show 274 using place-value blocks? How can you write each way you found?

### Lesson 1-2

© **Use Tools** Solve using place-value blocks.

How can you use place-value blocks to show the number 1,500 in two different ways? Show each way using place value blocks. Then draw a picture of each way and record each in words.

### Lesson 1-3

© **Use Structure** Use what you know about place value and smaller numbers to complete this task.

The number of people watching a parade is shown in the place-value chart at the right. How can you use the place-value chart to show this number in expanded form? How can you show the number in word form?

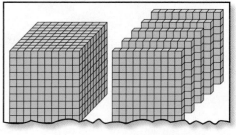

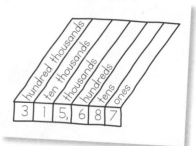

**Lesson 1-4**

© **Use Structure** Solve using a number line.

The vertical marks on the number line at the right are evenly spaced. What are the missing numbers? How did you decide? Write all the missing numbers on number line B of your recording sheet. Explain how you know what numbers to write.

2 ? 4 ? ?

**Lesson 1-5**

© **Reason** Solve using a number line.

The vertical marks on the number line at the right are evenly spaced. What are the two missing numbers? How did you decide? Then write all the numbers on number line B on your recording sheet and explain how you know what numbers to write.

0 ? 10 ? 20

**Lesson 1-6**

© **Reason** Use place value materials to complete this task.

I have a group of 345 pens and a group of 380 pens. How can you use place-value blocks and a place-value chart to find which group has more? Explain how you decided.

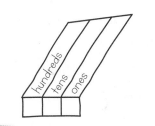

**Lesson 1-7**

© **Reason** The recording sheet shows the height of some of the world's highest waterfalls. How do you know which height is greatest? Put the numbers in order from greatest to least. Explain how you decided.

| Thousands | Hundreds | Tens | Ones |
|-----------|----------|------|------|
|           |          |      |      |
|           |          |      |      |
|           |          |      |      |

Ordered from greatest to least _____

**Lesson 1-8**

© **Use Tools** Solve any way you choose.

What numbers fit the following clues? It is a 2-digit, odd number. The digit in the tens place is greater than 3. The digit in the ones place is less than 5. Make an organized list of all of the possible numbers. How do you know you found them all?

**Common Core**

3.NBT.1 Use place value understanding to round whole numbers to the nearest 10 or 100. Also 3.NBT.2

# Representing Numbers

**Hands-On**
place-value blocks

## How can you read and write 3- and 4-digit numbers?

All numbers are made from the digits 0, 1, 2, 3, 4, 5, 6, 7, 8, and 9. Place value is the value of the place a digit has in a number.

Did you know that a two-humped camel weighs between 1,000 and 1,450 pounds?

This camel weighs 1,350 pounds.

---

**Another Example** **How can you show 1,350 on a place-value chart?**

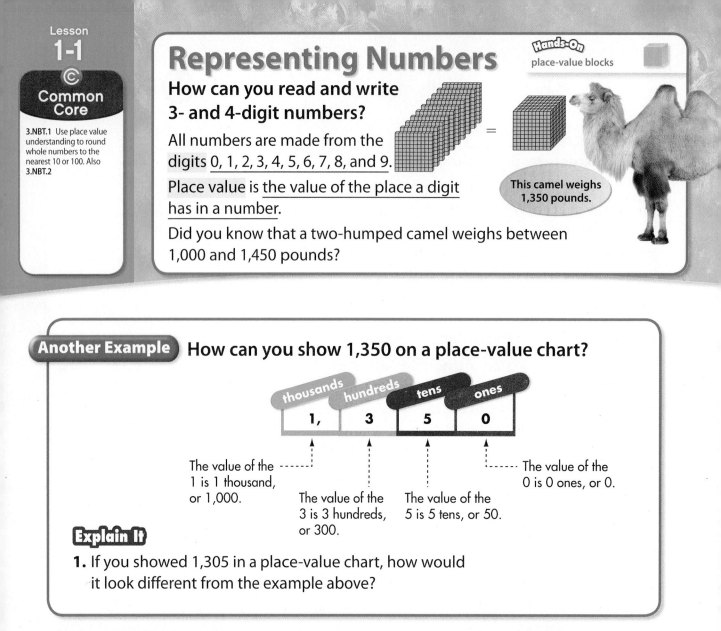

| thousands | hundreds | tens | ones |
|-----------|----------|------|------|
| 1, | 3 | 5 | 0 |

The value of the 1 is 1 thousand, or 1,000.

The value of the 3 is 3 hundreds, or 300.

The value of the 5 is 5 tens, or 50.

The value of the 0 is 0 ones, or 0.

**Explain It**

1. If you showed 1,305 in a place-value chart, how would it look different from the example above?

---

## Guided Practice*

**MATHEMATICAL PRACTICES**

### Do you know HOW?

Write each number in standard form.

1.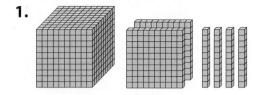

2. 8,000 + 500 + 30 + 9

3. eight hundred nine

4. two thousand, four hundred sixty-one

### Do you UNDERSTAND?

5. **Communicate** Explain the value of each digit in 6,835.

6. A horse weighs about 2,150 pounds. Write the number in two different ways.

7. **Use Tools** Write a 4-digit number that has a tens digit of 5, a hundreds digit of 2, and 6 for each of the other digits. Use place-value blocks to help you.

Animated Glossary, eTools
www.pearsonsuccessnet.com

DIGITAL

*For another example, see Set A on page 24.

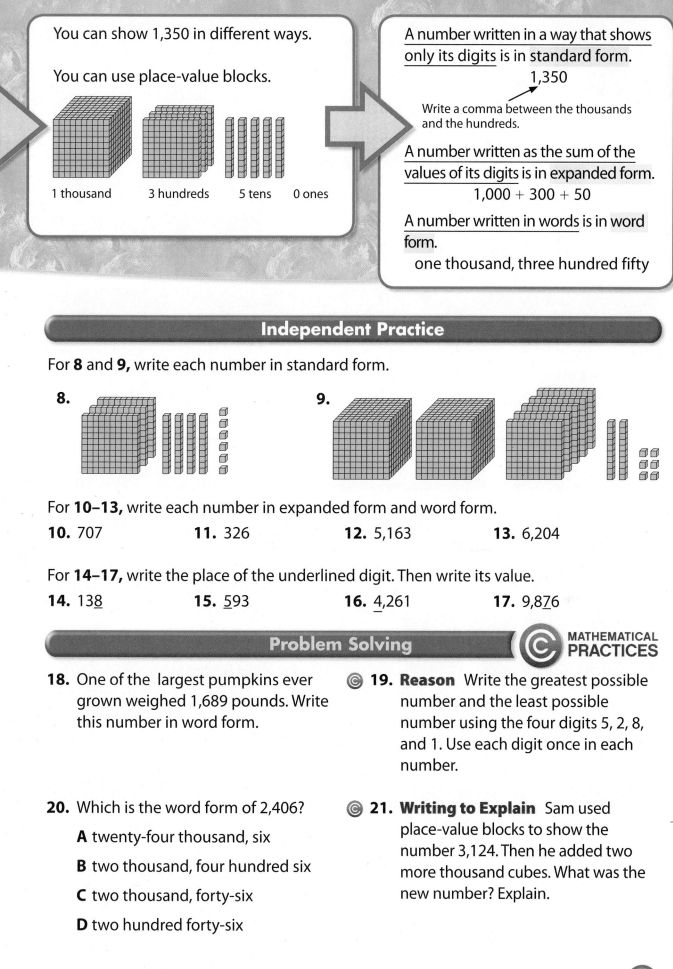

You can show 1,350 in different ways.

You can use place-value blocks.

1 thousand      3 hundreds      5 tens      0 ones

A number written in a way that shows only its digits is in standard form.

1,350

Write a comma between the thousands and the hundreds.

A number written as the sum of the values of its digits is in expanded form.

1,000 + 300 + 50

A number written in words is in word form.

one thousand, three hundred fifty

## Independent Practice

For **8** and **9,** write each number in standard form.

8.

9.

For **10–13,** write each number in expanded form and word form.

**10.** 707          **11.** 326          **12.** 5,163          **13.** 6,204

For **14–17,** write the place of the underlined digit. Then write its value.

**14.** 13<u>8</u>          **15.** <u>5</u>93          **16.** <u>4</u>,261          **17.** 9,8<u>7</u>6

## Problem Solving

MATHEMATICAL PRACTICES

**18.** One of the largest pumpkins ever grown weighed 1,689 pounds. Write this number in word form.

ⓒ **19. Reason** Write the greatest possible number and the least possible number using the four digits 5, 2, 8, and 1. Use each digit once in each number.

**20.** Which is the word form of 2,406?

   **A** twenty-four thousand, six

   **B** two thousand, four hundred six

   **C** two thousand, forty-six

   **D** two hundred forty-six

ⓒ **21. Writing to Explain** Sam used place-value blocks to show the number 3,124. Then he added two more thousand cubes. What was the new number? Explain.

Lesson
1-2

Common Core

3.NBT.1 Use place value understanding to round whole numbers to the nearest 10 or 100.

# Ways to Name Numbers

Hands-On
place-value blocks

## How can you use and name numbers?

The Sunshine Skyway Bridge crosses Tampa Bay, Florida. The length of its longest span is shown in the picture at the right. What are some different ways to name this number?

1,200 feet

## Other Examples

**You can use numbers to name addresses and years.**

### Addresses

23105 Glen Avenue
Twenty-three thousand, one hundred five

### Years

July 4, 1776
Seventeen hundred seventy-six

## Guided Practice*

MATHEMATICAL
PRACTICES

### Do you know HOW?

Name the number that the model shows in two ways.

**1.**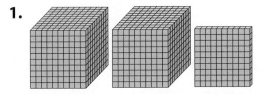

Name each number in two ways.

**2.** 3,500          **3.** 8,100

### Do you UNDERSTAND?

**4. Reason** In the example about the Sunshine Skyway Bridge, how are the two names for 1,200 the same? How are they different?

**5. Be Precise** The longest span of the Brooklyn Bridge in New York City is about 1,600 feet long. How can you name this number in two ways?

## Independent Practice

For **6–9,** name the number in two ways.

**6.** 5,200          **7.** 6,500          **8.** 9,800          **9.** 4,700

eTools
www.pearsonsuccessnet.com

*For another example, see Set B on page 24.*

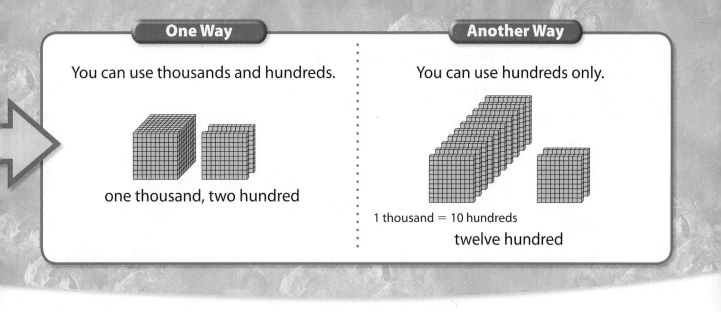

**One Way**

You can use thousands and hundreds.

one thousand, two hundred

**Another Way**

You can use hundreds only.

1 thousand = 10 hundreds

twelve hundred

---

In **10–12,** write each year in word form.

**10.** 1492 **11.** 1825 **12.** 1948

## Problem Solving

**MATHEMATICAL PRACTICES**

 **Be Precise** Use the table at the right for **13** and **14.**

**13.** Beth wrote down the address she heard: fifteen thousand, one hundred eight Allen Street. Which place has this address?

**14.** Write two names for the number in the address of Gibson's Market.

| Place | Address |
|---|---|
| Ace Sporting Goods | 1518 Allen Street |
| Central Post Office | 15008 Allen Street |
| Gibson's Market | 3900 Allen Street |
| Tops Bowling Center | 15108 Allen Street |

**15. Writing to Explain** Ana said, "I was born in the year nineteen hundred seventy-nine." Write the number to name the year. How does a number that names a year look different from a 4-digit number in standard form?

**16.** Which is another way to write the number 6,200?

**A** six hundred two

**B** six hundred two thousand

**C** sixty-two hundred

**D** sixty thousand, two hundred

**17.** There are 7,700 lakes in Florida that cover more than ten acres. Write two names for this number.

**18.** Social Studies Jonesborough, Tennessee, was founded in 1779. How can you write this year in word form?

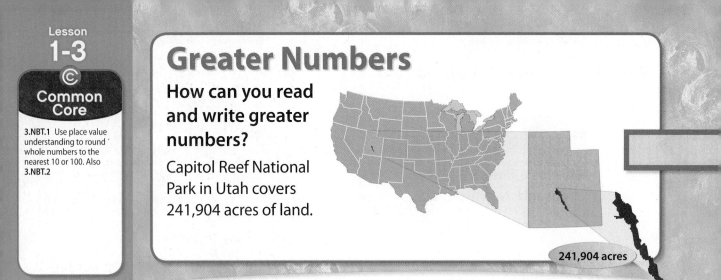
# Greater Numbers

**How can you read and write greater numbers?**

Capitol Reef National Park in Utah covers 241,904 acres of land.

241,904 acres

---

## Guided Practice*

**MATHEMATICAL PRACTICES**

### Do you know HOW?

For **1–3**, write each number in standard form.

**1.** three hundred forty-two thousand, six hundred seven

**2.** ninety-eight thousand, three hundred twenty

**3.** $500,000 + 40,000 + 600 + 90 + 3$

**4.** What is the value of the 9 in 379,050?

### Do you UNDERSTAND?

**5. Critique Reasoning** Ramos says the value of the digit 7 in 765,450 is 70,000. Do you agree? Why or why not?

**6. Writing to Explain** Describe how 130,434 and 434,130 are alike and how they are different.

---

## Independent Practice

Write each number in standard form.

**7.** twenty-seven thousand, five hundred fifty

**8.** $100,000 + 20,000 + 6,000 + 300 + 50$

Write each number in expanded form.

**9.** 46,354

**10.** 395,980

Write the place of the underlined digit. Then write its value.

**11.** 404,705    **12.** 163,254    **13.** 45,391    **14.** 283,971    **15.** 657,240

Animated Glossary
www.pearsonsuccessnet.com

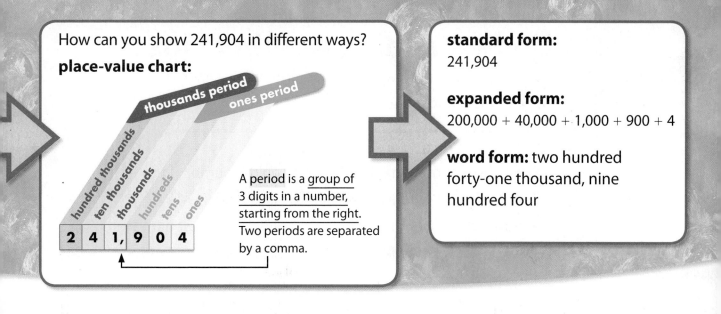

How can you show 241,904 in different ways?

**place-value chart:**

thousands period
ones period

hundred thousands
ten thousands
thousands
hundreds
tens
ones

| 2 | 4 | 1, | 9 | 0 | 4 |

A period is a group of 3 digits in a number, starting from the right. Two periods are separated by a comma.

**standard form:**
241,904

**expanded form:**
200,000 + 40,000 + 1,000 + 900 + 4

**word form:** two hundred forty-one thousand, nine hundred four

Find each missing number.

**16.** 26,305 = 20,000 + ▨ + 300 + 5

**17.** 81,960 = 80,000 + 1,000 + ▨ + 60

**18.** 400,000 + ▨ + 30 + 2 = 470,032

**19.** 118,005 = ▨ + 10,000 + 8,000 + 5

**20.** 300,000 + ▨ + 600 + 3 = 304,603

**21.** 200,000 + 4,000 + 60 + 3 = ▨

## Problem Solving

MATHEMATICAL
PRACTICES

Ⓒ **Reason** For **22–24**, use the table.

**22.** Write the population of each city in the table in expanded form.

**23.** Write the population of Des Moines, IA in word form.

| City Populations | |
|---|---|
| **City** | **Number of People** |
| Des Moines, IA | 193,886 |
| Taylorsville, UT | 58,048 |
| Akron, OH | 209,704 |

**24.** Which cities listed in the table have more than one hundred thousand people?

Ⓒ **25. Model** A new world record was once set when 303,628 dominos fell. Write 303,628 in expanded form.

**26.** Which is the word form of the number 505,920?

    **A** fifty-five thousand, ninety-two

    **B** five hundred five thousand, ninety-two

    **C** five thousand, five hundred ninety-two

    **D** five hundred five thousand, nine hundred twenty

Common
Core

3.NBT.1 Use place value understanding to round whole numbers to the nearest 10 or 100.

# Understanding Number Lines

How can you locate and write numbers on a number line?

Look at this number line.

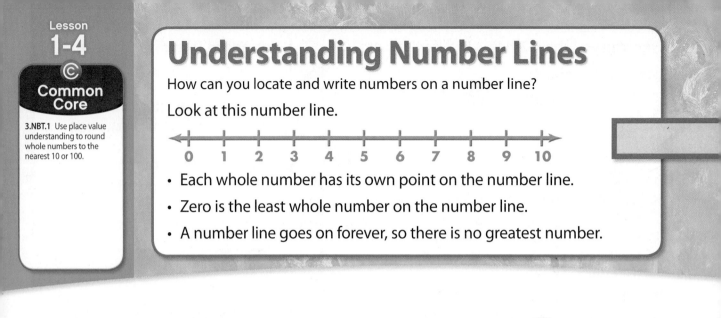

- Each whole number has its own point on the number line.
- Zero is the least whole number on the number line.
- A number line goes on forever, so there is no greatest number.

---

## Guided Practice*

MATHEMATICAL
PRACTICES

### Do you know HOW?

In **1** and **2**, write the number for each lettered point on the number line.

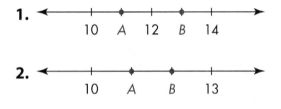

1.
```
    10   A   12   B   14
```

2.
```
    10   A    B   13
```

### Do you UNDERSTAND?

ⓒ **3. Reason** How are the number lines for Exercises 1 and 2 the same? How are they different?

ⓒ **4. Writing to Explain** Why are there 5 numbers on the number line in Exercise 1 and only 4 numbers on the number line in Exercise 2?

---

## Independent Practice

In **5–9**, write the number for each lettered point on the number line.

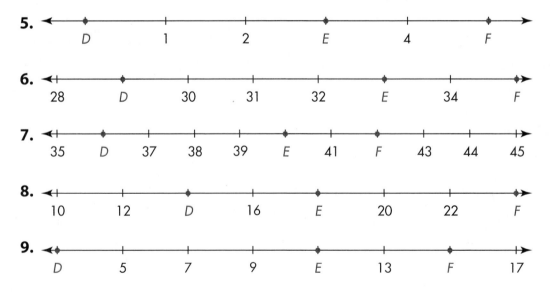

5.
```
    D       1       2       E       4       F
```

6.
```
  28      D    30    31    32    E    34    F
```

7.
```
  35   D   37   38   39   E   41   F   43   44   45
```

8.
```
  10      12    D    16    E    20    22    F
```

9.
```
   D    5    7    9    E    13    F    17
```

On a number line, the distance between any whole number and the next whole number is the same.

Both of these number lines show the numbers 5 through 9.

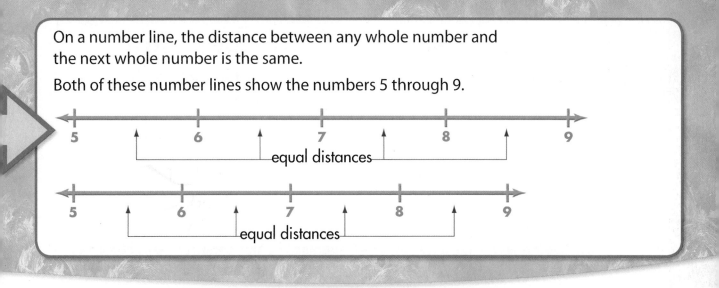

MATHEMATICAL
PRACTICES

**10.** In 1976, the world record was set for the "World's Longest Apple Peel," measuring at about 170 feet. Which lettered point best represents the length of the "World's Longest Apple Peel"?

©**11. Critique Reasoning** Maryanne marked and labeled the points on the number line below. Explain what is wrong with her work.

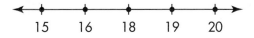

©**12. Critique Reasoning** Tito marked and labeled the points on the number line below. Explain what is wrong with his work.

**13.** Which lettered point on the number line represents 30?

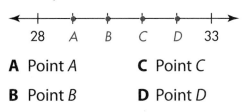

   **A** Point A      **C** Point C

   **B** Point B      **D** Point D

**14.** What number does Point C on the number line represent?

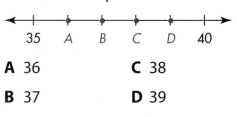

   **A** 36      **C** 38

   **B** 37      **D** 39

©**15. Writing to Explain** Explain why Points A and B both represent the number 6.

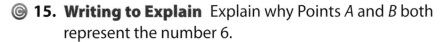

Common Core

3.NBT.1 Use place value understanding to round whole numbers to the nearest 10 or 100.

# Counting on the Number Line

## How can you complete the pattern on a number line?

What numbers do Points *A* and *B* represent?

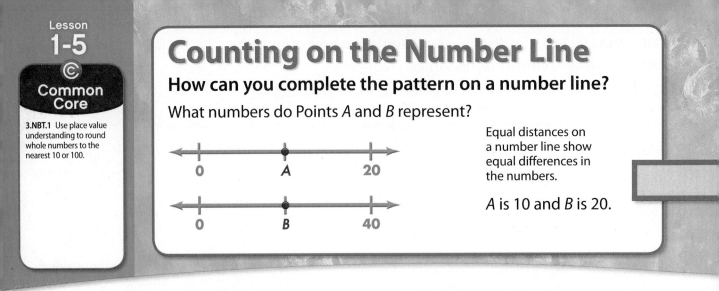

Equal distances on a number line show equal differences in the numbers.

*A* is 10 and *B* is 20.

---

## Guided Practice*

**MATHEMATICAL PRACTICES**

### Do you know HOW?

**1.** What whole numbers are missing on this part of a number line?

40 ▢ ▢ ▢ 45 ▢ ▢ · ▢ 50

**2.** What whole numbers are missing from this number line?

▢ 6 ▢ ▢ 15 18

### Do you UNDERSTAND?

© **3. Writing to Explain** Describe how you found the pattern in the number line in Exercise 2.

© **4. Reason** In the number line above, where you skip counted by tens, what will the next 3 numbers be after 100?

---

## Independent Practice

Write the missing whole numbers for each number line.

**5.** ▢ 10 ▢ ▢ ▢ 30 35 40

**6.** ▢ 6 10 14 ▢ ▢ ▢

**7.** ▢ 14 ▢ ▢ ▢ 42 49 56 ▢

**8.** ▢ 11 ▢ 17 20 23 ▢ ▢

**9.** 50 ▢ 150 ▢ ▢ ▢ 350

*For another example, see Set D on page 25.*

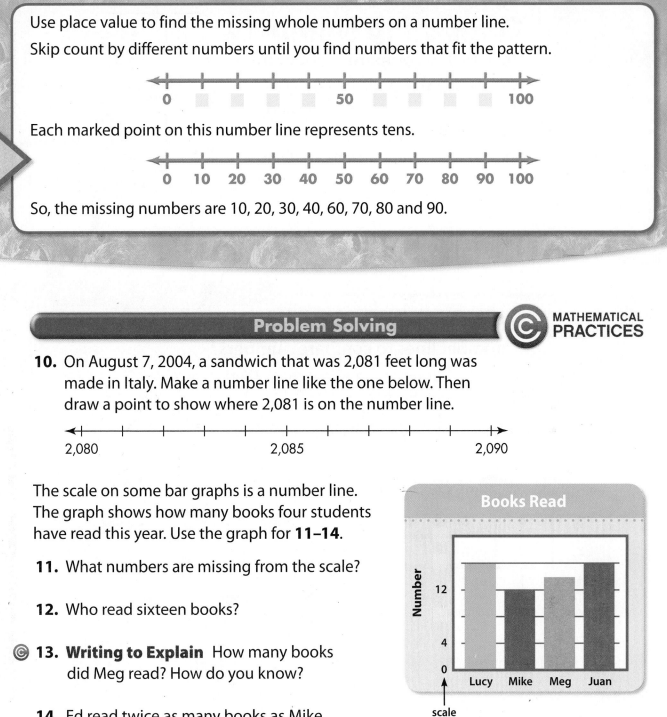

Use place value to find the missing whole numbers on a number line.

Skip count by different numbers until you find numbers that fit the pattern.

Each marked point on this number line represents tens.

So, the missing numbers are 10, 20, 30, 40, 60, 70, 80 and 90.

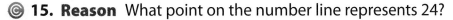

**Problem Solving**

10. On August 7, 2004, a sandwich that was 2,081 feet long was made in Italy. Make a number line like the one below. Then draw a point to show where 2,081 is on the number line.

2,080          2,085          2,090

The scale on some bar graphs is a number line. The graph shows how many books four students have read this year. Use the graph for **11–14**.

**Books Read**

11. What numbers are missing from the scale?

12. Who read sixteen books?

© 13. **Writing to Explain** How many books did Meg read? How do you know?

14. Ed read twice as many books as Mike. How many books did Ed read?

© 15. **Reason** What point on the number line represents 24?

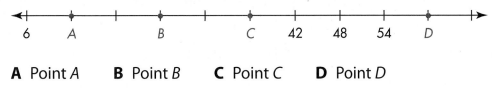

6     A          B          C     42     48     54     D

**A** Point A     **B** Point B     **C** Point C     **D** Point D

Lesson
**1-6**

ⓒ
**Common Core**

**3.NBT.1** Use place value understanding to round whole numbers to the nearest 10 or 100.

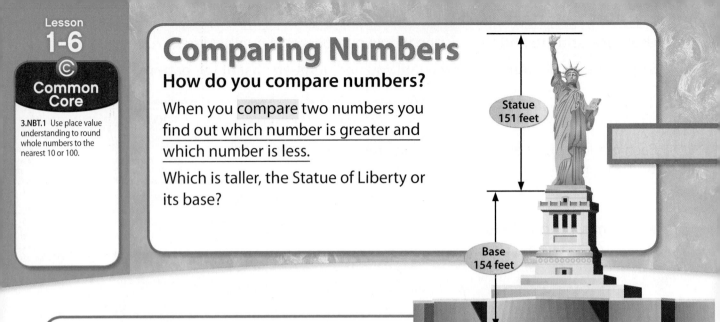

# Comparing Numbers

## How do you compare numbers?

When you compare two numbers you find out which number is greater and which number is less.

Which is taller, the Statue of Liberty or its base?

Statue
151 feet

Base
154 feet

---

**Another Example** **How can you use place-value charts and number lines to compare numbers?**

Compare 3,456 and 3,482 using a place-value chart. Then show these two numbers on a number line.

On a place-value chart, line up the digits by place value. Compare the digits starting from the left.

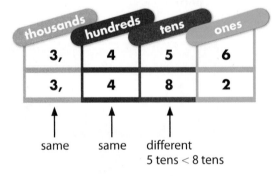

| thousands | hundreds | tens | ones |
|-----------|----------|------|------|
| 3, | 4 | 5 | 6 |
| 3, | 4 | 8 | 2 |

same · same · different
5 tens < 8 tens

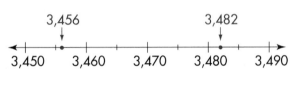

3,456          3,482
↓              ↓
3,450  3,460  3,470  3,480  3,490

On the number line, 3,456 is to the left of 3,482.

So 3,456 **is less than** 3,482.

3,456 < 3,482

**Explain It**

ⓒ **1. Reason** In this example, why don't you need to compare the digit in the ones place?

ⓒ **2. Reason** Why can't you tell which number is greater by just comparing the first digit in each number?

DIGITAL

Animated Glossary
www.pearsonsuccessnet.com

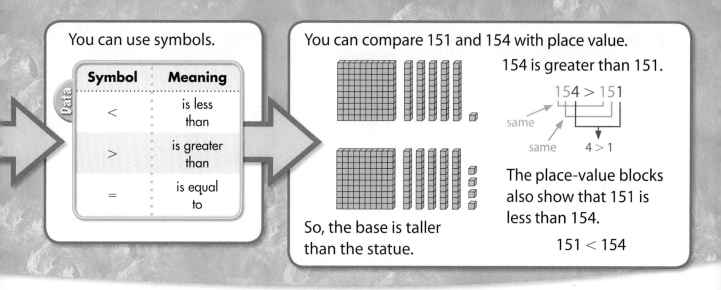

You can use symbols.

| Symbol | Meaning |
|--------|---------|
| < | is less than |
| > | is greater than |
| = | is equal to |

You can compare 151 and 154 with place value.

154 is greater than 151.

$154 > 151$

same

same   $4 > 1$

The place-value blocks also show that 151 is less than 154.

$151 < 154$

So, the base is taller than the statue.

---

## Guided Practice*

**MATHEMATICAL PRACTICES**

### Do you know HOW?

Compare the numbers. Use <, >, or =.

**1.**

141 ◯ 64

**2.**

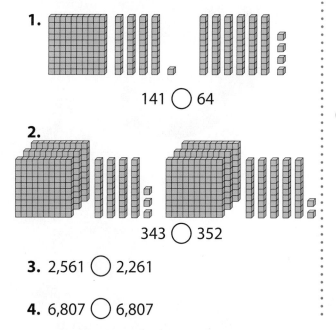

343 ◯ 352

**3.** 2,561 ◯ 2,261

**4.** 6,807 ◯ 6,807

### Do you UNDERSTAND?

**5. Critique Reasoning** Cara says that since 4 is greater than 1, the number 496 is greater than the number 1,230. Do you agree? Why or why not?

**6. Writing to Explain** The total height of the Statue of Liberty is 305 feet. The Washington Monument is 555 feet tall. Which is taller? Explain how you know.

**7.** Draw a number line to compare the numbers.

1,462 ◯ 1,521

---

## Independent Practice

Compare the numbers. Use <, >, or =.

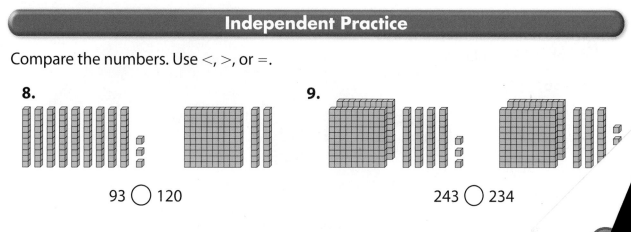

**8.**

93 ◯ 120

**9.**

243 ◯ 234

---

Compare the numbers. Use <, >, or =.

**10.** 679 ◯ 4,985

**11.** 9,642 ◯ 9,642

**12.** 5,136 ◯ 5,163

**13.** 8,204 ◯ 8,402

**14.** 3,823 ◯ 3,853

**15.** 2,424 ◯ 2,242

Write the missing digits to make each number sentence true.

**16.** ▢24 > 896

**17.** 6▢7 < 617

**18.** 29▢ = 2▢0

**19.** ▢,000 < 1,542

**20.** 3,▢12 > 3,812

**21.** 2,185 > 2,▢85

Use the pictures for **22** and **23**.

ⓒ **22. Communicate** Which is taller, the Washington Monument or the Great Pyramid in Egypt? How do you know?

**23.** Which is taller, the Gateway Arch or the Space Needle?

ⓒ **24. Reason** Mark is thinking of a 3-digit number. Rory is thinking of a 4-digit number. Whose number is greater? How do you know?

ⓒ **25. Use Structure** Suppose you are comparing 1,272 and 1,269. Do you need to compare the ones digits? Which number would be farther to the right on the number line? Explain.

**26.** Which number sentence is true if the number 537 replaces the box?

**A** 456 > ▢

**B** ▢ = 256

**C** 598 < ▢

**D** ▢ > 357

**Gateway Arch**
630 feet tall

**Space Needle**
605 feet tall

**Great Pyramid**
451 feet tall

**Washington Monument**
555 feet tall

# Algebra Connections

## Number Patterns

Remember that skip counting can be used to make a number pattern. Skip counting can also be used to find missing numbers in a given pattern.

Copy and complete. Write the number that completes each pattern.

**1.** 3, 6, 9, 12, ▨, 18

**2.** 14, ▨, 18, 20, 22, 24

**3.** 20, 30, ▨, 50, 60, 70

**4.** 25, 50, 75, 100, 125, ▨

**5.** 3, 8, 13, 18, 23, ▨

**6.** 9, 19, 29, ▨, 49, 59

**7.** 7, 9, 11, ▨, 15, 17

**8.** 12, ▨, 20, 24, 28

**9.** 90, 80, 70, ▨, 50, 40

**10.** 22, 20, 18, 16, ▨, 12

**11.** 86, 81, ▨, 71, 66, 61

**12.** 150, ▨, 100, 75, 50, 25

. . . . . . . . . . . . . . . . . . . . . . . . . . . . . . . . . . . . . . . . . . . . . . . . . . . . . . . . . . .

For **13** and **14**, copy and complete each pattern. Use the pattern to help solve the problem.

**13.** Rusty saw that the house numbers on a street were in a pattern. First he saw the number 101. Then he saw the numbers 103, 105, and 107. There was a missing number, and then the number 111. What was the missing number?

101, 103, 105, 107, ▨, 111

**14.** Alani was skip counting the pasta shapes she made. The numbers she said were 90, 95, 100, 105, 110, 115. She needed to say one more number in the count to finish counting the pasta. How many pasta shapes did Alani make?

90, 95, 100, 105, 110, 115, ▨

© **15. Write a Problem** Copy and complete the number pattern below. Write a real-world problem to match the number pattern.

5, 10, 15, 20, 25, 30, ▨

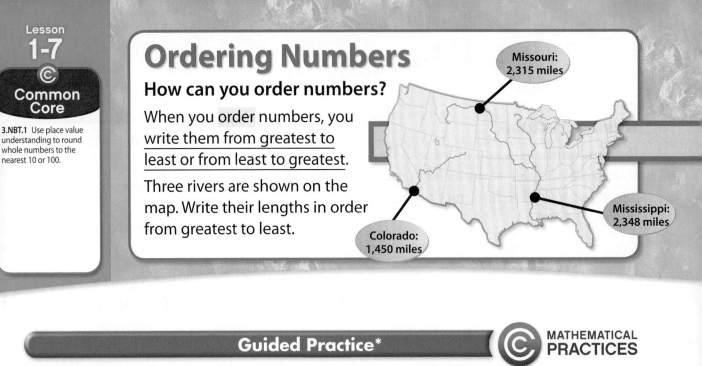

Lesson
1-7

© Common Core

3.NBT.1 Use place value understanding to round whole numbers to the nearest 10 or 100.

# Ordering Numbers

**How can you order numbers?**

When you order numbers, you write them from greatest to least or from least to greatest.

Three rivers are shown on the map. Write their lengths in order from greatest to least.

Missouri: 2,315 miles

Mississippi: 2,348 miles

Colorado: 1,450 miles

---

## Guided Practice*

© MATHEMATICAL PRACTICES

### Do you know HOW?

For **1** and **2**, order the numbers from least to greatest.

**1.** 769    679    697

**2.** 359    368    45

For **3** and **4**, order the numbers from greatest to least.

**3.** 4,334    809    4,350

**4.** 1,137    1,573    1,457

### Do you UNDERSTAND?

© **5. Construct Arguments** The length of another river has a 2 in the hundreds place. Can this river be longer than the Colorado? Why or why not?

**6.** Copy and complete the number line below to show the numbers 315, 305, and 319 in order.

```
 ←+————————————+————————————+→
  300          310          320
```

---

## Independent Practice

For **7–9**, order the numbers from least to greatest.

**7.** 6,743    6,930    6,395

**8.** 995    1,293    1,932

**9.** 8,754    8,700    8,792

For **10–12**, order the numbers from greatest to least.

**10.** 2,601    967    2,365

**11.** 3,554    3,454    3,459

**12.** 5,304    5,430    5,403

**13.** Copy and complete the number line below to show 1,020, 965, and 985 in order.

```
 ←+————————————+————————————+→
  950        1,000        1,050
```

DIGITAL

Animated Glossary
www.pearsonsuccessnet.com

*For another example, see Set E on page 25.

You can use a place-value chart to help you.

| thousands | hundreds | tens | ones |
|---|---|---|---|
| 1, | 4 | 5 | 0 |
| 2, | 3 | 4 | 8 |
| 2, | 3 | 1 | 5 |

↑ 1 < 2
So 1,450 is the least number.

↑ 3 = 3

↑ 4 > 1
So 2,348 is the greatest number.

The lengths of the rivers in order from greatest to least are:

Mississippi: 2,348 miles;
Missouri: 2,315 miles;
Colorado: 1,450 miles.

## Problem Solving

Use the pictures for **14–17**.

**14.** Which animal weighs 100 pounds more than a moose?

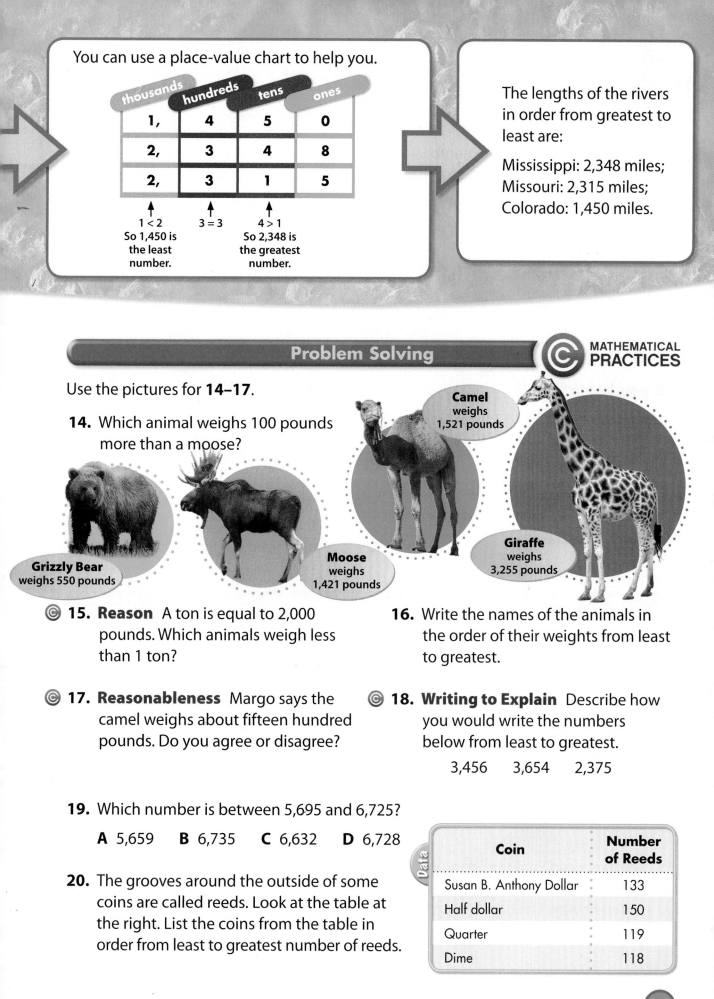

Camel weighs 1,521 pounds

**Grizzly Bear** weighs 550 pounds

**Moose** weighs 1,421 pounds

**Giraffe** weighs 3,255 pounds

Ⓒ **15. Reason** A ton is equal to 2,000 pounds. Which animals weigh less than 1 ton?

**16.** Write the names of the animals in the order of their weights from least to greatest.

Ⓒ **17. Reasonableness** Margo says the camel weighs about fifteen hundred pounds. Do you agree or disagree?

Ⓒ **18. Writing to Explain** Describe how you would write the numbers below from least to greatest.

3,456     3,654     2,375

**19.** Which number is between 5,695 and 6,725?

**A** 5,659     **B** 6,735     **C** 6,632     **D** 6,728

**20.** The grooves around the outside of some coins are called reeds. Look at the table at the right. List the coins from the table in order from least to greatest number of reeds.

| Data | Coin | Number of Reeds |
|---|---|---|
| | Susan B. Anthony Dollar | 133 |
| | Half dollar | 150 |
| | Quarter | 119 |
| | Dime | 118 |

Lesson
1-8

Common
Core

3.NBT.2 Fluently add and
subtract within 1000 using
strategies and algorithms
based on place value,
properties of operations,
and/or the relationship
between addition and
subtraction.

Problem Solving

# Make an Organized List

Randy is playing a game called
*Guess the Number*. What are all
the possible numbers that fit
the clues shown at the right?

You can make an organized
list to find all the possible
numbers.

## Clues

- It is a 3-digit even number.
- The digit in the hundreds
  place is greater than 8.
- The digit in the tens place
  is less than 2.

**Guided Practice***

MATHEMATICAL
PRACTICES

### Do you know HOW?

Make an organized list to solve.

1. Rachel has a quarter, a dime, a
   nickel, and a penny. She told her
   brother he could take two coins. List
   all the different pairs of coins her
   brother can take.

### Do you UNDERSTAND?

© 2. **Communicate** How did making
   an organized list help you solve
   Problem 1?

© 3. **Write a Problem** Write a problem
   that can be solved by making an
   organized list. Solve the problem.

**Independent Practice**

MATHEMATICAL
PRACTICES

For **4** and **5**, make an organized list to solve.

4. List all the 5-digit numbers that fit
   these clues.

   - The ten thousands digit is 7.
   - The thousands digit is less than 2.
   - The hundreds digit is greater than 7.
   - The tens digit and ones digit both
     equal 10 − 5.

5. Jen, Meg, and Emily are standing
   in line at the movies. How many
   different ways can they line up?
   List the ways.

### Applying Math Practices

- What am I asked to find?
- What else can I try?
- How are quantities related?
- How can I explain my work?
- How can I use math to model the
  problem?
- Can I use tools to help?
- Is my work precise?
- Why does this work?
- How can I generalize?

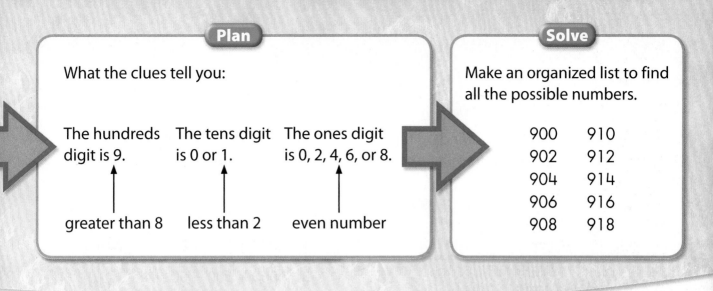

What the clues tell you:

| The hundreds digit is 9. | The tens digit is 0 or 1. | The ones digit is 0, 2, 4, 6, or 8. |
|---|---|---|
| ↑ | ↑ | ↑ |
| greater than 8 | less than 2 | even number |

Make an organized list to find all the possible numbers.

| | |
|---|---|
| 900 | 910 |
| 902 | 912 |
| 904 | 914 |
| 906 | 916 |
| 908 | 918 |

For **6–8**, use the table.

**6.** How many different sandwich choices are there if you want white bread?

**7.** How many different sandwich choices are there if you don't want turkey?

**8.** Suppose wheat bread was added as a bread choice. How many different sandwich choices would there be?

| Sandwich Choices | |
|---|---|
| **Bread Choices** | **Filling Choices** |
| White | Ham |
| Rye | Tuna |
| | Turkey |

**9.** Jeremy has tan pants and black pants. He also has three shirts: blue, green, and red. List all the different outfits that Jeremy can wear.

Ⓒ **10. Persevere** Dennis bought a 3-pound bag of apples for $3. He also bought some grapes for $4. How much did Dennis spend?

**11.** How many different ways can you make 15 cents using dimes, nickels, or pennies?

**A** 15 ways    **C** 6 ways

**B** 9 ways    **D** 3 ways

Ⓒ **12. Persevere** Carla bought 4 sheets of poster board. Each sheet cost $2. She paid with a $10 bill. Carla cut each sheet into 2 pieces. How many pieces does Carla have?

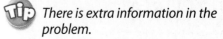 *There is extra information in the problem.*

Ⓒ **13. Reason** What is this 3-digit number?

- The hundreds digit is 3 less than 5.
- The tens digit is greater than 8.
- The ones digit is 1 less than the tens digit.

**Set A,** pages 6–7

Write the number below in standard form, expanded form, and word form.

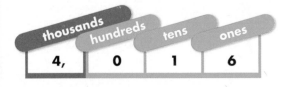

Standard form: 4,016

Expanded form: 4,000 + 10 + 6

Word form: four thousand, sixteen

**Remember** that the digit 0 is sometimes needed to hold a place in a number.

Write each number in standard form.

**1.** 1,000 + 5          **2.** 300 + 20 + 7

**3.** 7,000 + 800 + 60 + 4

**4.** 9,000 + 300 + 5

Write each number in expanded form and word form.

**5.** 8,214          **6.** 620

**Set B,** pages 8–9

Name 1,300 in two different ways.

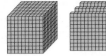
1 thousand + 3 hundreds
one thousand, three hundred

10 hundreds + 3 hundreds
thirteen hundred

**Remember** that 10 hundreds equal 1 thousand.

Name each number in two ways.

**1.** 1,700          **2.** 5,600

**3.** 4,800          **4.** 9,100

**Set C,** pages 10–11

Find the value of the 4 in 847,193.

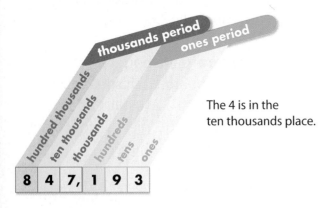

The 4 is in the ten thousands place.

The value of the 4 is 40,000.

**Remember** that 10 thousands equal 1 ten thousand.

Write the place of each underlined digit. Then write its value.

**1.** 341,791          **2.** 829,526

**3.** 570,890          **4.** 215,003

**5.** 197,206          **6.** 473,069

**7.** 628,174          **8.** 782,413

Look at these number lines. What numbers are shown by Points *A* and *B*?

Point *A* stands for 20.

Point *B* stands for 30.

Equal distances on a number line show equal differences in the numbers.

**Remember** to find a pattern that fits all of the points on the number line.

Write the number for each lettered point on the number line.

**1.** 
*A*  20  *B*  *C*  *D*  100  120  140

**2.** 
*E*  12  20  28  *F*  *G*  *H*

**3.** 
*J*  12  *K*  *L*  *M*  36  42  48  *N*

---

Compare 7,982 and 7,682.
Line up the digits by place value.
Compare the digits starting from the left.

| 7, | 9 | 8 | 2 |
|----|---|---|---|
| 7, | 6 | 8 | 2 |

same    different: 9 hundreds > 6 hundreds

7,982 > 7,682

**Remember,** when ordering numbers, compare one place at a time.

Compare. Use <, >, or =.

**1.** 479 ◯ 912    **2.** 1,156 ◯ 156

Write the numbers in order from greatest to least.

**3.** 393    182    229

**4.** 1,289    2,983    1,760

---

When you make an organized list to solve problems, follow these steps.

**Step 1**

Carefully read the clues or information from the problem.

**Step 2**

Choose one clue or piece of information and use it to start your list.

**Step 3**

Repeat step 2 until you have used all of the clues or information to make an organized list.

**Remember** that each item on your list must match all of the clues.

**1.** Pedro has a red marble, a blue marble, a yellow marble, and a green marble. He told Frank to take two marbles. How many different pairs of marbles can Frank take? List the pairs.

**Multiple Choice**

1. The place-value blocks show the number of students at a school. How many students are there? (1-1)

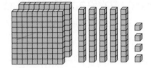

**A** 2,054

**B** 254

**C** 250

**D** 245

2. On Friday, 1,593 people watched the play *Cinderella*. On Saturday, 1,595 people watched, and on Sunday, 1,586 people watched. Which lists these numbers in order from least to greatest? (1-7)

**A** 1,586   1,593   1,595

**B** 1,586   1,595   1,593

**C** 1,593   1,595   1,586

**D** 1,595   1,593   1,586

3. Ryan adds the same number of basketball cards to his collection every week. The number line shows how his collection is growing. What number does Point *N* represent? (1-5)

```
82      87      92      L      N      107
```

**A** 94

**B** 97

**C** 100

**D** 102

4. What is the value of the 9 in the number 295,863? (1-3)

**A** 90

**B** 9,000

**C** 90,000

**D** 900,000

5. The students at summer camp marked their ages on a number line. Maria marked her age with the letter *M*. How old is Maria? (1-4)

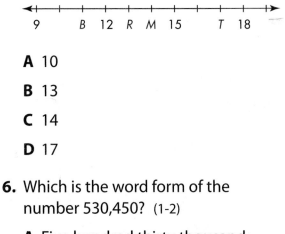

```
9      B   12   R   M   15      T   18
```

**A** 10

**B** 13

**C** 14

**D** 17

6. Which is the word form of the number 530,450? (1-2)

**A** Five hundred thirty thousand, forty-five

**B** Five hundred thirty thousand, four hundred fifty

**C** Five hundred thirty, four fifty

**D** Fifty-three thousand, four hundred fifty

7. Which is greater than 4,324? (1-6)

**A** 4,342

**B** 4,322

**C** 4,314

**D** 3,424

**8.** What point on the number line represents 43? (1-5)

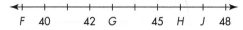

**9.** What is the value of the 7 in 107,695? (1-3)

**10.** Write the number 3,700 in word form. (1-2)

**11.** Carson used place-value blocks to show this number. What number can Carson write for the place-value blocks? (1-1)

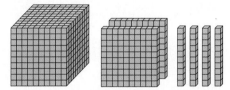

**12.** Hector used the following clues to find an unknown 4-digit number. My thousands digit is 3. My tens digit is one less than my hundreds digit. My hundreds digit is 7. The sum of my ones digit and my thousands digit is 5.

What is the number? (1-8)

**13.** Alex, Eric, Josh, and Tony are playing tennis. How many different groups of 2 can they make? (1-8)

**14.** A library has 11,400 fiction books, 11,413 nonfiction books, and 11,431 picture books. List the number of books in order from greatest to least. (1-7)

**15.** There are 1,568 students in Greenville and 1,705 students in Linden. Which town has a greater number of students? (1-6)

**16.** Jason marked and labeled the points on the number line below. What is wrong with his work? (1-4)

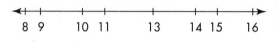

**17.** Use word form to name the number 1,300 in two different ways. (1-2)

**18.** Karen wants to make a sandwich. She can choose from rye bread, whole-wheat bread, or multi-grain bread. Karen can choose one ingredient from turkey, roast beef, tuna, or cheese to put on the bread. How many different sandwiches can she make? (1-8)

**19.** Parker used place-value blocks to show this number. Write the number in standard form, and in expanded form. (1-1)

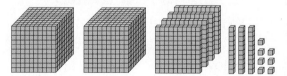

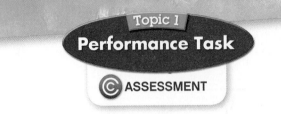
Use the information in the table to plan a vacation trip.

| Distance Between Cities | | |
| --- | --- | --- |
| **City 1** | **City 2** | **Number of Miles Between Cities** |
| San Francisco, CA | Denver, CO | 1,241 |
| Denver, CO | St. Louis, MO | 871 |
| Indianapolis, IN | Washington, D.C. | 605 |
| Dallas, TX | Boston, MA | 1,867 |

1. How far apart are San Francisco and Denver? Write the distance in standard form and expanded form.

2. On a separate sheet of paper, draw place-value blocks to show the distance between San Francisco and Denver. Label and explain your drawing.

3. Put the distances in the table in order from greatest to least. Is the distance between San Francisco and Denver either the greatest distance or the least distance? If not, how can you describe this distance?

4. The distance between which two cities is shown below?

5. Which lettered point best represents the distance between Dallas, TX and Boston, MA on the number line below? Explain how you know.

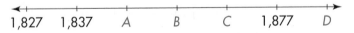

1,827   1,837   A       B       C    1,877   D

Topic
2

# Number Sense: Addition and Subtraction

▼ In recent years, how many missions from NASA's Jet Propulsion Lab have studied comets? You will find out in Lesson 2-2.

## Topic Essential Questions
- How can sums and differences be found mentally?
- How can sums and differences be estimated?

## Review What You Know!

### Vocabulary

Choose the best term from the box.

- hundreds      • subtract
- sum           • tens

1. In 259, the 2 is in the _?_ place.

2. When you _?_ you find the missing part.

3. The answer in addition is the _?_.

### Place Value

Copy and complete.

4. 35 = ▉ tens ▉ ones

5. 264 = ▉ hundreds ▉ tens ▉ ones

6. 302 = ▉ hundreds ▉ tens ▉ ones

### Addition Facts

Write each sum.

7. 7 + 6      8. 8 + 6      9. 9 + 9

### Subtraction Facts

Find each difference.

10. 9 − 5      11. 11 − 3      12. 16 − 7

13. Janika bought 3 books on Monday and 6 books on Tuesday. How many books did she buy in all?

© 14. **Writing to Explain** Derrick has 4 red, 2 blue, 2 green, 2 yellow, and 2 orange balloons. Explain how to skip count to find how many balloons he has in all.

# Interactive Learning

**Pose the problem.** Start each lesson by working together to solve problems. It will help you make sense of math.

## Applying Math Practices

- What am I asked to find?
- What else can I try?
- How are quantities related?
- How can I explain my work?
- How can I use math to model the problem?
- Can I use tools to help?
- Is my work precise?
- Why does this work?
- How can I generalize?

### Lesson 2-1

© **Generalize** Solve. Use the cups at the right.

In the top row of cups, is the total for the two cups on the left the same as the total for the two cups on the right? Explain. In the second row of cups, is the total for the three cups on the left the same as the total for the three cups on the right? Explain.

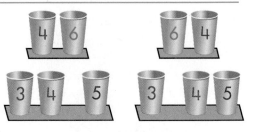

### Lesson 2-2

© **Use Tools** Solve. Use counters to help.

Ling made 14 hats to sell at the fair. She sold 6 of them. How many hats does Ling have now? Draw a picture to show how you found the answer.

### Lesson 2-3

© **Reason** Solve using mental math.

The school store sold 36 pencils last week and 23 pencils this week. How many pencils were sold in all? Explain how you found the answer using mental math.

**Lesson 2-4**

Ⓒ **Reason** Solve using mental math.

You want to buy an item that was originally $63. If you get the discount at the right, what is the sale price? Explain how you found the answer using mental math.

DISCOUNT:
$17 off
original price

**Lesson 2-5**

Ⓒ **Reason** Think about ways to find numbers that tell about how much or how many.

Suppose you have 27 stickers. How might you describe for someone *about how many* stickers you have? Use a number line to show that your answer is reasonable.

20 21 22 23 24 25 26 27 28 29 30

**Lesson 2-6**

Ⓒ **Reasonableness** Solve. You only need an estimate.

Do the two sun bears together weigh more than the female black bear? Without finding the exact values, tell how you can decide.

| Type of Bear | Weight | |
|---|---|---|
| | Female | Male |
| Sun Bear | 78 pounds | 95 pounds |
| Black Bear | 215 pounds | 345 pounds |

**Lesson 2-7**

Ⓒ **Reasonableness** Solve. You only need an estimate.

Sara collected 356 cans. Pierre collected 117 cans. About how many more cans did Sara collect? Without finding the exact values, tell how you can decide.

**Lesson 2-8**

Ⓒ **Use Structure** What can I write on the left side of the balance that will have the same value as what is on the right side? Find 5 different answers!

?     7 − 4

**Lesson 2-9**

Ⓒ **Reasonableness** One of the choices at the right is the correct answer. Without finding the exact answer to the problem, choose the correct answer and explain your choice.

Heidi has 19 stickers. Wendy has 28 stickers. How many stickers do the girls have together?

**A.** Wendy has 9 more stickers than Heidi.

**B.** The girls have 47 stickers.

**C.** The girls have 37 stickers

© Common Core

3.NBT.2 Fluently add and subtract within 1000 using strategies and algorithms based on place value, properties of operations, and/or the relationship between addition and subtraction. Also 3.OA.9

# Addition Meaning and Properties

## What are some ways to think about addition?

You can use addition to join groups.

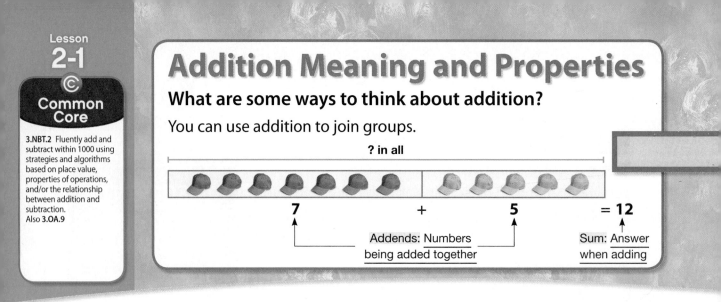

? in all

$$7 \quad + \quad 5 \quad = 12$$

Addends: Numbers being added together

Sum: Answer when adding

---

**Another Example** What is another way to think about addition?

Marda has two pieces of ribbon. One is 4 inches long and the other is 3 inches long. How many inches of ribbon does Marda have all together?

You can use a number line to think about addition.

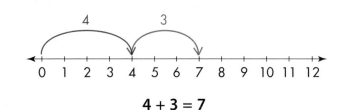

$$4 + 3 = 7$$

All together, Marda has 7 inches of ribbon.

3 inches

4 inches

---

## Guided Practice*

© **MATHEMATICAL PRACTICES**

### Do you know HOW?

Write each missing number.

1. ▢ $+ 9 = 9$

2. $4 + 6 = 6 +$ ▢

3. $(2 +$ ▢$) + 6 = 2 + (3 + 6)$

### Do you UNDERSTAND?

© 4. **Reason** Why does it make sense that the Commutative Property is also called the *order property*?

© 5. **Critique Reasoning** Ralph says you can rewrite $(4 + 5) + 2$ as $9 + 2$. Do you agree? Why or why not?

DIGITAL

Animated Glossary
www.pearsonsuccessnet.com

*For another example, see Set A on page 58.

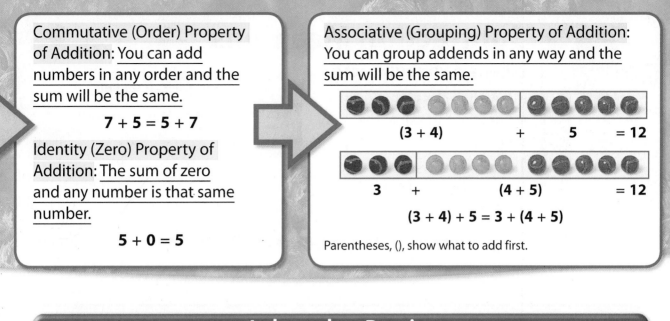

**Commutative (Order) Property of Addition:** You can add numbers in any order and the sum will be the same.

$$7 + 5 = 5 + 7$$

**Identity (Zero) Property of Addition:** The sum of zero and any number is that same number.

$$5 + 0 = 5$$

**Associative (Grouping) Property of Addition:** You can group addends in any way and the sum will be the same.

(3 + 4)    +    5    = 12

3    +    (4 + 5)    = 12

$$(3 + 4) + 5 = 3 + (4 + 5)$$

Parentheses, (), show what to add first.

## Independent Practice

Write each missing number.

**6.** ☐ $+ 8 = 8 + 2$

**7.** $19 +$ ☐ $= 19$

**8.** $(3 +$ ☐ $) + 2 = 2 + 8$

**9.** $4 + (2 + 3) = 4 +$ ☐

**10.** $7 + 3 =$ ☐ $+ 7$

**11.** ☐ $+ 25 = 25$

**12.** $(3 +$ ☐ $) + 6 = 3 + (4 + 6)$

**13.** $(6 + 2) +$ ☐ $= 8 + 7$

**14.** $(7 +$ ☐ $) + 6 = 7 + 6$

**15.** $(5 + 6) + 3 =$ ☐ $+ (5 + 6)$

## Problem Solving

ⓒ **MATHEMATICAL PRACTICES**

ⓒ **16. Use Structure** What property of addition is shown in the number sentence $3 + (6 + 5) = (6 + 5) + 3$? Explain.

**17.** Draw objects of 2 different colors to show that $4 + 3 = 3 + 4$.

ⓒ **18. Model** A lionfish has 13 spines on its back, 2 near the middle of its underside, and 3 on its underside near its tail. Write two different number sentences to find how many spines a lionfish has in all. What property did you use?

ⓒ **19. Model** Which number sentence matches the picture?

**A** $3 + 8 = 11$

**B** $11 + 0 = 11$

**C** $11 - 8 = 3$

**D** $11 - 3 = 8$

0 1 2 3 4 5 6 7 8 9 10 11 12

© Common Core

3.NBT.2 Fluently add and subtract within 1000 using strategies and algorithms based on place value, properties of operations, and/or the relationship between addition and subtraction.

# Subtraction Meanings

**Hands-On** counters

## When do you subtract?

Ms. Aydin's class is making school flags to sell at the school fair.

The table shows how many flags several students have made so far.

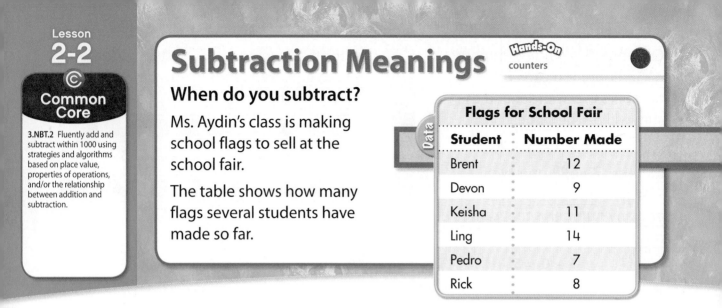

| Flags for School Fair | |
|---|---|
| **Student** | **Number Made** |
| Brent | 12 |
| Devon | 9 |
| Keisha | 11 |
| Ling | 14 |
| Pedro | 7 |
| Rick | 8 |

---

**Another Example** **Subtract to find a missing addend.**

Rick plans on making 13 flags. How many more flags does he need?

The parts and the whole show how addition and subtraction are related.

13 flags in all

| 8 | ? |
|---|---|

A **fact family** is a group of related facts using the same numbers.

The missing part is 5. This means Rick needs to make 5 more flags.

$8 + \boxed{\phantom{0}} = 13$

You can write a fact family when you know the parts and the whole.

$5 + 8 = 13 \qquad 8 + 5 = 13$
$13 - 8 = 5 \qquad 13 - 5 = 8$

The **difference** is the answer when subtracting two numbers.

---

## Guided Practice*

© **MATHEMATICAL PRACTICES**

### Do you know HOW?

Use the table to write and solve a number sentence.

1. How many more flags has Ling made than Devon?

2. How many more flags must Pedro make to have 15 in all? to have the same number as Ling?

### Do you UNDERSTAND?

© 3. **Model** Ling sold 8 of the flags she had made. Write a number sentence to find how many flags she has left. Then solve the problem.

© 4. **Write a Problem** Write and solve a word problem that can be solved by subtracting.

DIGITAL Animated Glossary, eTools
www.pearsonsuccessnet.com

*For another example, see Set B on page 58.

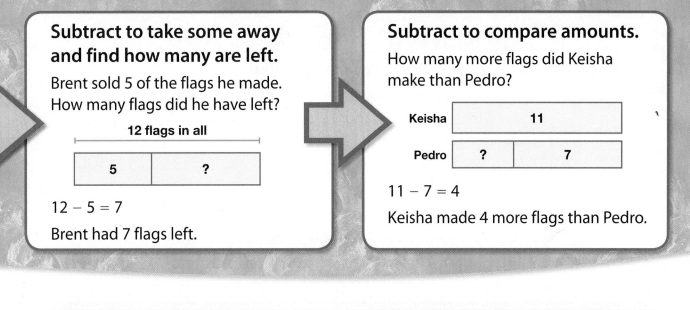

**Subtract to take some away and find how many are left.**

Brent sold 5 of the flags he made. How many flags did he have left?

12 flags in all

| 5 | ? |
|---|---|

$12 - 5 = 7$

Brent had 7 flags left.

**Subtract to compare amounts.**

How many more flags did Keisha make than Pedro?

| Keisha | 11 | |
|---|---|---|

| Pedro | ? | 7 |
|---|---|---|

$11 - 7 = 4$

Keisha made 4 more flags than Pedro.

## Independent Practice

Write a number sentence for each situation. Solve.

**5.** Pat has 15 pins. Chris has 9 pins. How many more pins does Pat have than Chris?

| Pat | 15 |
|---|---|

| Chris | 9 | ? |
|---|---|---|

**6.** How many more orange flags than green flags are there?

## Problem Solving

**7.** Ching had 12 pies to sell. After she sold some of the pies, she had 4 pies left. How many pies had Ching sold?

**8.** A pole holding a state flag is 10 feet tall. The height of the flag is 4 feet. How many feet taller is the pole than the flag?

**9.** The Jet Propulsion Lab had 9 missions between 2003 and 2006. Two of these missions were to study comets. How many of these missions did not study comets?

**10.** Kevin has 17 spelling words to learn this week. He already knows how to spell 9 of the words. How many words does he still need to learn?

© **11. Model** Rob had 17 pens. After he gave some of them to his friend, he had 8 pens. Which number sentence shows one way to find how many pens Rob gave to his friend?

**A** $17 + 8 = $ ▢     **B** $8 - 1 = $ ▢     **C** $17 - 1 = $ ▢     **D** $17 - $ ▢ $ = 8$

© Common Core

3.NBT.2 Fluently add and subtract within 1000 using strategies and algorithms based on place value, properties of operations, and/or the relationship between addition and subtraction.

# Using Mental Math to Add

## How can you add with mental math?

Dr. Gomez recorded how many whales, dolphins, and seals she saw. How many whales did she see during the two weeks?

Find $25 + 14$.

**Marine Animals Seen**

| Animal | Week 1 | Week 2 |
|---|---|---|
| Whales | 25 | 14 |
| Dolphins | 28 | 17 |
| Seals | 34 | 18 |

**Another Example** How can you make tens to add mentally?

How many dolphins did Dr. Gomez see during the two weeks?

You can make a ten to help you find $28 + 17$.

**Think**
- Break apart 17.
  $17 = 2 + 15$
  - Add 2 to 28
    $2 + 28 = 30$
  - Add 15 to 30.
    $30 + 15 = 45$

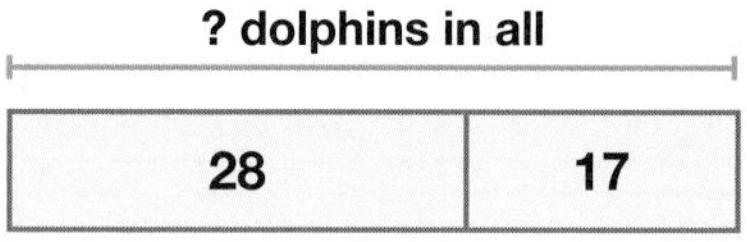

? dolphins in all

| 28 | 17 |
|---|---|

$28 + 17 = 45$

Dr. Gomez saw 45 dolphins.

**Explain It**

© 1. **Reason** How does knowing that $17 = 2 + 15$ help you find $28 + 17$ mentally?

2. What is another way to make a 10 to add $28 + 17$?

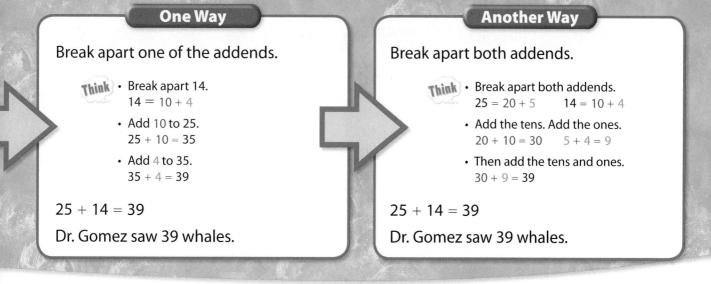

Break apart one of the addends.

Think • Break apart 14.
14 = 10 + 4

• Add 10 to 25.
25 + 10 = 35

• Add 4 to 35.
35 + 4 = 39

25 + 14 = 39

Dr. Gomez saw 39 whales.

Break apart both addends.

Think • Break apart both addends.
25 = 20 + 5    14 = 10 + 4

• Add the tens. Add the ones.
20 + 10 = 30    5 + 4 = 9

• Then add the tens and ones.
30 + 9 = 39

25 + 14 = 39

Dr. Gomez saw 39 whales.

## Guided Practice*

### MATHEMATICAL PRACTICES

### Do you know HOW?

**1.** Make a ten to add 38 + 26.

38 + 26
26 = 2 + 24
38 + ▢ = 40
40 + ▢ = 64
38 + 26 = ▢

**2.** Use breaking apart to add 25 + 12.

25 + 12
12 = 10 + 2
25 + 10 = ▢
▢ + 2 = 37
25 + 12 = ▢

### Do you UNDERSTAND?

© **3. Generalize** Compare the One Way and Another Way examples above. How are they the same? How are they different?

© **4. Reason** To find 37 + 28, you could add 37 + 30 = 67. Then what should you do next?

© **5. Persevere** Use breaking apart or making tens to find how many seals Dr. Gomez saw during the two weeks. Explain which method you used.

## Independent Practice

**Leveled Practice** Use breaking apart to add mentally.

**6.** 72 + 18
18 = 10 + ▢
72 + ▢ = 82
82 + ▢ = 90
72 + 18 = ▢

**7.** 34 + 25
25 = 20 + ▢
34 + ▢ = 54
▢ + 5 = 59
34 + 25 = ▢

**8.** 53 + 36
36 = ▢ + 6
53 + ▢ = 83
▢ + 6 = 89
53 + 36 = ▢

**Leveled Practice** Make a ten to add mentally.

**9.** 47 + 9

9 = ☐ + 6

47 + ☐ = 50

☐ + 6 = 56

47 + 9 = ☐

**10.** 55 + 37

37 = 5 + ☐

☐ + 5 = 60

60 + ☐ = 92

55 + 37 = ☐

**11.** 49 + 29

29 = ☐ + 28

49 + ☐ = 50

50 + ☐ = 78

49 + 29 = ☐

Find each sum using mental math.

**12.** 35 + 26

**13.** 50 + 42

**14.** 43 + 4

**15.** 71 + 13

**16.** 52 + 44

**17.** 7 + 54

**18.** 63 + 12

**19.** 62 + 34

**20.** 37 + 9

**21.** 5 + 38

**22.** 65 + 15

**23.** 33 + 23

**Problem Solving**

MATHEMATICAL
**PRACTICES**

**24.** How long can a python be?

**25.** What is the total length of the iguana?

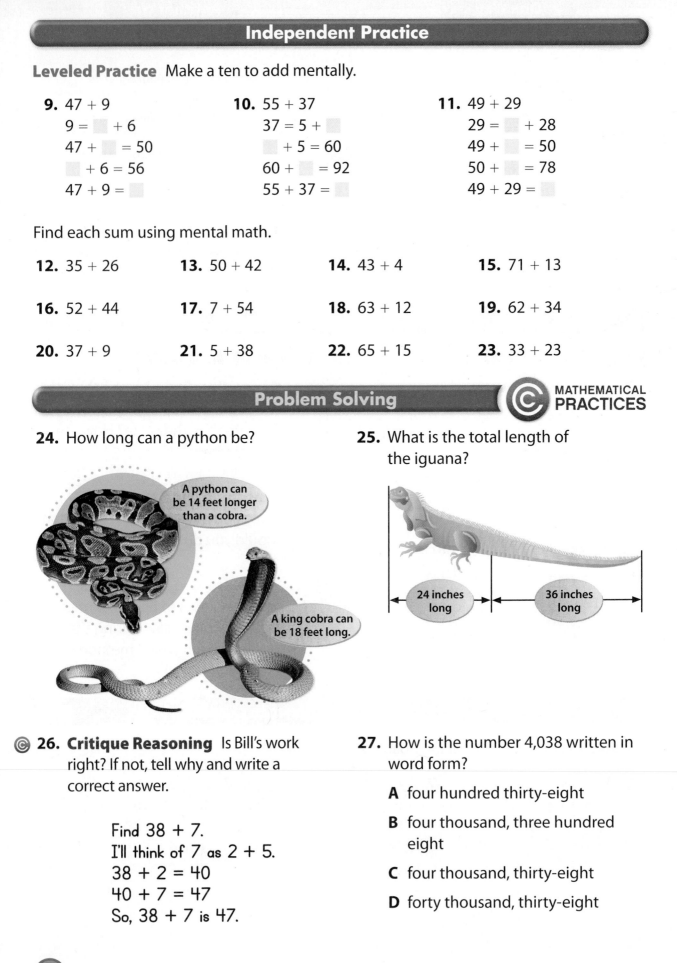

A python can be 14 feet longer than a cobra.

A king cobra can be 18 feet long.

24 inches long

36 inches long

**26. Critique Reasoning** Is Bill's work right? If not, tell why and write a correct answer.

Find 38 + 7.
I'll think of 7 as 2 + 5.
38 + 2 = 40
40 + 7 = 47
So, 38 + 7 is 47.

**27.** How is the number 4,038 written in word form?

**A** four hundred thirty-eight

**B** four thousand, three hundred eight

**C** four thousand, thirty-eight

**D** forty thousand, thirty-eight

## Adding with Mental Math

Use **tools**
**Place-Value Blocks**

Show two ways to make a ten to add 27 + 38.

**Step 1** ▭ Go to the
Place-Value Blocks eTool.
Click on the Two-part
workspace icon. In the
top space, show 27 with
place-value blocks. Show
38 in the bottom space.

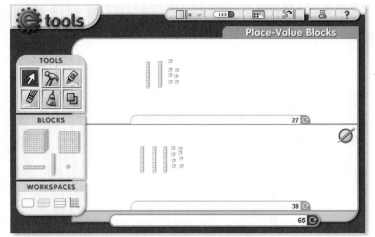

**Step 2** ↗ Use the arrow tool
to select ones from the
bottom space and drag
them to the top space.
Do this until you make a ten on top. The odometers show that
you have 30 + 35 = 65. So, 27 + 38 = 65, and 30 + 35 = 65.

**Step 3** Use the arrow tool to
move the blocks back
to show 27 + 38. Then
select ones from the
top space and drag
them to the bottom
space until you make a
ten on the bottom. The
odometers show that
you have 25 + 40 = 65.
So, 27 + 38 = 65, and
25 + 40 = 65.

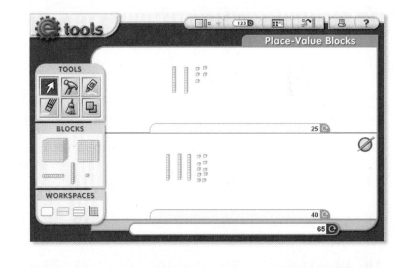

### Practice

Use the Place-Value Blocks eTool. Find two ways to
make a ten to add.

**1.** 47 + 29 = ▢ + ▢ = 76
47 + 29 = ▢ + ▢ = 76

**2.** 58 + 36 = ▢ + ▢ = 94
58 + 36 = ▢ + ▢ = 94

Common
Core

3.NBT.2 Fluently add and subtract within 1000 using strategies and algorithms based on place value, properties of operations, and/or the relationship between addition and subtraction.

# Using Mental Math to Subtract

## How can you subtract with mental math?

The store is having a sale on jackets. A jacket is on sale for $17 less than the original price. What is the sale price?

You can use mental math to subtract and solve this problem.

$52
$17 off!

---

## Guided Practice*

MATHEMATICAL PRACTICES

### Do you know HOW?

In **1–8**, find each difference using mental math.

**1.** 26 − 18

**2.** 34 − 19

**3.** 73 − 16

**4.** 45 − 27

**5.** 67 − 28

**6.** 83 − 39

**7.** 46 − 18

**8.** 49 − 19

### Do you UNDERSTAND?

© **9. Reason** In the One Way example above, why do you add 3 to 32 instead of subtract 3 from 32?

© **10. Communicate** Suppose a coat has an original price of $74 and it is on sale for $18 less than the original price. What is the sale price of the coat? How can you use mental math to solve this problem?

---

## Independent Practice

In **11–30**, find each difference using mental math.

**11.** 28 − 19

**12.** 66 − 18

**13.** 39 − 17

**14.** 68 − 11

**15.** 52 − 9

**16.** 75 − 12

**17.** 29 − 18

**18.** 49 − 18

**19.** 64 − 15

**20.** 43 − 16

**21.** 97 − 14

**22.** 86 − 13

**23.** 31 − 14

**24.** 98 − 17

**25.** 57 − 18

**26.** 72 − 19

**27.** 53 − 39

**28.** 27 − 19

**29.** 82 − 27

**30.** 73 − 39

*For another example, see Set D on page 59.

## Problem Solving

**MATHEMATICAL PRACTICES**

© **31. Communicate** The giant Rafflesia flower can be as wide as shown in the picture. One petal can be 18 inches wide. How can you use mental math to find how much wider the whole flower is than one petal?

**36 in.**

© **32. Critique Reasoning** To subtract $57 - 16$, Tom added 4 to each number, while Saul added 3 to each number. Will both methods work to find the correct answer? Explain.

In **33** and **34**, use the photo below.

**33. a** What is the sale price of the jeans? Describe one way you can use mental math to find the answer.

    **b** Maria bought two pairs of jeans. What was the total sale price of the jeans Maria bought?

© **34. Model** Which number sentence shows the original price of two pairs of jeans?

    **A** $46 + 46 = \square$

    **B** $46 + 18 = \square$

    **C** $18 + 18 = \square$

    **D** $46 - 18 = \square$

© **35. Model** Eva saved $38. She bought a book for $17. Which number sentence shows one way to find how much money Eva had left?

    **A** $38 + 17 = \square$

    **B** $38 - 17 = \square$

    **C** $\square - 38 = 17$

    **D** $\square - 17 = 38$

$46
SALE!
Take $18 off
the original price

Lesson
2-5

ⓒ
Common
Core

3.NBT.1 Use place value
understanding to round
whole numbers to the
nearest 10 or 100.

# Rounding

## How can you round numbers?

To the nearest 10, about how
many rocks does Tito have?

Round 394 to the nearest ten.
To round, <u>replace a number
with a number that tells
about how many.</u>

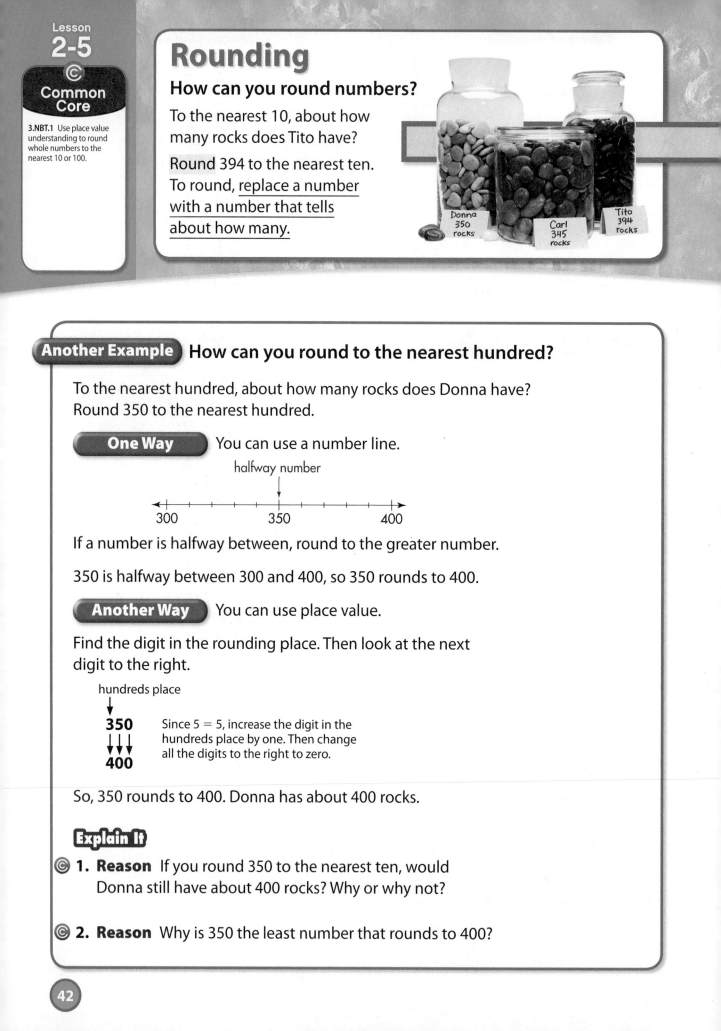

Donna
350
rocks

Carl
345
rocks

Tito
394
rocks

**Another Example** **How can you round to the nearest hundred?**

To the nearest hundred, about how many rocks does Donna have?
Round 350 to the nearest hundred.

**One Way** You can use a number line.

halfway number

300       350       400

If a number is halfway between, round to the greater number.

350 is halfway between 300 and 400, so 350 rounds to 400.

**Another Way** You can use place value.

Find the digit in the rounding place. Then look at the next
digit to the right.

hundreds place

**350**
↓↓↓
**400**

Since 5 = 5, increase the digit in the
hundreds place by one. Then change
all the digits to the right to zero.

So, 350 rounds to 400. Donna has about 400 rocks.

### Explain It

ⓒ **1. Reason** If you round 350 to the nearest ten, would
Donna still have about 400 rocks? Why or why not?

ⓒ **2. Reason** Why is 350 the least number that rounds to 400?

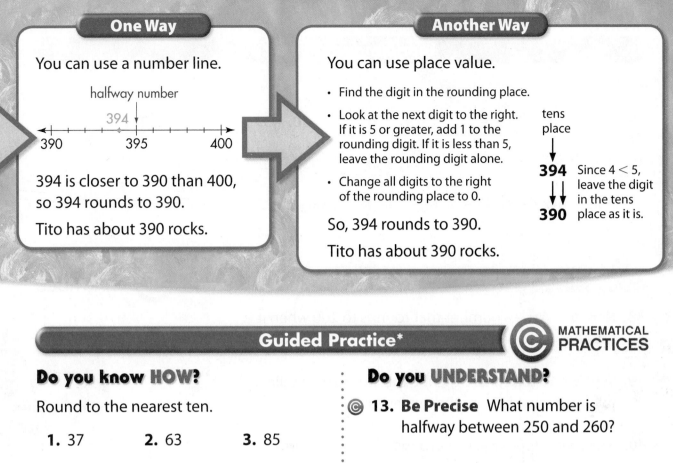

## One Way

You can use a number line.

halfway number
394 ↓

390    395    400

394 is closer to 390 than 400, so 394 rounds to 390.

Tito has about 390 rocks.

## Another Way

You can use place value.

- Find the digit in the rounding place.
- Look at the next digit to the right. If it is 5 or greater, add 1 to the rounding digit. If it is less than 5, leave the rounding digit alone.
- Change all digits to the right of the rounding place to 0.

So, 394 rounds to 390.

Tito has about 390 rocks.

tens place
↓
**394**  Since 4 < 5,
↓↓↓  leave the digit
↓↓↓  in the tens
**390**  place as it is.

---

## Guided Practice*

**MATHEMATICAL PRACTICES**

### Do you know HOW?

Round to the nearest ten.

**1.** 37      **2.** 63      **3.** 85

**4.** 654     **5.** 305     **6.** 752

Round to the nearest hundred.

**7.** 557     **8.** 149     **9.** 552

**10.** 207    **11.** 888    **12.** 835

### Do you UNDERSTAND?

Ⓒ **13. Be Precise** What number is halfway between 250 and 260?

Ⓒ **14. Reason** If Tito adds one more rock to his collection, about how many rocks will he have, rounded to the nearest ten? rounded to the nearest hundred? Explain your answer.

Ⓒ **15. Writing to Explain** Tell what you would do to round 46 to the nearest ten.

---

## Independent Practice

Round to the nearest ten.

**16.** 45      **17.** 68      **18.** 98      **19.** 24      **20.** 55

**21.** 249     **22.** 732     **23.** 235     **24.** 805     **25.** 703

**26.** Round 996 to the nearest ten. Explain your answer.

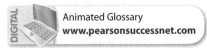
Animated Glossary
www.pearsonsuccessnet.com

Round to the nearest hundred.

**27.** 354    **28.** 504    **29.** 470    **30.** 439    **31.** 682

**32.** 945    **33.** 585    **34.** 850    **35.** 702    **36.** 870

**37.** Round 954 to the nearest hundred. Explain your answer.

**Problem Solving**

MATHEMATICAL
PRACTICES

© **38. Reason** Write a number that rounds to 200 when it is rounded to the nearest hundred.

293 steps

© **39. Writing to Explain** Describe the steps you would follow to round 439 to the nearest ten.

© **40. Reason** Suppose you are rounding to the nearest hundred. What is the greatest number that rounds to 600? What is the least number that rounds to 600?

© **41. Reason** A 3-digit number has the digits 2, 5, and 7. To the nearest hundred, it rounds to 800. What is the number?

**42.** To the nearest hundred dollars, a computer game costs $100. Which could **NOT** be the actual cost of the game?

A $89        C $110

B $91        D $150

**43.** What is the standard form of 700 + 40?

A 740        C 470

B 704        D 407

**44.** There are 293 steps to the top of the Leaning Tower of Pisa in Italy. To the nearest hundred, about how many steps are there?

# Algebra Connections

## Greater, Less, or Equal

Remember that the two sides of a number sentence can be equal or unequal. A symbol $>$, $<$, or $=$ tells how the sides compare. Using estimation or repeated reasoning can help you tell if one side is greater.

**Example**: $6 + 2 \bigcirc 8 + 1$

**Think** Is $6 + 2$ more than $8 + 1$?

Since $6 + 2 = 8$, 8 is already less than $8 + 1$. Write "$<$."

$$6 + 2 \enclose{circle}{<} 8 + 1$$

**Tip**

| $>$ | $<$ | $=$ |
|---|---|---|
| is greater than | is less than | is equal to |

© **Reason** Copy and complete. Replace the circle with $<$, $>$, or $=$. Check your answers.

1. $3 + 4 \bigcirc 2 + 7$     2. $9 + 1 \bigcirc 5 + 4$     3. $5 + 3 \bigcirc 6 + 3$

4. $2 + 9 \bigcirc 1 + 8$     5. $4 + 6 \bigcirc 4 + 7$     6. $8 + 6 \bigcirc 9 + 5$

7. $18 + 2 \bigcirc 16 + 4$     8. $15 + 5 \bigcirc 10 + 8$     9. $14 + 4 \bigcirc 12 + 4$

10. $17 + 3 \bigcirc 20 + 1$     11. $21 + 2 \bigcirc 19 + 2$     12. $27 + 3 \bigcirc 26 + 4$

For **13** and **14**, copy and complete each number sentence. Use it to help solve the problem.

13. Al and Jiro had some toy animals. Al had 8 lizards and 3 frogs. Jiro had 11 lizards and 2 frogs. Who had more toy animals?

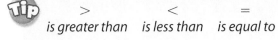

Al's toys     Jiro's toys

☐ + ☐ ◯ ☐ + ☐

© 15. **Write a Problem** Write a problem using this number sentence: $9 + 2 > 4 + 5$.

14. The number below each block tells how many are in a set. Val used all of the small and large cylinders. Jen used all of the small and large cubes. Who used more blocks?

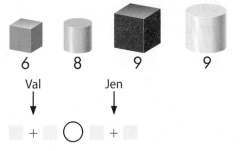

6     8     9     9

Val     Jen

☐ + ☐ ◯ ☐ + ☐

Lesson
2-6

Common Core

3.NBT.2 Fluently add and subtract within 1000 using strategies and algorithms based on place value, properties of operations, and/or the relationship between addition and subtraction.
Also 3.NBT.1, 3.OA.8

# Estimating Sums

**How can you estimate sums?**

Do the two pandas together weigh more than 500 pounds?

You can estimate to find out about how much the two pandas weigh.

Estimate 255 + 322.

Female
255
pounds

Male
322
pounds

---

**Another Example** **How can you estimate sums to the nearest ten?**

A panda eats a lot of bamboo in a week. Suppose one panda ate 148 pounds of bamboo and another ate 173 pounds. About how much bamboo did the two pandas eat?

Round to the nearest ten to estimate the sum.

148 ⟶ 150
173 ⟶ 170

Find 150 + 170.

**Think**
15 tens + 17 tens = 32 tens
32 tens = 320

The pandas ate about 320 pounds of bamboo.

**Explain It**

© 1. **Generalize** How is rounding to the nearest ten to estimate a sum similar to rounding to the nearest hundred?

© 2. **Reason** Which estimate do you think is closest to the actual sum, rounding to the nearest ten, or to the nearest hundred?

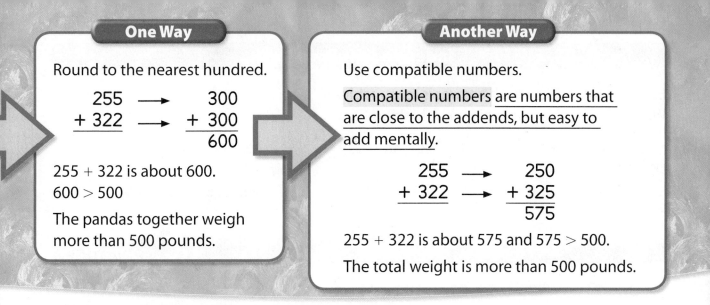

**One Way**

Round to the nearest hundred.

$$255 \longrightarrow 300$$
$$+\ 322 \longrightarrow +\ 300$$
$$\overline{\phantom{+\ 322} 600}$$

255 + 322 is about 600.

600 > 500

The pandas together weigh more than 500 pounds.

**Another Way**

Use compatible numbers.

Compatible numbers are numbers that are close to the addends, but easy to add mentally.

$$255 \longrightarrow 250$$
$$+\ 322 \longrightarrow +\ 325$$
$$\overline{\phantom{+\ 322} 575}$$

255 + 322 is about 575 and 575 > 500.

The total weight is more than 500 pounds.

---

## Guided Practice*  MATHEMATICAL PRACTICES

### Do you know HOW?

Round to the nearest ten to estimate.

**1.** 28 + 46  **2.** 75 + 17

Round to the nearest hundred to estimate.

**3.** 114 + 58  **4.** 198 + 426

Use compatible numbers to estimate.

**5.** 136 + 437  **6.** 654 + 253

### Do you UNDERSTAND?

© **7. Reason** If both addends are rounded up, will the estimate be greater than or less than the actual sum?

© **8. Construct Arguments** By rounding to the same place, everyone gets the same answer. Is this true if compatible numbers are used to estimate? Explain.

---

## Independent Practice

In **9–12**, round to the nearest ten to estimate.

**9.** 18 + 43  **10.** 75 + 72  **11.** 39 + 102  **12.** 376 + 295

In **13–16**, round to the nearest hundred to estimate.

**13.** 403 + 179  **14.** 462 + 251  **15.** 64 + 403  **16.** 539 + 399

In **17–20**, use compatible numbers to estimate.

**17.** 75 + 26  **18.** 167 + 27  **19.** 108 + 379  **20.** 145 + 394

Animated Glossary
www.pearsonsuccessnet.com

DIGITAL

Estimate to decide if each answer is reasonable.
Write *yes* or *no*. Then explain your thinking.

**21.** 32 + 58 = 70

**22.** 83 + 46 = 129

**23.** 55 + 64 = 99

**24.** 105 + 23 = 308

**25.** 713 + 118 = 831

**26.** 328 + 365 = 693

**Problem Solving**

MATHEMATICAL
PRACTICES

**Social Studies** In **27–29**, use the table at the right.

**27.** Which city is farthest from Gainesville?

**28.** Mr. Tyson drove from Gainesville to Tampa and back again. To the nearest ten miles, about how many miles did he drive?

**29.** Mr. Tyson drove from Tallahassee to Gainesville to Cocoa. To the nearest ten miles, about how many miles in all did he drive?

| Distance from Gainesville, FL | |
| --- | --- |
| **City** | **Miles Away** |
| Cocoa, FL | 165 miles |
| Miami, FL | 333 miles |
| Orlando, FL | 114 miles |
| Tallahassee, FL | 148 miles |
| Tampa, FL | 129 miles |

**30. Estimation** Round to the nearest hundred to estimate how many musicians in all are in the world's largest accordion band and the world's largest trombone band.

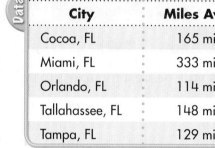

| World's Largest Bands | |
| --- | --- |
| Trombone | 284 musicians |
| Accordion | 625 musicians |

**31. Reason** Why might you round to the nearest ten instead of the nearest hundred when you estimate a sum?

**32. Communicate** How could you use rounding to estimate 268 + 354?

**33.** Write the number 3,500 in word form in two different ways.

**34.** How could you use compatible numbers to estimate 229 + 672?

**35. Think About the Structure** Jared has 138 marbles. Manny has 132 marbles. Which number sentence is best to estimate how many marbles they have in all?

**A** 38 + 32 = 70

**B** 100 + 100 = 200

**C** 108 + 102 = 210

**D** 140 + 130 = 270

# Mixed Problem Solving

© **Persevere**  Read the story and answer the questions.

## We Can't Wait!

Jamie and her sisters stared out the front window of their home. They were talking about all the good stories their grandmother always tells them when she visits. About 10 minutes ago, their dad had called home from the airport. He said that he was exactly 26 blocks away. He needed to make one more stop 12 blocks farther away. Then he would come home.

When Dad finally came around the street corner, the sisters jumped off the sofa and ran to the door. Dad arrived at the door with some grocery bags, a suitcase, and a special visitor. Soon the family would be hearing many good stories.

1. What conclusion can you draw?

2. When the sisters were staring out of the window, their dad had called about 10 minutes ago. Write a number of minutes that rounds to 10 minutes.

3. To the nearest 10 blocks, about how many blocks away from home was Dad when he called home?

4. To the nearest 10 blocks, about how many blocks did Dad travel from his last stop to home?

5. Look at the table below.

   Write the distances in order from least to greatest.

| Place | Distance from Home |
|---|---|
| Bakery | 38 blocks |
| Bank | 12 blocks |
| Grocery Store | 21 blocks |
| Toy Store | 26 blocks |

Data

© 6. **Use Structure**  Jamie earned some money doing chores. She wants to put 70 cents in her bank. What are two different ways she could use coins to make 70 cents? Make an organized list to help solve the problem.

Common
Core

**3.NBT.2** Fluently add and subtract within 1000 using strategies and algorithms based on place value, properties of operations, and/ or the relationship between addition and subtraction.
Also 3.NBT.1, 3.OA.8

# Estimating Differences

## How can you estimate differences?

All of the tickets for a concert were sold. So far, 126 people have arrived at the concert. About how many people who have tickets have not arrived?

Since you need to find *about* how many, you can estimate.

Estimate 493 − 126 by rounding.

**493 tickets sold**

---

**Another Example** **How can you use compatible numbers to estimate differences?**

The Perry family is taking a car trip. The trip is 372 miles long. So far, the family has traveled 149 miles. About how many miles are left to travel?

Use compatible numbers to estimate 372 − 149.

Remember:  Compatible numbers are numbers that are close and easy to work with.

$$
\begin{array}{r}
372 \longrightarrow 375 \\
- 149 \longrightarrow - 150 \\
\hline
225
\end{array}
$$

The Perry family still has about 225 miles to travel.

**Explain It**

1. **Reason**  How are the numbers 375 and 150 easy to work with?

2. Use a different pair of compatible numbers to estimate 372 − 149.

3. **Construct Arguments**  Is an estimate enough to solve this problem? Why or why not?

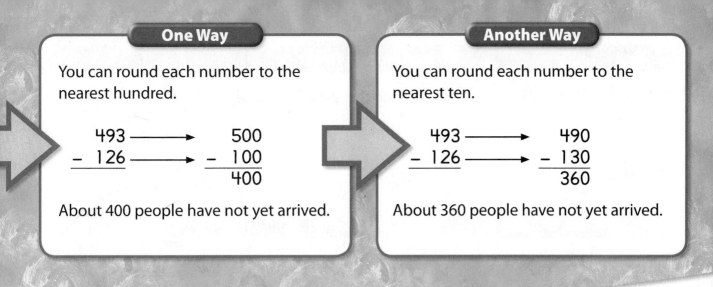

## One Way

You can round each number to the nearest hundred.

$$493 \longrightarrow 500$$
$$- \ 126 \longrightarrow - \ 100$$
$$\overline{400}$$

About 400 people have not yet arrived.

## Another Way

You can round each number to the nearest ten.

$$493 \longrightarrow 490$$
$$- \ 126 \longrightarrow - \ 130$$
$$\overline{360}$$

About 360 people have not yet arrived.

## Guided Practice*

MATHEMATICAL PRACTICES

### Do you know HOW?

In **1** and **2**, round to the nearest hundred to estimate each difference.

**1.** 321 − 112      **2.** 255 − 189

In **3** and **4**, round to the nearest ten to estimate each difference.

**3.** 579 − 214      **4.** 216 − 97

In **5** and **6**, use compatible numbers to estimate each difference.

**5.** 328 − 207      **6.** 472 − 148

### Do you UNDERSTAND?

© **7. Reason** In the problem above, which way of rounding gives an estimate that is closer to the actual difference? Explain why.

© **8. Communicate** The theater sold 415 tickets to the comedy show. So far, 273 people have arrived at the show. About how many more people are expected to arrive? Tell which estimation method you used and how you found your answer.

## Independent Practice

In **9–11**, round to the nearest hundred to estimate each difference.

**9.** 186 − 75      **10.** 704 − 369      **11.** 291 − 93

In **12–17**, round to the nearest ten to estimate each difference.

**12.** 88 − 32      **13.** 149 − 95      **14.** 361 − 117

**15.** 75 − 41      **16.** 86 − 38      **17.** 227 − 121

In **18–23**, use compatible numbers to estimate each difference.

**18.** 77 − 28

**19.** 202 − 144

**20.** 611 − 168

**21.** 512 − 205

**22.** 342 − 153

**23.** 904 − 31

**Problem Solving**

MATHEMATICAL
**PRACTICES**

Use the table for **24–27**.

**24.** The concert hall sold 28 fewer tickets for the Sunday concert than for the Friday concert. About how many tickets were sold for the Sunday concert?

**25.** About how many tickets in all were sold for Thursday and Friday?

| Grand Concert Hall | |
| --- | --- |
| **Day of Concert** | **Number of Tickets Sold** |
| Wednesday | 506 |
| Thursday | 323 |
| Friday | 251 |
| Saturday | 427 |
| Sunday | |

© **26. Think About the Structure** About how many more tickets were sold for the Wednesday concert than for the Friday concert? Write a number sentence that uses numbers rounded to the nearest ten to estimate how many more. Explain your answer.

© **27. Model** Which number sentence shows the best way to estimate how many fewer tickets were sold for the Friday concert than the Thursday concert?

**A** 400 − 200 = 200

**B** 300 − 300 = 0

**C** 325 − 200 = 125

**D** 325 − 250 = 75

© **28. Communicate** About how many feet longer was a *Brachiosaurus* than a *T. rex*? Use compatible numbers to estimate. Explain your answer.

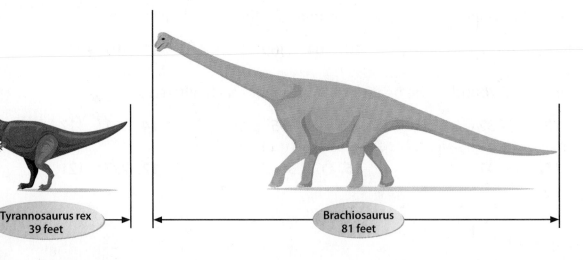

Tyrannosaurus rex
39 feet

Brachiosaurus
81 feet

# Mixed Problem Solving

The length of one year on a planet is the total time for the planet to make one complete trip around the Sun.

1. About how many fewer Earth days is a year on Mercury than a year on Earth?

2. About how many more Earth days is a year on Mars than a year on Earth?

| Length of Year | |
| --- | --- |
| **Planet** | **Length of Year** (in Earth Days) |
| Mercury | 88 |
| Venus | 225 |
| Earth | 365 |
| Mars | 687 |
| Jupiter | 4,330 |
| Saturn | 10,756 |
| Uranus | 30,687 |
| Neptune | 60,190 |

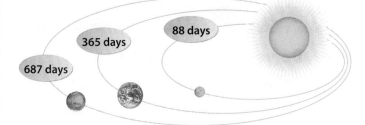

3. Which planet has a digit 6 with a value of sixty thousand in the length of its year?

4. Which planet has a year that is about six thousand Earth days more than Jupiter's?

5. **Be Precise** Which space object listed in the table at the right has an average surface temperature closest to Mercury's?

| Space Object | Average Surface Temperature |
| --- | --- |
| Mercury | 332°F |
| Earth | 59°F |
| The Moon | 225°F |
| Venus | 854°F |

6. Write the average surface temperatures in order from least to greatest.

7. **Use Tools** Meg's favorite planet has at least 5 letters in its name. The length of its year is less than 10,000 Earth days. List all the planets that fit these clues. Make an organized list to help solve the problem.

Common
Core

**3.NBT.2** Fluently add and subtract within 1000 using strategies and algorithms based on place value, properties of operations, and/or the relationship between addition and subtraction.

# Making Sense of Addition and Subtraction Equations

## How do equations work?

The pan balance shows $20 + 9 = 29$. An equation is a number sentence that uses an equal sign (=) to show that the value to its left is the same as the value to its right.

20 + 9 = 29

---

## Guided Practice*

**MATHEMATICAL PRACTICES**

### Do you know HOW?

In **1** and **2**, decide if the two sides are equal. If yes, write =. If no, write ≠ (not equal).

**1.** $7 - 3 \bigcirc 4$      **2.** $14 \bigcirc 8 + 8$

In **3–6**, find the value for $n$ that makes the equation true.

**3.** $9 + n = 11$      **4.** $8 = 12 - n$

**5.** $10 + n = 17$      **6.** $n - 3 = 6$

### Do you UNDERSTAND?

**7. Construct Arguments** Explain why the equation $9 + 7 = 16$ is true.

**8.** What is the value of $n$ in $5 = 5 + n$?

**9. Critique Arguments** Sue says that the value of $n$ in the equation below is 12. Is she correct? Why or why not?
$9 = n + 3$

---

## Independent Practice

In **10–13**, decide if the two sides are equal. If yes, write =. If no, write ≠ (not equal).

**10.** $13 \bigcirc 0 + 12$    **11.** $9 - 4 \bigcirc 13$    **12.** $22 + 9 \bigcirc 31$    **13.** $45 \bigcirc 50 - 5$

In **14–21**, find the value for $n$ that makes the equation true.

**14.** $18 = 11 + n$    **15.** $n - 4 = 6$    **16.** $25 = 19 + n$    **17.** $16 - n = 7$

**18.** $1 + n = 1$    **19.** $21 = n - 2$    **20.** $n = 32 + 6$    **21.** $4 = 5 - n$

DIGITAL

Animated Glossary
www.pearsonsuccessnet.com

*For another example, see Set F on page 59.*

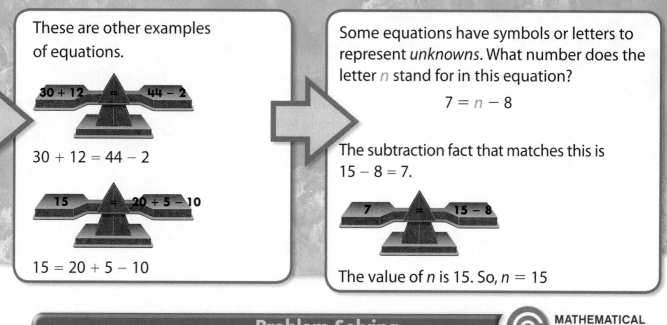

These are other examples of equations.

30 + 12 = 44 − 2

15 = 20 + 5 − 10

Some equations have symbols or letters to represent *unknowns*. What number does the letter *n* stand for in this equation?

$$7 = n - 8$$

The subtraction fact that matches this is $15 - 8 = 7$.

The value of *n* is 15. So, $n = 15$

## Problem Solving

For **22** and **23**, copy and complete the equation shown below each problem. Use it to solve the problem.

**22.** Nate has 10 river stones. Chen has 26 river stones. How many more river stones does Chen have than Nate?
$10 + n = 26$

**23.** Tania collected 8 fewer leaves than Gwen. Tania collected 12 leaves. How many leaves did Gwen collect?
$n - 8 = 12$

© **24. Model** Ana has 5 stamps. Ana's sister has *n* stamps. Together they have 16 stamps. Write an equation to model the problem. How many stamps does Ana's sister have?

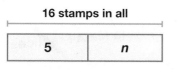

16 stamps in all

| 5 | n |
|---|---|

**25.** Dean helps at the family restaurant. He keeps a record of the hours he works. How many hours in all did he work on Monday and Wednesday?

| Dean's Work Hours | |
|---|---|
| **Days** | **Hours** |
| Monday | 6 |
| Tuesday | 5 |
| Wednesday | 8 |

© **26. Write a Problem** Write and solve a problem to match the equation below.
$48 = 20 + n$

© **28. Reasonableness** Stan added $36 + 29$ and got 515. Explain why his answer is NOT reasonable.

**27.** Which value for *n* makes the equation below true?
$n - 6 = 10$

**A** $n = 4$      **C** $n = 16$

**B** $n = 12$     **D** $n = 17$

**Common Core**

**3.NBT.2** Fluently add and subtract within 1000 using strategies and algorithms based on place value, properties of operations, and/or the relationship between addition and subtraction.
Also **3.OA.8**

Problem Solving

# Reasonableness

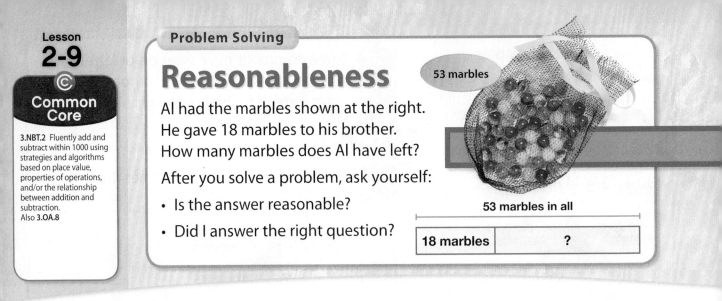

53 marbles

Al had the marbles shown at the right. He gave 18 marbles to his brother. How many marbles does Al have left?

After you solve a problem, ask yourself:

- Is the answer reasonable?
- Did I answer the right question?

53 marbles in all

| 18 marbles | ? |

---

## Guided Practice*

 MATHEMATICAL PRACTICES

### Do you know HOW?

1. Rosita is reading a book that is 65 pages long. She has 27 pages left to read. How many pages has she already read?

65 pages in all

| ? | 27 |

### Do you UNDERSTAND?

2. **Communicate** Describe how to check that your answer is reasonable and that you have answered the right question.

3. **Write a Problem** Write and solve a problem. Check that your answer is reasonable.

---

## Independent Practice

MATHEMATICAL PRACTICES

**Reasonableness** Solve. Then check that your answer is reasonable.

4. James is reading a book that is 85 pages long. He read 35 pages yesterday and 24 pages today. How many pages did James read in the two days?

? pages in all

| 35 | 24 |

**Applying Math Practices**

- What am I asked to find?
- What else can I try?
- How are quantities related?
- How can I explain my work?
- How can I use math to model the problem?
- Can I use tools to help?
- Is my work precise?
- Why does this work?
- How can I generalize?

5. Kyle had 56 model cars. He gave his brother 36 of them. How many model cars does Kyle have now?

*For another example, see Set G on page 59.

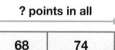

| Jim's Answer | Sally's Answer | Pablo's Answer |
|---|---|---|

**Jim's Answer**

53 − 18 = 35
Al's brother has
35 marbles.

53 − 18 is about
50 − 20, or 30.

35 is close to 30,
so 35 is reasonable.

The number 35 is
reasonable, but Jim
did not answer the
right question.

**Sally's Answer**

53 − 18 = 45
Al has 45 marbles left.

53 − 18 is about
50 − 20, or 30.

45 is not close to 30,
so 45 is not reasonable.

Sally answered the
right question, but
the number 45 is not
reasonable.

**Pablo's Answer**

53 − 18 = 35
Al has 35 marbles left.

53 − 18 is about
50 − 20, or 30.

35 is close to 30,
so 35 is reasonable.

The number 35 is
reasonable, and Pablo
did answer the right
question.

**Independent Practice**

MATHEMATICAL
**PRACTICES**

© **Reasonableness** Use the table to solve **6–8**.
Estimate, then check that your answer is reasonable.

**6.** How many points were scored all
together in Games 1 and 2?

? points in all

| 68 | 74 |
|---|---|

Data

| Total Points Scored | |
|---|---|
| **Games** | **Points** |
| Game 1 | 68 |
| Game 2 | 74 |
| Game 3 | 89 |

**7.** There were 39 points scored in the
first half of Game 1. How many points
were scored in the second half?

68 points in all

| 39 | ? |
|---|---|

© **8. Estimation** About how many
points were scored all together
in the three games?

? points in all

| 70 | 70 | 90 |
|---|---|---|

**9.** Carl practices the piano 45 minutes
each day. Today, he practiced
15 minutes after school and
10 minutes before dinner. How
much time does he still need
to practice?

A 70 minutes    C 35 minutes

B 60 minutes    D 20 minutes

**10.** Carrie has 15 pennies. Her brother
has 10 more pennies than Carrie.
How many pennies do they have
in all?

A 40 pennies    C 10 pennies

B 25 pennies    D 5 pennies

Set A, pages 32–33

Use the Associative Property of Addition.

$(2 + \boxed{\phantom{5}}) + 1 = 2 + (5 + 1)$    You can group addends
$(2 + 5) + 1 = 2 + (5 + 1)$    in any way and the sum will be the same.

Use the Commutative Property of Addition.

$7 + \boxed{\phantom{6}} = 6 + 7$    You can add numbers in any order
$7 + 6 = 6 + 7$    and the sum will be the same.

**Remember** the Identity Property of Addition: the sum of any number and zero is that same number.

Write each missing number.

1. $(2 + 3) + 5 = 2 + (3 + \boxed{\phantom{5}})$

2. $\boxed{\phantom{5}} + 0 = 6$

3. $(1 + \boxed{\phantom{5}}) + 6 = 1 + (4 + 6)$

Set B, pages 34–35

Write a number sentence, then solve.

Anthony has 10 flags. He gives 7 flags to his friends to wave during a parade on the 4$^{th}$ of July. How many flags does Anthony have left?

| 10 flags in all | |
|:---:|:---:|
| 7 | ? |

$10 - 7 = 3$

Anthony has 3 flags left.

**Remember** that you can subtract to find how many are left, to compare, or to find a missing addend.

Write a number sentence, then solve.

1. A band has eight members. Five of the band members sing. How many do not sing?

Set C, pages 36–38, 42–44, 46–48

Round 867 to the nearest hundred.

hundreds place

867
↓↓↓
900

Since 6 > 5, increase the digit in the hundreds place by one. Then change all the digits to the right to zero.

867 rounds to 900.

Estimate $478 + 134$.

Use compatible numbers.

$\begin{array}{r} 478 \longrightarrow 470 \\ + 134 \longrightarrow + 130 \\ \hline 600 \end{array}$

**Remember** that you can break apart addends to use mental math.

Find each sum using mental math.

1. $30 + 56$      2. $45 + 19$

In **3–8**, estimate each sum.
Round to the nearest hundred.

3. $367 + 319$      4. $732 + 110$

Round to the nearest ten.

5. $98 + 42$      6. $459 + 213$

Use compatible numbers.

7. $372 + 123$      8. $211 + 164$

Use mental math to find 83 − 16.

20 is easier to subtract than 16.
So, add 4 to each number and then subtract.

$$83 + 4 = 87 \text{ and } 16 + 4 = 20$$
$$87 - 20 = 67 \text{ so } 83 - 16 = 67$$

**Remember** to change each number in the same way.

Find each difference using mental math.

**1.** 56 − 14   **2.** 31 − 5

Estimate 486 − 177.

Round each number to the nearest hundred.

$$
\begin{array}{r}
486 \longrightarrow 500 \\
- \ 177 \longrightarrow - \ 200 \\
\hline
300
\end{array}
$$

Or use compatible numbers.

$$
\begin{array}{r}
486 \longrightarrow 500 \\
- \ 177 \longrightarrow - \ 175 \\
\hline
325
\end{array}
$$

**Remember** to check place value when rounding.

For **1–4**, estimate each difference.

Round to the nearest hundred.

**1.** 367 − 319   **2.** 872 − 110

Use compatible numbers.

**3.** 472 − 228   **4.** 911 − 347

In an equation, the value on the left is equal to the value on the right.

What is the value of $n$ that makes the equation $4 + n = 12$ true?

You can think about an addition fact.
Since $4 + 8 = 12$, then the value of $n = 8$.

**Remember** that you can think of an addition or subtraction fact to find the value of $n$.

Find the value for $n$ that makes each equation true.

**1.** $7 + n = 15$   **2.** $6 = 10 - n$

Carla's book has 87 pages. She read 49 pages. How many pages are left to read?

Estimate: 87 − 49 is about 90 − 50, or 40.
        87 − 49 = 38.

Carla has 38 pages to read. The answer is reasonable because it is close to the estimate.

**Remember** to check if your answer is reasonable.

**1.** Lucy has 45 tulips. There are 27 red tulips. The rest are yellow. How many yellow tulips does Lucy have?

**Multiple Choice**

 **ASSESSMENT**

1. To the nearest ten pounds, Riley weighs 90 pounds. Which could be her weight? (2-5)

   **A** 84 pounds

   **B** 86 pounds

   **C** 95 pounds

   **D** 98 pounds

2. Mario wants to have 15 insects in his collection. He has 8 insects. Which number sentence shows a way to find how many more insects Mario needs to collect? (2-2)

   **A** $15 - 7 = $ ▨

   **B** $15 - $ ▨ $= 7$

   **C** $8 + 15 = $ ▨

   **D** $8 + $ ▨ $= 15$

3. Rex has 252 football cards and 596 baseball cards. Which number sentence shows the best estimate of how many cards Rex has in all, using compatible numbers? (2-6)

   **A** $300 + 550 = 850$

   **B** $300 + 500 = 800$

   **C** $250 + 550 = 800$

   **D** $250 + 600 = 850$

4. Tom had $41. He spent $17. Which is the best estimate of how much he had left? (2-7)

   **A** $60

   **B** $30

   **C** $20

   **D** $10

5. Which number sentence is shown? (2-2)

   **A** $3 + 7 = 10$

   **B** $17 - 7 = 10$

   **C** $7 + 3 = 10$

   **D** $10 - 7 = 3$

6. Tropical Fish Warehouse had 98 goldfish on Monday. By Friday, they had sold 76 of the goldfish. How many goldfish had not been sold? Use mental math to solve. (2-4)

   **A** 22

   **B** 32

   **C** 38

   **D** 174

7. Which number sentence can be used to find how many erasers in all? (2-1)

   **A** $8 + 6 = 14$

   **B** $9 + 6 = 15$

   **C** $9 + 5 = 14$

   **D** $3 + 6 = 9$

8. Mr. Kipper's class collected $453 for the local animal shelter. What is $453 rounded to the nearest hundred? (2-5)

9. Ava swam for 39 minutes on Saturday and 49 minutes on Sunday. To find 39 + 49, Ava made a ten, as shown below. What is the missing number? (2-3)

   $39 + 49 = 40 + \boxed{\phantom{0}} = 88$

10. Find the value for n that will make the following equation true. (2-8)

    $18 = 9 + n$

11. Lee drove 348 miles on Monday and 135 miles on Tuesday. Is 313 miles a reasonable answer for how much farther Lee drove on Monday than on Tuesday? Explain your answer. (2-9)

12. Find the value for n that will make the following equation true. (2-8)

    $22 - n = 9$

13. To subtract 62 − 17 mentally, Talia subtracted 62 − 20 = 42 first. What should Talia do next to find the difference? (2-4)

14. Kaitlyn read a 48-page book. Her sister read a 104-page book. Give an estimate for the total number of pages the sisters read. (2-6)

15. Shawn had 342 cards. He gave 128 cards to his sister. Estimate how many cards he had left. Round to the nearest ten to estimate your answer. (2-7)

16. A zoo has 52 kinds of snakes and 12 kinds of lizards. Estimate how many more kinds of snakes than lizards are in the zoo. (2-7)

17. Kal spent 28 minutes on math homework and 43 minutes on science homework. Use mental math to find how much more time he spent on science than on math. (2-4)

18. Round to the nearest hundred to estimate the difference 398 − 129. (2-7)

19. What property of addition is shown in the number sentence 3 + 9 = 9 + 3? Explain. (2-1)

20. Celia has $26 and Juan has $12. Use breaking apart to find how much money Celia and Juan have together. (2-3)

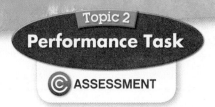
Mrs. Carlton is in charge of the school carnival. She bought all the items shown on the shopping list.

1. Meg used 6 of the poster board sheets to make signs for the carnival. How many sheets of poster board are left? On a separate piece of paper, draw and label a picture and write a number sentence to explain.

**School Carnival Shopping List**

| | |
|---|---|
| 5 | rolls of tickets |
| 18 | sheets of poster board |
| 84 | balloons |
| 364 | small prizes |
| 248 | large prizes |

2. Which property of addition will let you add the number of rolls of tickets to the number of sheets of poster board in any order and get the same sum of items?

3. There are 75 tickets on each roll of tickets. The first hour of the carnival, 30 tickets were sold from one roll. Use mental math to find how many tickets were left on the roll. Explain your thinking.

4. Miguel used all the balloons to decorate the booths and needed 16 more balloons to finish the job. Use mental math to find how many balloons he needed in all. Then explain your thinking.

5. Estimate how many small prizes and large prizes were bought for the carnival. Explain the method you used to estimate.

6. Estimate how many more small prizes were bought than large prizes. Explain the method you used to estimate.

7. Sarah, Maria and Ken each took home 3 balloons at the end of the carnival. How many balloons did they take home in all? Write a number sentence to show how you solved the problem.

### Topic 3

# Using Place Value to Add and Subtract

▼ How much fresh and processed fruit does a person eat in a year? You will find out in Lesson 3-9.

## Review What You Know!

### Vocabulary

Choose the best term from the box.

- difference
- estimate
- order
- regroup

1. When you trade 1 ten for 10 ones, you _?_.

2. The answer in subtraction is the _?_.

3. When you find an answer that is close to the exact answer, you _?_.

### Estimating Differences

Round to the nearest ten to estimate each difference.

**4.** 255 − 104    **5.** 97 − 61    **6.** 302 − 38

Round to the nearest hundred to estimate each difference.

**7.** 673 − 250    **8.** 315 − 96    **9.** 789 − 713

### Compatible Numbers

©**10. Writing to Explain** Use compatible numbers to estimate the difference 478 − 123. Explain why the numbers you chose are compatible.

**11.** How is rounding to estimate an answer different from using compatible numbers?

**Topic Essential Question**
- What are standard procedures for adding and subtracting whole numbers?

# Interactive Learning

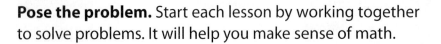

**Pose the problem.** Start each lesson by working together to solve problems. It will help you make sense of math.

Lesson 3-1

Ⓒ **Reason**  Solve any way you choose. Think about place value.

Find the sum of 327 + 241. Show all of your work.

$$327 + 241$$

Lesson 3-2

Ⓒ **Use Tools**  Solve using place-value blocks.

Use place-value blocks to find the sum of 146 + 247. Explain how you found the answer.

Lesson 3-3

Ⓒ **Use Tools**  Solve using any techniques you have learned.

Suppose a bus drives 276 miles on Monday and 248 miles on Tuesday. How many miles does the bus travel in all? Explain how you found the answer.

Lesson 3-4

Ⓒ **Generalize**  Solve. Use what you learned in the previous lesson to help.

The pet store has 162 goldfish, 124 angel fish, and 53 puffer fish. How many fish are there in all? How might an estimate help you solve the problem? Explain.

Puffer fish
53

Angel fish
124

Goldfish
162

Lesson 3-5

Ⓒ **Use Tools**  Solve. Draw a picture to help, and then write a number sentence.

An aquarium has 25 guppies and 18 goldfish in it. How many fish live in the aquarium? Show all of your work.

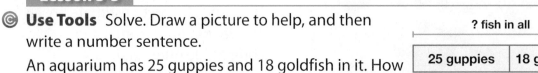

? fish in all

| 25 guppies | 18 goldfish |

### Lesson 3-6

© **Reason** Solve any way you choose. Think about place value.

How can you find the difference of 534 − 108 by breaking the problem into several smaller subtraction problems?

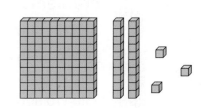

### Lesson 3-7

© **Use Tools** Solve using place value blocks.

Use place-value blocks to find 246 − 153. Explain how you found the answer.

### Lesson 3-8

© **Use Tools** Solve using any techniques you have learned.

Last year there were 347 houses for sale in Mill County. Of these, 162 were sold. How many houses were not sold? Explain how you found the answer.

$$347 - 162$$

### Lesson 3-9

© **Generalize** Solve using what you learned in previous lessons.

A community center needs to raise $302 to buy a printer. So far, it has raised $164. How much more does the center need to raise? Explain how you found the answer.

### Lesson 3-10

© **Model** Solve. Use the Problem-Solving Recording Sheet to help.

The Jackson School has 2 floors and 600 students. If 200 students are on the first floor, how many students are on the second floor? Use your Problem-Solving Recording Sheet to complete your work.

Name _____
Problem-Solving Recording Sheet      Teaching Tool 1
Problem:

Find?        Know?        Strategies?

**Common Core**

3.NBT.2 Fluently add and subtract within 1000 using strategies and algorithms based on place value, properties of operations, and/or the relationship between addition and subtraction.

# Adding with an Expanded Algorithm

**How can you break large addition problems into smaller ones?**

Find the sum 243 + 179.

Each digit in each number can be modeled with place-value blocks. You can use place value to add the numbers.

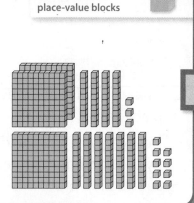

**Hands-On** place-value blocks

---

## Guided Practice*

**MATHEMATICAL PRACTICES**

### Do you know HOW?

In **1** and **2**, name the value of the digits in these numbers.

**1.** the 7 in 700    **2.** the 4 in 542

**3.** Complete these steps to find 375 + 412.

| Hundreds | Tens | Ones | Total |
|----------|------|------|-------|
| 300 | 70 | 5 | |
| + 400 | + 10 | + 2 | |

**4.** Find 308 + 494.

### Do you UNDERSTAND?

**5. Reason** How are the three problems in the example related to the 3-digit problem you started with?

**6. Communicate** Suppose you were adding 405 + 527. What would the tens problem be? Why?

**7.** Write the problems you could use to find 623 + 281.

---

## Independent Practice

In **8** and **9**, complete the steps to find each sum.

**8.** 550 + 423

| Hundreds | Tens | Ones | Total |
|----------|------|------|-------|
| 500 | 50 | 0 | |
| + 400 | + 20 | + 3 | |

**9.** 546 + 232

| Hundreds | Tens | Ones | Total |
|----------|------|------|-------|
| 500 | 40 | 6 | |
| + 200 | + 30 | + 2 | |

In **10–15**, find each sum.

**10.** 185 + 613.    **11.** 730 + 168.    **12.** 645 + 314.

**13.** 315 + 251.    **14.** 288 + 103.    **15.** 561 + 332.

eTools
www.pearsonsuccessnet.com

DIGITAL

*For another example, see Set A on page 92.

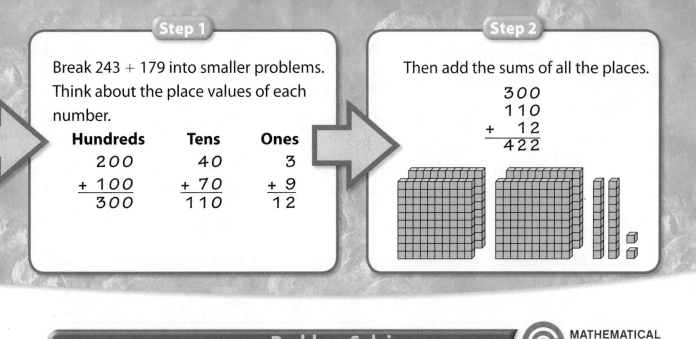

Break 243 + 179 into smaller problems. Think about the place values of each number.

| Hundreds | Tens | Ones |
|---|---|---|
| 200 | 40 | 3 |
| + 100 | + 70 | + 9 |
| 300 | 110 | 12 |

Then add the sums of all the places.

```
  300
  110
+  12
  422
```

## Problem Solving

© **MATHEMATICAL PRACTICES**

**16.** John read a book with 377 pages. Jess read a book with 210 pages. How many pages in all did they read?

© **17. Persevere** Anne made a necklace with 176 beads. Lynn made one with 254 beads. How many beads did they use in all?

**18.** There are 431 people watching a soccer game at a stadium. Then, 245 more people arrive. How many people are at the soccer game now?

© **19. Reason** Bill needs to find 318 + 230. Into what three smaller problems can he break this addition?

© **20. Writing to Explain** Paulo wants to add the points his favorite basketball team scored in the last two games. The team scored 137 points and 112 points. Describe how Paulo can add these numbers using smaller problems.

© **21. Communicate** Leah wants to find the sum 335 + 420. She wants to break the problem into easier problems. Does she need to find a sum for the ones? Explain.

© **22. Persevere** A movie theater sold 275 tickets on Monday and 226 tickets on Tuesday. How many tickets did the movie theater sell in all?

**23.** Which of the following shows the sum of the hundreds, tens, and ones for 331 + 516?

  **A** 800 + 40 + 6

  **B** 800 + 40 + 7

  **C** 700 + 40 + 8

  **D** 400 + 80 + 8

Lesson
**3-2**

ⓒ
**Common
Core**

3.NBT.2 Fluently add and subtract within 1000 using strategies and algorithms based on place value, properties of operations, and/or the relationship between addition and subtraction.

# Models for Adding 3-Digit Numbers

**Hands-On**
place-value blocks

## How can you add 3-digit numbers with place-value blocks?

You can add whole numbers by using place value to break them apart.

Find 143 + 285.

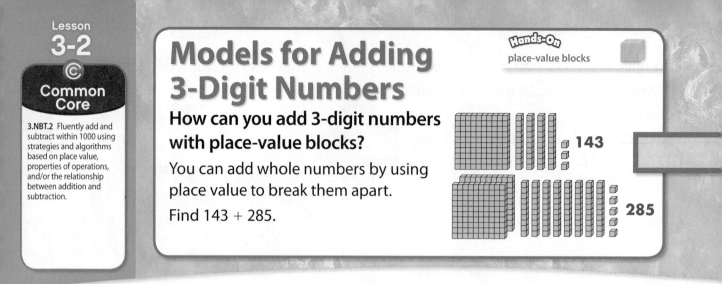

**143**

**285**

---

**Another Example** **How do you add with two regroupings?**

Find 148 + 276.

**Step 1** Add the ones.
8 ones + 6 ones = 14 ones

Regroup.
14 ones = 1 ten 4 ones

**Step 2** Add the tens.
1 ten + 4 tens + 7 tens = 12 tens

Regroup.
12 tens = 1 hundred 2 tens

**Step 3** Add the hundreds.
1 hundred + 1 hundred +
2 hundreds = 4 hundreds

So, 148 + 276 = 424.

**Explain It**

**1.** Why did you need to regroup two times?

ⓒ **2. Reason** Why didn't you regroup hundreds?

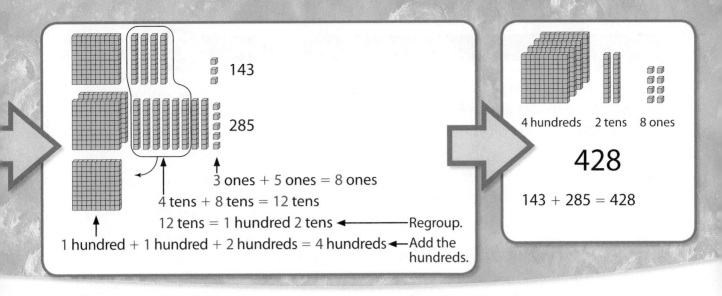

143

285

3 ones + 5 ones = 8 ones
4 tens + 8 tens = 12 tens
12 tens = 1 hundred 2 tens ◄——— Regroup.
1 hundred + 1 hundred + 2 hundreds = 4 hundreds ◄— Add the hundreds.

4 hundreds  2 tens  8 ones

428

143 + 285 = 428

---

## Guided Practice*

MATHEMATICAL PRACTICES

### Do you know HOW?

**1.** Write the problem and find the sum.

Use place-value blocks or draw pictures to find each sum.

**2.** 256 + 162    **3.** 138 + 29

### Do you UNDERSTAND?

**4. Model** How do you know when you need to regroup?

**5.** Mr. Wu drove 224 miles yesterday. He drove 175 miles today. Use place-value blocks or draw pictures to find how many miles he drove in all.

---

## Independent Practice

Write each problem and find the sum.

**6.**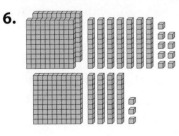

**7.**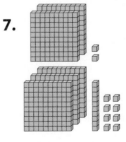

Find each sum. Use place-value blocks or draw pictures to help.

**8.** 635 + 222    **9.** 337 + 152    **10.** 359 + 211    **11.** 358 + 243

eTools
www.pearsonsuccessnet.com

For **12–15**, use the table at the right. Use place-value blocks or draw a picture to help.

 **Tip** *You can draw squares to show hundreds, lines to show tens, and ×s to show ones.*

**12.** Estimate about how many tickets in all were sold for the three rides on Saturday.

© **13. Writing to Explain** Without adding, how can you tell whether more tickets were sold in the two days for the Ferris wheel or the swings?

| Number of Tickets Sold | | |
|---|---|---|
| Ride | Saturday | Sunday |
| Ferris Wheel | 368 | 406 |
| Roller Coaster | 486 | 456 |
| Swings | 138 | 251 |

**14.** How many Ferris wheel tickets were sold in the two days?

**15.** How many roller coaster tickets were sold in the two days?

© **16. Reason** Mike wants to use place-value blocks to show 237 + 153. He has 8 tens blocks. Is that enough to show the sum? Explain.

**17.** One kind of pecan tree produces about 45 pecans in each pound of nuts. If you have one pound of these pecans and one pound of the kind of pecan shown below, how many pecans do you have?

© **18. Writing to Explain** Is the sum of two 3-digit numbers always a 3-digit number? Explain how you know.

**19.** Which number sentence do these place-value blocks show?

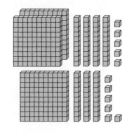

**A** 254 + 163 = 417

**B** 245 + 136 = 381

**C** 245 + 163 = 408

**D** 254 + 136 = 390

There are about 60 pecans in one pound of this kind of nut.

**20.** At a busy airport, 228 flights landed between noon and 3:00 P.M. On the same day 243 flights landed at that airport between 3:00 P.M. and 6:00 P.M. How many flights in all landed between noon and 6:00 P.M.?

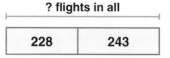

? flights in all

| 228 | 243 |
|---|---|

## Going Digital

### Adding with Regrouping

Use  tools

### Place-Value Blocks

Use the Place-Value Blocks eTool to add 367 + 175 by regrouping.

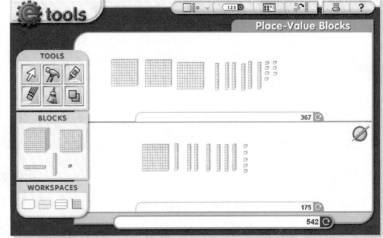

**Step 1**  Go to the Place-Value Blocks eTool. Click on the Two-part workspace icon. In the top space, show 367 with place-value blocks. Show 175 in the bottom space.

**Step 2** Use the arrow tool to move the ones from 175 to the top space. Then use the glue tool to select 10 ones. Click on the group of 10 ones to make one ten.

**Step 3** Use the arrow tool to move the tens from 175 to the top space. Use the glue tool to select 10 tens. Click on the group of 10 tens to make one hundred.

**Step 4** Use the arrow tool to move the hundred from 175 to the top space. Look at the blocks to find the sum, 367 + 175 = 542.

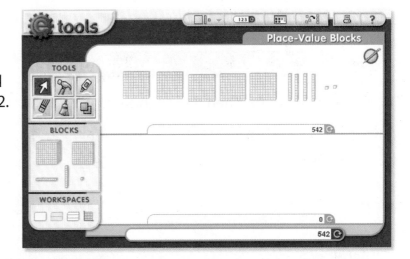

### Practice

Use the Place-Value Blocks eTool to find the sums by regrouping.

**1.** 248 + 374      **2.** 459 + 178      **3.** 566 + 293      **4.** 675 + 189

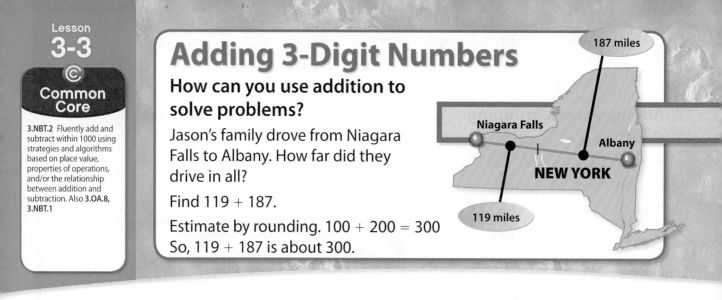

© Common Core

3.NBT.2 Fluently add and subtract within 1000 using strategies and algorithms based on place value, properties of operations, and/or the relationship between addition and subtraction. Also 3.OA.8, 3.NBT.1

# Adding 3-Digit Numbers

How can you use addition to solve problems?

Jason's family drove from Niagara Falls to Albany. How far did they drive in all?

Find 119 + 187.

Estimate by rounding. 100 + 200 = 300
So, 119 + 187 is about 300.

187 miles

Niagara Falls

Albany

**NEW YORK**

119 miles

## Guided Practice*

© MATHEMATICAL PRACTICES

### Do you know HOW?

Estimate. Then find each sum. Use place-value blocks or drawings to help.

1.  126
    + 171

2.  415
    + 168

3. 445 + 524

4. 394 + 97

### Do you UNDERSTAND?

© **5. Reasonableness** In the example about Jason's family, is the answer 306 miles reasonable? Explain.

6. Ms. Lane drove 278 miles on Tuesday and 342 miles on Wednesday. Write and solve a number sentence to find how far she drove in all.

## Independent Practice

For **7–24**, estimate. Then find each sum.

7.  347
    + 325

8.  136
    + 252

9.  564
    + 283

10.  231
     + 344

11.  324
     + 589

12.  441
     + 399

13.  333
     + 207

14.  127
     + 554

15.  271
     + 531

16.  426
     + 396

17. 324 + 68

18. 709 + 94

19. 496 + 275

20. 526 + 307

21. 438 + 233

22. 582 + 230

23. 494 + 313

24. 207 + 238

 *For another example, see Set B on page 92.*

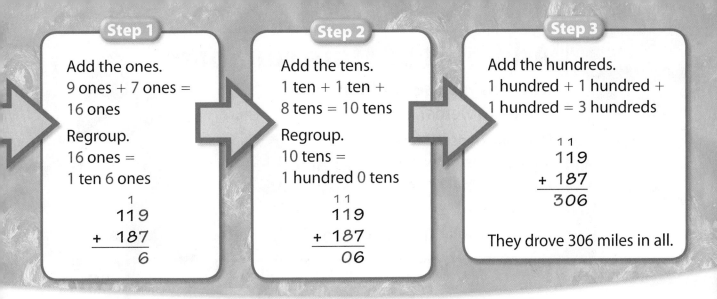

Add the ones.
9 ones + 7 ones =
16 ones

Regroup.
16 ones =
1 ten 6 ones

$$\begin{array}{r} \overset{1}{11\,9} \\ +\;\;187 \\ \hline 6 \end{array}$$

Add the tens.
1 ten + 1 ten +
8 tens = 10 tens

Regroup.
10 tens =
1 hundred 0 tens

$$\begin{array}{r} \overset{1\,1}{11\,9} \\ +\;\;187 \\ \hline 06 \end{array}$$

Add the hundreds.
1 hundred + 1 hundred +
1 hundred = 3 hundreds

$$\begin{array}{r} \overset{1\,1}{11\,9} \\ +\;\;187 \\ \hline 306 \end{array}$$

They drove 306 miles in all.

## Problem Solving

**MATHEMATICAL PRACTICES**

**Use Tools** For **25–28**, use the table at the right.

**25. a** Write a number sentence to find how many labels the first and second grades collected in all.

　**b** Estimate the answer.

　**c** Solve the problem.

　**d** Is your answer reasonable? Explain.

**26. Reason** Without finding the exact sum, how do you know that Grades 2 and 3 together collected more labels than Grade 4?

**27.** Write the number of labels collected from least to greatest.

**28.** Which number sentence shows how many labels Grades 1 and 4 collected in all?

　**A** 385 + 479 =

　**B** 385 + 564 =

　**C** 294 + 479 + 564 =

　**D** 385 + 294 + 479 + 564 =

**29.** The tallest roller coaster in the world is called Kingda Ka. It is 192 feet higher than the first Ferris wheel. How tall is Kingda Ka?

**Soup Labels Collected**

| Grades | Number |
| --- | --- |
| Grade 1 | 385 |
| Grade 2 | 294 |
| Grade 3 | 479 |
| Grade 4 | 564 |

*Data*

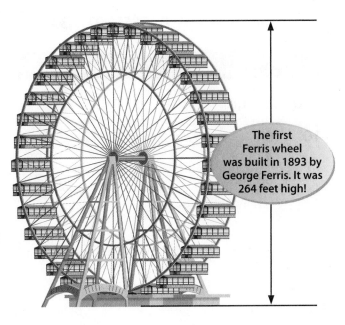

The first Ferris wheel was built in 1893 by George Ferris. It was 264 feet high!

Common
Core

**3.NBT.2** Fluently add and subtract within 1000 using strategies and algorithms based on place value, properties of operations, and/or the relationship between addition and subtraction. Also **3.OA.8**

# Adding 3 or More Numbers

## How can you use addition to solve problems?

Different kinds of birds are for sale at a pet store. How many birds are for sale in all?

Canaries
137

Parrots
18

Parakeets
155

- Find $137 + 155 + 18$.
- Estimate: $140 + 160 + 20 = 320$

---

## Guided Practice*

MATHEMATICAL
PRACTICES

### Do you know HOW?

Find each sum.

1.  36
    47
  + 35

2.  247
    362
  +  49

3.  273
    82
  + 124

4.  59
    506
    302
  +  24

5. $9 + 46 + 24$

6. $385 + 97 + 34$

### Do you UNDERSTAND?

For **7–9**, look at the example above.

7. **Reason** Why is there a 2 above the tens place in Step 2?

8. **Reasonableness** How can you tell that 310 birds is a reasonable answer?

9. Suppose the pet store gets 46 lovebirds to sell. Write and solve a number sentence to show how many birds are for sale now.

---

## Independent Practice

Find each sum.

10.  64
     42
   + 88

11.  307
     37
   + 234

12.  602
     125
   + 231

13.  246
     54
     233
   + 205

14.  303
     128
     63
   + 149

15. $164 + 68 + 35$

16. $32 + 9 + 46 + 8$

17. $125 + 36 + 124 + 239$

*For another example, see Set B on page 92.*

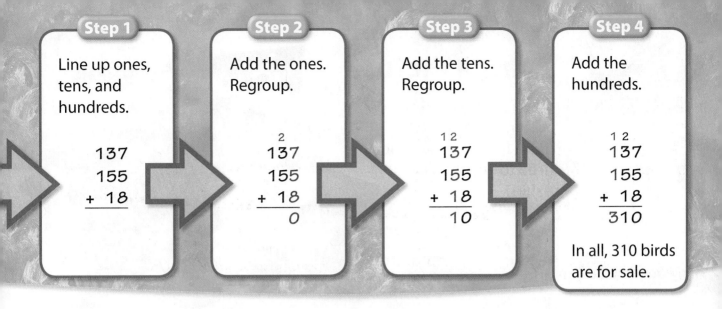

| Step 1 | Step 2 | Step 3 | Step 4 |
|--------|--------|--------|--------|
| Line up ones, tens, and hundreds. | Add the ones. Regroup. | Add the tens. Regroup. | Add the hundreds. |

**Step 1**

```
  137
  155
+  18
```

**Step 2**

```
    2
  137
  155
+  18
────
    0
```

**Step 3**

```
  1 2
  137
  155
+  18
────
   10
```

**Step 4**

```
  1 2
  137
  155
+  18
────
  310
```

In all, 310 birds are for sale.

---

## Problem Solving

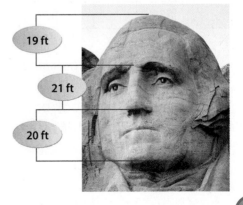

MATHEMATICAL PRACTICES

Calories are used to measure the energy in food. Use the picture for **18** and **19**.

**18.** Karin had cereal, a glass of milk, and a banana for breakfast. Follow these steps to find how many calories were in the food she ate.

banana: 105 calories
bowl of dry cereal: 110 calories
glass of milk: 150 calories

  **a** Write a number sentence to show how to solve the problem.

  **b** Estimate the answer.

  **c** Solve the problem.

  **d** Use the estimate to explain why your answer is reasonable.

© **19. Reason** Compare the number of calories in a glass of milk with the number of calories in a banana. Use $>$, $<$, or $=$.

© **20. Reasonableness** Meg said that $95 + 76 + 86$ is greater than 300. Explain why her answer is not reasonable.

**21.** Use the picture to find the size of President Washington's head carved in Mt. Rushmore.

**22.** Ramos has 225 pennies, 105 nickels, and 65 dimes. How many coins does he have?

  **A** 385 coins    **C** 980 coins

  **B** 395 coins    **D** 3,815 coins

19 ft

21 ft

20 ft

**Common Core**

**3.NBT.2** Fluently add and subtract within 1000 using strategies and algorithms based on place value, properties of operations, and/or the relationship between addition and subtraction. Also **3.OA.8**

Problem Solving

# Draw a Picture

David wants to buy some soccer souvenirs. How much money does David need to buy shorts and a shirt?

Pennant $12

Poster $10

Shorts $15

Shirt $19

---

## Guided Practice*

MATHEMATICAL PRACTICES

### Do you know HOW?

**1.** Use the picture above. Cal bought a poster and a pennant. Copy and complete the diagram to find how much money he spent.

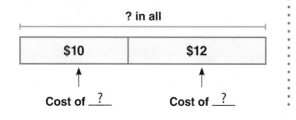

? in all

| $10 | $12 |

Cost of ___?___   Cost of ___?___

### Do you UNDERSTAND?

**2.** Look at the diagram for Problem 1.

  **a** What does each box show?

  **b** What does the line above the whole rectangle show?

**3. Write a Problem** Write and solve a problem that can be solved by drawing a picture.

---

## Independent Practice

MATHEMATICAL PRACTICES

**4.** David's dad spent $27 for tickets to the baseball game. He also spent $24 on food. About how much did he spend?

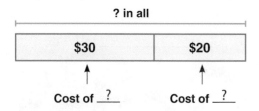

? in all

| $30 | $20 |

Cost of ___?___   Cost of ___?___

**5. Writing to Explain** Look back at the diagram for Problem 4. Why are the numbers in the diagram $30 and $20 instead of $27 and $24?

**Applying Math Practices**

- What am I asked to find?
- What else can I try?
- How are quantities related?
- How can I explain my work?
- How can I use math to model the problem?
- Can I use tools to help?
- Is my work precise?
- Why does this work?
- How can I generalize?

*For another example, see Set E on page 93.

Draw a diagram to show what you know.

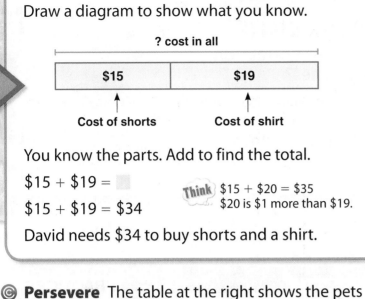

? cost in all

| $15 | $19 |

Cost of shorts     Cost of shirt

You know the parts. Add to find the total.

$15 + $19 = $\boxed{\phantom{00}}$

**Think** $15 + $20 = $35
$20 is $1 more than $19.

$15 + $19 = $34

David needs $34 to buy shorts and a shirt.

Make sure the answer is reasonable.

Estimate.

$15 + $19 is about $20 + $20, or $40.

The answer is reasonable because $34 is close to $40.

© **Persevere** The table at the right shows the pets owned by third graders at Smith School. Use the table for **6–8**. For **6** and **7**, copy and complete the diagram. Answer the question.

**Data**

| Students' Pets | |
|---|---|
| Pets | Number of Students |
| Cats | 18 |
| Dogs | 22 |
| Fish | 9 |
| Hamsters | 7 |
| Snakes | 2 |

**6.** How many students have fish or hamsters?

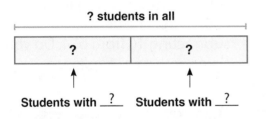

? students in all

| ? | ? |

Students with ＿?＿    Students with ＿?＿

**7.** How many students have cats, dogs, or snakes?

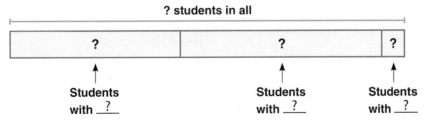

? students in all

| ? | ? | ? |

Students with ＿?＿     Students with ＿?＿     Students with ＿?＿

© **8. Model** Draw a diagram to find about how many students have cats or dogs.

© **9. Estimation** At the aquarium, Janet counted 12 sand sharks, 9 zebra sharks, and 11 nurse sharks. About how many sharks did Janet count?

**A** 50 sharks     **B** 30 sharks     **C** 20 sharks     **D** 15 sharks

Lesson
3-6

Common
Core

3.NBT.2 Fluently add and
subtract within 1000 using
strategies and algorithms
based on place value,
properties of operations,
and/or the relationship
between addition and
subtraction.

# Subtracting with an Expanded Algorithm

**How can you break large subtraction problems into smaller ones?**

Drew scored fewer points than Marco in a game of *Digit Derby*. Marco's score is 462 points. How many more points than Drew's is Marco's score? Find 462 − 181.

Marco
Score: 462

Drew
Score: 181

**Think** "I can subtract 100, then 80, and then 1."

---

## Guided Practice*

**MATHEMATICAL PRACTICES**

### Do you know HOW?

1. Follow these steps to find 374 − 236.

   First subtract 200.
   Then, subtract 30.
   Then, subtract 4.
   Then, subtract 2.

In **2** and **3**, find each difference.

2. 674 − 332      3. 369 − 175

### Do you UNDERSTAND?

ⓒ 4. **Use Structure** Why do you need to record the numbers you subtract at each step?

ⓒ 5. **Reason** Ana is trying to find 634 − 210. She decides to start by subtracting 10 from 634. Do you agree with Ana? Explain.

---

## Independent Practice

**Leveled Practice** In **6–9**, follow the steps to find each difference.

6. 738 − 523

   First subtract 500.
   Then, subtract 20.
   Then, subtract 3.

7. 755 − 315

   First subtract 300.
   Then, subtract 10.
   Then, subtract 5.

8. 336 − 217

   First subtract 200.
   Then, subtract 10.
   Then, subtract 6.
   Then, subtract 1.

9. 643 − 281

   First subtract 200.
   Then, subtract 40.
   Then, subtract 40.
   Then, subtract 1.

In **10–15**, find each difference.

10. 398 − 146      11. 455 − 182      12. 865 − 506

13. 794 − 355      14. 675 − 384      15. 472 − 154

*For another example, see Set A on page 92.

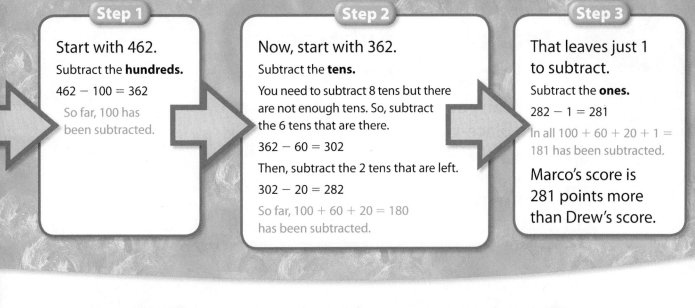

**Step 1**

Start with 462.

Subtract the **hundreds.**

$462 - 100 = 362$

So far, 100 has been subtracted.

**Step 2**

Now, start with 362.

Subtract the **tens.**

You need to subtract 8 tens but there are not enough tens. So, subtract the 6 tens that are there.

$362 - 60 = 302$

Then, subtract the 2 tens that are left.

$302 - 20 = 282$

So far, $100 + 60 + 20 = 180$ has been subtracted.

**Step 3**

That leaves just 1 to subtract.

Subtract the **ones.**

$282 - 1 = 281$

In all $100 + 60 + 20 + 1 = 181$ has been subtracted.

Marco's score is 281 points more than Drew's score.

## Problem Solving

**MATHEMATICAL PRACTICES**

**16.** Dan and Beth go bowling. Dan gets a score of 87. Beth gets a score of 128. How much greater is Beth's score than Dan's score?

**17.** Beth bowls one more game to see if she can tie her record. Her record is a score of 165. She needs 37 more to do this. What is Beth's score right now?

ⓒ **18. Writing to Explain** Suppose you want to subtract a 3-digit number from another 3-digit number. Why can the problem be made easier by breaking it into smaller problems and doing repeated subtraction?

**19.** Mr. Brown sells flowers. He has 417 red roses and 232 yellow roses. How many more red roses than yellow roses does Mr. Brown have?

    **A**  175        **C**  185

    **B**  184        **D**  225

**20.** There are 128 students in the school lunchroom. Near the end of lunch, 53 students leave. How many students are left in the cafeteria?

ⓒ **21. Communicate** Owen needs to find $345 - 124$. He decides to subtract in steps. What number do you think he should subtract first? Why?

ⓒ **22. Persevere** Don's book has 316 pages. He read 50 pages last week. He read another 71 pages this week. How many more pages does Don have left to read?

ⓒ **23. Reason** Liz wants to find the difference $623 - 411$. She has subtracted the hundreds and tens so far. How much has she subtracted so far? How much does she still need to subtract?

 *Think about the hidden question.*

Lesson
3-7

© 
Common
Core

3.NBT.2 Fluently add and
subtract within 1000 using
strategies and algorithms
based on place value,
properties of operations,
and/or the relationship
between addition and
subtraction. Also 3.OA.8

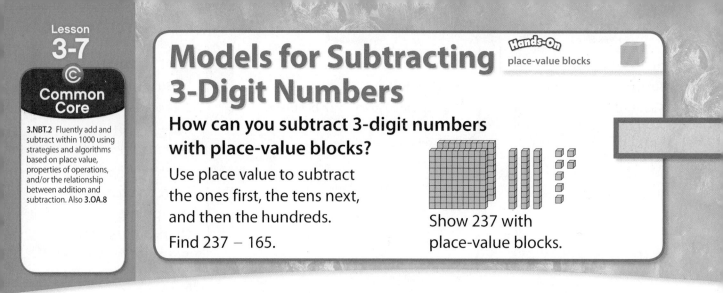

# Models for Subtracting 3-Digit Numbers

**Hands-On**
place-value blocks

## How can you subtract 3-digit numbers with place-value blocks?

Use place value to subtract
the ones first, the tens next,
and then the hundreds.

Find 237 − 165.

Show 237 with
place-value blocks.

---

## Guided Practice*

© **MATHEMATICAL PRACTICES**

### Do you know HOW?

In **1–6**, use place-value blocks or draw
pictures to subtract.

**1.**  249
      − 187

**2.**  261
      − 134

**3.**  158
      −  76

**4.**  384
      − 182

**5.** 173 − 158     **6.** 325 − 213

### Do you UNDERSTAND?

© **7. Communicate** In the example
above, why do you need to regroup
1 hundred into 10 tens?

© **8. Model** Colby saved $256 doing
jobs in the neighborhood. He
bought a computer printer for
$173. How much money did he
have left? Draw a picture to help
you subtract.

---

## Independent Practice

In **9–18**, use place-value blocks
or draw pictures to subtract.

**Tip** You can draw squares to show hundreds, lines to show
tens, and Xs to show ones. This picture shows 127.

☐  ――――――  × ×
   ――――――  × × × × ×

**9.**  347
      − 263

**10.**  196
       − 149

**11.**  218
       − 117

**12.**  251
       − 132

**13.**  423
       − 291

**14.**  123
       −  81

**15.**  265
       −  84

**16.**  539
       − 275

**17.**  376
       − 153

**18.**  417
       − 308

eTools
www.pearsonsuccessnet.com

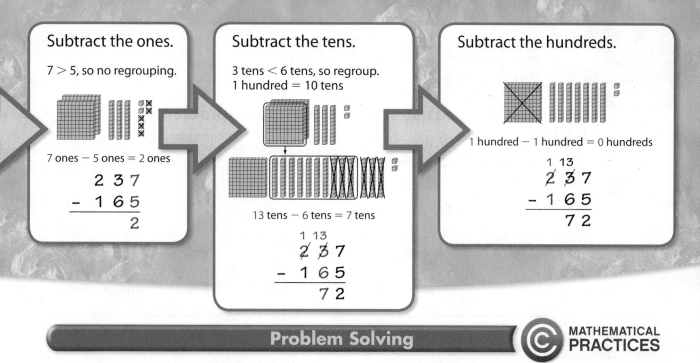

**Subtract the ones.**

7 > 5, so no regrouping.

7 ones − 5 ones = 2 ones

```
  2 3 7
− 1 6 5
------
      2
```

**Subtract the tens.**

3 tens < 6 tens, so regroup.
1 hundred = 10 tens

13 tens − 6 tens = 7 tens

```
  1 13
  2 3̶ 7
− 1 6 5
------
    7 2
```

**Subtract the hundreds.**

1 hundred − 1 hundred = 0 hundreds

```
  1 13
  2̶ 3̶ 7
− 1 6 5
------
    7 2
```

---

## Problem Solving

For **19–21**, use the table at the right.

**19.** The Wen family drove from Cincinnati to Cleveland. Then the family drove to Chicago. How many miles did the family drive in all?

**Trip Distances**

| Trip | Miles |
|------|-------|
| Cleveland to Chicago | 346 |
| Cincinnati to Cleveland | 249 |
| Washington, D.C., to Cleveland | 372 |

Data

© **20. Persevere** The Miller family is driving from Washington, D.C., to Cleveland and then to Cincinnati. So far the Millers have traveled 127 miles. How many miles are left in their trip?

© **21. Writing to Explain** Which city is farther from Cleveland, Chicago or Washington, D.C.? How much farther? Explain your answer.

© **22. Reason** In the United States, students go to school about 180 days per year. Students in Japan go to school about 60 days more per year than students in the United States. About how many days per year do students in Japan attend school?

**23.** An amusement park ride can hold 120 people. There were 116 people on the ride and 95 people waiting in line. Which number sentence can be used to find how many people in all were on the ride or waiting in line?

**A** $116 − 95 =$ ▢

**B** $120 + 116 + 95 =$ ▢

**C** $116 + 95 =$ ▢

**D** $120 − 95 =$ ▢

© Common Core

3.NBT.2 Fluently add and subtract within 1000 using strategies and algorithms based on place value, properties of operations, and/or the relationship between addition and subtraction. Also 3.OA.8, 3.NBT.1

# Subtracting 3-Digit Numbers

Hands-On
place-value blocks

## How can you use subtraction to solve problems?

Mike and Linda are playing a game. How many more points does Mike have than Linda?

Find 528 − 341.

Estimate: 530 − 340 = 190

MIKE  528      341  LINDA

---

**Another Example**  How do you subtract with two regroupings?

Find 356 − 189.
Estimate: 400 − 200 = 200

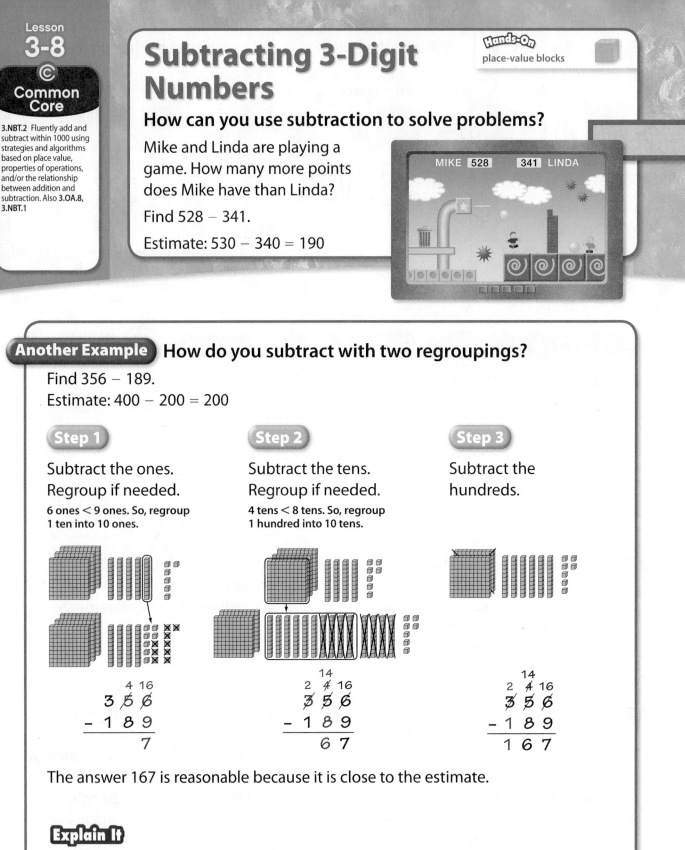

**Step 1**

Subtract the ones. Regroup if needed.

6 ones < 9 ones. So, regroup 1 ten into 10 ones.

```
      4 16
  3 5̶ 6̶
−  1 8 9
─────────
        7
```

**Step 2**

Subtract the tens. Regroup if needed.

4 tens < 8 tens. So, regroup 1 hundred into 10 tens.

```
         14
   2  4̶ 16
  3̶ 5̶ 6̶
−  1 8 9
─────────
      6 7
```

**Step 3**

Subtract the hundreds.

```
         14
   2  4̶ 16
  3̶ 5̶ 6̶
−  1 8 9
─────────
    1 6 7
```

The answer 167 is reasonable because it is close to the estimate.

**Explain It**

1. Why do you need to regroup both a ten and a hundred?

© 2. **Reason** How is 3 hundreds 5 tens 6 ones the same as 3 hundreds 4 tens 16 ones? How is 3 hundreds 4 tens 16 ones the same as 2 hundreds 14 tens 16 ones?

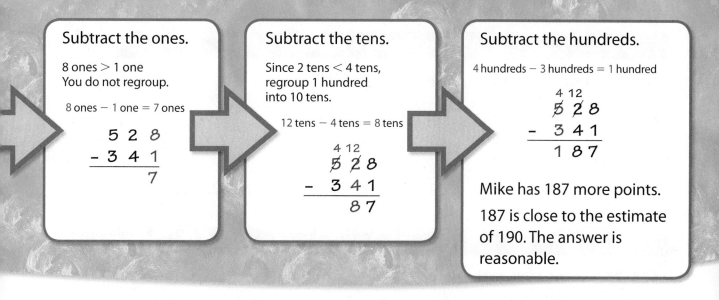

**Subtract the ones.**

8 ones > 1 one
You do not regroup.

8 ones − 1 one = 7 ones

$$
\begin{array}{r}
5\ 2\ 8 \\
-\ 3\ 4\ 1 \\
\hline
7
\end{array}
$$

**Subtract the tens.**

Since 2 tens < 4 tens, regroup 1 hundred into 10 tens.

12 tens − 4 tens = 8 tens

$$
\begin{array}{r}
4\ 12 \\
\cancel{5}\ \cancel{2}\ 8 \\
-\ 3\ 4\ 1 \\
\hline
8\ 7
\end{array}
$$

**Subtract the hundreds.**

4 hundreds − 3 hundreds = 1 hundred

$$
\begin{array}{r}
4\ 12 \\
\cancel{5}\ \cancel{2}\ 8 \\
-\ 3\ 4\ 1 \\
\hline
1\ 8\ 7
\end{array}
$$

Mike has 187 more points.

187 is close to the estimate of 190. The answer is reasonable.

---

## Guided Practice*

**MATHEMATICAL PRACTICES**

### Do you know HOW?

In **1–6**, subtract. Use place-value blocks, if you wish.

**1.**  374
      − 176

**2.**  431
      − 145

**3.**  568
      − 269

**4.**  327
      − 238

**5.** 574 − 86

**6.** 410 − 257

### Do you UNDERSTAND?

Ⓒ **7. Communicate** In the example above, explain how to decide if regrouping is needed.

**8.** At the end of their game, Lora had 426 points, and Lou had 158 points. How many more points did Lora have than Lou?

   **a** Write a number sentence.

   **b** Estimate the answer.

   **c** Solve the problem.

   **d** Explain why your answer is reasonable.

---

## Independent Practice

Estimate. Then find each difference. Check answers for reasonableness.

**9.**  385
      − 296

**10.**  276
       − 97

**11.**  516
       − 238

**12.**  629
       − 453

**13.**  948
       − 569

eTools
www.pearsonsuccessnet.com

DIGITAL

Estimate and subtract. Check answers for reasonableness.

**14.**   392
        − 195

**15.**   754
        − 476

**16.**   819
        − 652

**17.**   123
        −  84

**18.**   435
        − 367

**19.** 236 − 78

**20.** 568 − 362

**21.** 147 − 58

**22.** 952 − 794

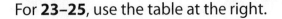

**MATHEMATICAL PRACTICES**

For **23–25**, use the table at the right.

**23.** Follow the steps below to find how many more swimmers signed up for the first session at Oak Pool than for the first session at Park Pool.

  **a** Write a number sentence that can be used to solve the problem.

  **b** Estimate the answer.

  **c** Solve the problem.

  **d** Explain why your answer is reasonable.

Ⓒ **25. Write a Problem** Write a problem using the data in the table. Include too much information.

| Swim Class Enrollment | | |
|---|---|---|
| **Pool** | **Number of Swimmers** | |
| | **1st session** | **2nd session** |
| Oak | 763 | 586 |
| Park | 314 | 179 |
| River | 256 | 63 |

Ⓒ **24. Persevere** At River Pool, late enrollments added 29 swimmers to the second session. The total number of swimmers enrolled in the second session is how many fewer than in the first?

**Tip** *What addition sentence can help?*

**26.** The world's largest basket is the building in the photo. It is 186 feet tall from the base to the top of the handles. What is the height of the handles?

186 ft

103 ft

**27.** Ana made 14 hats. After giving some hats to Ty's family and some to Liv's family, she had 3 hats left. If she gave Ty's family 6 hats, which of these shows one way to find how many hats Ana gave to Liv's family?

  **A** $14 + 3 − 6 =$

  **B** $14 − 3 − 6 =$

  **C** $14 − 3 + 6 =$

  **D** $14 + 3 + 6 =$

# Algebra Connections

## Using Properties to Complete Number Sentences

The properties of addition can help you find missing numbers.

**Commutative (Order) Property** You can add numbers in any order and the sum will be the same. Example: $4 + 3 = 3 + 4$

**Identity (Zero) Property** The sum of any number and zero is that same number. Example: $9 + 0 = 9$

**Associative (Grouping) Property** You can group addends in any way and the sum will be the same. Example: $(5 + 2) + 3 = 5 + (2 + 3)$

**Example:** $26 + \blacksquare = 26$

**Think** 26 plus what number is equal to 26?

You can use the Identity Property.

$26 + 0 = 26$

**Example:**
$36 + (14 + 12) = (36 + \blacksquare) + 12$

**Think** What number makes the two sides equal?

Use the Associative Property.

$36 + (14 + 12) = (36 + 14) + 12$

Copy and complete. Write the missing number.

**1.** $19 + \blacksquare = 19$

**2.** $15 + 32 = 32 + \blacksquare$

**3.** $28 + (17 + 32) = (28 + \blacksquare) + 32$

**4.** $\blacksquare + 27 = 27$

**5.** $\blacksquare + 8 = 8 + 49$

**6.** $(16 + 14) + \blacksquare = 16 + (14 + 53)$

**7.** $(\blacksquare + 9) + 72 = 96 + (9 + 72)$

**8.** $\blacksquare + 473 = 473$

· · · · · · · · · · · · · · · · · · · · · · · · · · · · · · · · · · · · · · · · · · · · · · · · · · · ·

© **Be Precise** For **9** and **10**, copy and complete the number sentence. Use it to help solve the problem.

**9.** Vin walked 9 blocks from home to the library. Then he walked 5 blocks farther to the store. Later he walked the same path back to the library. How many more blocks would he need to walk to his home?

$9 + 5 = 5 + \blacksquare$

$\blacksquare$ blocks

**10.** Bo scored 7 points in each of two tosses in a game. Then he made one more toss. He had the same total score as Ed. Ed scored 8 points in one toss and 7 points in each of two tosses. How many points did Bo score on his last toss?

$7 + 7 + \blacksquare = 8 + 7 + 7$

$\blacksquare$ points

Lesson
3-9

© Common Core

3.NBT.2 Fluently add and subtract within 1000 using strategies and algorithms based on place value, properties of operations, and/or the relationship between addition and subtraction.

# Subtracting Across Zero

## How do you subtract from a number with one or more zeros?

How much more does the club need?

Find:   305    305:
      − 178

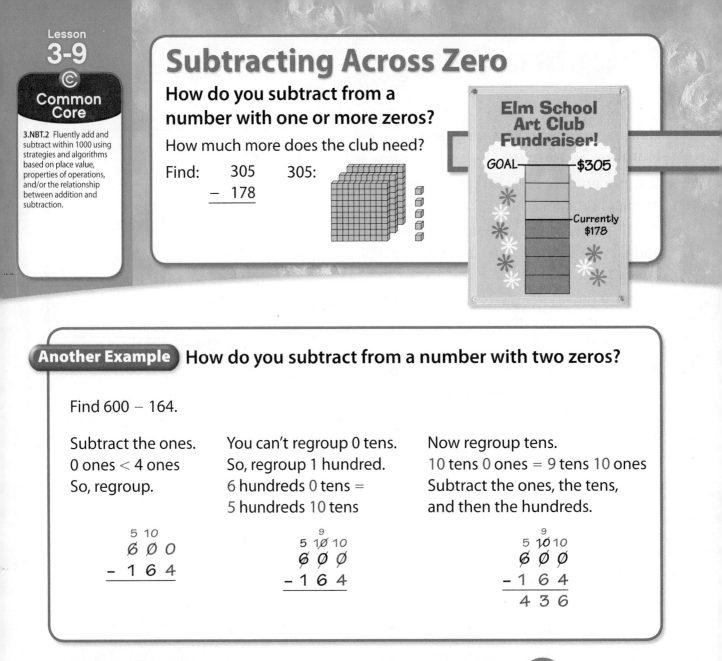

**Elm School Art Club Fundraiser!**

GOAL——$305

Currently $178

---

**Another Example** How do you subtract from a number with two zeros?

Find 600 − 164.

| Subtract the ones. | You can't regroup 0 tens. | Now regroup tens. |
|---|---|---|
| 0 ones < 4 ones | So, regroup 1 hundred. | 10 tens 0 ones = 9 tens 10 ones |
| So, regroup. | 6 hundreds 0 tens = | Subtract the ones, the tens, |
|  | 5 hundreds 10 tens | and then the hundreds. |

$$\begin{array}{r} \overset{5\ 10}{\cancel{6}\ \cancel{0}\ 0} \\ -\ 1\ 6\ 4 \\ \hline \end{array}$$

$$\begin{array}{r} \overset{\quad\ 9}{\overset{5\ 10\ 10}{\cancel{6}\ \cancel{0}\ \cancel{0}}} \\ -\ 1\ 6\ 4 \\ \hline \end{array}$$

$$\begin{array}{r} \overset{\quad\ 9}{\overset{5\ 10\ 10}{\cancel{6}\ \cancel{0}\ \cancel{0}}} \\ -\ 1\ 6\ 4 \\ \hline 4\ 3\ 6 \end{array}$$

---

**Guided Practice***

© MATHEMATICAL PRACTICES

### Do you know HOW?

In **1–6**, find each difference.

1.   402
   − 139

2.   300
   − 157

3.   607
   − 439

4.   820
   − 167

**5.** 200 − 74

**6.** 501 − 186

### Do you UNDERSTAND?

© **7. Use Structure** In the examples above, why do you write 10 above the 0 in the tens place?

© **8. Critique Reasoning** Lia says that she needs to regroup every time she subtracts from a number with a zero. Do you agree? Explain.

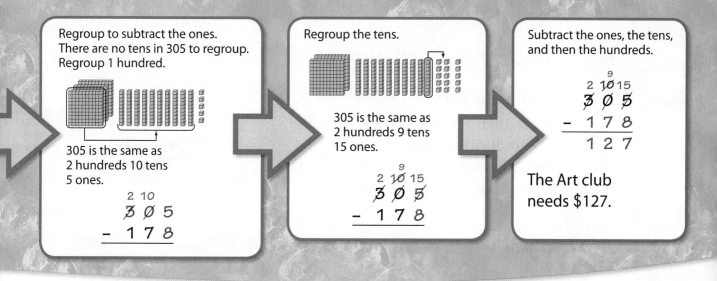

Regroup to subtract the ones. There are no tens in 305 to regroup. Regroup 1 hundred.

305 is the same as 2 hundreds 10 tens 5 ones.

$$\begin{array}{r} \overset{2\ 10}{\cancel{3}\ \cancel{0}\ 5} \\ -\ 1\ 7\ 8 \end{array}$$

Regroup the tens.

305 is the same as 2 hundreds 9 tens 15 ones.

$$\begin{array}{r} \overset{9}{\overset{2\ \cancel{10}\ 15}{\cancel{3}\ \cancel{0}\ \cancel{5}}} \\ -\ 1\ 7\ 8 \end{array}$$

Subtract the ones, the tens, and then the hundreds.

$$\begin{array}{r} \overset{9}{\overset{2\ \cancel{10}\ 15}{\cancel{3}\ \cancel{0}\ \cancel{5}}} \\ -\ 1\ 7\ 8 \\ \hline 1\ 2\ 7 \end{array}$$

The Art club needs $127.

## Independent Practice

In **9–18**, find each difference.

**9.** 203
− 157

**10.** 400
− 371

**11.** 304
− 95

**12.** 401
− 282

**13.** 500
− 64

**14.** 600
− 439

**15.** 306
− 248

**16.** 705
− 123

**17.** 800
− 74

**18.** 900
− 506

## Problem Solving

Ⓒ **MATHEMATICAL PRACTICES**

Ⓒ **19. Model** The average person eats about 126 pounds of fresh fruit in a year. Write a number sentence to help you find how many pounds of processed fruit you eat. Then solve.

> An average person eats a total of about 280 pounds of fresh and processed fruit each year.

Ⓒ **20. Writing to Explain** The Art Club needs 605 beads. A large bag of beads has 285 beads. A small bag of beads has 130 beads. Will one large bag and one small bag be enough beads? Explain.

**21.** Dina counted 204 items on the library cart. There were 91 fiction books, 75 nonfiction books, and some magazines. Which number sentence shows one way to find the number of magazines?

**A** 204 − 91 − 75 =

**C** 204 − 91 + 75 =

**B** 204 + 91 + 75 =

**D** 204 + 91 − 75 =

Lesson
**3-10**

**Common Core**

**3.OA.8** Solve two-step word problems using the four operations. Represent these problems using equations with a letter standing for the unknown quantity. Assess the reasonableness of answers using mental computation and estimation strategies including rounding. Also **3.NBT.2**

**Problem Solving**

# Draw a Picture and Write a Number Sentence

There are two lunch periods at Central School. If 221 students eat during the first lunch period, how many students eat during the second lunch period?

**Central School**
**Grades K-6**
**458 Students**

---

**Another Example** **Are there other types of subtraction situations?**

There are 85 students in Grade 2. That is 17 more students than in Grade 3. How many students are in Grade 3?

### Plan and Solve

Draw a diagram to show what you know.

| Gr. 2 | 85 | |
|---|---|---|

| Gr. 3 | ? | 17 |
|---|---|---|

There are 17 more students in Grade 2 than in Grade 3. Subtract to find the number of students in Grade 3.

Write a number sentence.

$85 - 17 = \blacksquare$

### Answer

$$\begin{array}{r} {\scriptstyle 7\ 15} \\ \cancel{8}\ \cancel{5} \\ -\ 1\ 7 \\ \hline 6\ 8 \end{array}$$

There are 68 students in Grade 3.

### Check

Make sure the answer is reasonable.

$85 - 17$ is about $90 - 20$, or 70.

68 is close to 70, so 68 is reasonable.

The number 68 is reasonable, and the question in the problem was answered.

### Explain It

**1.** Harry wrote $17 + \blacksquare = 85$ for the diagram above. Is his number sentence correct? Why or why not?

**2. Reason** Grade 4 has 72 students. There are 12 more students in Grade 5 than in Grade 4. Would you add or subtract to find the number of students in Grade 5? Write and solve a number sentence.

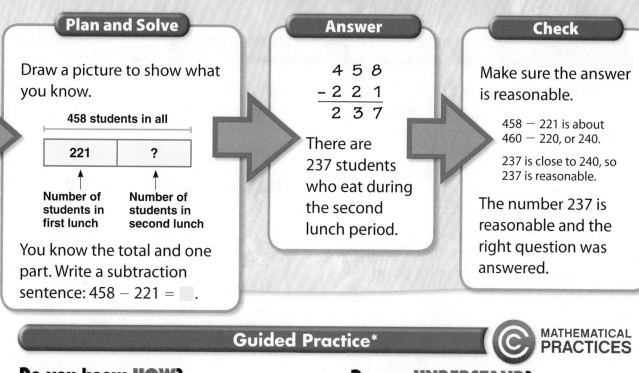

**Plan and Solve**

Draw a picture to show what you know.

258 students in all *(458 students in all)*

| 221 | ? |

↑ Number of students in first lunch  ↑ Number of students in second lunch

You know the total and one part. Write a subtraction sentence: 458 − 221 = ☐.

**Answer**

$$\begin{array}{r} 4\ 5\ 8 \\ -\ 2\ 2\ 1 \\ \hline 2\ 3\ 7 \end{array}$$

There are 237 students who eat during the second lunch period.

**Check**

Make sure the answer is reasonable.

458 − 221 is about 460 − 220, or 240.

237 is close to 240, so 237 is reasonable.

The number 237 is reasonable and the right question was answered.

## Guided Practice*

MATHEMATICAL PRACTICES

### Do you know HOW?

1. A total of 254 people entered a bicycle race. So far 135 people have finished the race. How many people are still racing?

254 people in all

| 135 | ? |

### Do you UNDERSTAND?

© 2. **Writing to Explain** How do you know what operation to use to solve Problem 1?

© 3. **Write a Problem** Write a problem that can be solved by adding or subtracting. Then give your problem to a classmate to solve.

## Independent Practice

MATHEMATICAL PRACTICES

4. The height of Capote Falls is 175 feet. The height of Madrid Falls is 120 feet. Write and solve a number sentence to find how much taller Capote Falls is than Madrid Falls.

| Capote Falls | 175 | |
|---|---|---|
| Madrid Falls | 120 | ? |

**Applying Math Practices**

- What am I asked to find?
- What else can I try?
- How are quantities related?
- How can I explain my work?
- How can I use math to model the problem?
- Can I use tools to help?
- Is my work precise?
- Why does this work?
- How can I generalize?

*For another example, see Set E on page 93.

In the United States House of Representatives, the number of representatives each state has depends upon the number of people who live in the state.

Use the table at the right for **5–7**.

Ⓒ **5. Persevere** Copy and complete the diagram below. New York has 14 more representatives than Michigan. How many representatives does New York have?

| U.S. Representatives as of 2010 | |
|---|---|
| **State** | **Number** |
| California | 53 |
| Florida | 25 |
| Michigan | 15 |
| Texas | 32 |

*Data*

? representatives in New York

| 15 | 14 |
|---|---|

**6.** Draw a diagram to find how many more representatives Texas has than Florida.

**7.** Which pair of states has more representatives: California and Michigan or Florida and Texas?

**8.** When the House of Representatives started in 1789, there were 65 members. Now there are 435 members. How many more members are there now?

Ⓒ **9. Reason** There are 50 states in the United States. Each state has 2 senators. Write and solve a number sentence to find the total number of senators.

Ⓒ **Think About the Structure**

**10.** Max exercised 38 minutes on Monday and 25 minutes on Tuesday. Which number sentence shows how long he exercised on the two days?

**A** $40 + 30 = $ ▓

**B** $40 - 30 = $ ▓

**C** $38 - 25 = $ ▓

**D** $38 + 25 = $ ▓

**11.** Nancy had $375 in the bank. She took $200 out to buy a scooter that cost $185. Which number sentence shows how much money is left in the bank?

**A** $\$375 + \$185 = $ ▓

**B** $\$375 - \$185 = $ ▓

**C** $\$375 - \$200 = $ ▓

**D** $\$375 + \$185 + \$200 = $ ▓

## Subtracting with Regrouping

Use  tools
**Place-Value Blocks**

Use the Place-Value Blocks eTool to subtract 324 − 168.

**Step 1** Go to the Place-Value Blocks eTool. Click on the two-part workspace icon. In the top space, show 324 with place-value blocks.

**Step 2**  Use the hammer tool to break one of the tens blocks into 10 ones. Then use the arrow tool to take away 8 ones and move them to the bottom workspace.

**Step 3** Use the hammer tool to break one of the hundreds blocks into 10 tens. Then take away the 6 tens in 168 and move them to the bottom workspace.

**Step 4** Use the arrow tool to take away the hundred block in 168. To find the difference, look at all of the blocks that are left.

324 − 168 = 156

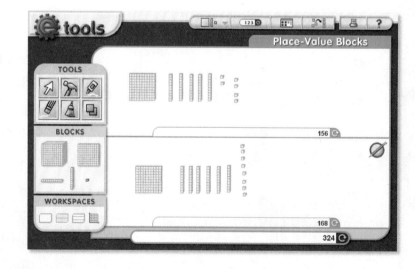

## Practice

Use the Place-Value Blocks eTool to subtract.

**1.** 445 − 176    **2.** 318 − 142    **3.** 546 − 259    **4.** 600 − 473

**Set A, pages 66–67, 78–79**

Follow the steps to find 674 + 215.

**Step 1:** Break 674 and 215 into easier problems.

| Hundreds | Tens | Ones |
|---|---|---|
| 600 | 70 | 4 |
| + 200 | + 10 | + 5 |
| 800 | 80 | 9 |

**Step 2:** Add all the sums.

```
        800
         80
      +   9
Total →  889
```

To subtract, you can follow similar steps.
Break the large subtraction problem into
smaller ones.

**Remember** to think about the
place values of each number.

Follow the steps to find 421 + 390.

| 1. Hundreds | Tens | Ones |
|---|---|---|
| 400 | 20 | 1 |
| + 300 | + 90 | + 0 |

**Total**

Find the sum or difference.

**2.** 274 + 326      **3.** 563 + 156

**4.** 527 − 414      **5.** 732 − 351

**6.** 376 − 265      **7.** 947 − 655

**Set B, pages 68–70, 72–73, 74–75**

Find 125 + 168.

Show 125 and 168 with place-value blocks.

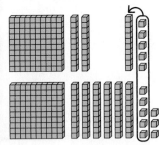

5 ones + 8 ones = 13 ones
Regroup.
13 ones = 1 ten 3 ones

1 ten + 2 tens + 6 tens =
9 tens

1 hundred + 1 hundred =
2 hundreds

So, 125 + 168 = 293.

Find 43 + 187 + 238.
Estimate: 40 + 190 + 240 = 470

```
  1  1
     4 3      Line up ones, tens, and hundreds.
  1 8 7      Then add each column. Regroup
+ 2 3 8      as needed.
  4 6 8      The answer 468 is close to 470,
             so 468 is reasonable.
```

**Remember** to add ones, then tens,
then hundreds.

Find each sum. Use place-value
blocks or draw a picture to help.

**1.** 265 + 116

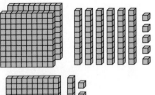

Find each sum.

| **2.** | 718 | **3.** | 139 |
|---|---|---|---|
| | + 156 | | 209 |
| | | | + 55 |

Find 236 − 127.

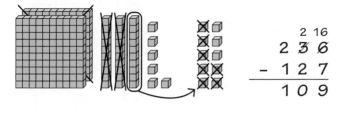

$$\begin{array}{r} \overset{2}{\phantom{2}}\overset{16}{\phantom{1}} \\ 2\ \cancel{3}\ \cancel{6} \\ -\ 1\ 2\ 7 \\ \hline 1\ 0\ 9 \end{array}$$

**Remember** to subtract ones, then tens, and then hundreds.

Use place-value blocks or draw pictures to subtract.

1.  $\begin{array}{r} 435 \\ -\ 217 \\ \hline \end{array}$   2.  $\begin{array}{r} 255 \\ -\ 161 \\ \hline \end{array}$

Find 306 − 129.

Estimate: 300 − 100 = 200

$$\begin{array}{r} \overset{2}{\phantom{2}}\overset{10}{\phantom{1}} \\ \cancel{3}\ \cancel{0}\ 6 \\ -\ 1\ 2\ 9 \\ \hline \end{array}$$
There are no tens. Regroup hundreds.

$$\begin{array}{r} \overset{9}{\phantom{0}} \\ 2\ \overset{10}{\cancel{1}}\ \overset{16}{\phantom{0}} \\ \cancel{3}\ \cancel{0}\ \cancel{6} \\ -\ 1\ 2\ 9 \\ \hline 1\ 7\ 7 \end{array}$$
Regroup tens.

177 is close to 200, so the answer is reasonable.

**Remember** that when you need to regroup tens, but have 0 tens, regroup hundreds first.

Find each difference.

1.  $\begin{array}{r} 308 \\ -\ 125 \\ \hline \end{array}$   2.  $\begin{array}{r} 397 \\ -\ 138 \\ \hline \end{array}$

3. 200 − 136   4. 854 − 296

At the school picnic, 234 students took part in the events. Of those students, 136 students were in the potato sack races. The other students were in the 3-legged races. How many students were in the 3-legged races?

| 234 students in all ||
| 136 | ? |

You know the total and one part, so you can subtract to find the other part: 234 − 136 = ☐.

234 − 136 = 98
98 students were in the 3-legged races.

**Remember** that drawing a picture of the problem can help you write a number sentence.

Draw a picture. Write a number sentence and solve.

1. A total of 293 people entered a running race. So far, 127 people have finished the race. How many people are still racing?

2. Jason had 35 trading cards. Then he bought 27 more. How many in all does he have now?

**Multiple Choice**

1. Mrs. Wesley bought 325 drinks for a picnic. She bought 135 cartons of milk, 95 bottles of water, and some bottles of juice. Which number sentence shows one way to find how many bottles of juice she bought? (3-8)

   **A** $325 - 135 + 95 = $ ▢

   **B** $325 - 135 - 95 = $ ▢

   **C** $325 + 135 - 95 = $ ▢

   **D** $325 + 135 + 95 = $ ▢

2. What regrouping is shown? (3-7)

   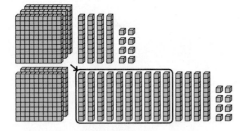

   **A** 3 hundreds 4 tens 8 ones as 2 hundreds 3 tens 18 ones

   **B** 3 hundreds 4 tens 8 ones as 2 hundreds 14 tens 8 ones

   **C** 2 hundreds 4 tens 8 ones as 1 hundreds 14 tens 8 ones

   **D** 2 hundreds 4 tens 8 ones as 2 hundreds 3 tens 18 ones

3. Texas has 254 counties. Georgia has 159 counties. How many more counties does Texas have than Georgia? (3-8)

   **A** 195   **C** 105

   **B** 145   **D** 95

4. Which picture shows the problem? Nessie saw 23 deer and 17 squirrels at a national park. How many more deer did she see than squirrels? (3-10)

   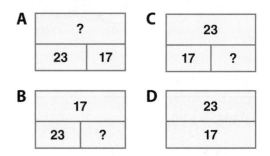

5. Trisha had 300 prize tickets. She cashed in 237 prize tickets to get a stuffed animal. How many prize tickets did Trisha have left? (3-9)

   **A** 173   **C** 137

   **B** 163   **D** 63

6. The Aztec Ruins monument has about 318 acres. Gilla Cliff Dwellings has about 553 acres. Which is reasonable for the total size for these two national monuments in New Mexico? (3-3)

   **A** 971 acres, because 318 + 553 is about 400 + 600 = 1,000

   **B** 871 acres, because 318 + 553 is about 300 + 600 = 900

   **C** 771 acres, because 318 + 553 is about 300 + 500 = 800

   **D** 671 acres, because 318 + 553 is about 200 + 500 = 700

**7.** Write the sum of the hundreds, tens, and ones for 256 + 341. (3-1)

**8.** What addition sentence is shown? (3-2)

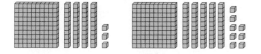

**9.** Between 6 A.M. and 10 A.M., 389 trucks and 599 cars crossed a bridge. How many vehicles is this in all? (3-3)

**10.** Tricia spent $35 on a toy bed, $48 on a toy dresser, and $24 on a table. How much did she spend in all? (3-4)

**11.** Cindy picked 9 roses and then 14 daisies. What number correctly replaces the question mark in the diagram? (3-5)

| ? flowers in all | |
| --- | --- |
| 9 roses | 14 daisies |

**12.** Cristina scored 485 points on a video game. Olivia scored 196 points. How many more points did Cristina score than Olivia? (3-8)

**13.** Al had $205. He spent $67 on a bike. How much did he have left? (3-9)

**14.** Luke wants to find the difference 175 − 134. He has subtracted the hundreds and tens so far. What is the sum of the two numbers he has subtracted? How much does he still need to subtract? (3-6)

**15.** There are 630 students at Portman Elementary School. There are 148 students in Grade 3. How many students at Portman Elementary School are not in Grade 3? (3-10)

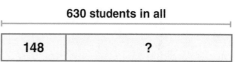

| 630 students in all | |
| --- | --- |
| 148 | ? |

**16.** Write the two numbers shown below with place-value blocks. Explain what regroupings you will need to do to find the sum of the two numbers. (3-2)

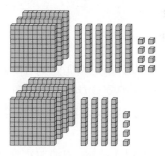

**17.** Melissa had 138 coins in her coin collection. She added 114 coins to her collection on Tuesday and another 25 coins on Friday. How many coins in all did Melissa have in her collection at the end of the week? (3-4)

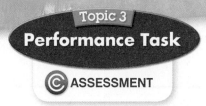

ASSESSMENT

You have won 500 tickets at a video arcade. You can cash in the tickets for prizes. You plan on using as many tickets as possible to get lots of prizes.

The table below shows the prizes that are available at the arcade. Use the information in the table to choose your prizes.

| Arcade Prizes | | | |
| --- | --- | --- | --- |
| Prize | Number of Tickets | Prize | Number of Tickets |
| Clock Radio | 138 | Calculator | 36 |
| CD Player | 162 | China Doll | 94 |
| Action Figures | 75 | Wristwatch | 159 |
| Comic Books | 14 | Cell Phone | 83 |
| Desk Set | 27 | Mystery Book | 22 |
| Model Airplane | 46 | Photo Album | 40 |

1. Make a Prize Log like the one shown below to record your choices and how many tickets you will have left.

| Prize | Number of Tickets | Tickets Left |
| --- | --- | --- |
| CD Player | 162 | 500 − 162 = 338 |
| China Doll | 94 | 338 − 94 = 244 |
| Cell Phone | 83 | 244 − 83 = 161 |

2. Choose one subtraction you made in your chart under "Tickets Left." On a separate sheet of paper, draw place-value blocks to show how you subtracted. Did you regroup? Explain.

3. Use a diagram to solve the subtraction you modeled in question 2.

4. Write the smaller subtraction problems you could use to solve the subtraction problem you chose in question 2.

5. Suppose you wanted to get the CD player, wristwatch and photo album. How many tickets in all would you need?

## Topic 4 Meanings of Multiplication

▼ Monarch butterflies have bright orange wings. How many wings does each monarch butterfly have? You will find out in Lesson 4-4.

**Topic Essential Questions**
- What are different meanings of multiplication?
- How are addition and multiplication related?

## Review What You Know!

### Vocabulary

Choose the best term from the box.

- add
- skip count
- equal groups
- subtract

1. If you combine groups to find how many in all, you __?__.

2. __?__ have the same number of items.

3. When you say the numbers 2, 4, 6, 8, you __?__.

### Equal Groups

Are the groups equal? Write *yes* or *no*.

4.

5.

### Adding

Find each sum.

6. 5 + 5 + 5          7. 7 + 7

8. 3 + 3 + 3          9. 2 + 2 + 2 + 2

10. 6 + 6 + 6         11. 9 + 9 + 9

### Repeated Addition

© 12. **Writing to Explain** Draw a picture to show how to solve 8 + 8 + 8 = ▢. Then copy and complete the number sentence.

# Interactive Learning

**Pose the problem.** Start each lesson by working together to solve problems. It will help you make sense of math.

## Applying Math Practices

- What am I asked to find?
- What else can I try?
- How are quantities related?
- How can I explain my work?
- How can I use math to model the problem?
- Can I use tools to help?
- Is my work precise?
- Why does this work?
- How can I generalize?

---

### Lesson 4-1

© **Use Tools** Solve any way you choose. Use counters to help.

Ms. Witt bought 3 boxes of finger paints with 5 jars of paint in each box. What is the total number of jars Ms. Witt bought?

---

### Lesson 4-2

© **Use Tools** Solve any way you choose. Use counters to represent the problem.

Mark puts sports cards in an album. He puts 4 rows of cards on each page. He puts 3 cards in each row. How many cards are on each page?

**Lesson 4-3**

© **Generalize** Solve. Look for what's the same in each.

Cathy has arranged some shells in two different arrays. One array has 2 rows with 6 shells in each row. The other array has 6 rows with 2 shells in each row. Do both arrays have the same number of shells? Explain. Write a multiplication sentence for each.

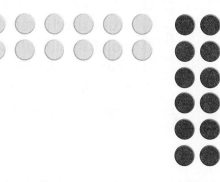

**Lesson 4-4**

© **Communicate** Use what you know about multiplication to complete this task.

Write a real-world multiplication story that can be solved by finding 4 × 5. Then give the answer to your problem in a complete sentence.

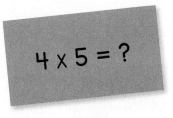

$4 \times 5 = ?$

**Lesson 4-5**

© **Communicate** Solve. Then write an explanation of how you solved the problem. You can use words, pictures, numbers, and symbols to explain.

Kay needs to buy the bicycle helmet at the right. She earns $9 each week babysitting. How long will it take Kay to earn the money she needs?

$25

Common
Core

3.OA.1 Interpret products
of whole numbers, e.g.,
interpret 5 × 7 as the total
number of objects in
5 groups of 7 objects each....
Also 3.OA.3, 3.OA.5

# Multiplication as Repeated Addition

## How can you find the total number of objects in equal groups?

Jessie used 3 bags to bring home the goldfish she won at a Fun Fair. She put the same number of goldfish in each bag. How many goldfish did she win?

**Hands-On**
counters

8 goldfish
in each bag

---

## Guided Practice*

**MATHEMATICAL PRACTICES**

### Do you know HOW?

Copy and complete. Use counters.

**1.** ○○  ○○
○○  ○○

2 groups of ☐
4 + 4 = ☐
2 × ☐ = ☐

**2.** ●● ●● ●●
●● ●● ●●

☐ groups of 5
5 + ☐ + ☐ = ☐
3 × ☐ = ☐

### Do you UNDERSTAND?

**3.** Can you write 3 + 3 + 3 + 3 as a multiplication sentence? Explain.

Ⓒ **4. Reason** Can 3 + 5 + 6 = 14 be written as a multiplication sentence? Explain.

Ⓒ **5. Model** Write an addition sentence and a multiplication sentence to solve this problem:

Jessie bought 4 packages of colorful stones to put in the fish bowl. There were 6 stones in each package. How many stones did Jessie buy?

---

## Independent Practice

Ⓒ **Use Tools** Copy and complete. Use counters or draw a picture to help.

**6.** ○○○  ○○○
○○○  ○○○

2 groups of ☐
6 + ☐ = ☐
2 × ☐ = ☐

**7.** ●●● ●●● ●●●
●●● ●●● ●●●

3 groups of ☐
7 + ☐ + ☐ = ☐
3 × ☐ = ☐

Animated Glossary, eTools
www.pearsonsuccessnet.com

DIGITAL

*For another example, see Set A on page 110.

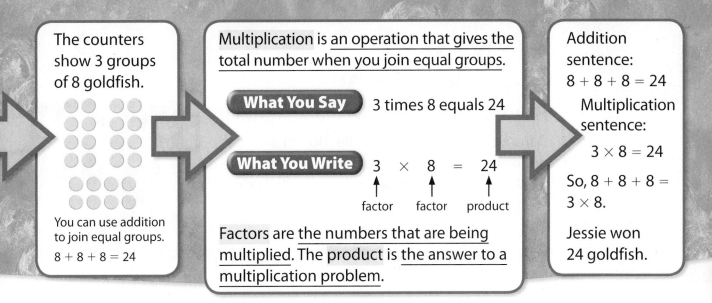

The counters show 3 groups of 8 goldfish.

You can use addition to join equal groups.

$8 + 8 + 8 = 24$

Multiplication is an operation that gives the total number when you join equal groups.

**What You Say** 3 times 8 equals 24

**What You Write**

$$3 \quad \times \quad 8 \quad = \quad 24$$
factor     factor     product

Factors are the numbers that are being multiplied. The product is the answer to a multiplication problem.

Addition sentence:

$8 + 8 + 8 = 24$

Multiplication sentence:

$3 \times 8 = 24$

So, $8 + 8 + 8 = 3 \times 8$.

Jessie won 24 goldfish.

---

Copy and complete each number sentence. Use counters or draw a picture to help.

**8.** $2 + 2 + 2 + 2 = 4 \times \square$

**9.** $\square + \square + \square = 3 \times 7$

**10.** $9 + \square + \square = \square \times 9$

**11.** $6 + 6 + 6 + 6 + 6 = \square \times \square$

© **Persevere** Write $+$, $-$, or $\times$ for each $\square$.

**12.** $4 \ \square \ 3 = 12$

**13.** $3 \ \square \ 6 = 9$

**14.** $4 \ \square \ 4 = 0$

**15.** $6 \ \square \ 4 = 10$

**16.** $5 \ \square \ 3 = 2$

**17.** $2 \ \square \ 4 = 8$

---

## Problem Solving

© MATHEMATICAL PRACTICES

**18.** What number sentence shows how to find the total number of erasers?

**A** $5 + 5 = \square$    **C** $15 + 5 = \square$

**B** $15 - 5 = \square$    **D** $3 \times 5 = \square$

© **19. Model** Write an addition sentence and a multiplication sentence to solve the problem below.

Maria has 6 new flashlights. Each flashlight takes 3 batteries. How many batteries will Maria need for the flashlights?

© **20. Communicate** Luke says that you can add or multiply to join groups. Is he correct? Explain.

**21.** Which picture shows 3 groups of 2?

**A** ♥♥ ♥♥ ♥♥

**B** ▲▲ ▲▲ ▲▲

**C** ☆☆☆☆☆ ☆☆☆☆☆

**D** ◇◇ ◇◇ ◇◇

Common
Core

**3.OA.3** Use multiplication and division within 100 to solve word problems in situations involving equal groups, arrays, and measurement quantities, ... Also **3.OA.1, 3.OA.5**

# Arrays and Multiplication

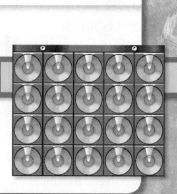

Hands-On
counters

## How does an array show multiplication?

Dana keeps her entire CD collection in a holder on the wall. The holder has 4 rows. Each row holds 5 CDs. How many CDs are in Dana's collection?

The CDs are in an array. An array shows objects in equal rows.

---

## Guided Practice*

MATHEMATICAL PRACTICES

### Do you know HOW?

In **1** and **2**, write a multiplication sentence for each array.

**1.** ●●●●
●●●●

**2.** ○○○
○○○
○○○
○○○
○○○

In **3** and **4**, draw an array to show each multiplication fact. Write the product.

**3.** 3 × 6          **4.** 5 × 4

### Do you UNDERSTAND?

© **5. Be Precise** Look at the example above. What does the first factor in the multiplication sentence tell you about the array?

© **6. Model** Mia puts 4 rows with 7 cookies in each row on a platter. Draw an array to find the total number of cookies.

---

## Independent Practice

In **7–9**, write a multiplication sentence for each array.

**7.** ●●●●●●
●●●●●●
●●●●●●

**8.** ○○○○
○○○○
○○○○
○○○○

**9.** ●●●●●●●

In **10–14**, draw an array to show each multiplication fact. Write the product.

**10.** 3 × 3      **11.** 5 × 6      **12.** 1 × 8      **13.** 4 × 3      **14.** 2 × 9

Animated Glossary, eTools
www.pearsonsuccessnet.com
DIGITAL

*For another example, see Set B on page 110.

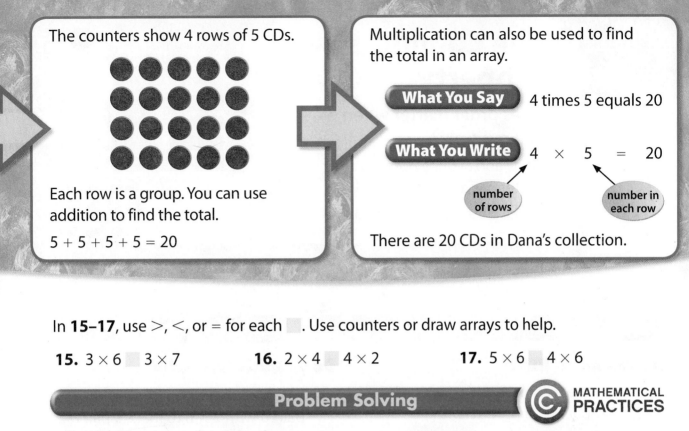

The counters show 4 rows of 5 CDs.

Each row is a group. You can use addition to find the total.

$5 + 5 + 5 + 5 = 20$

Multiplication can also be used to find the total in an array.

**What You Say**    4 times 5 equals 20

**What You Write**    $4 \times 5 = 20$

number of rows          number in each row

There are 20 CDs in Dana's collection.

In **15–17**, use >, <, or = for each ▢. Use counters or draw arrays to help.

**15.** $3 \times 6$ ▢ $3 \times 7$          **16.** $2 \times 4$ ▢ $4 \times 2$          **17.** $5 \times 6$ ▢ $4 \times 6$

## Problem Solving

**MATHEMATICAL PRACTICES**

**18.** Which array on the right shows equal groups of 3 in each row?

© **19. Communicate** How does an array show equal groups?

© **20. Model** Mr. Lopez planted Elm trees on his farm in 3 rows. He planted 6 trees in each row. Write an addition sentence and a multiplication sentence to find the total number of trees.

© **21. Reason** Margo has 23 pictures. Can she use all of the pictures to make an array with exactly two equal rows? Why or why not?

**22.** Dan bought the stamps shown at the right. Which number sentence shows one way to find how many stamps Dan bought?

**A** $4 + 5 =$ ▢

**B** $5 \times 4 =$ ▢

**C** $5 + 4 =$ ▢

**D** $5 - 4 =$ ▢

# The Commutative Property

## Does order matter when you multiply?

Libby and Sydney both say their poster has more stickers.

Which poster has more stickers?

Hands-On
counters

Libby's poster

Sydney's poster

---

## Guided Practice*

© MATHEMATICAL PRACTICES

### Do you know HOW?

Write a multiplication sentence for each array. Compare their products.

**1.**

Draw an array and give the product for each fact.

**2.** $5 \times 2$ $\qquad$ $2 \times 5$

Copy and complete.

**3.** $6 \times 4 = 24$ so $4 \times 6 =$ ▢

### Do you UNDERSTAND?

**4.** What multiplication fact can be paired with $2 \times 6$ to make a pair of facts showing the Commutative Property of Multiplication?

© **5. Communicate** Why is the Commutative Property of Multiplication sometimes called the *order property*?

**6.** Scott puts some sports stickers in rows. He makes 6 rows with 5 stickers in each row. If he put the same stickers in 5 equal rows, how many stickers would be in each row?

---

## Independent Practice

In **7** and **8**, write a multiplication sentence for each array in the pair. Compare their products.

**7.**

**8.**

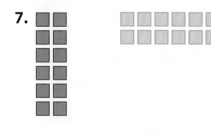

Animated Glossary, eTools
www.pearsonsuccessnet.com

*For another example, see Set B on page 110.*

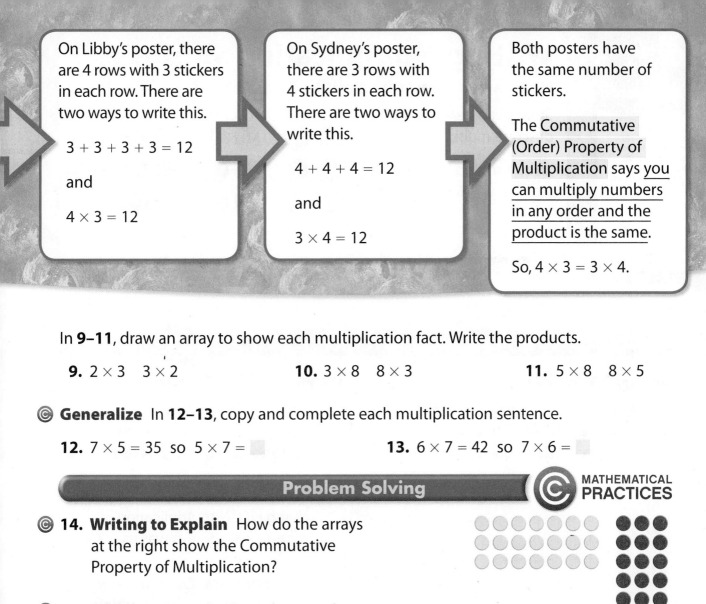

On Libby's poster, there are 4 rows with 3 stickers in each row. There are two ways to write this.

$3 + 3 + 3 + 3 = 12$

and

$4 \times 3 = 12$

On Sydney's poster, there are 3 rows with 4 stickers in each row. There are two ways to write this.

$4 + 4 + 4 = 12$

and

$3 \times 4 = 12$

Both posters have the same number of stickers.

The Commutative (Order) Property of Multiplication says you can multiply numbers in any order and the product is the same.

So, $4 \times 3 = 3 \times 4$.

In **9–11**, draw an array to show each multiplication fact. Write the products.

**9.** $2 \times 3$   $3 \times 2$

**10.** $3 \times 8$   $8 \times 3$

**11.** $5 \times 8$   $8 \times 5$

© **Generalize** In **12–13**, copy and complete each multiplication sentence.

**12.** $7 \times 5 = 35$ so $5 \times 7 = $

**13.** $6 \times 7 = 42$ so $7 \times 6 = $

### Problem Solving

© **MATHEMATICAL PRACTICES**

© **14. Writing to Explain** How do the arrays at the right show the Commutative Property of Multiplication?

© **15. Critique Arguments** Taylor says that the product of $7 \times 2$ is the same as the product of $2 \times 7$. Is he correct? Explain.

© **16. Model** Show the Commutative Property of Multiplication by drawing two arrays. Each array should have at least 2 rows and show a product of 6.

**17.** Miguel has 5 rows of stickers. There are 3 stickers in each row. Write an addition and a multiplication sentence to show how many stickers he has.

**18.** Candice arranged 32 berries in the array shown. What other array can she use for the berries?

  **A** 3 rows of 4 berries

  **B** 5 rows of 4 berries

  **C** 3 rows of 8 berries

  **D** 8 rows of 4 berries

© Common Core

3.OA.3 Use multiplication and division within 100 to solve word problems in situations involving equal groups, arrays, and measurement quantities, ... Also 3.OA.1, 3.OA.5

# Writing Multiplication Stories

## How can you describe a multiplication fact?

Stories can be written to describe multiplication facts.

Write a multiplication story for $3 \times 6 = $ ▢.

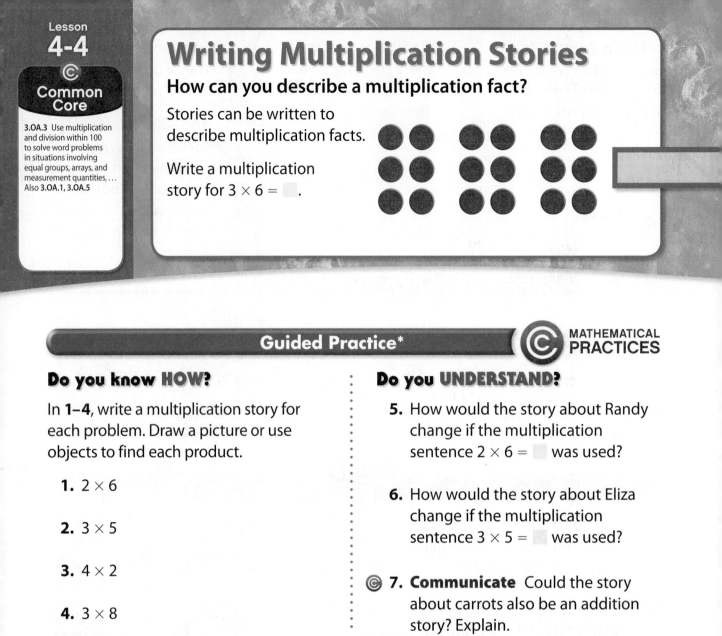

---

**Guided Practice***

© MATHEMATICAL PRACTICES

### Do you know HOW?

In **1–4**, write a multiplication story for each problem. Draw a picture or use objects to find each product.

**1.** $2 \times 6$

**2.** $3 \times 5$

**3.** $4 \times 2$

**4.** $3 \times 8$

### Do you UNDERSTAND?

**5.** How would the story about Randy change if the multiplication sentence $2 \times 6 = $ ▢ was used?

**6.** How would the story about Eliza change if the multiplication sentence $3 \times 5 = $ ▢ was used?

© **7. Communicate** Could the story about carrots also be an addition story? Explain.

---

**Independent Practice**

Write a multiplication story for each problem. Draw a picture or use objects to find each product.

**8.** $7 \times 3$    **9.** $2 \times 9$    **10.** $4 \times 5$

Write a multiplication story for each picture. Use the picture to find the product.

**11.**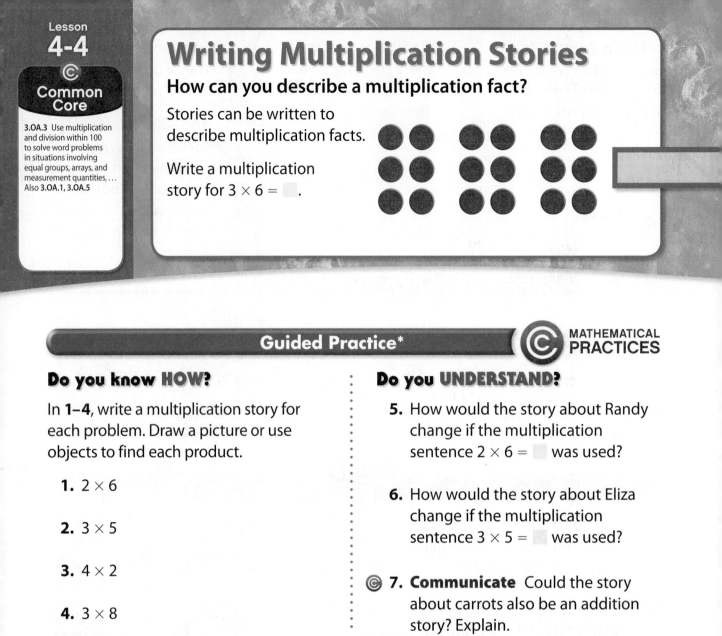

**12.**

*For another example, see Set C on page 111.*

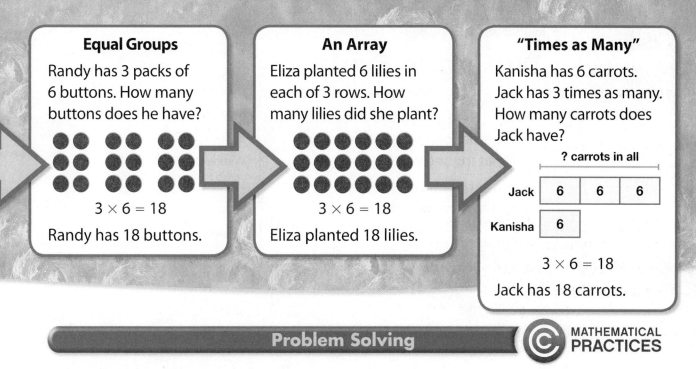

**Equal Groups**

Randy has 3 packs of 6 buttons. How many buttons does he have?

$3 \times 6 = 18$

Randy has 18 buttons.

**An Array**

Eliza planted 6 lilies in each of 3 rows. How many lilies did she plant?

$3 \times 6 = 18$

Eliza planted 18 lilies.

**"Times as Many"**

Kanisha has 6 carrots. Jack has 3 times as many. How many carrots does Jack have?

? carrots in all

| Jack | 6 | 6 | 6 |

| Kanisha | 6 |

$3 \times 6 = 18$

Jack has 18 carrots.

**Problem Solving**

Ⓒ **MATHEMATICAL PRACTICES**

Ⓒ **Communicate** For **13–15**, describe each story as an addition story, a subtraction story, or a multiplication story.

**13.** Kay has 6 pencils. She gave 4 of them to her friend. How many pencils does Kay have left?

**14.** Kay has 6 pencils. She bought 4 more pencils at the school store. How many pencils does Kay have now?

**15.** Kay has 6 bags of pencils. There are 2 pencils in each bag. How many pencils does Kay have?

**16.** A soccer team traveled to a soccer game in 4 vans. All four vans were full. Each van held 7 players. How many players went to the game?

**A** 47          **C** 24

**B** 28          **D** 11

Ⓒ **17. Model** Steve has some packages of balloons. There are 8 balloons in each package. He has 24 balloons in all. Draw a picture to find how many packages of balloons Steve has.

**18.** A group of 12 monarch butterflies is getting ready to migrate. How many wings will be moving when the group flies away?

Each monarch butterfly has 4 bright orange wings and 6 legs.

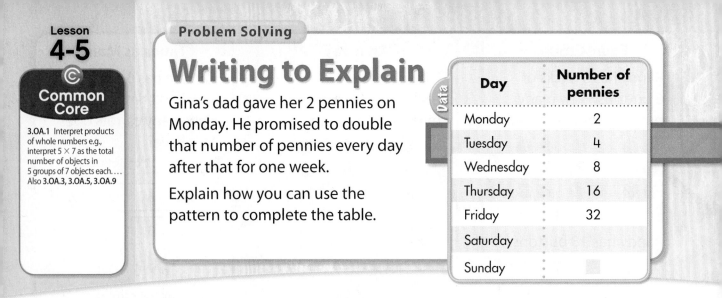

## Lesson
## 4-5

**Common Core**

3.OA.1 Interpret products of whole numbers e.g., interpret 5 × 7 as the total number of objects in 5 groups of 7 objects each.... Also 3.OA.3, 3.OA.5, 3.OA.9

**Problem Solving**

# Writing to Explain

Gina's dad gave her 2 pennies on Monday. He promised to double that number of pennies every day after that for one week.

Explain how you can use the pattern to complete the table.

| Day | Number of pennies |
|---|---|
| Monday | 2 |
| Tuesday | 4 |
| Wednesday | 8 |
| Thursday | 16 |
| Friday | 32 |
| Saturday | |
| Sunday | |

## Guided Practice*

MATHEMATICAL PRACTICES

### Do you know HOW?

© 1. **Communicate** Brian bought 3 packs of baseball cards. There are 4 cards in each pack. How many baseball cards did he buy? Explain how you can solve this problem.

### Do you UNDERSTAND?

2. If the pattern in the table above continued, how many pennies would Gina get next Monday?

© 3. **Write a Problem** Write a problem. Explain how to solve it using words, pictures, numbers, or symbols.

## Independent Practice

MATHEMATICAL PRACTICES

4. Pam is setting up tables and chairs. She puts 4 chairs at each table.

   **a** Explain how the number of chairs changes as the number of tables changes.

   **b** Copy and complete the table.

| Number of Tables | 1 | 2 | 3 | 4 | 5 |
|---|---|---|---|---|---|
| Number of Chairs | 4 | 8 | 12 | | |

**Applying Math Practices**

- What am I asked to find?
- What else can I try?
- How are quantities related?
- How can I explain my work?
- How can I use math to model the problem?
- Can I use tools to help?
- Is my work precise?
- Why does this work?
- How can I generalize?

© 5. **Model** Aaron cut a log into 5 pieces. How many cuts did he make? Explain how you found the answer.

*For another example, see Set D on page 111.*

**Complete the table. Use *words*, *pictures*, *numbers*, or *symbols* to write a math explanation.**

The number of pennies doubles each day. That means that Gina will get 2 times as many pennies as she got the day before.

So, I need to double 32.
32 + 32 = 64 pennies
Gina will get 64 pennies on Saturday.

Then, I need to double 64.
64 + 64 = 128 pennies
Gina will get 128 pennies on Sunday.

| Day | Number of Pennies |
| --- | --- |
| Monday | 2 |
| Tuesday | 4 |
| Wednesday | 8 |
| Thursday | 16 |
| Friday | 32 |
| Saturday | 64 |
| Sunday | 128 |

**6. Persevere** Copy and complete the table below. Then describe how the table helps you explain the pattern.

**Cost of School Play Tickets**

| Number of Tickets | Cost |
| --- | --- |
| 1 | $5 |
| 2 | $10 |
| 3 | $15 |
| 4 | |
| 5 | |

**7.** Hank earns $4 for raking lawns and $6 for mowing lawns. How much will Hank earn if he mows and rakes 2 lawns?

**8. Model** Jake planted trees in a row that is 20 feet long. He planted a tree at the beginning of the row. Then he planted a tree every 5 feet. How many trees did he plant in this row? Draw a picture to explain.

**9. Use Structure** Alexandra bought 5 bags of oranges. There were 6 oranges in each bag. Then she gave 4 oranges away. Which number sentence shows how many oranges Alexandra bought?

**A** $5 + 6 = $ ▪

**B** $5 \times 6 = $ ▪

**C** $(5 \times 6) - 4 = $ ▪

**D** $(5 + 6) - 4 = $ ▪

**10. Use Structure** Tara ran 5 miles on Monday and 4 miles on Tuesday. Teresa ran 3 miles on Monday and 6 miles on Tuesday. Which number sentence shows how far Tara ran in all?

**A** $3 + 6 = $ ▪

**B** $5 + 4 = $ ▪

**C** $5 - 4 = $ ▪

**D** $5 + 4 + 3 + 6 = $ ▪

**Set A,** pages 100–101

Find the total number of counters.

There are 3 groups of 2 counters.

You can use addition to join groups.

$2 + 2 + 2 = 6$

You can also multiply to join equal groups.

$3 \times 2 = 6$

So, $2 + 2 + 2 = 3 \times 2$.

**Remember** that multiplication is a quick way of joining equal groups.

Copy and complete.

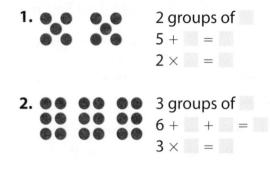

1. 2 groups of ▢
   $5 + ▢ = ▢$
   $2 \times ▢ = ▢$

2. 3 groups of ▢
   $6 + ▢ + ▢ = ▢$
   $3 \times ▢ = ▢$

**Set B,** pages 102–105

Draw an array to show $2 \times 3$.
Then write the product.

This array shows
2 rows of 3.

■ ■ ■  2 rows
■ ■ ■  3 in each row

$3 + 3 = 6$ or $2 \times 3 = 6$.

Draw an array to show $3 \times 2$.

This array shows
3 rows of 2.

■ ■  3 rows
■ ■  2 in each row
■ ■

$2 + 2 + 2 = 6$ or $3 \times 2 = 6$.

The **Commutative (Order) Property of Multiplication** says you can multiply numbers in any order and the product is the same.

$2 \times 3 = 3 \times 2$.

**Remember** to use the Commutative (Order) Property of Multiplication.

Draw an array to show each fact. Write the product.

**1.** $2 \times 4$    **2.** $3 \times 5$    **3.** $4 \times 4$

**4.** $7 \times 3$    **5.** $1 \times 6$    **6.** $2 \times 8$

Copy and complete each number sentence. Draw an array to help.

**7.** $5 \times ▢ = 10$    **8.** $3 \times ▢ = 21$

   $2 \times ▢ = 10$        $7 \times ▢ = 21$

**9.** $2 \times ▢ = 12$    **10.** $4 \times ▢ = 24$

   $6 \times ▢ = 12$        $6 \times ▢ = 24$

Write a multiplication story for 3 × 5.

Draw a picture to find the product.

Jessica is putting pretzels into 3 bags. She will put 5 pretzels in each bag. How many pretzels does Jessica have in all?

Jessica has 15 pretzels.

**Remember** that your multiplication story should always end with a question.

Write a multiplication story for each. Draw a picture to find each product.

**1.** 3 × 9    **2.** 5 × 6    **3.** 7 × 2

Write a multiplication story for each picture. Use the picture to find the product.

**4.**

**5.** ⬤⬤⬤⬤⬤
⬤⬤⬤⬤⬤
⬤⬤⬤⬤⬤

You can use words, pictures, numbers, or symbols to explain an answer. When you explain your answer to a problem, be sure that you:

• clearly show your explanation using words, pictures, numbers, or symbols.

• tell what the numbers mean in your explanation.

• tell why you took certain steps.

**Remember** that another person should be able to follow your explanation.

Solve. Explain how you found each answer.

**1.** Gina earns $3 for making dinner and $5 for changing the sheets on her bed. How much will Gina earn in one week if she makes dinner 3 times and changes the sheets one time?

**2.** Jack is setting up tables for a party. Each table has 6 chairs. How many chairs does he need for 10 tables?

**Multiple Choice**

1. Which has the same value as 5 × 2? (4-1)

   A 5 + 2

   B 2 + 2 + 2 + 2

   C 2 + 2 + 2 + 5

   D 2 + 2 + 2 + 2 + 2

2. For the 4th of July, Ron put flags in his yard as shown below. Which number sentence could be used to find how many flags Ron put in his yard? (4-2)

   A 5 + 4 =

   B 4 × 5 =

   C 4 + 5 =

   D 5 − 4 =

3. Which story could be solved with 7 × 8? (4-4)

   A Ben bought 7 bags of apples. Each bag had 8 apples. How many apples did Ben buy?

   B Rob has 7 red fish and 8 orange fish. How many fish does Rob have in all?

   C Tao had 8 math problems to solve. He has solved 7 of them. How many does he have left?

   D Max has 7 pages in his album. He has 8 pictures. How many pictures can he put on each page?

4. Which number makes the second number sentence true? (4-3)

   9 × 7 = 63
   7 × ▢ = 63

   A 63

   B 56

   C 9

   D 7

5. Which is a multiplication sentence for this repeated addition? (4-1)

   6 + 6 + 6 + 6 + 6

   A 1 × 6

   B 4 × 6

   C 5 × 6

   D 6 × 6

6. Alice is buying paper cups for the picnic. Each package has 8 cups. How does the number of cups change as the number of packages increases by 1? (4-5)

   | Packages | 1 | 2 | 3 | 4 | 5 |
   |----------|---|---|---|---|---|
   | Cups | 8 | 16 | 24 | 32 | 40 |

   A There are 40 more cups for each additional package.

   B There are 40 fewer cups for each additional package.

   C There are 8 more cups for each additional package.

   D There are 8 fewer cups for each additional package.

**7.** Write a repeated addition sentence for $8 \times 6$. (4-1)

**8.** Mrs. Salinas planted her flowers as shown in the picture below. Write a number sentence that best shows how many she planted. (4-2)

**9.** Write a story that could be solved with $3 \times 9$. (4-4)

**10.** The Carroll family replaced the tiles on their kitchen floor. A $5 \times 4$ array of tiles fit the area. How many tiles did they use? (4-2)

**11.** How can knowing that $5 \times 13 = 65$ help you find the answer to $13 \times 5$? Explain. (4-3)

**12.** Complete the number sentence. (4-1)

$7 + 7 + 7 + 7 + 7 + 7 = \boxed{\phantom{0}} \times 7$

**13.** Hamid is putting books on shelves. Each shelf holds 9 books. How does the number of books change as the number of shelves increases by 1? (4-5)

| Shelves | 1 | 2 | 3 | 4 | 5 |
|---------|---|---|----|----|----|
| Books | 9 | 18 | 27 | 36 | 45 |

**14.** Write the number that makes the second number sentence true. (4-3)

$5 \times 4 = 20$
$4 \times \boxed{\phantom{0}} = 20$

**15.** Can you write $2 + 3 + 4 = 9$ as a multiplication sentence? Explain. (4-1)

**16.** A marching band has 3 rows of band members. There are 8 students in each row. How many students are in the band? Draw a picture to help. (4-2)

**17.** Mason has 4 boxes of granola bars. There are 5 granola bars in each box. Write and solve a multiplication sentence to find how many granola bars Mason has. (4-4)

**18.** Julianna earns $3 for walking dogs and $5 for washing dogs. How much will Julianna earn if she walks 2 dogs and washes 4 dogs? Explain how you can find the answer using a table. (4-5)

| Walking Dogs | $3 | $6 | | |
|---|---|---|---|---|
| Washing Dogs | $5 | $10 | $15 | $20 |

You want to make a design using tiles. You have 24 tiles to use. Your design must be set up in rows and have the same number of tiles in each row.

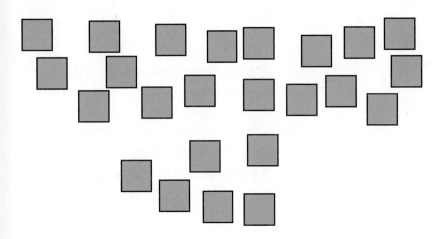

1. Draw a picture of some of the different arrangements you can make. Make at least 2 drawings.

2. Choose one arrangement that you will use for your design. Draw a circle around that design. Write a repeated addition sentence for the array.

3. Look at the repeated addition sentence that you wrote. Write the repeated addition sentence as a multiplication sentence.

4. Write a multiplication story to go with your number sentence.

5. Write a multiplication sentence for each of the tile designs shown below. Explain how the tile designs show the Commutative Property of Multiplication.

DOMAIN Operations and Algebraic Thinking

Topic 5

# Multiplication Facts: Use Patterns

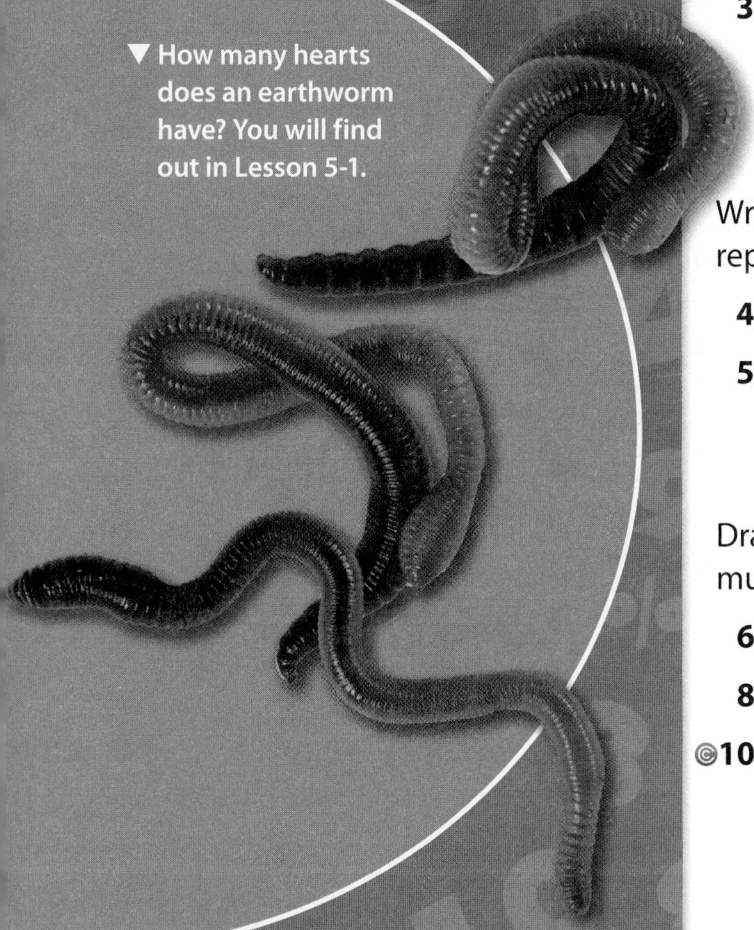

▼ How many hearts does an earthworm have? You will find out in Lesson 5-1.

**Topic Essential Question**
- What patterns can be used to find certain multiplication facts?

## Review What You Know!

### Vocabulary

Choose the best term from the box.

- factors
- sum
- product
- equal

1. When you add to combine numbers, another name for the total is the _?_.
2. In the number sentence $5 \times 7 = 35$, the number 35 is called _?_.
3. Multiplication can be used to join _?_ groups.

### Multiplication

Write a multiplication sentence for each repeated addition.

4. $6 + 6 + 6 + 6 + 6 + 6 = 36$
5. $8 + 8 + 8 + 8 + 8 = 40$

### Arrays

Draw an array of dots to model each multiplication fact.

6. $2 \times 7$
7. $5 \times 4$
8. $1 \times 9$
9. $3 \times 4$
10. **Writing to Explain** Adam arranged some cups in 4 rows with 7 cups in each row. He wrote $7 + 7 + 7 + 7$ to find the total number of cups. Pat says Adam should find the total by writing $4 \times 7$. Who is correct? Explain.

# Interactive Learning

**Pose the problem.** Start each lesson by working together to solve problems. It will help you make sense of math.

### Applying Math Practices
- What am I asked to find?
- What else can I try?
- How are quantities related?
- How can I explain my work?
- How can I use math to model the problem?
- Can I use tools to help?
- Is my work precise?
- Why does this work?
- How can I generalize?

## Lesson 5-1

© **Look for Patterns**  Solve any way you choose.

How can you find how many legs there are all together in a group of 9 chickens? 8 chickens? 7 chickens? Show how you found the solution.

## Lesson 5-2

© **Use Tools**  Solve any way you choose.

Maria bought 4 packages of bottled water. There are 9 bottles in each package. How many bottles did she buy? Show how you found the solution.

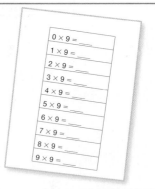

## Lesson 5-3

© **Generalize**  Solve any way you choose.

Jackson has ? bowls. He puts 1 apple in each bowl. How many apples does he use? Tell how you decided.

**Lesson 5-4**

Ⓒ **Look for Patterns** Solve. Use the hundred chart to help.

How many fingers are there on three hands? Four hands? Five hands? Describe patterns you found.

| 1 | 2 | 3 | 4 | 5 | 6 | 7 | 8 | 9 | 10 |
|---|---|---|---|---|---|---|---|---|---|
| 11 | 12 | 13 | 14 | 15 | 16 | 17 | 18 | 19 | 20 |
| 21 | 22 | 23 | 24 | 25 | 26 | 27 | 28 | 29 | 30 |
| 31 | 32 | 33 | 34 | 35 | 36 | 37 | 38 | 39 | 40 |
| 41 | 42 | 43 | 44 | 45 | 46 | 47 | 48 | 49 | 50 |
| 51 | 52 | 53 | 54 | 55 | 56 | 57 | 58 | 59 | 60 |
| 61 | 62 | 63 | 64 | 65 | 66 | 67 | 68 | 69 | 70 |
| 71 | 72 | 73 | 74 | 75 | 76 | 77 | 78 | 79 | 80 |
| 81 | 82 | 83 | 84 | 85 | 86 | 87 | 88 | 89 | 90 |
| 91 | 92 | 93 | 94 | 95 | 96 | 97 | 98 | 99 | 100 |

**Lesson 5-5**

Ⓒ **Look for Patterns** Solve any way you choose.

Duke runs 10 miles each week. How many miles will he run in 6 weeks? 7 weeks? 8 weeks? Describe patterns you found.

$0 \times$ _____ = _____

$1 \times$ _____ = _____

$2 \times$ _____ = _____

$3 \times$ _____ = _____

$4 \times$ _____ = _____

$5 \times$ _____ = _____

$6 \times$ _____ = _____

$7 \times$ _____ = _____

$8 \times$ _____ = _____

$9 \times$ _____ = _____

$10 \times$ _____ = _____

**Lesson 5-6**

Ⓒ **Generalize** Solve any way you choose. Look for basic facts.

Find each product at the right. What patterns do you see in the products? What generalizations can you make about problems like this?

$5 \times 30 =$ _____,
$2 \times 40 =$ _____,
$9 \times 20 =$ _____.

**Lesson 5-7**

Ⓒ **Model** Solve any way you choose.

Pablo bought 2 red notebooks, 3 green notebooks, and 3 blue notebooks. How many notebooks did he buy in all? If each notebook cost $5, what was the total cost? Show how you found the solution.

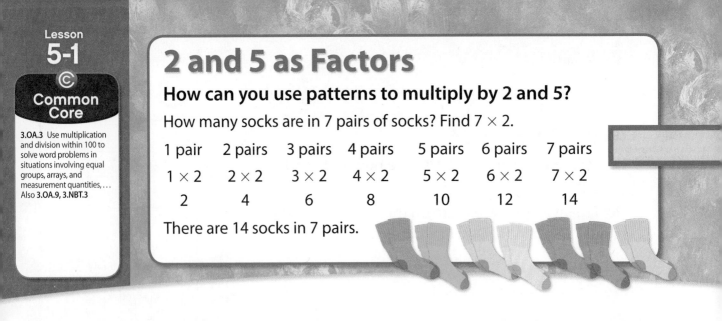

# 2 and 5 as Factors

## How can you use patterns to multiply by 2 and 5?

How many socks are in 7 pairs of socks? Find $7 \times 2$.

| 1 pair | 2 pairs | 3 pairs | 4 pairs | 5 pairs | 6 pairs | 7 pairs |
|--------|---------|---------|---------|---------|---------|---------|
| $1 \times 2$ | $2 \times 2$ | $3 \times 2$ | $4 \times 2$ | $5 \times 2$ | $6 \times 2$ | $7 \times 2$ |
| 2 | 4 | 6 | 8 | 10 | 12 | 14 |

There are 14 socks in 7 pairs.

© Common Core

3.OA.3 Use multiplication and division within 100 to solve word problems in situations involving equal groups, arrays, and measurement quantities, …
Also 3.OA.9, 3.NBT.3

## Other Examples

### What are the patterns in multiples of 2 and 5?

The products for the 2s facts are multiples of 2.
The products for the 5s facts are multiples of 5.
Multiples are the products of a number and other whole numbers.

**2s Facts**

| | |
|---|---|
| $0 \times 2 = 0$ | $5 \times 2 = 10$ |
| $1 \times 2 = 2$ | $6 \times 2 = 12$ |
| $2 \times 2 = 4$ | $7 \times 2 = 14$ |
| $3 \times 2 = 6$ | $8 \times 2 = 16$ |
| $4 \times 2 = 8$ | $9 \times 2 = 18$ |

**5s Facts**

| | |
|---|---|
| $0 \times 5 = 0$ | $5 \times 5 = 25$ |
| $1 \times 5 = 5$ | $6 \times 5 = 30$ |
| $2 \times 5 = 10$ | $7 \times 5 = 35$ |
| $3 \times 5 = 15$ | $8 \times 5 = 40$ |
| $4 \times 5 = 20$ | $9 \times 5 = 45$ |

**Patterns for 2s Facts**

- Multiples of 2 are even numbers. Multiples of 2 end in 0, 2, 4, 6, or 8.

- Each multiple of 2 is 2 more than the one before it.

**Patterns for 5s Facts**

- Each multiple of 5 ends in 0 or 5.

- Each multiple of 5 is 5 more than the one before it.

**Explain It**

1. Is 83 a multiple of 2? a multiple of 5? How do you know?

© 2. **Reason** How can patterns help you find $10 \times 2$?

How many fingers are on 7 gloves?

**Choose an Operation** Find $7 \times 5$.

$$1 \times 5 = 5$$
$$2 \times 5 = 10$$
$$3 \times 5 = 15$$
$$4 \times 5 = 20$$
$$5 \times 5 = 25$$
$$6 \times 5 = 30$$
$$7 \times 5 = 35$$

There are 35 fingers on 7 gloves.

## Guided Practice*

MATHEMATICAL PRACTICES

### Do you know HOW?

Find each product.

**1.** $2 \times 6$    **2.** $2 \times 3$    **3.** $7 \times 2$

**4.** $5 \times 3$    **5.** $5 \times 5$    **6.** $6 \times 5$

**7.** $\begin{array}{r} 4 \\ \times 2 \\ \hline \end{array}$    **8.** $\begin{array}{r} 5 \\ \times 2 \\ \hline \end{array}$    **9.** $\begin{array}{r} 8 \\ \times 5 \\ \hline \end{array}$

### Do you UNDERSTAND?

© **10. Generalize** How can you skip count to find the number of socks in 9 pairs? in 10 pairs?

© **11. Generalize** How can you skip count to find how many fingers are on 9 gloves? on 10 gloves?

© **12. Use Structure** Bert says that $2 \times 8$ is 15. How can you use patterns to know that his answer is wrong?

## Independent Practice

For **13–22**, find each product.

**13.** $2 \times 2$    **14.** $5 \times 2$    **15.** $3 \times 5$    **16.** $8 \times 2$    **17.** $9 \times 5$

**18.** $\begin{array}{r} 3 \\ \times 5 \\ \hline \end{array}$    **19.** $\begin{array}{r} 2 \\ \times 4 \\ \hline \end{array}$    **20.** $\begin{array}{r} 4 \\ \times 5 \\ \hline \end{array}$    **21.** $\begin{array}{r} 9 \\ \times 2 \\ \hline \end{array}$    **22.** $\begin{array}{r} 5 \\ \times 7 \\ \hline \end{array}$

**23.** Find 5 times 6.      **24.** Multiply 2 by 5.

**25.** Find the product of 7 and 5.      **26.** Find $6 \times 2$.

DIGITAL   Animated Glossary
www.pearsonsuccessnet.com

*For another example, see Set A on page 134.      Lesson 5-1   

Compare. Use <, >, or =.

**27.** $2 \times 5 \bigcirc 5 \times 2$

**28.** $4 \times 5 \bigcirc 5 \times 6$

**29.** $2 \times 5 \bigcirc 2 \times 4$

**30.** $6 \times 5 \bigcirc 5 \times 5$

**31.** $9 \times 5 \bigcirc 5 \times 9$

**32.** $7 \times 2 \bigcirc 2 \times 9$

## Problem Solving

**MATHEMATICAL PRACTICES**

For **33–35**, use the table at the right.

**33.** How much does it cost to bowl three games without renting shoes?

**34.** Maru rented some bowling shoes. She also bowled two games. How much money did she spend?

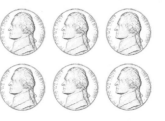

| Bowling | |
|---|---|
| Cost per game | $5 |
| Daily shoe rental | $2 |

**35.** Wendy paid for 2 games with a twenty-dollar bill. How much change did she get back?

**36. Writing to Explain** Eric has some nickels. He says they are worth exactly 34 cents. Can you tell if he is correct or not? Why or why not?

**37.** April has the coins shown below.

**38.** Use the picture below. How many hearts do 3 earthworms have?

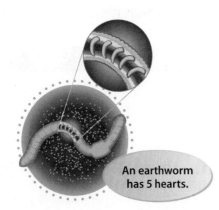

An earthworm has 5 hearts.

April counted the value of these coins in cents. Which list shows numbers she would have named?

**A** 5, 10, 16, 20, 25, 26

**B** 5, 10, 15, 22, 25, 32

**C** 5, 10, 15, 20, 25, 30

**D** 10, 15, 22, 25, 30, 35

**39. Reason** What two 1-digit factors could you multiply to get a product of 30?

**40. Persevere** Jake went bowling. On his first turn, he knocked down 2 pins. On his second turn, he knocked down 2 times as many. So far, how many pins in all has he knocked down?

## Meanings of Multiplication

Use  tools

### Counters

**Step 1** Go to the Counters eTool. Select a counter shape. Make 4 groups of counters with 3 counters in each group. The odometer tells how many counters in all. Write a number sentence: $4 \times 3 = 12$.

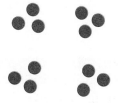

**Step 2**  Use the broom tool to clear the workspace. Show 3 groups with 8 counters in each and write a number sentence: $3 \times 8 = 24$.

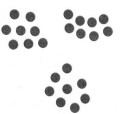

**Step 3**  Select the array workspace. Drag the button to show 7 rows with 6 counters in each row. Write a number sentence: $7 \times 6 = 42$.

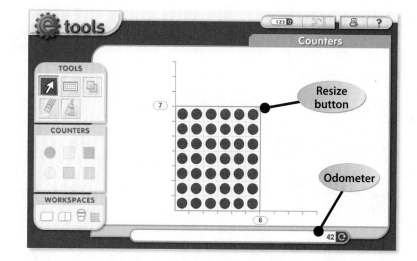

---

## Practice

Use the Counters eTool to draw counters. Write a number sentence.

**1.** 5 groups with 3 counters in each

**2.** 7 groups with 4 counters in each

**3.** 8 rows with 6 counters in each

**4.** 9 rows with 5 counters in each

Lesson
5-2

Common
Core

3.OA.9 Identify arithmetic patterns (including patterns in the addition table or multiplication table), and explain them using properties of operations.... Also 3.OA.3, 3.OA.7, 3.OA.8

# 9 as a Factor

### How can patterns be used to find 9s facts?

The owner of a flower shop puts 9 roses in each package. How many roses are in 8 packages?

Use patterns to find $8 \times 9$.

| 9s Facts | |
|---|---|
| $0 \times 9 =$ | $0$ |
| $1 \times 9 =$ | $9$ |
| $2 \times 9 =$ | $18$ |
| $3 \times 9 =$ | $27$ |
| $4 \times 9 =$ | $36$ |
| $5 \times 9 =$ | $45$ |
| $6 \times 9 =$ | $54$ |
| $7 \times 9 =$ | $63$ |
| $8 \times 9 =$ | |
| $9 \times 9 =$ | |

## Guided Practice*

MATHEMATICAL
PRACTICES

### Do you know HOW?

Find each product.

**1.** $9 \times 2$   **2.** $5 \times 9$   **3.** $7 \times 9$

**4.** $4 \times 9$   **5.** $2 \times 8$   **6.** $6 \times 9$

**7.** $\begin{array}{r} 3 \\ \times\ 9 \\ \hline \end{array}$   **8.** $\begin{array}{r} 5 \\ \times\ 5 \\ \hline \end{array}$   **9.** $\begin{array}{r} 8 \\ \times\ 9 \\ \hline \end{array}$

### Do you UNDERSTAND?

**10. Generalize** Use the patterns above to find $9 \times 9$. Then explain how you found the product.

**11. Critique Reasoning** Paul thinks that $3 \times 9$ is 24. Use a 9s pattern to show that he is wrong.

## Independent Practice

Find each product.

**12.** $9 \times 0$   **13.** $5 \times 8$   **14.** $9 \times 4$   **15.** $8 \times 9$

**16.** $9 \times 9$   **17.** $1 \times 9$   **18.** $5 \times 9$   **19.** $2 \times 9$

**20.** $7 \times 9$   **21.** $5 \times 2$   **22.** $6 \times 5$   **23.** $9 \times 1$

**24.** $\begin{array}{r} 6 \\ \times\ 9 \\ \hline \end{array}$   **25.** $\begin{array}{r} 9 \\ \times\ 5 \\ \hline \end{array}$   **26.** $\begin{array}{r} 9 \\ \times\ 7 \\ \hline \end{array}$   **27.** $\begin{array}{r} 9 \\ \times\ 2 \\ \hline \end{array}$

**28.** $\begin{array}{r} 7 \\ \times\ 9 \\ \hline \end{array}$   **29.** $\begin{array}{r} 8 \\ \times\ 2 \\ \hline \end{array}$   **30.** $\begin{array}{r} 0 \\ \times\ 9 \\ \hline \end{array}$   **31.** $\begin{array}{r} 2 \\ \times\ 3 \\ \hline \end{array}$

*For another example, see Set A on page 134.

## One Way

Use these patterns. Start with $1 \times 9 = 9$.

The ones digit decreases by 1 each time. So the ones digit in the product after 63 is 2.

The tens digit increases by 1 each time. So the tens digit in the product after 63 is 7.

$8 \times 9 = 72$

There are 72 roses in 8 packages.

## Another Way

Use these patterns to find the product.

The tens digit is 1 less than the factor being multiplied by 9.

$$8 - 1 = 7$$

$$8 \times 9 = 72$$

The digits of the product have a sum of 9.

$$7 + 2 = 9$$

There are 72 roses in 8 packages.

---

Copy and complete. Use $+$, $-$, or $\times$.

**32.** $2 \times 6 = 10 \; \square \; 2$

**33.** $5 \times 7 = 45 \; \square \; 10$

**34.** $9 \times 9 = 80 \; \square \; 1$

**35.** $20 - 2 = 2 \; \square \; 9$

**36.** $9 \; \square \; 3 = 30 - 3$

**37.** $9 \; \square \; 1 = 2 \; \square \; 5$

---

### Problem Solving

**MATHEMATICAL PRACTICES**

The library is having a used book sale. For **38–41**, use the table at the right.

**38.** How much do 4 hardcover books cost?

**39. Reason** How much more would Chico spend if he bought 3 books on CDs rather than 3 hardcover books?

**40. Be Precise** Maggie bought only paperback books. The clerk told her she owed $15. How does Maggie know that the clerk made a mistake?

**41. Writing to Explain** Mr. Lee bought 2 books on CDs and 9 paperback books. Did he spend more on CDs or on paperback books? Tell how you know.

| Library Book Sale | |
| --- | --- |
| Paperback Books | $2 |
| Hardcover Books | $5 |
| Books on CDs | $9 |

**42. Persevere** The owner of a flower shop counted the flowers in groups of 9. Which list shows the numbers he named?

9 sunflowers in each vase.

**A** 9, 19, 29, 39, 49, 59

**C** 18, 27, 36, 45, 56, 65

**B** 6, 12, 18, 24, 36, 42

**D** 9, 18, 27, 36, 45, 54

Lesson
5-3

©
Common
Core

3.OA.9 Identify arithmetic
patterns (including patterns
in the addition table or
multiplication table),
and explain them using
properties of operations....
Also 3.OA.3, 3.OA.8

# Multiplying with 0 and 1

## What are the patterns in multiples of 1 and 0?

Kira has 8 plates with 1 orange on each plate.
How many oranges does Kira have?

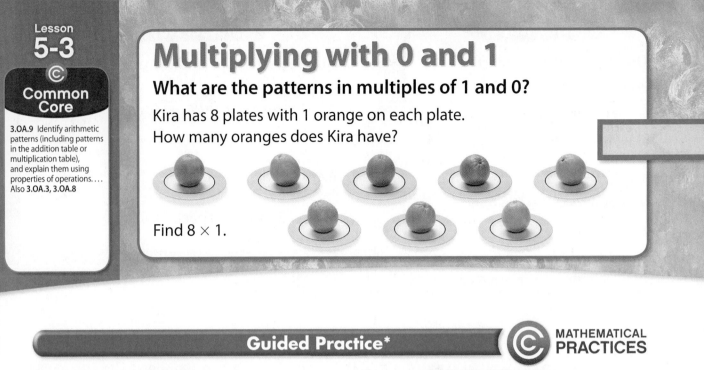

Find 8 × 1.

---

## Guided Practice*

© MATHEMATICAL
PRACTICES

### Do you know HOW?

Find each product.

**1.** 1 × 7     **2.** 5 × 0     **3.** 5 × 1

**4.** 0 × 0     **5.** 1 × 1     **6.** 8 × 1

**7.**   7     **8.**   1     **9.**   0
  × 0         × 9         × 6

### Do you UNDERSTAND?

© **10. Construct Arguments** How can
you use the properties above to
find 375 × 1 and 0 × 754?

© **11. Model** Draw an array to show that
1 × 8 = 8.

© **12. Persevere** Chad has 6 plates.
There is 1 apple and 0 grapes on
each plate. How many apples are
there? How many grapes are there?

---

## Independent Practice

Find each product.

**13.** 0 × 4     **14.** 1 × 6     **15.** 1 × 3     **16.** 3 × 0     **17.** 4 × 1

**18.** 0 × 9     **19.** 1 × 3     **20.** 1 × 7     **21.** 0 × 7     **22.** 8 × 0

**23.**   8     **24.**   0     **25.**   1     **26.**   9     **27.**   0
  × 1         × 2         × 2         × 0         × 1

Animated Glossary
www.pearsonsuccessnet.com

DIGITAL

*For another example, see Set B on page 134.*

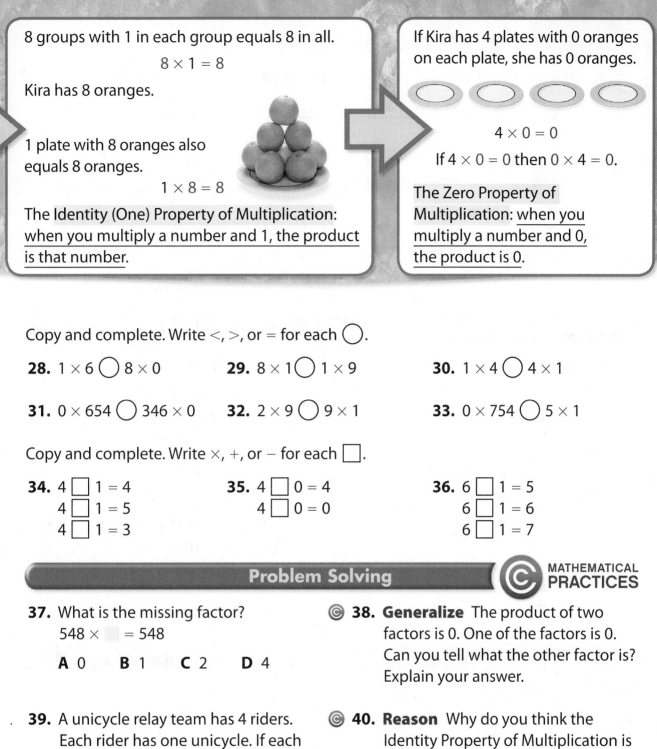

8 groups with 1 in each group equals 8 in all.

$$8 \times 1 = 8$$

Kira has 8 oranges.

1 plate with 8 oranges also equals 8 oranges.

$$1 \times 8 = 8$$

The Identity (One) Property of Multiplication: when you multiply a number and 1, the product is that number.

If Kira has 4 plates with 0 oranges on each plate, she has 0 oranges.

$$4 \times 0 = 0$$

If $4 \times 0 = 0$ then $0 \times 4 = 0$.

The Zero Property of Multiplication: when you multiply a number and 0, the product is 0.

Copy and complete. Write <, >, or = for each $\bigcirc$.

**28.** $1 \times 6 \bigcirc 8 \times 0$

**29.** $8 \times 1 \bigcirc 1 \times 9$

**30.** $1 \times 4 \bigcirc 4 \times 1$

**31.** $0 \times 654 \bigcirc 346 \times 0$

**32.** $2 \times 9 \bigcirc 9 \times 1$

**33.** $0 \times 754 \bigcirc 5 \times 1$

Copy and complete. Write $\times$, $+$, or $-$ for each $\square$.

**34.** $4 \square 1 = 4$
$4 \square 1 = 5$
$4 \square 1 = 3$

**35.** $4 \square 0 = 4$
$4 \square 0 = 0$

**36.** $6 \square 1 = 5$
$6 \square 1 = 6$
$6 \square 1 = 7$

## Problem Solving

MATHEMATICAL PRACTICES

**37.** What is the missing factor?

$548 \times \blacksquare = 548$

**A** 0   **B** 1   **C** 2   **D** 4

Ⓒ **38. Generalize** The product of two factors is 0. One of the factors is 0. Can you tell what the other factor is? Explain your answer.

**39.** A unicycle relay team has 4 riders. Each rider has one unicycle. If each unicycle has 1 wheel, how many wheels does the team have?

Ⓒ **40. Reason** Why do you think the Identity Property of Multiplication is sometimes called the One Property of Multiplication?

**41.** Tickets for a school concert are free to students. The cost is $1 for each adult. What is the total cost of tickets for 2 adults and 5 students?

**A** $7   **B** $5   **C** $2   **D** $1

**42.** The children in the 3rd-grade classes are having a bicycle parade. There are 5 rows of bikes with 8 bikes in each row. How many bikes in all are in the parade?

© **Common Core**

**3.OA.9** Identify arithmetic patterns (including patterns in the addition table or multiplication table), and explain them using properties of operations.... Also **3.OA.3, 3.OA.8**

# Patterns for Facts

## What are the patterns for multiples of 2, 5, and 9?

A multiple is the product of any two whole numbers.

○ multiples of 2

□ multiples of 5

△ multiples of 9

| 1 | ②  | 3 | ④  | 5 | ⑥  | 7 | ⑧  | △9 | ⑩ |
|---|---|---|---|---|---|---|---|---|---|
| 11 | ⑫ | 13 | ⑭ | 15 | ⑯ | 17 | △⑱ | 19 | ⑳ |
| 21 | ㉒ | 23 | ㉔ | 25 | ㉖ | △27 | ㉘ | 29 | ㉚ |
| 31 | ㉜ | 33 | ㉞ | 35 | △㊱ | 37 | ㊳ | 39 | ㊵ |

---

## Guided Practice*

© **MATHEMATICAL PRACTICES**

### Do you know HOW?

In **1** through **4**, skip count to find the number that comes next.

**1.** 2, 4, 6, 8, ▨

**2.** 20, 22, 24, ▨

**3.** 20, 25, 30, ▨

**4.** 36, 45, 54, ▨

In **5** through **8**, find the product.

**5.** $9 \times 1$

**6.** $2 \times 8$

**7.** $5 \times 4$

**8.** $2 \times 4$

### Do you UNDERSTAND?

© **9. Generalize** In the chart above, what pattern do you see for the numbers that have both red circles and green squares?

© **10. Look for Patterns** Why is 63 not a multiple of 2? Explain using the pattern for multiples of 2.

**11.** Leah has 9 pairs of socks. How many socks does she have in all?

---

## Independent Practice

In **12** through **15**, skip count to find the number that comes next.

**12.** 18, 27, 36, ▨

**13.** 12, 14, 16, ▨

**14.** 5, 10, 15, ▨

**15.** 88, 90, 92, ▨

In **16** through **30**, find each product.

**16.** $2 \times 6$

**17.** $5 \times 3$

**18.** $5 \times 2$

**19.** $5 \times 8$

**20.** $9 \times 8$

**21.** $2 \times 7$

**22.** $5 \times 7$

**23.** $9 \times 3$

**24.** $9 \times 6$

**25.** $2 \times 5$

**26.** $2 \times 3$

**27.** $5 \times 9$

**28.** $5 \times 6$

**29.** $9 \times 9$

**30.** $5 \times 5$

DIGITAL
Animated Glossary
www.pearsonsuccessnet.com

*For another example, see Set C on page 134.

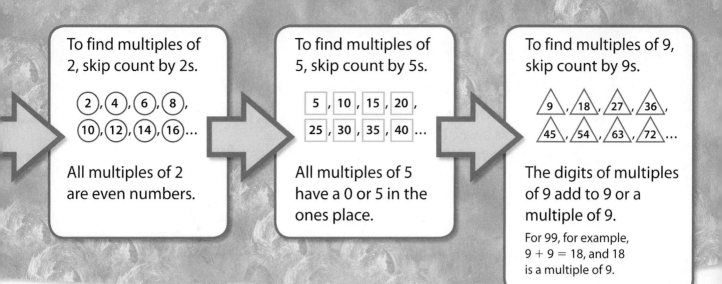

To find multiples of 2, skip count by 2s.

(2), (4), (6), (8),
(10), (12), (14), (16)...

All multiples of 2 are even numbers.

To find multiples of 5, skip count by 5s.

5, 10, 15, 20,
25, 30, 35, 40 ...

All multiples of 5 have a 0 or 5 in the ones place.

To find multiples of 9, skip count by 9s.

9, 18, 27, 36,
45, 54, 63, 72 ...

The digits of multiples of 9 add to 9 or a multiple of 9.

For 99, for example, 9 + 9 = 18, and 18 is a multiple of 9.

## Problem Solving

© **MATHEMATICAL PRACTICES**

**31.** How many arms do 9 starfish have

    **a**   if each starfish has 6 arms?

    **b**   if each starfish has 7 arms?

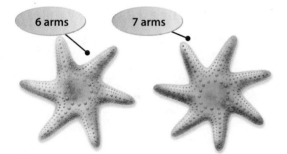

6 arms      7 arms

**32.** In wheelchair basketball, players use sports chairs that have 2 large wheels and 5 small wheels. If there are 9 players, how many

    **a**   large wheels do the sports chairs have?

    **b**   small wheels do the sports chairs have?

    **c**   wheels do the sports chairs have in all?

**33.** Jody is working on her model train. She adds 9 pieces of track. Each piece of track is attached with 4 screws. How many screws does she need in all?

    **A**   18 screws    **C**   54 screws

    **B**   36 screws    **D**   72 screws

**34.** Pedro is making a poster for each of his 5 friends. Each poster will have 4 stickers. How many stickers will Pedro need? Skip count by 5s to find the answer. Then, write the multiplication sentence.

© **35. Persevere** Use the digits 3, 4, and 6 to make as many 3-digit numbers as you can. Put the numbers in order from least to greatest.

© **36. Use Tools** Which numbers are in order from least to greatest?

    **A**   352  759  935

    **B**   532  543  352

    **C**   652  759  523

    **D**   732  452  935

Lesson
5-5

Common
Core

3.OA.9 Identify arithmetic patterns (including patterns in the addition table or multiplication table), and explain them using properties of operations.... Also 3.OA.3, 3.NBT.3, 3.OA.8

# 10 as a Factor

## What are the patterns in multiples of 10?

Greg wants to train for a race that is 10 weeks away. The chart shows his training schedule. How many miles will Greg run to train for the race?

**Choose the Operation**
Find $10 \times 10$.

| Weekly Schedule | |
|---|---|
| **Activity** | **Miles** |
| Swimming | 4 miles |
| Running | 10 miles |
| Biking | 9 miles |

---

## Guided Practice*

### Do you know HOW?

Find each product.

**1.** $2 \times 10$      **2.** $6 \times 10$

**3.**   10
   $\times \, 1$

**4.**   10
   $\times \, 3$

**5.**   10
   $\times \, 7$

### Do you UNDERSTAND?

**6. Writing to Explain** Is 91 a multiple of 10? Explain.

**7. Generalize** How many miles will Greg bike in 10 weeks?

---

## Independent Practice

Find each product.

**8.** $4 \times 10$    **9.** $9 \times 10$    **10.** $10 \times 6$    **11.** $5 \times 5$    **12.** $10 \times 10$

**13.** $5 \times 10$    **14.** $8 \times 2$    **15.** $7 \times 10$    **16.** $2 \times 5$    **17.** $1 \times 10$

**18.** $5 \times 3$    **19.** $10 \times 2$    **20.** $5 \times 9$    **21.** $3 \times 10$    **22.** $10 \times 8$

**23.**   6
   $\times \, 5$

**24.**   10
   $\times \, 1$

**25.**   10
   $\times \, 9$

**26.**   2
   $\times \, 9$

**27.**   10
   $\times \, 5$

**28.**   10
   $\times \, 2$

**29.**   7
   $\times \, 2$

**30.**   10
   $\times \, 4$

**31.**   10
   $\times \, 8$

**32.**   0
   $\times \, 6$

**33.**   5
   $\times \, 8$

**34.**   10
   $\times \, 0$

**35.**   10
   $\times \, 3$

**36.**   5
   $\times \, 7$

**37.**   10
   $\times \, 7$

**10s Facts**

| | |
|---|---|
| $0 \times 10 = 0$ | $5 \times 10 = 50$ |
| $1 \times 10 = 10$ | $6 \times 10 = 60$ |
| $2 \times 10 = 20$ | $7 \times 10 = 70$ |
| $3 \times 10 = 30$ | $8 \times 10 = 80$ |
| $4 \times 10 = 40$ | $9 \times 10 = 90$ |
| | $10 \times 10 =$ |

Data

**Use patterns to find the product.**

- Write the factor you are multiplying by 10.
- Write a zero to the right of that factor. A multiple of 10 will always have a zero in the ones place.

$$10 \times 10 = 100$$

Greg will run 100 miles.

---

## Problem Solving

MATHEMATICAL
**PRACTICES**

Use the table at the right for **38** and **39**. It shows the food that was bought for 70 third graders for a school picnic.

| Food Item | Number of Packages | Number in Each Package |
|---|---|---|
| Hot dogs | 8 | 10 |
| Rolls | 10 | 9 |
| Juice boxes | 7 | 10 |

Data

**38.** Find the total number of each item bought.

  **a** Hot dogs

  **b** Rolls

  **c** Juice boxes

ⓒ **39. Persevere** How many extra juice boxes were bought?

ⓒ **40. Writing to Explain** Look at the table at the top of page 128. Greg multiplied $5 \times 10$ to find how many more miles he biked than swam in the 10 weeks. Does that make sense? Why or why not?

ⓒ **41. Model** Mai had 3 packs of pens. Each pack had 10 pens. She gave 5 pens to Ervin. How many pens did she have left? Draw a picture to help solve the problem.

ⓒ **42. Reason** Raul has only dimes in his pocket. Could he have exactly 45 cents? Explain.

**43.** Kimmy bought 7 tickets for a concert. Each ticket cost $10. What was the total cost of the tickets Kimmy bought?

**44.** Which sign makes the number sentence true?

$$8 \; \square \; 5 = 40$$

  **A** +        **C** ×

  **B** −        **D** ÷

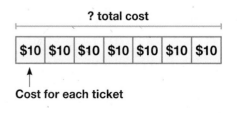

? total cost

| $10 | $10 | $10 | $10 | $10 | $10 | $10 |

Cost for each ticket

Lesson
5-6

ⓒ
Common
Core

3.NBT.3 Multiply one-digit whole numbers by multiples of 10 in the range 10–90 (e.g., 9 × 80, 5 × 60) using strategies based on place value and properties of operations.

# Multiplying by Multiples of 10

## What is a rule for multiplying by a multiple of 10?

You can use basic multiplication facts to multiply by multiples of 10.

Find 5 × 30.

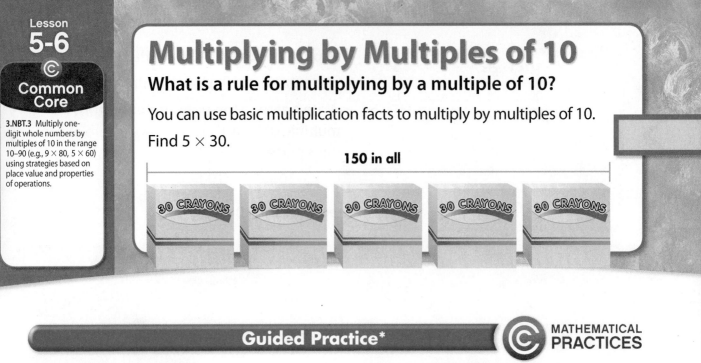

150 in all

---

Guided Practice*

ⓒ MATHEMATICAL
PRACTICES

## Do you know HOW?

In **1** and **2**, copy and complete each sentence.

**1.** 2 × 7 =

    2 × 70 =

**2.** 5 × 4 =

    5 × 40 =

In **3–6**, use basic facts to find each product.

**3.** 5 × 70

**4.** 2 × 40

**5.** 9 × 20

**6.** 5 × 50

## Do you UNDERSTAND?

**7.** What basic fact can you use to find the product of 5 × 90?

ⓒ **8. Generalize** How can you find the product of 9 × 80? Explain.

ⓒ **9. Reason** Sue wants to find the product of 30 × 2, but knows only the product of 2 × 30. What property of multiplication could she use to help solve her problem? Explain.

---

**Independent Practice**

**Leveled Practice** In **10–12**, copy and complete each sentence.

**10.** 2 × 6 =

    2 × 60 =

**11.** 5 × 8 =

    5 × 80 =

**12.** 9 × 4 =

    9 × 40 =

In **13–22**, find each product.

**13.** 2 × 30    **14.** 60 × 9    **15.** 90 × 7    **16.** 8 × 20    **17.** 80 × 5

**18.** 90 × 2    **19.** 30 × 9    **20.** 20 × 4    **21.** 50 × 7    **22.** 9 × 90

Find 5 × 30.

Multiply by the digit in the tens place.

Multiply:
5 × 3 = 15

Write one zero after the product.

5 × 3$\underline{0}$ = 15$\underline{0}$

So, 5 × 30 = 150.

Sometimes, the basic fact makes the rule look different.
Try 5 × 60.

Multiply by the digit in the tens place.

Multiply:
5 × 6 = 30

Write one zero after the product.

5 × 6$\underline{0}$ = 30$\underline{0}$

So, 5 × 60 = 300.

When the product of a basic fact ends in zero, the answer will have two zeros.

## Problem Solving

MATHEMATICAL
PRACTICES

**23. Reasonableness** Adam says the product of 2 × 50 equals 100. Dan says the product is 1,000. Who is correct?

**24.** Juanita buys 7 sheets of postage stamps at the post office. Each sheet has 20 stamps. How many stamps does she buy in all?

**25.** Hanna has 9 spools of ribbon. Each spool has 60 yards of ribbon. How many yards of ribbon does she have in all?

? yards

| 60 | 60 | 60 | 60 | 60 | 60 | 60 | 60 | 60 |

**26. Persevere** Ali and his family are going to the amusement park. Each adult ticket costs $30 and each child's ticket costs $20. If there are 2 adults and 5 children, how much will the tickets cost?

**27.** Which value for $n$ makes the equation below true?

9 × $n$ = 630

**A** $n = 30$     **C** $n = 80$

**B** $n = 70$     **D** $n = 90$

**28.** Allie bought 210 red beads and 137 green beads. How many beads did she buy in all?

**A** 173     **C** 347

**B** 247     **D** 474

**29. Reason** Is there a basic fact that would help you find 5 × 10? Explain.

**30. Communicate** Explain why there are two zeros in the product of 5 × 40.

Common
Core

3.OA.3 Use multiplication and division within 100 to solve word problems in situations involving equal groups, arrays, and measurement quantities, … Also 3.OA.8

**Problem Solving**

# Two-Question Problems

Sometimes you must use the answer to one problem to solve another problem.

**Problem 1:** Four girls and five boys went to the movies. How many children went to the movies?

**Problem 2:** Children's movie tickets cost $5 each. What was the total cost of the tickets for these children?

**Movie Plex**
Admit One
Child
$5

**Movie Plex**
Admit One
Child
$5

---

## Guided Practice*

**MATHEMATICAL
PRACTICES**

### Do you know HOW?

**1a.** A movie ticket for an adult costs $9. How much do 3 adult tickets cost?

? Total cost

| $9 | $9 | $9 |
|----|----|----|

**b.** Mr. Jones paid for 3 adult tickets with $40. How much change will he get?

$40

| $27 | ? |
|-----|---|

### Do you UNDERSTAND?

**2.** What operations were used to solve Problems 1a and 1b? Tell why.

© **3. Reason** Why must you solve Problem 1a before solving Problem 1b?

© **4. Communicate** Write 2 problems that use the answer from the first problem to solve the second one.

---

## Independent Practice

**5a.** Jared bought a baseball cap for $12 and a T-shirt for $19. How much did the items cost all together?

?

| $12 | $19 |
|-----|-----|

**b.** Suppose Jared paid with a $50 bill. How much change should he get?

$50

| $31 | ? |
|-----|---|

**Applying Math Practices**

- What am I asked to find?
- What else can I try?
- How are quantities related?
- How can I explain my work?
- How can I use math to model the problem?
- Can I use tools to help?
- Is my work precise?
- Why does this work?
- How can I generalize?

*For another example, see Set F on page 135.*

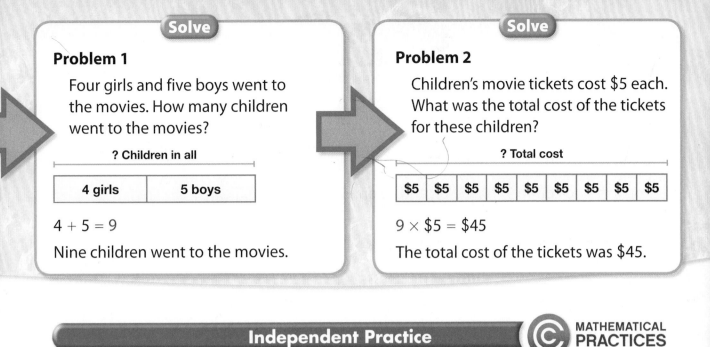

**Solve**

## Problem 1

Four girls and five boys went to the movies. How many children went to the movies?

**? Children in all**

| 4 girls | 5 boys |
|---------|--------|

$4 + 5 = 9$

Nine children went to the movies.

**Solve**

## Problem 2

Children's movie tickets cost $5 each. What was the total cost of the tickets for these children?

**? Total cost**

| $5 | $5 | $5 | $5 | $5 | $5 | $5 | $5 | $5 |
|----|----|----|----|----|----|----|----|----|

$9 \times \$5 = \$45$

The total cost of the tickets was $45.

---

### Independent Practice

© **MATHEMATICAL PRACTICES**

© **Reason** Cara and some friends bought gifts in a museum shop. The gifts were from Hawaii. In **6–8**, use the answer from the first problem to solve the second problem.

**6a.** Cara bought a poster and a shirt. How much did her gifts cost?

**b.** Cara gave the clerk $30. How much change should she get?

**7a.** Dan bought 3 cups. How much did Dan spend on cups?

**b.** Dan also bought a CD. How much did Dan spend in all?

**8a.** Teri bought the most expensive and the least expensive gift. How much did she spend?

**b.** Teri's sister bought a CD. How much did the two girls spend in all?

$15   $9   $20   $2

© **9.** **Persevere** On Monday, Roberta swam 10 laps. On Tuesday, she swam twice as many laps as on Monday. Which pair of number sentences can be used to find:

**a** how many laps Roberta swam on Tuesday?
**b** how many laps Roberta swam in all?

**A** $2 \times 10 = 20$
$20 + 10 = 30$

**B** $2 \times 10 = 20$
$20 - 10 = 10$

**C** $10 + 2 = 12$
$12 + 10 = 22$

**D** $10 + 2 = 12$
$12 - 10 = 2$

**Set A,** pages 118–120, 122–123

Find 8 × 5.

You can use patterns to multiply by 5s.

- You can skip count: 5, 10, 15, 20, and so on.
- Each multiple of 5 ends with a 0 or a 5.
- Each multiple of 5 is 5 more than the one before it.

$$8 \times 5 = 40$$

**Remember** that making a table and using a pattern can help you to multiply by 2, 5 or 9.

Find each product.

**1.** 2 × 4    **2.** 5 × 4    **3.** 5 × 9

**4.** 2 × 3    **5.** 9 × 4    **6.** 3 × 5

**Set B,** pages 124–125

**Identity Property of Multiplication:**
When you multiply a number and 1, the product is that number.

$$1 \times 6 = 6 \qquad 12 \times 1 = 12$$

**Zero Property of Multiplication:**
When you multiply a number and 0, the product is 0.

$$0 \times 6 = 0 \qquad 12 \times 0 = 0$$

**Remember** that you can think about an array with 1 row when you multiply by 1.

Find each product.

**1.** 7 × 0    **2.** 1 × 10    **3.** 0 × 9

**4.** 3 × 1    **5.** 7 × 0    **6.** 1 × 5

**Set C,** pages 126–127

Find 2 × 10.

When you multiply a number by 2, the product is always even.

$$2 \times 6 = 12$$

$$2 \times 9 = 18$$

$$2 \times 10 = 20$$

When you multiply a number by 5, the product always ends in 0 or 5.

$$5 \times 2 = 10$$

$$5 \times 3 = 15$$

$$5 \times 4 = 20$$

**Remember** you can solve some multiplication problems by using patterns of multiples.

**1.** 6 × 5      **2.** 9 × 8

**3.** 9 × 6      **4.** 2 × 3

**5.** 2 × 7      **6.** 5 × 7

**7.** 9 × 5      **8.** 2 × 5

**9.** 5 × 8      **10.** 9 × 3

**11.** 9 × 2      **12.** 5 × 2

**13.** 9 × 4      **14.** 2 × 2

Find $7 \times 10$.

To find the product:

- Write the factor you are multiplying by 10.

- To the right of that factor, write a zero in the ones place.

$$7 \times 10 = 70$$

**Remember** that a multiple of 10 will always have a zero in the ones place.

Find each product.

**1.** $3 \times 10$      **2.** $5 \times 10$

**3.** $10 \times 2$      **4.** $10 \times 6$

Use basic multiplication facts to multiply by multiples of 10.

Multiply by the digit in the tens place. Then, write one zero in the product.

Find $4 \times 60 \rightarrow$ Multiply $4 \times 6 = 24$.

Write one zero after 24.

$$4 \times 60 = 240$$

So, $4 \times 60 = 240$.

**Remember** when the product of a basic fact has a zero, the answer will have an extra zero.

Write the basic fact. Then find the product.

**1.** $9 \times 80$      **2.** $2 \times 50$

**3.** $6 \times 50$      **4.** $2 \times 90$

**5.** $70 \times 5$      **6.** $50 \times 3$

**7.** $40 \times 9$      **8.** $20 \times 7$

In two-question problems, you must solve one problem before you can solve the other.

**Problem 1:** A family of 2 adults and 3 children went to an air show. How many family members went to the air show?
$2 + 3 = 5$

**Problem 2:** Each pass to the air show cost $10. How much did the family spend on passes for the air show?
$5 \times \$10 = \$50$

The family spent a total of $50.

**Remember** to solve the first problem before you try to solve the second problem.

**1. a** For lunch, Julia bought a sandwich for $8 and a glass of juice for $3. How much did her lunch cost?

    **b** Julia paid with a $20 bill. How much change will she get?

**Multiple Choice**

1. Which symbol makes the number sentence true? (5-3)

   $5 \times 0 \bigcirc 2 \times 1$

   **A** $>$

   **B** $<$

   **C** $=$

   **D** $\times$

2. The 3rd graders at Willow School were put in 9 groups of 10. How many 3rd graders were there? (5-5)

   **A** 19

   **B** 90

   **C** 99

   **D** 900

3. Mrs. Oritz can make 40 cookies out of one batch of dough. If she makes 5 batches of dough, how many cookies can she make? (5-6)

   **A** 8

   **B** 20

   **C** 200

   **D** 2,000

4. Each flower has 5 petals.

   If Stephanie counted the petals in groups of 5, which list shows numbers she could have named? (5-4)

   **A** 12, 15, 18, 30

   **B** 15, 20, 34, 40

   **C** 15, 20, 25, 30

   **D** 10, 12, 14, 16

5. Todd has 7 aquariums. Each aquarium has 9 fish. What is the total number of fish? (5-2)

   **A** 63

   **B** 62

   **C** 27

   **D** 21

6. Len has 3 rolls of quarters. Ryan has 8 rolls. How many more rolls does Ryan have than Len? Each roll has $10 worth of quarters. In these rolls of quarters, how much more money does Ryan have than Len? (5-7)

   **A** Ryan has 11 more rolls, so he has $110 more than Len.

   **B** Ryan has 5 more rolls, so he has $55 more than Len.

   **C** Ryan has 5 more rolls, so he has $50 more than Len.

   **D** Ryan has 6 more rolls, so he has $60 more than Len.

7. Which of these best describes all of the snake lengths? (5-1)

   | Snake | Length in Feet |
   | --- | --- |
   | Black Mamba | 14 |
   | King Cobra | 16 |
   | Taipan | 10 |

   **A** They are all greater than 12.

   **B** They are all less than 15.

   **C** They are all multiples of 5.

   **D** They are all multiples of 2.

**8.** Emma fills three vases with flowers. The table given below shows the number of flowers in each vase. The number of flowers are multiples of what number? (5-2)

| Vase | Flowers |
|------|---------|
| Blue | 18 |
| Green | 27 |
| Red | 36 |

**9.** Melvin stacked boxes in 3 groups of 10. How many boxes did Melvin stack? (5-5)

**10.** Use >, < or = to make the number sentence true. (5-3)

$9 \times 0 \bigcirc 4 \times 1$

**11.** Mona brought 6 crates of bottled water to the race. Otis brought 8 crates of bottled water. How many more crates did Otis bring than Mona? Each crate had 8 bottles of water. In these crates, how many more bottles of water did Otis bring than Mona? (5-7)

**12.** Alberto has 9 bags. Each bag has 9 balls of yarn. How many balls of yarn does Alberto have? (5-2)

**13.** Rina draws some stars for her poster.

Each star has 5 points. Rina counts the number of points in groups of 5. Skip count to find the number that comes next. (5-4)

5, 10, 15, 20, 25, ?

**14.** Elisabeth has 7 baskets. She places 50 oranges in each basket. How many oranges does she have in all? (5-6)

**15.** Tara helped her dad finish the laundry. She folded 7 pairs of socks. How many socks did Tara fold in all? (5-1)

**16.** Jorge wants to draw 2 pictures of a goldfish for each of his 9 friends. How many goldfish will Jorge need to draw in all? Skip count by 2s to find the answer. Then, write the multiplication sentence. (5-4)

**17.** Students from the 3rd and 4th grade class went on a picnic together. There was room for a group of 10 students at each picnic table. There were a total of 8 groups of students. How many students went to the picnic in all? (5-5)

**18.** Jimmy is going to the water park with his family. Each adult ticket costs $30, and each child's ticket costs $20. If there are 7 children and 4 adults, how much will the tickets cost in all? (5-6)

**19.** The product of two numbers is the same as one of the factors. How can you use properties of multiplication to determine what the factors are? (5-3)

ASSESSMENT

You are selling boxes of cards to raise money for your soccer team. Cards of different sizes come in boxes of 5, 9, and 10. Each soccer player wants to sell at least $100 worth of boxes.

| Boxes of Cards | Price of Box |
|---|---|
| Set of 5 small cards | $2 |
| Set of 9 medium cards | $5 |
| Set of 10 large cards | $6 |

1. Decide how many of each box of cards you would like to sell.

2. Make a chart to show how many cards in all for each set you will sell, and the total cost for each set of boxes.

3. Explain how you decided how many of each kind of box to sell.

4. Suppose you counted the total number of cards for each set of boxes in multiples. Write a list of the numbers you would name for each set of boxes.

5. Suppose the set of 5 small cards is out of stock. Decide how many of each box of 9 medium cards and 10 large cards you would like to sell to earn at least $100.

6. Suppose the set of 9 medium cards is out of stock. Decide how many of each box of 5 small cards and 10 large cards you would like to sell to earn at least $100?

138 Topic 5

Topic
6

# Multiplication Facts: Use Known Facts

▼ How long does Comet Encke take to orbit the Sun? You will find out in Lesson 6-2.

## Review What You Know!

### Vocabulary

Choose the best term from the box.

- addend
- array
- factor
- multiply

1. When you put together equal groups to get the total number, you __?__.

2. When numbers are multiplied, each number is called a(n) __?__.

3. When you display objects in rows and columns, you make a(n) __?__.

### Multiplication

Find each product.

4. $3 \times 2$      5. $4 \times 5$      6. $7 \times 2$

7. $6 \times 1$      8. $8 \times 0$      9. $5 \times 9$

### Arrays

Draw an array for each multiplication fact.

10. $6 \times 2$              11. $4 \times 9$

12. Write a multiplication number sentence for the array shown at the right. Explain why you used the numbers you did.

©13. **Writing to Explain** Is an array for $2 \times 9$ the same as or different from an array for $9 \times 2$? Draw a picture and explain your answer.

**Topic Essential Question**
• How can unknown multiplication facts be found using known facts?

# Interactive Learning

**Pose the problem.** Start each lesson by working together to solve problems. It will help you make sense of math.

## Applying Math Practices

- What am I asked to find?
- What else can I try?
- How are quantities related?
- How can I explain my work?
- How can I use math to model the problem?
- Can I use tools to help?
- Is my work precise?
- Why does this work?
- How can I generalize?

### Lesson 6-1

© **Use Tools** Use the array at the right to complete this task.

Find two ways to break apart the array at the right into two arrays. What multiplication sentence can you write for each array? What is the total? Tell how you decided.

### Lesson 6-2

© **Use Tools** Solve any way you choose. Use counters to build an array.

There are 3 rows of pictures on a wall. Each row has 6 pictures. How many pictures are on the wall?

### Lesson 6-3

© **Use Tools** Solve any way you choose. Use counters to build and break apart an array.

Ed made 8 key chains with 12 links in a chain each week for 4 weeks. How many key chains did Ed make in all?

**Lesson 6-4**

Ⓒ **Use Tools** Solve any way you choose. Use counters to build and break apart an array.

Students set up 6 rows of seats for a music concert. They put 6 seats in each row. What is the total number of seats?

**Lesson 6-5**

Ⓒ **Use Tools** Solve any way you choose. Use counters to build and break apart an array.

There are 8 rows of prizes for the raffle. There are 6 prizes in each row. How many prizes are there in all?

**Lesson 6-6**

Ⓒ **Generalize** Solve. Try to discover two different ways to find the total.

Gina has 2 quilt sections. Each section has 5 rows with 3 squares in each row. How many squares are in both sections? Explain how you found the solution.

**Lesson 6-7**

Ⓒ **Be Precise** Solve any way you choose. Use counters if needed.

Alfredo buys 6 bags of oranges. Each bag contains 5 oranges. How many oranges does Alfredo buy in all?

**Lesson 6-8**

Ⓒ **Persevere** Solve any way you choose. Show how you found the answer.

Delia is tying strings onto balloons. She has green and blue balloons and red and yellow string. How many possible combinations of a balloon and a piece of string can Delia make? Show each combination.

**Lesson 6-9**

Ⓒ **Model** Solve using skills you have learned previously. Show how you found the solution.

At the craft store, Nan bought 3 bottles of glitter that cost $5 each. She bought twice as many bottles of glue that cost $2 each. How much did Nan spend in all?

Lesson
6-1

Common
Core

3.OA.5 Apply properties
of operations as strategies
to multiply and divide....
Also 3.OA.3

# The Distributive Property

## How can you break up a multiplication fact?

Maria wants to set up 7 rows of 4 chairs for a meeting. She wants to know how many chairs are needed, but does not know the product $7 \times 4$.

Hands-On
counters

---

## Guided Practice*

MATHEMATICAL
PRACTICES

### Do you know HOW?

Copy the array and separate the rows into two smaller arrays. Write the new facts.

1. ( ☐ × ☐ ) and ( ☐ × ☐ )

Use the smaller arrays and the Distributive Property to find each missing factor. You may use counters to help.

2. ☐ × 4 = ( ☐ × 4 ) + ( 5 × 4 )

### Do you UNDERSTAND?

3. What is another way Maria could break up the array for $7 \times 4$? Draw a picture of the two new arrays and write the new facts.

© 4. **Reason** Rafael broke up an array for $6 \times 3$ into two new arrays that both look the same. Draw a picture of these two arrays.

© 5. **Reason** Ann broke up a large array into two smaller arrays. The two smaller arrays show $1 \times 8$ and $4 \times 8$. What was the large array that Ann started with?

---

## Independent Practice

In **6** and **7**, copy each array and separate the rows into two smaller arrays. Write the new facts.

6. ( ☐ × ☐ ) and ( ☐ × ☐ )

7. ( ☐ × ☐ ) and ( ☐ × ☐ )

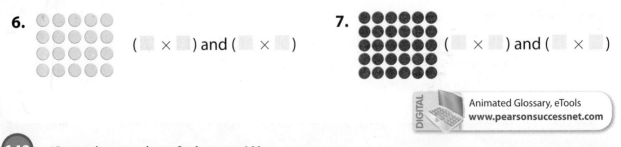

DIGITAL
Animated Glossary, eTools
www.pearsonsuccessnet.com

*For another example, see Set A on page 164.

Maria thinks of **7** rows of 4 chairs as **5** rows of 4 chairs and another **2** rows of 4 chairs.

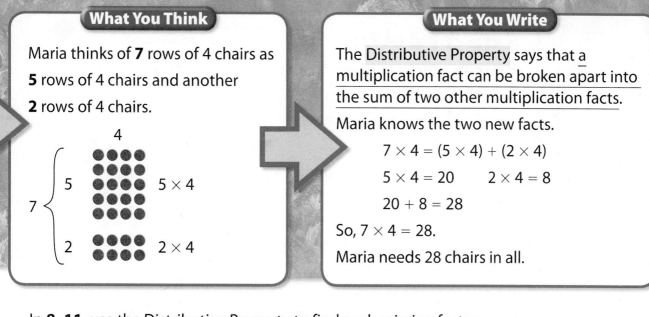

The Distributive Property says that a multiplication fact can be broken apart into the sum of two other multiplication facts.

Maria knows the two new facts.

$$7 \times 4 = (5 \times 4) + (2 \times 4)$$

$$5 \times 4 = 20 \qquad 2 \times 4 = 8$$

$$20 + 8 = 28$$

So, $7 \times 4 = 28$.

Maria needs 28 chairs in all.

In **8–11**, use the Distributive Property to find each missing factor. You may use counters and arrays to help.

**8.** $6 \times 8 = (4 \times \boxed{\phantom{0}}) + (2 \times 8)$

**9.** $10 \times 3 = (\boxed{\phantom{0}} \times 3) + (2 \times 3)$

**10.** $\boxed{\phantom{0}} \times 7 = (3 \times 7) + (2 \times \boxed{\phantom{0}})$

**11.** $8 \times \boxed{\phantom{0}} = (\boxed{\phantom{0}} \times 8) + (4 \times 8)$

---

## Problem Solving

© **12. Use Structure** Paige has 7 toy horses. Lexi has 5 times as many. How many toy horses does Lexi have?

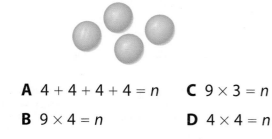

© **13. Critique Reasoning** Fred wants to separate the rows of the array below into a $2 \times 4$ array and a $3 \times 4$ array. Can he do this? Explain.

© **14. Communicate** Explain how you can break a $9 \times 6$ array into two smaller arrays. What are the new facts?

© **15. Reason** How can you use $3 \times 5 = 15$ to help you find $6 \times 5$?

© **16. Model** Which equation shows how to find 9 times the number of marbles shown below?

**17.** David has 10 packs of juice boxes. Each pack contains 9 juice boxes. Kara gives David 2 more packs of 9 juice boxes. How many juice boxes does David have now?

**A** $4 + 4 + 4 + 4 = n$    **C** $9 \times 3 = n$

**B** $9 \times 4 = n$    **D** $4 \times 4 = n$

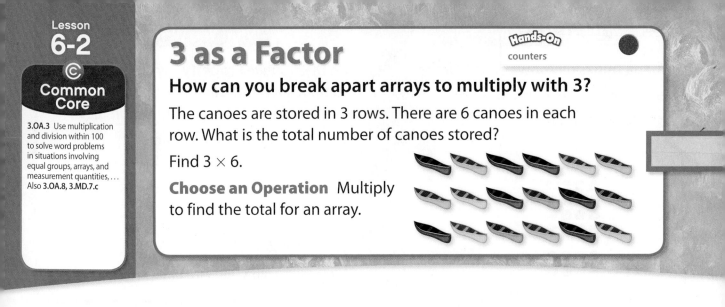

## Lesson 6-2

**Common Core**

3.OA.3 Use multiplication and division within 100 to solve word problems in situations involving equal groups, arrays, and measurement quantities, ... Also 3.OA.8, 3.MD.7.c

# 3 as a Factor

**Hands-On** counters

### How can you break apart arrays to multiply with 3?

The canoes are stored in 3 rows. There are 6 canoes in each row. What is the total number of canoes stored?

Find $3 \times 6$.

**Choose an Operation** Multiply to find the total for an array.

---

## Guided Practice*

**MATHEMATICAL PRACTICES**

### Do you know HOW?

In **1–6**, multiply. You may use counters or draw pictures to help.

**1.** $3 \times 4$      **2.** $3 \times 10$

**3.** $3 \times 5$      **4.** $3 \times 9$

**5.**   $\begin{array}{r} 12 \\ \times\ 3 \\ \hline \end{array}$      **6.**   $\begin{array}{r} 3 \\ \times\ 6 \\ \hline \end{array}$

### Do you UNDERSTAND?

**7. Use Structure** How can you use $2 \times 8 = 16$ to find $3 \times 8$?

**8.** Selena arranged plants in 3 rows at the community garden. She put 6 plants in each row. How many plants in all did Selena arrange into the rows?

---

## Independent Practice

In **9–28**, find the product. You may draw pictures to help.

**9.** $3 \times 2$    **10.** $4 \times 9$    **11.** $10 \times 3$    **12.** $2 \times 9$    **13.** $1 \times 3$

**14.** $8 \times 3$    **15.** $2 \times 7$    **16.** $5 \times 3$    **17.** $0 \times 3$    **18.** $3 \times 8$

**19.** $\begin{array}{r} 7 \\ \times\ 3 \\ \hline \end{array}$    **20.** $\begin{array}{r} 9 \\ \times\ 8 \\ \hline \end{array}$    **21.** $\begin{array}{r} 3 \\ \times\ 3 \\ \hline \end{array}$    **22.** $\begin{array}{r} 5 \\ \times\ 4 \\ \hline \end{array}$    **23.** $\begin{array}{r} 3 \\ \times\ 9 \\ \hline \end{array}$

**24.** $\begin{array}{r} 1 \\ \times\ 3 \\ \hline \end{array}$    **25.** $\begin{array}{r} 6 \\ \times\ 3 \\ \hline \end{array}$    **26.** $\begin{array}{r} 9 \\ \times\ 5 \\ \hline \end{array}$    **27.** $\begin{array}{r} 3 \\ \times\ 4 \\ \hline \end{array}$    **28.** $\begin{array}{r} 3 \\ \times\ 7 \\ \hline \end{array}$

**DIGITAL** eTools www.pearsonsuccessnet.com

*For another example, see Set B on page 164.*

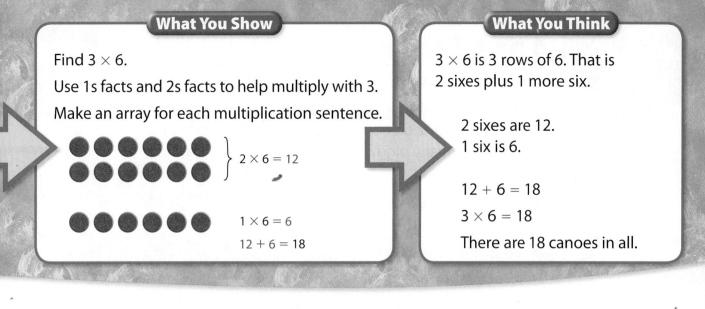

Find 3 × 6.

Use 1s facts and 2s facts to help multiply with 3.

Make an array for each multiplication sentence.

2 × 6 = 12

1 × 6 = 6
12 + 6 = 18

3 × 6 is 3 rows of 6. That is 2 sixes plus 1 more six.

2 sixes are 12.
1 six is 6.

12 + 6 = 18
3 × 6 = 18

There are 18 canoes in all.

## Problem Solving

MATHEMATICAL
PRACTICES

For **29** and **30**, use the table at the right.

**29.** What is the total number of stamps in a package of car stamps and a package of outer space stamps?

ⓒ **30. Use Tools** Cara bought 1 package of reptile stamps. What is the total number of reptile stamps she bought? Draw an array.

**Data**

| Number of Stamps in Different Packages | | |
|---|---|---|
| Kind of Stamp | Number of Rows | Number in Each Row |
| Dinosaurs | 3 | 7 |
| Cars | 3 | 9 |
| Outer Space | 3 | 8 |
| Reptiles | 5 | 6 |

ⓒ **31. Generalize** Suppose you need to find 3 × 9.

   **a** What two multiplication facts can help you find 3 × 9?

   **b** How could you use 3 × 9 to help you find 9 × 3?

**32.** It takes about 3 years for Comet Encke to orbit the Sun. About how many years will it take Comet Encke to orbit the Sun 5 times?

   **A** About 5 years

   **B** About 10 years

   **C** About 15 years

   **D** About 20 years

ⓒ **33. Use Structure** Mr. Torres had packages of tomatoes on the counter. Each package had 3 tomatoes in it.

If Mr. Torres counted the tomatoes in groups of 3, which list shows numbers he could have named?

   **A** 6, 12, 16, 19   **C** 3, 6, 10, 13

   **B** 6, 9, 12, 15   **D** 3, 7, 11, 15

Lesson
6-3

Common
Core

3.OA.3 Use multiplication
and division within 100
to solve word problems
in situations involving
equal groups, arrays, and
measurement quantities, ...
Also 3.OA.5, 3.OA.8,
3.MD.7.c

# 4 as a Factor

Hands-On
counters

## How can you use doubles to multiply with 4?

Anna painted piggy banks to sell at the student art show.
She painted a bank on each of the 7 days of the week for
4 weeks. How many piggy banks did she paint in all?

Find $4 \times 7$.

**Choose an Operation** Multiply
to find the total for an array.

---

## Guided Practice*

MATHEMATICAL
PRACTICES

### Do you know HOW?

In **1–6**, multiply. You may use counters
or draw pictures to help.

**1.** $4 \times 6$     **2.** $5 \times 4$

**3.** $4 \times 9$     **4.** $1 \times 4$

**5.** $\begin{array}{r} 1 \\ \times\,4 \\ \hline \end{array}$     **6.** $\begin{array}{r} 10 \\ \times\,4 \\ \hline \end{array}$

### Do you UNDERSTAND?

**7. Reason** Besides the way shown
above, what is another way to break
apart $4 \times 7$ using facts you know?

**8. Use Structure** You know $2 \times 8 = 16$.
How can you find $4 \times 8$?

**9.** Nolan made lamps to sell at the
school art show. He made 9 lamps
each week for 4 weeks. How many
lamps did Nolan make in all?

---

## Independent Practice

In **10–29**, find the product. You may draw pictures to help.

**10.** $4 \times 8$    **11.** $3 \times 8$    **12.** $4 \times 3$    **13.** $6 \times 4$    **14.** $9 \times 6$

**15.** $4 \times 4$    **16.** $5 \times 9$    **17.** $1 \times 4$    **18.** $0 \times 4$    **19.** $2 \times 10$

**20.** $3 \times 4$    **21.** $2 \times 8$    **22.** $4 \times 5$    **23.** $7 \times 4$    **24.** $4 \times 1$

**25.** $\begin{array}{r} 2 \\ \times\,4 \\ \hline \end{array}$   **26.** $\begin{array}{r} 7 \\ \times\,4 \\ \hline \end{array}$   **27.** $\begin{array}{r} 9 \\ \times\,4 \\ \hline \end{array}$   **28.** $\begin{array}{r} 10 \\ \times\,7 \\ \hline \end{array}$   **29.** $\begin{array}{r} 4 \\ \times\,8 \\ \hline \end{array}$

DIGITAL
eTools
www.pearsonsuccessnet.com

*For another example, see Set B on page 164.*

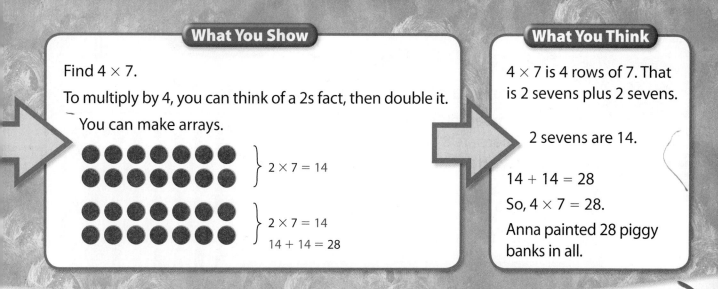

## What You Show

Find $4 \times 7$.

To multiply by 4, you can think of a 2s fact, then double it.

You can make arrays.

$2 \times 7 = 14$

$2 \times 7 = 14$
$14 + 14 = 28$

## What You Think

$4 \times 7$ is 4 rows of 7. That is 2 sevens plus 2 sevens.

2 sevens are 14.

$14 + 14 = 28$
So, $4 \times 7 = 28$.
Anna painted 28 piggy banks in all.

---

## Problem Solving

MATHEMATICAL PRACTICES

For **30** and **31**, use the table at the right for the supplies James needs to buy for the Trail Walk trip.

**30.** What is the total number of cereal bars he needs to buy?

© **31. Persevere** How many more apples than juice drinks does James need?

| Trail Walk Trip Supplies | | |
|---|---|---|
| Item | Number of Packages Needed | Number of Items in Each Package |
| Apples | 2 | 8 |
| Cereal Bars | 4 | 6 |
| Juice Drinks | 4 | 3 |

© **32. Be Precise** Martin studied slugs in science class. He learned that each slug has 4 feelers. That evening, he saw 8 slugs. How many feelers did the slugs have in all?

© **33. Construct Arguments** Lila had 9 weeks of rock climbing lessons. She had 4 lessons each week. Explain why Lila can use $4 \times 9$ to find the product $9 \times 4$.

© **34. Reason** Which of these best describes all the numbers on the shirts?

**A** They are all even numbers.

**B** They are all multiples of 3.

**C** They are all greater than 10.

**D** They are all 2-digit numbers.

© **35. Use Structure** Bess had boxes of candles on the table. Each box had 4 candles in it.

If Bess counted the candles in groups of 4, which list shows numbers she could have named?

**A** 8, 12, 16, 20    **C** 4, 6, 12, 14

**B** 8, 12, 14, 18    **D** 4, 8, 10, 14

© Common Core

**3.OA.3** Use multiplication and division within 100 to solve word problems in situations involving equal groups, arrays, and measurement quantities, ...
Also **3.OA.8, 3.MD.7.c**

# 6 and 7 as Factors

**Hands-On**
counters

## How can you break apart arrays to multiply?

The members of the band march in 6 equal rows. There are 8 band members in each row. How many are in the band?

Find 6 × 8.

**Choose an Operation** Multiply to find the total for an array.

---

**Another Example** How can you break apart arrays to multiply by 7?

The singers in the chorus are standing in equal rows.
There are 8 singers in each row. There are 7 rows.
How many singers are in the chorus?

**What You Show**

Find 7 × 8.

Use 5s facts and 2s facts to help multiply by 7.
Make an array for each multiplication sentence.

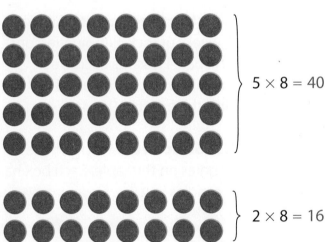

$5 \times 8 = 40$

$2 \times 8 = 16$

**What You Think**

7 × 8 is 7 rows of 8.

That is 5 eights plus 2 eights.

5 eights are 40.
2 eights are 16.

$40 + 16 = 56$

So, $7 \times 8 = 56$.

The chorus has 56 singers.

**Explain It**

1. What other multiplication facts might help to find 7 × 8?

2. How could you use 5 × 7 and 2 × 7 to find 7 × 7?

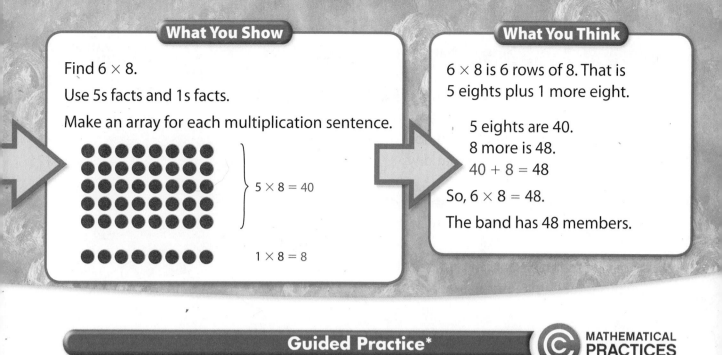

Find 6 × 8.

Use 5s facts and 1s facts.

Make an array for each multiplication sentence.

5 × 8 = 40

1 × 8 = 8

6 × 8 is 6 rows of 8. That is 5 eights plus 1 more eight.

5 eights are 40.
8 more is 48.
40 + 8 = 48

So, 6 × 8 = 48.

The band has 48 members.

---

## Guided Practice*

MATHEMATICAL
PRACTICES

### Do you know HOW?

In **1–6**, multiply. You may draw pictures or use counters to help.

**1.** 6 × 10

**2.** 7 × 6

**3.** $\begin{array}{r} 7 \\ \times\ 7 \\ \hline \end{array}$

**4.** $\begin{array}{r} 9 \\ \times\ 7 \\ \hline \end{array}$

**5.** Find 4 times 7.

**6.** Multiply 6 and 5.

### Do you UNDERSTAND?

**7. Model** Draw a picture of two arrays that show that 6 × 9 is equal to 5 × 9 plus 1 × 9. Explain your drawing.

**8.** The students who are graduating are standing in 7 equal rows. There are 9 students in each row. How many students are graduating?

---

## Independent Practice

In **9–23**, find the product. You may draw pictures to help.

**9.** 6 × 7

**10.** 7 × 9

**11.** 9 × 6

**12.** 8 × 7

**13.** 6 × 4

**14.** 6 × 6

**15.** 10 × 7

**16.** 8 × 6

**17.** 7 × 7

**18.** 7 × 3

**19.** $\begin{array}{r} 5 \\ \times\ 7 \\ \hline \end{array}$

**20.** $\begin{array}{r} 3 \\ \times\ 6 \\ \hline \end{array}$

**21.** $\begin{array}{r} 4 \\ \times\ 7 \\ \hline \end{array}$

**22.** $\begin{array}{r} 7 \\ \times\ 8 \\ \hline \end{array}$

**23.** $\begin{array}{r} 10 \\ \times\ 6 \\ \hline \end{array}$

DIGITAL
eTools
www.pearsonsuccessnet.com

**24.** The National Toy Train Museum has 5 large layouts for trains. One day, each layout had the same number of trains. Use the picture on the right to find how many trains were on display at the museum that day.

6 trains in each layout

© **25. Critique Reasoning** Marge says that $1 \times 0$ is equal to $1 + 0$. Is she correct? Why or why not?

**26.** Miguel had the baskets of oranges shown below. Each basket held 6 oranges.

If Miguel counted the oranges in groups of 6, which list shows the numbers he would have named?

**A** 6, 12, 21, 26, 32          **C** 12, 16, 20, 24, 28

**B** 6, 11, 16, 21, 26          **D** 6, 12, 18, 24, 30

© **27. Model** Nan made the arrays shown to find $6 \times 3$. Explain how to change the arrays to find $7 \times 3$. Use objects and draw a picture.

For **28** and **29**, use the drawings of the trains below.

© **28. Reason** A group of tourists needs 7 rows of seats in Car 5 of the Réseau train.

  **a** How many seats will they need?

  **b** How many seats are left on this train for other passengers?

© **29. Estimation** Use rounding to the nearest ten to find about how many seats in all are on the Réseau and the Sud-Est trains.

| Réseau 377 total seats | Car 1 | Car 2 | Car 3 | Car 4 | Car 5 |
|---|---|---|---|---|---|
| | 3 seats each row | 3 seats each row | 3 seats each row | 4 seats each row | 4 seats each row |

| Sud-Est 345 total seats | Car 1 | Car 2 | Car 3 | Car 4 | Car 5 |
|---|---|---|---|---|---|
| | 3 seats each row | 3 seats each row | 3 seats each row | 4 seats each row | 4 seats each row |

# Algebra Connections

## Missing Operations

In a number sentence with the = symbol, both sides of the number sentence must have the same value. An operation symbol such as +, −, or × tells how to find that value. Reasoning can help you decide which operation symbol is missing.

**Example:** 72 = 8 ☐ 9

**Think** 72 is equal to 8 (plus or minus or multiplied by) 9?

Since 8 × 9 = 72, write "×."

72 = 8 ☒ 9

Copy and complete. Replace the square with +, −, or ×. Check your answers.

**1.** 9 ☐ 36 = 45

**2.** 24 ☐ 17 = 7

**3.** 16 = 2 ☐ 8

**4.** 8 = 32 ☐ 24

**5.** 7 ☐ 5 = 35

**6.** 50 = 12 ☐ 38

**7.** 18 = 9 ☐ 2

**8.** 64 ☐ 36 = 28

**9.** 30 = 6 ☐ 5

**10.** 47 ☐ 37 = 84

**11.** 63 = 9 ☐ 7

**12.** 12 ☐ 1 = 12

For **13** and **14**, copy and complete the number sentence below each problem. Use it to help find your answer.

**13.** Lisa had some pens left after she gave 27 pens to her friends. She started with a package of 36 pens. What operation can you use to find the number of pens Lisa had left?

9 = 36 ☐ 27

**14.** The picture below shows the number of each kind of button in a package. What operation can you use to find the total number of buttons in one package?

45 = 5 ☐ 9

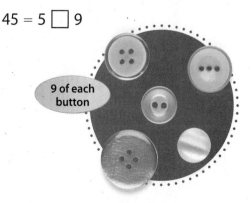

9 of each button

**15. Write a Problem** Write a problem using the number sentence below.

48 = 26 + 22

© Common Core

3.OA.3 Use multiplication and division within 100 to solve word problems in situations involving equal groups, arrays, and measurement quantities, . . . Also **3.MD.7.c**

# 8 as a Factor

## How can you use doubles to multiply with 8?

At the school fun fair, students try to toss a table tennis ball into a bowl. There are 8 rows of bowls. There are 8 bowls in each row. How many bowls are there in all?

**Choose an Operation** Multiply to find the total for an array. Find $8 \times 8$.

---

## Guided Practice*

**MATHEMATICAL PRACTICES**

### Do you know HOW?

In **1–6**, multiply.

**1.** $8 \times 7$

**2.** $8 \times 4$

**3.** $6 \times 8$

**4.** $10 \times 8$

**5.** $\begin{array}{r} 9 \\ \times\ 8 \\ \hline \end{array}$

**6.** $\begin{array}{r} 8 \\ \times\ 3 \\ \hline \end{array}$

### Do you UNDERSTAND?

© **7. Use Structure** How could the fact that $5 \times 8 = 40$ help you find $8 \times 8$?

© **8. Use Structure** How can you use $4 \times 7$ to find $8 \times 7$?

**9.** Mrs. Reyes needs to order bricks for her garden. She needs 8 rows of bricks. Each row will have 7 bricks. How many bricks in all should Mrs. Reyes order?

---

## Independent Practice

In **10–27**, find the product.

**10.** $8 \times 4$

**11.** $1 \times 8$

**12.** $2 \times 9$

**13.** $5 \times 7$

**14.** $8 \times 2$

**15.** $8 \times 6$

**16.** $5 \times 9$

**17.** $8 \times 5$

**18.** $0 \times 8$

**19.** $4 \times 9$

**20.** $\begin{array}{r} 10 \\ \times\ 8 \\ \hline \end{array}$

**21.** $\begin{array}{r} 3 \\ \times\ 7 \\ \hline \end{array}$

**22.** $\begin{array}{r} 8 \\ \times\ 8 \\ \hline \end{array}$

**23.** $\begin{array}{r} 2 \\ \times\ 4 \\ \hline \end{array}$

**24.** $\begin{array}{r} 9 \\ \times\ 8 \\ \hline \end{array}$

**25.** Find 6 times 9.

**26.** Multiply 8 and 1.

**27.** Find 9 times 8.

*For another example, see Set C on page 164.*

Use 2s facts to find $8 \times 8$.

$8 \times 8$ is 4 groups of 2 eights.

$\left.\begin{array}{l} \bullet\bullet\bullet\bullet\bullet\bullet\bullet\bullet \\ \bullet\bullet\bullet\bullet\bullet\bullet\bullet\bullet \end{array}\right\} 2 \times 8 = 16$

$\left.\begin{array}{l} \bullet\bullet\bullet\bullet\bullet\bullet\bullet\bullet \\ \bullet\bullet\bullet\bullet\bullet\bullet\bullet\bullet \end{array}\right\} 2 \times 8 = 16$

$\left.\begin{array}{l} \bullet\bullet\bullet\bullet\bullet\bullet\bullet\bullet \\ \bullet\bullet\bullet\bullet\bullet\bullet\bullet\bullet \end{array}\right\} 2 \times 8 = 16$

$\left.\begin{array}{l} \bullet\bullet\bullet\bullet\bullet\bullet\bullet\bullet \\ \bullet\bullet\bullet\bullet\bullet\bullet\bullet\bullet \end{array}\right\} 2 \times 8 = 16$

$16 + 16 + 16 + 16 = 64$

Double a 4s fact to find $8 \times 8$.

$8 \times 8$ is 4 eights plus 4 eights.

$\left.\begin{array}{l} \bullet\bullet\bullet\bullet\bullet\bullet\bullet\bullet \\ \bullet\bullet\bullet\bullet\bullet\bullet\bullet\bullet \\ \bullet\bullet\bullet\bullet\bullet\bullet\bullet\bullet \\ \bullet\bullet\bullet\bullet\bullet\bullet\bullet\bullet \end{array}\right\} 4 \times 8 = 32$

$\left.\begin{array}{l} \bullet\bullet\bullet\bullet\bullet\bullet\bullet\bullet \\ \bullet\bullet\bullet\bullet\bullet\bullet\bullet\bullet \\ \bullet\bullet\bullet\bullet\bullet\bullet\bullet\bullet \\ \bullet\bullet\bullet\bullet\bullet\bullet\bullet\bullet \end{array}\right\} 4 \times 8 = 32$

Double the product.
$32 + 32 = 64$

So, $8 \times 8 = 64$.
There are 64 bowls in all.

## Problem Solving

MATHEMATICAL
PRACTICES

For **28–30**, find the total number of tiles.

**28.** Mischa bought 8 boxes of orange tiles.

**29.** Aaron bought 6 boxes of yellow tiles.

**30.** Liz bought 7 boxes of green tiles.

8 tiles in each box

9 tiles in each box

7 tiles in each box

© **31. Critique Reasoning** Sophi says, "To find $8 \times 8$, I can find $2 \times 8$ and double it." Do you agree? Explain.

For **32** and **33**, use the table at the right.

© **32. Reason** The total amount of money Nate spent at the clothing sale is $(2 \times \$9) + \$42$. What did he buy?

**33.** Willa bought a shirt and a sweater. She had $14 left. How much money did she start with?

| Clothing Sale | |
| --- | --- |
| Shirt | $23 |
| Belt | $9 |
| Sweater | $38 |
| Pair of jeans | $42 |

© **34. Use Structure** Ms. Vero had boxes of crayons in a closet. Each box had 8 crayons in it. If Ms. Vero counted the crayons in groups of 8, which list shows the numbers she would have named?

**A** 8, 16, 28, 32, 40, 48          **C** 16, 20, 24, 28, 32, 36

**B** 8, 14, 18, 24, 32, 40          **D** 8, 16, 24, 32, 40, 48

**35.** During the California Gold Rush, miners sometimes paid $10 for a glass of water. What was the total cost if 8 miners each bought one glass of water?

**Lesson**
**6-6**

**Common Core**

3.OA.3 Use multiplication and division within 100 to solve word problems in situations involving equal groups, arrays, and measurement quantities, ... Also 3.OA.5, 3.OA.8

# Multiplying with 3 Factors

### How can you multiply 3 numbers?

Drew is joining 3 sections of a quilt. Each section has 2 rows with 4 squares in each row. How many squares in all are in these 3 sections?

Find $3 \times 2 \times 4$.

---

## Guided Practice*

**MATHEMATICAL PRACTICES**

### Do you know HOW?

In **1–6**, multiply. You may use objects or draw a picture to help.

**1.** $2 \times 4 \times 2$

**2.** $3 \times 4 \times 3$

**3.** $2 \times 2 \times 3$

**4.** $2 \times 5 \times 2$

**5.** $3 \times 2 \times 4$

**6.** $2 \times 6 \times 2$

### Do you UNDERSTAND?

**7. Reason** In the example above, if you find $3 \times 4$ first, do you get the same product? Explain.

**8.** Sara has 4 quilt pieces. Each piece has 3 rows with 3 squares in each row. How many squares are in Sara's quilt pieces?

---

## Independent Practice

In **9–16**, find the product. You may draw a picture to help.

**9.** $2 \times 3 \times 2$

**10.** $5 \times 2 \times 2$

**11.** $3 \times 6 \times 1$

**12.** $3 \times 3 \times 2$

**13.** $2 \times 2 \times 2$

**14.** $2 \times 3 \times 4$

**15.** $3 \times 3 \times 3$

**16.** $6 \times 2 \times 2$

In **17–22**, write the missing number.

**17.** $3 \times (2 \times 5) = 30$, so $(3 \times 2) \times 5 = \boxed{\phantom{0}}$

**18.** $5 \times (7 \times 2) = (5 \times 7) \times \boxed{\phantom{0}}$

**19.** $4 \times (2 \times 2) = 16$, so $(4 \times 2) \times 2 = \boxed{\phantom{0}}$

**20.** $8 \times (3 \times 6) = (8 \times 3) \times \boxed{\phantom{0}}$

**21.** $(7 \times 3) \times 4 = \boxed{\phantom{0}} \times (3 \times 4)$

**22.** $5 \times (2 \times 9) = (5 \times \boxed{\phantom{0}}) \times 9$

Animated Glossary
www.pearsonsuccessnet.com

DIGITAL

*For another example, see Set D on page 165.*

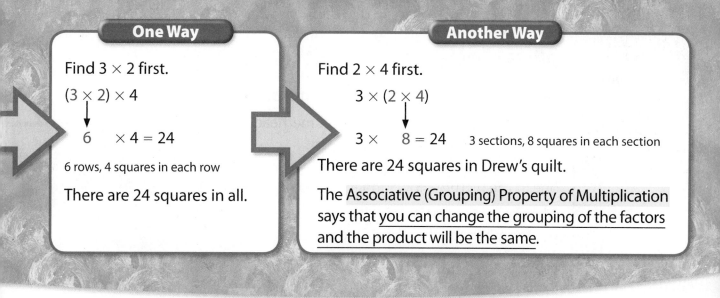

**One Way**

Find 3 × 2 first.

(3 × 2) × 4

6 × 4 = 24

6 rows, 4 squares in each row

There are 24 squares in all.

**Another Way**

Find 2 × 4 first.

3 × (2 × 4)

3 × 8 = 24    3 sections, 8 squares in each section

There are 24 squares in Drew's quilt.

The Associative (Grouping) Property of Multiplication says that you can change the grouping of the factors and the product will be the same.

## Problem Solving

MATHEMATICAL
PRACTICES

For **23–25**, find the total number of eggs.

**23.** There are 8 mockingbird nests at a park. Each nest has 5 eggs.

**24.** At another park, there are 3 mockingbird nests with 4 eggs in each nest, and 2 more nests with 3 eggs in each.

Ⓒ **25. Estimation** About how many eggs would you find in 10 nests?

Mockingbirds lay 3 to 5 eggs.

Ⓒ **26. Critique Reasoning** Anita says the product of 5 × 2 × 3 is less than 20. Do you agree? Explain.

For **27** and **28**, use the table at the right.

**27.** Ellis bought 3 packs of baseball cards and 2 packs of basketball cards. How many cards did he buy in all?

**28.** Mandy bought 1 pack of each of the four kinds of cards. What is the total number of cards she bought?

| Sports Card Sale | |
| --- | --- |
| Kind of Cards | Number of Cards in Each Pack |
| Baseball | 8 |
| Basketball | 5 |
| Football | 7 |
| Hockey | 6 |

Ⓒ **29. Use Structure** Which number makes this number sentence true?

4 × (3 × 2) = (4 × ▢ ) × 2

**A** 12        **B** 7        **C** 3        **D** 2

Common Core

3.OA.3 Use multiplication and division within 100 to solve word problems in situations involving equal groups, arrays, and measurement quantities, . . .
Also 3.OA.8

# Multiplication Facts

## How do you use strategies to multiply?

A scientist is on a boat studying hammerhead sharks. The length of the boat equals the total length of 6 sharks like the one in the picture. How long is the boat?

**Choose an Operation** Multiply to put together equal groups. Find $6 \times 5$.

An adult hammerhead shark is about 5 yards long.

---

## Guided Practice*

MATHEMATICAL PRACTICES

### Do you know HOW?

In **1–6**, multiply.

**1.** $6 \times 4$

**2.** $9 \times 3$

**3.** $3 \times 2$

**4.** $5 \times 8$

**5.**  $\begin{array}{r} 1 \\ \times\ 4 \\ \hline \end{array}$

**6.**  $\begin{array}{r} 9 \\ \times\ 8 \\ \hline \end{array}$

### Do you UNDERSTAND?

**7. Reason** In the example above, what other facts could you use to find $6 \times 5$?

**8. Use Structure** To find $9 \times 5$, how could knowing $7 \times 5 = 35$ help you?

**9.** Each angel shark has 7 fins. Mr. Park is studying 4 angel sharks. How many fins in all do the sharks have?

---

## Independent Practice

**Leveled Practice** In **10** and **11**, use a pattern to find the product. Write the numbers you count.

**10.** $7 \times 5$

**11.** $9 \times 2$

**Leveled Practice** In **12–16**, use known facts to find the product. List the facts you use.

**12.** $5 \times 9$

**13.** $7 \times 8$

**14.** $3 \times 6$

**15.** $8 \times 4$

**16.** $9 \times 7$

In **17–21**, find the product.

**17.**  $\begin{array}{r} 3 \\ \times\ 2 \\ \hline \end{array}$

**18.**  $\begin{array}{r} 10 \\ \times\ 4 \\ \hline \end{array}$

**19.**  $\begin{array}{r} 7 \\ \times\ 6 \\ \hline \end{array}$

**20.**  $\begin{array}{r} 6 \\ \times\ 5 \\ \hline \end{array}$

**21.**  $\begin{array}{r} 2 \\ \times\ 8 \\ \hline \end{array}$

*For another example, see Sets B and C on page 164.

## One Way

Use a pattern to find $6 \times 5$.

$6 \times 5$ means 6 groups of 5. Count by 5s.

| | ? | | | | |
|---|---|---|---|---|---|
| 5 | 5 | 5 | 5 | 5 | 5 |

5  10  15  20  25  30

So, $6 \times 5 = 30$.

The boat is 30 yards long.

## Another Way

Use known facts to find $6 \times 5$.

Use 2s facts and 4s facts to help.

$\left.\right\}$ $2 \times 5 = 10$

$\left.\right\}$ $4 \times 5 = 20$

$10 + 20 = 30$

The boat is 30 yards long.

## Problem Solving

MATHEMATICAL
**PRACTICES**

**Science** Use the pictures for **22–24**.

**Black Tip Shark**
About 2 yards long

**22.** Ms. Dell is on a boat studying whale sharks. The length of the boat equals the total length of 2 whale sharks like the one in the picture. How long is the boat?

**23.** Mr. Marks is studying 3 black tip sharks and 4 tiger sharks. What is the total length of the 7 sharks?

**24. Critique Reasoning** Mrs. Kent says that the total length of 4 whale sharks is greater than the total length of 7 tiger sharks. Is she correct? Explain your thinking.

**Tiger Shark**
About 4 yards long

**25. Communicate** Explain how you can find $7 \times 3$ using a counting pattern.

**26.** Hal counted the number of fish in 3 fish tanks. There were 7 fish in each fish tank. How many fish were in the 3 fish tanks?

**Whale Shark**
About 7 yards long

**A** 21

**B** 24

**C** 27

**D** 37

Common
Core

3.OA.3 Use multiplication and division within 100 to solve word problems in situations involving equal groups, arrays, and measurement quantities, …

# Multiplying to Find Combinations

## How can you find the number of possible combinations?

At his dental checkup Jay will get one toothbrush and one kind of floss. How many different combinations can he choose from?

Floss

Toothbrushes

---

## Guided Practice*

**MATHEMATICAL PRACTICES**

### Do you know HOW?

For **1** and **2**, find the number of possible combinations. Use objects, pictures, or multiplication.

1. Choose one of the letters A or B and one of the numbers 1 or 2.

2. Choose one of the letters A or B and one of the numbers 1, 2, 3, or 4.

### Do you UNDERSTAND?

3. **Writing to Explain** In Exercises 1 and 2, does it matter whether you choose the letter first or the number first? Explain.

4. **Reason** In the example above, if a third kind of dental floss is offered, how many combinations can Jay choose from?

---

## Independent Practice

For **5** and **6**, use the table to find the number of possible combinations.

5. Choose one color counter and one color tile.

6. Choose a coin and a bill.

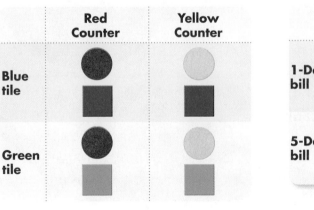

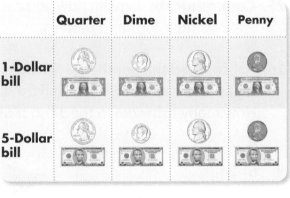

---

eTools
www.pearsonsuccessnet.com

*For another example, see Set E on page 165.

Use objects or pictures.

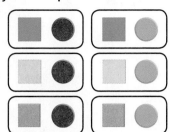

Jay has 6 combinations of one toothbrush and one dental floss to choose from.

Multiply.

The picture has 3 rows. Each row has 2 combinations.

$$3 \times 2 = 6$$

There are 6 combinations.

**Remember:** You can also make an organized list to find all the possible combinations.

---

For **7** and **8**, find the number of possible combinations.
Use objects, pictures, or multiplication.

**7.** Choose one kind of pet: dog, cat, or rabbit, and one pet sitter: Jill, Marta, or Dave.

**8.** Choose one of 3 hats and one of 8 books to bring on a camping trip.

---

## Problem Solving

MATHEMATICAL
PRACTICES

**© 9. Model** Wanda is choosing a shirt and pants. She has 4 different color shirts: green, pink, red, and yellow. She has 3 different color pants: blue, white, and black. How many different combinations of a shirt and pants can she make? Use an organized list.

**10.** Social Studies The state courts of Florida have 983 judges in all, and 599 of the judges are circuit judges. How many of the judges are not circuit judges? Show your work.

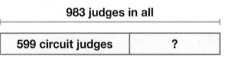

| 983 judges in all | |
|---|---|
| 599 circuit judges | ? |

**© 11. Construct Arguments** Nelson is buying sneakers. He can choose red, black, blue, or white shoe color. He can choose orange or yellow stripe color. How many different combinations of one shoe color and one stripe color are there? Explain your answer.

**12.** Theo wants to choose one sandwich and one drink for lunch. There are 3 kinds of sandwiches: peanut butter, tuna, and turkey. There are 3 kinds of drinks: grape juice, milk, and orange juice. How many different combinations of a sandwich and a drink are there?

**A** 3      **C** 9

**B** 6      **D** 12

Common Core

3.OA.3 Use multiplication and division within 100 to solve word problems in situations involving equal groups, arrays, and measurement quantities, ...
Also 3.MD.8

**Problem Solving**

# Multiple-Step Problems

Some word problems have hidden questions that need to be answered before you can solve the problem.

Keisha bought 2 yards of felt to make some puppets. Tanya bought 6 yards of felt. The felt cost $3 a yard. How much did the two girls spend on felt?

$3
per yard

## Another Example

Keisha plans to make 3 puppets. Tanya will make 3 times as many puppets as Keisha. Each puppet needs 2 buttons for its eyes. How many buttons will Tanya need?

**Find and solve the hidden question.**

How many puppets will Tanya make?

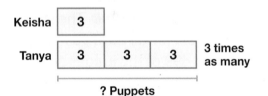

$3 \times 3$ puppets = 9 puppets

Tanya will make 9 puppets.

**Use the answer to the hidden question to solve the problem.**

How many buttons will Tanya need?

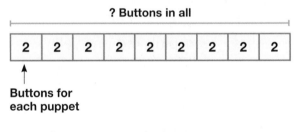

$9 \times 2$ buttons = 18 buttons

Tanya will need 18 buttons.

## Explain It

**1. Construct Arguments** Philip wrote $3 + 3 + 3 = $ ▢ instead of $3 \times 3 = $ ▢ for the diagram for the hidden question. Is his number sentence correct? Why or why not?

**2. Model** What number sentences could you write to find how many buttons both girls need? Explain your thinking.

**Find and solve the hidden question.**

How much felt did the girls buy in all?

? Yards in all

| 2 yards | 6 yards |
|---------|---------|

2 yards + 6 yards = 8 yards

The girls bought 8 yards of felt.

**Use the answer to the hidden question to solve the problem.**

How much did the girls spend in all?

? Total cost

| $3 | $3 | $3 | $3 | $3 | $3 | $3 | $3 |
|----|----|----|----|----|----|----|----|

8 × $3 = $24

The two girls spent $24 on felt.

---

## Guided Practice*

### Do you know HOW?

1. Keisha bought glue for $3, sequins for $6, and lace for $4 to decorate her puppets. She paid for these items with a $20 bill. How much change should she get?

    **Tip** *The hidden question is "What is the total cost of the three items?"*

### Do you UNDERSTAND?

2. Describe another way to solve the problem above about buying felt.

Ⓒ 3. **Write a Problem** Write a problem that has a hidden question. Then solve your problem.

---

## Independent Practice

Ⓒ 4. **Model** The library has 4 videos and some books about dinosaurs. There are 5 times as many books as videos. After 3 of the books were checked out, how many were left? The diagram below helps you answer the hidden question. Draw a diagram and solve the problem.

| Videos | 4 |
|--------|---|

| Books | 4 | 4 | 4 | 4 | 4 |
|-------|---|---|---|---|---|

5 times as many

? Books

**Applying Math Practices**

- What am I asked to find?
- What else can I try?
- How are quantities related?
- How can I explain my work?
- How can I use math to model the problem?
- Can I use tools to help?
- Is my work precise?
- Why does this work?
- How can I generalize?

---

Use the pictures for **5–8**.

© **5. Use Tools** Craig bought 2 bags of oranges. After he ate 3 of the oranges, how many oranges were left?

**Tip** *First find how many oranges Craig bought.*

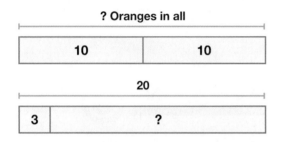

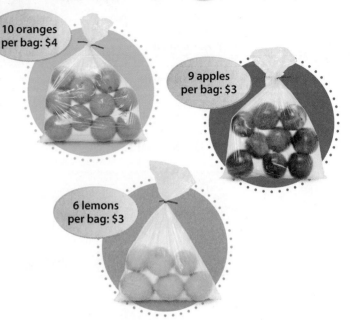

10 oranges per bag: $4

9 apples per bag: $3

6 lemons per bag: $3

**6.** Delia bought 2 bags of lemons and 3 bags of apples. How much did she spend on fruit?

**7.** Mrs. Evans bought 2 bags of oranges and 2 bags of lemons. How many pieces of fruit did she buy?

**8.** Mr. Day bought a bag each of apples, oranges, and lemons. He paid with a $20 bill. What change should he get?

© **9. Writing to Explain** Which costs more, 30 oranges or 30 lemons? How much more? Explain how you found your answer.

---

© **Think About the Structure**

**10.** Al had $38. He spent $4 on an action figure and $10 on a board game. Which number sentence shows how much money Al has left?

**A** $38 + $4 + $10 = ■

**B** $38 − ($4 + $10) = ■

**C** $38 − $4 = ■

**D** 38 + $10 = ■

**11.** Jose has 4 action figures. His brother has 3 times as many action figures. Which number sentence shows how many figures the boys have in all?

**A** 4 + 3 = ■

**B** 4 × 3 = ■

**C** 4 − 3 = ■

**D** 4 + (3 × 4) = ■

# Going Digital

## Using Known Facts

Use  tools

**Counters**

Use known facts to find $4 \times 6$ and $6 \times 7$.

**Step 1** ▢▢ Go to the Counters eTool. Select the two-part workspace. Use $2 \times 6$ to find $4 \times 6$. Select a counter. Show two rows of 6 counters in the left side. Look at the odometer. You see that $2 \times 6 = 12$. Show the same rows on the right side. There are 4 rows of 6 counters in all. $4 \times 6 = 24$, and $12 + 12 = 24$.

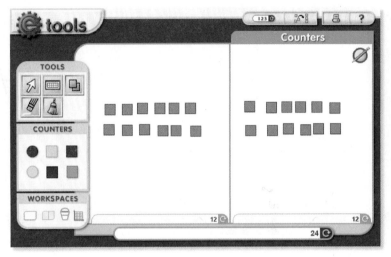

**Step 2** 🧹 Use the broom tool to clear one side of the workspace. Select the other side and use the broom tool again, to clear it. Use $5 \times 7$ and $1 \times 7$ to find $6 \times 7$. Show 5 rows of 7 counters on one side of the workspace. Look at the odometer to find that $5 \times 7 = 35$. Show 1 row of 7 counters on the other side. There are 6 rows of 7 counters in all. $6 \times 7 = 42$, and $35 + 7 = 42$.

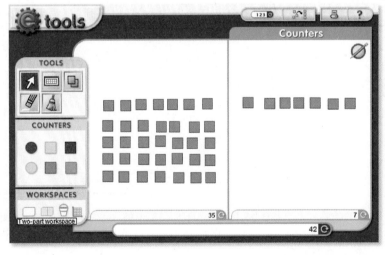

## Practice

Use the Counters eTool and known facts to find each product. Explain how you found the product.

**1.** $4 \times 9$

**2.** $8 \times 8$

**3.** $6 \times 8$

**4.** $7 \times 7$

© INTERVENTION

Using the Distributive Property, you can break the array for $4 \times 5$ into smaller arrays. What are the new facts?

$$4 \times 5 \quad = \quad (3 \times 5) + (1 \times 5)$$

**Remember** that you can break an array into facts you know.

Separate the rows in the array to break them into two smaller arrays. Write the new facts.

**1.**

$$3 \times 9 = (\quad \times 9) + (\quad \times 9)$$

Find $3 \times 7$.

You can break an array into facts you know.

$3 \times 7$
3 groups of 7

$2 \times 7 = 14$

$1 \times 7 = 7$

Add the products: $14 + 7 = 21$

So, $3 \times 7 = 21$.

Find $4 \times 6$.

Think of a 2s fact, then double the product.

$4 \times 6 \quad \begin{cases} 2 \times 6 = 12 \\ 2 \times 6 = 12 \end{cases}$

Add the products: $12 + 12 = 24$

So, $4 \times 6 = 24$.

**Remember** that you can draw arrays and use facts you already know to help you multiply.

Find the product.

**1.** $3 \times 8$   **2.** $3 \times 9$   **3.** $6 \times 3$

**4.** $4 \times 3$   **5.** $4 \times 8$   **6.** $6 \times 4$

**7.** $\begin{array}{r} 3 \\ \times 3 \\ \hline \end{array}$   **8.** $\begin{array}{r} 3 \\ \times 5 \\ \hline \end{array}$   **9.** $\begin{array}{r} 10 \\ \times 3 \\ \hline \end{array}$

**10.** $\begin{array}{r} 2 \\ \times 4 \\ \hline \end{array}$   **11.** $\begin{array}{r} 4 \\ \times 10 \\ \hline \end{array}$   **12.** $\begin{array}{r} 9 \\ \times 4 \\ \hline \end{array}$

Find $7 \times 6$. Use 5s facts and 2s facts.

$5 \times 6 = 30$

$30 + 12 = 42$

$2 \times 6 = 12$

So, $7 \times 6 = 42$.

Find $8 \times 6$. Double a 4s fact.

$8 \times 6 \quad \begin{cases} 4 \times 6 = 24 \\ 4 \times 6 = 24 \end{cases}$

Add the products: $24 + 24 = 48$

So, $8 \times 6 = 48$.

**Remember** that you can use known facts to multiply with 6, 7, or 8.

Find the product.

**1.** $7 \times 9$   **2.** $8 \times 7$   **3.** $6 \times 9$

**4.** $3 \times 6$   **5.** $7 \times 4$   **6.** $8 \times 6$

**7.** $\begin{array}{r} 8 \\ \times 7 \\ \hline \end{array}$   **8.** $\begin{array}{r} 6 \\ \times 2 \\ \hline \end{array}$   **9.** $\begin{array}{r} 3 \\ \times 8 \\ \hline \end{array}$

Find $4 \times 5 \times 2$.

The Associative Property of Multiplication states that you can change the grouping of the factors and the product will be the same.

| One Way | Another Way |
|---|---|
| $4 \times (5 \times 2)$ | $(4 \times 2) \times 5$ |
| $4 \times 10 = 40$ | $8 \times 5 = 40$ |

So, $4 \times 5 \times 2 = 40$.

**Remember** you may draw a picture to help you multiply 3 factors.

Find the product.

**1.** $3 \times 2 \times 5$     **2.** $5 \times 2 \times 6$

**3.** $1 \times 9 \times 8$     **4.** $7 \times 2 \times 5$

**5.** $2 \times 2 \times 4$     **6.** $4 \times 3 \times 2$

Find the number of possible combinations of one color: red, blue, or green; and one shape: star or square.

Make an array.

You can multiply.
2 rows with 3 combinations in each row
$2 \times 3 = 6$

In all, there are 6 combinations.

**Remember** that the order does not matter when you count combinations.

Find the number of possible combinations.

**1.** Choose one drink: milk or juice; and one side dish: a baked potato, corn, or green beans.

**2.** Choose a backpack, soft suitcase, or hard suitcase, and then choose one of 5 colors.

Some problems have hidden questions.

Jeff charged $10 to wash a car and $7 to walk a dog. How much money did Jeff earn for washing 6 cars and walking 1 dog?

Find and solve the hidden question.
How much money did Jeff earn washing 6 cars?
$6 \times \$10 = \$60$
Then solve the problem.
How much money in all did Jeff earn?
$\$60 + \$7 = \$67$, so Jeff earned $67.

**Remember** to carefully read the order in which things happen.

**1.** At the fair, Bonnie wants to get 2 rings and 1 pen. Each ring costs 8 tickets, and each pen costs 6 tickets. How many tickets in all does she need?

**2.** Ty bought 2 bags of apples. Each bag had 10 apples. He used 4 apples. How many apples did he have left?

**Multiple Choice**

1. Martin walked the Oak Hill Trail 7 times. The trail is 8 miles long. How many miles in all did he walk on the trail? (6-4)

   **A** 78

   **B** 56

   **C** 54

   **D** 15

2. There are 3 periods in a hockey game. How many periods are there in 5 hockey games? (6-2)

   **A** 8

   **B** 12

   **C** 15

   **D** 18

3. Which shows a way to find $4 \times 6$? (6-3)

   **A** $4 + 6$

   **B** $6 + 6 + 6$

   **C** $2 \times 6$ plus $2 \times 6$

   **D** $2 \times 6$ plus $3 \times 6$

4. Jon bought 3 boxes of greeting cards. Each box had 8 cards. He sent out 20 cards. Which shows one way to find how many cards are left? (6-9)

   **A** Multiply 3 by 8 and then subtract 20.

   **B** Multiply 3 by 20 and then subtract 8.

   **C** Multiply 5 by 8 and then add 20.

   **D** Multiply 3 by 8 and then add 20.

5. If you count the muffins below in groups of 6, which list shows numbers you would name? (6-7)

   **A** 6, 12, 16, 24, 32, 40

   **B** 6, 12, 18, 24, 30, 36

   **C** 12, 18, 24, 32, 38, 44

   **D** 12, 18, 24, 30, 36, 42

6. Sven feeds his fish 2 food pellets 3 times a day. How many pellets does he feed them in 7 days? (6-6)

   **A** 13

   **B** 14

   **C** 21

   **D** 42

7. What number makes the number sentence true? (6-6)
   $6 \times (3 \times 2) = (6 \times 3) \times \quad$

   **A** 2

   **B** 6

   **C** 9

   **D** 54

8. Mr. Hernandez bought 8 bags of limes. Each bag had 4 limes. How many limes did he buy? (6-3)

   **A** 32

   **B** 28

   **C** 24

   **D** 12

9. Tia can buy one of 4 books and one of 4 bookmarks. How many different combinations of one book and one bookmark can she choose? (6-8)

10. Mrs. Chavez put new light switch covers in her house. She put in 4 plastic covers and 2 wooden covers. Each cover had 2 screws. How many screws did she use? (6-9)

11. A marching band was in a parade. The band members marched in 8 rows. There were 6 band members in each row. Explain how the fact that $5 \times 6 = 30$ can help you find $8 \times 6$. (6-5)

12. Tasha has 6 bags with 9 carrots in each. How many carrots does she have in all? (6-4)

13. The Cougars basketball team has 8 players. The coach ordered 3 shirts for each player. How many shirts did he order? (6-5)

14. Tony can choose one main dish: steak, chicken, or fish. He can choose one side dish: peas, corn, squash, beans, potatoes, okra, or spinach. How many different combinations of one main dish and one side dish are there? (6-8)

15. Could you multiply a number by 2 and get a product of 15? Explain. (6-7).

16. Separate the rows in the array to break them into two smaller arrays. Write the new facts. (6-1)

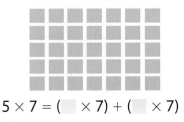

$5 \times 7 = (\phantom{x} \times 7) + (\phantom{x} \times 7)$

17. Mrs. Kent drives 3 miles 6 times a week for her job. How many miles is this in all? Explain how you found your answer. (6-2)

18. Explain how you can break a $6 \times 7$ array into two smaller arrays. What are the new facts? (6-1)

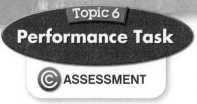
You and some friends are making baked goods for a school bake sale.
The chart shows the number of trays and the number of items
on each tray.

| Baked Goods | Number of Trays | Number on Each Tray |
|---|---|---|
| Blueberry Muffins | 4 | 6 |
| Strawberry Tarts | 6 | 5 |
| Granola Bars | 8 | 4 |

1. Choose one kind of baked goods that you will bring to the sale.
   Then draw an array to show the number of items in all.

2. Write a multiplication number sentence for the array that
   you drew.

3. Explain two different ways you could break apart the arrays
   to solve your number sentence. Draw a picture of the arrays.

4. Suppose two of your friends make trays of blueberry muffins as
   shown in the chart above. Write a multiplication number sentence
   to show the number of muffins in all.

5. Trina brings in some trays of peach tarts to the sale. The array below
   shows the number of trays and number of tarts on each tray. How
   many peach tarts does Trina bring?

## Topic 7

# Meanings of Division

▼ About how many baseballs are used during one inning of a major league game? You will find out in Lesson 7-5.

## Review What You Know!

### Vocabulary

Choose the best term from the box.

- array
- difference
- factor
- product

**1.** The answer in multiplication is the _?_.

**2.** In $3 \times 5 = 15$, 5 is a(n) _?_.

**3.** When objects are placed in equal rows they form a(n) _?_.

### Subtraction

Subtract.

| **4.** | **5.** | **6.** |
|---|---|---|
| $21 - 7$ | $15 - 5$ | $27 - 9$ |
| $14 - 7$ | $10 - 5$ | $18 - 9$ |
| $7 - 7$ | $5 - 5$ | $9 - 9$ |

### Multiplication Facts

**7.** $5 \times 4$    **8.** $7 \times 3$    **9.** $3 \times 8$

**10.** $9 \times 2$    **11.** $6 \times 5$    **12.** $4 \times 7$

**13.** $6 \times 7$    **14.** $8 \times 4$    **15.** $5 \times 9$

### Equal Groups

© **16. Writing to Explain** The picture has 9 counters. Describe why this picture doesn't show equal groups. Then show how to change the drawing so it does show equal groups.

### Topic Essential Questions

- What are different meanings of division?
- How is division related to other operations?

# Interactive Learning

**Pose the problem.** Start each lesson by working together to solve problems. It will help you make sense of math.

### Applying Math Practices

- What am I asked to find?
- What else can I try?
- How are quantities related?
- How can I explain my work?
- How can I use math to model the problem?
- Can I use tools to help?
- Is my work precise?
- Why does this work?
- How can I generalize?

**Lesson 7-1**

© **Use Tools** Solve. Use counters if you want.

Four friends picked 20 apples. They want to share them equally. How many apples should each person get? Show how you found the answer.

**Lesson 7-2**

© **Use Tools** Solve. Use counters if you want.

Li made 12 tacos. He wants to give 2 tacos each to some of his friends. How many friends can get tacos? Show how you found the answer.

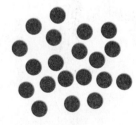

**Lesson 7-3**

© **Use Structure** Use what you already know about a multiplication table to solve.

Use a multiplication table to find $18 \div 3$.

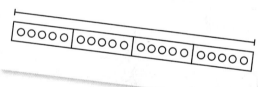

| x | 0 | 1 | 2 | 3 | 4 | 5 | 6 | 7 | 8 | 9 | 10 |
|---|---|---|---|---|---|---|---|---|---|---|----|
| 0 | 0 | 0 | 0 | 0 | 0 | 0 | 0 | 0 | 0 | 0 | 0 |
| 1 | 0 | 1 | 2 | 3 | 4 | 5 | 6 | 7 | 8 | 9 | 10 |
| 2 | 0 | 2 | 4 | 6 | 8 | 10 | 12 | 14 | 16 | 18 | 20 |
| 3 | 0 | 3 | 6 | 9 | 12 | 15 | 18 | 21 | 24 | 27 | 30 |
| 4 | 0 | 4 | 8 | 12 | 16 | 20 | 24 | 28 | 32 | 36 | 40 |
| 5 | 0 | 5 | 10 | 15 | 20 | 25 | 30 | 35 | 40 | 45 | 50 |
| 6 | 0 | 6 | 12 | 18 | 24 | 30 | 36 | 42 | 48 | 54 | 60 |
| 7 | 0 | 7 | 14 | 21 | 28 | 35 | 42 | 49 | 56 | 63 | 70 |
| 8 | 0 | 8 | 16 | 24 | 32 | 40 | 48 | 56 | 64 | 72 | 80 |
| 9 | 0 | 9 | 18 | 27 | 36 | 45 | 54 | 63 | 72 | 81 | 90 |
| 10 | 0 | 10 | 20 | 30 | 40 | 50 | 60 | 70 | 80 | 90 | 100 |

**Lesson 7-4**

Ⓒ **Reason** Use what you already know about addition, subtraction, multiplication, and division to write and solve an equation to find the answer to this problem. Is more than one equation possible?

Kenny was asked to hand out 24 crayons equally to the 4 students at his table. How many crayons should each student get? Let *n* represent the unknown value.

**Lesson 7-5**

Ⓒ **Reason** Use what you have learned about division to complete this task.

Write a real-world division story for the number sentence shown at the right. Then write another real-world story that shows a different way to think about division.

$8 \div 2 = \underline{\hspace{1cm}}$

**Lesson 7-6**

Ⓒ **Model** Use the recording sheet to solve these problems.

Leo spilled ink on his paper. The ink covered up part of his picture of a tile floor. The tile floor was in the shape of a rectangle. There were 18 tiles in the whole floor. How many tiles were in each row? How did you decide?

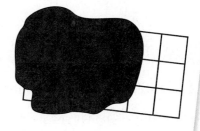

Lesson
**7-1**

**Common Core**

3.OA.2 Interpret whole-number quotients of whole numbers, e.g., interpret 56 ÷ 8 as the number of objects in each share when 56 objects are partitioned equally into 8 shares, or as a number of shares when 56 objects are partitioned into equal shares of 8 objects each.... Also **3.OA.3, 3.OA.4**

# Division as Sharing

**Hands-On** counters ●

## How many are in each group?

Three friends have 12 toys to share equally. How many toys will each person get?

Think of putting 12 toys into 3 equal groups.

Division is an operation that is used to find how many equal groups or how many are in each group.

---

## Guided Practice*

© **MATHEMATICAL PRACTICES**

### Do you know **HOW?**

Use counters or draw a picture to solve.

**1.** 15 bananas, 3 boxes
How many bananas in each box?

**2.** 16 plants, 4 pots
How many plants in each pot?

### Do you **UNDERSTAND?**

© **3. Model** Copy and complete the division sentence. Use the picture to help.

```
        18
┌──────┬──────┬──────┐
│  ?   │  ?   │  ?   │        18 ÷ 3 =
└──────┴──────┴──────┘
```

© **4. Communicate** Can 12 grapes be shared equally among 5 children? Explain.

---

## Independent Practice

Use counters or draw a picture to solve.

**5.** 18 marbles, 6 sacks
How many marbles in each sack?

**6.** 36 stickers, 4 people
How many stickers for each person?

**7.** 16 crayons, 2 people
How many crayons for each person?

**8.** 12 pictures, 4 pages
How many pictures on each page?

**9.** 24 bottles, 4 cases
How many bottles in each case?

**10.** 27 CDs, 9 packages
How many CDs in each package?

Complete each division sentence.

**11.**
```
      12
┌──────┬──────┐
│  ?   │  ?   │        12 ÷ 2 =
└──────┴──────┘
```

**12.**
```
              16
┌──┬──┬──┬──┬──┬──┬──┬──┐
│? │? │? │? │? │? │? │? │   16 ÷ 8 =
└──┴──┴──┴──┴──┴──┴──┴──┘
```

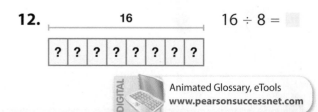

DIGITAL  Animated Glossary, eTools
www.pearsonsuccessnet.com

*For another example, see Set A on page 184.*

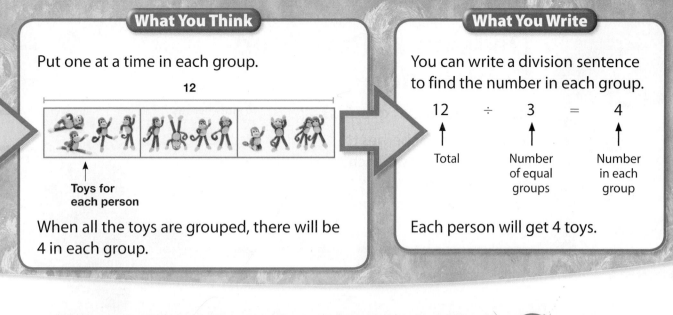

Put one at a time in each group.

12

Toys for
each person

When all the toys are grouped, there will be
4 in each group.

You can write a division sentence
to find the number in each group.

12 ÷ 3 = 4

Total     Number     Number
of equal    in each
groups     group

Each person will get 4 toys.

## Problem Solving

MATHEMATICAL
PRACTICES

© **13. Writing to Explain** Jim is putting 18 pens into equal groups.
He says that there will be more pens in each of 2 equal
groups than in each of 3 equal groups. Is he correct? Explain.

© **14. Persevere** Joy has 12 shells. She gives 2 to her mom. Then
she and her sister share the rest equally. How many shells
does Joy get? How many shells does her sister get?

**15.** Three astronauts were on each *Apollo* spacecraft. How many
astronauts in all were on the nine *Apollo* spacecrafts that
orbited the Moon?

© **16. Model** Max has the stickers shown. He wants
to put an equal number of stickers on each
of 2 posters. Which number sentence shows
how to find the number of stickers Max
should put on each poster?

**A** $14 + 2 =$

**B** $14 \times 2 =$

**C** $14 - 2 =$

**D** $14 \div 2 =$

**17.** The flag bearers march in 9 rows with 5 people in each row.
Each person is carrying one flag. Write a number sentence to
show how many flags there are.

Lesson
7-2

Common
Core

3.OA.2 Interpret whole-number quotients of whole numbers, e.g., interpret 56 ÷ 8 as the number of objects in each share when 56 objects are partitioned equally into 8 shares, or as a number of shares when 56 objects are partitioned into equal shares of 8 objects each.... Also 3.OA.3, 3.OA.4

# Division as Repeated Subtraction

**Hands-On**
counters ●

## How many equal groups?

June has 10 strawberries to serve to her guests. If each guest eats 2 strawberries, how many guests can June serve?

10 strawberries

2 | ? guests →

↑
**Strawberries for each guest**

---

## Guided Practice*

**© MATHEMATICAL PRACTICES**

### Do you know HOW?

Use counters or draw a picture to solve.

**1.** 16 gloves
2 gloves in each pair
How many pairs?

**2.** 15 tennis balls
3 balls in each can
How many cans?

### Do you UNDERSTAND?

© **3. Use Tools** Suppose June had 12 strawberries and each guest ate 2 strawberries. How many guests could she serve? Use counters or draw a picture to solve.

© **4. Model** Show how you can use repeated subtraction to find how many groups of 4 there are in 20. Then write the division sentence for the problem.

---

## Independent Practice

© **Use Tools** Use counters or draw a picture to solve.

**5.** 12 wheels
4 wheels on each wagon
How many wagons?

**6.** 30 markers
5 markers in each package
How many packages?

**7.** 8 apples
4 apples in each bag
How many bags?

**8.** 18 pencils
2 pencils on each desk
How many desks?

DIGITAL  eTools
www.pearsonsuccessnet.com

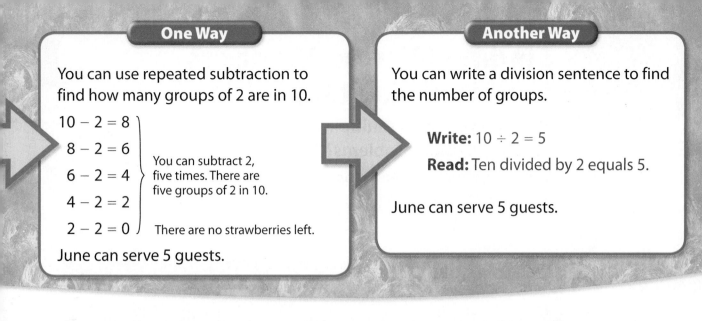

You can use repeated subtraction to find how many groups of 2 are in 10.

$10 - 2 = 8$
$8 - 2 = 6$
$6 - 2 = 4$
$4 - 2 = 2$
$2 - 2 = 0$

You can subtract 2, five times. There are five groups of 2 in 10.

There are no strawberries left.

June can serve 5 guests.

You can write a division sentence to find the number of groups.

**Write:** $10 \div 2 = 5$

**Read:** Ten divided by 2 equals 5.

June can serve 5 guests.

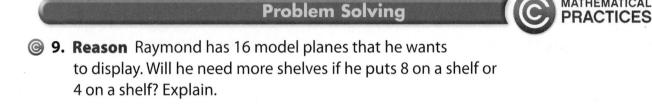

## Problem Solving

**MATHEMATICAL PRACTICES**

9. **Reason** Raymond has 16 model planes that he wants to display. Will he need more shelves if he puts 8 on a shelf or 4 on a shelf? Explain.

**Use Tools** For **10–12**, match each problem to a picture or a repeated subtraction. Then write the division sentence to solve.

**10.** 24 books
6 in a box
How many boxes?

**11.** 24 books
3 in a box
How many boxes?

**12.** 24 books
8 in a box
How many boxes?

a
24 books
? boxes
3
Books in a box

b  $24 - 8 = 16$
$16 - 8 = 8$
$8 - 8 = 0$

c
24 books
? boxes
6
Books in a box

13. **Be Precise** In 1999, the United States Mint began circulating state quarters. New quarters for 5 states are released each year. How many years will it take for quarters to be released for all 50 states? Write a number sentence to solve.

14. **Model** Toni has 6 tulips and 6 daisies. She wants to put 4 flowers in each vase. Which number sentence shows how many vases she needs?

**A** $12 + 4 = 16$ **B** $12 - 4 = 8$ **C** $6 \times 4 = 24$ **D** $12 \div 4 = 3$

Lesson
7-3

Common
Core

3.OA.6 Understand
division as an unknown-
factor problem....
Also 3.OA.4, 3.OA.9

# Finding Missing Numbers in a Multiplication Table

## How can you use a multiplication table to solve division problems?

Write a missing factor equation and then use a multiplication table.

Find $15 \div 3$.

**Think**

$15 \div 3 = n$

$3 \times n = 15$

3 times what number equals 15?

| x | 0 | 1 | 2 | 3 | 4 | 5 |
|---|---|---|---|---|---|---|
| 0 | 0 | 0 | 0 | 0 | 0 | 0 |
| 1 | 0 | 1 | 2 | 3 | 4 | 5 |
| 2 | 0 | 2 | 4 | 6 | 8 | 10 |
| 3 | 0 | 3 | 6 | 9 | 12 | 15 |

---

## Guided Practice*

**MATHEMATICAL PRACTICES**

### Do you know HOW?

In **1** through **4**, find the value for $n$ that makes the equation true. Use a multiplication table to help.

**1.** $18 \div 3 = n$
$3 \times n = 18$

**2.** $24 \div 6 = n$
$6 \times n = 24$

**3.** $81 \div 9 = n$

**4.** $20 \div 4 = n$

### Do you UNDERSTAND?

© **5. Use Tools** Where in a multiplication table do you find the two factors in a multiplication problem?

**6.** How can you use a multiplication table to solve division problems?

**7.** When using the multiplication table to answer Exercise 2, were multiples of 6 always even or odd?

---

## Independent Practice

**Leveled Practice** In **8** through **16**, find the value for $n$ that makes the equation true. Use a multiplication table to help.

**8.** $45 \div 9 = n$
$9 \times n = 45$

**9.** $21 \div 3 = n$
$3 \times n = 21$

**10.** $36 \div 9 = n$
$9 \times n = 36$

**11.** $28 \div 4 = n$

**12.** $32 \div 8 = n$

**13.** $56 \div 7 = n$

**14.** $36 \div 6 = n$

**15.** $18 \div 9 = n$

**16.** $35 \div 5 = n$

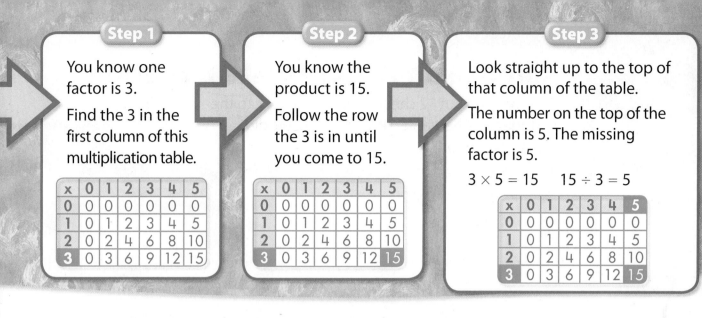

### Step 1
You know one factor is 3.

Find the 3 in the first column of this multiplication table.

| x | 0 | 1 | 2 | 3 | 4 | 5 |
|---|---|---|---|---|---|---|
| 0 | 0 | 0 | 0 | 0 | 0 | 0 |
| 1 | 0 | 1 | 2 | 3 | 4 | 5 |
| 2 | 0 | 2 | 4 | 6 | 8 | 10 |
| 3 | 0 | 3 | 6 | 9 | 12 | 15 |

### Step 2
You know the product is 15.

Follow the row the 3 is in until you come to 15.

| x | 0 | 1 | 2 | 3 | 4 | 5 |
|---|---|---|---|---|---|---|
| 0 | 0 | 0 | 0 | 0 | 0 | 0 |
| 1 | 0 | 1 | 2 | 3 | 4 | 5 |
| 2 | 0 | 2 | 4 | 6 | 8 | 10 |
| 3 | 0 | 3 | 6 | 9 | 12 | 15 |

### Step 3
Look straight up to the top of that column of the table.

The number on the top of the column is 5. The missing factor is 5.

$3 \times 5 = 15 \qquad 15 \div 3 = 5$

| x | 0 | 1 | 2 | 3 | 4 | 5 |
|---|---|---|---|---|---|---|
| 0 | 0 | 0 | 0 | 0 | 0 | 0 |
| 1 | 0 | 1 | 2 | 3 | 4 | 5 |
| 2 | 0 | 2 | 4 | 6 | 8 | 10 |
| 3 | 0 | 3 | 6 | 9 | 12 | 15 |

## Problem Solving

MATHEMATICAL PRACTICES

For **17–19**, use the multiplication table at the right.

| x | 0 | 1 | 2 | 3 | 4 | 5 | 6 | 7 |
|---|---|---|---|---|---|---|---|---|
| 0 | 0 | 0 | 0 | 0 | 0 | 0 | 0 | 0 |
| 1 | 0 | 1 | 2 | 3 | 4 | 5 | 6 | 7 |
| 2 | 0 | 2 | 4 | 6 | 8 | 10 | 12 | 14 |
| 3 | 0 | 3 | 6 | 9 | 12 | 15 | 18 | 21 |
| 4 | 0 | 4 | 8 | 12 | 16 | 20 | 24 | 28 |
| 5 | 0 | 5 | 10 | 15 | 20 | 25 | 30 | 35 |
| 6 | 0 | 6 | 12 | 18 | 24 | 30 | 36 | 42 |
| 7 | 0 | 7 | 14 | 21 | 28 | 35 | 42 | 49 |
| 8 | 0 | 8 | 16 | 24 | 32 | 40 | 48 | 56 |
| 9 | 0 | 9 | 18 | 27 | 36 | 45 | 54 | 63 |

**17. Critique Reasoning** Bill used a multiplication table to find the value of *n* in $12 \div 6 = n$. His answer was 3. Do you agree? Why or why not?

**18.** Mrs. Sanchez had 27 pencils to distribute equally to 9 children. How many pencils did each child get?

**19. Use Structure** Write two division facts and two multiplication facts using the numbers 7, 9, and 63.

**20. Reason** Anna has 72 jars of pickles. She can place 8 jars into a carton. How many cartons will she need? What if she could place 9 jars in a carton?

**21.** Mr. Baker had a basket of apples. He made 5 pies with the apples. He used 5 apples to make each pie. When he was done, he had 3 apples left over. Before he started baking how many apples were in the basket?

**22. Reason** Manny has 64 beans. He wants to plant them equally in 8 pots. How many seeds should he plant in each pot?

**23.** Carlos fed his pig, Daisy, 42 pounds of food in 6 days. If Daisy ate an equal amount of food each day, how many pounds of food did she eat each day?

**A** 6     **B** 8     **C** 9     **D** 12

Lesson
**7-4**

© Common Core

**3.OA.4** Determine the unknown whole number in a multiplication or division equation relating three whole numbers.... Also **3.OA.6**

Problem Solving

# Choose an Appropriate Equation

Kara handed out 12 sheets of paper equally to the 6 students at her table. How many sheets did each student get?

Choose an equation that shows the problem.

**A** $6 + 12 = n$      **C** $12 \times n = 6$

**B** $n = 12 \div 6$      **D** $12 - 6 = n$

---

## Guided Practice*

© MATHEMATICAL PRACTICES

### Do you know HOW?

Choose the equation that shows the problem.

1. At another table, the students are equally sharing 20 colored pencils. Each student has 4 of them. How many students are there?

   **A** $20 \div 2 = n$      **C** $20 = 4 + n$
   **B** $n \times 4 = 20$      **D** $20 - n = 4$

### Do you UNDERSTAND?

© 2. **Persevere** Write a different equation that could be used to solve Problem 1.

© 3. **Reason** Could there ever be a division equation and a multiplication equation that could both work to solve a problem? Explain.

---

## Independent Practice

© MATHEMATICAL PRACTICES

© 4. **Use Structure** Kayla has 15 stickers to give equally to 3 friends. How many stickers will each friend get? Choose an equation that shows the problem.

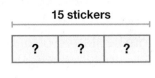

15 stickers

| ? | ? | ? |

   **A** $15 - 3 = n$      **C** $3 \times n = 15$
   **B** $n = 3 \times 15$      **D** $3 + n = 15$

5. Six students each need 3 crayons. How many crayons are needed in all?

**Applying Math Practices**

- What am I asked to find?
- What else can I try?
- How are quantities related?
- How can I explain my work?
- How can I use math to model the problem?
- Can I use tools to help?
- Is my work precise?
- Why does this work?
- How can I generalize?

## Understand and Plan

Draw a picture to show what you know.

12 sheets in all

| ? | ? | ? | ? | ? | ? |

You know how many in all and the number of groups.

You need to find the size of each group.

## Solve

Look at the four equations. Choose the one that shows the situation.

**A** $6 + 12 = n$ No, 6 and 12 are not being joined

**B** $n = 12 \div 6$ Yes, this one works. 6 groups, 12 in all

**C** $12 \times n = 6$ No, this would mean 12 groups of something.

**D** $12 - 6 = n$ No, this would mean 6 fewer than 12.

---

© **Use Structure** For **6–11** choose the equation that shows the problem.

**6.** Omar exercises 10 hours each week. He exercises 2 hours each day. How many days does Omar exercise each week?

    **A** $10 \div 2 = n$     **C** $10 - 2 = n$
    **B** $n = 10 \times 2$     **D** $10 + 2 = n$

**7.** Mrs. Santos has a vegetable garden. She buys 24 tomato plants and 18 pepper plants for her garden. How many plants does she buy altogether?

    **A** $24 - 18 = n$     **C** $n + 18 = 24$
    **B** $24 \div n = 18$     **D** $n = 24 + 18$

**8.** Jason helps his grandfather pack peaches on his farm. He packs 30 peaches in each box. Each tray in the box holds 6 peaches. How many trays are in the box?

    **A** $n = 30 \div 6$     **C** $30 - n = 6$
    **B** $6 \times 30 = n$     **D** $30 = n + 6$

**9.** The electronics store has a section for video games. There are 6 shelves, with 9 games on each shelf. How many video games does the store have?

    **A** $9 \div n = 6$     **C** $n = 9 + 6$
    **B** $9 \times 6 = n$     **D** $9 - n = 6$

**10.** Carl delivers 56 newspapers each morning. He has already delivered 18 papers. How many papers does he have left to deliver?

    **A** $56 + n = 18$     **C** $n = 56 \div 18$
    **B** $56 - 18 = n$     **D** $18 \times n = 56$

**11.** A patchwork quilt has 3 rows of squares. There are 5 squares in each row. How many quilt squares are in the quilt?

    **A** $3 + 5 = n$     **C** $3 \times 5 = n$
    **B** $3 + n = 5$     **D** $5 \div 3 = n$

© **12. Persevere** Matt has 5 boxes of oatmeal like the one shown at the right. Lindsay gives Matt 2 more boxes of oatmeal with 8 packets in each box. How many packets of oatmeal does Matt have now?

Instant Oatmeal

8 packets

Lesson
7-5

© Common Core

**3.OA.3** Use multiplication and division within 100 to solve word problems in situations involving equal groups, arrays, and measurement quantities, . . . Also **3.OA.4**

# Writing Division Stories

Hands-On
counters

## What is the main idea of a division story?

Mrs. White asked her students to write a division story for $15 \div 3 = $ .

Mike and Kia decided to write stories about putting roses in vases.

---

### Guided Practice*

© MATHEMATICAL PRACTICES

#### Do you know HOW?

Write a division story for each number sentence. Then use counters or draw a picture to solve.

**1.** $8 \div 4 = $

**2.** $10 \div 2 = $

**3.** $20 \div 5 = $

**4.** $14 \div 7 = $

#### Do you UNDERSTAND?

© **5. Persevere** How are Mike's and Kia's stories alike? How are the two stories different?

© **6. Writing to Explain** When you write a division story, what two pieces of information do you need to include? What kind of information do you ask for?

---

### Independent Practice

© **Use Tools** Write a division story for each number sentence. Then use counters or draw a picture to solve.

**7.** $18 \div 3 = $     **8.** $25 \div 5 = $     **9.** $16 \div 4 = $     **10.** $30 \div 6 = $

© **11. Reason** Choose two of the stories you wrote for the exercises above. For each, tell whether you found the number in each group or the number of equal groups.

DIGITAL
eTools
www.pearsonsuccessnet.com

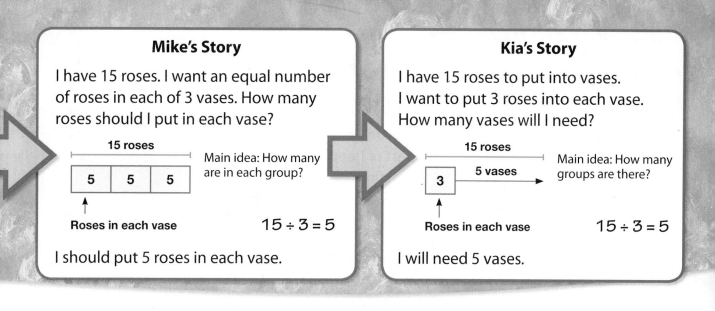

**Mike's Story**

I have 15 roses. I want an equal number of roses in each of 3 vases. How many roses should I put in each vase?

15 roses

| 5 | 5 | 5 |

Roses in each vase

Main idea: How many are in each group?

$15 \div 3 = 5$

I should put 5 roses in each vase.

**Kia's Story**

I have 15 roses to put into vases. I want to put 3 roses into each vase. How many vases will I need?

15 roses

5 vases

3

Roses in each vase

Main idea: How many groups are there?

$15 \div 3 = 5$

I will need 5 vases.

---

## Problem Solving

MATHEMATICAL PRACTICES

The table shows the number of players needed for each kind of sports team. Use the table for **12–15**.

There are 36 third graders at sports camp who want to play on different teams.

| Sports Team | Number |
| --- | --- |
| Baseball | 9 players |
| Basketball | 5 players |
| Doubles Tennis | 2 players |

**12.** If everyone wants to play baseball, how many teams will there be?

**13. Writing to Explain** Could everyone play basketball at the same time? Why or why not?

**14. Persevere** Twenty of the third graders went swimming. The rest of them played doubles tennis. How many doubles tennis teams were there?

**15.** Two baseball teams are playing a game. At the same time, two basketball teams are playing a game. The rest of the campers are playing tennis. How many campers are playing tennis?

**16. Reasonableness** Carmen rides her bike to school from 3 to 5 times a week. Which is a reasonable number of times Carmen will ride her bike in 4 weeks?

**A** More than 28

**B** From 12 to 20

**C** From 14 to 28

**D** Fewer than 12

**17. Model** In one inning, each baseball was used for 7 pitches. Write a number sentence that shows the total number of pitches thrown that inning.

4 baseballs are used each inning.

Lesson
**7-6**

**Common Core**

3.OA.3 Use multiplication and division within 100 to solve word problems in situations involving equal groups, arrays, and measurement quantities, ... Also **3.OA.4, 3.OA.6**

**Problem Solving**

# Use Objects and Draw a Picture

Naomi spilled some ink on her paper. The ink covered up part of her picture of a tile floor. The entire floor was shaped like a rectangle covered by 24 square tiles. How many tiles were in each row?

**Hands-On**

square tiles

grid paper

---

## Guided Practice*

**MATHEMATICAL PRACTICES**

### Do you know HOW?

Solve. Use objects or draw a picture.

**1.** Paint covered part of a tile floor. The square floor had 16 tiles. How many tiles had paint on them?

### Do you UNDERSTAND?

**2. Communicate** What strategy did you use to find the number of tiles covered by paint in Exercise 1?

**3. Write a Problem** Write and solve a problem that you can solve by using objects or drawing a picture.

---

## Independent Practice

**MATHEMATICAL PRACTICES**

Solve. Use objects or draw a picture.

**4. Persevere** Kim painted part of a tiled section of a wall. The whole section of tiles was shaped like a rectangle. There were 27 square tiles. How many tiles were in each row?

### Applying Math Practices

- What am I asked to find?
- What else can I try?
- How are quantities related?
- How can I explain my work?
- How can I use math to model the problem?
- Can I use tools to help?
- Is my work precise?
- Why does this work?
- How can I generalize?

DIGITAL

eTools
www.pearsonsuccessnet.com

*For another example, see Set E on page 185.*

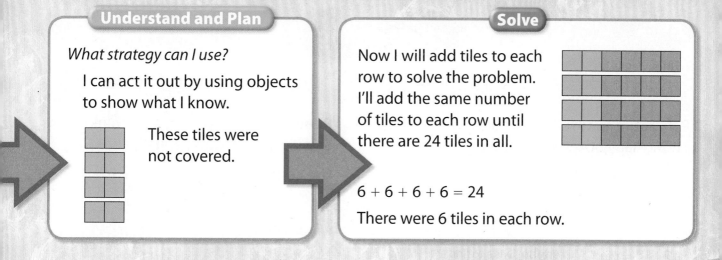

*What strategy can I use?*

I can act it out by using objects to show what I know.

These tiles were not covered.

Now I will add tiles to each row to solve the problem. I'll add the same number of tiles to each row until there are 24 tiles in all.

$6 + 6 + 6 + 6 = 24$

There were 6 tiles in each row.

---

**5.** Some glue spilled on Ana's drawing of a tile floor. The glue covered up some of the tiles. The tile floor was shaped like a rectangle. There were 20 square tiles in the whole floor. How many of the tiles had glue on them?

© **6. Look for Patterns** Joyce wants to make a design using the pattern of square tiles shown below. She wants to use this pattern four times. How many white tiles does she need?

© **7. Model** Jeff's family took a car trip for a summer vacation. The family drove 362 miles to a national park. Then the family drove 174 miles to hike in the mountains. How many miles did the family drive all together?

| ? miles in all | |
|---|---|
| 362 miles | 174 miles |

© **Think About the Structure**

**8.** Which of the following can be used to find how many days there are in 8 weeks?

**A** $8 \times 7$      **B** $8 \div 2$      **C** $8 + 7$      **D** $8 - 2$

**9.** Mrs. Clay bought 28 picture frames packed equally into 4 boxes. Which number sentence shows how to find the number of frames in each box?

**A** $28 - 4 = $      **B** $28 + 4 = $      **C** $28 \times 4 = $      **D** $28 \div 4 = $

**Set A,** pages 172–175

© INTERVENTION

There are 12 toys. If 4 toys are put in each box, how many boxes are needed?

$12 - 4 = 8$    Use repeated subtraction to find
$8 - 4 = 4$     how many groups.
$4 - 4 = 0$     You can subtract 4 three times.

$12 \div 4 = 3$    You can also divide to find the
number of groups.

Three boxes are needed.

**Remember** that you can also think of division as sharing equally.

Use counters or draw a picture to solve each problem.

1. 6 books
   3 shelves
   How many books are on each shelf?

2. 18 students
   2 students in each group
   How many groups are there?

**Set B,** pages 176–177

Use a multiplication table to find $10 \div 2$.
$10 \div 2 = n$          $2 \times n = 10$

| × | 1 | 2 | 3 | 4 | 5 | 6 | 7 |
|---|---|---|---|---|---|---|---|
| **1** | 1 | 2 | 3 | 4 | 5 | 6 | 7 |
| **2** | 2 | 4 | 6 | 8 | 10 | 12 | 14 |
| **3** | 3 | 6 | 9 | 12 | 15 | 18 | 21 |
| **4** | 4 | 8 | 12 | 16 | 20 | 24 | 28 |
| **5** | 5 | 10 | 15 | 20 | 25 | 30 | 35 |

Find the **2** in the first column of the table, and go across the row to 10. Then go up in the column with the 10 to find the missing factor.

$2 \times 5 = 10$          $10 \div 2 = 5$

**Remember** that you can look for a missing factor in the top row or the left column.

Find the value for $n$ that makes the equation true.

1. $14 \div 2 = n$          2. $18 \div 6 = n$
   $2 \times n = 14$           $6 \times n = 18$

3. $35 \div 7 = n$          4. $16 \div 4 = n$

5. $30 \div 6 = n$          6. $28 \div 4 = n$

**Set C,** pages 178–179

Tom has 12 apples to put into bags. Each bag holds 4 apples. How many bags can Tom fill?

Look at the four equations. Choose the one that shows the situation.

**A** $12 + 4 = n$          **C** $12 - 4 = n$

**B** $12 \div 4 = n$          **D** $12 \times n = 4$

Tom can find equal groups of apples by dividing.

**Remember** that you can draw a picture to show what you know.

Choose the equation that shows the problem.

1. Emily made 20 muffins. She put 4 muffins in each box. How many boxes could Emily fill?

   **A** $20 + 4 = n$          **C** $20 \div 4 = n$

   **B** $20 - 4 = n$          **D** $20 \times n = 4$

Write a division story for 20 ÷ 5.

If 20 children form 5 equal teams, how many children are on each team?

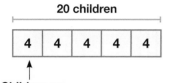

20 children

Children on each team

20 ÷ 5 = 4

There are 4 children on each team.

**Remember** that division stories can ask for the number in each group or the number of equal groups.

Write a division story for each number sentence. Draw a picture to help.

**1.** 15 ÷ 3 =

**2.** 21 ÷ 7 =

**3.** 24 ÷ 6 =

**4.** 30 ÷ 5 =

Some blue paint spilled on a tile floor. The tile floor was in the shape of a square. There were 9 tiles in the whole floor. How many of the tiles had blue paint on them?

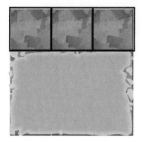

Draw a picture to show what you know.

Finish the picture to solve. Show 9 tiles in all.

Six tiles had blue paint on them.

**Remember** to check that your picture matches the information in the problem.

**1.** Carmela painted over a part of some tiles. The whole group of tiles was in the shape of a rectangle. There were 28 tiles in the whole group. How many tiles did Carmela paint over?

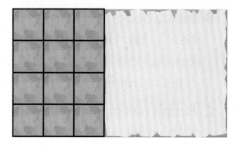

**Multiple Choice**

Ⓒ ASSESSMENT

**1.** Martin has 12 pinecones. His birdfeeder design uses 3 pinecones. Which equation shows how many birdfeeders he can make? (7-4)

**A** $12 + 3 = n$

**B** $12 ÷ 3 = n$

**C** $12 - 3 = n$

**D** $12 × 3 = n$

**2.** Which story could be solved with $20 ÷ 4$? (7-5)

**A** Harold caught 20 fish. All but 4 of them were catfish. How many of the fish were something other than catfish?

**B** Becky bought 20 bags of crystal beads. Each bag had 4 crystal beads. How many crystal beads did she buy?

**C** Batina has made 20 doll dresses. If she makes 4 more, how many doll dresses will she have made?

**D** Coach Sid has 20 baseballs. Each group needs 4 balls for the practice drill. How many groups can he form?

**3.** Five friends have 15 pencils to share equally. Which number sentence shows how many pencils each friend will get? (7-1)

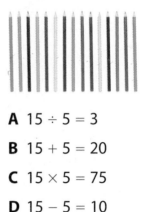

**A** $15 ÷ 5 = 3$

**B** $15 + 5 = 20$

**C** $15 × 5 = 75$

**D** $15 - 5 = 10$

**4.** Mrs. Vincent bought 16 kiwis for her 4 children to share equally. How many kiwis will each child get? (7-1)

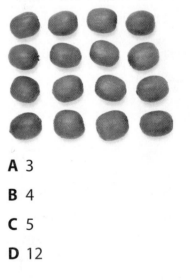

**A** 3

**B** 4

**C** 5

**D** 12

**5.** Mason wants to find $28 ÷ 4$. Which missing factor equation can he use to help solve the problem? (7-3)

**A** $28 + n = 4$

**B** $28 - n = 4$

**C** $4 × n = 28$

**D** $28 × n = 4$

**6.** What division sentence is shown by the repeated subtraction? (7-2)

$$15 - 3 = 12$$
$$12 - 3 = 9$$
$$9 - 3 = 6$$
$$6 - 3 = 3$$
$$3 - 3 = 0$$

**7.** The pet store had 24 parakeets to put equally in 8 cages. How many birds should be put in each cage? (7-1)

24 parakeets

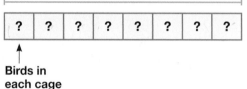

↑
**Birds in each cage**

**8.** While on vacation, Ginny bought 20 postcards. She can put 4 postcards on each page in her memory book. How many pages will Ginny fill with her postcards? (7-3)

**9.** Write a story that could be solved with $36 \div 6$. (7-5)

**10.** The pictures below are examples of a triangle in several different positions.

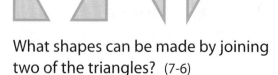

What shapes can be made by joining two of the triangles? (7-6)

**11.** In 2007, the United States Mint began circulating $1 coins with past Presidents of the United States on them. New $1 coins for 4 Presidents are released each year. How many years will it take for $1 coins to be released for the first 36 Presidents? Write a number sentence to solve. (7-2)

**12.** Carli is using a multiplication table to find the value of $n$ that makes the equation $21 \div 3 = n$ true. Her answer is 8. Do you agree? Explain. (7-3)

**13.** A rug is covering up some of the tiles of a tile floor. The tile floor is shaped like a rectangle. There are 42 square tiles in the whole floor. How many of the tiles have a rug covering them? (7-6)

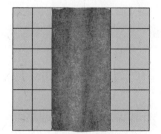

**14.** Ken has 6 rows of shells with 5 shells in each row. He wants to find the total number of shells he has. He decides to use the equation $6 \times 5 = n$ to show the problem. Is he correct? Explain. (7-4)

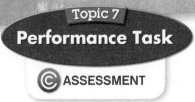
James needs help setting up his rock collection. James has collected 36 rocks. He can set the rocks up in different-sized display boxes. The boxes hold 4, 6, or 9 rocks each.

Copy the table below on a separate piece of paper. Complete the table by following the instructions at the top to draw arrays of 36 rocks in equal groups.

| Display Boxes | | |
|---|---|---|
| **Box 1**<br>**4 rocks per box** | **Box 2**<br>**6 rocks per box** | **Box 3**<br>**9 rocks per box** |
| | | |

1.  Choose a box. Write a division sentence to show how the rocks are divided. Then write a repeated subtraction to show how to find the quotient.

2.  Which type of box requires the most number of boxes to display all of the rocks?

3.  Can James use 2 different box types to display all 36 rocks? Explain.

4.  Suppose you have a rock collection of 27 rocks. Which box would you use to display the rocks? Write a division story to explain how you would display the rocks.

5.  How many boxes would James need if he had 54 rocks and wanted to put them in boxes that hold 9 rocks? What about boxes that hold 6 rocks?

## Topic 8 Division Facts

▼ A mosaic is a type of art made with tiles. How does this mosaic show multiplication and division? You will find out in Lesson 8-1.

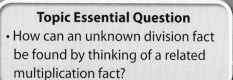

**Topic Essential Question**
• How can an unknown division fact be found by thinking of a related multiplication fact?

# Review What You Know!

## Vocabulary

Choose the best term from the box.

- addends
- difference
- factors
- product

**1.** The numbers you multiply are ＿?＿.

**2.** The answer in a subtraction problem is the ＿?＿.

**3.** The answer in a multiplication problem is the ＿?＿.

## Fact Families

Copy and complete each fact family.

**4.** $7 + 6 =$ ▢     $13 - 6 =$ ▢
$6 + 7 =$ ▢     ▢ $- 7 = 6$

**5.** $8 +$ ▢ $= 17$     $17 - 8 =$ ▢
$9 + 8 =$ ▢     ▢ $- 9 = 8$

**6.** Write the fact family for 2, 6, and 8.

## Multiplication

Copy and complete.

**7.** $6 \times 8 =$ ▢ $\times 6$

**8.** $10 \times$ ▢ $= 0$

**9.** ▢ $\times 1 = 7$

**10.** **Writing to Explain** Explain how to find how many items are in 3 groups if there are 4 items in each group. Draw a picture to help.

# Topic 8  Interactive Learning

**Pose the problem.** Start each lesson by working together to solve problems. It will help you make sense of math.

### Applying Math Practices

- What am I asked to find?
- What else can I try?
- How are quantities related?
- How can I explain my work?
- How can I use math to model the problem?
- Can I use tools to help?
- Is my work precise?
- Why does this work?
- How can I generalize?

---

### Lesson 8-1

ⓒ **Use Structure**  Solve using counters.

Use 24 counters to make an array with 3 equal rows. Write as many multiplication and division sentences as you can to describe the array. Tell why you think you found all of them.

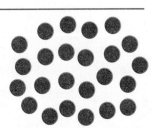

---

### Lesson 8-2

ⓒ **Use Structure**  Solve. Think about multiplication to help.

Kara is putting 30 toys into 5 party bags. She puts the same number of toys into each bag. How many toys are in each bag? Write and solve a division problem. Show your work.

___ × ___ = ___   ___ ÷ ___ = ___

___ × ___ = ___   ___ ÷ ___ = ___

---

### Lesson 8-3

ⓒ **Use Structure**  Solve. Think about multiplication to help.

There are 18 children in a ballet class. They are standing in rows of 6 for a dance recital. How many rows of children are there? Write and solve a division problem. Show your work.

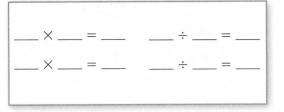

6 × ___ = 18

## Lesson 8-4

© **Use Structure**  Solve. Think about multiplication to help.

The art teacher put 72 crayons in a bucket. The crayons came in boxes with 8 crayons in each box. How many boxes of crayons were there? Write and solve a division sentence for this problem. Show your work.

## Lesson 8-5

© **Model**  Solve any way you choose. Show your work.

Three girls and four boys went to the amusement park. The total cost of their tickets was $42. They paid the same amount for each ticket. What was the cost of each ticket?

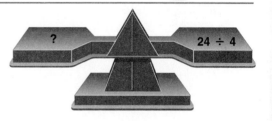

Worlds of Fun

Total cost of tickets:

$42

## Lesson 8-6

© **Use Structure**  What can I write on the left side of the balance that will have the same value as what is on the right side? Find 5 different answers!

?          24 ÷ 4

## Lesson 8-7

© **Model**  Use counters to solve each problem. Make a sketch of your work to show how you solved each problem.

5 ÷ 1

5 ÷ 5

## Lesson 8-8

© **Use Structure**  Solve. Use multiplication or division basic facts.

A tour bus to a national park holds 56 people. Once they arrive at the park, there will be 7 tour guides to lead equal groups of people. How many people will be in each tour group?

**56 people**

## Lesson 8-9

© **Model**  Solve. Use the bar diagram to help.

At the community garden, 32 pounds of green beans have been picked. They will be shared by 4 families. If each family gets the same amount, how many pounds of beans will each family get?

32 pounds

| ? | ? | ? | ? |

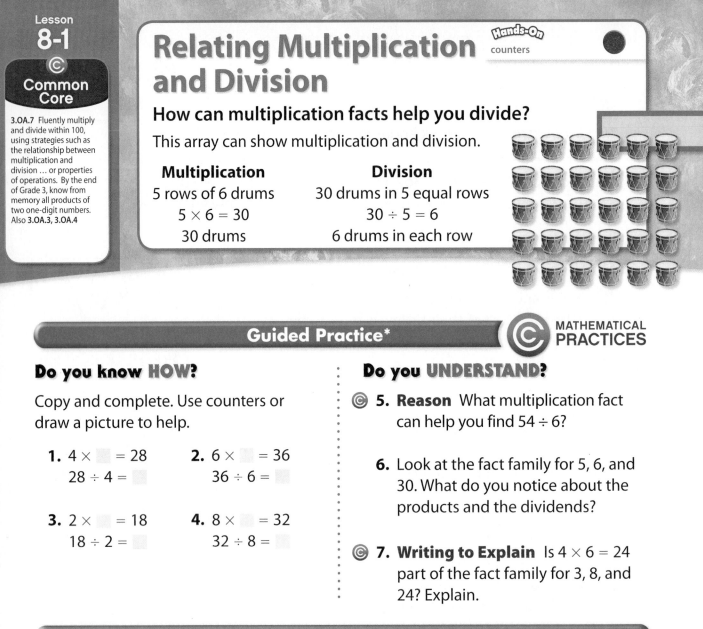

Lesson
8-1

Common Core

3.OA.7 Fluently multiply and divide within 100, using strategies such as the relationship between multiplication and division ... or properties of operations. By the end of Grade 3, know from memory all products of two one-digit numbers. Also **3.OA.3, 3.OA.4**

# Relating Multiplication and Division

**Hands-On** counters

## How can multiplication facts help you divide?

This array can show multiplication and division.

**Multiplication**
5 rows of 6 drums
$5 \times 6 = 30$
30 drums

**Division**
30 drums in 5 equal rows
$30 \div 5 = 6$
6 drums in each row

## Guided Practice*

**MATHEMATICAL PRACTICES**

### Do you know HOW?

Copy and complete. Use counters or draw a picture to help.

**1.** $4 \times \_ = 28$
$28 \div 4 = \_$

**2.** $6 \times \_ = 36$
$36 \div 6 = \_$

**3.** $2 \times \_ = 18$
$18 \div 2 = \_$

**4.** $8 \times \_ = 32$
$32 \div 8 = \_$

### Do you UNDERSTAND?

**5. Reason** What multiplication fact can help you find $54 \div 6$?

**6.** Look at the fact family for 5, 6, and 30. What do you notice about the products and the dividends?

**7. Writing to Explain** Is $4 \times 6 = 24$ part of the fact family for 3, 8, and 24? Explain.

## Independent Practice

**Use Tools** Copy and complete. Use counters or draw a picture to help.

**8.** $8 \times \_ = 16$
$16 \div 8 = \_$

**9.** $5 \times \_ = 35$
$35 \div 5 = \_$

**10.** $6 \times \_ = 48$
$48 \div 6 = \_$

**11.** $9 \times \_ = 36$
$36 \div 9 = \_$

**12.** $3 \times \_ = 27$
$27 \div 3 = \_$

**13.** $8 \times \_ = 56$
$56 \div 8 = \_$

**14.** $\_ \times 7 = 42$
$42 \div 7 = \_$

**15.** $\_ \times 8 = 72$
$72 \div 8 = \_$

**16.** $\_ \times 9 = 45$
$45 \div 9 = \_$

**17.** Write the fact family for 5, 8, and 40.

Animated Glossary, eTools
www.pearsonsuccessnet.com

A fact family shows how multiplication and division are related.

Fact family for 5, 6, and 30:

$5 \times 6 = 30$    $30 \div 5 = 6$

$6 \times 5 = 30$    $30 \div 6 = 5$

dividend    divisor    quotient

The **dividend** is the number of objects to be divided.

The **divisor** is the number by which another number is divided.

The **quotient** is the answer to a division problem.

## Problem Solving

**18. Writing to Explain** Why does the fact family for $2 \times 2 = 4$ have only two facts?

**Use Structure** For **19** and **20**, write the rest of the fact family for each array.

19.

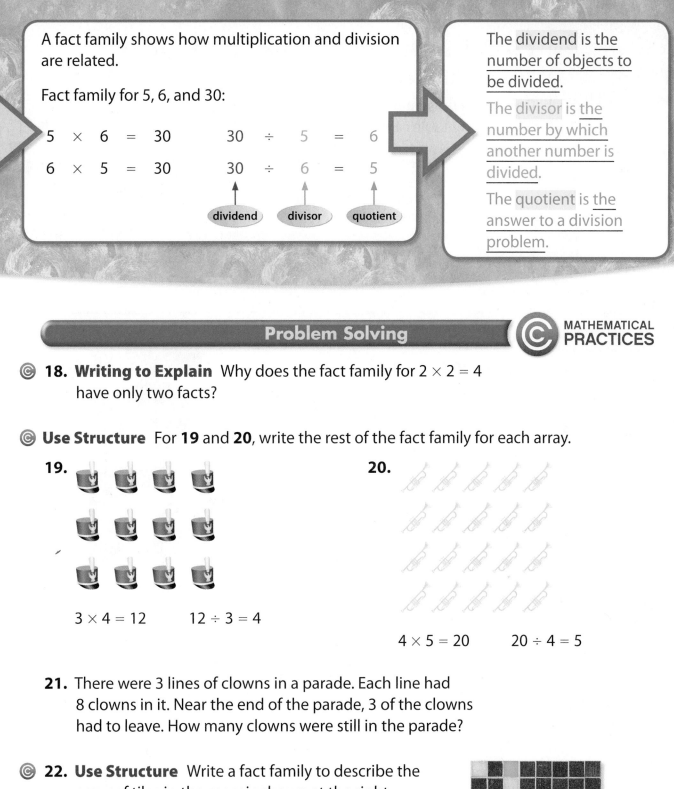

$3 \times 4 = 12$    $12 \div 3 = 4$

20.

$4 \times 5 = 20$    $20 \div 4 = 5$

**21.** There were 3 lines of clowns in a parade. Each line had 8 clowns in it. Near the end of the parade, 3 of the clowns had to leave. How many clowns were still in the parade?

**22. Use Structure** Write a fact family to describe the array of tiles in the mosaic shown at the right.

**23. Reason** Which number for $n$ makes this equation true?

$n \div 3 = 9$

**A** 3          **B** 12          **C** 18          **D** 27

Lesson
8-2

ⓒ
Common
Core

3.OA.7 Fluently multiply
and divide within 100,
using strategies such as the
relationship between
multiplication and
division ... or properties
of operations. By the end
of Grade 3, know from
memory all products of
two one-digit numbers.
Also 3.OA.3, 3.OA.4

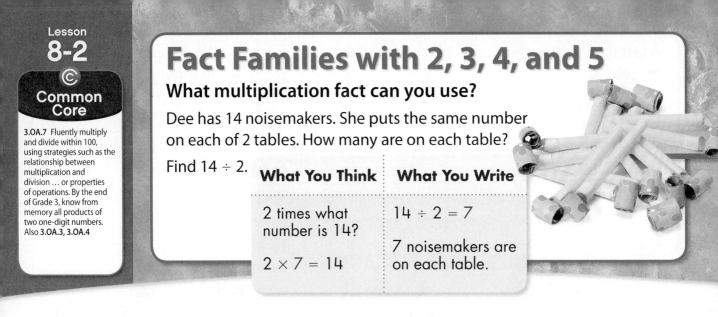

# Fact Families with 2, 3, 4, and 5

## What multiplication fact can you use?

Dee has 14 noisemakers. She puts the same number on each of 2 tables. How many are on each table?

Find 14 ÷ 2.

| What You Think | What You Write |
|---|---|
| 2 times what number is 14? | 14 ÷ 2 = 7 |
| 2 × 7 = 14 | 7 noisemakers are on each table. |

---

**Another Example** **What is another way to write a division problem?**

Dee is making balloon animals for her party. She has 24 balloons. It takes 4 balloons to make each animal. How many balloon animals can she make?

4 times what number is 24?
4 × 6 = 24

There are two ways to write a division problem.

24 ÷ 4 = 6
↑     ↑     ↑
dividend   divisor   quotient

$$6 \leftarrow \text{quotient}$$
$$\text{divisor} \rightarrow 4\overline{)24} \leftarrow \text{dividend}$$

Dee can make 6 balloon animals.

### Explain It

1. Copy and complete the fact family.

   4 × 6 = 24
   24 ÷ 4 = 6

2. How do you know what multiplication fact to use to find 24 ÷ 4?

ⓒ 3. **Critique Reasoning** Dee says she could make more than 10 balloon animals if she used only 3 balloons to make each animal. Do you agree? Why or why not?

Dee has 40 stickers. She puts 5 stickers on each bag. How many bags can she decorate?

Find $40 \div 5$.

| What You Think | What You Write |
|---|---|
| What number times 5 is 40? | $40 \div 5 = 8$ |
| $8 \times 5 = 40$ | Dee can decorate 8 bags. |

Dee wants to put 15 cups in 3 stacks on the table. How many cups will she put in each stack?

Find $15 \div 3$.

| What You Think | What You Write |
|---|---|
| 3 times what number is 15? | $15 \div 3 = 5$ |
| $3 \times 5 = 15$ | Dee will put 5 cups in each stack. |

## Guided Practice*

MATHEMATICAL PRACTICES

### Do you know HOW?

In **1–4,** copy and complete each fact family.

**1.** $2 \times 7 = 14$
$14 \div 2 = 7$

**2.** $3 \times 2 = 6$
$6 \div 3 = 2$

**3.** $5 \times 8 = 40$
$40 \div 5 = 8$

**4.** $4 \times 1 = 4$
$4 \div 1 = 4$

In **5–10**, find each quotient.

**5.** $27 \div 3$ **6.** $16 \div 4$ **7.** $40 \div 4$

**8.** $2\overline{)18}$ **9.** $4\overline{)28}$ **10.** $5\overline{)30}$

### Do you UNDERSTAND?

**11.** Identify the dividend, divisor, and quotient in Exercise 10.

**12. Construct Arguments** How can you tell without dividing that $15 \div 3$ has a greater quotient than $15 \div 5$?

**13. Reason** How can you use multiplication to help you find 36 divided by 4?

**14.** Dee has planned 4 games for her party. If she has 12 prizes, how many prizes can she give for each game?

## Independent Practice

In **15–29,** find each quotient.

**15.** $10 \div 2$ **16.** $25 \div 5$ **17.** $21 \div 3$ **18.** $18 \div 3$

**19.** $2\overline{)16}$ **20.** $5\overline{)45}$ **21.** $3\overline{)24}$ **22.** $4\overline{)36}$

**23.** $12 \div 4$ **24.** $50 \div 5$ **25.** $4\overline{)16}$ **26.** $5\overline{)40}$

**27.** Find 12 divided by 2. **28.** Divide 20 by 5. **29.** Find 32 divided by 4.

In **30–35,** find each missing number.

**30.** $2 \times \boxed{\phantom{0}} = 8$

**31.** $15 \div 3 = \boxed{\phantom{0}}$

**32.** $\boxed{\phantom{0}} \div 3 = 2$

**33.** $7 \times 4 = \boxed{\phantom{0}}$

**34.** $\boxed{\phantom{0}} \times 5 = 40$

**35.** $32 \div \boxed{\phantom{0}} = 8$

In **36–38,** write < or > to compare.

**36.** $4 \times 2 \bigcirc 4 \div 2$

**37.** $2 \times 3 \bigcirc 6 \div 2$

**38.** $5 + 8 \bigcirc 5 \times 8$

## Problem Solving

MATHEMATICAL
PRACTICES

**© 39. Writing to Explain** Joey says, "I can't solve $8 \div 2$ by using the fact $2 \times 8 = 16$." Do you agree or disagree? Explain.

**© 40. Persevere** Anna wants to make one array with 2 rows of 8 tiles and another array with 3 rows of 5 tiles. How many tiles does she need all together?

**© 41. Model** You might use as much as 2 gallons of water when you brush your teeth. There are 16 cups in 1 gallon. Write an addition sentence to show about how many cups of water you might use when you brush your teeth.

**© 42. Reason** Bob has 15 pennies and 3 dimes. Miko has the same amount of money, but she has only nickels. How many nickels does Miko have?

**43.** Which number sentence is in the same fact family as $3 \times 6 = 18$?

**A** $3 \times 3 = 9$

**B** $2 \times 9 = 18$

**C** $6 \div 3 = 2$

**D** $18 \div 6 = 3$

**44.** Mike bought 3 bags of marbles with 5 marbles in each bag. He gave 4 marbles to Marsha. How many marbles did Mike have left?

**A** 11  **C** 19

**B** 15  **D** 21

**© 45. Writing to Explain** Sammy wants to buy one remote control car for $49 and three small cars for $5 each. What is the total amount he will spend? Explain.

**46.** Annie helped her friend set up 40 chairs for a meeting. They set up the chairs in 5 equal rows. Write a division sentence to show the number of chairs in each row. What multiplication fact could you use to help you divide?

# Algebra Connections

## Using Multiplication Properties

Remember to use the properties of multiplication to help you complete number sentences.

**Commutative (Order) Property**  You can multiply factors in any order and the product is the same.
$5 \times 9 = 9 \times 5$

**Identity (One) Property**  When you multiply a number and 1, the product is that number.  $1 \times 8 = 8$

**Zero Property**  When you multiply a number and 0, the product is 0.  $0 \times 7 = 0$

**Associative (Grouping) Property**  You can change the grouping of the factors, and the product is the same.  $(3 \times 2) \times 4 = 3 \times (2 \times 4)$

**Example**:   $\times 8 = 0$

**Think**  What number multiplied by 8 is equal to 0?

You can use the Zero Property.
$0 \times 8 = 0$

**Example**:
$6 \times (9 \times 7) = (6 \times \phantom{9}) \times 7$

**Think**  What number makes the two sides equal?

Use the Associative Property.
$6 \times (9 \times 7) = (6 \times 9) \times 7$

Copy and complete with the number that makes the two sides equal.

**1.** $10 \times \phantom{x} = 10$

**2.** $6 \times 8 = 8 \times \phantom{x}$

**3.** $6 \times (2 \times 5) = (6 \times \phantom{x}) \times 5$

**4.** $\phantom{x} \times 9 = 0$

**5.** $\phantom{x} \times 7 = 7 \times 5$

**6.** $(4 \times 3) \times \phantom{x} = 4 \times (3 \times 8)$

**7.** $6 \times \phantom{x} = 9 \times 6$

**8.** $\phantom{x} \times 9 = 9$

**9.** $(\phantom{x} \times 7) \times 2 = 5 \times (7 \times 2)$

. . . . . . . . . . . . . . . . . . . . . . . . . . . . . . . . . . . . . . . . . . . . . . . . . . . . . . . . . . . . . . .

Ⓒ **Persevere**  In **10** and **11,** copy and complete the number sentence. Solve the problem.

**10.** Hal and Den each have copies of the same photos. Hal arranges 5 photos on each of 6 pages in 2 albums. Den needs 5 pages in 2 albums for the same photos. How many photos are on each page in Den's albums?

$(6 \times 5) \times 2 = (5 \times \phantom{x}) \times 2$

**11.** Gemma filled 3 pages in her sticker album. On each page, she made 3 rows of stickers with 5 stickers in each row. Complete the number sentence. Then solve to find how many stickers in all are on the 3 pages.

$3 \times (3 \times 5) = (3 \times \phantom{x}) \times 5$

Ⓒ **12. Write a Problem**  Write a problem to match the following number sentence.

$\phantom{x} \times 9 = 9 \times 3$

Common
Core

3.OA.7 Fluently multiply
and divide within 100,
using strategies such as
the relationship between
multiplication and
division . . . or properties
of operations. By the end
of Grade 3, know from
memory all products of
two one-digit numbers.
Also 3.OA.3

# Fact Families with 6 and 7

## How do you divide with 6 and 7?

There are 48 dogs entered in a dog show. The judge wants 6 dogs in each group. How many groups will there be?

**Choose an Operation** Divide to find how many groups.

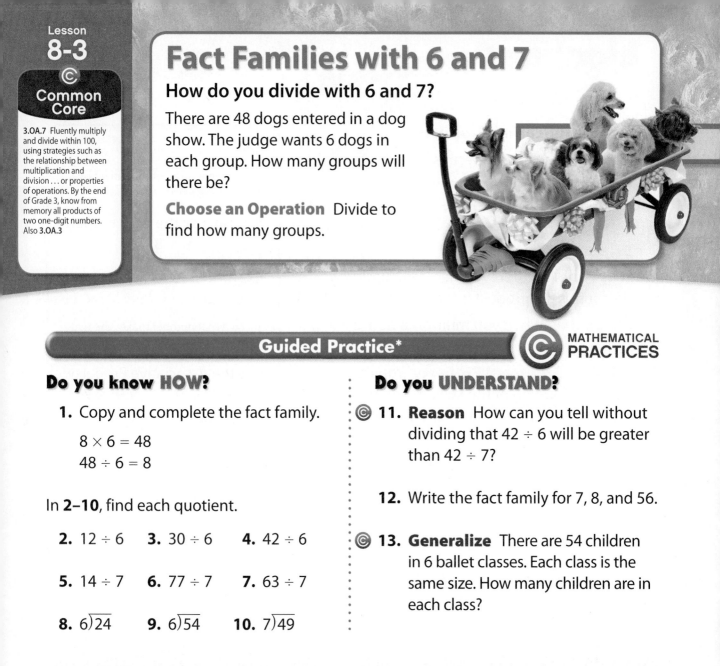

---

## Guided Practice*

**MATHEMATICAL PRACTICES**

### Do you know HOW?

**1.** Copy and complete the fact family.

$8 \times 6 = 48$
$48 \div 6 = 8$

In **2–10**, find each quotient.

**2.** $12 \div 6$ **3.** $30 \div 6$ **4.** $42 \div 6$

**5.** $14 \div 7$ **6.** $77 \div 7$ **7.** $63 \div 7$

**8.** $6\overline{)24}$ **9.** $6\overline{)54}$ **10.** $7\overline{)49}$

### Do you UNDERSTAND?

**11. Reason** How can you tell without dividing that $42 \div 6$ will be greater than $42 \div 7$?

**12.** Write the fact family for 7, 8, and 56.

**13. Generalize** There are 54 children in 6 ballet classes. Each class is the same size. How many children are in each class?

---

## Independent Practice

Find each quotient.

**14.** $18 \div 6$ **15.** $6 \div 6$ **16.** $21 \div 7$ **17.** $36 \div 6$ **18.** $70 \div 7$

**19.** $6\overline{)48}$ **20.** $5\overline{)30}$ **21.** $7\overline{)56}$ **22.** $7\overline{)35}$ **23.** $6\overline{)36}$

**24.** $6\overline{)42}$ **25.** $7\overline{)63}$ **26.** $6\overline{)18}$ **27.** $7\overline{)42}$ **28.** $3\overline{)21}$

**29.** Find 49 divided by 7. **30.** Divide 45 by 5. **31.** Find 56 divided by 7.

**32.** Find 60 divided by 6. **33.** Divide 28 by 7. **34.** Find 48 divided by 6.

 *For another example, see Set B on page 214.*

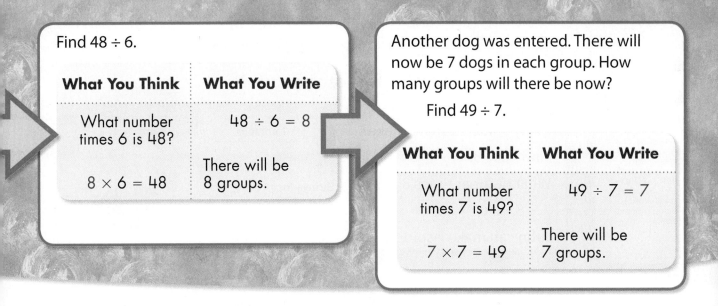

Find 48 ÷ 6.

| What You Think | What You Write |
|---|---|
| What number times 6 is 48?  8 × 6 = 48 | 48 ÷ 6 = 8  There will be 8 groups. |

Another dog was entered. There will now be 7 dogs in each group. How many groups will there be now?

Find 49 ÷ 7.

| What You Think | What You Write |
|---|---|
| What number times 7 is 49?  7 × 7 = 49 | 49 ÷ 7 = 7  There will be 7 groups. |

## Problem Solving

MATHEMATICAL PRACTICES

Use the pictures below for **35–38**.

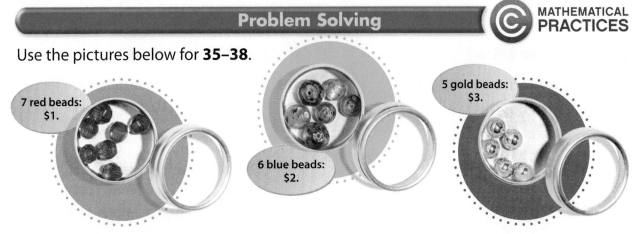

7 red beads: $1.

6 blue beads: $2.

5 gold beads: $3.

**35.** Rita needs 15 gold beads for an art project.

  **a** How many packages of beads does she need?

  **b** How much do the beads cost?

**36.** Eve bought 2 packages of red beads and 2 packages of blue beads.

  **a** How many beads did she buy?

  **b** How much did she spend?

© **37. Writing to Explain** Guy bought 28 red beads and 18 blue beads. How many packages did he buy? Explain how you solved the problem.

© **38. Be Precise** Andy bought exactly 35 beads, all the same color. Which color beads could he have bought? Explain your thinking.

© **39. Persevere** There are 6 rafts on the river. Each raft holds 8 people. Which number sentence is in the fact family for these numbers?

  **A** 48 − 6 = 42    **C** 48 + 6 = 54

  **B** 48 ÷ 6 = 8    **D** 48 − 8 = 40

© **40. Persevere** The school auditorium has 182 seats. People are sitting in 56 of the seats. Which is the best estimate of the number of seats that do **NOT** have people sitting in them?

  **A** 20   **B** 120   **C** 240   **D** 250

**Lesson 8-4**

©
**Common Core**

**3.OA.7** Fluently multiply and divide within 100, using strategies such as the relationship between multiplication and division … or properties of operations. By the end of Grade 3, know from memory all products of two one-digit numbers. Also **3.OA.3**

# Fact Families with 8 and 9

## What multiplication fact can you use?

John has 56 straws. How many spiders can he make?

Find 56 ÷ 8.

What number times 8 is 56?

$7 \times 8 = 56$

John can make 7 spiders.

56 straws

8    ? spiders →

Straws for each spider

To make each spider, you need 8 straws.

---

## Guided Practice*

© MATHEMATICAL PRACTICES

### Do you know HOW?

Find each quotient.

**1.** 16 ÷ 8     **2.** 64 ÷ 8     **3.** 36 ÷ 9

**4.** 27 ÷ 9     **5.** 45 ÷ 9     **6.** 63 ÷ 9

**7.** 8)24     **8.** 8)72     **9.** 8)8

### Do you UNDERSTAND?

© **10. Reason** What multiplication fact could you use to find 18 ÷ 9?

© **11. Reason** Carla and Jeff each use 72 straws. Carla makes animals with 9 legs. Jeff makes animals with 8 legs. Who makes more animals? Explain.

---

## Independent Practice

Find each quotient.

**12.** 32 ÷ 8     **13.** 28 ÷ 7     **14.** 18 ÷ 9     **15.** 48 ÷ 8     **16.** 81 ÷ 9

**17.** 5)45     **18.** 9)54     **19.** 7)56     **20.** 4)28     **21.** 8)56

**22.** 9)27     **23.** 9)72     **24.** 8)16     **25.** 8)64     **26.** 8)48

**27.** Find 90 divided by 9.     **28.** Divide 40 by 8.     **29.** Find 56 divided by 8.

**30.** Find 81 divided by 9.     **31.** Divide 45 by 9.     **32.** Find 80 divided by 8.

**33.** Write fact families for the numbers in **30** and **31**. How are the fact families different?

*For another example, see Set B on page 214.*

Luz made 9 animals. She used 54 straws. She used the same number of straws for each animal. How many straws did Luz use for each animal?

Find 54 ÷ 9.

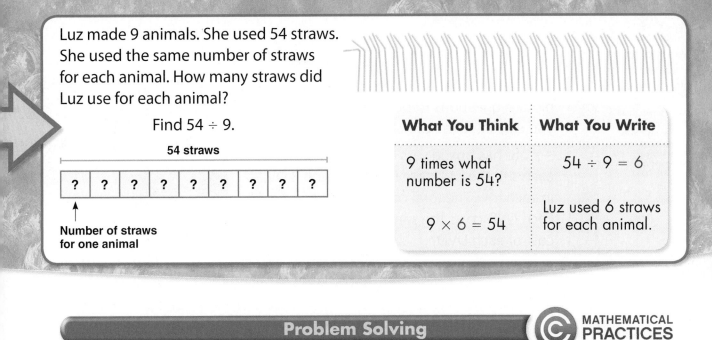

**54 straws**

| ? | ? | ? | ? | ? | ? | ? | ? | ? |

↑
Number of straws for one animal

| What You Think | What You Write |
|---|---|
| 9 times what number is 54? | 54 ÷ 9 = 6 |
| 9 × 6 = 54 | Luz used 6 straws for each animal. |

## Problem Solving

MATHEMATICAL
PRACTICES

Write < or > to compare.

**34.** 36 ÷ 9 ◯ 9

**35.** 65 ◯ 8 × 8

**36.** 63 ÷ 9 ◯ 8

Use the ticket prices at the right for **37–39**.

© **37. Writing to Explain** Mr. Stern bought 4 children's tickets and 2 adult tickets. How much more did he spend for the adult tickets than the children's tickets? Explain.

**38.** What is the total cost of 2 children's tickets and 2 adult tickets?

**Playhouse Ticket Prices**

| Type of Ticket | Price of Ticket |
|---|---|
| Child | $4 |
| Youth | $8 |
| Adult | $9 |

© **39. Reason** The clerk at the playhouse sold $72 worth of adult tickets. Ten people bought adult tickets online. Did more people buy tickets at the playhouse or online? Tell how you know.

© **40. Persevere** Which number sentence is **NOT** in the same fact family as the others?

**A** 8 × 4 = 32

**B** 32 ÷ 8 = 4

**C** 2 × 4 = 8

**D** 4 × 8 = 32

© **41. Model** The London Underground has 12 lines. The District line is 8 times as long as the East London line. Use the diagram to write a number sentence to find the length of the East London line.

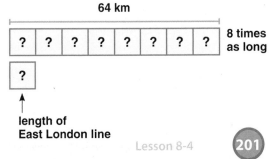

**64 km**

| ? | ? | ? | ? | ? | ? | ? | ? | 8 times as long |

| ? |

↑
length of East London line

Lesson
8-5

Common Core

3.OA.3 Use multiplication and division within 100 to solve word problems in situations involving equal groups, arrays, and measurement quantities, ... Also 3.OA.4, 3.OA.8

**Problem Solving**

# Multiple-Step Problems

You have learned that some problems have hidden questions to be answered before you can solve the problem.

A store has boxed sets of DVDs for sale. In each set, the DVDs are in 2 rows with 3 DVDs in each row. The total cost of a boxed set is $54. Each DVD costs the same amount. What is the cost of each DVD?

$54

DVD Set

---

**Guided Practice\***

MATHEMATICAL PRACTICES

## Do you know HOW?

Answer the hidden question. Then solve.

1. **Persevere** Twelve friends went camping. All except 4 of them went on a hike. The hikers carried 32 water bottles. Each hiker carried the same number of water bottles. How many water bottles did each hiker carry?

   HINT: Hidden Question—How many friends went on the hike?

## Do you UNDERSTAND?

2. How do you know what the hidden question is in the problem above?

3. What operations did you use to solve Exercise 1?

4. **Write a Problem** Write a problem that can be solved by finding and answering a hidden question.

---

**Independent Practice**

MATHEMATICAL PRACTICES

Solve. Answer the hidden question first.

5. **Persevere** Mrs. Lum bought 6 rolls of pink ribbon and some rolls of yellow ribbon. The total cost of the rolls of ribbon was $27. Each roll cost $3. How many rolls of yellow ribbon did Mrs. Lum buy?

   HINT: Hidden Question—What is the total number of rolls of ribbon Mrs. Lum bought?

### Applying Math Practices

- What am I asked to find?
- What else can I try?
- How are quantities related?
- How can I explain my work?
- How can I use math to model the problem?
- Can I use tools to help?
- Is my work precise?
- Why does this work?
- How can I generalize?

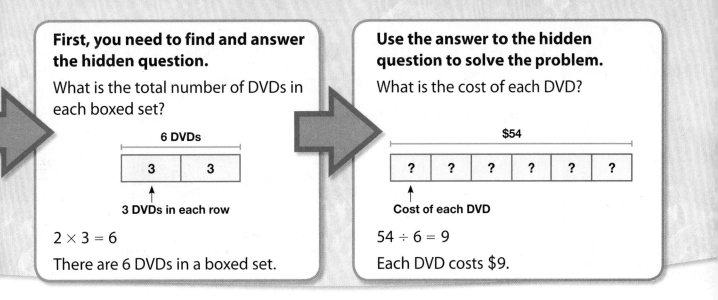

**First, you need to find and answer the hidden question.**

What is the total number of DVDs in each boxed set?

6 DVDs

| 3 | 3 |

↑
3 DVDs in each row

$2 \times 3 = 6$

There are 6 DVDs in a boxed set.

**Use the answer to the hidden question to solve the problem.**

What is the cost of each DVD?

$54

| ? | ? | ? | ? | ? | ? |

↑
Cost of each DVD

$54 \div 6 = 9$

Each DVD costs $9.

---

© **6. Persevere** Mr. Alton wants to buy tickets for a show. The tickets are for seats in 3 rows with 3 seats in each row. The total cost of the tickets is $81. Each ticket costs the same. What is the cost of one ticket?

© **7. Reason** Seven students went bowling. Four of the students bowled 1 game each, and three of the students bowled 2 games each. The cost was $5 per game. How much money in all did the students spend on bowling? Explain.

**8.** Use the table at the right. Mrs. Casey bought one adult and one child admission ticket. Then she bought one adult ticket and one child ticket for a boat ride. What was the total amount Mrs. Casey spent? Explain how you found your answer.

**Data**

| County Fair | | |
|---|---|---|
| **Kind of Ticket** | **Adult** | **Child** |
| Admission | $8 | $4 |
| Boat Rides | $2 | $1 |

© **9. Think About the Structure** Elio had $36 in his wallet. He used $9 to buy a book. Which number sentence shows how to find the amount of money he has left?

**A** $36 + 9 = \;$

**B** $36 - 9 = \;$

**C** $36 \times 9 = \;$

**D** $39 \div 9 = \;$

© **10. Think About the Structure** Martin raked 3 lawns yesterday and 4 lawns today. He earned a total of $42. He earned the same amount for each lawn. Which number sentence shows one way to find how much he earned for each lawn he raked?

**A** $42 - 4 = \;$

**B** $42 + 4 = \;$

**C** $42 \times 3 = \;$

**D** $42 \div 7 = \;$

Lesson
8-6

Common
Core

3.OA.3 Use multiplication
and division within 100
to solve word problems
in situations involving
equal groups, arrays, and
measurement quantities, …
Also 3.OA.4

# Making Sense of Multiplication and Division Equations

## How do multiplication and division equations work?

The pan balance shows $35 \div 7 = 5$.
Remember, in an equation, the symbol $=$
means "is equal to". It tells you that the value
to its left is the same as the value to its right.

**35 ÷ 7 = 5**

---

## Guided Practice*

MATHEMATICAL
PRACTICES

### Do you know HOW?

In **1–3**, decide if the two sides are equal.
If yes, write $=$. If no, write $\neq$ (not equal).

**1.** $8 \div 2 \bigcirc 4$　　　**2.** $18 \bigcirc 9 \times 8$

**3.** $10 + 40 \bigcirc 7 \times 5$

In **4–7**, find the value for $n$ that makes
the equation true.

**4.** $9 \times n = 27$　　　**5.** $8 = 40 \div n$

**6.** $8 \times n = 4 \times 8$　　　**7.** $n \div 3 = 9$

### Do you UNDERSTAND?

**8. Construct Arguments** Explain
why $25 = 5 \times 5$ is a true equation.

**9.** What is the value of $n$ in $8 = 56 \div n$?

**10. Critique Arguments** Sawyer says
that the value of $n$ in the equation
below is 24. Is she correct? Why or
why not?
$12 = n \times 3$

---

## Independent Practice

In **11–13**, decide if the two sides are equal. If yes, write $=$. If no, write $\neq$ (not equal).

**11.** $89 \bigcirc 8 \times 9$　　　**12.** $30 \div 3 \bigcirc 10$　　　**13.** $0 + 7 \bigcirc 35 \div 5$

In **14–21**, find the value for $n$ that makes the equation true.

**14.** $10 \times n = 70$　　**15.** $n = 18 \div 6$　　**16.** $45 \div 9 = n$　　**17.** $n \times 9 = 36$

**18.** $8 \times n = 64$　　**19.** $42 \div n = 7$　　**20.** $10 = 20 \div n$　　**21.** $9 \times 8 = n \times 8$

*For another example, see Set D on page 215.

These are other examples of equations.

$16 \div 4 = 2 \times 2$

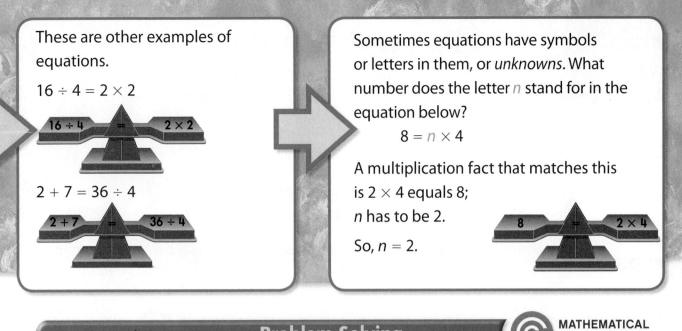

$2 + 7 = 36 \div 4$

Sometimes equations have symbols or letters in them, or *unknowns*. What number does the letter *n* stand for in the equation below?

$$8 = n \times 4$$

A multiplication fact that matches this is $2 \times 4$ equals 8; *n* has to be 2.

So, $n = 2$.

---

## Problem Solving

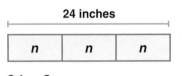MATHEMATICAL PRACTICES

For **22** and **23**, copy and complete the equation shown below each problem. Use it to solve the problem.

**22.** Carlos has a poster that is 24 inches long. He wants to divide it into 3 equal parts. What will be the length of each part?

24 inches

| n | n | n |
|---|---|---|

$24 \div 3 = n$

**23.** A baker is decorating 5 cakes. He is using 9 chocolate flowers for decorating each cake. How many flowers will he need to decorate all the cakes?

$n = 5 \times 9$

n

| 9 | 9 | 9 | 9 | 9 |
|---|---|---|---|---|

Ⓒ **24. Model** Noriko wants to buy 72 stamps. The stamps come in sheets like the one shown below. If the letter *n* stands for the number of sheets she needs to buy, write an equation that shows how to find the number of sheets Noriko needs. Find the value of *n*.

Ⓒ **25. Write a Problem** Write and solve a problem to match the equation below.

$63 \div n = 7$

**26.** James wants to give an equal number of his 45 stickers to each of his 5 friends. Which equation shows how to find the number of stickers each friend will get?

**A** $n = 45 \div 9$  **C** $n = 45 + 5$

**B** $n = 45 - 5$  **D** $n = 45 \div 5$

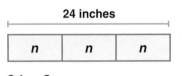

© Common Core

**3.OA.3** Use multiplication and division within 100 to solve word problems in situations involving equal groups, arrays, and measurement quantities, ... Also **3.OA.4, 3.OA.5**

# Dividing with 0 and 1

## How do you divide with 1 or 0?

3 groups of 1.

### Dividing by 1

Find 3 ÷ 1

What number times 1 is 3?

$3 \times 1 = 3$

So, $3 \div 1 = 3$.

**Rule:** Any number divided by 1 is itself.

---

## Guided Practice*

© MATHEMATICAL PRACTICES

### Do you know HOW?

Find each quotient.

**1.** 8 ÷ 8      **2.** 2 ÷ 1      **3.** 0 ÷ 5

**4.** 1)8      **5.** 6)6      **6.** 10)0

### Do you UNDERSTAND?

© **7. Reason** How can you tell without dividing that 375 ÷ 375 = 1?

© **8. Writing to Explain** Describe how you can find 0 ÷ 267, without dividing.

---

## Independent Practice

Find each quotient.

**9.** 7 ÷ 7      **10.** 0 ÷ 4      **11.** 10 ÷ 1      **12.** 0 ÷ 6      **13.** 10 ÷ 10

**14.** 4 ÷ 1      **15.** 7 ÷ 1      **16.** 0 ÷ 8      **17.** 5 ÷ 5      **18.** 5 ÷ 1

**19.** 14 ÷ 2      **20.** 70 ÷ 7      **21.** 56 ÷ 7      **22.** 24 ÷ 4      **23.** 90 ÷ 9

**24.** 6)36      **25.** 7)49      **26.** 8)64      **27.** 9)81      **28.** 5)20

**29.** 7)56      **30.** 8)48      **31.** 7)42      **32.** 5)25      **33.** 4)32

**34.** Divide 0 by 9.      **35.** Find 9 divided by 9.      **36.** Find 6 divided by 1.

**37.** Divide 3 by 3.      **38.** Find 0 divided by 8.      **39.** Find 7 divided by 1.

*For another example, see Set E on page 215.

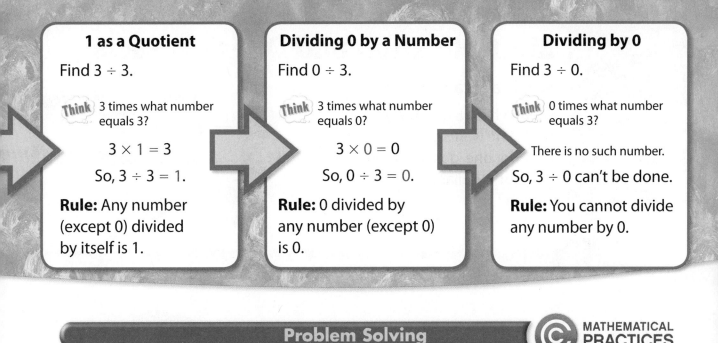

| **1 as a Quotient** | **Dividing 0 by a Number** | **Dividing by 0** |
|---|---|---|
| Find $3 \div 3$. | Find $0 \div 3$. | Find $3 \div 0$. |
| **Think** 3 times what number equals 3? | **Think** 3 times what number equals 0? | **Think** 0 times what number equals 3? |
| $3 \times 1 = 3$ | $3 \times 0 = 0$ | There is no such number. |
| So, $3 \div 3 = 1$. | So, $0 \div 3 = 0$. | So, $3 \div 0$ can't be done. |
| **Rule:** Any number (except 0) divided by itself is 1. | **Rule:** 0 divided by any number (except 0) is 0. | **Rule:** You cannot divide any number by 0. |

## Problem Solving

© MATHEMATICAL PRACTICES

In **40–43**, copy and complete. Use $<$, $>$, or $=$.

**40.** $3 \div 3 \bigcirc 3 \times 0$

**41.** $17 \div 17 \bigcirc 1 \div 1$

**42.** $0 \div 6 \bigcirc 0 \div 1$

**43.** $6 \times 1 \bigcirc 6 \div 1$

© **Reason** Use the sign at the right for **44–47**.

**44.** Paul hiked one trail 3 times for a total distance of 12 miles. Which trail did he hike?

**45.** Addie hiked 3 different trails for a total distance of 11 miles. Which trails did she hike?

**46.** Yoko hiked the blue trail once and the green trail twice. How many miles did she hike on the green trail?

**47.** Marty hiked one trail 4 times. He hiked more than 10 miles but less than 16 miles. Which trail did he hike? Explain.

Blue · 3 Miles
White · 5 Miles
Red · 2 Miles
Green · 4 Miles

© **48. Be Precise** Real-life objects are 12 times the size of the miniature versions in Queen Mary's dollhouse. How tall is a real-life painting if it is 1 inch tall in the dollhouse?

© **49. Reason** Which number will make the number sentence below true?

$54 \div \boxed{\phantom{0}} = 9$

**A** 5 **B** 6 **C** 7 **D** 8

Lesson
8-8

Common
Core

3.OA.7 Fluently multiply
and divide within 100,
using strategies such as
the relationship between
multiplication and
division ... or properties
of operations. By the end
of Grade 3, know from
memory all products of
two one-digit numbers.
Also 3.OA.3, 3.OA.4

# Multiplication and Division Facts

## What fact can you use?

Sabrina has 28 quarters in her bank. She wants to trade all of them for one-dollar bills. How many one-dollar bills will she get?

There are 4 quarters in one dollar.

---

## Guided Practice*

 MATHEMATICAL PRACTICES

### Do you know HOW?

In **1–6**, copy and complete.

**1.** $45 \div 5 =$ ▨
   $5 \times$ ▨ $= 45$

**2.** $3 \times$ ▨ $= 21$
   $21 \div 3 =$ ▨

**3.** $6 \times$ ▨ $= 30$
   $30 \div 6 =$ ▨

**4.** $32 \div 8 =$ ▨
   $8 \times$ ▨ $= 32$

**5.** $56 \div 7 =$ ▨
   $7 \times$ ▨ $= 56$

**6.** $27 \div$ ▨ $= 3$
   ▨ $\times 3 = 27$

### Do you UNDERSTAND?

© **7. Writing to Explain** Why can both number sentences, $28 \div 4 =$ ▨ and ▨ $\times 4 = 28$, be used to solve the problem above?

© **8. Reason** Sabrina found 8 more quarters in her desk. Including the quarters that were in her bank, how many one-dollar bills can she trade for her quarters now?

---

## Independent Practice

In **9–29**, find the product or quotient.

**9.** $36 \div 4$  **10.** $8 \times 8$  **11.** $15 \div 5$  **12.** $7 \times 5$  **13.** $6 \times 4$

**14.** $9 \div 9$  **15.** $24 \div 3$  **16.** $5 \times 5$  **17.** $9 \times 2$  **18.** $16 \div 4$

**19.**  $\begin{array}{r} 3 \\ \times\ 4 \\ \hline \end{array}$  **20.** $6\overline{)36}$  **21.**  $\begin{array}{r} 9 \\ \times\ 6 \\ \hline \end{array}$  **22.** $9\overline{)63}$  **23.**  $\begin{array}{r} 7 \\ \times\ 7 \\ \hline \end{array}$

**24.** Find 42 divided by 7.  **25.** Multiply 6 and 3.  **26.** Divide 56 by 8.

**27.** Multiply 8 and 5.  **28.** Divide 72 by 9.  **29.** Multiply 4 and 5.

*For another example, see Set F on page 215.*

How many groups of 4 are in 28?

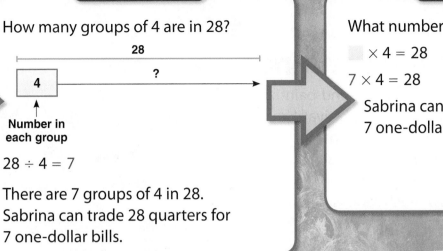

28 ÷ 4 = 7

There are 7 groups of 4 in 28.
Sabrina can trade 28 quarters for
7 one-dollar bills.

What number times 4 equals 28?

$\square \times 4 = 28$

$7 \times 4 = 28$

Sabrina can trade 28 quarters for
7 one-dollar bills.

## Problem Solving

**MATHEMATICAL PRACTICES**

For **30–33**, use the recipe at the right.

**30.** How many cups of peanuts would
Eric need to make 5 batches of
trail mix?

**31.** How many batches of trail mix can
be made with 16 cups of peanuts,
12 cups of raisins, and 8 cups of
walnuts?

**Eric's Trail Mix**

Makes one batch.

Ingredients:
4 cups peanuts
3 cups raisins
2 cups walnuts

**ⓒ 32. Reason** Eric needs 27 cups of trail
mix. How many batches will he
need to make? Explain.

**33.** Eric spends $30 on the ingredients
for 5 batches of trail mix. What is
the cost of the ingredients he needs
for one batch?

**34.** Little League Baseball began in 1939
in Pennsylvania. There were 3 teams
with 10 players on each team. How
many players were there all together?
Explain your work.

**35.** Today, there are 9 players on a
baseball team. How many players
are there on 4 teams?

**36.** Jesse has 40 nickels. He wants
to trade them for quarters. One
quarter is worth 5 nickels. How
many quarters should Jesse get?

    **A** 7    **B** 8    **C** 9    **D** 10

**37.** Which number is missing from this
fact family?

$42 \div 6 = \square$      $6 \times \square = 42$

$42 \div \square = 6$      $\square \times 6 = 42$

    **A** 4    **B** 5    **C** 6    **D** 7

Lesson
**8-9**

© **Common Core**

3.OA.3 Use multiplication
and division within 100
to solve word problems
in situations involving
equal groups, arrays, and
measurement quantities, …

**Problem Solving**

# Draw a Picture and Write a Number Sentence

Jeff is setting up the sand-painting
booth at the school carnival. He
put the sand from one bag of
sand into 5 buckets. If each
bucket has the same amount of
sand, how much sand is in each bucket?

45 pounds
of sand

**Another Example** **Are there other types of division situations?**

Alison is setting up the prize booth. She has 48 prizes. She
will put 8 prizes in each row. How many rows can she make?

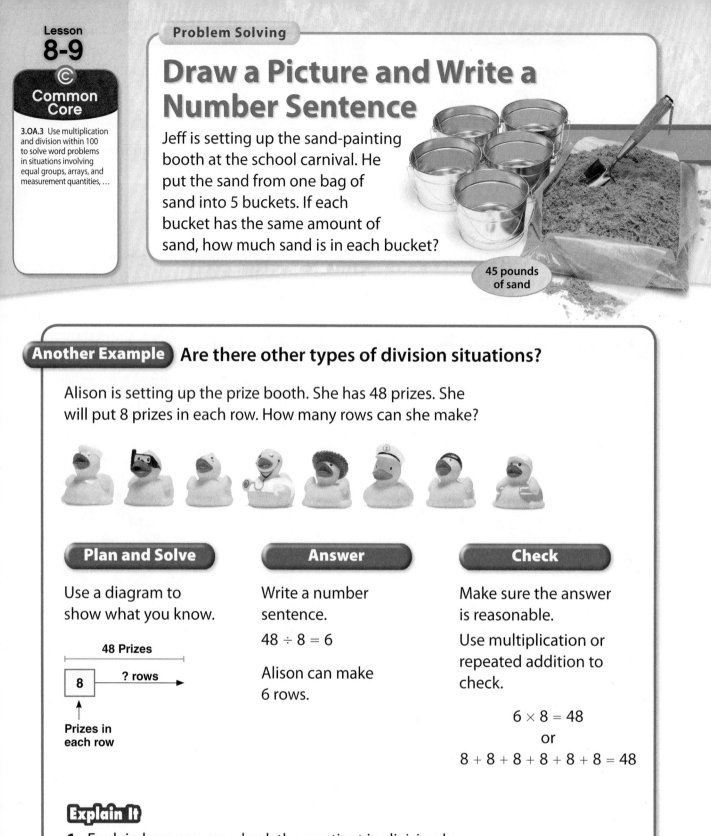

**Plan and Solve**

Use a diagram to
show what you know.

48 Prizes

| 8 | ? rows → |

↑
Prizes in
each row

**Answer**

Write a number
sentence.

$48 \div 8 = 6$

Alison can make
6 rows.

**Check**

Make sure the answer
is reasonable.

Use multiplication or
repeated addition to
check.

$6 \times 8 = 48$

or

$8 + 8 + 8 + 8 + 8 + 8 = 48$

**Explain It**

1. Explain how you can check the quotient in division by
   using either multiplication or addition.

© 2. **Reason** If Alison wants fewer than 6 rows of prizes,
   should she put more or fewer prizes in each row?
   Explain your thinking.

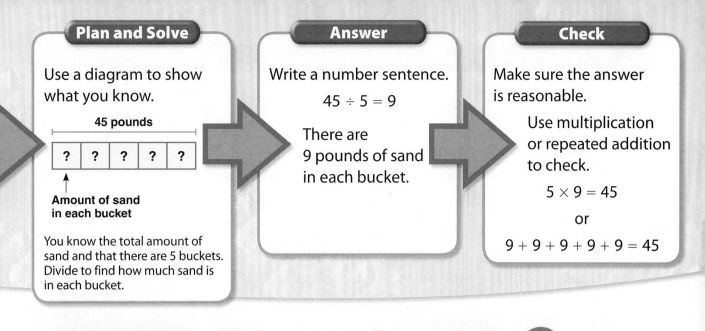

## Plan and Solve

Use a diagram to show what you know.

**45 pounds**

| ? | ? | ? | ? | ? |

↑
**Amount of sand in each bucket**

You know the total amount of sand and that there are 5 buckets. Divide to find how much sand is in each bucket.

## Answer

Write a number sentence.

$45 \div 5 = 9$

There are 9 pounds of sand in each bucket.

## Check

Make sure the answer is reasonable.

Use multiplication or repeated addition to check.

$5 \times 9 = 45$

or

$9 + 9 + 9 + 9 + 9 = 45$

---

## Guided Practice*

**MATHEMATICAL PRACTICES**

### Do you know HOW?

**1. Model** Larry and Pat made 18 posters. Each made the same number. How many did each make? Write a number sentence and solve.

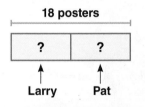

**18 posters**

| ? | ? |

↑        ↑
**Larry    Pat**

### Do you UNDERSTAND?

**2. Communicate** What operation did you use for Problem 1? Tell why.

**3. Write a Problem** Write a real-world problem that you can solve by subtracting. Draw a diagram. Write a number sentence and solve.

---

## Independent Practice

**MATHEMATICAL PRACTICES**

**Model** For **4** and **5**, draw a diagram to show what you know. Then write a number sentence and solve.

**4.** There are 8 cars on a Ferris wheel. Each car holds 3 people. How many people can ride the Ferris wheel at the same time?

**5.** There were 24 children in a relay race. There were 6 teams in all. How many children were on each team?

**6.** Austin is 8 years old. Grace is twice as old as Austin. How old is Grace?

**Applying Math Practices**

- What am I asked to find?
- What else can I try?
- How are quantities related?
- How can I explain my work?
- How can I use math to model the problem?
- Can I use tools to help?
- Is my work precise?
- Why does this work?
- How can I generalize?

---

*For another example, see Set G on page 215.*

Use the table at the right for **7** and **8**.
Solve each problem.

| Cost of Tickets | |
| --- | --- |
| Adult | $10 |
| Youth | $5 |
| Child | $3 |

© **7. Persevere** Mr. Niglio bought 2 youth tickets and 2 adult tickets. He gave the clerk a $50 bill. How much change did he get back?

© **8. Reason** Dan, Sue, and Joe each bought a different kind of ticket. Dan spent the least. Sue spent twice as much as Joe. How much did Joe spend?

© **Persevere** For **9** and **10**, use the animal pictures at the right. Write a number sentence and solve.

**9.** About how many hours is a sloth awake each day?

 *There are 24 hours in a day.*

**10.** About how many hours is a koala bear awake each day?

 *There are 7 days in a week.*

Koala bears are awake about 28 hours each week.

Sloths sleep about 20 hours each day.

© **Think About the Structure**

**11.** Alma bought 2 bracelets for $6 at the craft fair. Each bracelet cost the same amount. Which number sentence shows how to find the cost of each bracelet?

**A** $2 \times \$6 = $ ■

**B** $2 + \$6 = $ ■

**C** $\$6 - 2 = $ ■

**D** $\$6 \div 2 = $ ■

**12.** Tomas bought a book for $4, crayons for $2, and a pen for $1. He gave the clerk $10. Which number sentence shows how to find his change?

**A** $\$4 + \$2 + \$1 = $ ■

**B** $\$4 \times \$2 \times \$1 = $ ■

**C** $\$10 - \$6 = $ ■

**D** $\$10 - (\$4 + \$2 + \$1) = $ ■

# Algebra Connections

## Use Reasoning to Compare

Remember that the two sides of a number sentence can be equal or unequal. A symbol such as >, <, or = tells how the sides compare. Estimation or reasoning can help you tell if one side is greater without doing any computations.

 **Tip**  > means *is greater than*
< means *is less than*
= means *is equal to*

**Example:** $10 \div 2 \bigcirc 8 \div 2$

**Think** Each whole is being divided into 2 equal groups. The greater whole will have a greater number of items in each group.

Since 10 is greater than 8, the quotient on the left side is greater. Write the symbol >.

$10 \div 2 \enspace \gtrdot \enspace 8 \div 2$

In **1–12,** copy and complete by writing >, <, or =.

**1.** $20 \div 5 \bigcirc 25 \div 5$

**2.** $12 \div 3 \bigcirc 12 \div 4$

**3.** $3 \times 18 \bigcirc 3 \times 21$

**4.** $0 \div 9 \bigcirc 2 \times 3 \times 2$

**5.** $19 + 19 \bigcirc 2 \times 19$

**6.** $100 \times 0 \bigcirc 473 + 106$

**7.** $1 \times 53 \bigcirc 1 \times 43$

**8.** $9 \bigcirc 36 \div 4$

**9.** $9 \div 3 \bigcirc 18 \div 3$

**10.** $16 \div 2 \bigcirc 1 + 9$

**11.** $35 \div 5 \bigcirc 2 + 3$

**12.** $24 \div 4 \bigcirc 24 \div 2$

---

© **Reason** In **13** and **14,** copy and complete the number sentence below each problem. Use it to help explain your answer.

**13.** Mara and Bobby each have 40 pages to read. Mara will read 4 pages each day. Bobby will read 5 pages each day. Who needs more days to read 40 pages?

Mara       Bobby

$\square \div \square \bigcirc \square \div \square$

**14.** Tim had a board that was 12 feet long. He cut the board into 3 equal pieces. Ellen had a board that was 18 feet long. She cut the board into 3 equal pieces. Who had the longer pieces?

© **15. Write a Problem** Write a problem described by $16 \div 2 > 14 \div 2$.

**Set A,** pages 192–193

Use the array to help you find the fact family for 4, 7, and 28.

☆☆☆☆☆☆☆
☆☆☆☆☆☆☆
☆☆☆☆☆☆☆
☆☆☆☆☆☆☆

| **Multiplication** | **Division** |
|---|---|
| $4 \times 7 = 28$ | $28 \div 4 = 7$ |
| $7 \times 4 = 28$ | $28 \div 7 = 4$ |

**Remember** that a fact family shows how multiplication and division are related.

Copy and complete.

**1.** $3 \times \ \square = 27$    **2.** $\square \times 7 = 49$
   $27 \div 3 = \square$        $49 \div 7 = \square$

**3.** $7 \times \square = 56$    **4.** $5 \times \square = 25$
   $56 \div 7 = \square$        $25 \div 5 = \square$

**Set B,** pages 194–196, 198–201

Hanna read 21 pages of a book in 3 days. If Hanna read the same number of pages each day, how many pages did she read each day?

Find $21 \div 3$.

**Think**  What number times 3 equals 21?

$7 \times 3 = 21$

Write: $21 \div 3 = 7$

Hanna read 7 pages each day.

**Remember** to think of a related multiplication fact to solve a division problem.

Find each quotient.

**1.** $27 \div 3$     **2.** $36 \div 6$

**3.** $32 \div 4$     **4.** $63 \div 7$

**5.** $50 \div 5$     **6.** $8 \div 2$

**7.** $18 \div 9$     **8.** $64 \div 8$

**Set C,** pages 202–203

Mrs. Davis needs 32 apples for baking. Each box of apples has 2 rows. There are 4 apples in each row. How many boxes of apples will Mrs. Davis use?

**Step 1** Find the number of apples in one box.

   2 rows × 4 apples per row
   $2 \times 4 = 8$

**Step 2** Divide the total number of apples needed by the number in each box.

   $32 \div 8 = 4$
   She will use 4 boxes.

**Remember** that some problems have hidden questions that you must answer before you can solve the problem.

**1.** Tickets for the play cost $3 for students and $5 for adults. Myra bought tickets for 3 students and 3 adults. How much money did Myra spend on the tickets?

What is the value of *n* that makes the equation $4 \times n = 16$ true?

You can think about a multiplication fact. Since $4 \times 4 = 16$, then the value of $n = 4$.

**Remember** that you can think of a multiplication or division fact to find the value of *n*.

**1.** Find the value for *n* that makes

$$42 \div n = 7 \text{ true.}$$

**Set E,** pages 206–207

Find $8 \div 1$, $8 \div 8$, and $0 \div 8$.

When any number is divided by 1, the quotient is that number. **$8 \div 1 = 8$**

When any number (except 0) is divided by itself, the quotient is 1. **$8 \div 8 = 1$**

When zero is divided by any number (except 0), the quotient is 0. **$0 \div 8 = 0$**

**Remember** that you cannot divide any number by 0.

Find each quotient.

**1.** $4 \div 1$     **2.** $7 \div 7$     **3.** $0 \div 5$

**4.** $1\overline{)5}$     **5.** $3\overline{)0}$     **6.** $9\overline{)9}$

**7.** $6\overline{)6}$     **8.** $1\overline{)7}$     **9.** $4\overline{)0}$

**Set F,** pages 208–209

Mrs. Reed had 18 grapes. She gave each of her 3 children an equal number of grapes. How many grapes did each child get?

**Using division facts:**
$18 \div 3 = 6$ (6 groups of 3 in 18.)

**Using multiplication facts:**
$3 \times 6 = 18$ (Each child got 6 grapes.)

**Remember** that you can use multiplication and division facts to solve problems.

Find the product or quotient.

**1.** $5 \times 3$          **2.** $14 \div 7$

**3.** $63 \div 9$          **4.** $7 \times 7$

**5.** $9 \times 5$          **6.** $25 \div 5$

**Set G,** pages 210–212

Carl has 48 balloons to tie in 6 equal groups. How many balloons will be in each group?

Draw a diagram to show what you know.

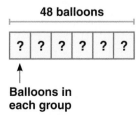

$48 \div 6 = 8$
There will be 8 balloons in each group.

**Remember** to read carefully.

Draw a diagram and write a number sentence to solve.

**1.** A roller coaster has 8 cars that each hold 5 people. How many people can ride the roller coaster at one time?

**Multiple Choice**

1. Which number makes both number sentences true? (8-1)

   $9 \times \square = 54$
   $54 \div 9 = \square$

   A 8

   B 7

   C 6

   D 5

2. Which number sentence is true? (8-7)

   A $6 \div 6 = 0$

   B $5 \div 1 = 1$

   C $0 \div 4 = 4$

   D $7 \div 1 = 7$

3. Nancy has 4 CDs. Each CD has 8 songs. Which number sentence is in the same fact family as $4 \times 8 = 32$? (8-2)

   A $32 \div 4 = 8$

   B $32 - 8 = 24$

   C $8 - 4 = 4$

   D $2 \times 4 = 8$

4. Gavin has 7 pages of his picture album filled. Each page has 6 pictures, for a total of 42 pictures. Which number sentence is **NOT** in the same fact family as the others? (8-3)

   A $7 \times 6 = 42$

   B $6 \times 7 = 42$

   C $42 \div 7 = 6$

   D $5 \times 7 = 35$

5. Mrs. Hendrix bought 45 pounds of modeling clay. She wants to divide it evenly among her 5 art classes. How many pounds of modeling clay will each class get? (8-2)

   A 40

   B 9

   C 8

   D 7

6. Beth bought a box of dog treats. The box had 48 treats. If Beth gives her dog 6 treats a day, how many days will the box of treats last? (8-3)

   A 6

   B 7

   C 8

   D 9

7. What number makes this equation true? (8-6)

   $n \div 9 = 8$

   A $n = 81$

   B $n = 72$

   C $n = 17$

   D $n = 8$

8. Which number sentence is in the same fact family as $16 \div 8 = 2$? (8-4)

   A $16 \div 4 = 4$

   B $16 - 8 = 8$

   C $2 \times 8 = 16$

   D $8 \times 8 = 64$

**Constructed Response**

**9.** Neil has 30 nails and 6 boards. Write a number sentence that shows how many nails he can put in each board if he puts the same number in each. (8-9)

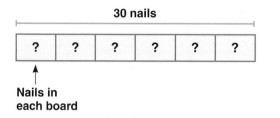

30 nails

| ? | ? | ? | ? | ? | ? |

↑
Nails in each board

**10.** The drawing below shows how Janet planted 18 daisies in her flowerbed.

$6 \times 3 = 18$

Write a division sentence that can be written using the drawing of Janet's daisies. (8-1)

**11.** Martin has 20 quarters in his piggy bank. He wants to trade them for dollars. There are 4 quarters in one dollar. How many dollars can Martin get? (8-8)

**12.** What is the quotient of $24 \div 8$? (8-4)

**13.** Mrs. Manchez bought 3 boxes of tissue. How many rooms will get a box of tissue if she puts 1 box in each room? (8-7)

**14.** A league has 7 basketball teams. Each team has 8 players, for a total of 56 players. Write a multiplication fact that uses these three numbers. (8-4)

**15.** Boxes of muffins have 3 rows with 3 muffins in each row. Mrs. Lee needs 45 muffins for the open house. How many boxes of muffins should she buy? (8-5)

**16.** Shawna buys tickets to a movie for a group. There are 4 adults and 4 children in the group. Adult's tickets cost $9 each. Children's tickets cost $7 each. How much does she pay for all tickets? (8-5)

**17.** Ben made 8 pancakes for his friends. If he gives 1 pancake to each friend, how many friends will get a pancake? (8-7)

**18.** Rachel has a ribbon that is 36 inches long. She wants to divide it into 4 equal parts. What will be the length of each part? (8-6)

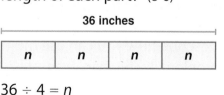

36 inches

| n | n | n | n |

$36 \div 4 = n$

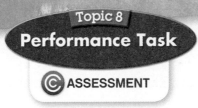

You have 36 stamps that you want to put into a stamp album. Stamp albums are made with either 4 or 6 pages. You need to decide which album you will use in order to have an equal number of stamps on each page.

1. How can you arrange the stamps into equal groups? Draw a picture of the different arrangements you can make for each album.

2. Choose one album that you will use for your collection. Write a division sentence and a multiplication sentence to describe your stamp arrangement.

3. Your friend found a 9-page album for the 36 stamps. Each page still needs an equal number of stamps. In an equation, *n* can stand for the number of stamps on each page. Find the value of *n* in the equation $36 \div n = 9$. How many stamps will be on each page of the 9-page album?

4. Write two fact families for 36.

5. Describe how you can use multiplication to solve a division problem. Include an example.

Topic
9

# Understanding Fractions

▼ Is the flag of Nigeria made up of equal parts? You will find out in Lesson 9-1.

## Vocabulary

Choose the best term from the box.

- compare
- greater
- less
- multiply

1. The number 219 is __?__ than the number 392.

2. The number 38 is __?__ than the number 19.

3. When you decide if 15 has more tens or fewer tens than 24, you __?__ the numbers.

## Arrays

Find the product for each array.

4. ○ ○ ○
   ○ ○ ○

5. ● ● ● ●
   ● ● ● ●
   ● ● ● ●

## Compare Numbers

Compare. Write >, <, or =.

6. 427 ◯ 583

7. 910 ◯ 906

8. 139 ◯ 136

9. 4,500 ◯ 4,500

10. 693 ◯ 734

11. 1,050 ◯ 1,005

© 12. **Writing to Explain** Which number is greater, 595 or 565? Explain which digits you used to decide.

**Topic Essential Question**
- What are different interpretations of a fraction?

# Interactive Learning

**Pose the problem.** Start each lesson by working together to solve problems. It will help you make sense of math.

### Applying Math Practices
- What am I asked to find?
- What else can I try?
- How are quantities related?
- How can I explain my work?
- How can I use math to model the problem?
- Can I use tools to help?
- Is my work precise?
- Why does this work?
- How can I generalize?

## Lesson 9-1

ⓒ **Use Tools** Use grid paper to solve this problem.

How many ways can you find to divide a 4 × 4 region into two equal parts? Show each way on grid paper. Explain how you know that the parts are equal.

## Lesson 9-2

ⓒ **Model** Solve. Look for more than one way.

Pat made a garden in the shape of a rectangle and divided it into 6 same-size pieces. She planted flowers on 4 of the pieces. What might Pat's garden have looked like?

## Lesson 9-3

ⓒ **Use Tools** Solve. Fold your paper to make 4 boxes to record your work.

How can you show the fraction $\frac{5}{8}$ using counters? Can you find more than one way? Explain.

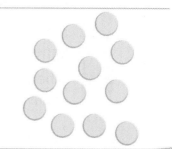

**MATHEMATICAL PRACTICES**

Lesson 9-4

© **Use Tools** Solve. Use counters to help.

Darren used $\frac{1}{4}$ of a carton of eggs to make breakfast. A carton has 12 eggs. How many eggs did he use? Tell how you decided.

Lesson 9-5

© **Be Precise** Solve. Use the paper strips to help you decide.

Each of your paper strips is 1 whole unit. Fold one of your strips in half once. Fold the other strip in half twice. Open the strips. What fractions can be used to name the fold lines? Tell how you decided.

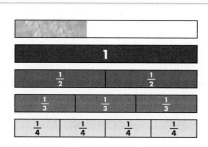

Lesson 9-6

© **Model** Use the fraction strips for 1 whole, 1 half, 1 third, and 1 fourth to estimate.

Work with a partner to take turns shading some fractional amount of a paper strip. Exchange with your partner and estimate whether the amount of each strip shaded is about 1 whole, $\frac{1}{2}$, $\frac{1}{3}$, or $\frac{1}{4}$. Use the known fraction strips to check.

Lesson 9-7

© **Use Tools** Use fraction strips to solve this problem.

How can you use fractions strips to show $\frac{3}{4}$? Tell how you decided.

Lesson 9-8

© **Look for Patterns** Solve any way you choose.

At the florist's shop, 5 out of every 7 roses sold are red roses. If the florist sold 28 roses, how many of them were red?

Lesson
## 9-1
**Common Core**

3.NF.1 Understand a
fraction 1/b as the quantity
formed by 1 part when a
whole is partitioned into b
equal parts; understand a
fraction a/b as the quantity
formed by a parts of size 1/b.

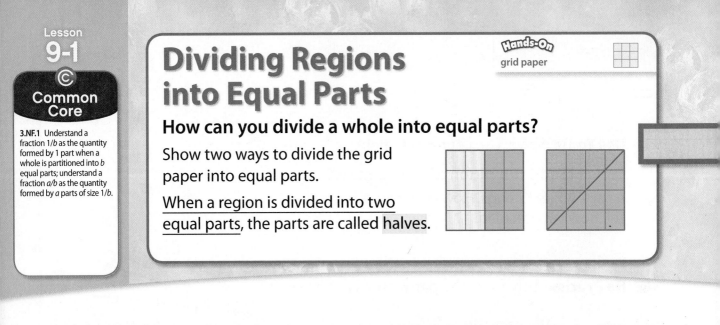

# Dividing Regions into Equal Parts

**Hands-On**
grid paper

## How can you divide a whole into equal parts?

Show two ways to divide the grid paper into equal parts.

When a region is divided into two equal parts, the parts are called halves.

---

## Other Examples

The parts do not need to be the same shape, but they must be equal in area.

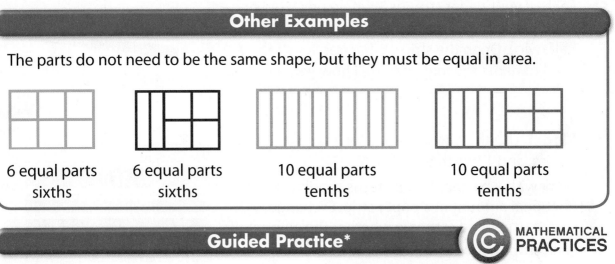

| 6 equal parts | 6 equal parts | 10 equal parts | 10 equal parts |
| sixths | sixths | tenths | tenths |

---

## Guided Practice*

**MATHEMATICAL PRACTICES**

### Do you know HOW?

In **1–4**, tell if each shows equal or unequal parts. If the parts are equal, name them.

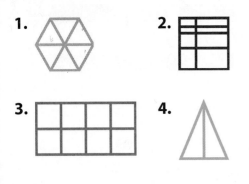

1.
2.
3.
4.

### Do you UNDERSTAND?

© 5. **Communicate** In the examples on grid paper above, explain how you know the two parts are equal.

© 6. **Use Tools** Use grid paper. Draw a picture to show sixths.

7. Amar divided his garden into equal areas, as shown below. What is the name of the equal parts of the whole?

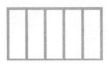
Animated Glossary, eTools
www.pearsonsuccessnet.com

Here are some names of equal parts of a whole.

| | | | |
|---|---|---|---|
| 2 equal parts **halves** | 3 equal parts **thirds** | 4 equal parts **fourths** | 5 equal parts **fifths** |
| 6 equal parts **sixths** | 8 equal parts **eighths** | 10 equal parts **tenths** | 12 equal parts **twelfths** |

## Independent Practice

In **8–11**, tell if each shows equal or unequal parts. If the parts are equal, name them.

**8.**

**9.**

**10.**

**11.**

In **12–15**, use grid paper. Draw a region showing the equal parts named.

**12.** fourths    **13.** halves    **14.** tenths    **15.** eighths

## Problem Solving

MATHEMATICAL
PRACTICES

In **16–18**, use the table of flags.

© **16. Reason** The flag of this nation has more than three parts. The parts are equal. Which nation is this?

**17.** The flag of Nigeria is made up of equal parts. What is the name of the parts of this flag?

**18.** Which flag does **NOT** have equal parts?

**19.** Which shape does **NOT** show equal parts?

**Flags of Different Nations**

| Nation | Flag |
|---|---|
| Mauritius | |
| Nigeria | |
| Poland | |
| Seychelles | |

A    B    C    D

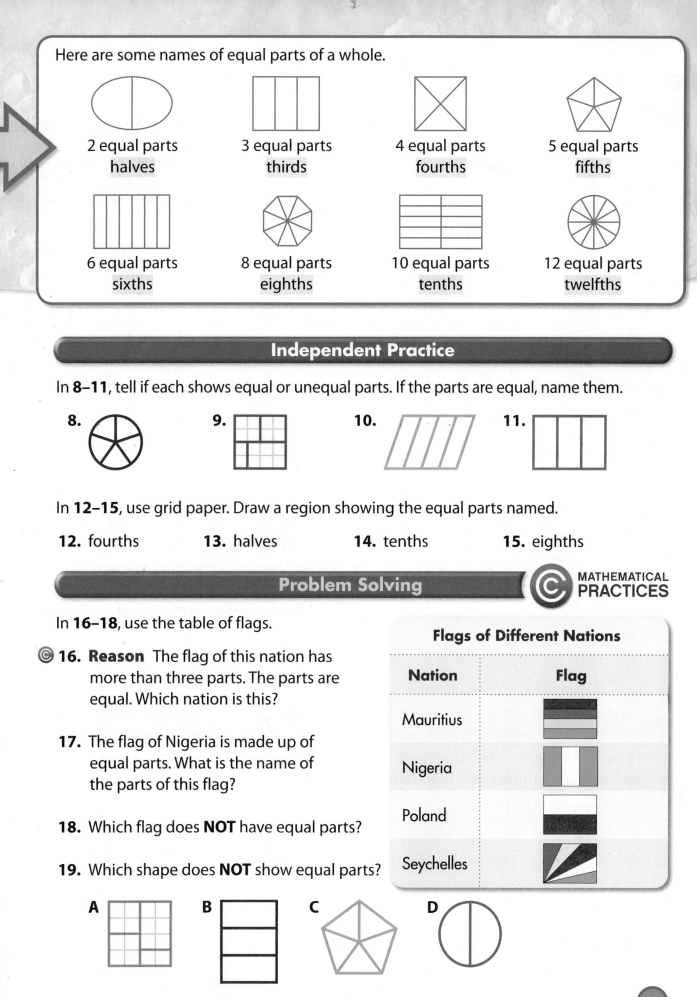

Lesson
9-2

Common
Core

3.NF.1 Understand a
fraction 1/b as the quantity
formed by 1 part when a
whole is partitioned into b
equal parts; understand a
fraction a/b as the quantity
formed by a parts of size 1/b.

# Fractions and Regions
## How can you show and name part of a region?

Mr. Kim served part of a pan of fruit bars to friends. What does each part of the whole pan represent? What part was served? What part was left?

A fraction is a symbol that names equal parts of a whole. A fraction with a numerator of 1 is a unit fraction.

---

## Guided Practice*

 MATHEMATICAL PRACTICES

### Do you know HOW?

In **1–3**, use the figure below.

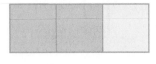

1. Write the unit fraction that represents each part of the whole.

2. How many parts are orange?

3. What fraction of the whole is orange?

### Do you UNDERSTAND?

4. In the example above, what fraction names *all* of the parts in the pan of bars?

© 5. **Reason** Mrs. Gupta bought a pizza. The picture shows what part of it she ate. What fraction of the whole pizza is each piece? How many pieces did she eat? What fraction of the whole pizza did she eat?

---

## Independent Practice

In **6–9**, write the unit fraction that represents each part of the whole. Write the number of green parts and the fraction of the whole that is green.

6.    7.    8.    9.

10. Draw a rectangle that shows 4 equal parts. Shade $\frac{2}{4}$ of the rectangle.

11. Draw a circle that shows 6 equal parts. Shade $\frac{1}{6}$ of the circle.

Animated Glossary
www.pearsonsuccessnet.com

There are 6 equal pieces in the whole, so each piece is $\frac{1}{6}$.

There are 2 pieces missing, so two $\frac{1}{6}$ pieces were served.

There are 4 pieces left, so four $\frac{1}{6}$ pieces are left.

The numerator <u>shows how many equal parts are described</u>.

The denominator <u>shows the total number of equal parts in a whole.</u>

$\frac{1}{6}$ ←——— Numerator
←——— Denominator

$\frac{2}{6}$ of the pan of fruit bars was served.

$\frac{4}{6}$ of the pan of fruit bars was left.

---

**Problem Solving**

MATHEMATICAL
PRACTICES

For **12–15,** use the sign at the right.

**12.** Ben and his friends ordered a medium pizza. What unit fraction does each slice represent?

**13.** Aida's family bought a large pizza. The family ate 4 slices of the pizza. What fraction of the pizza was left?

**14.** Tami's family bought 3 small pizzas. Leo's family bought 2 medium pizzas. How much more did Tami's family spend than Leo's family?

© **15. Model** Which costs more, 6 small pizzas or 4 large pizzas? Show your comparison using dollar amounts and the > symbol.

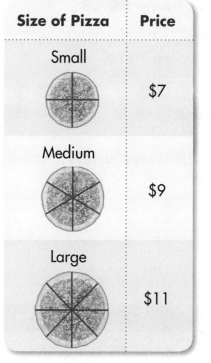

| Size of Pizza | Price |
|---|---|
| Small | $7 |
| Medium | $9 |
| Large | $11 |

© **16. Construct Arguments** A pan of cornbread is divided into 6 unequal parts. Alana serves 2 of the parts. Is it reasonable to say she has served $\frac{2}{6}$ of the cornbread? Explain.

**17.** Look at the grid at the right. What fraction of the grid is white?

**A** $\frac{3}{8}$      **C** $\frac{5}{8}$

**B** $\frac{8}{8}$      **D** $\frac{5}{6}$

Lesson
**9-3**
Ⓒ
**Common Core**

3.NF.1 Understand a fraction 1/*b* as the quantity formed by 1 part when a whole is partitioned into *b* equal parts; understand a fraction *a*/*b* as the quantity formed by *a* parts of size 1/*b*.

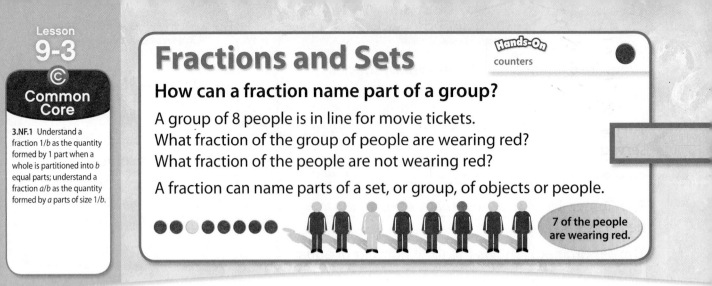

# Fractions and Sets

**Hands-On** counters

## How can a fraction name part of a group?

A group of 8 people is in line for movie tickets.
What fraction of the group of people are wearing red?
What fraction of the people are not wearing red?

A fraction can name parts of a set, or group, of objects or people.

7 of the people are wearing red.

---

## Guided Practice*

MATHEMATICAL **PRACTICES**

### Do you know HOW?

In **1** and **2**, write the fraction of the counters that are red.

**1.**

**2.**

In **3** and **4**, draw counters to show the fraction given.

**3.** $\frac{1}{3}$

**4.** $\frac{3}{8}$

### Do you UNDERSTAND?

Ⓒ **5. Communicate** In the example above, why is the denominator the same for the part of the group wearing red and for the part not wearing red?

**6.** A group of 6 students is waiting for a bus. Five of them are wearing jackets. What unit fraction represents 1 student in the group? What fraction of the students in the group are wearing jackets?

---

## Independent Practice

In **7–9**, write the fraction of the counters that are yellow.

**7.**

**8.**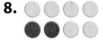

**9.**

In **10–12**, draw a picture of the set described.

**10.** 4 shapes, $\frac{3}{4}$ of the shapes are circles

**11.** 8 shapes, $\frac{5}{8}$ of the shapes are triangles

**12.** 2 shapes, $\frac{1}{2}$ of the shapes are squares

*For another example, see Set A on page 238.

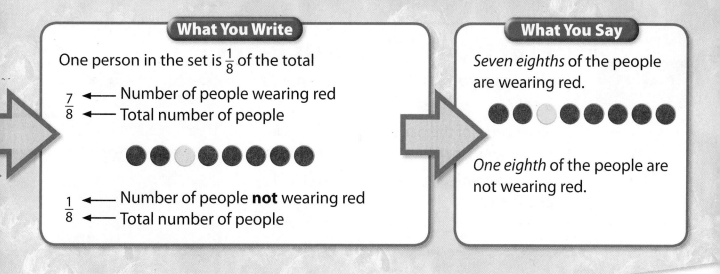

One person in the set is $\frac{1}{8}$ of the total

$\frac{7}{8}$ ◄— Number of people wearing red
◄— Total number of people

$\frac{1}{8}$ ◄— Number of people **not** wearing red
◄— Total number of people

*Seven eighths* of the people are wearing red.

*One eighth* of the people are not wearing red.

## Problem Solving

**MATHEMATICAL PRACTICES**

For **13–15**, write the fraction of the group of buttons described.

**13.** Pink buttons

**14.** Blue buttons

**15.** Buttons with only two holes

In **16** and **17**, draw a picture to show each fraction of a set.

**16.** Flowers: $\frac{3}{4}$ are yellow

**17.** Apples: $\frac{1}{2}$ are green

**18.** The picture below shows six statues of children. How many are statues of girls?

$\frac{3}{6}$ of the statues are statues of girls.

Ⓒ **19. Model** Zeke has 4 times as many pens as Don. If Zeke has 24 pens, how many does Don have? Solve $4 \times n = 24$.

**20.** What fraction of the flower petals have fallen off the flower?

**A** $\frac{3}{5}$

**B** $\frac{2}{8}$

**C** $\frac{8}{10}$

**D** $\frac{2}{10}$

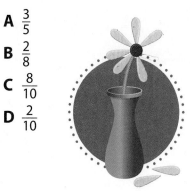

3.NF.1 Understand a fraction 1/b as the quantity formed by 1 part when a whole is partitioned into *b* equal parts; understand a fraction *a/b* as the quantity formed by *a* parts of size 1/b.

# Fractional Parts of a Set

How can you find a fractional part of a set?

Sam used $\frac{1}{4}$ of the package of batteries for his camera. How many batteries did he use?

<u>A fraction with a numerator of 1</u> is called a unit fraction.

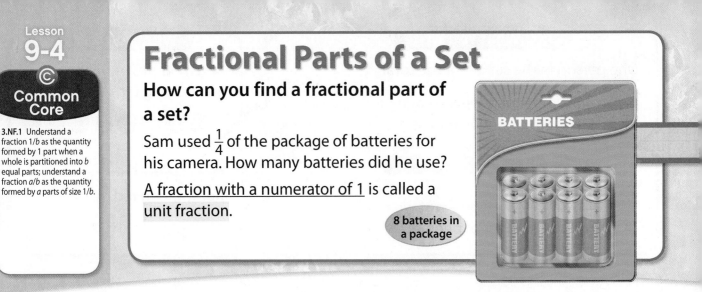

BATTERIES

8 batteries in a package

---

## Guided Practice*

MATHEMATICAL PRACTICES

### Do you know HOW?

1. Find $\frac{1}{2}$ of 12 eggs.

$\frac{1}{2}$ of 12 = ▨

2. Find $\frac{1}{4}$ of 8 apples. You may draw a picture to help.

$\frac{1}{4}$ of 8 = ▨

### Do you UNDERSTAND?

3. **Reason** In the example above, why do you put the batteries into 4 equal groups?

4. **Generalize** Suppose there are 12 batteries in a package. How many batteries are in $\frac{1}{4}$ package?

5. Thelma used $\frac{1}{3}$ of a bag of bows to wrap gifts. There were 9 bows in the bag. How many bows did she use?

---

## Independent Practice

**Leveled Practice** In **6–8**, use the picture to help find the part of the set.

6. Find $\frac{1}{3}$ of 15 grapes.

$\frac{1}{3}$ of 15 = ▨

7. Find $\frac{1}{2}$ of 14 peanuts.

$\frac{1}{2}$ of 14 = ▨

8. Find $\frac{1}{4}$ of 16 cherries.

$\frac{1}{4}$ of 16 = ▨

9. Find $\frac{1}{6}$ of 18.

10. Find $\frac{1}{3}$ of 21.

11. Find $\frac{1}{2}$ of 20.

DIGITAL

Animated Glossary
www.pearsonsuccessnet.com

*For another example, see Set B on page 238.

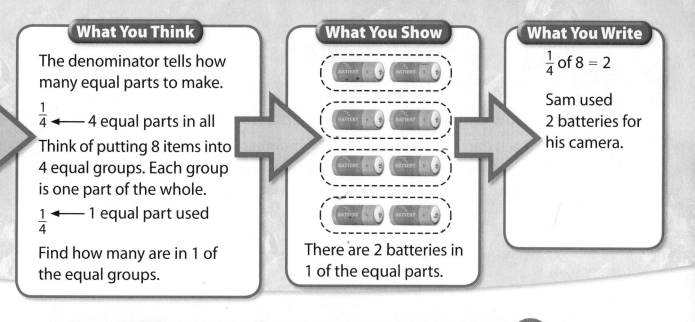

**What You Think**

The denominator tells how many equal parts to make.

$\frac{1}{4}$ ←— 4 equal parts in all

Think of putting 8 items into 4 equal groups. Each group is one part of the whole.

$\frac{1}{4}$ ←— 1 equal part used

Find how many are in 1 of the equal groups.

**What You Show**

There are 2 batteries in 1 of the equal parts.

**What You Write**

$\frac{1}{4}$ of 8 = 2

Sam used 2 batteries for his camera.

---

## Problem Solving

MATHEMATICAL PRACTICES

12. 🎵 **Music** The band room has 18 instruments. One third of them are brass. How many brass instruments are there?

13. Dave buys 2 cases of juice boxes. Each case has 4 packs. Each pack has 2 juice boxes. How many juice boxes does Dave buy?

14. Summer lasts $\frac{1}{4}$ of a year. How many months does summer last? (Hint: A year has 12 months.)

15. Write a number that will round to 850 when rounded to the nearest ten.

🔍 **Science** The snowy orchid grows wild in nature. The table at the right shows the total number of petals on different numbers of snowy orchid flowers. Use the table for **16** and **17**.

16. How many petals do 9 orchid flowers have?

| Number of Snowy Orchid Flowers | Total Number of Petals |
|---|---|
| 1 | 6 |
| 3 | 18 |
| 6 | 36 |
| 9 | |

© 17. **Model** Let *n* stand for the number of petals for 9 flowers. Write an equation to represent how to find the total number of petals.

18. If you divide 36 by 6, what fraction of 36 are you finding? Find the answer.

19. Which shows $\frac{1}{8}$ of 24 oranges?

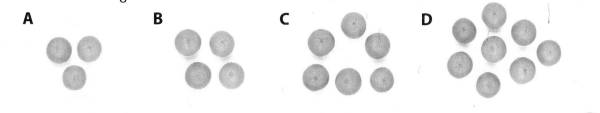

A          B          C          D

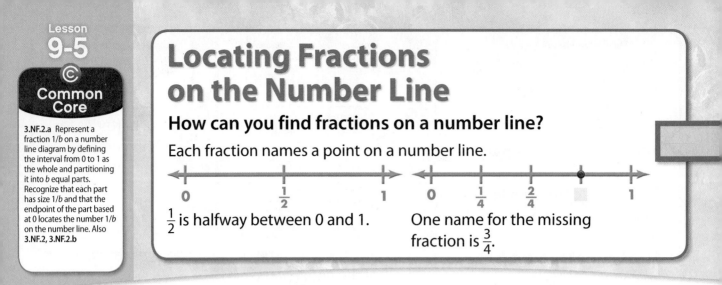

Lesson
9-5

© Common Core

3.NF.2.a Represent a fraction 1/b on a number line diagram by defining the interval from 0 to 1 as the whole and partitioning it into b equal parts. Recognize that each part has size 1/b and that the endpoint of the part based at 0 locates the number 1/b on the number line. Also 3.NF.2, 3.NF.2.b

# Locating Fractions on the Number Line

## How can you find fractions on a number line?

Each fraction names a point on a number line.

$\frac{1}{2}$ is halfway between 0 and 1.

One name for the missing fraction is $\frac{3}{4}$.

---

### Guided Practice*

**MATHEMATICAL PRACTICES**

#### Do you know HOW?

Write the missing fractions or mixed numbers for each number line.

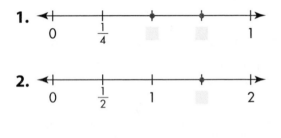

1.

2.

#### Do you UNDERSTAND?

**3.** Name a fraction between 0 and 1.

**4.** What mixed number would come after $2\frac{1}{4}$ on a number line that was divided into fourths?

© **5. Construct Arguments** Chris says that $1\frac{1}{4}$ comes after $1\frac{1}{2}$ on a number line. Do you agree? Why or why not?

---

### Independent Practice

In **6–8,** write the missing fractions or mixed numbers for each number line.

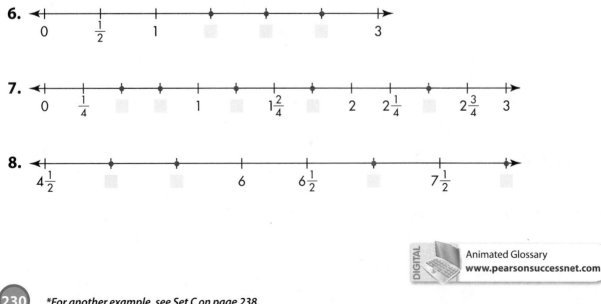

6.

7.

8.

Animated Glossary
www.pearsonsuccessnet.com

*For another example, see Set C on page 238.

Mixed numbers are <u>numbers that have a whole number part and a fraction part.</u> You can use mixed numbers to name points on a number line.

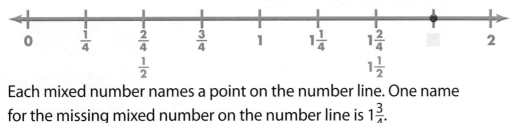

| 0 | $\frac{1}{4}$ | $\frac{2}{4}$ $\frac{1}{2}$ | $\frac{3}{4}$ | 1 | $1\frac{1}{4}$ | $1\frac{2}{4}$ $1\frac{1}{2}$ | | 2 |

Each mixed number names a point on the number line. One name for the missing mixed number on the number line is $1\frac{3}{4}$.

---

## Problem Solving

The number line below shows how many miles different places are from the campground. Use the number line for **9** and **10**.

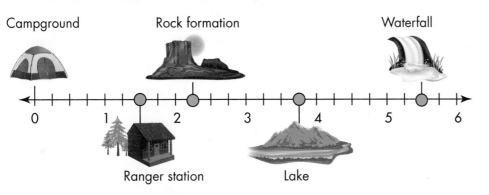

**9.** How many miles from the campground is the ranger station?

**10.** What is $3\frac{3}{4}$ miles from the campground?

© **11. Use Tools** Which letter on the ruler below could represent the number of centimeters that Iceland's shore grows in a year?

A   B   C   D

1   2   3   4

**CENTIMETERS**

The shore of Iceland grows between 2 and 3 centimeters each year!

**ICELAND**

**12.** Which number makes this number sentence true?

☐ × 8 = 56

**A** 8          **B** 7          **C** 6          **D** 5

© Common Core

**3.NF.2.a** Represent a fraction 1/b on a number line diagram by defining the interval from 0 to 1 as the whole and partitioning it into *b* equal parts. Recognize that each part has size 1/b and that the endpoint of the part based at 0 locates the number 1/b on the number line.

# Benchmark Fractions

## How do you estimate parts?

Mr. Anderson is harvesting wheat on his farm. About what part of the wheat field does he still need to harvest?

---

## Guided Practice*

© MATHEMATICAL PRACTICES

### Do you know HOW?

**1.** Estimate the fractional part that is yellow. Use a benchmark fraction.

**2.** What benchmark fraction should be written at point *P*?

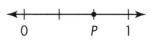

### Do you UNDERSTAND?

© **3. Reason** In the example above, what benchmark fraction can you use for the part of the wheat field that Mr. Anderson has harvested?

**4.** Geena is raking the leaves in her yard. About what part of the yard still needs to be raked?

---

## Independent Practice

In **5–7**, estimate the fractional part that is green. Use a benchmark fraction.

**5.** **6.** **7.** _____

In **8–11**, what benchmark fraction is closest to each point? Choose from the benchmark fractions $\frac{1}{2}$, $\frac{1}{3}$, $\frac{2}{3}$, $\frac{1}{4}$, and $\frac{3}{4}$.

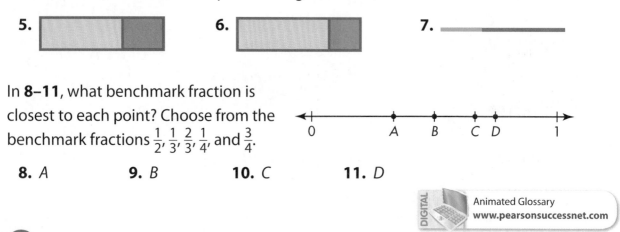

**8.** *A*  **9.** *B*  **10.** *C*  **11.** *D*

You can use benchmark fractions to estimate fractional parts.

Benchmark fractions <u>are commonly used fractions.</u>
Some benchmark fractions are $\frac{1}{4}$, $\frac{1}{3}$, $\frac{1}{2}$, $\frac{2}{3}$, and $\frac{3}{4}$.

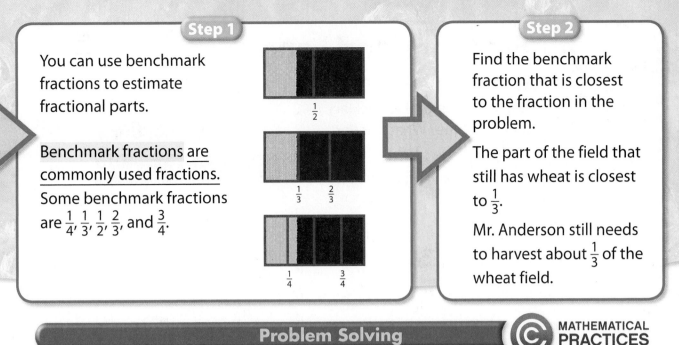

$\frac{1}{2}$

$\frac{1}{3}$   $\frac{2}{3}$

$\frac{1}{4}$   $\frac{3}{4}$

Find the benchmark fraction that is closest to the fraction in the problem.

The part of the field that still has wheat is closest to $\frac{1}{3}$.

Mr. Anderson still needs to harvest about $\frac{1}{3}$ of the wheat field.

## Problem Solving

**MATHEMATICAL PRACTICES**

In **12–14**, estimate the part of each garden that has flowers.

**12.** Garden A

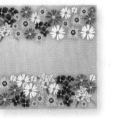

**13.** Garden B

**14.** Garden C

Use the table at the right for **15–17**.

**15.** In which months did the garden sell more tickets— May and June combined or July and August combined?

**16. Estimation** About how many tickets in all were sold in the four months? Explain how you estimated.

**17.** Which shows the numbers in the table from least to greatest?

  **A** 583, 947, 815, 726

  **B** 947, 815, 726, 583

  **C** 947, 726, 815, 583

  **D** 583, 726, 815, 947

© **18. Reason** What fraction of your body's bones are **NOT** in your feet? Use the picture at the right.

| Children's Garden Tickets Sold | |
| --- | --- |
| May | 583 |
| June | 947 |
| July | 815 |
| August | 726 |

One fourth of your body's bones are in your feet.

Common
Core

3.NF.2.b Represent a
fraction *a/b* on a number
line diagram by marking
off *a* lengths 1/*b* from 0.
Recognize that the resulting
interval has size *a/b* and
that its endpoint locates
the number *a/b* on the
number line.

# Fractions and Length

**Hands-On**
fraction strips

## How can a fraction name part of a length?

What fraction of this necklace length is blue? What fraction is not blue?

A fraction can name part of a length.

---

## Guided Practice*

**MATHEMATICAL PRACTICES**

### Do you know HOW?

In **1** and **2**, write the unit fraction that represents each part of the length. What fraction of the length is shown?

**1.**

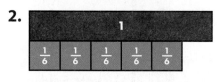

**2.**

### Do you UNDERSTAND?

**3. Communicate** In the example above, how do the fraction strips help you solve the problem?

**4.** What fraction of the ribbon length below is green? What fraction of the ribbon length is not green?

---

## Independent Practice

In **5–8**, write the unit fraction that represents each part of the length. What fraction of the length is shown?

**5.**

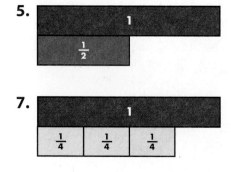

**6.**

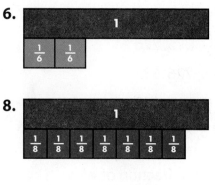

**7.**

**8.**

eTools
www.pearsonsuccessnet.com

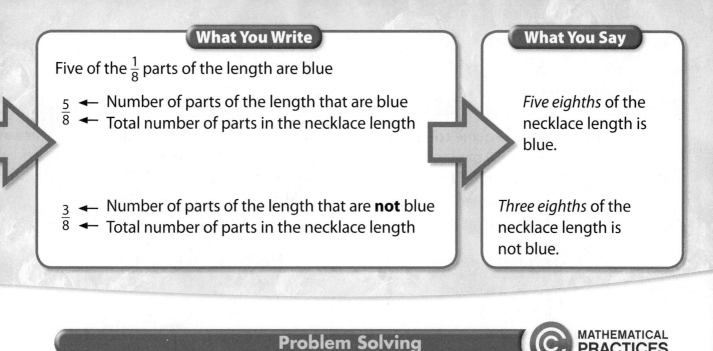

Five of the $\frac{1}{8}$ parts of the length are blue

$\frac{5}{8}$ ← Number of parts of the length that are blue
← Total number of parts in the necklace length

*Five eighths* of the necklace length is blue.

$\frac{3}{8}$ ← Number of parts of the length that are **not** blue
← Total number of parts in the necklace length

*Three eighths* of the necklace length is not blue.

## Problem Solving

**MATHEMATICAL PRACTICES**

For **9** and **10**, what fraction of each length of yarn is green?

**9.**

**10.**

**11. Estimation** Nick wants to buy two items. He estimated that the total cost of the items is $100. One item costs $58. What is one reasonable price of the other item?

**12.** For her part in the school play, Carmen must memorize 10 lines. Each line has about 10 words. About how many words does Carmen need to memorize?

**13.** Nia painted $\frac{6}{8}$ of a fence rail. The rest of the fence rail was painted by her brother. What fraction of the rail was painted by Nia's brother?

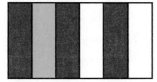

Ⓒ **14. Reason** Rashad colored $\frac{3}{6}$ of a flag red and $\frac{1}{6}$ of the same flag green. What fraction of the flag was **NOT** colored?

**15.** Which group shows fewer than $\frac{2}{4}$ of the shapes shaded?

**A** ◆ ◇ ◆ ◇

**C** ◆ ◆ ◆ ◆

**B** ◆ ◇ ◆ ◆

**D** ◆ ◇ ◇ ◇

Lesson
**9-8**

Common
Core

**3.OA.3** Use multiplication and division within 100 to solve word problems in situations involving equal groups, arrays, and measurement quantities, e.g., by using drawings and equations with a symbol for the unknown number to represent the problem.

**Problem Solving**

# Make a Table and Look for a Pattern

A video game company tested 20 games. Three of the games did not work. If 120 games are tested, how many of them might not work?

---

## Guided Practice*

MATHEMATICAL
**PRACTICES**

### Do you know HOW?

Copy and complete the table to solve.

1. Ms. Simms is buying bags of blocks. Out of the 10 blocks in each bag, 3 are cubes. If she buys 50 blocks, how many cubes will she get?

| Cubes | 3 | | | | |
|---|---|---|---|---|---|
| Total Blocks | 10 | | | | |

### Do you UNDERSTAND?

2. Look at the example above. If the video game store bought 50 games, about how many games might not work? Explain.

3. **Write a Problem** Write a problem that can be solved by making a table and using a pattern. Then solve the problem.

---

## Independent Practice

MATHEMATICAL
**PRACTICES**

**Persevere** Copy and complete the table to solve.

4. Erasers are sold in packages of 6. In each package, 2 of the erasers are pink. How many pink erasers will Andrea get if she buys 30 erasers?

| Pink Erasers | 2 | | | | |
|---|---|---|---|---|---|
| Total Erasers | 6 | | | | |

**Applying Math Practices**

- What am I asked to find?
- What else can I try?
- How are quantities related?
- How can I explain my work?
- How can I use math to model the problem?
- Can I use tools to help?
- Is my work precise?
- Why does this work?
- How can I generalize?

Make a table.

Then, write in the information you know.

| Might Not Work | 3 | | | | | |
|---|---|---|---|---|---|---|
| Total Games | 20 | | | | | |

Extend the table. Look for a pattern to help. Then find the answer in the table.

| Might Not Work | 3 | 6 | 9 | 12 | 15 | 18 |
|---|---|---|---|---|---|---|
| Total Games | 20 | 40 | 60 | 80 | 100 | 120 |

If 120 games are tested, 18 might not work.

Copy and complete the tables in **5** and **7**. Use the tables to help solve.

**5.** Sue planted 8 daffodil bulbs. Two of the bulbs didn't grow. Suppose that pattern continues and Sue plants 32 bulbs. How many bulbs most likely won't grow?

| Didn't Grow | 2 | | | |
|---|---|---|---|---|
| Total Bulbs | 8 | | | |

© **6. Reason** Look back at Problem 5. Suppose Sue decided to plant 20 daffodil bulbs.

  **a** How many bulbs would most likely not grow?

  **b** How many bulbs would most likely grow?

**7.** Sue planted 9 tulip bulbs of mixed colors. When the bulbs grew, there were 4 red tulips. Suppose that pattern continues and Sue plants 36 bulbs. How many of the tulips will likely be red? How many will **NOT** be red?

| Red Tulips | 4 | | | |
|---|---|---|---|---|
| Total Tulips | 9 | | | |

© **8. Reason** Tad planted 15 tulips in a row. He followed the pattern shown below. What is the color of the last tulip in the row?

© **9. Reason** See Problem 8. Suppose Tad planted 30 tulips in this pattern. How many would be red?

**10.** World Tours takes 5 vans of tourists to New York. Each van holds 7 tourists. There are 16 more tourists from World Tours flying to New York. Which equation represents the total number of tourists from World Tours that will arrive in New York?

  **A** $5 + 7 + 16 = n$    **B** $7 - 5 + 16 = n$    **C** $5 \times 7 - 16 = n$    **D** $5 \times 7 + 16 = n$

**Set A,** pages 222–227

What fraction of the triangles are pink?

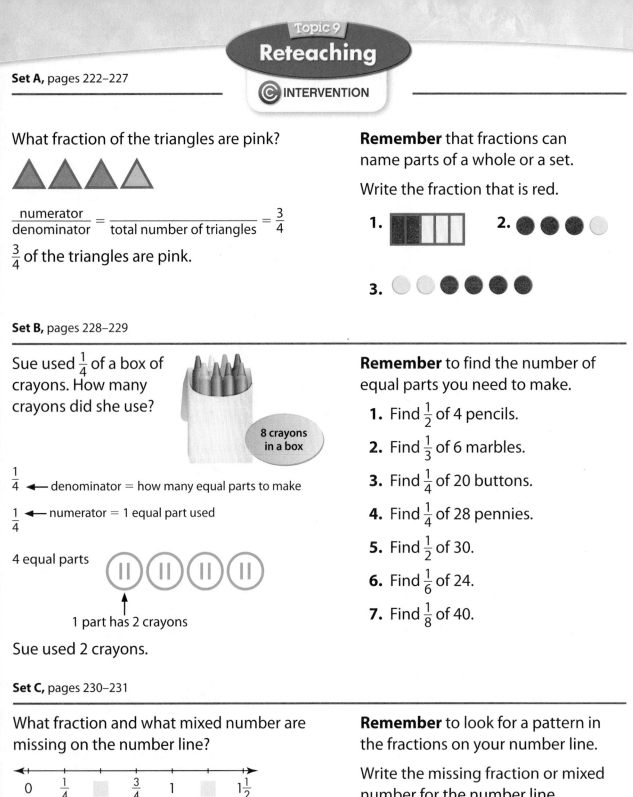

$$\frac{\text{numerator}}{\text{denominator}} = \frac{}{\text{total number of triangles}} = \frac{3}{4}$$

$\frac{3}{4}$ of the triangles are pink.

**Remember** that fractions can name parts of a whole or a set.

Write the fraction that is red.

1.

2.

3.

**Set B,** pages 228–229

Sue used $\frac{1}{4}$ of a box of crayons. How many crayons did she use?

8 crayons in a box

$\frac{1}{4}$ ◄— denominator = how many equal parts to make

$\frac{1}{4}$ ◄— numerator = 1 equal part used

4 equal parts

1 part has 2 crayons

Sue used 2 crayons.

**Remember** to find the number of equal parts you need to make.

1. Find $\frac{1}{2}$ of 4 pencils.

2. Find $\frac{1}{3}$ of 6 marbles.

3. Find $\frac{1}{4}$ of 20 buttons.

4. Find $\frac{1}{4}$ of 28 pennies.

5. Find $\frac{1}{2}$ of 30.

6. Find $\frac{1}{6}$ of 24.

7. Find $\frac{1}{8}$ of 40.

**Set C,** pages 230–231

What fraction and what mixed number are missing on the number line?

0    $\frac{1}{4}$    ▨    $\frac{3}{4}$    1    ▨    $1\frac{1}{2}$

Each section of the number line is $\frac{1}{4}$.

So $\frac{2}{4}$ or $\frac{1}{2}$, and $1\frac{1}{4}$ are missing.

**Remember** to look for a pattern in the fractions on your number line.

Write the missing fraction or mixed number for the number line.

1.

0    $\frac{1}{4}$    $\frac{2}{4}$    ▨    1    $1\frac{1}{4}$    ▨    ▨

Lisa is raking the leaves in her yard. About what part of the yard has she raked?

Find the benchmark fraction that is closest to the fraction in the problem.

Try $\frac{1}{2}, \frac{1}{3}, \frac{2}{3}, \frac{1}{4},$ or $\frac{3}{4}.$

Lisa has raked about $\frac{1}{4}$ of the yard.

**Remember** that benchmark fractions are commonly used fractions such as $\frac{1}{4}, \frac{1}{3}, \frac{1}{2}, \frac{2}{3},$ and $\frac{3}{4}.$

Estimate the fractional part that is yellow. Use a benchmark fraction.

**1.**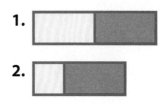

**2.**

---

What fraction of the length of the 1 strip do the other strips show?

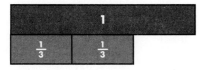

Two $\frac{1}{3}$ strips show $\frac{2}{3}$ of the 1 strip.

**Remember** that fraction strips divide the whole strip into equal parts.

What fraction of the length of the 1 strip do the other strips show?

**1.**

**2.**

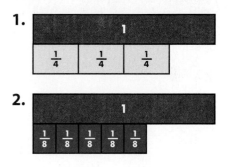

---

Make a table and find a pattern to solve.

Each bag of 20 marbles has 4 green marbles. If Ed buys 80 marbles, how many are green?

Make a table. Look for a pattern.

| Green | 4 | 8 | 12 | 16 |
|-------|-----|-----|-----|-----|
| Total | 20 | 40 | 60 | 80 |

16 marbles are green.

**Remember** that making a table can help you find a pattern.

**1.** Each box of pens has 2 red pens. How many red pens will you get if you buy 40 pens?

| Red | 2 | | | | |
|-------|-----|-----|-----|-----|-----|
| Total | 8 | | | | |

**Multiple Choice**

**1.** What is the name of the equal parts of the whole pizza? (9-1)

**A** Thirds

**B** Fourths

**C** Sixths

**D** Eighths

**2.** The stage was divided into equal parts. What unit fraction represents each part of the whole? What fraction names the part of the stage used for flute players? (9-2)

| Clarinets | Trombones | Clarinets |
|-----------|-----------|-----------|
| Flutes | Triangles | Flutes |

**A** $\frac{1}{8}, \frac{2}{8}$

**B** $\frac{1}{6}, \frac{2}{6}$

**C** $\frac{1}{6}, \frac{4}{6}$

**D** $\frac{1}{4}, \frac{2}{4}$

**3.** Blair bought the fruit shown below. What fraction of the pieces of fruit are oranges? (9-3)

**A** $\frac{3}{8}$

**B** $\frac{3}{6}$

**C** $\frac{5}{8}$

**D** $\frac{4}{6}$

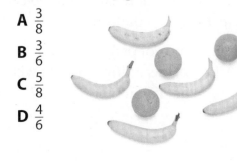

**4.** James bought a bag of 12 dinner rolls. He used $\frac{1}{6}$ of the bag. How many dinner rolls did James use? (9-4)

**A** 2

**B** 4

**C** 6

**D** 8

**5.** Mick glued a wire onto the middle of a board. What fraction of the length of board has wire glued to it? (9-7)

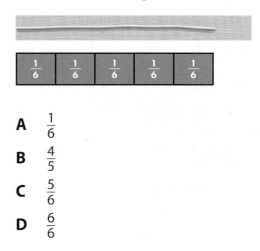

**A** $\frac{1}{6}$

**B** $\frac{4}{5}$

**C** $\frac{5}{6}$

**D** $\frac{6}{6}$

**6.** Jane likes to ride her bicycle to school. She rides about $1\frac{1}{4}$ miles each way. Which point represents $1\frac{1}{4}$ on the number line below? (9-5)

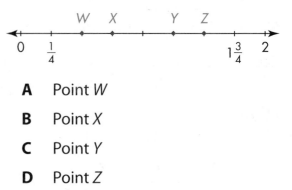

**A** Point *W*

**B** Point *X*

**C** Point *Y*

**D** Point *Z*

**7.** Ms. Rodriquez planted 24 tulips in her flowerbed. Of the tulips, $\frac{1}{3}$ are red. How many tulips are red? (9-4)

**8.** Allison is buying packages of sliced meat for the picnic. Each package has 20 slices of meat. Out of the 20 slices, 5 are turkey. If Allison buys 80 slices, how many are turkey? (9-8)

| Turkey Slices | 5 | 10 | | |
|---|---|---|---|---|
| Total Slices | 20 | 40 | 60 | 80 |

**9.** Explain what a unit fraction is. Give an example of a unit fraction in your explanation. (9-2)

**10.** About how much of Trenton's garden is corn? (9-6)

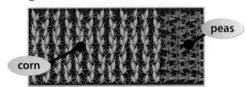

**11.** Danny and Latisha were running in a long race. Danny did not make it halfway. Latisha almost made it to the finish line. What are two possible benchmark fractions that can be used to describe how far each person ran? (9-6)

**12.** Four friends guessed the length in inches of a Guiana striped scorpion. The number line shows their guesses. Ty's guess was correct. Which number did Ty guess? (9-5)

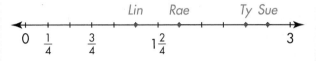

**13.** What fraction of the counters below are red? (9-3)

**14.** Draw a picture of a rectangle that has been divided into 4 equal parts. (9-1)

**15.** Emily painted a design for her friend. She drew a rectangle and then painted $\frac{2}{6}$ of its length red and $\frac{2}{6}$ yellow. What fraction of the rectangle did Emily not paint? (9-7)

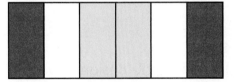

**16.** John wants to buy some construction paper. Each package has 50 pieces of paper, of which 12 pieces are blue. How many pieces of blue paper will there be in 250 pieces of construction paper? (9-8)

| Blue Pieces of Paper | 12 | | | | |
|---|---|---|---|---|---|
| Total Pieces of Paper | 50 | | | | |

## Part A

This is a map of different places from Jeff's home.

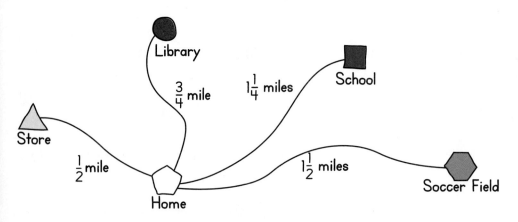

1. Copy and complete the number line below. Write the fractions, whole numbers, and mixed numbers from the map onto the number line.

2. Put a point for each distance from the map on the number line. Label each point with the name of its location from the map.

0                                                                                 2

## Part B

You are making tile designs. Two different designs are below. Trace each design on paper and follow the directions.

**Design A:** Color a fraction of the tiles blue.

**Design B:** Color a fraction of the design yellow.

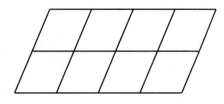

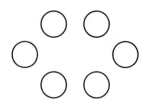

1. Below each design, write the fraction that you colored.

2. What unit fraction represents each equal part of Design A?

Topic
**10**

# Fraction Comparison and Equivalence

▼ What fraction of Earth's land surface is desert? You will find out in Lesson 10-5.

## Review What You Know!

### Vocabulary

Choose the best term from the box.

- factor
- order
- group
- separate

1. When you subtract, you __?__ a group from the whole.

2. A number line helps show numbers in __?__.

3. When you divide, you find how many are in each equal __?__.

### Identify Fractions

Write the fraction of the counters that are yellow.

4. ●●●● ●○○○

5. ●●● ●○○

### Division

Divide.

6. $14 \div 2$     7. $4 \div 4$

8. $9 \div 3$     9. $10 \div 5$

10. $12 \div 6$    11. $24 \div 8$

12. **Writing to Explain** Benji put 6 eggs into 2 equal groups. Explain how to find the number of eggs in each group.

**Topic Essential Question**
- What are different ways to compare fractions?

# Interactive Learning

**Pose the problem.** Start each lesson by working together to solve problems. It will help you make sense of math.

## Lesson 10-1

ⓒ **Use Tools**  Solve. Use fraction strips to help.

Jo and Dan both walk to school. Jo lives $\frac{5}{8}$ mile from school. Dan lives $\frac{2}{8}$ mile from school. Who walks the shorter distance to school? Tell how you decided. Write a number sentence that compares the distances.

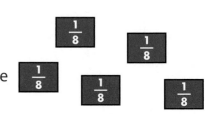

## Lesson 10-2

ⓒ **Reason**  Solve using fractions strips.

Carrie and Alan both have the same amount of vegetables to eat. Carrie has eaten $\frac{1}{4}$ of her serving of vegetables. Alan has eaten $\frac{1}{3}$ of his serving. Who has eaten more vegetables? Tell how you decided.

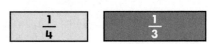

## Lesson 10-3

ⓒ **Reason**  Solve any way you choose.

Tell whether each of these fractions is closer to 0 or closer to 1. Tell how you decided.

$$\frac{1}{3}, \frac{1}{4}, \frac{3}{8}, \frac{5}{6}, \frac{3}{4}, \frac{1}{6}$$

## Lesson 10-4

ⓒ **Reason**  Solve using a number line to help.

Each person in Rosie's art class got bags of flour to make modeling clay. The bags were labeled $\frac{1}{4}$ lb, $\frac{2}{4}$ lb, and $\frac{3}{4}$ lb. The teacher wanted to organize the bags according to their weights and line them up. She started with the $\frac{1}{4}$ lb bag and told the students to line up their bags with her bag as if on a number line. Where will each of the bags go?

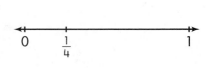

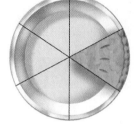
## Lesson 10-5

ⓒ **Use Tools** Use fraction strips to complete this task.

Erica skipped $\frac{3}{4}$ of the length of the sidewalk in front of her apartment building. How many fractions can you find that name this same amount? Tell how you decided.

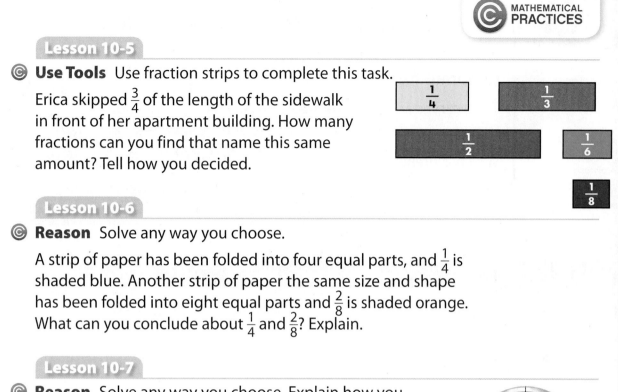

## Lesson 10-6

ⓒ **Reason** Solve any way you choose.

A strip of paper has been folded into four equal parts, and $\frac{1}{4}$ is shaded blue. Another strip of paper the same size and shape has been folded into eight equal parts and $\frac{2}{8}$ is shaded orange. What can you conclude about $\frac{1}{4}$ and $\frac{2}{8}$? Explain.

## Lesson 10-7

ⓒ **Reason** Solve any way you choose. Explain how you decided.

Jacy ate 6 pieces of pie during the week. Each piece was $\frac{1}{6}$ of the pie. How much pie is left?

## Lesson 10-8

ⓒ **Reason** Solve any way you choose. Tell how you decided.

Marie, Liz, and Tyler are each putting tiles on a wall. Each wall is the same size. Marie has $\frac{2}{6}$ of her wall tiled. Liz has $\frac{5}{8}$ of her wall tiled. Tyler has $\frac{1}{4}$ of his wall tiled. Who has the greatest part of the wall tiled? Who has the least part of the wall tiled?

## Lesson 10-9

ⓒ **Model** Solve. Draw a picture to help.

You are responsible for setting up markers at equal distances along a 2-mile racecourse. You also need to place a marker at the start line and one at the finish line. What is one way to place the markers? How many markers will you need?

Common
Core

3.NF.3.d Compare two
fractions with the same
numerator or the same
denominator by reasoning
about their size. Recognize
that comparisons are
valid only when the two
fractions refer to the same
whole. Record the results
of comparisons with the
symbols >, =, or <, and
justify the conclusions, e.g.,
by using a visual fraction
model. Also 3.NF.3.a

# Using Models to Compare Fractions: Same Denominator

Hands-On
fraction strips

$\frac{1}{6}$

## How can you compare fractions with the same denominator?

Two scarves are the same size. One scarf is $\frac{4}{6}$ green, and the other scarf is $\frac{2}{6}$ green.

Which is greater, $\frac{4}{6}$ or $\frac{2}{6}$?

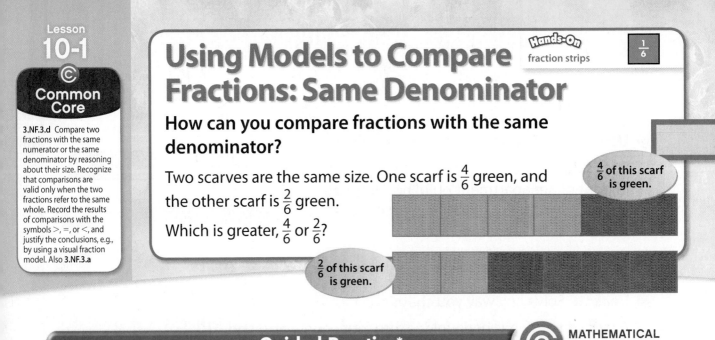

$\frac{4}{6}$ of this scarf is green.

$\frac{2}{6}$ of this scarf is green.

---

### Guided Practice*

© MATHEMATICAL PRACTICES

**Do you know HOW?**

In **1** and **2**, compare. Write >, <, or =. Use fraction strips to help.

1.
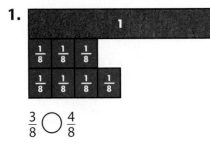

$\frac{3}{8} \bigcirc \frac{4}{8}$

2. $\frac{3}{6} \bigcirc \frac{2}{6}$

**Do you UNDERSTAND?**

© 3. **Reason** Use the example above. How can models show that if two fractions have the same denominator, the fraction with the greater numerator is greater?

4. Two ribbons are the same length. Each has a pink part and a yellow part. One ribbon is $\frac{2}{4}$ pink, and the other is $\frac{3}{4}$ pink. Which fraction is greater, $\frac{2}{4}$ or $\frac{3}{4}$?

---

### Independent Practice

In **5** and **6**, compare. Write >, <, or =. Use fraction strips to help.

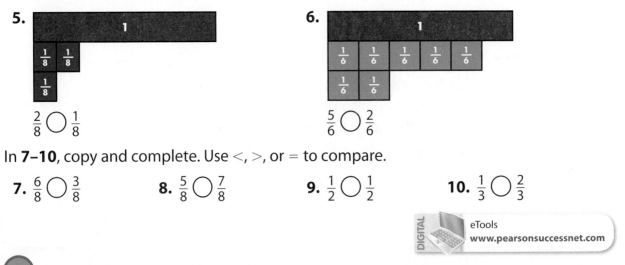

5.

$\frac{2}{8} \bigcirc \frac{1}{8}$

6.

$\frac{5}{6} \bigcirc \frac{2}{6}$

In **7–10**, copy and complete. Use <, >, or = to compare.

7. $\frac{6}{8} \bigcirc \frac{3}{8}$    8. $\frac{5}{8} \bigcirc \frac{7}{8}$    9. $\frac{1}{2} \bigcirc \frac{1}{2}$    10. $\frac{1}{3} \bigcirc \frac{2}{3}$

DIGITAL
eTools
www.pearsonsuccessnet.com

You can use fraction strips.

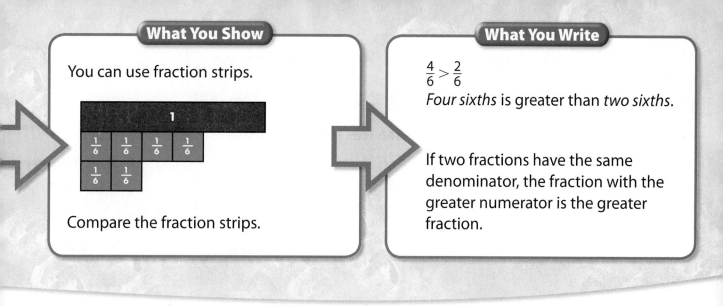

Compare the fraction strips.

$\frac{4}{6} > \frac{2}{6}$

*Four sixths* is greater than *two sixths*.

If two fractions have the same denominator, the fraction with the greater numerator is the greater fraction.

## Problem Solving

**MATHEMATICAL PRACTICES**

For **11** and **12**, the drawing shows four fence posts that are partly painted. Copy and complete each number sentence to compare painted parts of the fence posts.

**11.** Fence posts painted green:

$\frac{2}{6} \bigcirc \frac{1}{6}$

**12.** Fence posts painted yellow:

$\frac{3}{4} \bigcirc \frac{2}{4}$

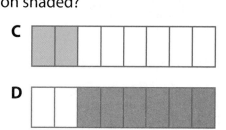

ⓒ **13. Reason** The table at the right shows the money that Roy has saved. He wants to buy a kit that costs $54.

**a** Use an estimate to decide if he has saved enough to buy the kit. Explain.

**b** How much money has Roy saved so far?

**c** How much more money does he need to buy the kit?

**Money Saved**

| Month | Amount |
|---|---|
| June | $12 |
| July | $13 |
| August | $21 |

**14.** Which picture shows more than $\frac{5}{8}$ of the region shaded?

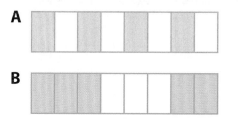

**A**

**C**

**B**

**D**

Common Core

3.NF.3.d Compare two fractions with the same numerator … by reasoning about their size. Recognize that comparisons are valid only when the two fractions refer to the same whole. Record the results of comparisons with the symbols >, =, or <, and justify the conclusions, e.g., by using a visual fraction model. Also 3.NF.3.a

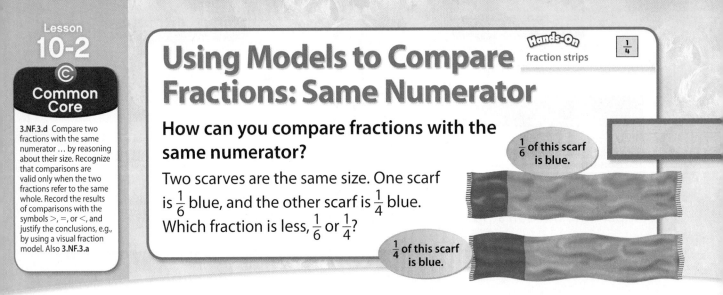

# Using Models to Compare Fractions: Same Numerator

**Hands-On** fraction strips   $\frac{1}{4}$

## How can you compare fractions with the same numerator?

Two scarves are the same size. One scarf is $\frac{1}{6}$ blue, and the other scarf is $\frac{1}{4}$ blue. Which fraction is less, $\frac{1}{6}$ or $\frac{1}{4}$?

$\frac{1}{6}$ of this scarf is blue.

$\frac{1}{4}$ of this scarf is blue.

---

## Guided Practice*

**MATHEMATICAL PRACTICES**

### Do you know HOW?

In **1** and **2**, compare. Write >, <, or =. Use fraction strips to help.

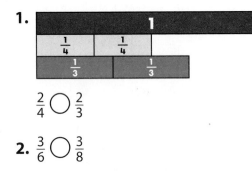

1.

$\frac{2}{4} \bigcirc \frac{2}{3}$

2. $\frac{3}{6} \bigcirc \frac{3}{8}$

### Do you UNDERSTAND?

© **3. Critique Reasoning** Julia says that $\frac{1}{8}$ is greater than $\frac{1}{4}$ because 8 is greater than 4. Is she correct? Explain.

© **4. Reason** Nico has 3 glasses of juice. All of the glasses are the same size. The first glass is $\frac{3}{8}$ full of juice, the second glass is $\frac{3}{4}$ full of juice, and the third glass is $\frac{3}{6}$ full of juice. Which glass contains the most juice? Explain.

---

## Independent Practice

In **5** and **6**, compare. Write >, <, or =. Use fraction strips to help.

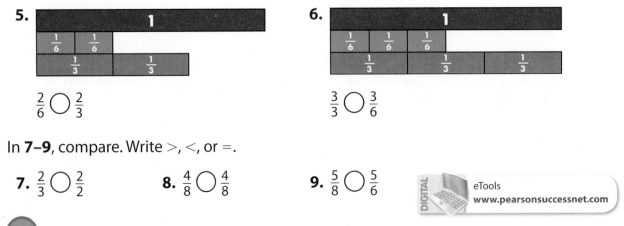

5.

$\frac{2}{6} \bigcirc \frac{2}{3}$

6.

$\frac{3}{3} \bigcirc \frac{3}{6}$

In **7–9**, compare. Write >, <, or =.

7. $\frac{2}{3} \bigcirc \frac{2}{2}$    8. $\frac{4}{8} \bigcirc \frac{4}{8}$    9. $\frac{5}{8} \bigcirc \frac{5}{6}$

**DIGITAL** eTools
www.pearsonsuccessnet.com

*For another example, see Set B on page 266.

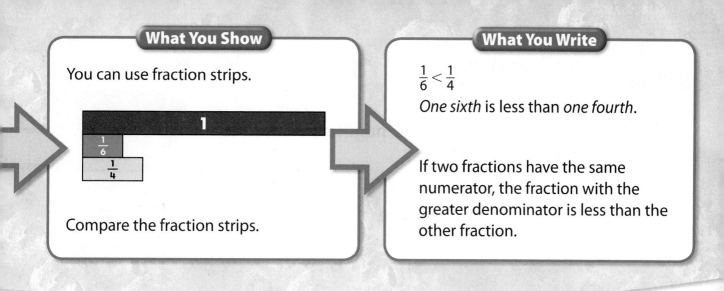

## What You Show

You can use fraction strips.

| 1 |
|---|

$\frac{1}{6}$

$\frac{1}{4}$

Compare the fraction strips.

## What You Write

$\frac{1}{6} < \frac{1}{4}$

*One sixth* is less than *one fourth*.

If two fractions have the same numerator, the fraction with the greater denominator is less than the other fraction.

---

**Problem Solving**

 **MATHEMATICAL PRACTICES**

**10.** There are 4 people in Sarah's family and 6 people in Mike's family. Both families buy the same size carton of milk to share equally. How much milk do Sarah and Mike each get? Who gets more milk? Explain your answer.

© **11. Writing to Explain** Li ran for $\frac{1}{2}$ hour on Monday, $\frac{1}{3}$ hour on Tuesday, and $\frac{1}{4}$ hour on Wednesday. On which day did Li run for the most amount of time? Explain.

© **12. Reason** An apple pie and a blueberry pie are the same size. The apple pie is cut into 3 equal pieces. The blueberry pie is cut into 4 equal pieces. Maria has 1 piece of apple pie. Hamza has 1 piece of blueberry pie. Who has the smaller piece of pie?

© **13. Model** There are 3 girls and 5 boys on Max's team. There are 3 girls and 3 boys on Marco's team. Which number sentence compares the fraction of girls on Max's team to the fraction of girls on Marco's team?

**A** $\frac{3}{3} > \frac{3}{5}$      **C** $\frac{3}{6} > \frac{3}{8}$

**B** $\frac{3}{3} < \frac{3}{5}$      **D** $\frac{3}{8} < \frac{3}{6}$

© **14. Critique Reasoning** Mario has two pieces of paper that are the same size. He colors 4 parts of each paper blue as shown to the right. Mario says that the blue area on the first paper is the same as the blue area on the second paper. Is he correct? Explain.

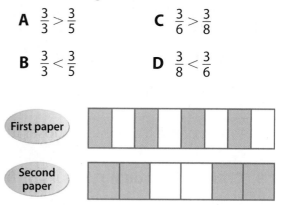

First paper

Second paper

© Common Core

3.NF.3.d Compare two fractions with the same numerator or the same denominator by reasoning about their size. . . . Record the results of comparisons with the symbols >, =, or <, and justify the conclusions, e.g., by using a visual fraction model.

# Comparing Fractions Using Benchmarks

**How can benchmark numbers be used to compare fractions?**

Keri wants to buy $\frac{2}{6}$ of a container of bulk peanuts.

Alan wants to buy $\frac{2}{3}$ of the same size container of the same kind of peanuts. Who will buy more peanuts?

Full

Roasted Peanuts

---

## Guided Practice*

© MATHEMATICAL PRACTICES

### Do you know HOW?

In **1–3**, choose from the fractions $\frac{1}{8}, \frac{1}{4}, \frac{6}{8}$, and $\frac{3}{4}$. Use fraction strips to help.

1. Which fractions are closer to 0 than to 1?

2. Which fractions are closer to 1 than to 0?

3. Use two of the fractions to write a true statement: ▨ < ▨.

### Do you UNDERSTAND?

4. Tina used benchmark numbers to decide that $\frac{3}{8}$ is less than $\frac{7}{8}$. Do you agree? Explain.

© 5. **Reason** Write two fractions with a denominator of 6 that are closer to 0 than to 1.

© 6. **Reason** Write two fractions with a denominator of 8 that are closer to 1 than to 0.

---

## Independent Practice

In **7–9**, choose from the fractions $\frac{2}{3}, \frac{7}{8}, \frac{1}{4}, \frac{2}{6}$.

7. Which of the fractions are closer to 0 than to 1?

8. Which of the fractions are closer to 1 than to 0?

© 9. **Critique Reasoning** Rahul says that $\frac{2}{6} < \frac{2}{3}$ because $\frac{2}{6}$ is less than $\frac{1}{2}$, and $\frac{2}{3}$ is greater than $\frac{1}{2}$. Is he correct? Explain.

In **10–12**, use benchmark numbers to compare. Write <, >, or =.

10. $\frac{5}{8} \bigcirc \frac{7}{8}$

11. $\frac{5}{8} \bigcirc \frac{2}{8}$

12. $\frac{3}{4} \bigcirc \frac{3}{6}$

*For another example, see Set C on page 267.

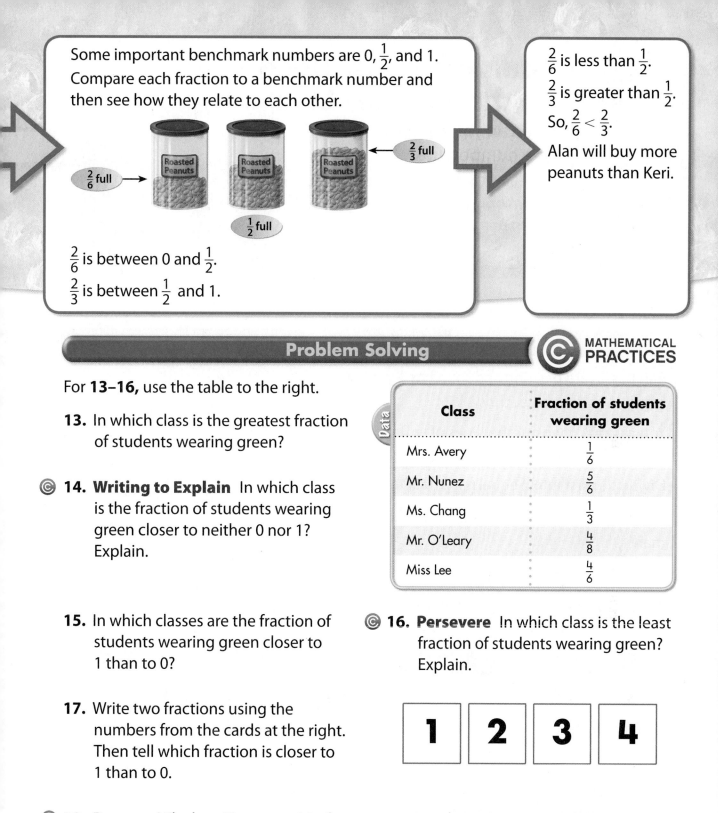

Some important benchmark numbers are 0, $\frac{1}{2}$, and 1. Compare each fraction to a benchmark number and then see how they relate to each other.

$\frac{2}{6}$ full →

$\frac{2}{3}$ full

$\frac{1}{2}$ full

$\frac{2}{6}$ is between 0 and $\frac{1}{2}$.

$\frac{2}{3}$ is between $\frac{1}{2}$ and 1.

$\frac{2}{6}$ is less than $\frac{1}{2}$.
$\frac{2}{3}$ is greater than $\frac{1}{2}$.
So, $\frac{2}{6} < \frac{2}{3}$.
Alan will buy more peanuts than Keri.

## Problem Solving

MATHEMATICAL PRACTICES

For **13–16,** use the table to the right.

**13.** In which class is the greatest fraction of students wearing green?

ⓒ **14. Writing to Explain** In which class is the fraction of students wearing green closer to neither 0 nor 1? Explain.

**Data**

| Class | Fraction of students wearing green |
|---|---|
| Mrs. Avery | $\frac{1}{6}$ |
| Mr. Nunez | $\frac{5}{6}$ |
| Ms. Chang | $\frac{1}{3}$ |
| Mr. O'Leary | $\frac{4}{8}$ |
| Miss Lee | $\frac{4}{6}$ |

**15.** In which classes are the fraction of students wearing green closer to 1 than to 0?

ⓒ **16. Persevere** In which class is the least fraction of students wearing green? Explain.

**17.** Write two fractions using the numbers from the cards at the right. Then tell which fraction is closer to 1 than to 0.

| **1** | **2** | **3** | **4** |

ⓒ **18. Reason** Nika has 40 erasers. 10 of them are yellow, 3 are green, 8 are red, and the rest are blue. How many blue erasers does Nika have?

**19.** Mr. Popov has 24 pencils that he will give to 8 students. Each student will receive the same number of pencils. How many pencils will each student receive?

**A** 2    **B** 3    **C** 16    **D** 32

©
Common
Core

3.NF.3.d Compare two
fractions with the same
numerator or the same
denominator by reasoning
about their size. Recognize
that comparisons are
valid only when the two
fractions refer to the same
whole. Record the results
of comparisons with the
symbols >, =, or <, and
justify the conclusions...
Also 3NF.3.a

# Comparing Fractions on the Number Line

**How can you compare fractions on a number line?**

Talia has two different lengths of red and blue ribbon. Does Talia have more red ribbon or more blue ribbon?

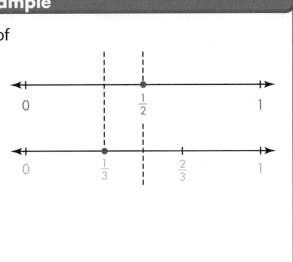

$\frac{1}{3}$ yard

$\frac{2}{3}$ yard

---

## Other Example

Ben has $\frac{1}{2}$ yard of string and John has $\frac{1}{3}$ yard of string. Who has more string?

You can draw two number lines of equal length to compare. Mark 0 and 1.

Divide the first into 2 equal parts. Mark $\frac{1}{2}$.

Divide the second into 3 equal parts and mark $\frac{1}{3}$.

$\frac{1}{2}$ is farther to the right than $\frac{1}{3}$.

$\frac{1}{2} > \frac{1}{3}$   Ben has more string than John.

*(number lines showing 0, $\frac{1}{2}$, 1 and 0, $\frac{1}{3}$, $\frac{2}{3}$, 1)*

---

## Guided Practice*

**MATHEMATICAL PRACTICES**

### Do you know HOW?

Compare. Write <, >, or =. Use number lines to help.

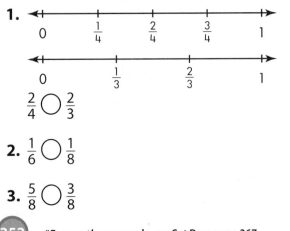

**1.**

0    $\frac{1}{4}$    $\frac{2}{4}$    $\frac{3}{4}$    1

0    $\frac{1}{3}$    $\frac{2}{3}$    1

$\frac{2}{4} \bigcirc \frac{2}{3}$

**2.** $\frac{1}{6} \bigcirc \frac{1}{8}$

**3.** $\frac{5}{8} \bigcirc \frac{3}{8}$

### Do you UNDERSTAND?

© **4. Use Structure** What do you notice when the denominators in the two fractions that you are comparing are the same?

© **5. Write a Problem** Write a problem that compares two fractions with different numerators.

*For another example, see Set D on page 267.

You can use a number line to compare $\frac{1}{3}$ and $\frac{2}{3}$.

The farther to the right a fraction is on the number line, the greater the fraction.

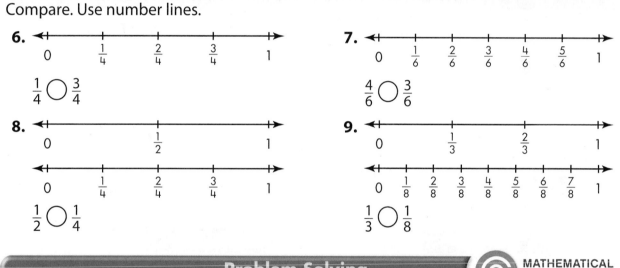

On the number line, $\frac{2}{3}$ is farther to the right, than $\frac{1}{3}$.

$$\frac{2}{3} > \frac{1}{3}$$

Talia has more blue ribbon than red ribbon.

## Independent Practice

Compare. Use number lines.

**6.**

| | | | | |
|---|---|---|---|---|
| 0 | $\frac{1}{4}$ | $\frac{2}{4}$ | $\frac{3}{4}$ | 1 |

$\frac{1}{4} \bigcirc \frac{3}{4}$

**7.**

| | | | | | | |
|---|---|---|---|---|---|---|
| 0 | $\frac{1}{6}$ | $\frac{2}{6}$ | $\frac{3}{6}$ | $\frac{4}{6}$ | $\frac{5}{6}$ | 1 |

$\frac{4}{6} \bigcirc \frac{3}{6}$

**8.**

| | | |
|---|---|---|
| 0 | $\frac{1}{2}$ | 1 |

| | | | | |
|---|---|---|---|---|
| 0 | $\frac{1}{4}$ | $\frac{2}{4}$ | $\frac{3}{4}$ | 1 |

$\frac{1}{2} \bigcirc \frac{1}{4}$

**9.**

| | | |
|---|---|---|
| 0 | $\frac{1}{3}$ | $\frac{2}{3}$ | 1 |

| | | | | | | | |
|---|---|---|---|---|---|---|---|
| 0 | $\frac{1}{8}$ | $\frac{2}{8}$ | $\frac{3}{8}$ | $\frac{4}{8}$ | $\frac{5}{8}$ | $\frac{6}{8}$ | $\frac{7}{8}$ | 1 |

$\frac{1}{3} \bigcirc \frac{1}{8}$

## Problem Solving

Ⓒ MATHEMATICAL PRACTICES

Ⓒ **10. Reason** Scott ate $\frac{2}{8}$ of a fruit bar. Anne ate $\frac{4}{8}$ of a fruit bar. Who ate more of the fruit bar, Scott or Anne? Draw a number line to help explain your answer.

Ⓒ **11. Be Precise** Matt and Adara have identical pieces of cardboard for an art project. Matt uses $\frac{2}{3}$ of his piece. Adara uses $\frac{2}{6}$ of her piece. Who uses more, Matt or Adara? Draw two number lines to help explain your answer.

**12.** Some friends are sharing a pizza. Nicole ate $\frac{2}{8}$ of the pizza. Chris ate $\frac{3}{8}$ of the pizza. Mike ate $\frac{1}{8}$ of the pizza. Johan ate $\frac{2}{8}$ of the pizza. Who ate the most pizza?

| | | | | | | | |
|---|---|---|---|---|---|---|---|
| 0 | $\frac{1}{8}$ | $\frac{2}{8}$ | $\frac{3}{8}$ | $\frac{4}{8}$ | $\frac{5}{8}$ | $\frac{6}{8}$ | $\frac{7}{8}$ | 1 |

**A** Nicole          **B** Chris          **C** Mike          **D** Johan

© Common Core

3.NF.3.a Understand two fractions as equivalent (equal) if they are the same size, or the same point on a number line.
Also 3.NF.3.b

# Finding Equivalent Fractions

## How can different fractions name the same part of a whole?

Sonya has decorated $\frac{1}{2}$ of the border. What are two other ways to name $\frac{1}{2}$?

$\frac{1}{2}$ of the border

Different fractions can name the same part of a whole.

---

**Another Example** How can you write a fraction in simplest form?

Fractions that name the same part of a whole are called equivalent fractions. Division facts that you know will help you find equivalent fractions.

Mario has colored $\frac{4}{6}$ of a border. What is the simplest form of $\frac{4}{6}$?

The simplest form of a fraction is a fraction with a numerator and denominator that cannot be divided by the same divisor, except 1.

$\frac{4}{6}$ of the length of the border

### One Way

Use models.

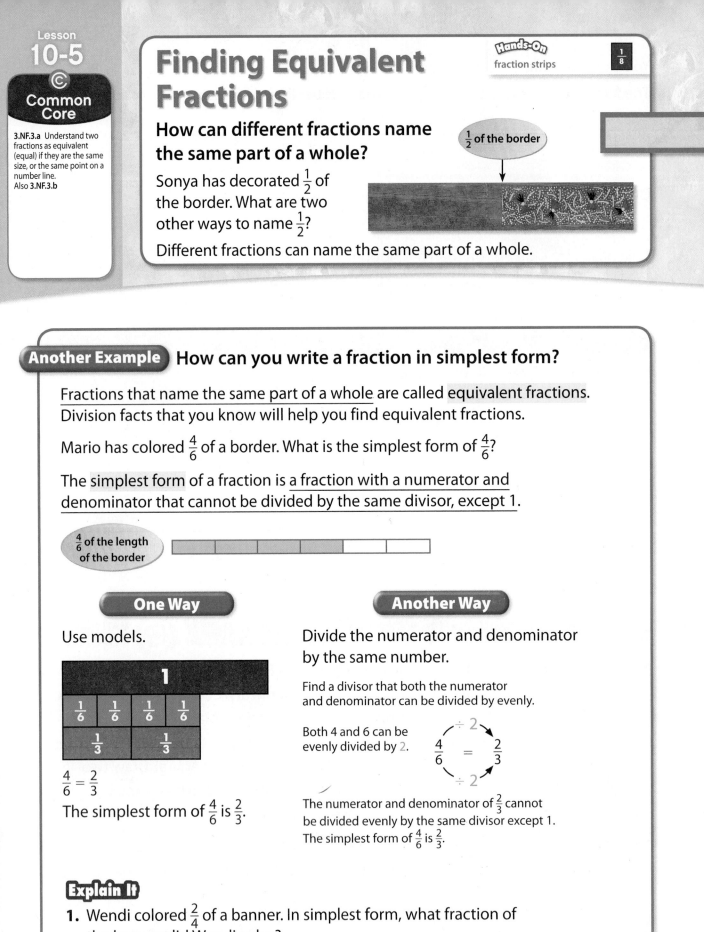

$\frac{4}{6} = \frac{2}{3}$

The simplest form of $\frac{4}{6}$ is $\frac{2}{3}$.

### Another Way

Divide the numerator and denominator by the same number.

Find a divisor that both the numerator and denominator can be divided by evenly.

Both 4 and 6 can be evenly divided by 2.

$$\frac{4}{6} = \frac{2}{3}$$

$\div 2$

The numerator and denominator of $\frac{2}{3}$ cannot be divided evenly by the same divisor except 1. The simplest form of $\frac{4}{6}$ is $\frac{2}{3}$.

**Explain It**

1. Wendi colored $\frac{2}{4}$ of a banner. In simplest form, what fraction of the banner did Wendi color?

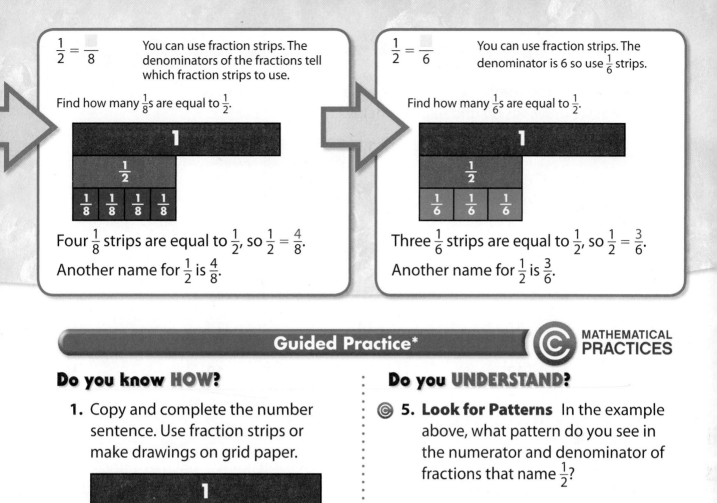

$\frac{1}{2} = \frac{\square}{8}$ You can use fraction strips. The denominators of the fractions tell which fraction strips to use.

Find how many $\frac{1}{8}$s are equal to $\frac{1}{2}$.

Four $\frac{1}{8}$ strips are equal to $\frac{1}{2}$, so $\frac{1}{2} = \frac{4}{8}$.
Another name for $\frac{1}{2}$ is $\frac{4}{8}$.

$\frac{1}{2} = \frac{\square}{6}$ You can use fraction strips. The denominator is 6 so use $\frac{1}{6}$ strips.

Find how many $\frac{1}{6}$s are equal to $\frac{1}{2}$.

Three $\frac{1}{6}$ strips are equal to $\frac{1}{2}$, so $\frac{1}{2} = \frac{3}{6}$.
Another name for $\frac{1}{2}$ is $\frac{3}{6}$.

## Guided Practice*

MATHEMATICAL PRACTICES

### Do you know HOW?

1. Copy and complete the number sentence. Use fraction strips or make drawings on grid paper.

$\frac{1}{3} = \frac{\square}{6}$

Find the simplest form of each fraction.

2. $\frac{4}{8}$   3. $\frac{5}{8}$   4. $\frac{2}{4}$

### Do you UNDERSTAND?

Ⓒ 5. **Look for Patterns** In the example above, what pattern do you see in the numerator and denominator of fractions that name $\frac{1}{2}$?

6. Vijay folded a rope into fourths. Then he showed $\frac{1}{4}$ of the length. Write $\frac{1}{4}$ one other way.

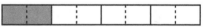

## Independent Practice

In **7–9**, copy and complete each number sentence. Use fraction strips or make drawings on grid paper to help.

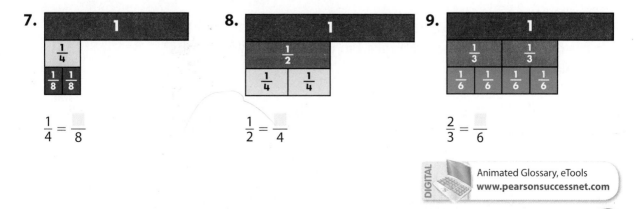

7. $\frac{1}{4} = \frac{\square}{8}$

8. $\frac{1}{2} = \frac{\square}{4}$

9. $\frac{2}{3} = \frac{\square}{6}$

DIGITAL   Animated Glossary, eTools
www.pearsonsuccessnet.com

For **10–11**, copy and complete each number sentence. Use fraction strips or make drawings on grid paper to help.

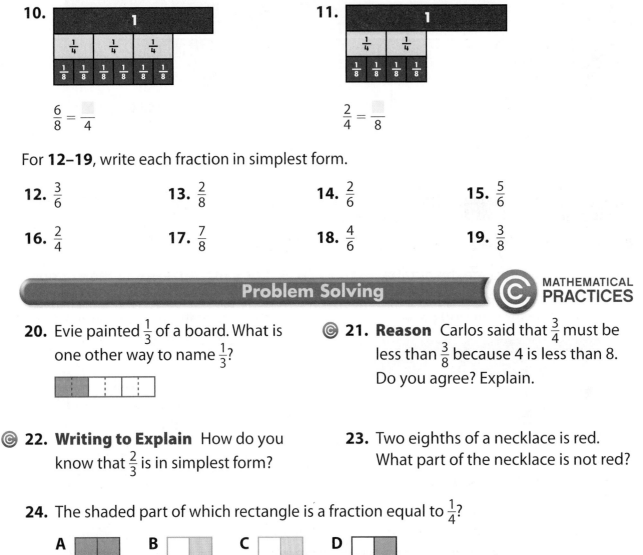

**10.**

| 1 |
|---|

| $\frac{1}{4}$ | $\frac{1}{4}$ | $\frac{1}{4}$ |

| $\frac{1}{8}$ | $\frac{1}{8}$ | $\frac{1}{8}$ | $\frac{1}{8}$ | $\frac{1}{8}$ | $\frac{1}{8}$ |

$$\frac{6}{8} = \frac{\phantom{x}}{4}$$

**11.**

| 1 |
|---|

| $\frac{1}{4}$ | $\frac{1}{4}$ |

| $\frac{1}{8}$ | $\frac{1}{8}$ | $\frac{1}{8}$ | $\frac{1}{8}$ |

$$\frac{2}{4} = \frac{\phantom{x}}{8}$$

For **12–19**, write each fraction in simplest form.

**12.** $\frac{3}{6}$  **13.** $\frac{2}{8}$  **14.** $\frac{2}{6}$  **15.** $\frac{5}{6}$

**16.** $\frac{2}{4}$  **17.** $\frac{7}{8}$  **18.** $\frac{4}{6}$  **19.** $\frac{3}{8}$

© **MATHEMATICAL PRACTICES**

**20.** Evie painted $\frac{1}{3}$ of a board. What is one other way to name $\frac{1}{3}$?

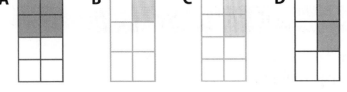

© **21. Reason** Carlos said that $\frac{3}{4}$ must be less than $\frac{3}{8}$ because 4 is less than 8. Do you agree? Explain.

© **22. Writing to Explain** How do you know that $\frac{2}{3}$ is in simplest form?

**23.** Two eighths of a necklace is red. What part of the necklace is not red?

**24.** The shaded part of which rectangle is a fraction equal to $\frac{1}{4}$?

**A**   **B**   **C**   **D**

© **25. Reasonableness** Jan reads 4 to 6 books every month. What is a reasonable number of books Jan would read in 7 months? Explain your answer.

**26.** In simplest form, what fraction of the Earth's land surface is desert? Use the picture.

**A** $\frac{1}{2}$   **B** $\frac{1}{3}$   **C** $\frac{1}{8}$   **D** $\frac{4}{6}$

About $\frac{2}{6}$ of Earth's land surface is desert.

## Circle Graphs

Kara earned $20 last week. The circle graph shows how she earned money and what part of the total was earned for each kind of job.

**Kara's Earnings**

The part for babysitting is half of the circle. Kara earned more by babysitting than by doing chores or lawn work.

One half of the $20 Kara earned was from babysitting.

$\frac{1}{2} = \frac{10}{20}$   So, Kara earned $10 by babysitting.

One fourth of the amount Kara earned was from doing chores, and one fourth was from doing lawn work.

$\frac{1}{4} = \frac{5}{20}$   Kara earned $5 doing chores and $5 doing lawn work.

### Practice

Tom spent a total of $12 on supplies for Hammy, his pet hamster.
For **1–5**, use the circle graph that Tom made.

**1.** Which item cost one fourth of the total? How much money is that?

**Supplies for Hammy**

**2.** How much did Tom spend on bedding?

**3.** Which item cost one sixth of the total? How much money is that?

**4.** List the items Tom bought from least to greatest cost.

**5.** How could thinking about a clock help Tom make the circle graph for Hammy's supplies?

For **6** and **7**, use the table at the right that shows the voting results for class color.

**6. a** What is the total number of votes?

   **b** Write a fraction that describes the votes for each color.

| Class Color | |
| --- | --- |
| **Color** | **Votes** |
| Blue | 9 |
| Green | 3 |
| Silver | 6 |

**7.** Make a circle graph showing the votes.

Common
Core

3.NF.3.a Understand two
fractions as equivalent
(equal) if they are the same
size, or the same point on a
number line.
Also 3.NF.3.b, 3.NF.3.c

# Equivalent Fractions and the Number Line

## What do equivalent fractions look like on a number line?

Sam and Nola are painting two boards that are the same size and the same shape. Is the amount painted by Sam equal to the amount painted by Nola?

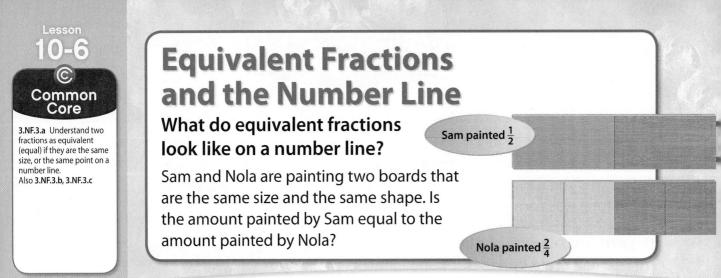

Sam painted $\frac{1}{2}$

Nola painted $\frac{2}{4}$

---

## Guided Practice*

MATHEMATICAL
PRACTICES

### Do you know HOW?

For **1** and **2**, write two fractions that name the location on the number line. You may use fraction strips to help.

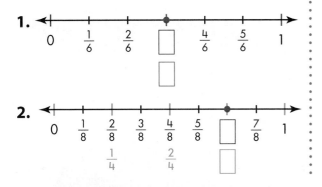

1.

0   $\frac{1}{6}$   $\frac{2}{6}$   ☐   $\frac{4}{6}$   $\frac{5}{6}$   1

☐

2.

0   $\frac{1}{8}$   $\frac{2}{8}$   $\frac{3}{8}$   $\frac{4}{8}$   $\frac{5}{8}$   ☐   $\frac{7}{8}$   1

$\frac{1}{4}$    $\frac{2}{4}$    ☐

### Do you UNDERSTAND?

© **3. Model** Draw a number line to show that $\frac{2}{8}$ and $\frac{1}{4}$ are equivalent fractions.

**4.** Anne painted $\frac{3}{6}$ of the same size board as Sam and Nola. Did she paint the same amount as Sam and Nola? Explain.

---

## Independent Practice

In **5–8**, write two fractions that name the location on the number line. You may use fraction strips to help.

5.

0   $\frac{1}{8}$   $\frac{2}{8}$   $\frac{3}{8}$   ☐   $\frac{5}{8}$   $\frac{6}{8}$   $\frac{7}{8}$   1

6.

0   $\frac{1}{6}$   ☐   $\frac{3}{6}$   $\frac{4}{6}$   $\frac{5}{6}$   1

7.

0    ☐    $\frac{2}{3}$    1

☐

8.

0    ☐    $\frac{2}{4}$    $\frac{3}{4}$    1

☐

*For another example, see Set E on page 268.*

You can use a number line to show $\frac{1}{2}$ and $\frac{2}{4}$.

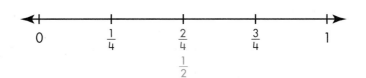

$$\frac{1}{2} = \frac{2}{4}$$

Sam and Nola painted the same amount.

Equivalent fractions are different names for the same point on a number line.

## Problem Solving

© **9. Model** Monica and Drew each had the same length of ribbon. Monica folded her piece of ribbon into fourths. She used $\frac{3}{4}$ of the ribbon to wrap a package. Drew folded his ribbon into eighths. He used $\frac{6}{8}$ of the ribbon to wrap his package. Who used more ribbon? Draw a number line to help explain your answer. Write a number sentence that describes what you found.

**Tip** *Use $>$, $<$, $=$ in your number sentence.*

© **10. Use Tools** Sophie and Zach each had a same-sized tube for a project. Sophie cut her tube into thirds. She used $\frac{2}{3}$ to build a tower. Zach cut his tube into sixths. He used $\frac{5}{6}$ of his tube to build a tower. Sophie said she and Zach each used the same amount of their tubes. Do you agree? Draw a number line and write a number sentence to show your answer.

**11.** Rachel cut 3 different pies into 6 equal pieces. How many pieces of pie did she have in all?

**12.** Rory had 40 slices of pizza to share. Each pizza was cut into 8 slices. How many pizzas did Rory have?

For **13** and **14**, choose the fraction that is **NOT** equivalent to the fraction given.

**13.** $\frac{2}{4}$

**A** $\frac{4}{8}$   **C** $\frac{1}{2}$

**B** $\frac{2}{8}$   **D** $\frac{3}{6}$

**14.** $\frac{5}{5}$

**A** $\frac{4}{4}$   **C** $\frac{5}{1}$

**B** $\frac{3}{3}$   **D** $\frac{2}{2}$

Lesson
10-7
©
**Common Core**

3.NF.3.c Express whole numbers as fractions, and recognize fractions that are equivalent to whole numbers. . . .

Hands-On
fraction strips

$\frac{1}{4}$

# Whole Numbers and Fractions

### Are there fraction names for whole numbers?

Lucy had a small box of crackers. She ate $\frac{1}{4}$ of the box in the morning and $\frac{1}{4}$ of the box after lunch. Then she ate $\frac{1}{4}$ of the box before dinner and $\frac{1}{4}$ of the box before bedtime. How much of the box of crackers did she eat in all?

Crackers

## Other Example

How many fourths are there in 2 wholes? Use a number line to find a fraction name for 2 using fourths.

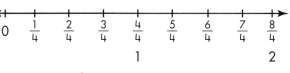

So, one fraction name for 2 is $\frac{8}{4}$.

All whole numbers have fraction names.

## Guided Practice*

© **MATHEMATICAL PRACTICES**

### Do you know HOW?

For **1–3,** copy and complete each number line.

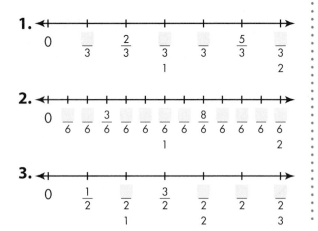

### Do you UNDERSTAND?

© 4. **Communicate** Explain how you know that $\frac{8}{8} = 1$.

© 5. **Use Structure** Write two fraction names for 3.

© 6. **Use Tools** Draw a number line to show that $\frac{4}{2} = 2$.

eTools
www.pearsonsuccessnet.com

*For another example, see Set F on page 268.*

You can use fraction strips to model how much of the box of crackers Lucy ate.

| 1 | | | |
|---|---|---|---|
| $\frac{1}{4}$ | $\frac{1}{4}$ | $\frac{1}{4}$ | $\frac{1}{4}$ |

Four $\frac{1}{4}$ fraction strips equal one whole fraction strip.

You can use a number line.

Whole numbers have equivalent fraction names. $\frac{4}{4} = 1$

So, Lucy ate $\frac{4}{4}$ or 1 whole box of crackers in all.

## Independent Practice

For **7** through **12**, write an equivalent fraction for each whole number.

**7.** 4　　　**8.** 1　　　**9.** 2　　　**10.** 5　　　**11.** 3　　　**12.** 6

For **13** through **17**, copy the number line and use the fraction name to divide the number line into equal parts. Label each part with a fraction.

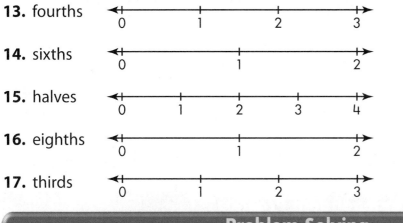

**13.** fourths

0　　1　　2　　3

**14.** sixths

0　　1　　2

**15.** halves

0　　1　　2　　3　　4

**16.** eighths

0　　1　　2

**17.** thirds

0　　1　　2　　3

## Problem Solving

MATHEMATICAL PRACTICES

**18.** There is $\frac{1}{2}$ of a chicken in each chicken dinner at Wings and Things Diner. How many whole chickens are in 6 chicken dinners?

© **19. Writing to Explain** What pattern do you notice in a fraction that is equivalent to 1 whole?

**20.** Wes completed $\frac{5}{8}$ of his science project on Saturday. On Sunday he completed $\frac{3}{8}$ of it. How much of the project did Wes complete over the weekend?

**A** $\frac{4}{14}$　　**B** $\frac{6}{8}$　　**C** $\frac{8}{8}$　　**D** $\frac{8}{4}$

© **21. Persevere** The kid's meal at Happy Time Diner comes with an apple slice that is $\frac{1}{4}$ of a whole apple. How many kid's meals would need to be ordered to have 3 whole apples?

Lesson
10-8

© 
Common
Core

3.NF.3 Explain equivalence
of fractions in special cases,
and compare fractions by
reasoning about their size.

# Using Fractions

## How can you compare and order fractions?

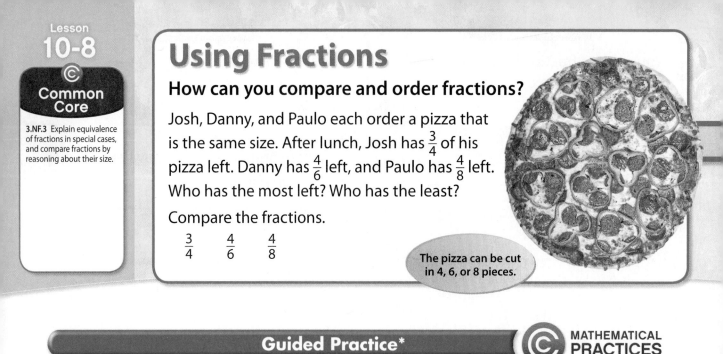

Josh, Danny, and Paulo each order a pizza that is the same size. After lunch, Josh has $\frac{3}{4}$ of his pizza left. Danny has $\frac{4}{6}$ left, and Paulo has $\frac{4}{8}$ left. Who has the most left? Who has the least?

Compare the fractions.

$$\frac{3}{4} \qquad \frac{4}{6} \qquad \frac{4}{8}$$

The pizza can be cut in 4, 6, or 8 pieces.

## Guided Practice*

© MATHEMATICAL
PRACTICES

### Do you know HOW?

In **1** and **2**, write the fractions in order from least to greatest.

**1.** $\frac{5}{6}$   $\frac{2}{3}$   $\frac{2}{4}$

| $\frac{1}{3}$ | $\frac{1}{3}$ | $\frac{1}{3}$ |
|---|---|---|
| $\frac{1}{4}$ | $\frac{1}{4}$ | $\frac{1}{4}$ | $\frac{1}{4}$ |
| $\frac{1}{6}$ | $\frac{1}{6}$ | $\frac{1}{6}$ | $\frac{1}{6}$ | $\frac{1}{6}$ | $\frac{1}{6}$ |

**2.** $\frac{1}{3}$   $\frac{3}{4}$   $\frac{3}{6}$

In **3–6**, copy and complete. Use <, >, or = to compare.

**3.** $\frac{4}{8} \bigcirc \frac{4}{6}$     **4.** $\frac{4}{4} \bigcirc \frac{2}{4}$

**5.** $\frac{3}{4} \bigcirc \frac{3}{6}$     **6.** $\frac{5}{8} \bigcirc \frac{5}{6}$

### Do you UNDERSTAND?

© **7. Communicate** Marco joins the boys for lunch and orders the same size pizza. After lunch, he has $\frac{2}{4}$ of his pizza left. Is this the same amount as any of the other boys? Explain.

© **8. Reason** Sue, Linda, and Jody are eating oranges. Sue eats $\frac{2}{6}$ orange, Jody eats $\frac{2}{4}$ orange, and Linda eats $\frac{2}{8}$ orange. Who eats the most of her orange? Who eats the least?

## Independent Practice

**9.** Copy and complete the number line by writing the missing fraction.

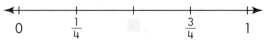

0     $\frac{1}{4}$         $\frac{3}{4}$     1

In **10–13**, copy and complete. Use <, >, or = to compare. Use the number line to help.

**10.** $\frac{3}{4} \bigcirc \frac{1}{2}$     **11.** $\frac{1}{4} \bigcirc \frac{2}{4}$     **12.** $\frac{2}{4} \bigcirc \frac{4}{8}$     **13.** $\frac{3}{6} \bigcirc \frac{4}{4}$

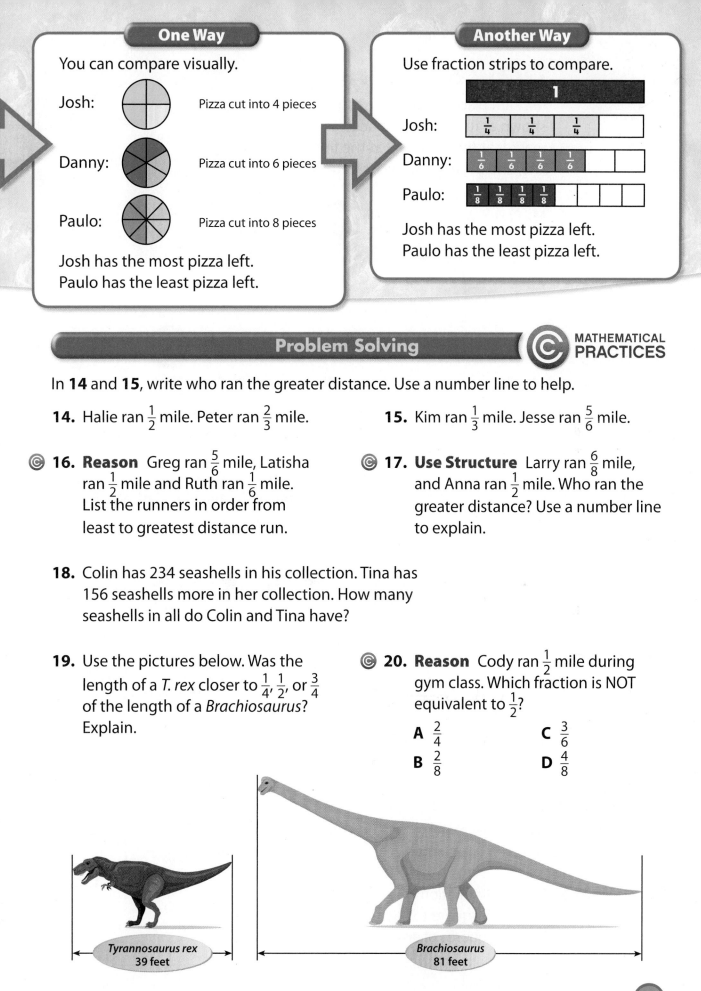

**One Way**

You can compare visually.

Josh: Pizza cut into 4 pieces

Danny: Pizza cut into 6 pieces

Paulo: Pizza cut into 8 pieces

Josh has the most pizza left.
Paulo has the least pizza left.

**Another Way**

Use fraction strips to compare.

| 1 |
|---|

Josh:

| $\frac{1}{4}$ | $\frac{1}{4}$ | $\frac{1}{4}$ | |

Danny:

| $\frac{1}{6}$ | $\frac{1}{6}$ | $\frac{1}{6}$ | $\frac{1}{6}$ | | |

Paulo:

| $\frac{1}{8}$ | $\frac{1}{8}$ | $\frac{1}{8}$ | $\frac{1}{8}$ | | | | |

Josh has the most pizza left.
Paulo has the least pizza left.

## Problem Solving

MATHEMATICAL
PRACTICES

In **14** and **15**, write who ran the greater distance. Use a number line to help.

**14.** Halie ran $\frac{1}{2}$ mile. Peter ran $\frac{2}{3}$ mile.

**15.** Kim ran $\frac{1}{3}$ mile. Jesse ran $\frac{5}{6}$ mile.

© **16. Reason** Greg ran $\frac{5}{6}$ mile, Latisha ran $\frac{1}{2}$ mile and Ruth ran $\frac{1}{6}$ mile. List the runners in order from least to greatest distance run.

© **17. Use Structure** Larry ran $\frac{6}{8}$ mile, and Anna ran $\frac{1}{2}$ mile. Who ran the greater distance? Use a number line to explain.

**18.** Colin has 234 seashells in his collection. Tina has 156 seashells more in her collection. How many seashells in all do Colin and Tina have?

**19.** Use the pictures below. Was the length of a *T. rex* closer to $\frac{1}{4}$, $\frac{1}{2}$, or $\frac{3}{4}$ of the length of a *Brachiosaurus*? Explain.

© **20. Reason** Cody ran $\frac{1}{2}$ mile during gym class. Which fraction is NOT equivalent to $\frac{1}{2}$?

**A** $\frac{2}{4}$  **C** $\frac{3}{6}$

**B** $\frac{2}{8}$  **D** $\frac{4}{8}$

*Tyrannosaurus rex*
39 feet

*Brachiosaurus*
81 feet

Lesson
10-9

Common
Core

3.NF.2 Understand a
fraction as a number on
the number line; represent
fractions on a number line
diagram.

## Problem Solving

# Draw a Picture

The racecourse is
5 kilometers long.

Mr. Park placed markers on the racecourse shown at the right. He placed a marker at the start line, at the finish line, and at each kilometer between.

How many markers did Mr. Park place?

**START**

---

## Guided Practice*

**MATHEMATICAL PRACTICES**

### Do you know HOW?

Draw a picture to solve.

1. A relay race team has 4 members. The race is 2 miles long. Each member runs an equal part of the race. How far does each member run?

### Do you UNDERSTAND?

© 2. **Reason** In the example above, what does the number line show?

© 3. **Write a Problem** Write and solve a problem that you can solve by drawing a picture.

---

## Independent Practice

**MATHEMATICAL PRACTICES**

For **4–6**, draw a picture to solve.

© 4. **Use Tools** Roy made a coat rack using a board that was 7 feet long. He put one hook at each end of the board. He also put a hook at each foot between the two ends. How many hooks in all did he use?

5. Nina put together 6 squares to make a rectangle. There are 3 rows of squares. Each row has 2 squares. How many small and large squares in all are in the rectangle?

© 6. **Persevere** Use the information in Exercise 5. If Nina added another square to each row, how many different squares of any size would there be?

**Applying Math Practices**

- What am I asked to find?
- What else can I try?
- How are quantities related?
- How can I explain my work?
- How can I use math to model the problem?
- Can I use tools to help?
- Is my work precise?
- Why does this work?
- How can I generalize?

*For another example, see Set H on page 269.*

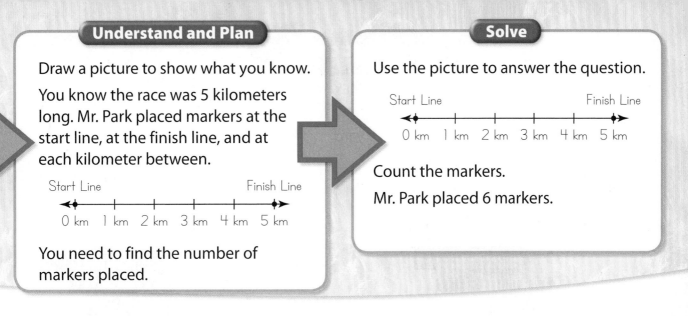

**Understand and Plan**

Draw a picture to show what you know.

You know the race was 5 kilometers long. Mr. Park placed markers at the start line, at the finish line, and at each kilometer between.

Start Line ———————— Finish Line
0 km  1 km  2 km  3 km  4 km  5 km

You need to find the number of markers placed.

**Solve**

Use the picture to answer the question.

Start Line ———————— Finish Line
0 km  1 km  2 km  3 km  4 km  5 km

Count the markers.

Mr. Park placed 6 markers.

---

© **7. Model** Heidi and Susan want to equally share $\frac{4}{8}$ feet of ribbon. What amount of ribbon should each girl get? Draw a number line to help solve the problem.

**8.** Mira's dad promised to add money to the amount Mira saves each week. How much does he add?

| Saved by Mira | $3 | $5 | $8 | $9 |
|---|---|---|---|---|
| Total Amount | $7 | $9 | $12 | $13 |

In **9** and **10,** use the menu board at the right.

© **9. Writing to Explain** How many different choices of 1 kind of sandwich and 1 topping can you make? Explain how you found your answer.

Build Your Own Sandwich
Choose chicken or beef and 1 topping.

Pickles • Tomatoes • Lettuce • Sauce

© **10. Persevere** Suppose you can choose white, wheat, or rye bread. How many different choices of 1 kind of sandwich, 1 kind of bread, and 1 kind of topping are there?

**11.** Members of the dog owners' club are building a fence around a square pen. The pen is 36 feet long on each side. They need to put a post at each corner and every 6 feet along each side. How many posts are needed?

**A** 16

**C** 24

**B** 20

**D** 28

**Set A,** pages 246–247

Alicia has $\frac{5}{6}$ yard of yarn and Emma has $\frac{4}{6}$ yard of yarn.

Who has more yarn, Alicia or Emma?

You can use fraction strips to compare.

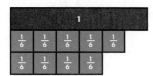

$\frac{5}{6} > \frac{4}{6}$

*Five sixths* is greater than *four sixths*.

Alicia has more yarn.

**Remember** that when two fractions have the same denominator, the fraction with the greater numerator is the greater fraction.

Compare. Write >, <, or =.

**1.** $\frac{6}{8} \bigcirc \frac{5}{8}$

**2.** $\frac{2}{6} \bigcirc \frac{1}{6}$

**3.** $\frac{5}{8} \bigcirc \frac{3}{8}$

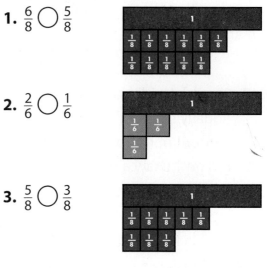

**Set B,** pages 248–249

Two ribbons are the same size. One ribbon is $\frac{2}{4}$ pink and the other is $\frac{2}{3}$ pink. Which fraction is less, $\frac{2}{4}$ or $\frac{2}{3}$?

You can use fraction strips to compare.

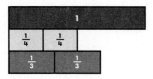

$\frac{2}{4} < \frac{2}{3}$

*Two fourths* is less than *two thirds*.

**Remember** that when two fractions have the same numerator, the fraction with the greater denominator is less than the other fraction.

Compare. Write <, >, or =.

**1.** $\frac{1}{4} \bigcirc \frac{1}{6}$

**2.** $\frac{3}{8} \bigcirc \frac{3}{4}$

**3.** $\frac{2}{6} \bigcirc \frac{2}{3}$

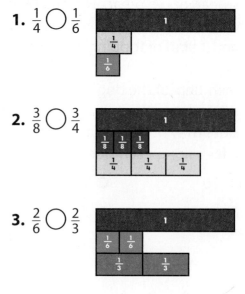

You can compare fractions using benchmark numbers such as 0, $\frac{1}{2}$, and 1.

In Chris' sock drawer, $\frac{2}{3}$ of the socks are white. In his sister's sock drawer, $\frac{2}{8}$ of the socks are white. They have the same number of socks. Who has more white socks?

$\frac{2}{3}$ is greater than $\frac{1}{2}$.

$\frac{2}{8}$ is less than $\frac{1}{2}$.

Chris has more white socks than his sister.

**Remember** you can compare each fraction to a benchmark fraction to see how they relate to each other.

1. Mike had $\frac{1}{8}$ of a candy bar. Sally had $\frac{4}{6}$ of a candy bar. Whose fraction of a candy bar was closer to 1? Closer to 0?

2. Paul compared two bags of rice. One weighed $\frac{5}{8}$ pound, and the other weighed $\frac{1}{2}$ pound. Which bag is heavier?

You can use a number line to compare fractions.

Which is greater, $\frac{3}{6}$ or $\frac{4}{6}$?

$\frac{4}{6}$ is farther to the right than $\frac{3}{6}$, so $\frac{4}{6}$ is greater.

You can also compare two fractions with the same numerator by drawing two number lines.

Which is greater, $\frac{2}{4}$ or $\frac{2}{3}$?

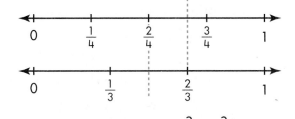

$\frac{2}{3}$ is farther to the right than $\frac{2}{4}$, so $\frac{2}{3}$ is greater.

**Remember** to draw two number lines that are equal in length when comparing fractions with different denominators.

Use number lines to compare.

1. $\frac{2}{6} \bigcirc \frac{3}{6}$

2. $\frac{3}{6} \bigcirc \frac{3}{4}$

3. $\frac{2}{3} \bigcirc \frac{2}{8}$

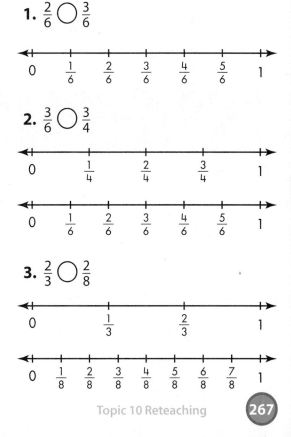

**Set E,** pages 254–256, 258–259

You can use fraction strips or a number line to find equivalent fractions.

What is another name for $\frac{3}{4}$?

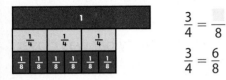

$$\frac{3}{4} = \frac{\blacksquare}{8}$$

$$\frac{3}{4} = \frac{6}{8}$$

Six $\frac{1}{8}$ strips are equal to three $\frac{1}{4}$ strips.

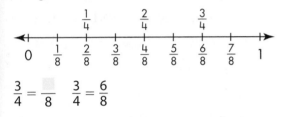

$$\frac{3}{4} = \frac{\blacksquare}{8} \qquad \frac{3}{4} = \frac{6}{8}$$

**Remember** that different fractions can name the same part of a whole.

Copy and complete each number sentence. Use fraction strips or a number line to help.

**1.** $\frac{1}{4} = \frac{\blacksquare}{8}$  **2.** $\frac{3}{4} = \frac{\blacksquare}{8}$

**3.** $\frac{4}{6} = \frac{\blacksquare}{3}$  **4.** $\frac{1}{2} = \frac{\blacksquare}{4}$

Use fraction strips or a number line to find an equivalent fraction for each of the following fractions.

**5.** $\frac{4}{8}$  **6.** $\frac{2}{6}$  **7.** $\frac{2}{8}$

**Set F,** pages 260–261

Sapna is baking a cake. She poured flour 6 times into a bowl using a $\frac{1}{3}$ cup container. How many cups of flour in all did Sapna pour into the bowl?

You can use fraction strips or a number line to find how many cups of flour Sapna poured into the bowl.

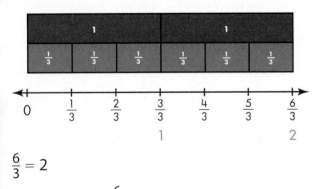

$$\frac{6}{3} = 2$$

Sapna poured $\frac{6}{3}$ or 2 cups of flour in the bowl.

**Remember** when you write whole numbers as fractions, the numerator can be greater than the denominator.

Write an equivalent fraction for each whole number. Use fraction strips or a number line to help.

**1.** 3  **2.** 2

**3.** 5  **4.** 1

**5.** 6  **6.** 10

**7.** Three friends were sharing a pizza. Ray ate $\frac{3}{6}$ of the pizza. Monica ate $\frac{2}{6}$ of the pizza. Alex ate $\frac{1}{6}$ of the pizza. How much of the pizza did they eat in all?

A salad dressing recipe uses $\frac{3}{8}$ cup vinegar, $\frac{3}{4}$ cup oil, and $\frac{1}{2}$ cup water. Which ingredient represents the least amount?

Use fraction strips to compare.

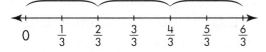

$$\frac{3}{8} < \frac{1}{2} < \frac{3}{4}$$

So, vinegar represents the least amount.

**Remember** to use models and reasoning to help you compare and order fractions.

Compare. Write <, >, or =.

1. $\frac{1}{4} \bigcirc \frac{1}{3}$      2. $\frac{1}{2} \bigcirc \frac{2}{6}$

3. $\frac{1}{2} \bigcirc \frac{2}{4}$      4. $\frac{3}{4} \bigcirc \frac{5}{8}$

Solve.

5. Mike, Bev, and Rhoda ride their bikes from their homes directly to school each morning. Mike rides $\frac{7}{8}$ mile, Rhoda rides $\frac{4}{6}$ mile, and Bev rides $\frac{1}{2}$ mile. Who lives closest to school?

Draw a picture to solve.

Three friends share a string that is 2 yards long. How much string does each friend get?

Draw a picture to show what you know. The string is 2 yards long. The three friends want to share the string by dividing it into 3 equal parts.

Use the picture to answer the question.

Each friend gets $\frac{2}{3}$ yard of string.

**Remember** that the picture you draw needs to match the story.

Draw a picture to solve.

1. Six friends want to equally share 3 yards of yarn. How much yarn should each friend get?

2. Marie wants to space markers evenly along a 5-mile race course. She puts a marker at the start line. How far apart should the 21 markers be?

3. Eight students are painting 2 boards for a project. The students want to divide the work equally. How much of the board should each student paint?

**Multiple Choice**

1. Ellen used fraction strips to compare fractions. Which comparison is true? (10-2)

   A $\frac{3}{6} < \frac{3}{8}$

   B $\frac{3}{8} > \frac{3}{4}$

   C $\frac{3}{4} < \frac{3}{6}$

   D $\frac{3}{6} > \frac{3}{8}$

2. Miguel measured the lengths of two small fish. The fish were $\frac{3}{4}$ inch and $\frac{1}{4}$ inch long. Use the number line to find which is the correct symbol to compare the fractions. (10-4)

   $\frac{3}{4} \bigcirc \frac{1}{4}$

   ```
   ←+————+————+————+————+→
     0    1/4   2/4   3/4   1
   ```

   A    =          C    >

   B    ÷          D    <

3. During the time allowed, Delia swam $\frac{3}{6}$ of the length of the pool. Loren swam $\frac{4}{6}$ of it. Use the fraction strips to find which is the correct symbol to compare the fractions. (10-1)

   $\frac{3}{6} \bigcirc \frac{4}{6}$

   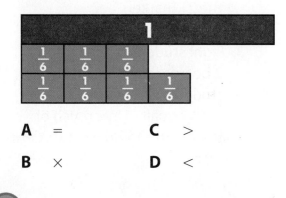

   A    =          C    >

   B    ×          D    <

4. Which lists the fractions in order from least to greatest? (10-8)

   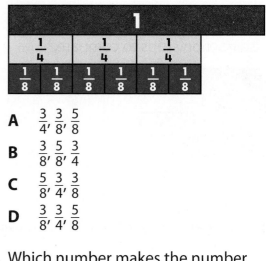

   A $\frac{3}{4}, \frac{3}{8}, \frac{5}{8}$

   B $\frac{3}{8}, \frac{5}{8}, \frac{3}{4}$

   C $\frac{5}{8}, \frac{3}{4}, \frac{3}{8}$

   D $\frac{3}{8}, \frac{3}{4}, \frac{5}{8}$

5. Which number makes the number sentence true? (10-5)

   $\frac{4}{6} = \frac{\blacksquare}{3}$

   A    1

   B    2

   C    3

   D    4

6. Lezlie hiked $\frac{3}{8}$ of a mile on Monday. On Wednesday, she hiked $\frac{3}{6}$ of a mile. She hiked $\frac{3}{4}$ of a mile on Friday. Use benchmark numbers to find which day Lezlie hiked the farthest? (10-3)

   A    Monday

   B    Wednesday

   C    Friday

   D    All 3 distances are equal

**7.** George wants to know if two pieces of wire are the same length. One wire is $\frac{6}{8}$ yard. The other is $\frac{3}{4}$ yard. Draw a number line to show they are the same length. (10-6)

**8.** Three friends were working on a project. Cindy completed $\frac{4}{8}$ of the project. Kim completed $\frac{3}{8}$ of the project. Sandy completed $\frac{1}{8}$ of the project. How much of the project did they complete all together? (10-7)

**9.** Sally, Ron, and Jerry shared some large sandwiches that were the same size and cut into eighths. Sally ate $\frac{5}{8}$ sandwiches, Ron ate $\frac{7}{8}$ sandwiches, and Jerry ate $\frac{3}{4}$ sandwiches. Who ate the most? Explain. (10-8)

**10.** Eight members of an origami club will make a paper chain together. The chain is 4 feet long. Each member will make an equal part of the chain. How much of the chain, in feet, will each member make? Draw a picture to solve. (10-9)

**11.** Fran painted $\frac{1}{2}$ of the fence around her house. What are two other ways to name $\frac{1}{2}$? (10-5)

**12.** There is $\frac{1}{4}$ of a pear in every container of fruit salad. How many whole pears are there in 8 containers of fruit salad? (10-7)

**13.** Two neighboring towns built a new bike path. The path is 8 miles long. They put up mile markers at the start and end of the path, and for every mile in between. How many mile markers did they put up on the bike path? Draw a picture to solve. (10-9)

**14.** Mark and Sidney had identical pieces of wood. Mark used $\frac{1}{3}$ of his piece of wood. Sidney used $\frac{5}{8}$ of her piece of wood. Who used more, Mark, or Sidney? Explain how you can tell using benchmark numbers. (10-3)

**15.** Jamal spent the day making a painting for his friend. At the end of the day, Jamal finished $\frac{1}{2}$ of the painting. If he is able to finish the same amount of painting each day, how long will it take Jamal to make 2 whole paintings? (10-7)

**16.** Jill finished reading $\frac{2}{3}$ of a book for a summer reading project. Ken read $\frac{2}{8}$ of a book for the same project. Who read more of their book? (10-4)

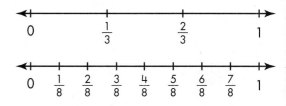

**17.** Meagan ate $\frac{3}{4}$ of a cookie. Write an equivalent fraction for the amount of cookie Meagan did not eat? (10-6)

The table below shows the shirt colors of all the students in two different classrooms.

| Shirt Color | Classroom A | Classroom B |
|:---:|:---:|:---:|
| Red | $\frac{1}{3}$ | $\frac{3}{8}$ |
| Blue | $\frac{2}{4}$ | $\frac{4}{8}$ |
| Yellow | $\frac{1}{6}$ | $\frac{1}{8}$ |

1. Write the fractions that show shirt colors for Classroom A from least to greatest.

2. Write the fractions that show shirt colors for Classroom B from greatest to least.

3. Which fraction of shirt color is closest to 0 in Classroom A? Which fraction of shirt color is closest to 1 in Classroom B?

4. Which shirt color is worn by the same fraction of students in each classroom? Use equivalent fractions to show your answer.

5. Write the fraction of students wearing blue shirts in Classroom A and Classroom B in simplest form.

6. Are more students wearing yellow shirts in Classroom A or Classroom B? Tell how you know?

7. Are more students wearing red shirts or yellow shirts in Classroom A? Draw two number lines to help compare the fractions.

8. Draw and label a number line to show the fraction of students wearing the different shirt colors in Classroom B. Which shirt color is worn the most in Classroom B? Explain how you know.

© DOMAIN **Geometry**

**Topic 11**

# Two-Dimensional Shapes and Their Attributes

▼ What shapes make up the front of this building? You will find out in Lesson 11-6.

mōdis

## Vocabulary

Choose the best term from the box.

- circle
- square
- hexagon
- triangle

**1.** A shape with 4 sides that are all the same length is called a __?__.

**2.** A shape with 6 sides is called a __?__.

**3.** A shape with 3 sides is called a __?__.

## Name Shapes

Write the name of each figure.

**4.**

**5.**

**6.**

**7.**

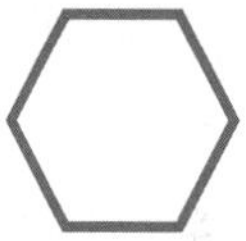

## Shapes

Write the number of sides each figure has.

**8.**

**9.**

**10.**

**11.**

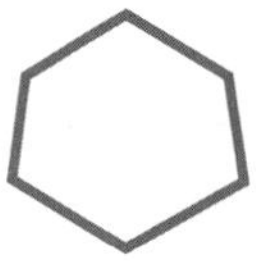

©**12. Writing to Explain** How are squares and triangles the same? How are they different?

**Topic Essential Question**
- How can two-dimensional shapes be described, analyzed, and classified?

# Interactive Learning

Hands-On
Minds-On

**Pose the problem.** Start each lesson by working together to solve problems. It will help you make sense of math.

## Lesson 11-1

ⓒ **Use Tools** Use your ruler to draw lines and answer each question.

Draw a number line from 10 to 12. Can you draw a line that crosses the number line at 1 point? 2 points? Can you draw a line that does not cross the number line? Explain.

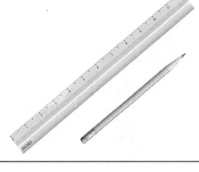

## Lesson 11-2

ⓒ **Use Tools** Solve using objects to represent line segments.

What are some different ways to make two line segments meet at their endpoints? Tell how they are alike and different.

## Lesson 11-3

ⓒ **Use Tools** Draw a shape on your dot paper to solve each riddle.

First riddle: I have 3 sides and 3 vertices. Two of my sides are the same length. Second riddle: I have 4 sides. None of my sides is the same length as any other.

## Lesson 11-4

ⓒ **Generalize** Solve. Try to find more than one way.

How can you sort the triangles into different groups? Describe each group.

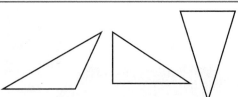

## Lesson 11-5

© **Use Structure** Solve. Try to find more than one way.

How can you sort the quadrilaterals into different groups? Describe each group.

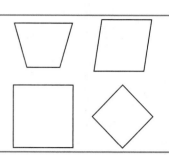

## Lesson 11-6

© **Persevere** Find as many ways as possible.

What shapes on the recording sheet can be combined to make hexagon H?

## Lesson 11-7

© **Persevere** Solve. Try cutting the square apart and rearrange the pieces. Keep trying!

Can you make a pentagon from a square?

## Lesson 11-8

© **Persevere** Solve. Don't stop until you find all answers.

The rug in Lance's room is a rectangle made up of squares. How many squares are on the rug?

## Lesson 11-9

© **Generalize** Look for what's the same and what's different. Justify your answer.

What is the same in all of these polygons? What is different?

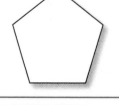

Each polygon has 4 sides.

Lesson
11-1

©
**Common Core**

**3.G.1** Understand that shapes in different categories . . . may share attributes, . . . and that the shared attributes can define a larger category. . . . Recognize rhombuses, rectangles, and squares as examples of quadrilaterals, and draw examples of quadrilaterals that do not belong to any of these subcategories.

# Lines and Line Segments

## What is important to know about lines?

Lines and parts of lines are used to describe shapes and solid figures.

•

A **point** is an exact position.

⟵——————⟶

A **line** is a set of points that is endless in two directions.

•——————•

A **line segment** is a part of a line with two endpoints.

---

**Guided Practice***

© **MATHEMATICAL PRACTICES**

### Do you know HOW?

In **1–4,** write the name for each.

1. •——————•

2.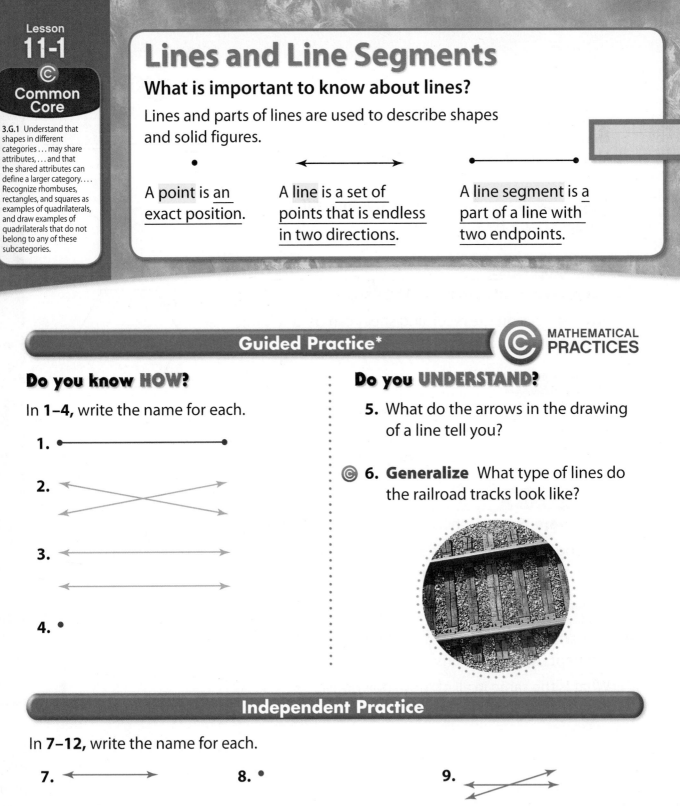

3. ⟵——————⟶

   ⟵——————⟶

4. •

### Do you UNDERSTAND?

5. What do the arrows in the drawing of a line tell you?

© **6. Generalize** What type of lines do the railroad tracks look like?

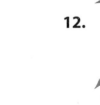

---

**Independent Practice**

In **7–12,** write the name for each.

7. ⟵——————⟶

8. •

9.

10.

11.

12.

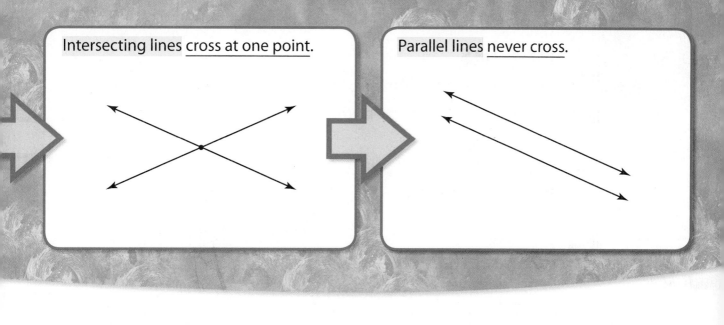

Intersecting lines cross at one point.

Parallel lines never cross.

In **13–16,** draw a picture of each.

**13.** Line segment    **14.** Line        **15.** Parallel lines    **16.** Intersecting lines

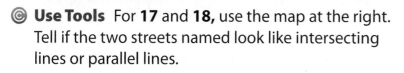
**Problem Solving**

**MATHEMATICAL PRACTICES**

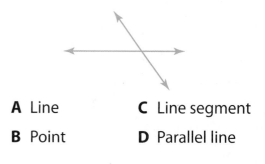

ⓒ **Use Tools** For **17** and **18,** use the map at the right. Tell if the two streets named look like intersecting lines or parallel lines.

**17.** Oak Street and Birch Street

**18.** Birch Street and Elm Street

ⓒ **19. Writing to Explain** Rosa bought 3 packs of 6 baseball cards. Luis bought 4 packs of 3 baseball cards. Who bought more baseball cards? Explain.

**20.** Look at the wings on the plane. What geometric term can you use to describe them? Explain.

**21.** Which best describes the place where these two lines intersect?

**A** Line          **C** Line segment

**B** Point         **D** Parallel line

**Common Core**

**3.G.1** Understand that shapes in different categories . . . may share attributes, . . . and that the shared attributes can define a larger category. . . . Recognize rhombuses, rectangles, and squares as examples of quadrilaterals, and draw examples of quadrilaterals that do not belong to any of these subcategories.

# Angles

## How do you describe angles?

You can describe an angle by the size of its opening.

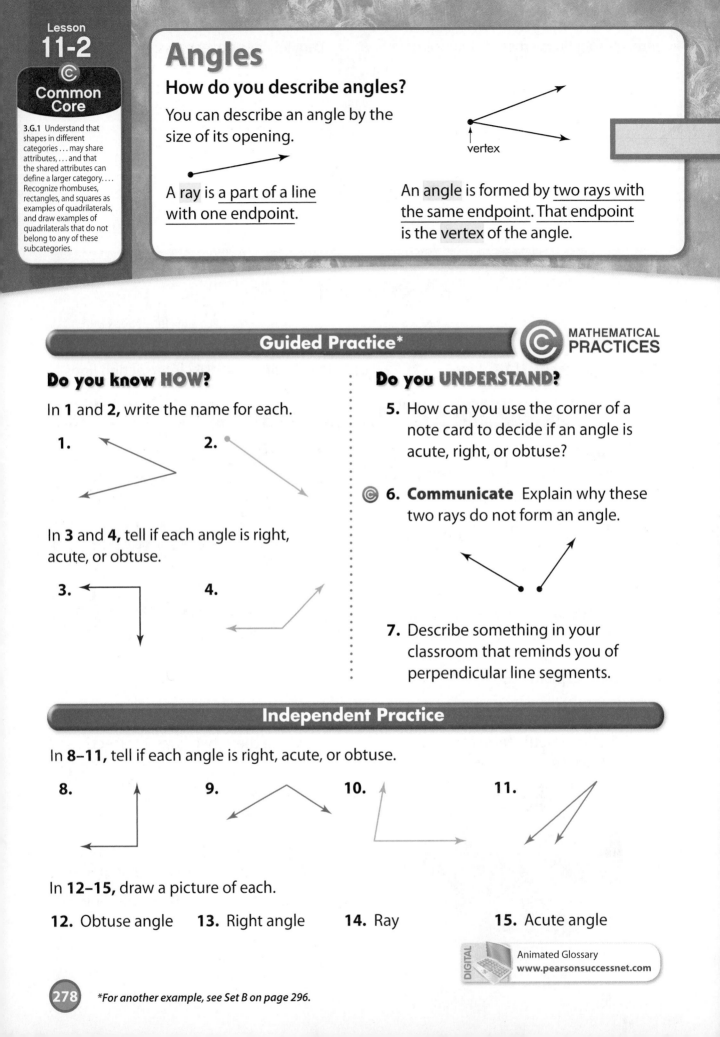

vertex

A ray is a part of a line with one endpoint.

An angle is formed by two rays with the same endpoint. That endpoint is the vertex of the angle.

---

## Guided Practice*

**MATHEMATICAL PRACTICES**

### Do you know HOW?

In **1** and **2**, write the name for each.

**1.**

**2.**

In **3** and **4**, tell if each angle is right, acute, or obtuse.

**3.**

**4.**

### Do you UNDERSTAND?

**5.** How can you use the corner of a note card to decide if an angle is acute, right, or obtuse?

**6. Communicate** Explain why these two rays do not form an angle.

**7.** Describe something in your classroom that reminds you of perpendicular line segments.

---

## Independent Practice

In **8–11**, tell if each angle is right, acute, or obtuse.

**8.**

**9.**

**10.**

**11.**

In **12–15**, draw a picture of each.

**12.** Obtuse angle   **13.** Right angle   **14.** Ray   **15.** Acute angle

Animated Glossary
www.pearsonsuccessnet.com

DIGITAL

*For another example, see Set B on page 296.*

A right angle makes a square corner.

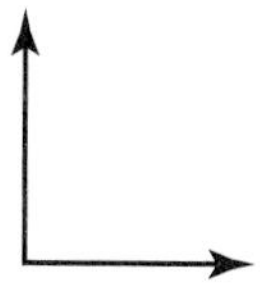

If two lines, line segments, or rays make a right angle, they are perpendicular.

An acute angle is an angle that is open less than a right angle.

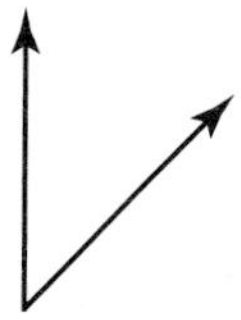

An obtuse angle is an angle that is open more than a right angle.

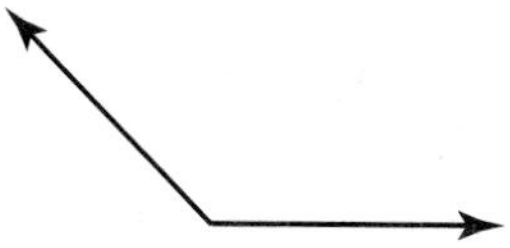

MATHEMATICAL PRACTICES

In **16–18**, tell what type of angle is formed by the hands of the clock. Then tell the time on each clock.

**16.**

**17.**

**18.**

© **19. Writing to Explain** Are all obtuse angles the same size? Draw a picture to explain your answer.

**20.** Which picture shows a pair of perpendicular line segments?

**A**     **B** 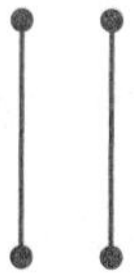    **C**     **D**

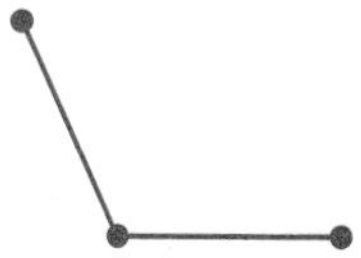

© **21. Reason** Are these lines parallel or intersecting? Explain.

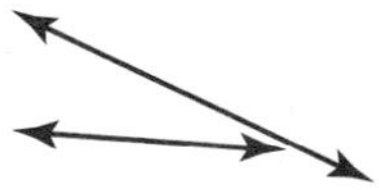

**Tip** *Remember that a line does not end.*

**22.** Which number is greater than 1,051?

**A** 1,005        **C** 947

**B** 1,073        **D** 1,021

**23.** Dori keeps her rock collection in boxes. She puts 8 rocks in each box. She has 5 boxes of rocks. How many rocks are in her collection?

© Common Core

**3.G.1** Understand that shapes in different categories . . . may share attributes, . . . and that the shared attributes can define a larger category. . . . Recognize rhombuses, rectangles, and squares as examples of quadrilaterals, and draw examples of quadrilaterals that do not belong to any of these subcategories.

# Polygons

## What is a polygon?

A polygon is a closed shape made up of line segments. Each line segment is a side of the polygon. The point where two sides meet is a vertex of the polygon. A line segment that connects two vertices that are not next to each other is a diagonal.

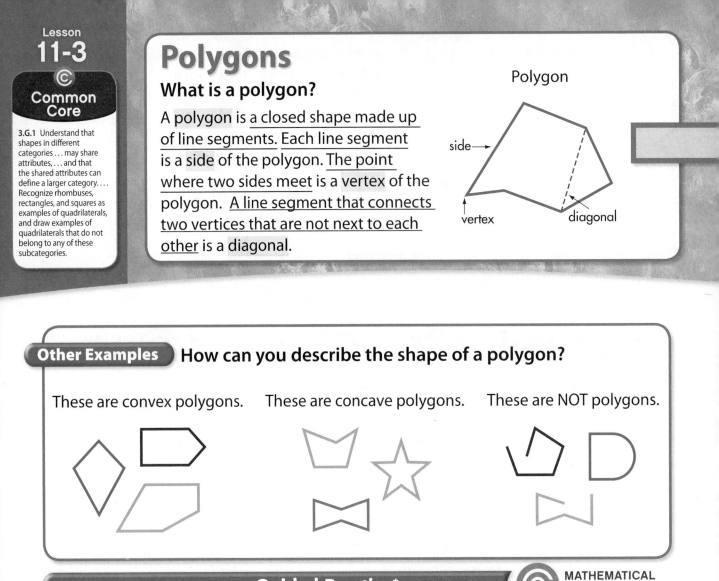

Polygon

side →

↑ vertex

diagonal

---

**Other Examples** **How can you describe the shape of a polygon?**

These are convex polygons.   These are concave polygons.   These are NOT polygons.

---

## Guided Practice*

© MATHEMATICAL PRACTICES

### Do you know HOW?

Name the polygon. Is it concave or convex?

**1.** 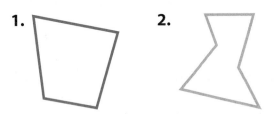     **2.**

Is each figure a polygon? If it is, trace it and draw its diagonals. If it is not, explain why.

**3.** 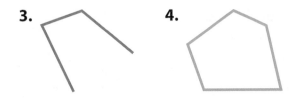     **4.**

### Do you UNDERSTAND?

© **5. Reason** Draw a polygon with 3 sides.

   **a** How many vertices are there?

   **b** How many angles are there?

   **c** What is the name of the polygon?

**6.** A decagon has 10 sides. How many angles does it have?

**7.** Describe an everyday object that is a model of a polygon. What is the name of the polygon?

Animated Glossary
www.pearsonsuccessnet.com
DIGITAL

Polygons are named for the number of sides they have. Two sides meet to form an angle at each vertex.

Some commonly used polygons are named and described in the table.

| Polygon | Number of Sides | Number of Vertices |
|---|---|---|
| Triangle | 3 | 3 |
| Quadrilateral | 4 | 4 |
| Pentagon | 5 | 5 |
| Hexagon | 6 | 6 |
| Octagon | 8 | 8 |
| Decagon | 10 | 10 |

## Independent Practice

In **8–11,** name the polygon.

**8.** **9.** **10.** **11.**

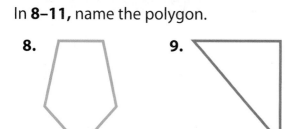
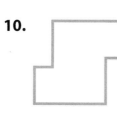

Is each figure in **12–15** a polygon? If so, name it. If not, explain.

**12.** **13.** **14.** **15.**

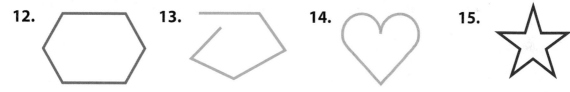

In **16–19,** trace each polygon. Then draw its diagonals.

**16.** **17.** **18.** **19.**

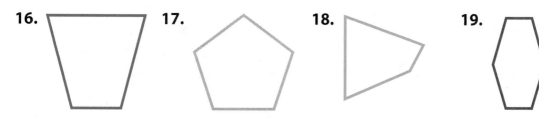

In **20–23,** describe each shape as convex or concave.

**20.** **21.** **22.** **23.**

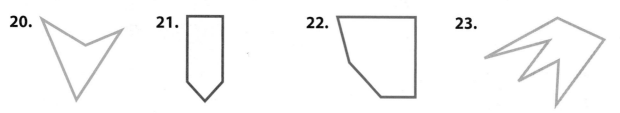

In **24–27,** name the polygon that each traffic sign looks most like.

**24.**

**25.**

**26.**

**27.**

© **28. Look for Patterns** Which polygon comes next in the pattern? Explain your answer.

**29.** Which polygon best describes the top of the box?

**30.** Which best describes this polygon?

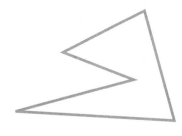

**A** Quadrilateral    **C** Pentagon

**B** Octagon    **D** Hexagon

**A** Octagon    **C** Hexagon

**B** Pentagon    **D** Quadrilateral

For **31–33,** use the illustration of the banana sculpture. The bananas on the front of the sculpture form a polygon with 3 sides.

**31.** Which polygon best describes the front of this sculpture?

**32.** How many vertices does the polygon have?

© **33. Construct Arguments** Does the polygon have diagonals? Explain why or why not.

© **34. Look for Patterns** Copy and complete by writing the missing number in each pattern.

**a** 25, 50, 75, 100, ▢, 150

**b** 75, 70, 65, 60, ▢, 50

# Mixed Problem Solving

Read the article below. Then, answer the questions.

**Not Just a Pretty Design**

The garden spider is finally still after about an hour of work. It is sitting near the center of the web it has made. It is waiting for an insect to become trapped. The insect will be its food.

The web looks like a bicycle wheel with spokes. The silk threads that come out from the center point are called radial threads. Other silk threads go across the spokes to make circle shapes, or spirals. These spiral threads are sticky.

A garden spider's web can be as wide as 16 inches. The radial threads in the web are between 5 and 10 inches long. There are hundreds of spiral threads. Some of the spiral threads are less than 1 inch long. Others can be as long as 2 inches.

You can see that the garden spider's web is more than just a pretty design. It is a complex trap with many parts.

> This garden spider's web has 30 radial threads.

1. In the last sentence of the article, what does the word *complex* mean?

2. What do you think will happen next?

3. Suppose a garden spider's web is 16 inches wide. About how many inches is it from the center to the outer edge?

In **4** and **5**, use the table.

ⓒ 4. **Use Tools** How much longer is a tarantula than a funnel-web spider?

ⓒ 5. **Model** Draw a Picture and Write a Number Sentence to solve this problem.

   Which kind of spider is about 80 millimeters longer than the black widow?

| Kind of Spider | Body Length in Millimeters |
| --- | --- |
| Black Widow | 19 |
| Funnel-web | 12 |
| Tarantula | 100 |
| Wolf | 25 |

Lesson
**11-4**

**Common Core**

3.G.1 Understand that shapes in different categories . . . may share attributes, . . . and that the shared attributes can define a larger category. . . . Recognize rhombuses, rectangles, and squares as examples of quadrilaterals, and draw examples of quadrilaterals that do not belong to any of these subcategories.

# Triangles

## How can you describe triangles?

Triangles can be described by their sides.

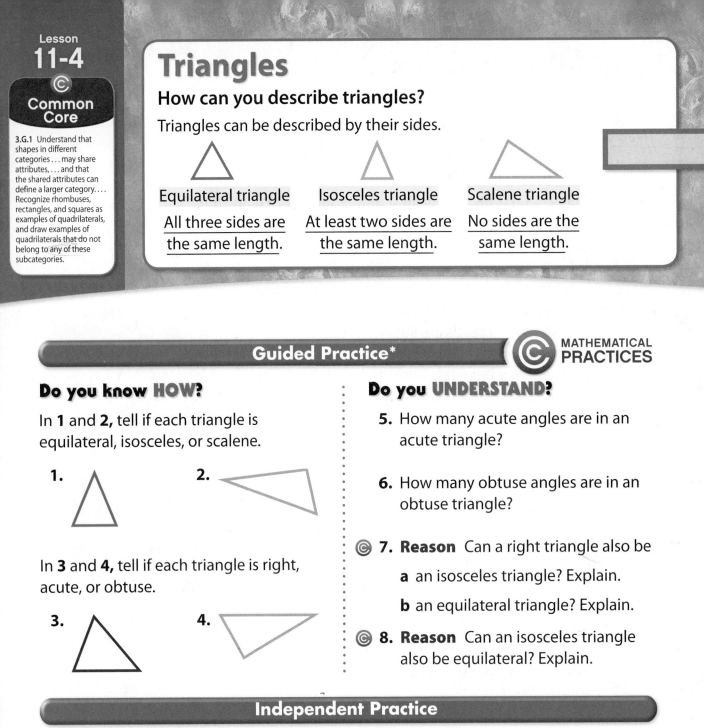

**Equilateral triangle**
All three sides are the same length.

**Isosceles triangle**
At least two sides are the same length.

**Scalene triangle**
No sides are the same length.

---

## Guided Practice*

**MATHEMATICAL PRACTICES**

### Do you know HOW?

In **1** and **2**, tell if each triangle is equilateral, isosceles, or scalene.

**1.**

**2.**

In **3** and **4**, tell if each triangle is right, acute, or obtuse.

**3.**

**4.**

### Do you UNDERSTAND?

**5.** How many acute angles are in an acute triangle?

**6.** How many obtuse angles are in an obtuse triangle?

Ⓒ **7. Reason** Can a right triangle also be

  **a** an isosceles triangle? Explain.

  **b** an equilateral triangle? Explain.

Ⓒ **8. Reason** Can an isosceles triangle also be equilateral? Explain.

---

## Independent Practice

In **9–12**, tell if each triangle is equilateral, isosceles, or scalene.
If a triangle has two names, give the name that best describes it.

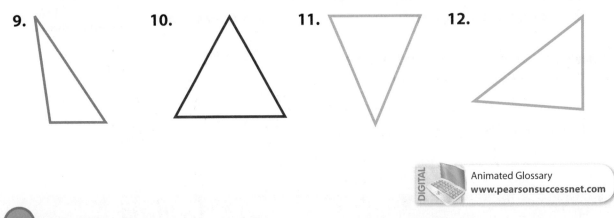

**9.**    **10.**    **11.**    **12.**

**Animated Glossary**
www.pearsonsuccessnet.com

DIGITAL

*For another example, see Set D on page 296.*

Triangles can be described by their angles.

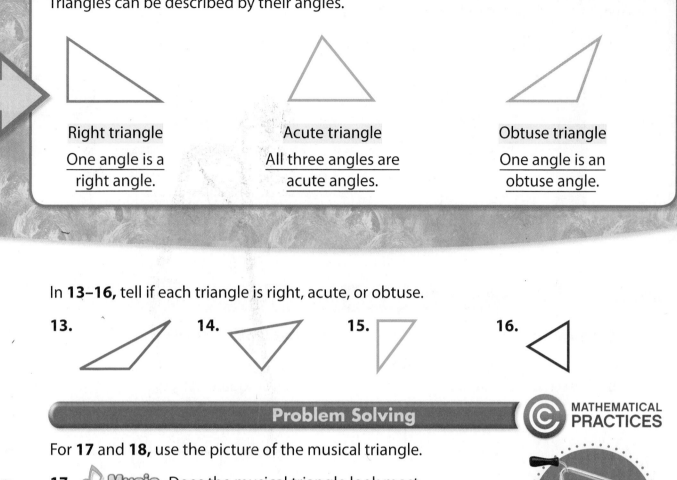

**Right triangle**
One angle is a
right angle.

**Acute triangle**
All three angles are
acute angles.

**Obtuse triangle**
One angle is an
obtuse angle.

In **13–16,** tell if each triangle is right, acute, or obtuse.

13.         14.         15.         16.

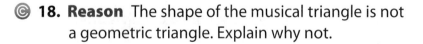

**Problem Solving**

**MATHEMATICAL
PRACTICES**

For **17** and **18,** use the picture of the musical triangle.

17. ♪ **Music** Does the musical triangle look most
like an equilateral triangle, an isosceles triangle,
or a scalene triangle?

Ⓒ 18. **Reason** The shape of the musical triangle is not
a geometric triangle. Explain why not.

19. Look at the sentence below.
Write the word that will make it true.

An obtuse triangle has one obtuse
angle and two ___?___ angles.

Ⓒ 20. **Use Structure** Draw a picture of a
rectangle. Show how you can make
one straight cut in the rectangle to
form two right triangles.

21. Which pair of triangle names best describes this pennant?

  **A** Equilateral triangle, acute triangle

  **B** Equilateral triangle, right triangle

  **C** Isosceles triangle, acute triangle

  **D** Isosceles triangle, obtuse triangle

Ⓒ 22. **Communicate** Why is it impossible for a triangle
to have two right angles?

**3.G.1** Understand that
shapes in different
categories . . . may share
attributes, . . . and that
the shared attributes can
define a larger category. . . .
Recognize rhombuses,
rectangles, and squares as
examples of quadrilaterals,
and draw examples of
quadrilaterals that do not
belong to any of these
subcategories.

# Quadrilaterals

## What are some special names for quadrilaterals?

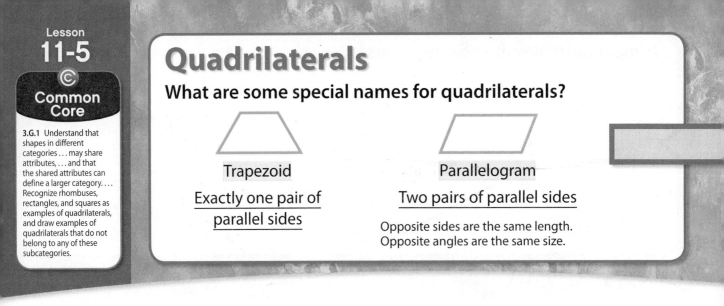

Trapezoid

Exactly one pair of
parallel sides

Parallelogram

Two pairs of parallel sides

Opposite sides are the same length.
Opposite angles are the same size.

---

### Guided Practice*

MATHEMATICAL
PRACTICES

#### Do you know HOW?

In **1–4,** write as many special names as
possible for each quadrilateral.

**1.** 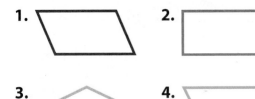      **2.**

**3.**      **4.**

#### Do you UNDERSTAND?

**5.** This figure is a rectangle, but it is
NOT a square. Why?

© **6. Reason** Draw two different
quadrilaterals that are not a
rectangle, square, or rhombus.

**7.** Why is a square a parallelogram?

---

### Independent Practice

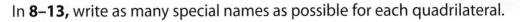

In **8–13,** write as many special names as possible for each quadrilateral.

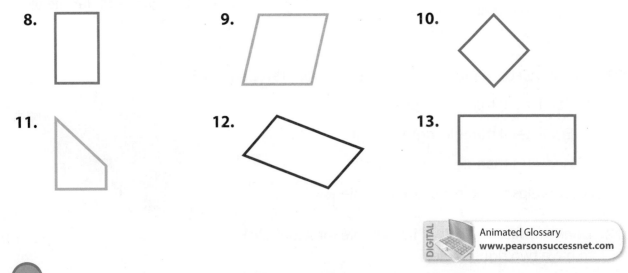

**8.**      **9.**      **10.**

**11.**      **12.**      **13.**

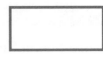

DIGITAL
Animated Glossary
www.pearsonsuccessnet.com

*For another example, see Set C on page 296.*

## Some quadrilaterals have more than one special name.

**Rectangle**

Four right angles

A *rectangle* is a special *parallelogram*.

**Rhombus**

All sides the same length

A *rhombus* is a special *parallelogram*.

**Square**

Four right angles and all sides the same length

A *square* is a special *parallelogram*. It is a combination of a *rectangle* and a *rhombus*.

---

In **14–17,** write the name that best describes the quadrilateral. Draw a picture to help.

**14.** A rectangle with all sides the same length

**15.** A quadrilateral with only one pair of parallel sides

**16.** A parallelogram with four right angles

**17.** A rhombus with four right angles

## Problem Solving

**MATHEMATICAL PRACTICES**

**18.** What is the shape of the wheels of this bike? How is this shape different from the wheels on most bikes?

© **19. Reason** I am a special quadrilateral with opposite sides the same length. What special quadrilateral could I be? (*Hint:* There is more than one correct answer.)

© **20. Construct Arguments** How are a rectangle and a rhombus alike? How are they different?

**21.** Sue bought a book for $12, two maps for $7 each, and postcards for $4. What was her total cost before tax?

**22.** Lee made this block tower. If he adds two more stories like those in the picture, how many blocks will be in the whole tower?

**A** 22 **B** 20 **C** 16 **D** 12

Common
Core

3.G.1 Understand that
shapes in different
categories . . . may share
attributes, . . . and that
the shared attributes can
define a larger category. . . .
Recognize rhombuses,
rectangles, and squares as
examples of quadrilaterals,
and draw examples of
quadrilaterals that do not
belong to any of these
subcategories.
Also 3.G.2

# Combining and Separating Shapes

## How can you combine or separate shapes to make other shapes?

Josey has these two right triangles that are exactly alike. She wants to put them together to make a new shape. Josey puts them together so that two sides match exactly. What shapes can she make?

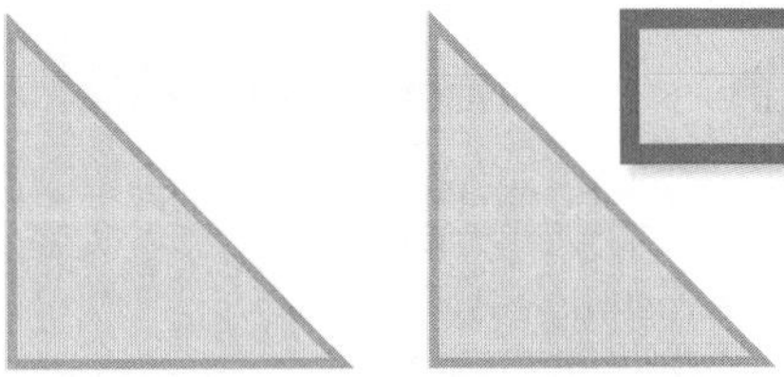

---

## Other Examples

### You can use diagonals to separate a shape into other shapes.

You can separate a hexagon into different kinds of triangles.

You can separate a pentagon into a triangle and a quadrilateral.

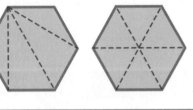

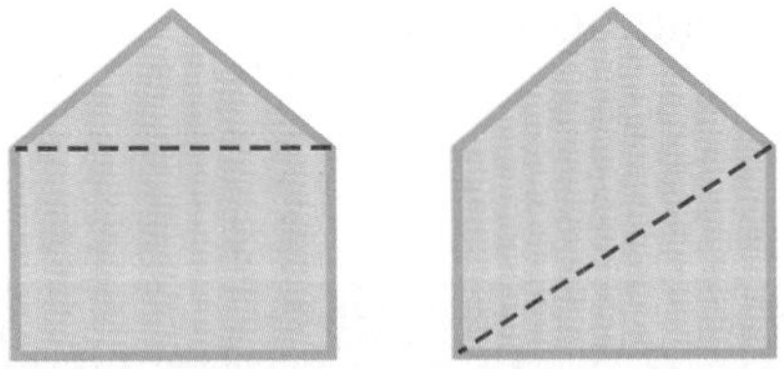

---

## Guided Practice*

**MATHEMATICAL PRACTICES**

### Do you know HOW?

1. What shape can you make by putting together two squares that are exactly alike? two pentagons? two hexagons? Remember to match up the sides.

In **2** and **3**, trace the polygons. Draw one diagonal to make new shapes. Name the new shapes you make.

2.

3.

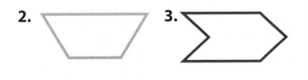

### Do you UNDERSTAND?

4. What other shape can you make with Josey's two right triangles shown above?

© 5. **Use Structure** Draw a hexagon. Separate it with one diagonal. What shapes did you make? Find another way to make different shapes using a different diagonal.

6. Kelly has a square sandwich. She wants to cut it into shapes using diagonals. What shapes could she make?

*For another example, see Set E on page 297.

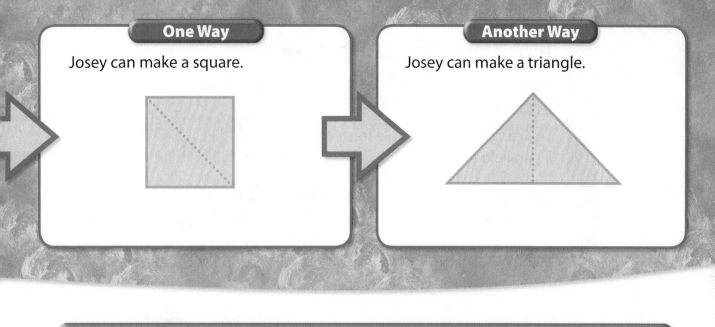

## One Way

Josey can make a square.

## Another Way

Josey can make a triangle.

## Independent Practice

In **7–9**, write the name of a polygon that can be made by matching two sides of the shapes.

**Tip** *There may be more than one way.*

**7.**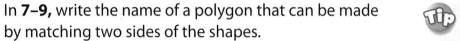

**8.**

**9.**

In **10–12**, trace the polygons. Draw two or more diagonals to make the new shapes named.

**10.**

3 triangles

**11.**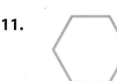

2 triangles and 1 rectangle

**12.**

4 triangles and 1 square

## Problem Solving

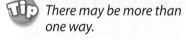
MATHEMATICAL PRACTICES

**13.** Mark has a rhombus, a rectangle, a triangle, a square, and a trapezoid.

    **a** Which two shapes can he put together to make a pentagon?

    **b** Which three shapes can he put together to make a hexagon?

**14.** Use the picture at the right. What two shapes make up the front of the Modis Tower?

© **15. Reason** Al drew all of a shape's diagonals. He made four small triangles. Which shape did he start with?

    **A** Triangle    **B** Pentagon    **C** Rectangle    **D** Hexagon

Modis Tower in Jacksonville, Florida

© **Common Core**

**3.G.1** Understand that shapes in different categories . . . may share attributes, . . . and that the shared attributes can define a larger category. . . . Recognize rhombuses, rectangles, and squares as examples of quadrilaterals, and draw examples of quadrilaterals that do not belong to any of these subcategories.
Also **3.G.2**

# Making New Shapes

### How can you use all the parts of a shape to make a new shape?

You can make a rectangle from a parallelogram.

---

## Guided Practice*

© **MATHEMATICAL PRACTICES**

### Do you know HOW?

In **1** and **2,** trace and carefully cut out each shape. Then cut along the dashed lines. Rearrange the pieces to make the new shape.

**1.** Start with a square. Make a different kind of rectangle.

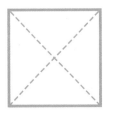

**2.** Start with a rectangle. Make a triangle.

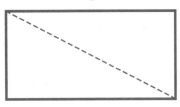

### Do you UNDERSTAND?

**3.** Suppose you cut the parallelogram above along a diagonal. Rearrange the pieces. What shape did you make?

**4.** What other shapes could you make from the four triangles in Exercise 1?

© **5. Construct Arguments** Sue cuts this parallelogram on the dashed lines.

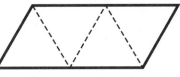

Can she rearrange the pieces to make one large triangle? Explain or draw a picture.

---

## Independent Practice

In **6–8,** suppose you cut each polygon along the dashed lines. Could you arrange the pieces to make the new shape? If so, draw the new shape.

**6.** A pentagon?

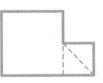

**7.** A parallelogram?

**8.** A square?

*For another example, see Set F on page 297.*

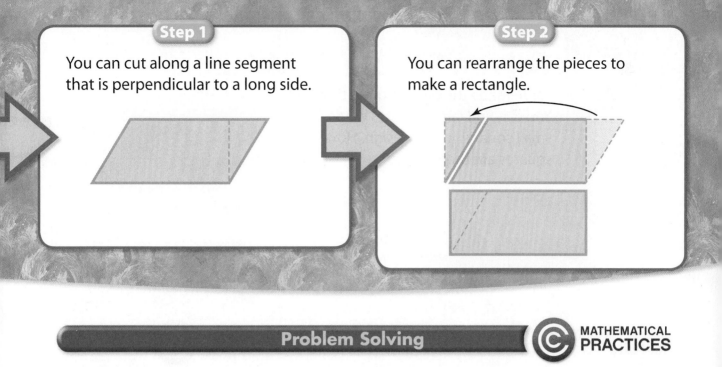

**Step 1**

You can cut along a line segment that is perpendicular to a long side.

**Step 2**

You can rearrange the pieces to make a rectangle.

---

**Problem Solving**

In **9** and **10**, trace and carefully cut out the shapes. Then cut along the dashed diagonals. Rearrange the pieces to make the new shape.

**9.** Start with this octagon. Make a triangle.

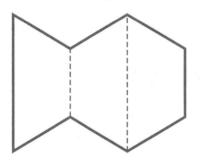

**10.** Start with this hexagon. Make a pentagon.

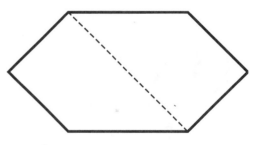

© **11. Model** Gifford School has 542 students. Larson School has *n* students. There are 928 students at Larson and Gifford schools. Write an equation and solve for *n* to find the number of students at Larson.

© **12. Be Precise** Orlando International Airport has 4 parallel runways. Draw a picture to show what the runways might look like on a map. Explain your reasoning.

**13.** Peter cuts a shape into two pieces. He rearranges them to make the shape at the right. Which shape did he start with?

A      B      C      D

3.G.2 Partition shapes into parts with equal areas. Express the area of each part as a unit fraction of the whole. *For example, partition a shape into 4 parts with equal area, and describe the area of each part as 1/4 of the area of the shape.*

Problem Solving

# Solve a Simpler Problem

Taryn made the tile design at the right. You can find large squares made up of small squares in her design. How many squares are there in all?

## Guided Practice*

**MATHEMATICAL PRACTICES**

### Do you know HOW?

1. Louise sees that this tile design has triangles made up of smaller triangles. How many triangles are there in all?

   (HINT: Make a list. Look for a large triangle as well as small triangles.)

### Do you UNDERSTAND?

2. In the example above, what simpler problems were used? Tell why these were used.

3. **Write a Problem** Write and solve a problem about shapes that you can solve by solving a simpler problem.

## Independent Practice

**MATHEMATICAL PRACTICES**

4. **Persevere** This design has rectangles that are several different sizes. How many rectangles are there in all?

   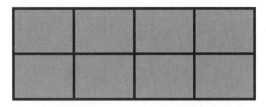

5. Four friends met and each person shook hands with everyone else once. How many handshakes in all were there?

   (Hint: First solve for 2 or 3 friends. Draw a picture and make a table to help.)

### Applying Math Practices

- What am I asked to find?
- What else can I try?
- How are quantities related?
- How can I explain my work?
- How can I use math to model the problem?
- Can I use tools to help?
- Is my work precise?
- Why does this work?
- How can I generalize?

*For another example, see Set G on page 297.*

I can solve a simpler problem.

**Step 1:** I can look for squares inside squares and count the number of each size square.

**Step 2:** Then I can add to find the total number of squares.

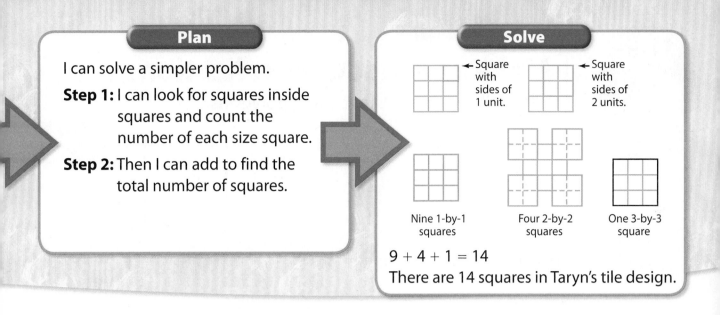

← Square with sides of 1 unit.

← Square with sides of 2 units.

Nine 1-by-1 squares

Four 2-by-2 squares

One 3-by-3 square

$9 + 4 + 1 = 14$

There are 14 squares in Taryn's tile design.

---

You may use a picture, a table, or a list to help solve **6–12.**

**6.** **Art** Isa made a paper chain. She used the pattern below.

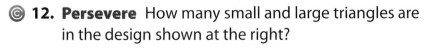

Isa ended with a yellow link. If she used 10 blue links, how many yellow links did she use?

**7.** The Nunez family is visiting the state aquarium. There are 2 adults and 3 children in the family. Adult tickets are $10 each and children's tickets are $6 each. A family ticket is $35 and admits 5 people. How much money will the Nunez's save by buying a family ticket?

**8.** Rachel had an apple. She cut it into two equal pieces. Then she cut each piece into two equal pieces. She ate one piece of apple. How many pieces did Rachel have left? Draw a picture to explain.

**© 9. Reason** Chris made 9 pancakes. He kept 3 pancakes and then gave an equal number to each of his two sisters. No pancakes were left. How many pancakes did each sister get?

**© 10. Look for Patterns** At a store's grand opening, the first customer gets a free mug, the second a poster, the third a pen, and the fourth a key ring. Then the pattern starts again. If the pattern continues, what item will the 18th customer get?

**11.** Three pizzas were cut into 8 slices each. Six friends ate all of the pizza, and each person ate the same number of slices. How many slices did each person eat?

**© 12. Persevere** How many small and large triangles are in the design shown at the right?

**A** 8      **B** 10      **C** 12      **D** 14

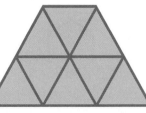

**Common Core**

**3.G.1** Understand that shapes in different categories . . . may share attributes, . . . and that the shared attributes can define a larger category. . . . Recognize rhombuses, rectangles, and squares as examples of quadrilaterals, and draw examples of quadrilaterals that do not belong to any of these subcategories.

**Problem Solving**

# Make and Test Generalizations
## What is the same in these three polygons?

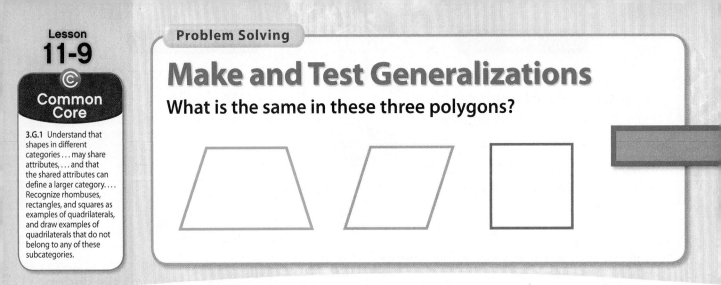

---

## Guided Practice*

**MATHEMATICAL PRACTICES**

### Do you know HOW?

In **1** and **2,** make and test a generalization for each set of polygons.

**1.**

**2.**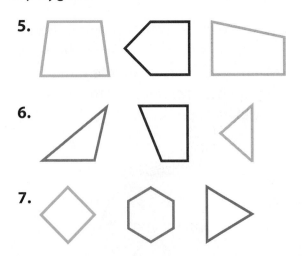

### Do you UNDERSTAND?

**3.** Look at the polygons above. All sides of the second and third polygons **are** the same length. So why is the friend's generalization incorrect?

Ⓒ **4. Write a Problem** Draw a set of polygons that are the same in some way. Ask a classmate to make a generalization.

---

## Independent Practice

**MATHEMATICAL PRACTICES**

In **5–7,** make a generalization for each set of polygons.

**5.**

**6.**

**7.**

### Applying Math Practices

• What am I asked to find?
• What else can I try?
• How are quantities related?
• How can I explain my work?
• How can I use math to model the problem?
• Can I use tools to help?
• Is my work precise?
• Why does this work?
• How can I generalize?

**Make a Generalization**

Your friend says that the sides are all the same length.

You say that they all have 4 sides.

**Test the Generalization**

Notice that the top and bottom of this polygon are not the same length. Your friend's generalization is not correct!

not the same length

You see that the first polygon has 4 sides. The second has 4 sides. So does the third. Your generalization is correct!

8. Mr. Redbird makes tables that have 3 legs and tables that have 4 legs. The tables that he made this month have 18 legs in all. How many tables of each kind did he make?

9. Anna earns $4 for each hour that she babysits. She babysat for 2 hours last week and 5 hours this week. How much did she earn in all?

10. How are the four numbers 18, 24, 16, and 40 alike?

11. Compare each sum to its addends in these number sentences:

$34 + 65 = 99$     $8 + 87 = 95$     $435 + 0 = 435$

Make a generalization about addends and sums for whole numbers.

© 12. **Critique Reasoning** Is the generalization below true? If not, explain or draw a picture to show why not.

If a shape is made up of line segments, then it is a polygon.

© 13. **Persevere** Ari gave his friends these clues about a secret number.

- The number has three digits.
- The hundreds digit is less than 3.
- The tens digit is twice the ones digit.
- The number is odd.

What are all of the possible secret numbers?

14. What is the same in these polygons?

A  All are convex.

B  All have two right angles.

C  All have only one acute angle.

D  All have four sides.

**Set A,** pages 276–277

Write the name for the following.

The lines cross at one point.
They are intersecting lines.

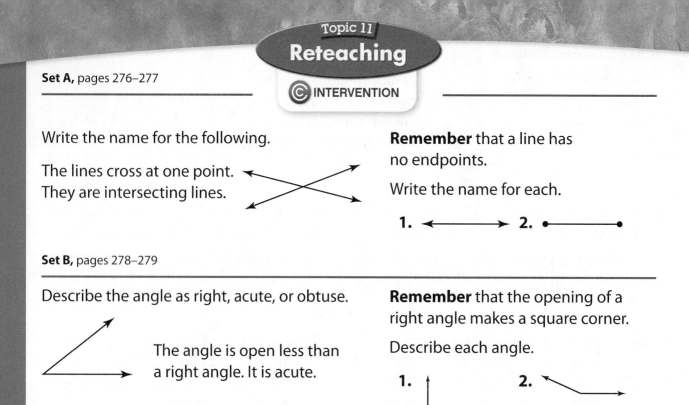

**Remember** that a line has no endpoints.

Write the name for each.

1. ← — — → 2. •— — —•

**Set B,** pages 278–279

Describe the angle as right, acute, or obtuse.

The angle is open less than a right angle. It is acute.

**Remember** that the opening of a right angle makes a square corner.

Describe each angle.

1.    2.

**Set C,** pages 280–282, 286–287

Is the shape a polygon? If it is a polygon, give its name. If not, explain why.

The shape is closed and is made up of line segments. It is a polygon.

The shape has 5 sides. It is a pentagon.

**Remember** that all quadrilaterals have four sides.

Is each shape a polygon? If so, give its name. If not, explain why.

1. ⬡     2. D

Write all possible names.

3. ▢     4. ⏢

**Set D,** pages 284–285

Tell if the triangle below is equilateral, isosceles, or scalene. Then tell if the triangle is right, acute, or obtuse.

None of the sides are the same length. One angle is obtuse.

The triangle is a scalene triangle.
The triangle is an obtuse triangle.

**Remember** that no sides of a scalene triangle are the same length.

Describe each triangle by its sides and by its angles.

1. △     2. ◿

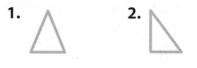

**Set E,** pages 288–289

Two trapezoids can make a hexagon.

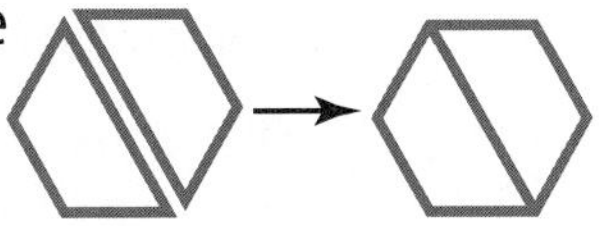

Draw a diagonal to separate a hexagon into a triangle and pentagon.

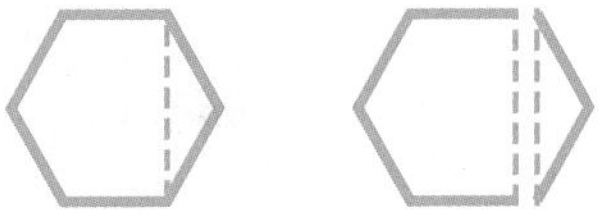

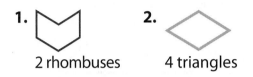

**Remember** a diagonal joins two vertices not next to each other.

Trace each polygon. Draw diagonals to make the new shapes.

**1.** 

2 rhombuses

**2.** 

4 triangles

**Set F,** pages 290–291

Tim cuts a square along one diagonal. Then he rearranges the pieces to make a new shape. What new shape can he make?

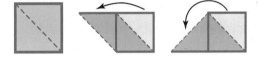

Tim can make a parallelogram or a triangle.

**Remember** to match the sides.

Can you make each shape named by cutting on the dashed lines? If so, show how.

**1.** a triangle

**2.** a square

**Set G,** pages 292–293

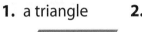

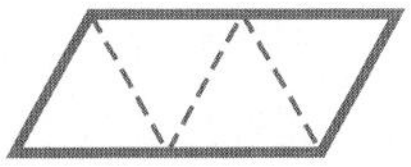

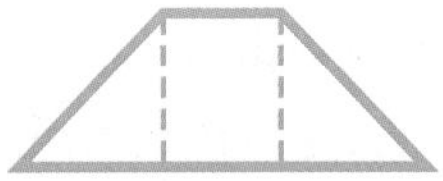

How many rectangles are in the design?

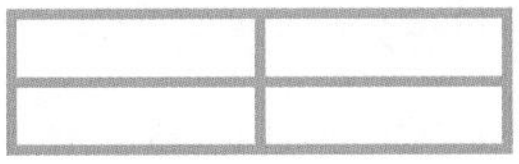

Count each kind of rectangle.

4 

2 

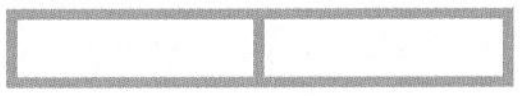

2 

1 

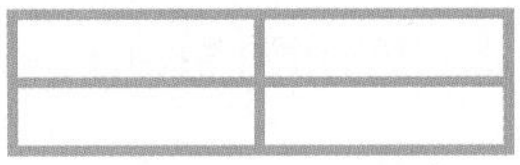

4 + 2 + 2 + 1 = 9 There are 9 rectangles.

**Remember** to use the answers to the simpler problems.

**1.** How many triangles are in the design below?

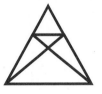

**Set H,** pages 294–295

Make and test a generalization for the shapes.

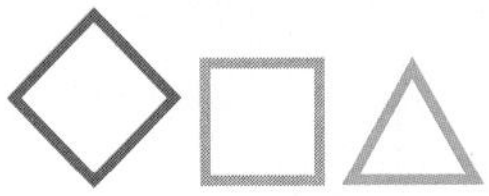

Make a generalization. *Each polygon has sides that are the same length.*

Test the generalization. *All of the polygons have sides that are the same length.*

**Remember** that a generalization must apply to the entire set.

Make and test a generalization.

**1.**

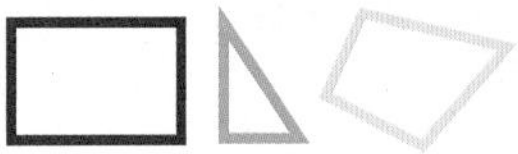

**Multiple Choice**

© ASSESSMENT

**1.** Latisha cut this trapezoid on the dashed line. She rearranged the pieces to make a new shape. Which new shape could she have made? (11-7)

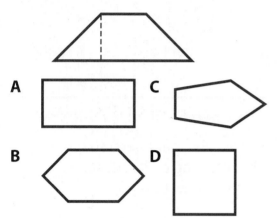

**A**

**C**

**B**

**D**

**2.** Which clock face below shows the hands forming an acute angle? (11-2)

**A**

**B**

**C**

**D**

**3.** Keenan bought a yo-yo in an unusually shaped box. Which best describes the shape of the top of the box? (11-3)

**A** Hexagon

**B** Pentagon

**C** Octagon

**D** Quadrilateral

**4.** Which best describes all three triangles? (11-9)

**A** They are acute.

**B** They are isosceles.

**C** They are obtuse.

**D** They are scalene.

**5.** Which shape is a polygon? (11-3)

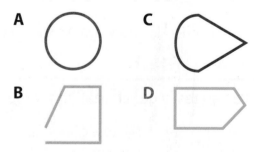

**A**

**C**

**B**

**D**

**6.** Four friends made shapes out of colored paper. Whose shape has only one set of parallel sides? (11-5)

Melissa          Nigel

Pat          Rahmi

**7.** Part of a nature trail map is shown below. Which two trails represent parallel lines? (11-1)

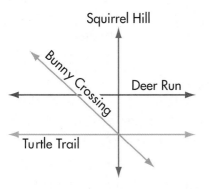

Squirrel Hill

Bunny Crossing

Deer Run

Turtle Trail

**8.** How many triangles in all are in this design? (11-8)

**9.** The students ran a course from the flag to the tree, to the trash can, and then back to the flag. What type of triangle did the course form? (11-4)

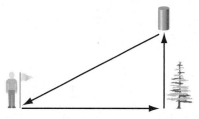

**10.** What two quadrilaterals did Kim use to make up the rug design? (11-5)

**11.** Rosa made a new shape by matching sides of these two triangles.

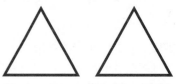

Describe a shape Rosa could have made. Draw a picture to help. (11-6)

**12.** How many diagonals does a pentagon have? Draw a picture to help. (11-3)

**13.** Name and draw a picture of a quadrilateral that is NOT a square, rectangle, or rhombus. (11-5)

Trace the patterns below on a separate sheet of paper. Then trace along the lines of the pattern to draw the shapes.

**1.** Draw a red hexagon. Then draw a blue rhombus inside the hexagon.

**2.** Draw a green trapezoid. How many triangles make up your trapezoid?

**3.** Draw a purple parallelogram. How many triangles make up your parallelogram?

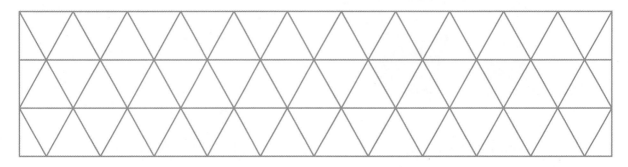

**4.** Draw a rectangle and then draw all of its diagonals. What new shapes did you make?

**5.** Can a right triangle also be an isosceles triangle? Draw a picture to support your answer.

**6.** Trace the pattern below on a separate sheet of paper. Look for right triangles that are the same size and shape. Draw as many shapes as you can that are made by putting together these right triangles. Write the names of the shapes you made.

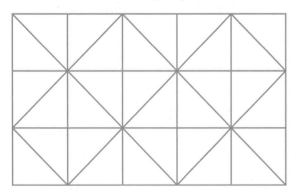

**7.** Use the pattern below that you traced on a separate sheet. Look for right triangles in the pattern. How many different-sized right triangles can you find in this pattern? Describe the size of each different triangle by counting how many of the smallest right triangles it contains.

Topic
**12** **Time**

▼ How long does the Hubble Telescope take to orbit Earth? You will find out in Lesson 12-2.

# Review What You Know!

## Vocabulary

Choose the best term from the box.

- hour
- minute
- o'clock
- day

1. Luz read the time. She saw that the time was nine __?__.

2. It takes about one __?__ for Anita to tie her shoelaces.

3. It takes about one __?__ for Tom to travel 50 miles on a train.

## Time

Write each time.

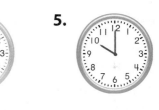

4.          5.

## Skip Counting

Skip count to find the missing numbers.

6. 9, 18, 27, ___, ___, 54

7. 5, 10, ___, ___, 25, 30

8. 10, ___, 30, 40, ___

9. 30, 60, ___, 120, ___

©10. **Writing to Explain** Draw a clock face. Draw the hour hand on the 8 and the minute hand on the 12. Write the time. Explain how to read the time on a clock.

**Topic Essential Question**
- How can lengths of time be measured and found?

# Interactive Learning

**Pose the problem.** Start each lesson by working together to solve problems. It will help you make sense of math.

### Applying Math Practices

- What am I asked to find?
- What else can I try?
- How are quantities related?
- How can I explain my work?
- How can I use math to model the problem?
- Can I use tools to help?
- Is my work precise?
- Why does this work?
- How can I generalize?

### Lesson 12-1

© **Use Tools** Use the clock face to show the given times and solve the problem.

Alana needs to call her friend at 7:15. Then she needs to leave for school at 7:30. How can you use your clock face to show these times? If she left for school at "half past 7," would the clock face change? Explain.

### Lesson 12-2

© **Be Precise** Solve. Tell how you decided your answer for this problem shows the exact time.

An airplane is scheduled to arrive at 8:47. How can you use a clock to show this time?

**Lesson 12-3**

ⓒ **Generalize** Solve. Tell how you decided.

A class is going to collect newspapers as part of a recycling project. They will collect newspapers for 3 weeks. How many days are in 3 weeks?

| | | | APRIL | | | |
|---|---|---|---|---|---|---|
| S | M | T | W | T | F | S |
| | | | 1 | 2 | 3 | 4 |
| 5 | 6 | 7 | 8 | 9 | 10 | 11 |
| 12 | 13 | 14 | 15 | 16 | 17 | 18 |
| 19 | 20 | 21 | 22 | 23 | 24 | 25 |
| 26 | 27 | 28 | 29 | 30 | | |

**Lesson 12-4**

ⓒ **Use Tools** Solve any way you choose. Use a clock face to help.

Denise went to see a movie. The movie started at 1:00 P.M. It ended at 2:35 P.M. How long did the movie last?

**Lesson 12-5**

ⓒ **Model** Solve any way you choose. Use a clock face to help.

Nina wants to arrive at the community center at 9:30 A.M. for an art class. It takes her 15 minutes to walk to the center, 15 minutes to get ready, and 30 minutes to make and eat breakfast. What time should she start making breakfast?

**Arrive at Community Center**

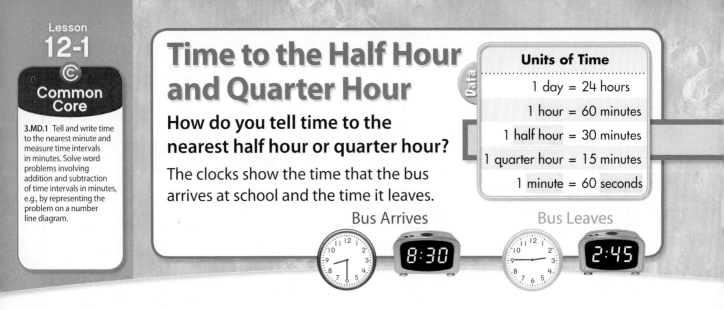

## Lesson 12-1

**Common Core**

3.MD.1 Tell and write time to the nearest minute and measure time intervals in minutes. Solve word problems involving addition and subtraction of time intervals in minutes, e.g., by representing the problem on a number line diagram.

# Time to the Half Hour and Quarter Hour

## How do you tell time to the nearest half hour or quarter hour?

The clocks show the time that the bus arrives at school and the time it leaves.

Bus Arrives · 8:30

Bus Leaves · 2:45

**Units of Time**

| | |
|---|---|
| 1 day | = 24 hours |
| 1 hour | = 60 minutes |
| 1 half hour | = 30 minutes |
| 1 quarter hour | = 15 minutes |
| 1 minute | = 60 seconds |

---

**Another Example** **How do you decide whether the time is A.M. or P.M.?**

The hours of the day between midnight and noon are A.M. hours.
The hours between noon and midnight are P.M. hours.

Would the time the bus arrives at school more likely be 8:30 A.M. or 8:30 P.M.?

8:30 P.M. is in the evening. The bus probably would not arrive at school in the evening. 8:30 A.M. is in the morning.

The bus would more likely arrive at school at 8:30 A.M.

Would the time the bus leaves school more likely be 2:45 A.M. or 2:45 P.M.?

2:45 A.M. is in the middle of the night. The bus probably would not be leaving school at that time. 2:45 P.M. is in the afternoon.

The bus would more likely leave school at 2:45 P.M.

### Explain It

1. Why might it be important to use A.M. or P.M. when you give a time?

2. Would you be more likely to leave your home to go to school at 8:15 A.M. or 8:15 P.M.?

3. Would you be more likely to eat lunch at 12:30 A.M. or 12:30 P.M.?

304

Tell the time the bus arrives.

Write 8:30 in three other ways.

When the minute hand is on the 6, you can say the time is "half past" the hour.

The bus arrives at *eight thirty*, or *half past eight*, or *30 minutes past eight*.

Tell the time the bus leaves.

Write 2:45 in three other ways.

When the minute hand is on the 9, you can say the time is "15 minutes to" or "quarter to" the hour.

The bus leaves at *two forty-five*, or *15 minutes to three*, or *quarter to three*.

---

## Guided Practice*

MATHEMATICAL PRACTICES

### Do you know HOW?

In **1** and **2**, write the time shown on each clock in two ways.

**1.**

**2.**

### Do you UNDERSTAND?

© **3. Reason** In the example above, why do you think the fraction word "quarter" is used for the time when the minute hand is on the 9?

**4.** The clock shows the time that Etta's skating lesson starts. What time does it start? Give the time in 3 ways.

---

## Independent Practice

In **5–7**, write the time shown on each clock in two ways.

**5.**

**6.**

**7.**

Animated Glossary
www.pearsonsuccessnet.com

*For another example, see Set A on page 316.*

In **8–10**, write the time shown on each clock in two ways.

**8.**

**9.**

**10.**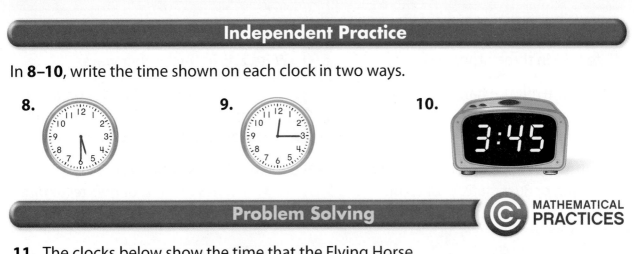

Ⓒ **MATHEMATICAL PRACTICES**

**11.** The clocks below show the time that the Flying Horse Carousel in Rhode Island opens and closes. What time does the carousel open? What time does it close?

Opens      Closes

Ⓒ **12. Construct Arguments** Mr. Boyd gave his students a math test at 10:45. Explain why this time is most likely an A.M. time.

For **13–16**, use the table at the right.

Ⓒ **13. Estimation** Whose bowling score was about 20 points less than Beth's?

**14.** Whose bowling score was 15 points more than Cal's?

**15.** What is the order of the friends' names from greatest to least score?

| Bowling Scores | |
|---|---|
| **Name** | **Score** |
| Cal | 63 |
| Beth | 78 |
| Rusty | 59 |
| Pang | 82 |

Ⓒ **16. Model** Write a number sentence that compares the total of Cal's and Beth's scores with the total of Rusty's and Pang's scores.

**17.** Ronaldo delivers a newspaper to the Hong family between 7:00 A.M. and 8:00 A.M. each day. Which clock shows a time between 7:00 A.M. and 8:00 A.M.?

**A**     **B**     **C**     **D**

## Roman Numerals

The symbols for numbers, or numerals, used by the ancient Romans are still seen today on some clock faces and buildings. They are used as page numbers at the front of many books, including this one.

| Data | Roman numeral | I | V | X | L | C | D | M |
|---|---|---|---|---|---|---|---|---|
| | Decimal value | 1 | 5 | 10 | 50 | 100 | 500 | 1,000 |

Our number system is called the decimal system. It is based on place value. Roman numerals are based on addition and subtraction.

How to read Roman numerals:

$VI = 5 + 1 = 6$  When the symbol for the smaller number is written to the right of the greater number, add. No more than three symbols for smaller numbers are used this way.

$IV = 5 - 1 = 4$  When the symbol for a smaller number is to the left of the greater number, subtract. No more than one symbol for a smaller number is used this way.

## Practice

Write each as a decimal number.

**1.** VII        **2.** XX        **3.** CV        **4.** XIV        **5.** LI

**6.** XXI        **7.** XIX        **8.** DC        **9.** CM        **10.** MC

Write each as a Roman numeral.

**11.** 15        **12.** 30        **13.** 9        **14.** 52        **15.** 60

**16.** 6        **17.** 110        **18.** 400        **19.** 550        **20.** 40

© **21. Use Structure** In Roman numerals, the year 1990 is written as MCMXC, and 2007 is written as MMVII. Write the current year using Roman numerals.

**22.** One movie was made in the year MMIV. Another movie was made in the year MCML. How many years passed between these years?

Lesson
**12-2**

© Common Core

**3.MD.1** Tell and write time to the nearest minute and measure time intervals in minutes. Solve word problems involving addition and subtraction of time intervals in minutes, e.g., by representing the problem on a number line diagram.

# Time to the Minute

## How do you tell time to the nearest minute?

The clock shows the time a train is scheduled to arrive at Pinewood Station. What time is the train scheduled to arrive? Give the time in digital form and in two other ways.

---

**Guided Practice\***

© **MATHEMATICAL PRACTICES**

### Do you know HOW?

In **1** and **2**, write the time shown on each clock in two ways.

**1.**

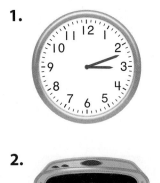

**2.**

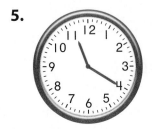

### Do you UNDERSTAND?

© **3. Reason** In the example above, why is 42 minutes past 12 the same as 18 minutes to 1? Explain.

**4.** The clock below shows the time that an airplane landed. Write the time in two ways.

---

**Independent Practice**

In **5–7**, write the time shown on each clock in two ways.

**5.**

**6.**

7:39

**7.**

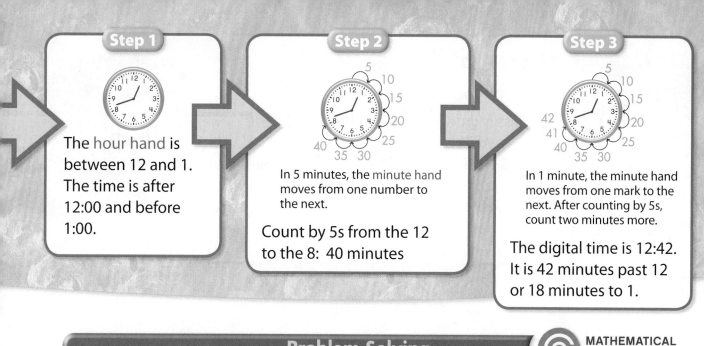

**Step 1**

The hour hand is between 12 and 1. The time is after 12:00 and before 1:00.

**Step 2**

In 5 minutes, the minute hand moves from one number to the next.

Count by 5s from the 12 to the 8: 40 minutes

**Step 3**

In 1 minute, the minute hand moves from one mark to the next. After counting by 5s, count two minutes more.

The digital time is 12:42. It is 42 minutes past 12 or 18 minutes to 1.

## Problem Solving

Ⓒ **MATHEMATICAL PRACTICES**

8. Toya's family went to see a movie. The clock shows the time that the movie ended. Write the digital time.

Ⓒ **9. Be Precise** The Hubble Space Telescope has been moving in its orbit for 1 hour. In 37 more minutes it will complete an orbit. How many minutes does it take the Hubble Space Telescope to complete 1 orbit?

For **10** and **11**, use the sign at the right.

Ⓒ **10. Reason** Roy says that a scarf and a hat together cost about the same as a blanket and a hat. Is his estimate reasonable? Explain.

11. What did Jorge buy at the sale if $19 + $19 + $19 + $23 stands for the total cost?

| Winter Sale | | |
|---|---|---|
| Blanket | | $19 |
| Hat | | $12 |
| Scarf | | $18 |
| Shovel | | $23 |

12. Ross walks his dog between 3:15 P.M. and 4:00 P.M. Which clock shows a time between 3:15 P.M. and 4:00 P.M.?

A          B          C          D

**Lesson**
# 12-3

**Common Core**

**3.MD.1** Tell and write time to the nearest minute and measure time intervals in minutes. Solve word problems involving addition and subtraction of time intervals in minutes, e.g., by representing the problem on a number line diagram.

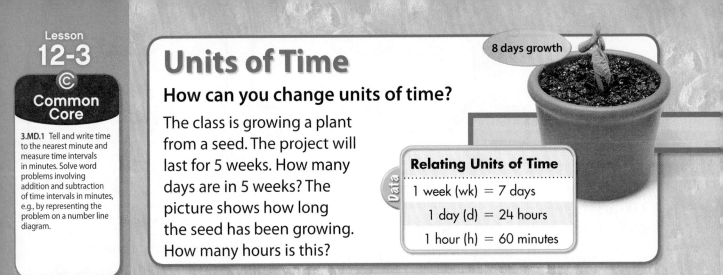

# Units of Time

## How can you change units of time?

The class is growing a plant from a seed. The project will last for 5 weeks. How many days are in 5 weeks? The picture shows how long the seed has been growing. How many hours is this?

**8 days growth**

**Relating Units of Time**

1 week (wk) = 7 days

1 day (d) = 24 hours

1 hour (h) = 60 minutes

---

## Guided Practice*

**MATHEMATICAL PRACTICES**

### Do you know HOW?

For **1–3**, copy and complete to change the units.

**1.** 8 weeks = ▢ days

**2.** 2 days = ▢ hours

**3.** How many days are in 2 weeks, 4 days?

### Do you UNDERSTAND?

**4.** In the example above, why do you multiply the number of weeks by 7?

Ⓒ **5. Reason** At the end of the first week, the class had worked on the science experiment for 6 hours. How many minutes did the class work on the experiment?

---

## Independent Practice

For **6–15**, copy and complete to change the units.

**6.** 3 hours = ▢ minutes

**7.** 5 days = ▢ hours

**8.** 4 hours = ▢ minutes

**9.** 7 weeks = ▢ days

**10.** 3 weeks = ▢ days

**11.** 7 days = ▢ hours

**12.** How many hours are in 3 days, 5 hours?

**13.** How many minutes are in 5 hours, 10 minutes?

**14.** How many days are in 10 weeks?

**15.** How many hours are in 9 days?

*For another example, see Set C on page 317.

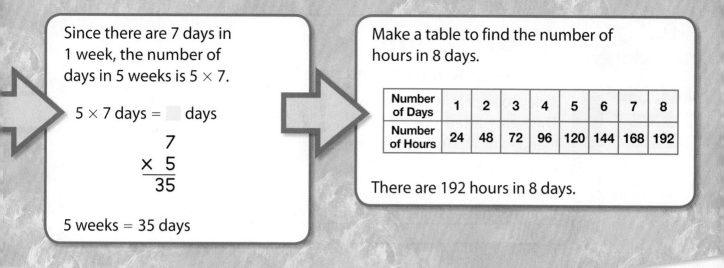

Since there are 7 days in 1 week, the number of days in 5 weeks is $5 \times 7$.

$5 \times 7$ days = ▢ days

$$\begin{array}{r} 7 \\ \times\ 5 \\ \hline 35 \end{array}$$

5 weeks = 35 days

Make a table to find the number of hours in 8 days.

| Number of Days | 1 | 2 | 3 | 4 | 5 | 6 | 7 | 8 |
|---|---|---|---|---|---|---|---|---|
| Number of Hours | 24 | 48 | 72 | 96 | 120 | 144 | 168 | 192 |

There are 192 hours in 8 days.

## Problem Solving

**MATHEMATICAL PRACTICES**

**16.** In 30 more minutes, the International Space Station will complete an orbit. It has been in this orbit for 1 hour. How many minutes does it take the International Space Station to complete 1 orbit?

**17.** A group of high school students helped to prepare samples of materials to send to the International Space Station in 2001. The samples were returned to Earth from space after 4 years. In what year were the samples returned?

For **18** and **19**, use the table at the right.

© **18. Be Precise** Astronauts at the International Space Station took a spacewalk to do tasks outside the station. They finished their tasks in less time than was planned. How many minutes of actual time did the astronauts need?

| Spacewalk | |
|---|---|
| **Planned Time** | 6 hours, 20 minutes |
| **Actual Time** | 5 hours, 54 minutes |

© **19. Writing to Explain** How many fewer minutes than planned did the astronauts need? Explain how you found your answer.

© **20. Communicate** A sailfish can swim as fast as 68 miles per hour. In 1 minute can a sailfish swim as far as 1 mile? Explain your answer.

**21.** What fraction of an hour is 20 minutes? Write your answer in simplest form.

**22.** How many days are in 6 weeks?

    **A** 42         **B** 36         **C** 13         **D** 7

Lesson
12-4

**Common Core**

3.MD.1 Tell and write time to the nearest minute and measure time intervals in minutes. Solve word problems involving addition and subtraction of time intervals in minutes, e.g., by representing the problem on a number line diagram.

# Elapsed Time

## How can you find elapsed time?

Janey took part in a charity walk. The walk started at 7:00 A.M. It ended at 11:20 A.M. How long did the walk last?

**Start**     **End**

**Elapsed time** is the total amount of time that passes from the starting time to the ending time.

---

### Guided Practice*

 **MATHEMATICAL PRACTICES**

#### Do you know **HOW?**

For **1–3**, find the elapsed time.

1. Start Time: 11:00 A.M.
   End Time: 5:00 P.M.

2. Start Time: 1:00 P.M.
   End Time: 4:45 P.M.

3. Start Time: 7:10 A.M.
   End Time: 8:00 A.M.

#### Do you **UNDERSTAND?**

4. **Reason** In the example above, why do you count the minutes by 5s as the minute hand moves to each number on the clock?

5. During the charity walk, lunch was served from 12:00 P.M. until 2:10 P.M. How long was lunch served?

6. A movie started at 2:30 P.M. and ran for 1 hour, 45 minutes. What time did the movie end?

---

### Independent Practice

For **7–15**, find the elapsed time.

7. Start Time: 6:30 P.M.
   End Time: 9:50 P.M.

8. Start Time: 11:00 A.M.
   End Time: 3:55 P.M.

9. Start Time: 5:40 P.M.
   End Time: 6:00 P.M.

10. Start Time: 8:10 A.M.
    End Time: 10:45 A.M.

11. Start Time: 9:15 A.M.
    End Time: 10:45 A.M.

12. Start Time: 10:00 A.M.
    End Time: 3:00 P.M.

13. Start Time: 3:20 P.M.
    End Time: 6:00 P.M.

14. Start Time: 7:30 A.M.
    End Time: 9:45 A.M.

15. Start Time: 12:45 P.M.
    End Time: 2:20 P.M.

Animated Glossary
www.pearsonsuccessnet.com

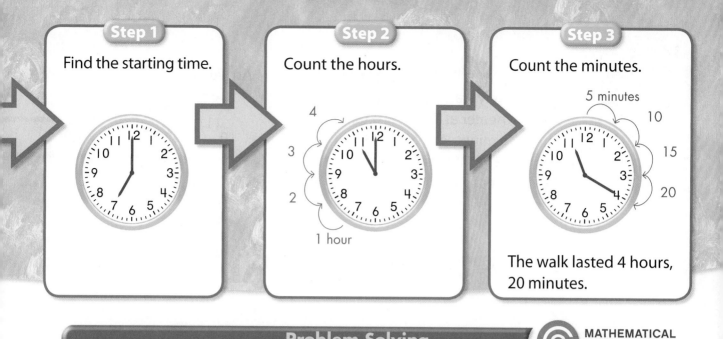

**Step 1**

Find the starting time.

**Step 2**

Count the hours.

**Step 3**

Count the minutes.

5 minutes

1 hour

The walk lasted 4 hours, 20 minutes.

## Problem Solving

MATHEMATICAL
PRACTICES

**16.** The picnic started at 12:10 P.M. and ended at 5:00 P.M. How long did the picnic last?

**17.** The baseball game started at 1:15 P.M. It lasted 2 hours, 45 minutes. What time did the game end?

For **18**, use the number line at right.

© **18. Model** The picnic started at 12:10 P.M. Kevin had arrived 30 minutes later. What time did Kevin arrive?

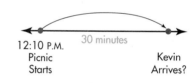

12:10 P.M.
Picnic
Starts

30 minutes

Kevin
Arrives?

Mrs. Flores keeps a list of the amount of time it takes for different items to bake. Use the table at the right for **19** and **20**.

**19.** Which items take less than $\frac{1}{2}$ hour to bake?

© **20. Estimation** About how many more minutes does it take to bake the pasta dish than to bake the granola bars?

| Item | Baking Time in Minutes |
|------|------------------------|
| Bread | 26 |
| Granola Bars | 21 |
| Pasta Dish | 48 |
| Vegetables | 24 |

© **21. Model** The train leaves Carlton at 9:25 A.M. and stops at Elgin at 10:55 A.M. How long is the ride?

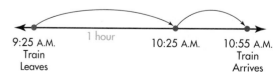

9:25 A.M.
Train
Leaves

1 hour

10:25 A.M.

10:55 A.M.
Train
Arrives

**A** 1 hour, 20 minutes    **C** 1 hour, 30 minutes

**B** 1 hour, 25 minutes    **D** 1 hour, 35 minutes

© Common Core

**3.MD.1** Tell and write time to the nearest minute and measure time intervals in minutes. Solve word problems involving addition and subtraction of time intervals in minutes, e.g., by representing the problem on a number line diagram.

Problem Solving

# Work Backward

Eric's family wants to arrive at the movie theater at 2:30 P.M. It takes them 30 minutes to travel to the theater, 15 minutes to get ready, and 30 minutes to eat lunch. What time should the family start eating lunch?

**Arrive at Theater**

---

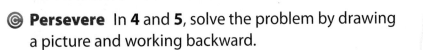
## Guided Practice*

© MATHEMATICAL PRACTICES

### Do you know HOW?

Solve the problem by drawing a picture and working backward.

**1.** The swim meet starts at 10:15 A.M. It takes Abby 15 minutes to walk to the pool. On her way, she needs 15 minutes to shop. It takes her 30 minutes to get ready. What time should Abby start getting ready?

### Do you UNDERSTAND?

**2.** In the example above, why do the arrows in the Solve step move to the left?

© **3. Write a Problem** Write a problem that you can solve by working backward.

---

## Independent Practice

© MATHEMATICAL PRACTICES

© **Persevere** In **4** and **5**, solve the problem by drawing a picture and working backward.

**4.** Emilio read the thermometer one evening. The temperature was 56°F. This temperature was 9°F less than the temperature that afternoon. The afternoon temperature was 7°F greater than the temperature in the morning. What was the temperature in the morning?

**5.** Jana's dentist appointment is at 4:30 P.M. It takes Jana 20 minutes to walk to the dentist's office, 20 minutes to get ready, and 30 minutes to clean her room. What time should she start cleaning her room?

**Applying Math Practices**

- What am I asked to find?
- What else can I try?
- How are quantities related?
- How can I explain my work?
- How can I use math to model the problem?
- Can I use tools to help?
- Is my work precise?
- Why does this work?
- How can I generalize?

*What do I know?*    Arrive 2:30 P.M.,
30 minutes to travel,
15 minutes to get
ready, 30 minutes
to eat lunch

*What am I being asked to find?*    The time the family
should start eating
lunch

Draw a picture to show each change.

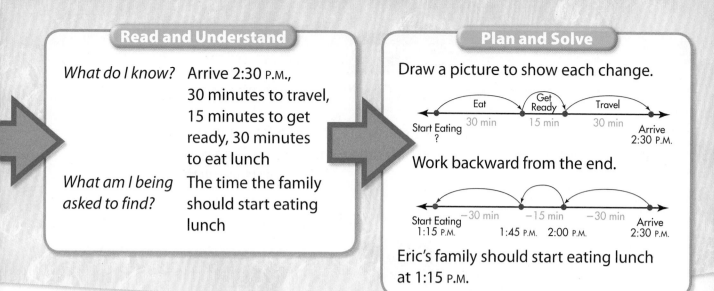

Work backward from the end.

Eric's family should start eating lunch
at 1:15 P.M.

---

© **6. Model** Use the number line above.
Eric's family decides to clean their
garage before eating lunch. It will
take them 45 minutes to clean.
They still plan to arrive at the movie
theater at 2:30 P.M. What time should
they start cleaning the garage?

© **7. Model** Lisa has soccer practice at
3:45 P.M. It takes her 10 minutes to
warm up and 15 minutes to get from
home to practice. What time should
Lisa leave home to get to practice on
time? Draw a number line to model
the problem.

© **8. Generalize** Wan-li drew these
polygons. What is the same in all
three polygons?

**9.** School starts at 8:15 A.M. It takes
Shane 15 minutes to walk to school,
20 minutes to eat, 15 minutes to
walk his dog, and 15 minutes to get
ready. What time should he get up?

**10.** A scientist recorded the data shown
in the table. About how long does
it take a Venus Flytrap to close after
an insect or spider lands on it?

   **A** Less than 1 second

   **B** More than 1 second

   **C** More than 1 minute

   **D** More than 2 minutes

| Time Prey Landed | Time Flytrap Closed |
|---|---|
| 2:07 | $\frac{1}{2}$ second after 2:07 |
| 2:49 | $\frac{3}{4}$ second after 2:49 |
| 2:53 | $\frac{1}{2}$ second after 2:53 |

**Set A,** pages 304–306

The clocks show the time that a movie starts. What time does the movie start? Write the time in at least 3 ways.

When the minute hand is on the 9, you can say "15 minutes to" the hour. You can also say "a quarter to" the hour.

The movie starts at <u>four forty-five</u>, or <u>15 minutes to five</u>, or <u>a quarter to five</u>.

**Remember** to find where the hour hand points and where the minute hand points to tell the time.

Write the time shown on each clock in two ways.

1.

2.

**Set B,** pages 308–309

What is the time to the nearest minute?

The hour hand is between 10 and 11. The time is after 10:00.

Count by 5s from the 12 to the 5.
5, 10, 15, 20, 25 minutes.

After counting by 5s, count the marks by 1.
5, 10, 15, 20, 25, 26, 27 minutes.

The digital time is 10:27.
It is 27 minutes past 10 or 33 minutes to 11.

**Remember** that for minutes, count numbers on the clock by 5s, then count marks by 1.

Write the time shown on each clock in two ways.

1.

2.

Change 9 weeks to days.

$\underbrace{9 \text{ weeks}}_{\text{Change to days.}} = \boxed{\phantom{0}} \text{ days}$

You know that 1 week equals 7 days.

Multiply: $9 \times 7 \text{ days} = 63 \text{ days}$

9 weeks = 63 days

**Remember** to use the correct factors for the units you are changing.

1. 6 hours = ▨ minutes
2. 2 weeks = ▨ days
3. 3 days = ▨ hours
4. 1 hour, 41 minutes = ▨ minutes
5. 2 days, 3 hours = ▨ hours
6. 3 hours, 15 minutes = ▨ minutes

How long does the hockey game last?
Start Time: 11:00 A.M.
End Time: 2:35 P.M.

- Find the starting time: **11:00 A.M.**
- Count the hours: **12, 1, 2.**
- Count the minutes: **5, 10, 15, 20, 25, 30, 35.**

The game lasted 3 hours, 35 minutes.

**Remember** to count hours and then minutes.

Find the elapsed time.

1. Start Time: 9:00 A.M.
   End Time: 12:15 P.M.

2. Start Time: 5:00 P.M.
   End Time: 9:50 P.M.

Jay's soccer practice begins at 10:00 A.M. He takes 30 minutes to walk to the field. He takes 10 minutes to walk his dog and 10 minutes to get ready. When should Jay start getting ready?

Work backward from the end using the opposite of each change.

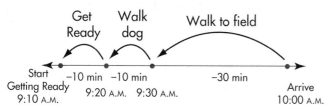

Jay should start getting ready at 9:10 A.M.

**Remember** to check your solution by working forward.

Solve by drawing a picture and working backward.

1. Hal needs to meet Lou at 1:00 P.M. It takes him 10 minutes to walk to Lou's house, 10 minutes to get ready, and 20 minutes to eat lunch. What time should Hal start eating lunch?

**Multiple Choice**

**1.** The clock below shows the time Levi arrived at the doctor's office. What time did he arrive? (12-2)

**A** 3:42

**B** 3:37

**C** 3:35

**D** 2:37

**2.** What is one way to write the time shown on the clock? (12-1)

**A** Quarter to 1

**B** 15 past 1

**C** Quarter past 2

**D** Quarter to 2

**3.** Anita got to school at 8:05 A.M. She was on the bus 15 minutes, stood at the bus stop for 10 minutes, and took 40 minutes to get ready after she got up. What time did Anita get up? (12-5)

**A** 9:10 A.M.

**B** 7:05 A.M.

**C** 7:00 A.M.

**D** 6:55 A.M.

**4.** Brad is going on vacation for 2 weeks. Which amount of time is greater than 2 weeks? (12-3)

**A** 5 days

**B** 7 days

**C** 14 days

**D** 18 days

**5.** Linda left her house at 12:40 P.M. She spent 15 minutes driving to the deli, 5 minutes waiting in line, and then 20 minutes eating her lunch. What time did she finish her lunch? (12-4)

**A** 12:55 P.M.

**B** 1:15 P.M.

**C** 1:20 P.M.

**D** 1:40 P.M.

**6.** Which of the following is a time that Jose would be asleep during the night? (12-1)

**A** 3:15 P.M.

**B** 11:45 P.M.

**C** 10:45 A.M.

**D** 12:30 P.M.

**7.** It was 3:00 P.M. Sandra had been at the bus station for 45 minutes. When did she arrive at the station? (12-4)

**A** 2:15 P.M.

**B** 2:30 P.M.

**C** 3:15 P.M.

**D** 3:45 P.M.

**8.** Judy says that she planted an apple seed 3 days ago. Her brother thinks she planted the seed less than 40 hours ago. Is Judy's brother correct? Explain your answer. (12-3)

**9.** Jon arrived home from school at the time shown on the clock.

What time did Jon arrive? (12-2)

**10.** Olivia left her house at 6:30 to go to the movies. What is another way to write 6:30? (12-1)

**11.** The Brown family boarded a train at 3:55 P.M. to go home from the county fair. It took them 25 minutes to get to the train station from the fair. They spent 1 hour, 15 minutes, at the fair. What time did they arrive at the fair? Draw a number line to model the problem. (12-5)

**12.** The concert in the park started at 11:15 A.M. and ended at 1:50 P.M. How long did the concert last? (12-4)

**13.** How many hours are in 4 days? (12-3)

**14.** The 3:00 P.M. temperature was 93°F. This was 8° warmer than the temperature at noon. The noon temperature was 13° warmer than the 9:00 A.M. temperature. What was the 9:00 A.M. temperature in °F? (12-5)

**15.** Jen was playing in a soccer game. The game started at 11:10 A.M. and ended at 12:40 P.M. How long did the game last? (12-4)

**16.** Reading hour at the library starts at the time shown on the clock. What time does reading hour begin? (12-1)

**17.** The game ended at 5:15 P.M. It lasted 2 hours 10 minutes. What time did the game start? (12-4)

**18.** Dan and his mom are going to a baseball game that starts at 7:05 P.M. Batting practice starts 90 minutes before the game starts. It takes 45 minutes for them to get to the ballpark. What time do Dan and his mom need to leave to see the start of batting practice? (12-5)

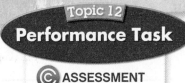
You need to arrive at the theater at exactly 12:15 P.M. for a movie. It takes you 30 minutes to walk to the theater, 40 minutes to get ready, and 30 minutes to walk your dog.

**1.** Write the time you should start each activity in two ways.

Arrive at theater

12:15 P.M.
a quarter after twelve

Start walking to theater

Start getting ready

Start walking dog

**2.** The bell rings at Addison gym every half hour. It last rang at 7:12 A.M. At what time will it ring again?

**3.** A plane leaves Chicago at 6:45 P.M. and arrives in Kansas City at 8:10 P.M. How long was the flight?

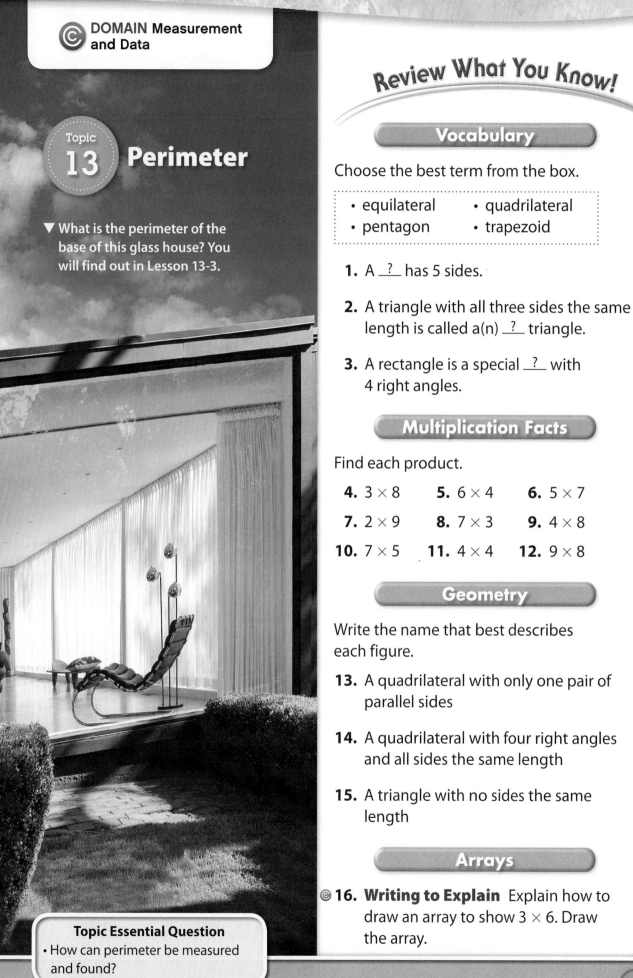

## Topic 13 Perimeter

▼ What is the perimeter of the base of this glass house? You will find out in Lesson 13-3.

# Review What You Know!

## Vocabulary

Choose the best term from the box.

- equilateral
- quadrilateral
- pentagon
- trapezoid

1. A __?__ has 5 sides.

2. A triangle with all three sides the same length is called a(n) __?__ triangle.

3. A rectangle is a special __?__ with 4 right angles.

## Multiplication Facts

Find each product.

4. $3 \times 8$   5. $6 \times 4$   6. $5 \times 7$

7. $2 \times 9$   8. $7 \times 3$   9. $4 \times 8$

10. $7 \times 5$   11. $4 \times 4$   12. $9 \times 8$

## Geometry

Write the name that best describes each figure.

13. A quadrilateral with only one pair of parallel sides

14. A quadrilateral with four right angles and all sides the same length

15. A triangle with no sides the same length

## Arrays

16. **Writing to Explain** Explain how to draw an array to show $3 \times 6$. Draw the array.

**Topic Essential Question**
- How can perimeter be measured and found?

# Interactive Learning

**Pose the problem.** Start each lesson by working together to solve problems. It will help you make sense of math.

### Applying Math Practices

- What am I asked to find?
- What else can I try?
- How are quantities related?
- How can I explain my work?
- How can I use math to model the problem?
- Can I use tools to help?
- Is my work precise?
- Why does this work?
- How can I generalize?

---

### Lesson 13-1

© **Use Tools** Solve using the diagram at the right.

Troy made this drawing of his garden. Each square in the grid has a side length of 1 foot. What is the distance around Troy's garden?

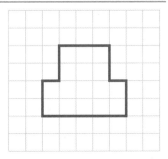

---

### Lesson 13-2

© **Use Tools** Solve. Choose a tool and a unit to use to find the perimeter.

Today you are designing a garden. Draw a closed shape for your garden design. Include a curved part in your design. Then find the perimeter of your drawing. Tell how you found the perimeter.

## Lesson 13-3

© **Generalize** Solve using any method you choose.
What is the perimeter of each shape? Explain how you found the perimeter of each.

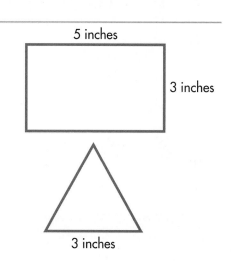

5 inches

3 inches

3 inches

## Lesson 13-4

© **Construct Arguments** Solve. Look for more than one answer.

The length of each straw is 1 unit. How can you use straws to make a shape that has a perimeter of 12 units? Record the shape you made and its perimeter on grid paper. Then find a different shape with a perimeter of 12 units.

## Lesson 13-5

© **Persevere** Solve. Use objects to help.
Erica has 25 markers. There are red, yellow, and blue markers. Erica has 4 more red markers than blue markers. She has the same number of blue markers as yellow markers. How many red markers does Erica have?

Lesson
**13-1**
© Common Core

**3.MD.8** Solve real world and mathematical problems involving perimeters of polygons, including finding the perimeter given the side lengths, finding an unknown side length, and exhibiting rectangles with the same perimeter and different areas or with the same area and different perimeters.

# Understanding Perimeter

## How do you find perimeter?

Gus wants to make a playpen for his dog and put a fence around it. He made drawings of two different playpens. What is the perimeter of the playpen in each drawing?

The distance around a figure is its perimeter.

**Hands-On** grid paper

scale: ⊢ = 1 foot

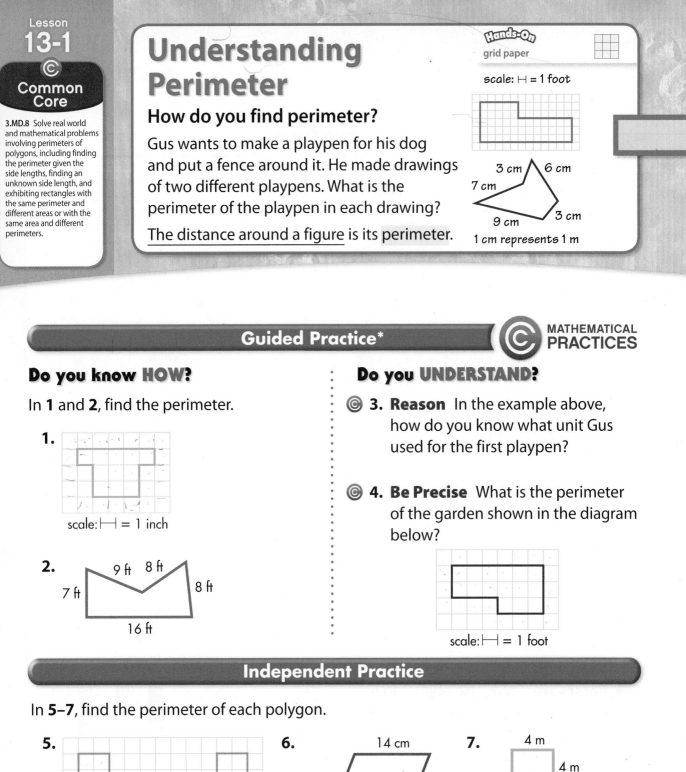

3 cm  6 cm
7 cm
9 cm  3 cm
1 cm represents 1 m

---

## Guided Practice*

**MATHEMATICAL PRACTICES**

### Do you know HOW?

In **1** and **2**, find the perimeter.

**1.**

scale: ⊢ = 1 inch

**2.**

9 ft  8 ft
7 ft      8 ft
16 ft

### Do you UNDERSTAND?

© **3. Reason** In the example above, how do you know what unit Gus used for the first playpen?

© **4. Be Precise** What is the perimeter of the garden shown in the diagram below?

scale: ⊢ = 1 foot

---

## Independent Practice

In **5–7**, find the perimeter of each polygon.

**5.**

scale: ⊢ = 1 m

**6.**

14 cm
11 cm      11 cm
14 cm

**7.**

4 m
4 m
8 m      6 m
6 m
6 m

In **8–10**, draw a figure with the given perimeter. Use grid paper.

**8.** 14 units     **9.** 8 units     **10.** 20 units

Animated Glossary, eTools
www.pearsonsuccessnet.com

*For another example, see Set A on page 334.*

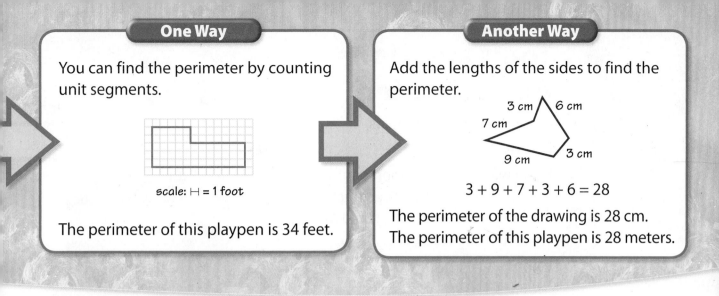

**One Way**

You can find the perimeter by counting unit segments.

scale: ⊢ = 1 foot

The perimeter of this playpen is 34 feet.

**Another Way**

Add the lengths of the sides to find the perimeter.

3 cm    6 cm

7 cm

9 cm    3 cm

$3 + 9 + 7 + 3 + 6 = 28$

The perimeter of the drawing is 28 cm. The perimeter of this playpen is 28 meters.

---

**Problem Solving**

**11.** Mr. Karas needs to find the perimeter of the playground to build a fence around it. What is the perimeter of the playground?

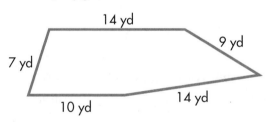

14 yd

9 yd

7 yd

10 yd    14 yd

**12.** Mike needs to find the perimeter of the pool so he knows how many tiles to put around the edge. What is the perimeter of the pool?

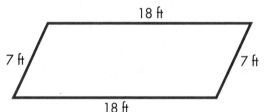

18 ft

7 ft    7 ft

18 ft

**© 13. Persevere** The distance around the outside of this maze is the same as the perimeter of a rectangle. The picture shows the lengths of the sides of the rectangle. What is the perimeter of the maze?

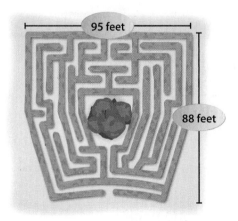

95 feet

88 feet

**14.** Jani has the magnet shown below.

What is the perimeter of Jani's magnet to the nearest inch? Use a ruler to measure.

**A** 2 in.    **B** 4 in.    **C** 5 in.    **D** 6 in.

**© 15. Communicate** Roberto has a magnet that is twice as long and twice as wide as Jani's magnet in Problem 14. Find the perimeter of Roberto's magnet. Explain your work.

Common Core

3.MD.8 Solve real world and mathematical problems involving perimeters of polygons, including finding the perimeter given the side lengths, finding an unknown side length, and exhibiting rectangles with the same perimeter and different areas or with the same area and different perimeters.

# Tools and Units for Perimeter

## How can you use tools to find perimeter?

Maria wants to put ribbon around a poster. She wants to find out how much ribbon she will need. What unit could Maria use? What tool could she use?

---

## Other Examples

A measuring tape can be used to measure a curve. A measuring tape measures in inches or feet.

If you do not have a measuring tape, you can wrap a string around the curve. Then mark the string and measure it with a yardstick or ruler.

---

## Guided Practice*

MATHEMATICAL PRACTICES

### Do you know HOW?

In **1** and **2**, choose a tool and unit.
Tools: ruler, yardstick, measuring tape
Units: feet, inches, yards, miles

1. Which tool and unit should be used to find the perimeter of a square swimming pool?

2. Which tool and unit should be used to find the perimeter of a sandbox with one curved side?

### Do you UNDERSTAND?

3. In the example above, what unit should Maria use if she were making a long banner instead of a poster?

4. **Construct Arguments** Why wouldn't you use a ruler or a yardstick to measure a mile?

5. Maria also wants to put ribbon around a small, round mirror. She doesn't have a tape measure. How could she find the distance around the mirror?

DIGITAL

Animated Glossary
www.pearsonsuccessnet.com

*For another example, see Set B on page 334.

A ruler is used to measure short distances, such as the length of a desk. A ruler measures in inches or feet.

A yardstick is used to measure medium distances, such as the length of a football field. A yardstick measures in inches, feet, or yards.

A mile is a measure of longer distances. It is too long to use a ruler or a yardstick. Most people can walk a mile in about 15 minutes.

Maria is measuring a short distance. She could use a ruler and measure in inches.

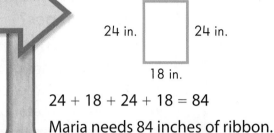

$24 + 18 + 24 + 18 = 84$

Maria needs 84 inches of ribbon.

## Independent Practice

In **6–8,** choose the best unit and tool for measuring the perimeter of each.

**6.** a square window

**7.** a round rug

**8.** a patio shaped like a rectangle

## Problem Solving

MATHEMATICAL
**PRACTICES**

In **9** and **10,** choose the best measuring tool and unit from the lists at the right.

**9.** Mr. Paz wants to put a railing around a deck that is shaped like a hexagon. Which tool and unit should he use to measure the perimeter of the deck?

**10.** Kelly wants to put ribbon around the edge of a round tablecloth. Which tool and unit should she use to measure the tablecloth?

| Tools | Units |
|---|---|
| Ruler | Inches |
| Yardstick | Feet |
| Measuring Tape | Yards |
| | Miles |

© **11. Reason** If you had only a 12-inch ruler, would you be able to measure the perimeter of a gymnasium? Explain.

© **12. Use Tools** Max wants to measure the perimeter of his shoe. What different tools and units could he use?

**13.** Which unit should be used to find the perimeter of a city?

    **A** inches      **B** feet      **C** yards      **D** miles

© **Common Core**

3.MD.8 Solve real world and mathematical problems involving perimeters of polygons, including finding the perimeter given the side lengths, finding an unknown side length, and exhibiting rectangles with the same perimeter and different areas or with the same area and different perimeters.

# Perimeter of Common Shapes

## How can you find the perimeter of common shapes?

Mr. Coe needs to find the perimeter of two swimming pool designs. One pool shape is a rectangle. The other pool shape is a square. What is the perimeter of each pool?

6 meters

10 meters

9 meters

---

## Guided Practice*

© **MATHEMATICAL PRACTICES**

### Do you know **HOW**?

For **1** and **2**, find the perimeter.

**1.** Rectangle

8 feet

4 feet

**2.** Square

5 cm

### Do you **UNDERSTAND**?

© **3. Generalize** How can you use multiplication and addition to find the perimeter of the rectangle above?

**4.** In Exercises **1** and **2**, explain how to find the missing lengths.

**5.** Darla drew an equilateral triangle. Each side was 9 inches long. What was the perimeter of the triangle?

---

## Independent Practice

In **6** and **7**, use an inch ruler to measure the lengths of the sides of the polygon. Find the perimeter.

**6.** Square

**7.** Rectangle

In **8** and **9**, find the perimeter of each polygon.

**8.** Rectangle

15 m

3 m

**9.** Equilateral triangle

4 yd

*For another example, see Set C on page 335.*

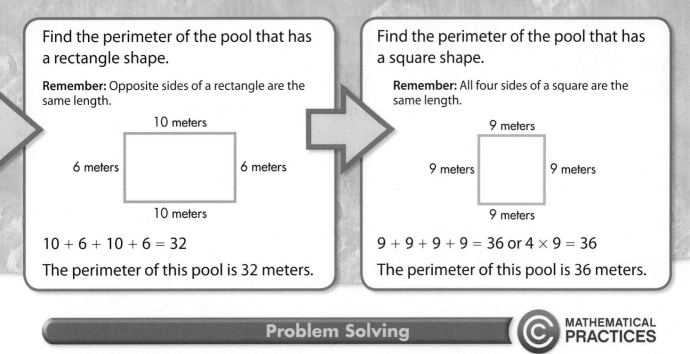

Find the perimeter of the pool that has a rectangle shape.

**Remember:** Opposite sides of a rectangle are the same length.

10 meters

6 meters          6 meters

10 meters

$10 + 6 + 10 + 6 = 32$

The perimeter of this pool is 32 meters.

Find the perimeter of the pool that has a square shape.

**Remember:** All four sides of a square are the same length.

9 meters

9 meters          9 meters

9 meters

$9 + 9 + 9 + 9 = 36$ or $4 \times 9 = 36$

The perimeter of this pool is 36 meters.

## Problem Solving

**© 10. Persevere** Cora uses ribbons to make three different sizes of bows. How much more ribbon does it take to make 2 large bows than 2 small bows? Explain how you found your answer.

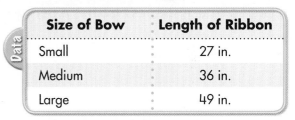

| Size of Bow | Length of Ribbon |
|---|---|
| Small | 27 in. |
| Medium | 36 in. |
| Large | 49 in. |

**11.** The base of the glass house to the right is a rectangle. What is the perimeter of the base of the glass house?

The base of the glass house is 56 feet long and 32 feet wide.

**12.** The base of a garage is 20 feet long and 15 feet wide. What is the perimeter of the base of the garage?

**13.** What is the perimeter of the cloth patch outlined below?

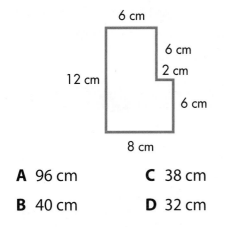

6 cm

6 cm

2 cm

12 cm

6 cm

8 cm

**A** 96 cm          **C** 38 cm

**B** 40 cm          **D** 32 cm

**© 14. Model** The perimeter of the figure below is 24 meters. What is the length of side *n*? Write an addition sentence to help.

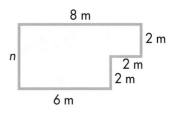

8 m

2 m

*n*

2 m

2 m

6 m

Lesson
**13-4**

© 
**Common Core**

**3.MD.8** Solve real world and mathematical problems involving perimeters of polygons, including finding the perimeter given the side lengths, finding an unknown side length, and exhibiting rectangles with the same perimeter and different areas or with the same area and different perimeters.

# Different Shapes with the Same Perimeter

Hands-On
grid paper

## What shapes can you make when you know the perimeter?

Kara wants to design a shape for her garden. She will use all of the fencing shown. What shape can she make?

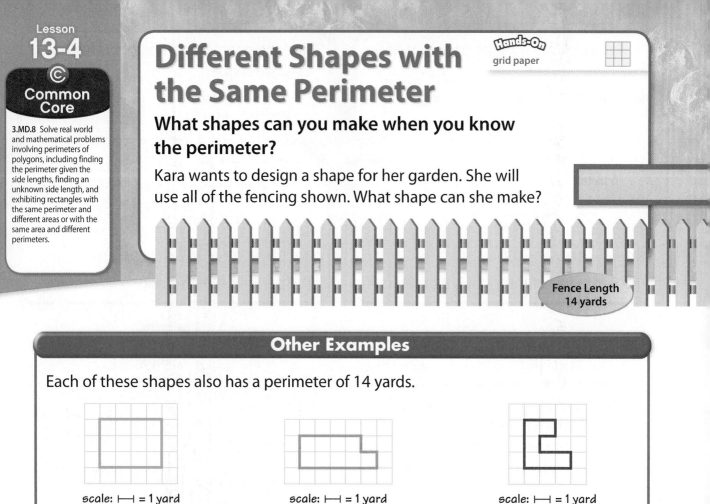

Fence Length 14 yards

## Other Examples

Each of these shapes also has a perimeter of 14 yards.

scale: ⊢—⊣ = 1 yard          scale: ⊢—⊣ = 1 yard          scale: ⊢—⊣ = 1 yard

## Guided Practice*

© **MATHEMATICAL PRACTICES**

### Do you know HOW?

Copy and complete each figure to show the given perimeter. Use grid paper.

**1.** A square
Perimeter = 16 ft

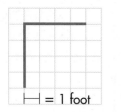

⊢—⊣ = 1 foot

**2.** A 6-sided figure
Perimeter = 10 m

⊢—⊣ = 1 meter

### Do you UNDERSTAND?

**3.** Look at the examples above. Describe the lengths of the sides of a third rectangle that has a perimeter of 14 yards.

© **4. Use Tools** Mike wants to design a shape for his garden. He wants to use exactly 18 meters of fencing. Draw a shape he can make. Use grid paper.

## Independent Practice

In **5–7**, draw a figure with each perimeter. Use grid paper.

**5.** 12 units          **6.** 4 units          **7.** 22 units

DIGITAL          eTools
www.pearsonsuccessnet.com

*For another example, see Set D on page 335.*

**Draw a picture or use straws to act out the problem.**

Each straw is 1 unit. Use 14 straws to make a shape. The perimeter of the shape is 14 units.

**Then describe the shape and the length of each side.**

The figure is a rectangle. Two sides are each 6 units long, and two sides are each 1 unit long.

**Check that the shape has the correct perimeter.**

Add the side lengths.
$6 + 1 + 6 + 1 = 14$ units

Kara needs exactly 14 yards of fencing to make a rectangle with sides that are 6 yards and 1 yard.

## Problem Solving

**MATHEMATICAL PRACTICES**

8. Darius wants to design a birthday card. He has exactly 18 inches of yarn that he wants to glue around the edge of the card. Draw a card design he can make. Use grid paper.

9. Draw 2 different shapes that have a perimeter of 24 units. Use grid paper to help.

Use the pictures at the right for **10** and **11**.

10. Aleesa bought one scarf and three hats. What was the total cost of these items?

11. How much more does a sweater cost than the mittens?

12. **Look for Patterns** Look for a pattern in the table. Copy and complete.

| Number of Tables | 1 | 2 | 3 | 4 | 5 | 6 |
|---|---|---|---|---|---|---|
| Number of Chairs | 8 | 16 | ▨ | 32 | ▨ | 48 |

Hat $7

Sweater $28

Scarf $16

Mittens $9

13. Which pair of shapes have the same perimeter?

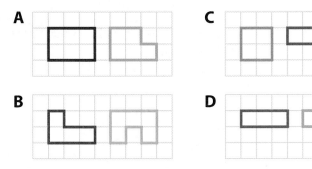

A    C

B    D

Lesson
**13-5**

© Common Core

3.MD.8 Solve real world and mathematical problems involving perimeters of polygons, including finding the perimeter given the side lengths, finding an unknown side length, and exhibiting rectangles with the same perimeter and different areas or with the same area and different perimeters.

Problem Solving

# Try, Check, and Revise

Tad, Holly, and Shana made 36 posters all together. Shana made 3 more posters than Holly.

Tad and Holly made the same number of posters. How many posters did Shana make?

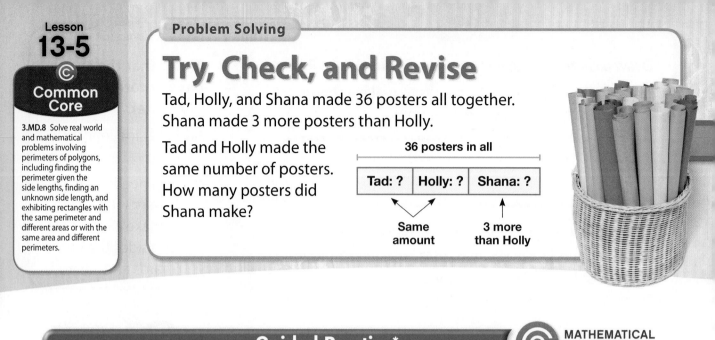

---

## Guided Practice*

**MATHEMATICAL PRACTICES**

### Do you know HOW?

**1.** Peg and Pat are sharing 64 crayons. Pat has 10 more crayons than Peg. How many crayons does each girl have?

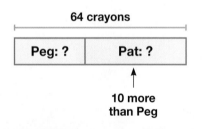

### Do you UNDERSTAND?

© **2. Construct Arguments** Look at the diagram for Exercise 1. Why aren't the two parts of the rectangle the same size?

© **3. Write a Problem** Write a problem that can be solved by using reasoning to make good tries.

---

## Independent Practice

**MATHEMATICAL PRACTICES**

For **4** and **5**, use the strategy Try, Check, and Revise.

**4.** Rectangles A and B have the same perimeter but are different shapes. Rectangle A is 5 inches long and 3 inches wide. Rectangle B is 6 inches longer than it is wide. What are the length and width of Rectangle B?

**5.** Hanna has 6 coins worth 50¢ in all. Some of the coins are nickels and some are dimes. What coins does Hanna have?

**Applying Math Practices**

- What am I asked to find?
- What else can I try?
- How are quantities related?
- How can I explain my work?
- How can I use math to model the problem?
- Can I use tools to help?
- Is my work precise?
- Why does this work?
- How can I generalize?

Use reasoning to make good tries.
Then check.

**Try:** 10 + 10 + 13 = 33

**Check:** 33 < 36
Too low, I need 3 more.

**Try:** 12 + 12 + 15 = 39

**Check:** 39 > 36
Too high, I need 3 less.

Revise, using what you know.

**Try:** 11 + 11 + 14 = 36

**Check:** 36 = 36
This is correct.

Shana made 14 posters.

Use the pictures at the right for **6–8**.

**6.** The clerk at the flower store puts all
the roses into two vases. One vase
has 2 more roses than the other vase.
How many roses are in each vase?

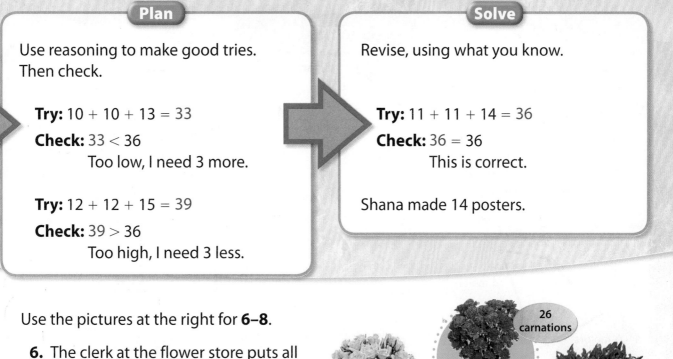

26 carnations

36 roses

42 irises

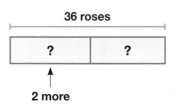

36 roses

? | ?

2 more

**7.** How many irises could be put into
each of 6 equal bouquets?

©  **8. Persevere** Edna, Jay, and Bob bought all of the carnations in
the flower store. Edna bought 2 more than Jay. Bob and Jay
bought the same number. How many carnations did Edna buy?

©  **9. Writing to Explain** Tamiya cut a 12-inch piece of string
into 3 equal parts. She also cut a 24-inch piece of ribbon
into 8 equal parts. Which was longer, a piece of the string
or a piece of the ribbon? Explain how you decided.

**10.** A rectangle has a perimeter of
48 inches. Which of the following
pairs of numbers could be the length
and width of the rectangle?

**A** 12 inches and 10 inches

**B** 8 inches and 6 inches

**C** 20 inches and 4 inches

**D** 15 inches and 5 inches

**11.** Kevin read that there are 22 types of
crocodiles and alligators in the world.
There are 6 more types of crocodiles
than alligators. How many types
of crocodiles are there? How many
types of alligators are there?

**Set A,** pages 324–325

What is the perimeter of the figure below?

Add the lengths of the sides to find the perimeter.

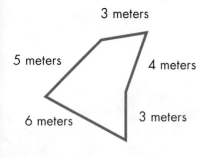

3 + 4 + 3 + 6 + 5 = 21 meters

The perimeter of the figure is 21 meters.

**Remember** the side on which you began adding so that you know where to stop.

Find the perimeter.

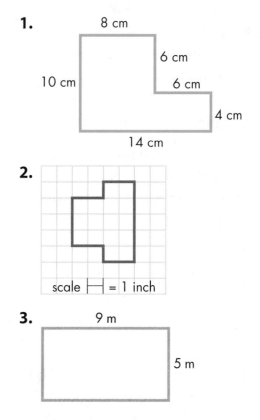

**1.**

**2.**

**3.**

**Set B,** pages 326–327

Ed wants to put a ribbon around a square picture. What tool and unit should he use to measure the perimeter of the picture?

Ed is measuring length, so he could choose a ruler, a yardstick, or a tape measure. He could measure in inches, feet, yards, or miles.

The square picture is small, so Ed should use a ruler and measure in inches.

**Remember** to choose a measuring tool and unit that are appropriate for what you are measuring.

Choose the best tool for measuring the perimeter of each.

**1.** a playground   **2.** a notebook

Choose the best unit for measuring the perimeter of each.

**3.** a flower pot    **4.** a house

What is the perimeter of the rectangle?

**Remember** that to find the perimeter, add the lengths of the sides.

Find the perimeter.

3 cm

6 cm

Opposite sides of a rectangle are the same length.

6 + 3 + 6 + 3 = 18

The perimeter is 18 centimeters.

**1.**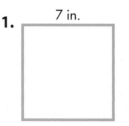

7 in.

**2.** A rectangle that is 5 m long and 9 m wide.

This shape has a perimeter of 10 yards.

scale: ⊢—⊣ = 1 yard

Draw another shape with a perimeter of 10 yards.

The perimeter of this shape is also 10 yards.

**Remember** that different shapes can have the same perimeter.

**1.** Draw a shape that has a perimeter of 8 units. Use grid paper.

**2.** Draw 2 different shapes that each have a perimeter of 16 units. Use grid paper.

Follow these steps for using Try, Check, and Revise to solve problems.

**Remember** to check each try.

Use Try, Check, and Revise to solve.

 **Step 1** Think to make a reasonable first try.

 **Step 2** Check, using information from the problem.

 **Step 3** Revise. Use your first try to make a reasonable second try. Check.

 **Step 4** Continue trying and checking until you find the correct answer.

**1.** Ray and Tony have 32 markers. Ray has 2 more markers than Tony. How many markers does each boy have?

**2.** The soccer club has 28 members. There are 4 more girls than boys. How many boys are members?

**Multiple Choice**

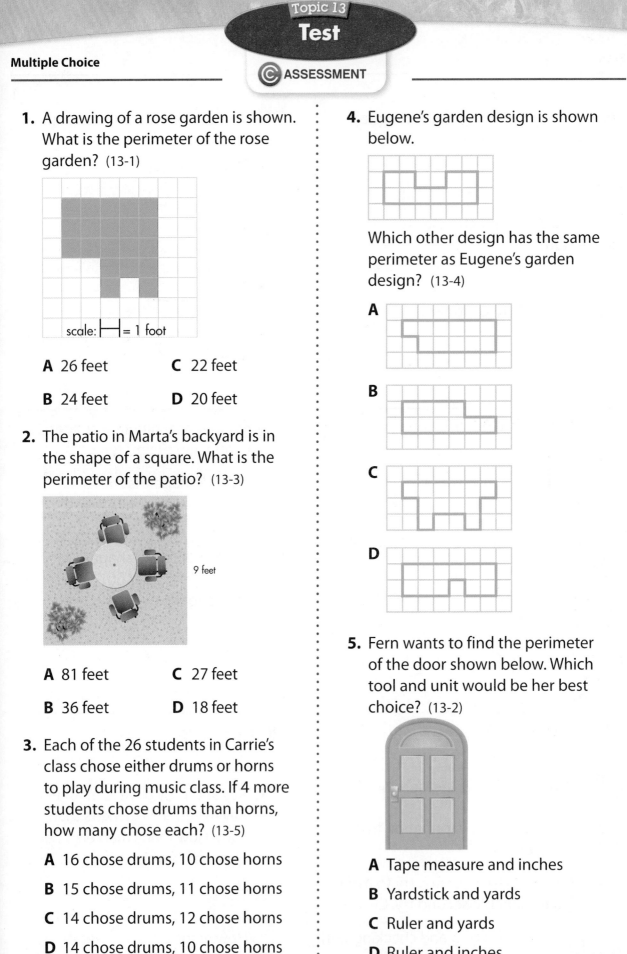

1. A drawing of a rose garden is shown. What is the perimeter of the rose garden? (13-1)

   scale: ⊢─⊣ = 1 foot

   **A** 26 feet     **C** 22 feet

   **B** 24 feet     **D** 20 feet

2. The patio in Marta's backyard is in the shape of a square. What is the perimeter of the patio? (13-3)

   9 feet

   **A** 81 feet     **C** 27 feet

   **B** 36 feet     **D** 18 feet

3. Each of the 26 students in Carrie's class chose either drums or horns to play during music class. If 4 more students chose drums than horns, how many chose each? (13-5)

   **A** 16 chose drums, 10 chose horns

   **B** 15 chose drums, 11 chose horns

   **C** 14 chose drums, 12 chose horns

   **D** 14 chose drums, 10 chose horns

4. Eugene's garden design is shown below.

   Which other design has the same perimeter as Eugene's garden design? (13-4)

   **A**

   **B**

   **C**

   **D**

5. Fern wants to find the perimeter of the door shown below. Which tool and unit would be her best choice? (13-2)

   **A** Tape measure and inches

   **B** Yardstick and yards

   **C** Ruler and yards

   **D** Ruler and inches

**6.** A drawing of Kimmy's vegetable garden is shown. What is the perimeter of the garden? (13-1)

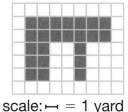

scale: ⊢⊣ = 1 yard

**7.** Benita's tool shed is in the shape of a rectangle. What is the perimeter of the tool shed? (13-3)

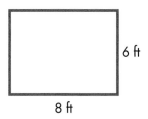

6 ft

8 ft

**8.** The third-grade students go on a field trip. Of the 321 students, there are 5 more girls than boys. How many girls are there? How many boys are there? (13-5)

**9.** Tina wants to put a ribbon around the mirror shown below. She needs to find how much ribbon to buy.

What measurement tool and unit would be a good choice? (13-2)

**10.** Robert's tile design is shown below.

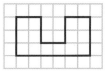

Draw another tile design that has the same perimeter as the design shown. (13-4)

**11.** Ms. Kent wants to put edging around her patio, which is shaped like a rectangle. She needs to measure the perimeter to make sure she buys enough edging. What tool should she use? What unit would be best? Explain. (13-2)

**12.** Use grid paper to draw a square with a perimeter of 24 units. Then draw a rectangle with a perimeter of 24 units. (13-4)

**13.** A drawing of the new park in the city is shown below. The city will put a fence up around the perimeter of the park. What is the perimeter of the park? (13-1)

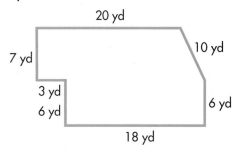

20 yd

7 yd

10 yd

3 yd

6 yd

6 yd

18 yd

1. Anna's rug is in the shape of a rectangle. Use an inch ruler to measure the lengths of the sides of the design of Anna's rug shown below. What is the perimeter of the design?

2. Use grid paper to draw a different rectangular rug design that has the same perimeter as Anna's rug design.

3. Shown below is a design of a rug with a perimeter of 28 feet. Use grid paper to draw another rug design that has a perimeter of 28 feet.

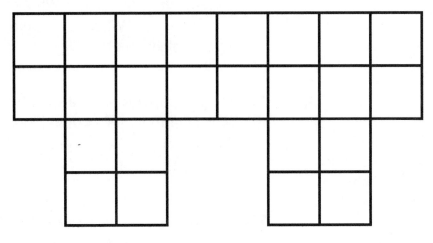

scale: ⊢————⊣ = 1 foot

4. The perimeter of the rug design shown below is 27 feet. What is the length of side *n*?

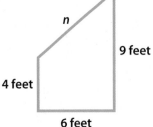

*n*

9 feet

4 feet

6 feet

5. Which measurement tool and unit would be a good choice for measuring the perimeter of a real rug? Explain your choice.

## Topic 14 Area

▼ Al Lopez Park is one of the most visited city parks in Tampa, Florida. What polygon does the park look like? You will find out in Lesson 14-1.

### Review What You Know!

#### Vocabulary

Choose the best term from the box.

- rectangle
- square
- height
- perimeter

**1.** The ? is the distance around a shape.

**2.** A shape that has 4 right angles and 4 equal sides is called a ?.

**3.** A shape that has 4 right angles and 2 pairs of parallel sides is called a ?.

#### Multiplication Facts

Find each product.

**4.** $6 \times 5$   **5.** $7 \times 9$   **6.** $8 \times 8$

**7.** $7 \times 4$   **8.** $3 \times 6$   **9.** $5 \times 4$

**10.** $4 \times 9$   **11.** $8 \times 5$   **12.** $9 \times 6$

**13.** $8 \times 4$   **14.** $3 \times 9$   **15.** $8 \times 7$

#### Shapes

Identify each shape.

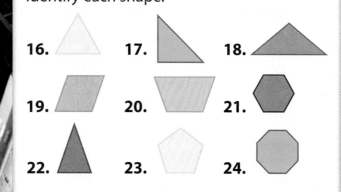

**16.**   **17.**   **18.**

**19.**   **20.**   **21.**

**22.**   **23.**   **24.**

**25. Writing to Explain** Explain how the shapes in Exercises 16–18 are alike and how they are different.

**Topic Essential Questions**
- What does area mean?
- What are different ways to find the area of a shape?

# Interactive Learning

**Pose the problem.** Start each lesson by working together to solve problems. It will help you make sense of math.

---

 **Lesson 14-1**

ⓒ **Reason** Solve using centimeter grid paper.

On your grid paper, draw a rectangle using grid lines for the sides of the rectangle. Then draw or trace a circle on your grid paper. How many square units are inside each shape? Explain how you decided.

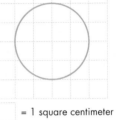

= 1 square centimeter

---

**Lesson 14-2**

ⓒ **Use Tools** Solve using 1-inch grid paper.

On your grid paper, create a region that has an area of 18 square inches. Why do you think we use squares instead of another shape to measure area?

= 1 square unit

---

**Lesson 14-3**

ⓒ **Reason** Solve using grid paper.

Trace the index card on the grid with small squares. What is the area? Then trace the same index card on the grid with the large squares. What is the area? Are the areas different? Explain.

---

**Lesson 14-4**

ⓒ **Generalize** Solve any way you choose.

Jorge is carpeting a room that is shaped like a square with dimensions shown at the right. How many square yards of carpet will Jorge need? Show how you found the answer.

6 yards

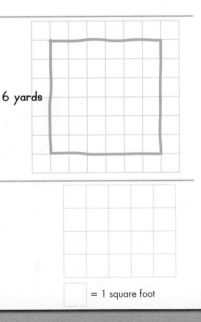

---

**Lesson 14-5**

ⓒ **Model** Solve using grid paper.

The new reading area in the library is a rectangle that is 8 feet by 9 feet. Mrs. Wallace has a rectangular piece of carpet that is 8 feet by 5 feet. What part of the reading area will be left uncarpeted?

= 1 square foot

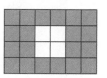
**Lesson 14-6**

ⓒ **Model**  Solve any way you choose.

Alex's parents are planning to tile their kitchen floor with 4 identical copies of the rectangular pattern shown at the right. Each square in this rectangle is 1 square foot. What is the total area of the shaded regions of all 4 rectangular patterns?

**Lesson 14-7**

ⓒ **Use Tools**  Solve using grid paper and the drawing at the right.

Alice's desk is shaped like the picture at the right. The length of each side is shown in feet. Find the area of Alice's desk without counting each square. Tell how you found the answer.

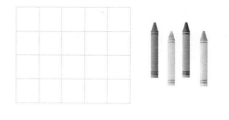

7 ft

3 ft

6 ft  4 ft

3 ft

3 ft

**Lesson 14-8**

ⓒ **Use Tools**  Use grid paper to help solve this problem.

How many different rectangles can you draw with an area of 12 square units? Do they each have the same perimeter? Explain.

**Lesson 14-9**

ⓒ **Model**  Use four different color crayons and grid paper to solve this problem.

Celinda wants to decorate one rectangular wall in her room with 4 different colors. She wants each color to cover the same amount of area. Draw a picture of this rectangular wall and use four colors to show how she could paint this wall. How can each part of the wall be labeled using a unit fraction?

**Lesson 14-10**

ⓒ **Use Tools**  Solve. Look for objects in your classroom.

What are three items you would measure using square inches or square centimeters? What are three items you would measure using square feet or square meters? What are three items you would measure using square miles or square kilometers? Explain your choices.

**Common Core**

**3.MD.5** Recognize area as an attribute of plane figures and understand concepts of area measurement. Also **3.MD.6**

# Covering Regions

## How do you measure area?

Emily made a collage in art class. She cut shapes to make her design.

What is the area of one of the shapes?

Area is <u>the number of square units needed to cover a region.</u>

---

## Guided Practice*

**MATHEMATICAL PRACTICES**

### Do you know HOW?

For **1** and **2**, count to find the area. Tell if the area is exact or an estimate.

**1.**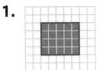

**2.**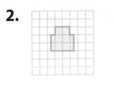

### Do you UNDERSTAND?

**3.** If the first shape above had two more rows of 4 squares, what would the new area be?

**4. Model** Make two different shapes that each have an area of 16 square units.

---

## Independent Practice

For **5** through **12**, count to find the area. Tell if the area is exact or an estimate.

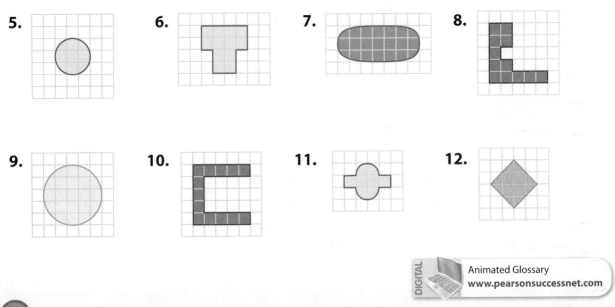

**5.**

**6.**

**7.**

**8.**

**9.**

**10.**

**11.**

**12.**

---

**DIGITAL**

Animated Glossary
www.pearsonsuccessnet.com

*For another example, see Set A on page 364.

Count the square units inside the shape. The exact count is the area of the shape.

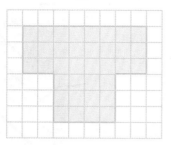

There are 36 squares inside the shape.

The area of the shape is 36 square units.

Sometimes you can estimate the area.

Count the squares inside the shape.

There are about 27 squares inside the shape.

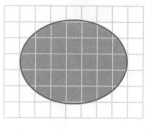

The area of the shape is about 27 square units.

---

## Problem Solving

**13. Persevere** Maggie bought 4 sketch pads and 2 boxes of art pencils. How much money did Maggie spend on her supplies?

$7 each

$4 per box

**14.** What would be a good estimate (in square units) of the green shaded area shown below?

   **A**  About 13

   **B**  About 10

   **C**  About 4

   **D**  About 2

**15.** A bookstore is having a sale. When customers buy 2 books, they get another book free. If Pat buys 8 books, how many books will he get for free?

For **16** and **17**, use the map at the right.

**16.** Which is the best estimate for the area of Al Lopez Park?

   **A**  About 160 square units

   **B**  About 125 square units

   **C**  About 27 square units

   **D**  About 6 square units

**17. Construct Arguments** Which polygon best describes the shape of Al Lopez Park?

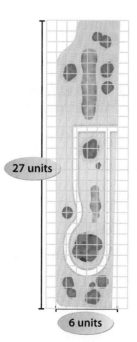

27 units

6 units

Lesson
**14-2**

**Common
Core**

**3.MD.5.a** A square with
side length 1 unit, called "a
unit square," is said to have
"one square unit" of area,
and can be used to measure
area.
Also **3.MD.5.b**

# Area and Units

## What types of units describe area?

Tran wants to make a bookmark for a paperback
book. He wants his bookmark to have an area of
20 square units. A square unit is a square with
sides that are each 1 unit long.

Should he use square centimeters or square inches
as a unit?

□ = 1 square unit

Hands-On
metric ruler

---

## Guided Practice*

MATHEMATICAL
**PRACTICES**

### Do you know HOW?

© **Use Tools** In **1–3**, use a ruler to draw.

**1.** Draw 1 square centimeter.

**2.** Draw 1 square inch.

**3.** Draw a square with sides that are
each 2 centimeters long. What is
the area of the figure?

### Do you UNDERSTAND?

**4.** Which of these shapes has an area
of 5 square centimeters? How do
you know?

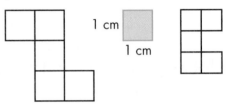

**5.** Beth made bookmarks for friends.
Alma's has an area of 8 square
inches. Tevan's has an area of
8 square centimeters. Whose
bookmark has a larger area?
Explain how you decided.

---

## Independent Practice

In **6–7**, use a ruler to make each drawing.

**6.** A figure with an area of
6 square centimeters.

**7.** A figure with an area of
6 square inches.

**8.** Mitch drew a pattern on the piece of
paper shown below. What is the area
of his drawing in square units?

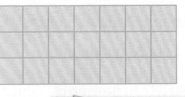

DIGITAL

Animated Glossary, eTools
www.pearsonsuccessnet.com

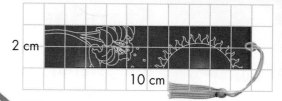

**2 in.**

**10 in.**

☐ = 1 square inch

The unit can be a square that has a length of 1 inch on each side. The area would be 20 square inches. That seems too large.

**2 cm**

**10 cm**

☐ = 1 square centimeter

The unit can be a square that has a length of 1 cm on each side. That seems more reasonable.

Tran should use square centimeters as the unit.

---

## Problem Solving

For **9** and **10**, use the picture at the right.

**9.** Suppose each square in the picture represents one square centimeter. What is the area of the blue shape?

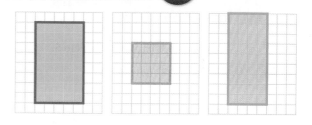

Ⓒ **10. Critique Reasoning** Maggie thinks that the area of two of the orange shapes is equal to the area of one of the green shapes. Do you agree? Explain.

**11.** Yasmeen is buying letter beads to make a bracelet that spells her name. The beads cost 8¢ each. How much money does Yasmeen need to buy the beads?

Ⓒ **12. Persevere** There were 24 grapes in a dish. Luke ate 6 grapes. Juan ate half of the grapes that were left. Then Luke ate all but two of the remaining grapes. Who ate the most grapes?

Ⓒ **13. Use Tools** On grid paper, make a shape with an area of 18 square centimeters.

**14.** What is the area of the shape Ben made with tile squares? Use the figure at the right.

    **A** 30 square inches

    **B** 32 square inches

    **C** 36 square inches

    **D** 40 square inches

☐ = 1 square inch

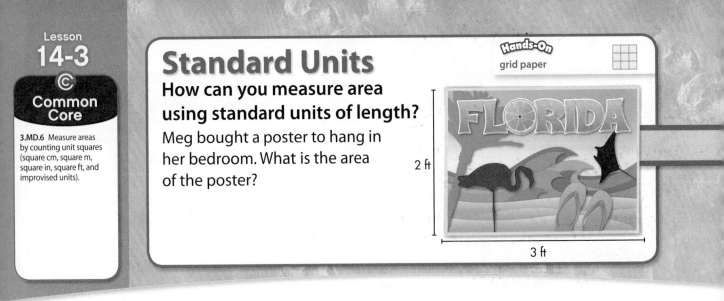

Common Core

3.MD.6 Measure areas by counting unit squares (square cm, square m, square in, square ft, and improvised units).

# Standard Units

Hands-On
grid paper

## How can you measure area using standard units of length?

Meg bought a poster to hang in her bedroom. What is the area of the poster?

2 ft

3 ft

---

## Guided Practice*

MATHEMATICAL PRACTICES

### Do you know HOW?

For **1** and **2**, count the square units. Then write the area.

**1.**

4 yd

3 yd

**2.**

2 m

6 m

### Do you UNDERSTAND?

**3. Reason** If the poster above measured 2 yards by 3 yards, what would its area be?

**4. Use Tools** Zoey has a picture on her wall that measures 8 inches by 10 inches. Use grid paper to find the area of the picture.

---

## Independent Practice

**Be Precise** For **5** through **10**, count the square units. Then write the area.

**5.**

4 km

4 km

**6.**

3 ft

3 ft

**7.**

3 in.

6 in.

**8.**

7 m

9 m

**9.**

5 cm

7 cm

**10.**

4 yd

5 yd

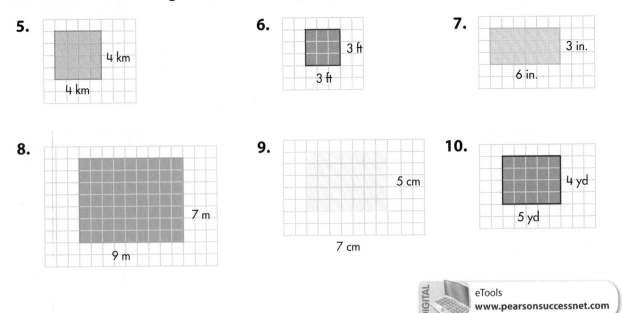

DIGITAL

eTools
www.pearsonsuccessnet.com

*For another example, see Set A on page 364.

Count the square units.

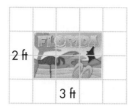

2 ft

3 ft

1 square unit = 1 square foot

The poster covers 6 of the square units.
The poster is measured in feet.

So, the area of the poster is 6 square feet.

**Standard Units of Length and Area**

| Unit | Square Unit |
| --- | --- |
| inch (in.) | square inch |
| foot (ft) | square foot |
| yard (yd) | square yard |
| mile (mi) | square mile |
| centimeter (cm) | square centimeter |
| meter (m) | square meter |
| kilometer (km) | square kilometer |

*Data*

---

## Problem Solving

Ⓒ **MATHEMATICAL PRACTICES**

Ⓒ **Use Tools** For **11** through **13**, use the picture at the right.

11. Mr. Sanchez grows three types of vegetables in his garden. What is the area of the section he uses to grow cucumbers?

12. Mr. Sanchez leaves one section unused each growing season. What is the area of the garden that is being left unused this season?

13. What is the area in square feet of the garden that is being used to grow crops?

**Mr. Sanchez's Garden**

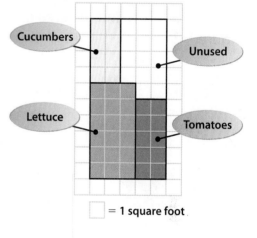

Cucumbers

Unused

Lettuce

Tomatoes

 = 1 square foot

Ⓒ 14. **Critique Reasoning** Brad says a square that has a length of 9 feet will have an area of 18 square feet. Why is Brad incorrect?

15. Amy bought $\frac{6}{8}$ pound of green grapes and $\frac{4}{8}$ pound of red grapes. Did she buy more green grapes or red grapes? Explain.

16. What is the area of the rectangle at the right?

   **A** 12 feet       **C** 12 square feet

   **B** 32 feet       **D** 32 square feet

4 ft

8 ft

17. Erica drew the shape shown at the right. What is the area of the shape?

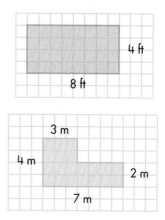

3 m

4 m

2 m

7 m

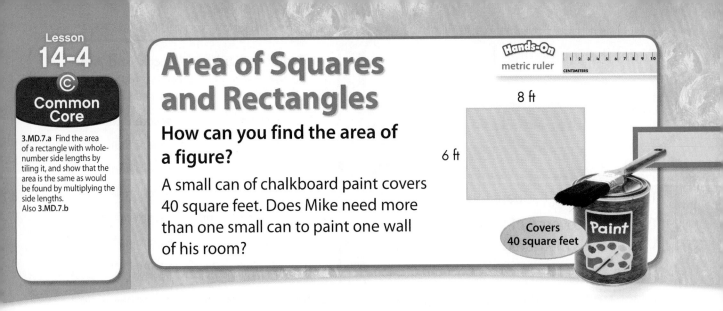

Common
Core

3.MD.7.a Find the area
of a rectangle with whole-
number side lengths by
tiling it, and show that the
area is the same as would
be found by multiplying the
side lengths.
Also 3.MD.7.b

# Area of Squares and Rectangles

## How can you find the area of a figure?

A small can of chalkboard paint covers 40 square feet. Does Mike need more than one small can to paint one wall of his room?

8 ft

6 ft

Hands-On
metric ruler

Covers
40 square feet

Paint

---

## Guided Practice*

MATHEMATICAL
PRACTICES

### Do you know HOW?

For **1** through **4**, find the area of each figure.

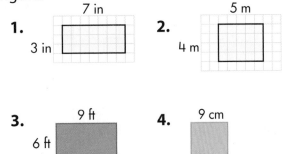

**1.**
7 in
3 in

**2.**
5 m
4 m

**3.**
9 ft
6 ft

**4.**
9 cm

### Do you UNDERSTAND?

**5. Communicate** What is the formula for the area of a square? Explain how you know.

**6.** Mike plans to paint another wall in his room blue. That wall measures 10 feet by 8 feet. How much area does Mike need to paint?

---

## Independent Practice

**Leveled Practice** In **7** and **8**, measure the sides, and find the area of each figure.

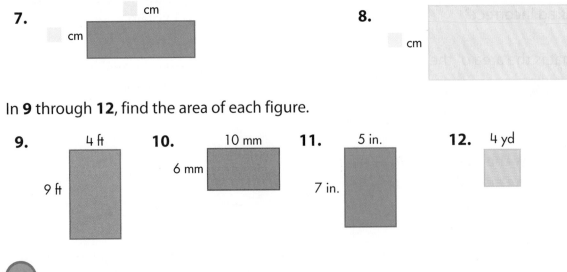

**7.**
cm
cm

**8.**
cm
cm

In **9** through **12**, find the area of each figure.

**9.**
4 ft
9 ft

**10.**
10 mm
6 mm

**11.**
5 in.
7 in.

**12.**
4 yd

*For another example, see Set C on page 365.

**One Way**

You can count the square units to find area.

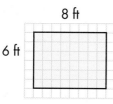

8 ft

6 ft

There are 48 square units.

The area of Mike's wall is 48 square feet.

**Another Way**

You can measure to find the length of each side and use a formula to find area.

Area = length × width

$A = \ell \times w$
$A = 8 \times 6$
$A = 48$

length

width

The area of Mike's wall is 48 square feet. He will need more than one small can of paint.

---

**Problem Solving**

 **MATHEMATICAL PRACTICES**

© **13. Reason** Jen's garden is 4 feet wide and has an area of 28 square feet. What is the length of the garden?

**14.** Diane drew a polygon with 4 sides and 1 set of parallel sides. What type of polygon did Diane draw?

**15.** Mr. Andre is putting tile down in his bathroom. The bathroom is 10 feet long and 5 feet wide. The tile costs $8 per square foot. How much will it cost Mr. Andre to tile his bathroom?

© **Use Tools** For **16** and **17**, use the map at the right.

**16.** What is the area of Lower Falls Gardens?

    **A** 11 square kilometers

    **B** 18 square kilometers

    **C** 20 square kilometers

    **D** 22 square kilometers

**17.** Which polygon best describes the shape of Lower Falls Gardens?

    **A** Triangle     **C** Quadrilateral

    **B** Pentagon     **D** Hexagon

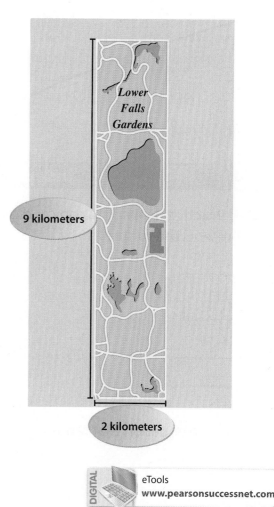

Lower Falls Gardens

9 kilometers

2 kilometers

DIGITAL eTools www.pearsonsuccessnet.com

Lesson
14-5

Common
Core

**3.MD.7c** ...Use area
models to represent the
distributive property in
mathematical reasoning.

# Area and the Distributive Property

## How can the area of rectangles represent the Distributive Property?

Gina wants to separate this rectangle into two small rectangles. Will the area of the large rectangle equal the sum of the areas of the two small rectangles? Use the Distributive Property to break apart facts to find the product.

$A = 7 \times 8$

---

### Guided Practice*

MATHEMATICAL
PRACTICES

#### Do you know HOW?

1. Copy and complete the equation that represents the picture.

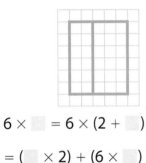

$6 \times \boxed{\phantom{0}} = 6 \times (2 + \boxed{\phantom{0}})$

$= (\boxed{\phantom{0}} \times 2) + (6 \times \boxed{\phantom{0}})$

#### Do you UNDERSTAND?

©  2. **Use Tools** Draw a picture on grid paper to show that
$7 \times 6 = 7 \times (3 + 3) = (7 \times 3) + (7 \times 3)$.

3. Describe a way to separate a $5 \times 6$ rectangle into two smaller rectangles.

---

### Independent Practice

**Leveled Practice** In **4** and **5**, copy and complete the equation that represents the picture.

4. $5 \times \boxed{\phantom{0}} = 5 \times (4 + \boxed{\phantom{0}}) = (\boxed{\phantom{0}} \times 4) + (5 \times \boxed{\phantom{0}})$

5. $3 \times \boxed{\phantom{0}} = \boxed{\phantom{0}} \times (4 + \boxed{\phantom{0}}) = (\boxed{\phantom{0}} \times 4) + (\boxed{\phantom{0}} \times \boxed{\phantom{0}})$

6. Write the equation that represents the picture.

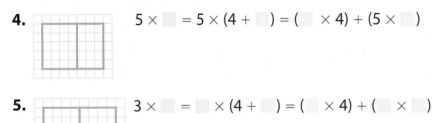

*For another example, see Set D on page 365.

Separate the 8-unit side into two parts.

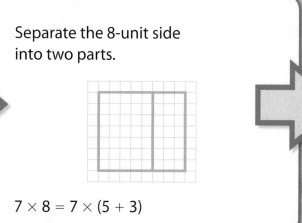

$7 \times 8 = 7 \times (5 + 3)$

$7 \times 8 = 7 \times (5 + 3) = (7 \times 5) + (7 \times 3)$

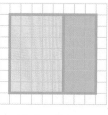

So, the area of the large rectangle is equal to the sum of the areas of the two small rectangles.

## Problem Solving

© **7. Generalize** Claudia sold 3 shells last week for $5 each and 2 more shells this week for $5 each. Show two ways to determine how much money she made in the two weeks.

**8.** Amit wrote a report about the tallest mountain peaks in the United States. He learned that Mt. McKinley, in Alaska, is the tallest mountain at twenty thousand, three hundred twenty feet. Write this number in standard form.

**9.** Kelly has 6 sheets of stickers, with 9 stickers on each sheet. Her aunt gives her 5 more sheets, with 10 stickers on each sheet. How many stickers does Kelly have in all.

© **10. Model** Daniel has a piece of cloth that is 7 feet by 9 feet. Explain how he could divide this large rectangle into two smaller rectangles.

© **11. Reasonableness** Chiya has a 6 × 8 sheet of tiles. Can she separate the sheet into two smaller sheets that are 6 × 5 and 6 × 3? Will they have the same total area?

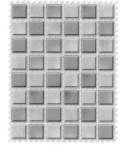

**12.** Mr. See's restaurant buys eggs in crates. Each crate contains 6 rows of eggs with 8 eggs in each row. Which equation shows how to find the number of eggs in a crate?

**A** $6 + 6 + 6 + 6 = n$

**B** $8 \times 6 = n$

**C** $8 \times 8 = n$

**D** $8 \times 4 = n$

Lesson
**14-6**

Common Core

3.MD.6 Measure areas by counting unit squares (square cm, square m, square in, square ft, and improvised units).
Also 3.MD.7, 3.MD.5.a

Problem Solving

# Solve a Simpler Problem

Janet wants to paint the door to her room. The shaded part of the figure shows the part of the door that needs paint.

= 1 square foot

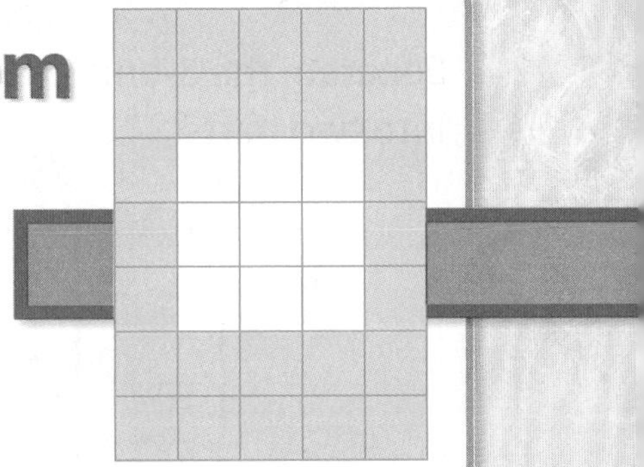

What is the area of the part of the door that needs paint?

## Guided Practice*

MATHEMATICAL PRACTICES

### Do you know HOW?

Solve. Use simpler problems.

1. Lil glued square beads on the shaded part of the frame. What is the area of the part she decorated?

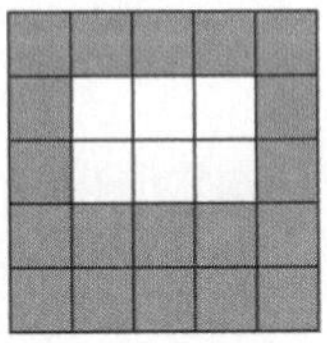

= 1 square inch

### Do you UNDERSTAND?

2. **Reason** What simpler problems did you use to solve Exercise 1?

3. **Write a Problem** Write a problem that you can solve by solving simpler problems. You may draw a picture to help.

## Independent Practice

MATHEMATICAL PRACTICES

For **4–8**, solve. Use simpler problems.

4. Reg wants to put tiles on a wall. The shaded part of the figure shows the part that needs tiles. What is the area of the shaded part?

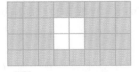

= 1 square foot

**A** 24 square feet

**B** 28 square feet

**C** 32 square feet

**D** 36 square feet

**Applying Math Practices**

- What am I asked to find?
- What else can I try?
- How are quantities related?
- How can I explain my work?
- How can I use math to model the problem?
- Can I use tools to help?
- Is my work precise?
- Why does this work?
- How can I generalize?



*For another example, see Set E on page 365.

*I can solve simpler problems.*

I can find the area of the whole rectangle and then the area of the square.

Then I can subtract to find the area of the shaded part.

Area of the whole rectangle
7 rows with 5 squares in each row
$7 \times 5 = 35$

Area of the square
3 rows with 3 squares in each row
$3 \times 3 = 9$

Subtract
$35 - 9 = 26$

The area of the part of the door that needs paint is 26 square feet.

**5. Persevere** Jim wants to tile the floor. The shaded part of the figure shows the part of the floor that needs tiles. What is the area of the shaded part?

= 1 square meter

**6.** Dan wants to paint the bottom of a pool. The shaded part of the figure shows the part that needs paint. What is the area of the shaded part?

= 1 square yard

**7.** Macy drew two designs. How much greater is the area of the yellow figure than the area of the green figure?

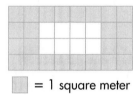
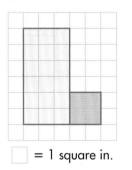

= 1 square in.

**8. Persevere** Mr. Eli grows vegetables in different fields on his farm. What is the total area of the corn and bean fields?

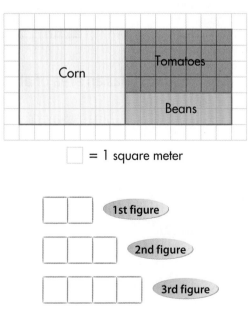

= 1 square meter

**9. Look for Patterns** Neva built these figures using toothpicks. If she continues the pattern, how many toothpicks in all will she use for the 4th figure? the 5th figure?

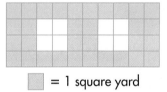

1st figure

2nd figure

3rd figure

C
Common
Core

**3.MD.7.d** Recognize area as additive. Find areas of rectilinear figures by decomposing them into non-overlapping rectangles and adding the areas of the non-overlapping parts, applying this technique to solve real world problems.

# Area of Irregular Shapes

**Hands-On**
metric ruler

CENTIMETERS

## How can you find the area of an irregular figure?

Mr. Fox is covering a miniature golf course hole with artificial grass. How many 1-foot squares of carpet will Mr. Fox need to cover the miniature golf course hole?

1-foot square of carpet

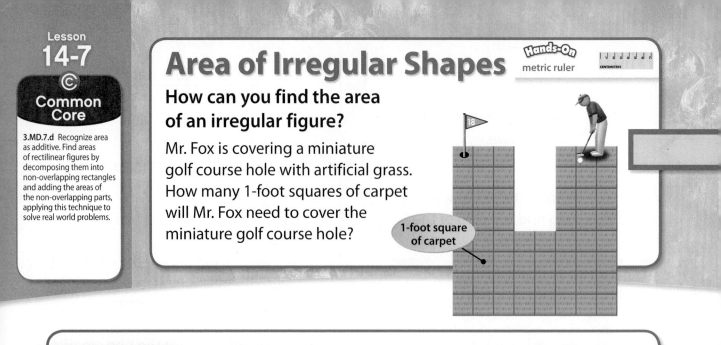

---

**Another Example** **How can you estimate area?**

Some shapes contain partial square units.

Estimate the area of the trapezoid to the right.

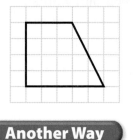

### One Way

Count the whole square units. Then estimate the number of units made from combining partial squares.

There are 14 whole square units. The partial square units make about 2 more square units.

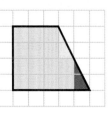

$14 + 2 = 16$

The trapezoid has an area of about 16 square units.

### Another Way

Draw a rectangle around the trapezoid and find the rectangle's area.
$A = 4 \times 5 = 20$

Find the area outside the trapezoid but inside the rectangle.

There are about 4 square units not in the trapezoid.

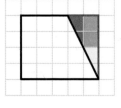

Subtract to find the difference between the two areas.

$20 - 4 = 16$

The trapezoid has an area of about 16 square units.

### Explain It

1. Why is the answer of 16 square units considered an estimate?

2. Can the trapezoid be divided into rectangles to find the area?

DIGITAL

eTools
www.pearsonsuccessnet.com

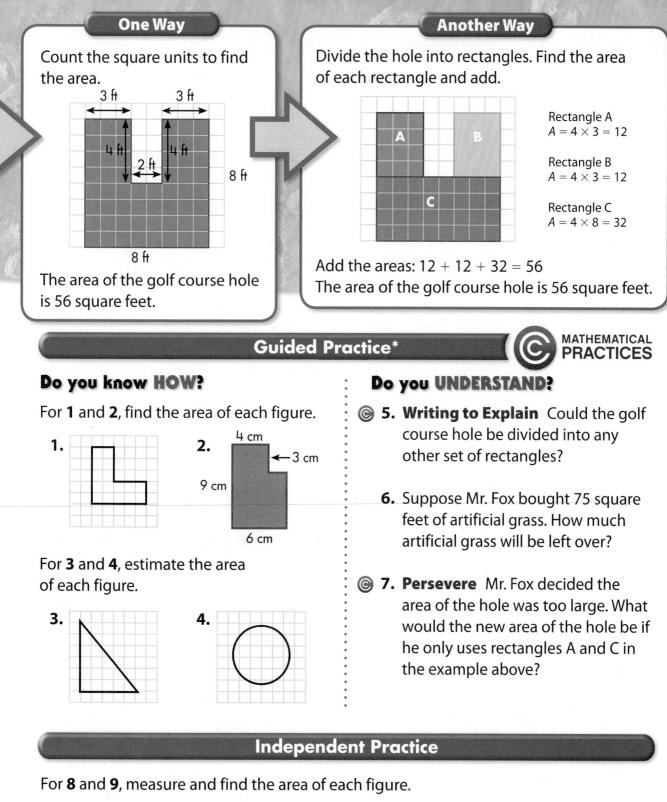

Count the square units to find the area.

3 ft        3 ft

4 ft    4 ft

2 ft

8 ft

8 ft

The area of the golf course hole is 56 square feet.

Divide the hole into rectangles. Find the area of each rectangle and add.

A        B

C

Rectangle A
$A = 4 \times 3 = 12$

Rectangle B
$A = 4 \times 3 = 12$

Rectangle C
$A = 4 \times 8 = 32$

Add the areas: $12 + 12 + 32 = 56$
The area of the golf course hole is 56 square feet.

## Guided Practice*

MATHEMATICAL
PRACTICES

### Do you know HOW?

For **1** and **2**, find the area of each figure.

**1.**

**2.**

4 cm

← 3 cm

9 cm

6 cm

For **3** and **4**, estimate the area of each figure.

**3.**

**4.**

### Do you UNDERSTAND?

© **5. Writing to Explain** Could the golf course hole be divided into any other set of rectangles?

**6.** Suppose Mr. Fox bought 75 square feet of artificial grass. How much artificial grass will be left over?

© **7. Persevere** Mr. Fox decided the area of the hole was too large. What would the new area of the hole be if he only uses rectangles A and C in the example above?

## Independent Practice

For **8** and **9**, measure and find the area of each figure.

**8.**
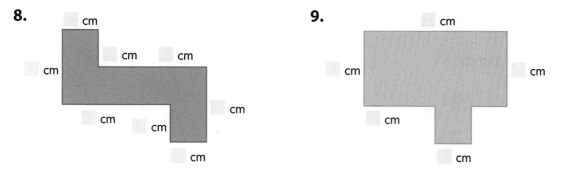

cm

cm      cm

cm

cm

cm

cm

**9.**

cm

cm                    cm

cm

cm

*For another example, see Set F on page 366.

For **10** through **13**, estimate the area of each figure.

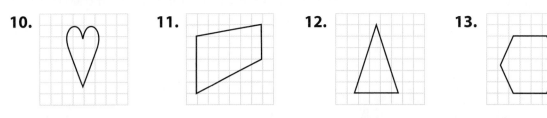

**10.** **11.** **12.** **13.**

---

**Problem Solving**

© **14. Think About the Structure** Jared drew the figure to the right on grid paper. Which is a way in which the figure could be divided to find the total area?

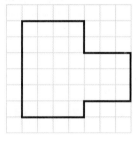

**A** $(6 \times 4) + (3 \times 3)$

**B** $(6 \times 4) + (6 \times 3)$

**C** $(6 \times 3) + (4 \times 3)$

**D** $(6 \times 7) - (4 \times 3)$

© **15. Persevere** Laurie's family is building a new house. The design for the house is shown to the right. Divide the design into two rectangles. What is the length and width of the large rectangle? What is the length and width of the small rectangle?

**Tip** 90' means 90 feet.

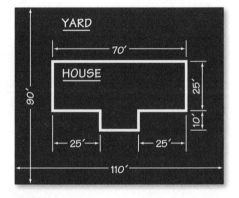

© **16. Use Tools** Mrs. Washington drew a triangle on grid paper. The base of the triangle is 6 units long. The triangle is 8 units tall. Draw a picture of Mrs. Washington's triangle on grid paper. Estimate the area.

© **17. Writing to Explain** Each student on a field trip got a sandwich, a salad, and a juice. If you know that there were 10 students on the field trip, would you be able to tell how much they paid for lunch in all? Why or why not?

© **18. Use Structure** Write the letter *n* to represent the unknown quantity in the phrase "six times a number is 24." Solve the equation.

**19.** Mandy designed a patch to add to her quilt. What fraction is colored blue?

**A** $\frac{2}{8}$

**B** $\frac{4}{8}$

**C** $\frac{8}{8}$

**D** $\frac{8}{4}$

Write each number in word form.

**1.** 3,914

**2.** 260,782

Order the numbers from greatest to least.

**3.** 608    643    640      **4.** 8,137    7,985    8,132

Round to the nearest hundred.

**5.** 298      **6.** 517      **7.** 136      **8.** 874      **9.** 625

Estimate and then find each sum or difference.
Check that your answer is reasonable.

**10.**    96
   + 48

**11.**    521
   − 73

**12.**    357
   + 496

**13.**    834
   + 159

**14.**    903
   − 624

**Error Search** Find each sum or difference that is not correct.
Write it correctly and explain the error.

**15.**    69
   + 35
    94

**16.**    338
   + 576
    814

**17.**    502
   − 142
    360

**18.**    149
   + 705
    854

**19.**    473
   − 298
    275

## Number Sense

MATHEMATICAL
PRACTICES

© **Reason** Write true or false for each statement.
If it is false, explain why.

**20.** The sum of 68 and 35 is less than 100.

**21.** The difference 225 − 157 is greater than 100.

**22.** The sum of 347 and 412 is greater than 700.

**23.** The difference 906 − 417 is less than 500.

**24.** The sum of 258 and 409 is less than 700.

**25.** The difference 519 − 398 is less than 100.

Lesson
14-8

Common
Core

3.MD.7.b Multiply side
lengths to find areas of
rectangles with whole-
number side lengths in
the context of solving real
world and mathematical
problems, and represent
whole-number products
as rectangular areas in
mathematical reasoning.
Also 3.MD.8

# Same Area, Different Perimeter

## Can rectangles have the same area but different perimeters?

In a video puzzle game, you have 16 castle tiles to make a rectangular castle and 16 water tiles for a moat. How can you completely surround the castle with water?

**Hands-On**
grid paper

16 castle tiles

16 water tiles

---

## Guided Practice*

**MATHEMATICAL PRACTICES**

### Do you know HOW?

For **1** through **4**, use grid paper to draw two different rectangles with the given area. Tell the dimensions and perimeter of each rectangle, and tell which one has the smaller perimeter.

**1.** 6 square feet    **2.** 36 square yards

**3.** 64 square meters    **4.** 80 square inches

### Do you UNDERSTAND?

**5. Reason** In the example above, what do you notice about the perimeter of the rectangles as the shape becomes more like a square?

**6. Use Structure** In Round 2 of the video puzzle game, you have 24 castle tiles. What is the fewest number of water tiles you will need to surround your castle?

---

## Independent Practice

For **7** through **10**, use grid paper to draw two different rectangles with the given area. Tell the dimensions and perimeter of each rectangle. Circle the one that has the smaller perimeter.

**7.** 9 square inches    **8.** 18 square feet    **9.** 30 square meters    **10.** 32 square centimeters

For **11** through **14**, describe a different rectangle with the same area as the one shown. Then tell which rectangle has a smaller perimeter.

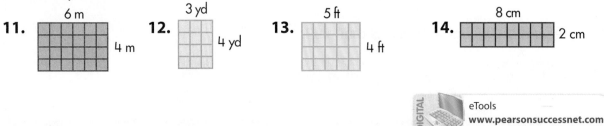

**11.**   6 m / 4 m    **12.**   3 yd / 4 yd    **13.**   5 ft / 4 ft    **14.**   8 cm / 2 cm

DIGITAL   eTools
www.pearsonsuccessnet.com

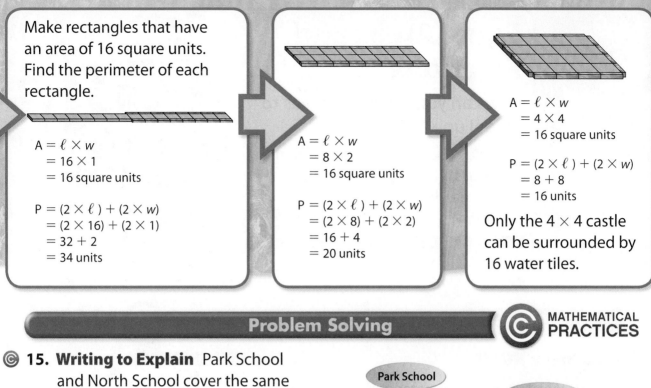

Make rectangles that have an area of 16 square units. Find the perimeter of each rectangle.

$A = \ell \times w$
$= 16 \times 1$
$= 16$ square units

$P = (2 \times \ell) + (2 \times w)$
$= (2 \times 16) + (2 \times 1)$
$= 32 + 2$
$= 34$ units

$A = \ell \times w$
$= 8 \times 2$
$= 16$ square units

$P = (2 \times \ell) + (2 \times w)$
$= (2 \times 8) + (2 \times 2)$
$= 16 + 4$
$= 20$ units

$A = \ell \times w$
$= 4 \times 4$
$= 16$ square units

$P = (2 \times \ell) + (2 \times w)$
$= 8 + 8$
$= 16$ units

Only the 4 × 4 castle can be surrounded by 16 water tiles.

## Problem Solving

**© 15. Writing to Explain** Park School and North School cover the same area. In physical education classes, each student runs one lap around the school. At which school do the students have to run farther?

Park School

North School

**© 16. Estimation** Sue bought 2 sweaters for $18 each and mittens for $11. About how much money will she get in change if she pays with 3 twenty-dollar bills?

**17.** The perimeter of rectangle P is 12 feet. The perimeter of rectangle Q is 18 feet. Both rectangles have the same area. Find the area and the dimensions of each rectangle.

**18.** Ms. Fisher is using 64 carpet tiles to make a reading area in her classroom. Each tile is a square that measures 1 foot by 1 foot. What is the length and width of the rectangular area she can make with the smallest possible perimeter?

**19.** Bella is putting down patches of sod to start a new lawn. She has 20 square yards of sod. Give the dimensions of two different rectangular regions that she can cover with the sod. What is the perimeter of each region?

**© 20. Reason** Which statement about the rectangles to the right is true?

**A** They both have the same width.

**B** They both have the same length.

**C** They both have the same perimeter.

**D** They both have the same area.

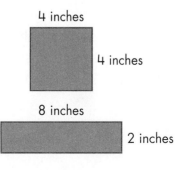

4 inches

4 inches

8 inches

2 inches

Lesson
# 14-9

ⓒ
**Common Core**

3.G.2 Partition shapes into parts with equal areas. Express the area of each part as a unit fraction of the whole.... Also 3.MD.5

# Equal Areas and Fractions

**Hands-On**
grid paper

## How can you use equal areas to model unit fractions?

Ben folds a square sheet of paper into four parts. All four parts have the same area. How can he label each part?

the whole

---

**Guided Practice***

ⓒ **MATHEMATICAL PRACTICES**

### Do you know HOW?

ⓒ **Use Tools** For **1–3**, use centimeter grid paper.

1. Draw a 6 × 3 rectangle. Then draw lines to separate the rectangle into 3 equal parts.

2. Draw another 6 × 3 rectangle. Draw lines to separate it into 3 equal parts another way.

3. In each rectangle, what fraction shows the area of one of the parts?

### Do you UNDERSTAND?

4. Draw a third way Ben could fold the paper in the example above into 4 equal parts.

5. Look at the rectangle you drew for Exercise 1. What is its area? What is the area of each part?

---

**Independent Practice**

For **6** and **7**, copy each drawing on centimeter grid paper.

6. Show two ways to separate the rectangle into 2 equal parts. What fraction shows the area of one of the parts?

7. Show two ways to separate the rectangle into 6 equal parts. What fraction shows the area of one of the parts?

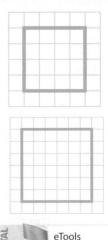

**DIGITAL**
eTools
www.pearsonsuccessnet.com

*For another example, see Set H on page 367.*

## One Way

Ben could fold the paper this way into four equal parts.

Since each part has the same area, it is $\frac{1}{4}$ of the whole.

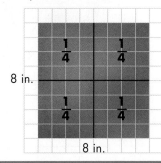

8 in.

8 in.

## Another Way

Ben could also fold the paper this way into four equal parts.

Since each part has the same area, it is $\frac{1}{4}$ of the whole.

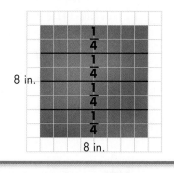

8 in.

8 in.

## Problem Solving

**MATHEMATICAL PRACTICES**

**8. Model** Mary made a cake to share equally among 8 people. Copy the picture below. Show how to divide the cake into 8 equal pieces. Label each piece using a unit fraction.

**9. Reason** Use the table below. Which animal can run 2 times as fast as the mule deer?

**Animal Sprint Speeds**

| Animal | Speed (mi per hr) |
|--------|------------------|
| Cheetah | 70 |
| Lion | 50 |
| Gray fox | 42 |
| Mule deer | 35 |

**10.** Noah's grandmother made a quilt for his bed. The quilt is made of 8 equal squares. What fraction of the quilt is one square?

**A** $\frac{1}{3}$  **B** $\frac{1}{4}$  **C** $\frac{1}{6}$  **D** $\frac{1}{8}$

**11. Persevere** Angie's teacher bought a crate of 48 apples at the market. She used 12 apples to make applesauce. Then she gave 25 apples to the students in her class. How many apples does she have left?

**12.** Kwan wants to plant half of his garden with flowers and half with vegetables. Copy the drawing on grid paper to show two ways he could do this.

**13. Writing to Explain** Look at how Casey and Pilar divided their pizzas. Who divided the pizza into equal parts? Explain.

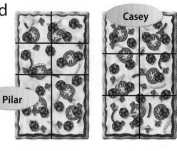

Casey

Pilar

Lesson
**14-10**

**Common Core**

3.MD.5 Recognize area as an attribute of plane figures and understand concepts of area measurement.

Problem Solving

# Selecting Appropriate Measurement Units and Tools

Which measurement unit and tool are the best choice for measuring the sides of a basketball court in order to find its area?

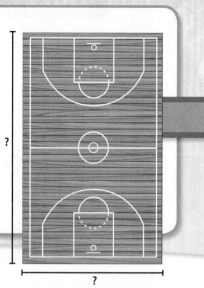

---

## Other Examples

Which measurement units would you choose to measure the area of these items?

notebook

The state of Wyoming

WYOMING

Cheyenne

- Square feet or square meters are much larger than the notebook.

- Square inches or square centimeters are smaller than the notebook and would be better to measure the area of something small.

- Square feet or square meters could be used but they are small compared to the size of the entire state of Wyoming.

- Square miles or square kilometers are larger and would be better to measure the area of something large.

---

## Guided Practice*

MATHEMATICAL PRACTICES

### Do you know HOW?

For **1** and **2**, name the measurement unit you would use to measure the area of each item.

   **1.** state of Florida    **2.** envelope

For **3** and **4**, name the measurement tool you would use to measure the area of each item.

   **3.** classroom floor    **4.** textbook cover

### Do you UNDERSTAND?

© **5. Reason** Give an example of an area that you would measure in square feet.

© **6. Reason** Give an example of an area that you would measure in square meters.

© **7. Reason** Give an example of a length that you would measure in inches or feet.

*For another example, see Set I on page 367.

A good measurement unit is usually:

- smaller than the amount to be measured
- large enough to make it easy to measure.

Think about these measurement tools:

inch ruler          centimeter ruler

yardstick          meter stick

- Square inches or square centimeters could be used to measure the basketball court, but they are small compared to the size of the court.
- Square feet or square meters are larger and would be better to use to measure the basketball court.

So, the appropriate measurement tool would be a yardstick or a meter stick.

## Independent Practice

**MATHEMATICAL PRACTICES**

For **8** through **11**, name the measurement unit you would use to measure the area of each item.

**8.** soccer field      **9.** large lake      **10.** cell phone      **11.** bedroom wall

For **12** through **15**, name the measurement tool you would use to measure the area of each item.

**12.** garage door      **13.** calculator      **14.** white board      **15.** postage stamp

**16.** What unit of measurement would you use to measure the area of a national park?

**17. Use Tools** Which measurement tool would you use to measure the length of a row boat? Explain your thinking.

**18.** Alexander is thinking of two whole numbers. The product of the two numbers is 28. Their difference is 3. What are the numbers?

**19. Reason** Mary has 3 hats, 4 scarves, and 2 pairs of gloves. How many different choices of 1 hat, 1 scarf, and 1 pair of gloves does she have?

**20.** Anna displayed 8 paintings in each of 4 rows. Which equation could NOT be used to find how many paintings she displayed in all?

   **A** $4 \times 8 = n$     **C** $8 \div n = 4$

   **B** $n \div 4 = 8$     **D** $8 + 8 + 8 + 8 = n$

**21. Use Structure** There are 250 horses entered in a show. All but 95 are jumpers. How many jumpers are entered?

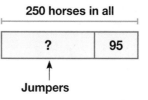

250 horses in all

| ? | 95 |
|---|----|

Jumpers

**Set A,** pages 342–343, 346–347

Count to find the area.

The shape fully covers 9 squares and partially covers 7 squares. Each partial cover is about one half of a square.

So, the shape has an area of about 13 square units.

You can use standard units of length to measure area.

If each unit in the grid above equals 1 square inch, then the shape has an area of about 13 square inches.

**Remember** you can count partial squares to estimate an area.

Count to find the area. Tell if the area is exact or an estimate.

**1.**

**2.**

Count the square units. Then write the area.

**3.**
4 in.

6 in.

**4.**
5 m

5 m

**Set B,** pages 344–345

The number of square units needed to cover the region inside a figure is its area.

Erica wants to make a wall poster that has an area of 30 square units. Should she use square inches or square centimeters as a unit?

A square centimeter is a square that has a length of 1 cm on each side.

An area of 30 square centimeters seems too small for a wall poster.

1 cm

A square inch is a square with 1-inch sides.

An area of 30 square inches seems more reasonable.

So, square inches is the better unit to use.

1 inch

**Remember** you can find the area of a figure by counting the number of square units in the figure.

**1.** Keisha made a painting with an area of 16 square inches. Anne's painting has an area of 16 square centimeters. Whose painting has a larger area?

**2.** Hasan wants to make an art design with an area of 50 square centimeters. If he makes his design on centimeter grid paper, how many squares would the design cover? Tell how you know.

Use a formula to find the area of the rectangle.

Area = length × width

$A = \ell \times w$
$A = 5 \times 4$
$A = 20$ square feet

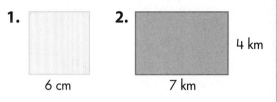
4 ft
5 ft

The area of the rectangle is 20 square feet.

**Remember** the terms *base* and *height* can be used for *length* and *width*.

Find the area of each shape.

1.

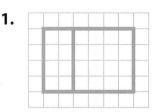

6 cm

2.

4 km

7 km

A large rectangle is separated into two rectangles. Compare the area of the large rectangle to the combined areas of the small rectangles.

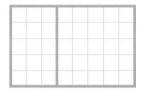

5 × 8 = 40
The area of the large rectangle is 40 square units.

Use the Distributive Property to break apart facts.

$5 \times 8 = 5 \times (5 + 3) = (5 \times 5) + (5 \times 3)$

The area of the large rectangle is equal to the area of the two small rectangles.

**Remember** to break apart facts to find the product.

Write an equation for each model.

1.

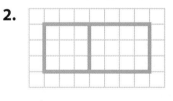

2.

Use simpler problems to find the area of the shaded part of the rectangle.

Find the area of the whole rectangle.
**5 × 7 = 35**

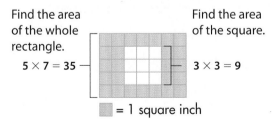

Find the area of the square.
**3 × 3 = 9**

= 1 square inch

Subtract: 35 − 9 = 26

The area of the shaded part of the rectangle is 26 square inches.

**Remember** to use the answers to the simpler problems.

Solve. Use simpler problems.

1. Walt wants to paint the shaded part of a wall. What is the area of the shaded part?

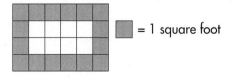

= 1 square foot

**Set F,** pages 354–356

You can divide a figure into rectangles to find the area.

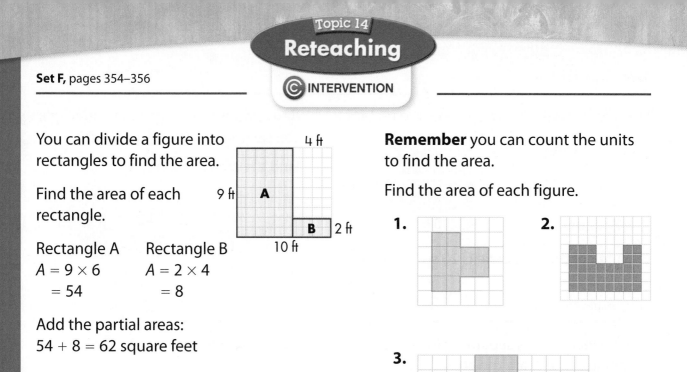

Find the area of each rectangle.

| Rectangle A | Rectangle B |
|---|---|
| $A = 9 \times 6$ | $A = 2 \times 4$ |
| $= 54$ | $= 8$ |

Add the partial areas:
$54 + 8 = 62$ square feet

**Remember** you can count the units to find the area.

Find the area of each figure.

**1.**

**2.**

**3.**

**Set G,** pages 358–359

Draw a different rectangle with the same perimeter as the one shown, and find its area.

8 ft

3 ft

$P = (2 \times \ell) + (2 \times w)$     $A = \ell \times w$
$= (2 \times 8) + (2 \times 3)$          $= 8 \times 3$
$= 16 + 6$                               $= 24$ square feet
$= 22$ ft

A 4 ft by 7 ft rectangle has the same perimeter.

$P = (2 \times 7) + (2 \times 4) = 22$ ft
$A = 7 \times 4$
$A = 28$ square feet

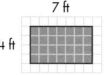

7 ft

4 ft

**Remember** that two rectangles can have the same area but different perimeters.

Draw two different rectangles with the perimeter listed. Find the area of each rectangle.

**1.** $P = 24$ feet

**2.** $P = 40$ centimeters

Draw two different rectangles with the area listed. Find the perimeter of each rectangle.

**3.** $A = 64$ square feet

**4.** $A = 80$ square yards

You can use equal areas to model unit fractions.

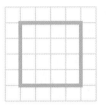

You can separate the square into 2 equal parts this way.

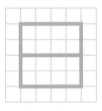

You can also separate the square into 2 equal parts this way.

Since each part has the same area it is $\frac{1}{2}$ of the whole.

**Remember** that equal parts have the same area.

Copy each figure on centimeter grid paper. Show two ways to separate the figure into equal parts. What fraction shows one of the parts?

**1.** 4 equal parts

**2.** 3 equal parts

**3.** 6 equal parts

Choose an appropriate measurement unit and tool to measure the area of a napkin.

- Square feet or square meters are too large compared to the size of a napkin.

- Square inches or square centimeters are smaller and easier to use.

The best tool would be an inch ruler or a centimeter ruler.

**Remember** a good measurement unit is smaller than the amount to be measured but large enough to make it easy to measure.

Name the measurement unit and tool you would use to measure the area of each item.

**1.** door          **2.** index card

**Multiple Choice**

ⓒ **ASSESSMENT**

1. Which measurement tool is the best choice for measuring the area of a football field? (14-10)

   **A**   Inch ruler

   **B**   Balance scale

   **C**   Yardstick

   **D**   Centimeter ruler

2. Mrs. Gee has 24 carpet squares. How should she arrange them so that she has the smallest perimeter? (14-8)

   **A**   12 by 2 rectangle

   **B**   1 by 24 rectangle

   **C**   8 by 3 rectangle

   **D**   4 by 6 rectangle

3. A diagram of Izzi's bedroom is shown below. What is the area of her room? (14-7)

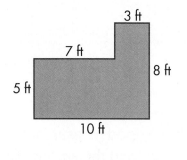

   **A**   44 square feet

   **B**   59 square feet

   **C**   74 square feet

   **D**   80 square feet

4. Which unit of measurement is best to use to measure the area of a large city? (14-10)

   **A**   Square centimeters

   **B**   Square meters

   **C**   Square yards

   **D**   Square miles

5. What is the area of the figure shown below? (14-1)

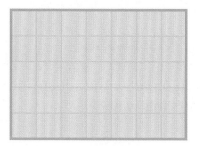

   **A**   25 square units

   **B**   30 square units

   **C**   35 square units

   **D**   40 square units

6. A picnic table is 9 feet long and 3 feet wide. What is the area of the rectangular surface of the table? (14-4)

   **A**   12 square feet

   **B**   18 square feet

   **C**   27 square feet

   **D**   39 square feet

**7.** A drawing of the floor in Curt's fort is shown below. What is the area of the fort's floor? (14-1)

**8.** Copy the figure below on grid paper. Show two ways to separate the figure into 8 equal parts. What fraction shows the area of one of the parts? (14-9)

**9.** Bill is making a poster with an area of 30 square inches. Jeff is making a poster with an area of 30 square centimeters. Phil thinks both the posters will be the same size. Is he correct? Explain. (14-2)

**10.** The large rectangle shown below has been separated into two small rectangles. Is the area of the large rectangle equal to the sum of the area of the two small rectangles? Write an equation to show how you know. (14-5)

**11.** Pepper's dog pen is shown below. What is the area of the dog pen? (14-3)

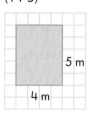

**12.** A swimming pool is drawn below. How many square feet of green tile are around the pool? (14-6)

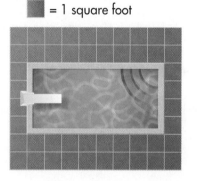

= 1 square foot

**13.** A diagram of Mark's garden is shown below. What is the area of the garden? (14-7)

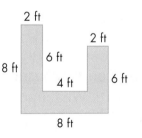

**14.** Meagan's playroom measures 6 feet by 9 feet. What is the area of the playroom? (14-3)

For **1** through **3,** use the banner below.

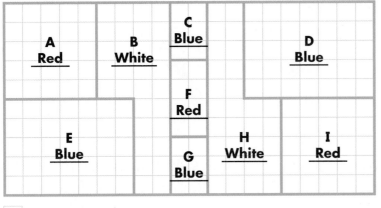

☐ = 1 square inch

1. Make a table like the one shown below. Complete the information for each section. The first part of the table has been started for you.

| Section | Color | Shape | Describe How to Find the Area | Area |
|---------|-------|-------|-------------------------------|------|
| A | Red | Square | | |
| | | | | |

2. What is the total area covered by each color?

3. What is the total area of the banner? What is its total perimeter?

4. Copy rectangle F on 1-inch grid paper and separate it into 4 equal parts. What fraction shows the area of one of the parts?

5. Copy rectangle D on 1-inch grid paper. Separate the 7-inch side in order to make a 5 × 4 rectangle and a 5 × 3 rectangle. Is the area of rectangle D equal to the sum of the areas of the two small rectangles? Write an equation to show how you know.

# Topic 15
# Liquid Volume and Mass

▼ Do you know how many grains of sand equal 1 gram? You will find out in Lesson 15-3.

## Review What You Know!

### Vocabulary

Choose the best term from the box.

- estimate
- fraction
- factor
- multiply

**1.** When you find $3 \times 4$, you __?__.

**2.** When you find a number that is about how many, you __?__.

**3.** If a whole is divided into equal parts, each part is a __?__ of the whole.

### Compare Measurements

Choose the greater amount.

**4.** 3 inches or 3 feet

**5.** 5 centimeters or 5 meters

### Add

Find each sum.

**6.** $400 + 57$

**7.** $100 + 100 + 36$

**8.** $10 + 10 + 5$

**9.** $1,000 + 1,000 + 1,000$

### Arrays

© **Writing to Explain** Use the array for **10** and **11**. Write an answer for each question.

**10.** How can you find the number of dots in the array?

**11.** Suppose there were 6 dots in each row. How could you find the number of dots in the array?

**Topic Essential Questions**
- What are the customary units for measuring capacity and weight?
- What are the metric units for measuring capacity and mass?

# Interactive Learning

**Pose the problem.** Start each lesson by working together to solve problems. It will help you make sense of math.

**Applying Math Practices**

- What am I asked to find?
- What else can I try?
- How are quantities related?
- How can I explain my work?
- How can I use math to model the problem?
- Can I use tools to help?
- Is my work precise?
- Why does this work?
- How can I generalize?

**1-Quart**

**1-Cup**

## Lesson 15-1

© **Reasonableness** Use measuring containers to complete this task.

The containers shown at the right are a 1-cup container and a 1-quart container. How much do you think the containers shown to you by your teacher hold? How can you check your estimate?

## Lesson 15-2

© **Reasonableness** Use measuring containers to complete this task.

The containers shown at the right are a 1-liter container and a 1-milliliter container. How much do you think the containers shown to you by your teacher hold? How can you check your estimates?

**About 1 Milliliter**

**About 1 Liter**

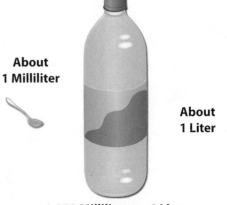

**1,000 Milliliters = 1 Liter**

### Lesson 15-3

© **Reasonableness** Use the objects you are shown to complete this task.

The objects shown at the right have a mass of about 1 gram and 1 kilogram. Using this information, what is the mass of the objects shown to you by your teacher? Tell how you made your estimates. How can you check?

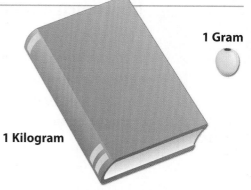

**1 Gram**

**1 Kilogram**

**1,000 Grams = 1 Kilogram**

### Lesson 15-4

© **Reasonableness** Use the objects you are shown to complete this task.

Using the information at the right, which unit of weight is more appropriate for stating the weight of the objects you are shown? Tell how you decided. How can you check?

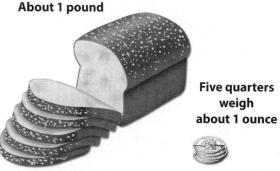

**About 1 pound**

**Five quarters weigh about 1 ounce**

**16 ounces = 1 pound**

### Lesson 15-5

© **Use Tools** Draw a picture to help you complete this task.

The animals at a pet store eat 80 kilograms of vegetables each day. How many kilograms of vegetables do they eat in one week?

| S | M | T | W | T | F | S |
|---|---|---|---|---|---|---|
| | | | | 1 | 2 | 3 |
| 4 | 5 | 6 | 7 | 8 | 9 | 10 |
| 11 | 12 | 13 | 14 | 15 | 16 | 17 |
| 18 | 19 | 20 | 21 | 22 | 23 | 24 |
| 25 | 26 | 27 | 28 | 29 | 30 | 31 |

**March**

Common
Core

3.MD.2 Measure
and estimate liquid
volumes . . . using standard
units of . . . liters (l). Add,
subtract, multiply, or divide
to solve one-step word
problems involving . . .
volumes that are given in
the same units, . . .

# Customary Units of Capacity

## What customary units describe how much a container holds?

The capacity of a container is the volume of a container measured in liquid units. What is the capacity of this pail?

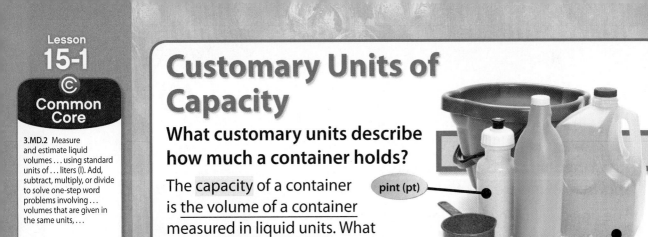

pint (pt)

cup (c)

quart (qt)

gallon (gal)

## Guided Practice*

MATHEMATICAL
PRACTICES

### Do you know HOW?

For **1** and **2**, choose the better estimate for each.

**1.**

1 c or 1 qt

**2.**

3 pt or 3 gal

### Do you UNDERSTAND?

**3. Reason** Why does it make sense to measure the pail above in gallons rather than in cups?

**4.** Find a container that you think holds about 1 gallon and another that holds about 1 cup. Then use measuring containers to see how well you estimated each capacity.

## Independent Practice

For **5–12**, choose the better estimate for each.

**5.**

1 pt or 1 gal

**6.**

1 c or 1 pt

**7.**

1 c or 1 pt

**8.**

1 c or 1 qt

**9.** kitchen sink

22 c or 22 qt

**10.** water glass

1 c or 1 qt

**11.** baby bottle

1 qt or 1 c

**12.** tea kettle

3 qt or 3 c

Animated Glossary
www.pearsonsuccessnet.com

DIGITAL

Cups, pints, quarts, and gallons are customary units of capacity.

Choose an appropriate unit and estimate.

The cup, pint, and quart are too small. Use gallons.

The pail looks like it will hold more than 1 gallon.

**Units of Capacity**

Data

1 pint = 2 cups

1 quart = 2 pints

1 gallon = 4 quarts

Measure the capacity of the pail.

Count how many times you can fill a gallon container and empty it into the pail.

The pail holds about 2 gallons.

For **13–16**, choose the better unit to measure the capacity of each.

**13.** teacup

pt or c

**14.** swimming pool

pt or gal

**15.** water bottle

pt or gal

**16.** pitcher of juice

c or qt

**Problem Solving**

**MATHEMATICAL PRACTICES**

Ⓒ **17. Writing to Explain** Can containers with different shapes have the same capacity? Why or why not?

Ⓒ **18. Reason** Look at the hat at the right. It is sometimes called a ten-gallon hat!

This ten-gallon hat has a capacity of about 3 quarts!

**a** Can this hat really hold 10 gallons? How do you know?

**b** Can this hat hold 1 gallon? How do you know?

**19.** Which measurement best describes the capacity of a bathtub?

**A** 50 cups

**B** 50 quarts

**C** 50 gallons

**D** 50 pints

**20.** Which of the objects below holds about 1 pint?

**A** bowl of soup

**B** punch bowl

**C** gas tank

**D** pool

Ⓒ **21. Persevere** Jeanne made 5 pitchers of lemonade. Each pitcher served 9 customers at her lemonade stand. If Jeanne had 1 pitcher of lemonade left, how many customers did Jeanne serve?

Lesson
15-2

© Common Core

3.MD.2 Measure and estimate liquid volumes . . . using standard units of . . . liters (l). Add, subtract, multiply, or divide to solve one-step word problems involving . . . volumes that are given in the same units, . . .

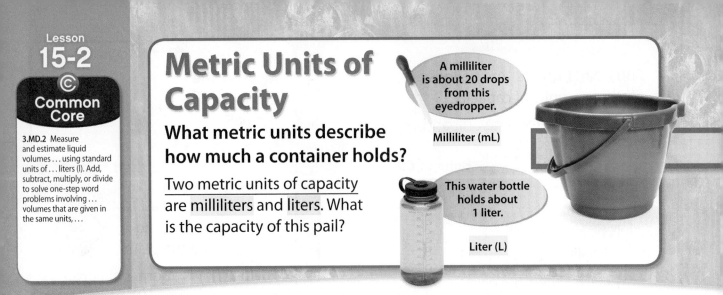

# Metric Units of Capacity

## What metric units describe how much a container holds?

Two metric units of capacity are milliliters and liters. What is the capacity of this pail?

A milliliter is about 20 drops from this eyedropper.

Milliliter (mL)

This water bottle holds about 1 liter.

Liter (L)

---

## Guided Practice*

© MATHEMATICAL PRACTICES

### Do you know HOW?

Choose the better estimate for each.

**1.**

250 mL or 2 L

**2.**

5 mL or 1 L

### Do you UNDERSTAND?

© **3. Writing to Explain** Suppose the capacity of the pail above is given in milliliters. Is this number greater or less than the number of liters? Explain.

**4.** Find a container that you predict will hold more than a liter and another that you predict will hold less than a liter. Then use a liter container to check your predictions.

---

## Independent Practice

In **5–12**, choose the better estimate for each.

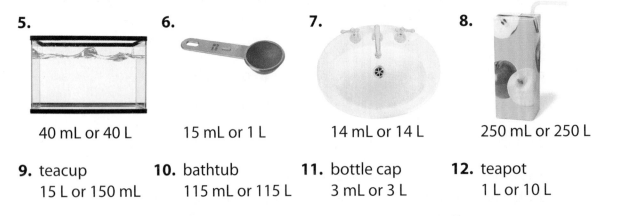

**5.**

40 mL or 40 L

**6.**

15 mL or 1 L

**7.**

14 mL or 14 L

**8.**

250 mL or 250 L

**9.** teacup
15 L or 150 mL

**10.** bathtub
115 mL or 115 L

**11.** bottle cap
3 mL or 3 L

**12.** teapot
1 L or 10 L

*For another example, see Set B on page 384.

## Step 1

Choose an appropriate unit and estimate.

**Units of Capacity**

1,000 milliliters = 1 liter

A milliliter is too small. So use liters.
The pail will hold several liters.

## Step 2

Measure the capacity.

Count how many times you can fill a liter container and empty it into the pail.

The pail holds about 8 liters.

---

For **13–16**, choose the unit you would use to measure the capacity of each.

**13.** soup can
mL or L

**14.** water pitcher
mL or L

**15.** swimming pool
mL or L

**16.** baby bottle
mL or L

---

## Problem Solving

MATHEMATICAL
PRACTICES

**Reasonableness** For **17–20**, is the capacity of each container more than a liter or less than a liter?

**17.** large pot

**18.** glass of juice

**19.** washing machine

**20.** mug

**21. Reason** Which cooler has a greater capacity? Explain your thinking.

**22.** Which measurement best describes the capacity of a can of paint?

**A** 4 mL

**C** 40 L

**B** 4 L

**D** 40 mL

Cooler B

Cooler A

A sandgrouse can soak up about enough water to fill a small perfume bottle.

**23. Reason** A sandgrouse can soak up water in its fluffy feathers. It can carry the water many kilometers to its chicks. Does a sandgrouse carry 20 milliliters of water or 2 liters of water?

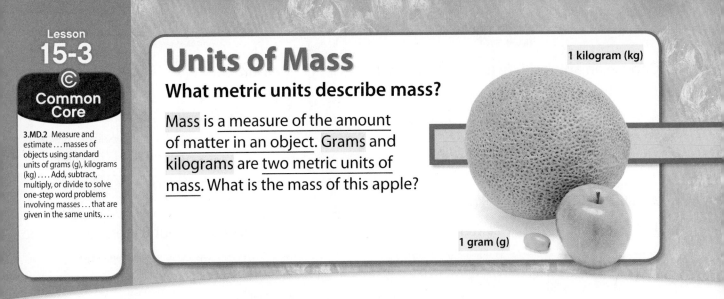

# Units of Mass

**What metric units describe mass?**

Mass is a measure of the amount of matter in an object. Grams and kilograms are two metric units of mass. What is the mass of this apple?

1 kilogram (kg)

1 gram (g)

**Lesson 15-3**

**Common Core**

3.MD.2 Measure and estimate . . . masses of objects using standard units of grams (g), kilograms (kg) . . . . Add, subtract, multiply, or divide to solve one-step word problems involving masses . . . that are given in the same units, . . .

---

## Guided Practice*

**MATHEMATICAL PRACTICES**

### Do you know HOW?

**Reasonableness** Choose the better estimate for each.

**1.** 5 g or 5 kg

**2.** 40 g or 4 kg

### Do you UNDERSTAND?

**3. Writing to Explain** There are 10 weights on the pan balance above. Why isn't the mass of the apple 10 grams?

**4.** Find an object that you think has a mass more than a kilogram and another that has a mass less than a kilogram. Then use a pan balance to see if you are correct.

---

## Independent Practice

For **5–12**, choose the better estimate for each.

**5.** 100 g or 10 kg

**6.** 15 g or 15 kg

**7.** 4 g or 400 g

**8.** 200 g or 2 kg

**9.** bicycle
2 kg or 12 kg

**10.** feather
1 g or 1 kg

**11.** horse
5 kg or 550 kg

**12.** penny
3 g or 300 g

Animated Glossary
www.pearsonsuccessnet.com

*For another example, see Set C on page 385.

## Step 1

Choose a unit and estimate.

> **Units of Mass**
> ..............
> 1,000 grams = 1 kilogram

The unit kilogram is too big. Use grams.

The mass of the apple is less than 1 kilogram but more than 1 gram.

## Step 2

Measure the mass of the apple.

Two 100-gram weights, six 10-gram weights, and two 1-gram weights balance with the apple.

The apple has a mass of 262 grams.

---

## Problem Solving

**MATHEMATICAL PRACTICES**

© **Use Tools** For **13–17**, choose the best tool to measure each.

**13.** the capacity of a glass

**14.** the temperature of water

**15.** the length of a box

**16.** the weight of a pear

**17.** the length of time you sleep

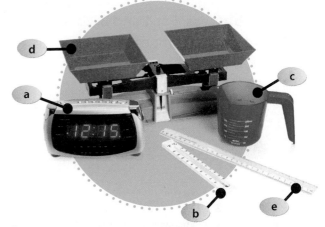

**18.** What is the mass of the orange?

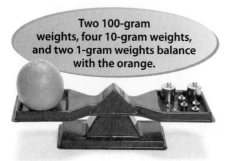

Two 100-gram weights, four 10-gram weights, and two 1-gram weights balance with the orange.

© **19. Reason** Correct the mistakes in the shopping list below.

Shopping List
2 L of apples
3 kg of milk
5 cm of flour

© **20. Use Structure** A bag holds 500 grams of sand. About how many grains of sand are in the bag?

There are about 1,000 grains of sand in 1 gram.

**21.** Which measurement best describes the mass of a rabbit?

**A** 2 grams

**B** 2 kilograms

**C** 2 liters

**D** 2 meters

3.MD.2 Measure and estimate . . . masses of objects using standard units of grams (g), kilograms (kg) . . . . Add, subtract, multiply, or divide to solve one-step word problems involving masses . . . that are given in the same units, . . .

# Units of Weight

### What customary units describe how heavy something is?

The weight of an object is a measure of how heavy the object is. What is the weight of this apple?

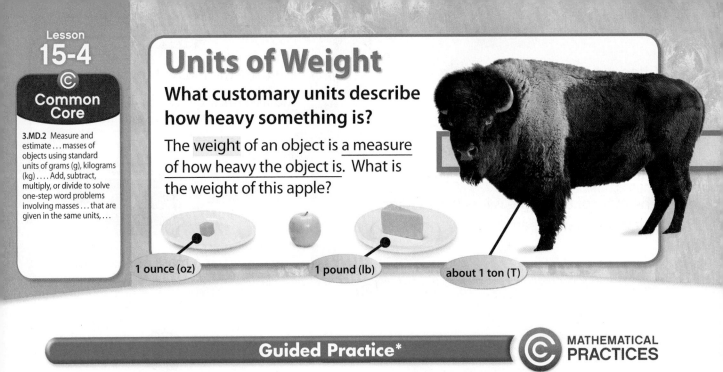

1 ounce (oz)　　　1 pound (lb)　　　about 1 ton (T)

---

## Guided Practice*

© **MATHEMATICAL PRACTICES**

### Do you know HOW?

© **Reasonableness** For **1** and **2**, choose the better estimate for each.

**1.**

1 oz or 1 lb

**2.**
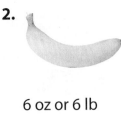
6 oz or 6 lb

### Do you UNDERSTAND?

© **3. Reason** If you buy a bag of 6 apples, what unit would you use for its weight? Explain.

**4.** Find an object that you think weighs about 1 pound and another that weighs about 1 ounce. Then weigh the objects to see how well you estimated.

---

## Independent Practice

For **5–12**, choose the better estimate for each.

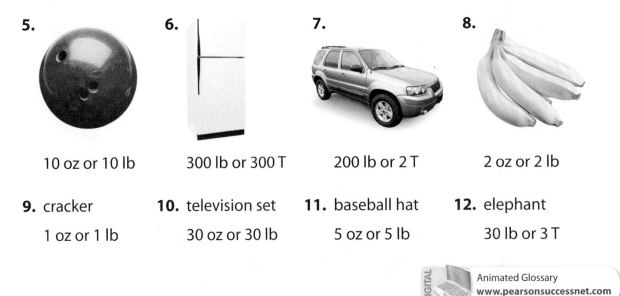

**5.**
10 oz or 10 lb

**6.**
300 lb or 300 T

**7.**
200 lb or 2 T

**8.**
2 oz or 2 lb

**9.** cracker
1 oz or 1 lb

**10.** television set
30 oz or 30 lb

**11.** baseball hat
5 oz or 5 lb

**12.** elephant
30 lb or 3 T

DIGITAL
Animated Glossary
www.pearsonsuccessnet.com

*For another example, see Set D on page 385.

Ounces, pounds, and tons are <u>units of weight</u>.

Choose a unit and estimate.

The units pound and ton are too big. Use ounces.

The apple weighs less than 1 pound but more than 1 ounce.

**Units of Weight**

Data

16 ounces = 1 pound

2,000 pounds = 1 ton

Weigh the apple.

Three stacks of three 1-ounce weights balance with the apple.

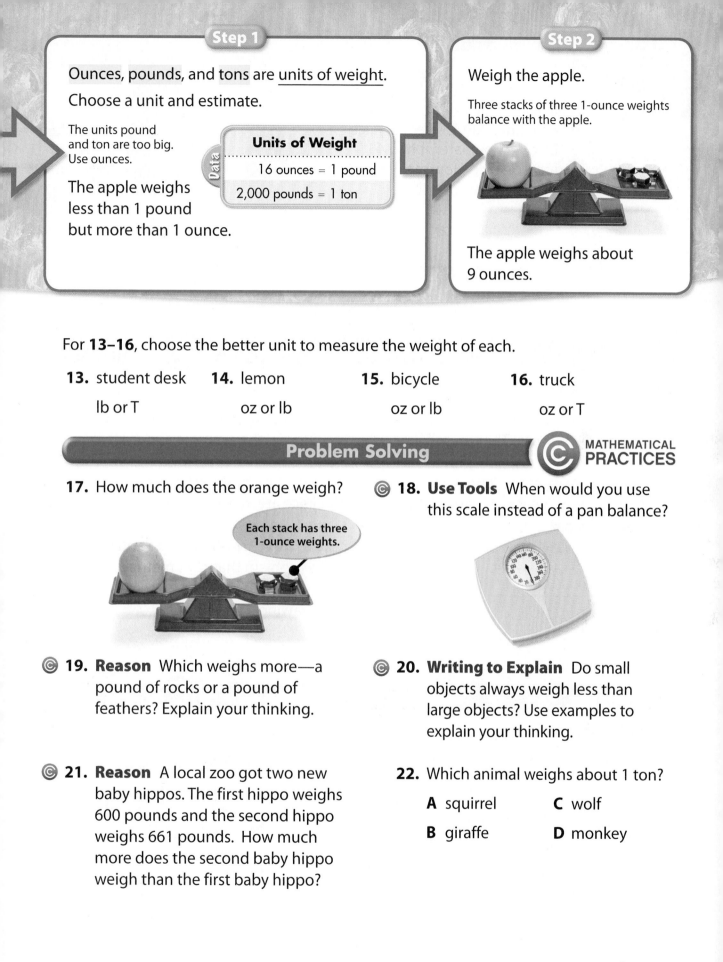

The apple weighs about 9 ounces.

For **13–16**, choose the better unit to measure the weight of each.

**13.** student desk

lb or T

**14.** lemon

oz or lb

**15.** bicycle

oz or lb

**16.** truck

oz or T

## Problem Solving

MATHEMATICAL
PRACTICES

**17.** How much does the orange weigh?

Each stack has three 1-ounce weights.

© **18. Use Tools** When would you use this scale instead of a pan balance?

© **19. Reason** Which weighs more—a pound of rocks or a pound of feathers? Explain your thinking.

© **20. Writing to Explain** Do small objects always weigh less than large objects? Use examples to explain your thinking.

© **21. Reason** A local zoo got two new baby hippos. The first hippo weighs 600 pounds and the second hippo weighs 661 pounds. How much more does the second baby hippo weigh than the first baby hippo?

**22.** Which animal weighs about 1 ton?

**A** squirrel     **C** wolf

**B** giraffe     **D** monkey

Lesson
**15-5**

© 
**Common Core**

3.MD.2 ... Add, subtract, multiply, or divide to solve one-step word problems involving masses or volumes that are given in the same units, e.g., by using drawings ... to represent the problem.

**Problem Solving**

# Draw a Picture

In a juice factory, one 50-liter container had 28 liters of juice in it. An hour later, it had 45 liters of juice. How many liters of juice were added?

28 liters to start

45 liters
an hour later

---

## Guided Practice*

© **MATHEMATICAL PRACTICES**

### Do you know HOW?

1. Alex buys a box of pudding mix and a box of cocoa. The mass of the box of pudding mix is 100 grams. The total mass of the 2 boxes is 550 grams. What is the mass of the box of cocoa?

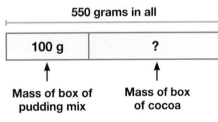

550 grams in all

| 100 g | ? |
|-------|---|

↑ Mass of box of pudding mix    ↑ Mass of box of cocoa

### Do you UNDERSTAND?

© 2. **Model** Suppose the 45 liters of juice in the example above were evenly divided into 9 batches. Draw a picture to show how many liters of juice are in each batch.

© 3. **Write a Problem** Write and solve a problem that uses metric units of capacity and can be solved by drawing a picture.

---

## Independent Practice

© **MATHEMATICAL PRACTICES**

© 4. **Be Precise** Peter has divided 120 liters of water equally in 3 containers. How many liters has he poured into each container?

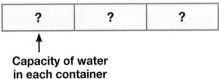

120 liters in all

| ? | ? | ? |
|---|---|---|

↑ Capacity of water in each container

**Applying Math Practices**

- What am I asked to find?
- What else can I try?
- How are quantities related?
- How can I explain my work?
- How can I use math to model the problem?
- Can I use tools to help?
- Is my work precise?
- Why does this work?
- How can I generalize?

5. Adeela pours 235 milliliters of milk in a glass and 497 milliliters of milk in a bottle. How many milliliters of milk has she poured in all?

*For another example, see Set E on page 385.

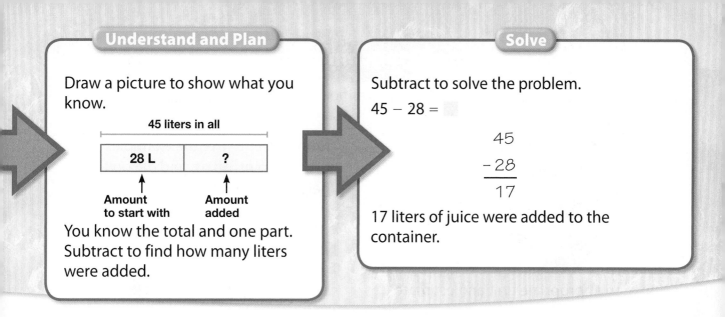

Draw a picture to show what you know.

45 liters in all

| 28 L | ? |
|------|---|

↑ Amount to start with   ↑ Amount added

You know the total and one part. Subtract to find how many liters were added.

Subtract to solve the problem.

45 − 28 =

$$\begin{array}{r} 45 \\ -\ 28 \\ \hline 17 \end{array}$$

17 liters of juice were added to the container.

---

© **Model** For **6** and **7,** draw a picture to help solve the problem.

**6.** Mr. Patel wants to pack 28 kilograms of potting soil into 4 boxes. He wants each box to have the same mass. How many kilograms of potting soil should he put in each box?

**7.** Laurie bought a 500 milliliter carton of cream. After using some of the cream, she had 245 milliliters left. How many milliliters of cream did she use?

Use the table for **8–10**. For **9**, copy and complete the picture. Answer the question.

**8.** Hector has poured the flour and salt needed to make a batch of modeling clay in a container. What is the total weight of both the ingredients?

© **9. Persevere** Beth has 63 ounces of salt in her mixing bowl. How many batches of modeling clay is she making?

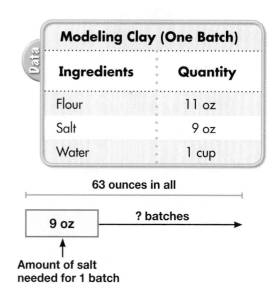

**Modeling Clay (One Batch)**

| Ingredients | Quantity |
|-------------|----------|
| Flour | 11 oz |
| Salt | 9 oz |
| Water | 1 cup |

63 ounces in all

| 9 oz | ? batches → |
|------|-------------|

↑ Amount of salt needed for 1 batch

**10.** Donna has 6 first aid kits. Each kit is 8 pounds. Which of these is the total weight of all of Donna's first aid kits?

**A** 14 lb   **B** 24 lb   **C** 48 lb   **D** 64 lb

© **11. Writing to Explain** Eric filled a container to the 20 L mark with juice an hour ago. The juice is now at the 15 L mark. How many liters of juice has been poured out of it? Explain how you know.

**Set A,** pages 374–375

What is the capacity of this teapot?

Choose an appropriate unit and estimate.

Gallon and quart are too big. The teapot holds more than 1 pint but fewer than 2 pints.

If you estimate using cups, the teapot looks like it holds about 3 cups.

**Remember** to use the examples of a cup, pint, quart, and gallon to help you estimate.

1 c or 1 qt          30 pt or 30 gal

**Set B,** pages 376–377

What is the capacity of this pitcher?

Choose an appropriate unit and estimate.

A milliliter is too small, so estimate using liters.

If you estimate using liters the pitcher looks like it will hold about 2 liters.

You can check your work by thinking about what you already know.

A liter is about the same size as a large water bottle. A pitcher usually holds more liquid than a water bottle. So, 2 liters seems like a good estimate.

**Remember** that more than one unit can be used to measure the capacity of a container.

Choose the better estimate.

**1.**

150 mL or 150 L

**2.**

5 mL or 5 L

**3.**

1 mL or 1 L

What is the mass of this bar of soap?

Choose a unit and estimate.

A kilogram is too much, so estimate using grams.

The bar of soap has about the same mass as 100 grapes, or about 100 grams.

**Remember** to use the examples of a gram and kilogram to help you estimate.

Choose the better estimate.

**1.** **2.**

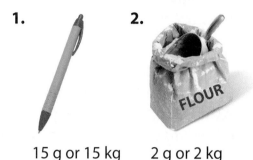

15 g or 15 kg      2 g or 2 kg

What is the weight of a tennis ball?

Choose a unit and estimate.

A tennis ball does not weigh as much as a ton or even a pound, so estimate using ounces.

The tennis ball weighs about as much as 4 small cubes of cheese, or about 4 ounces.

**Remember** to use the examples of an ounce, pound, and ton to help you estimate.

Choose the better estimate.

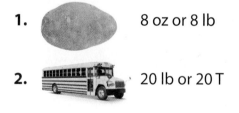

**1.**      8 oz or 8 lb

**2.**      20 lb or 20 T

There are 7 people on Ed's bowling team. Each own their own bowling ball. The mass of a bowling ball is 5 kilograms. What is the total mass of the team's bowling balls?

| ? kg in all | | | | | | |
|---|---|---|---|---|---|---|
| 5 kg | 5 kg | 5 kg | 5 kg | 5 kg | 5 kg | 5 kg |

$7 \times 5 =$ ▢      **The total mass of the**

$7 \times 5 = 35$      **the team's bowling**

**balls is 35 kg.**

**Remember** to draw pictures to show the information you know.

Draw a picture and then solve.

**1.** The water tank in Mary's yard holds 60 liters of water. She used 13 liters to water her plants. How many liters of water remain in the water tank?

**1.** Which unit would be best to measure the mass of a mouse? (15-3)

**A** Gram

**B** Kilogram

**C** Liter

**D** Milliliter

**2.** One serving of butter contains 90 mg of sodium. How many milligrams of sodium do 5 servings of butter contain? (15-5)

? milligrams

| 90 mg | 90 mg | 90 mg | 90 mg | 90 mg |
|-------|-------|-------|-------|-------|

**A** 540

**B** 450

**C** 360

**D** 45

**3.** Which is the best unit to measure the capacity of a swimming pool? (15-1)

**A** Cups

**B** Gallons

**C** Pints

**D** Quarts

**4.** Which of the following best describes the mass of an orange? (15-3)

**A** 20 kilograms

**B** 200 kilograms

**C** 20 grams

**D** 200 grams

**5.** Which of the following would you measure in milliliters? (15-2)

**A** Capacity of an aquarium

**B** Capacity of an eyedropper

**C** Capacity of a coffee pot

**D** Capacity of a bathtub

**6.** Which of the following best describes the capacity of a water balloon? (15-1)

**A** 2 cups

**B** 2 quarts

**C** 20 cups

**D** 20 pints

**7.** Which is the best estimate of the weight of a common adult raccoon? (15-4)

**A** 30 tons

**B** 300 pounds

**C** 30 pounds

**D** 30 ounces

**8.** Which is a metric unit that would be best to measure the capacity of a watering can? (15-2)

**A** Meter

**B** Liter

**C** Kilogram

**D** Quart

**9.** Name a customary unit that would be best to measure the capacity of a kitchen sink. (15-1)

Name the correct customary unit to complete each sentence.

**10.** The best estimate of the weight of an adult American bison is
1 _____. (15-4)

**11.** A basketball weighs about
20 _____. (15-4)

Name the correct metric unit to complete each sentence.

**12.** The mass of a bicycle is about
10 _____. (15-3)

**13.** The capacity of a sink is about
10 _____. (15-2)

**14.** Rory has 1 liter of water and wants to fill a household container with it. Name a container Rory can fill. (15-2)

**15.** A catsup bottle contains 24 fluid ounces of catsup. Marsha wants to fill 6 containers with the same amount of catsup in each container. How many fluid ounces of catsup will be in each container? Draw a picture to solve. (15-5)

**16.** Explain why it is better to use ounces than pounds to measure the weight of a bumble bee. (15-4)

**17.** The lines on the container below show its capacity in milliliters. Joanna filled the container to the 750 mL mark with milk. Then she used some of the milk. How many milliliters of milk did she use? (15-5)

**18.** Which container holds more, a half-gallon carton, or a 2-quart bottle? Explain your answer. (15-1)

**19.** What is the best tool to use to measure the mass of a grapefruit? (15-3)

**20.** Is the capacity of a recycling bin more than a liter or less than a liter? (15-2)

1. The winners of a blue ribbon are shown.

pumpkin

red pepper

Write a possible mass for each. Use grams or kilograms.

2. You need to decide which container of apple juice to buy. You need about 2 drinking glasses of apple juice for a recipe. Which container should you buy – the 250 mL or the 1 L of apple juice? Explain your answer.

3. Name something you would measure in gallons.

4. A recipe for pasta salad is shown. Which weighs more—the Swiss cheese cubes or the pasta?

5. What measurement would best describe the mass of the spinach leaves?

6. The recipe for fruit punch is shown. Which container would be best to use to hold the fruit punch—1 cup, 1 pint, 1 quart, 3 quarts, or 5 quarts? Why?

7. Will one recipe of fruit punch fit into a 1-gallon container? Explain.

8. Tom wants to make 5 batches of fruit punch. Draw a picture to show how much ginger ale he will use.

9. Holly wants to make 3 batches of pasta salad. Draw a picture to show how many ounces of cheddar cheese cubes she will use.

> **Pasta Salad**
> 1 lb of elbow pasta
> 4 ounces cheddar cheese cubes
> 6 ounces Swiss cheese cubes
> 2 cups spinach leaves
> 1 cup tomatoes, chopped
> $\frac{1}{3}$ cup Italian dressing

> **Fruit Punch**
> 1 quart orange juice
> 1 quart hot tea
> 1 quart ginger ale
> 1 pint apple juice
> 1 cup lemon juice
> $\frac{1}{2}$ cup honey

# Topic 16 Data

▼ How fast can a peregrine falcon fly? You will find out in Lesson 16-5.

## Review What You Know!

### Vocabulary

Choose the best term from the box.

- compare
- symbol
- data
- tally

1. A graph can be used to _?_ information.

2. _?_ from a survey can be used to make a graph.

3. A _?_ is a mark used to record data on a chart.

### Order Numbers

Write in order from least to greatest.

4. 56, 47, 93, 39, 10    5. 20, 43, 23, 19, 22

6. 24, 14, 54, 34, 4    7. 65, 33, 56, 87, 34

### Skip Counting

Find the next two numbers in each pattern. Write a rule for the pattern.

8. 5, 10, 15, 20, ▮, ▮

9. 2, 4, 6, 8, ▮, ▮

10. 10, 20, 30, 40, ▮, ▮

11. 4, 8, 12, 16, ▮, ▮

### Comparing

Ⓒ12. **Writing to Explain** Explain how to use place value to compare 326 and 345.

**Topic Essential Question**
- How can data be represented, interpreted, and analyzed?

# Interactive Learning  Hands-On Minds-On

**Pose the problem.** Start each lesson by working together to solve problems. It will help you make sense of math.

## Applying Math Practices

- What am I asked to find?
- What else can I try?
- How are quantities related?
- How can I explain my work?
- How can I use math to model the problem?
- Can I use tools to help?
- Is my work precise?
- Why does this work?
- How can I generalize?

---

### Lesson 16-1

© **Use Tools**  Use data collected to answer the question.

There are 10 pieces of paper in a bag, each with a number from 1 through 4. As each piece of paper is picked, use the number line on the recording sheet to keep track of each number by making a mark above the number. The paper is returned to the bag and repeated 20 times. Which number is picked most often from the bag?

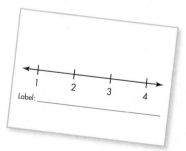

---

### Lesson 16-2

© **Reason**  Use data given by your class to answer the questions.

A shoe manufacturer wants to know the lengths to the nearest half-inch of third graders' feet. What information could your class send to them, and how can you organize to answer their questions like, "Are the lengths spread out evenly, or clumped around certain numbers"?  What value appears the most in the data?

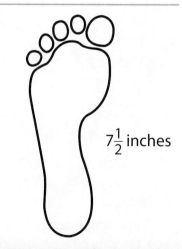

$7\frac{1}{2}$ inches

MATHEMATICAL
PRACTICES

**Lesson 16-3**

© **Use Tools** Use the given graph on the recording sheet to answer the question.

Students in Jorge's class took a survey of their favorite cereals. Then they made a graph to show the data. Jorge was absent on the day the class did this work. What can he learn by looking at the graph? Tell how you decided.

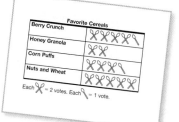

**Lesson 16-4**

© **Use Tools** Solve using the data on the recording sheet.

Mary is helping her teacher count new playground toys for the school. How can she put the data in a pictograph? What can you conclude from the graph?

| Basketballs | |
| Jump Ropes | |
| Bats | |
| Soccer Balls | |

Each 🏀 = 5 toys

**Lesson 16-5**

© **Use Tools** Solve using the data shown at the right.

Use the data about the number of pages read to make a bar graph. What conclusions can you make by looking at the bar graph? How did you decide?

| Student's Name | Number of Pages Read |
|---|---|
| Yoma | 25 |
| Don | 20 |
| Bonita | 20 |
| Adam | 15 |

_Data_

**Lesson 16-6**

© **Model** Solve any way you choose.

Compare the data shown in the bar graphs on the recording sheet. What are three conclusions you can draw from the data? Tell how you decided.

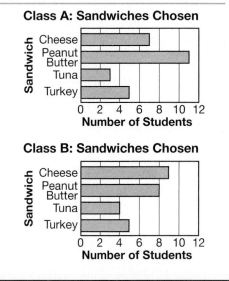

Class A: Sandwiches Chosen

Class B: Sandwiches Chosen

Common
Core

3.MD.4 Generate
measurement data by
measuring lengths using
rulers marked with halves
and fourths of an inch.
Show the data by making
a line plot, where the
horizontal scale is marked
off in appropriate units–
whole numbers, halves,
or quarters.

# Line Plots

## How can you use line plots?

For each day in April, Dara recorded the high temperature on a line plot. What temperature occurred as the high temperature most often in April?

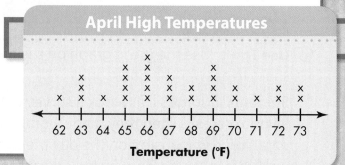

**April High Temperatures**

Temperature (°F)

---

## Guided Practice*

MATHEMATICAL
PRACTICES

### Do you know HOW?

The table below shows the results of the 3rd Grade long jump event. Use the data for **1** and **2**.

| 3rd Grade Long Jump | | | |
|---|---|---|---|
| Student | Distance (Inches) | Student | Distance (Inches) |
| 1 | 27 | 9 | 30 |
| 2 | 31 | 10 | 26 |
| 3 | 28 | 11 | 28 |
| 4 | 26 | 12 | 30 |
| 5 | 30 | 13 | 31 |
| 6 | 33 | 14 | 26 |
| 7 | 29 | 15 | 33 |
| 8 | 31 | 16 | 30 |

1. Make a line plot to show the data.

2. How many Xs should be drawn for the number of students who jumped 33 inches?

### Do you UNDERSTAND?

3. In the example above, what was the highest temperature recorded in April?

4. **Use Structure** Use the line plot below. Which high temperature occurred most often in August?

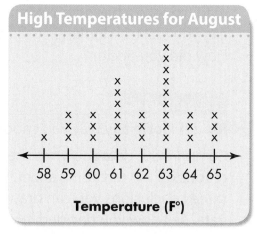

**High Temperatures for August**

Temperature (F°)

5. Using the line plot in Exercise 4, which high temperature occurred least often?

Animated Glossary
www.pearsonsuccessnet.com

*For another example, see Set A on page 406.

A line plot is a way to organize data on a number line.

To read a line plot, look at the numbers below the line. Then count the Xs above each number.

On Dara's line plot, each temperature is labeled below the line. Each X represents one day.

Since there are 2 Xs above the 68, the high temperature was 68° on two days.

Which temperature has the most Xs?

There are 5 Xs above the 66, so the high temperature was 66° on five days.

The temperature that occurred as the high temperature most often in April was 66°.

## Independent Practice

Amelia recorded the number of people riding in each of 18 cars that passed by. Use the data to the right for **6–8**.

**6.** Make a line plot to show the data.

**7.** How many Xs should be drawn for 3 people in a car?

**8.** Which number of people in each car occurred most often?

### Number of People in Each Car

| Car | Number of People | Car | Number of People | Car | Number of People |
|-----|------------------|-----|------------------|-----|------------------|
| 1 | 2 | 7 | 3 | 13 | 1 |
| 2 | 3 | 8 | 1 | 14 | 2 |
| 3 | 2 | 9 | 2 | 15 | 2 |
| 4 | 1 | 10 | 4 | 16 | 4 |
| 5 | 4 | 11 | 1 | 17 | 1 |
| 6 | 1 | 12 | 3 | 18 | 3 |

## Problem Solving

### MATHEMATICAL PRACTICES

Ⓒ **Be Precise** Use the line plot at the right for **9–11**. It shows how long it took each of 28 people to run a mile.

**9.** Which amount of time was used by the greatest number of people?

**10.** How many more people took 10 minutes than 5 minutes?

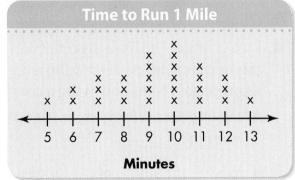

Time to Run 1 Mile

Minutes

**11.** Which was the longest time it took to run a mile?

    **A** 13 minutes      **C** 10 minutes

    **B** 12 minutes      **D** 5 minutes

Lesson
16-2

© Common Core

3.MD.4 Generate measurement data by measuring lengths using rulers marked with halves and fourths of an inch. Show the data by making a line plot, where the horizontal scale is marked off in appropriate units—whole numbers, halves, or quarters.

# Length and Line Plots

## How can line plots show data you have collected?

Serena measured the lengths of the pencils in her pencil box. How can she make a line plot to show these lengths?

| Lengths of Serena's Pencils | |
|---|---|
| **Color** | **Length** |
| Red | 6 in. |
| Blue | $4\frac{3}{4}$ in. |
| Green | $4\frac{3}{4}$ in. |
| Purple | $5\frac{1}{2}$ in. |
| Orange | $4\frac{3}{4}$ in. |
| Yellow | $4\frac{3}{4}$ in. |

---

## Guided Practice*

© MATHEMATICAL PRACTICES

### Do you know HOW?

**1.** Draw a line plot to show the data.

| Lengths of Sandy's Pencils | |
|---|---|
| **Color** | **Length** |
| Red | $6\frac{1}{4}$ in. |
| Blue | $3\frac{1}{4}$ in. |
| Green | $6\frac{3}{4}$ in. |
| Purple | $3\frac{3}{4}$ in. |
| Orange | $6\frac{3}{4}$ in. |
| Yellow | $6\frac{1}{2}$ in. |

### Do you UNDERSTAND?

**2.** What does the line plot tell you about Sandy's pencils?

© **3. Reason** Look at the chart for Sandy's pencils and the line plot you drew plotting their sizes. Compare them against the chart and line plot for the lengths of Serena's pencils.

   **A** Who has more pencils that are the same length, Serena or Sandy?

   **B** How can you tell whether Serena or Sandy has more pencils that are the same length?

---

## Independent Practice

**4.** Rico wants to organize his collection of paper chains. He measured the lengths of his paper chains and made a chart.

   **A** Use the data in Rico's chart to make a line plot.

   **B** What is the length of the longest paper chain? Shortest?

| Rico's Paper Chains | |
|---|---|
| **Number of Paper Chains** | **Length** |
| 3 | $6\frac{1}{2}$ in. |
| 2 | $7\frac{1}{2}$ in. |
| 4 | 8 in. |
| 1 | $8\frac{1}{2}$ in. |

Steps to make a line plot:

Draw a number line and choose a scale based on the lengths in the table. Mark halves and fourths.

The scale should show data values from the least to greatest.

Write a title for the line plot.

Mark an X for each length.

Serena can follow these steps to make a line plot. The line plot shows the lengths of her pencils.

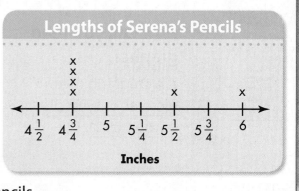

**Lengths of Serena's Pencils**

Inches

## Problem Solving

**MATHEMATICAL PRACTICES**

The line plot at the right shows the lengths in inches of pet hamsters in Mrs. Bell's class. Use the line plot to answer **5–8**.

**5. Use Tools** How many hamsters does the class have in all?

**6.** How long is the shortest hamster?

**Lengths of Mrs. Bell's Hamsters**

Inches

**7.** How long is the longest hamster?

**8. Writing to Explain** How do you know which length of hamster is the most common?

**Use Tools** For **9–11**, measure the lengths to the nearest quarter inch of 10 classroom objects that are between 1 and 6 inches long. Record your measurements.

**9.** Draw a line plot to show the data.

**10.** Based on the line plot, organize your data into a chart.

**11.** What was the greatest length? The least length? Which length occurred the most?

**12.** If a line plot has 3 Xs at 4 in., 1 X at 5 in., and 2 Xs at $3\frac{1}{2}$ in., which length is the most common?

**A** 3 in.          **C** 4 in.

**B** $3\frac{1}{2}$ in.          **D** 5 in.

3.MD.3 Draw a scaled picture graph and a scaled bar graph to represent a data set with several categories. Solve one- and two-step "how many more" and "how many less" problems using information presented in scaled bar graphs....

# Reading Pictographs and Bar Graphs

## How can you read graphs?

A pictograph uses pictures or symbols to show data.

The key explains what each picture represents.

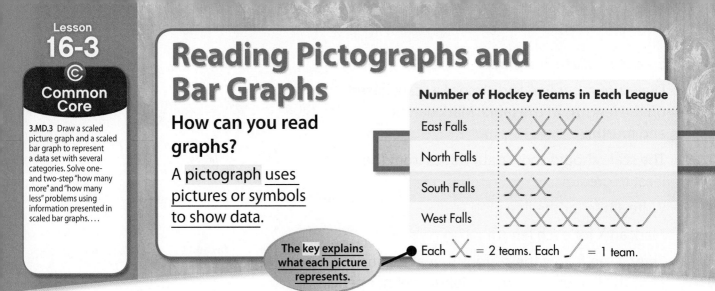

**Number of Hockey Teams in Each League**

| East Falls | ✗ ✗ ✗ ╱ |
| North Falls | ✗ ✗ ╱ |
| South Falls | ✗ ✗ |
| West Falls | ✗ ✗ ✗ ✗ ✗ ╱ |

Each ✗ = 2 teams. Each ╱ = 1 team.

---

**Another Example** **How can you read a bar graph?**

A bar graph uses bars to compare information. This bar graph shows the number of goals scored by different players on a hockey team.

The scale shows the units used.

On this graph, each grid line represents one unit. But only every other grid line is labeled: 0, 2, 4, and so on. For example, the line halfway between 4 and 6 represents 5 goals.

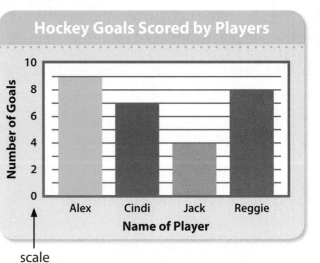

scale

How many goals did Cindi score?

Find Cindi's name. Use the scale to find how high the bar reaches. Cindi scored 7 goals.

Who scored the fewest goals?

Find the shortest bar. The bar for Jack is shortest. He scored the fewest goals.

### Explain It

1. Explain how to find how many more goals Alex scored than Cindi.

2. Who scored 8 goals?

3. How many goals in all did Alex and Reggie score?

How many teams are in the East Falls League?

Use the key.

Each ✕ represents 2 teams.

Each ╱ represents 1 team.

There are 3 ✕ and 1 ╱.

2 + 2 + 2 + 1 = 7

There are 7 teams in the East Falls League.

How many more teams does the East Falls League have than the South Falls League?

Compare the two rows.

East Falls League

3 more teams

South Falls League

The East Falls League has 3 more teams than the South Falls League.

## Guided Practice*

**MATHEMATICAL PRACTICES**

### Do you know HOW?

1. Which hockey league in the pictograph above has 5 teams?

2. Which league has the most teams? How many teams are in that league?

### Do you UNDERSTAND?

In **3** and **4**, use the pictograph above.

© 3. **Communicate** Explain how to find which league has the fewest teams.

4. How many teams in all are in the North Falls and West Falls Leagues?

## Independent Practice

In **5–7**, use the pictograph at the right.

5. Which area has lights on for the most hours in a week?

6. Which area of the Tri-Town Sports Center has lights on for 50 hours each week?

7. In one week, how many more hours are lights on in the exercise room than in the swimming pool?

**Tri-Town Sports Center**
**Number of Hours Lights Are on Each Week**

| | |
|---|---|
| Exercise Room | 💡💡💡💡💡💡💡💡 |
| Locker Room | 💡💡💡💡💡💡💡💡💡💡 |
| Swimming Pool | 💡💡💡💡💡 |
| Tennis Court | 💡💡💡💡💡 |

Each 💡 = 10 hours. Each ❘ = 5 hours.

Animated Glossary
www.pearsonsuccessnet.com

DIGITAL

In **8–12**, use the bar graph at the right.

**8.** How fast can a jack rabbit run?

**9.** Which animal has the greatest top running speed?

**10.** Which animal has a top running speed of 50 miles per hour?

**11.** How much greater is the top running speed of a coyote than that of a grizzly bear?

Ⓒ **12. Use Tools** Which animals have the same top running speed?

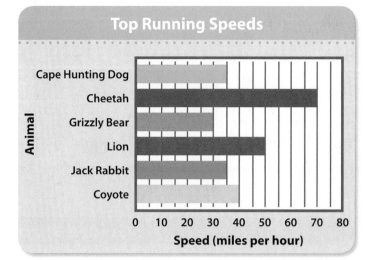

**Top Running Speeds**

In **13–15**, use the pictograph.

**13.** To the nearest 10,000, how many seats are in the Rose Bowl?

Ⓒ **14. Estimation** Which two stadiums have about the same number of seats?

Ⓒ **15. Writing to Explain** Maria says Soldier Field has about 6,000 seats. Is she correct? Explain.

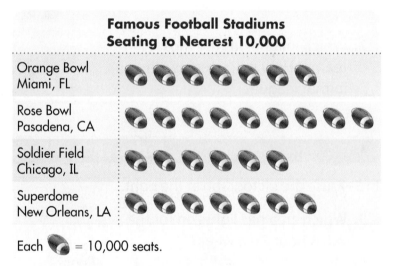

**Famous Football Stadiums
Seating to Nearest 10,000**

Each 🏈 = 10,000 seats.

In **16** and **17**, use the bar graph.

**16.** How many more soccer balls than basketballs are in the gym closet?

　**A** 8　　　　**C** 4

　**B** 5　　　　**D** 3

Ⓒ **17. Persevere** How many balls in all are in the gym closet?

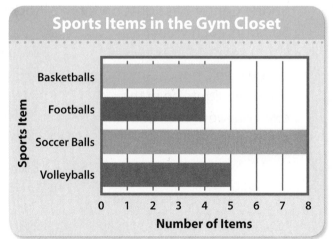

**Sports Items in the Gym Closet**

# Mixed Problem Solving

The government where you live uses money from the taxes that people pay to provide different kinds of services. The bar graph at the right shows how much money different departments in Park Town receive. Use the graph to answer the questions.

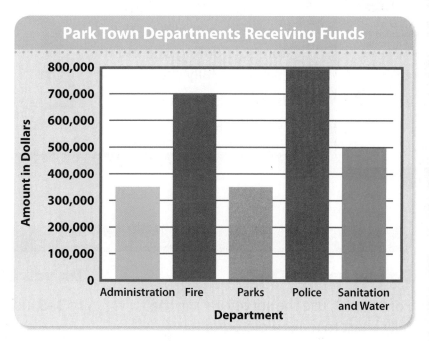

**Park Town Departments Receiving Funds**

1. Which service in Park Town will receive the most funds?

2. Which two departments will get the same amount?

© 3. **Be Precise** About how much money will the Sanitation and Water Department receive?

4. Which services will receive $500,000 or more in funds?

5. Use the table below that shows how the Police Department money is used.

| Police Department | |
| --- | --- |
| **Expenses** | **Amount** |
| Cars | $42,000 |
| Computers | $14,000 |
| Police Equipment | $88,000 |
| Salaries | $643,000 |
| Station Expenses | $13,000 |

Which expenses are less than $50,000?

© 6. **Model** The state representatives voted on a budget plan. Each representative has 1 vote. There were 86 votes for the plan and 34 votes against the plan. Write a number sentence to show how many representatives voted in all?

Lesson
16-4

C
Common
Core

**3.MD.3** Draw a scaled picture graph and a scaled bar graph to represent a data set with several categories. Solve one- and two-step "how many more" and "how many less" problems using information presented in scaled bar graphs. . . .

# Making Pictographs

## How do you make a pictograph?

Sam recorded the number of each kind of bicycle the store sold during one month. He made a tally chart.

Use the tally chart to make a pictograph.

| Kind of Bicycle | Tally | Number |
|---|---|---|
| Boy's | 卌 卌 | 10 |
| Girl's | 卌 卌 卌 卌 | 20 |
| Training | 卌 卌 卌 | 15 |
| Tricycle | 卌 卌 | 10 |

Data

---

 **Guided Practice***

C **MATHEMATICAL PRACTICES**

### Do you know HOW?

For **1** and **2**, use the survey data in the tally chart to make a pictograph.

| Which is your favorite school lunch? | | |
|---|---|---|
| **Lunch** | **Tally** | **Number** |
| Taco | ‖ | 2 |
| Pizza | 卌 ‖‖ | 8 |
| Salad | ‖‖ | 3 |
| Sandwich | 卌 ‖ | 6 |

Data

1. What is the title? What is the symbol for the key? How many votes will each symbol stand for?

2. List the lunch choices. Draw the symbols to complete the graph.

### Do you UNDERSTAND?

In **3–5**, use the pictograph above.

C 3. **Communicate** Explain the symbols that were used for the number of training bicycles that were sold.

C 4. **Persevere** Suppose 25 mountain bicycles were also sold. Draw symbols to show a row in the graph for mountain bicycles.

5. If the key was △ = 2 bicycles, how many symbols would be used for the boy's bicycles sold? How many symbols would be used for girl's bicycles sold?

---

## Independent Practice

| Goals Each Kickball Team Has Scored | | |
|---|---|---|
| **Team Name** | **Tally** | **Number** |
| Cubs | 卌 卌 | 10 |
| Hawks | 卌 卌 卌 卌 | 20 |
| Lions | 卌 卌 卌 卌 卌 卌 | 30 |
| Roadrunners | 卌 卌 卌 | 15 |

Data

For **6** and **7**, use the chart.

6. Make a pictograph to show the data.

7. Explain how you decided the number of symbols to draw to show the goals for the Roadrunners.

 *For another example, see Set C on page 407.*

Write a title for the pictograph.

The title is
Kinds of Bicycles Sold.

Choose a symbol for the key.
Decide what each symbol and
half-symbol will represent.

Each △ means 10 bicycles.

Each ◢ means 5 bicycles.

Set up the graph and
list the kinds of bicycles.
Decide how many
symbols you need for
each number sold.
Draw the symbols.

**Kinds of Bicycles Sold**

| | |
|---|---|
| Boy's | △ |
| Girl's | △ △ |
| Training | △ ◢ |
| Tricycle | △ |

Each △ = 10 bicycles.
Each ◢ = 5 bicycles.

---

## Problem Solving

Ed made a tally chart of the items he
picked from the plants in his garden.

© **8. Model** Make a pictograph to show
the data in Ed's chart. Write a title and
the key.

9. How many green peppers and red
peppers did Ed pick in all?

**Vegetables from Garden**

| Kind | Tally | Number of Items |
|---|---|---|
| Green Pepper | IIII | 4 |
| Red Pepper | II | 2 |
| Tomato | HHt | 5 |

© **10. Model** Ed's garden has a square shape. Each side
is 9 feet long. What is the area of Ed's garden?

In **11** and **12**, suppose you are going to make a
pictograph to show Simon's Book Shop data.

**11.** Choose a symbol to stand for 5 books
sold. Draw the row for fiction books sold.

© **12. Reason** Why is 5 a good number to use
in the key?

**Simon's Book Shop**

| Kind of Book | Number Sold |
|---|---|
| Fiction | 25 |
| Nonfiction | 40 |
| Poetry | 20 |
| Dictionary | 15 |

**13.** Marisol is making a pictograph
to show plant sales. There were
35 plants sold in June. How many
symbols should Marisol draw
for June?

**A** 5     **B** 7     **C** 11     **D** 35

Plants Sold at Garden Shop

Each 🌱 = 5 plants

© Common Core

3.MD.3 Draw a scaled picture graph and a scaled bar graph to represent a data set with several categories. Solve one- and two-step "how many more" and "how many less" problems using information presented in scaled bar graphs....

# Making Bar Graphs

## How do you make a bar graph?

Greg made a table to show the amount of money he saved each month.

Use the data in the table to make a bar graph on grid paper. A bar graph can make it easy to compare data.

**Hands-On**
grid paper

| Month | Amount Saved |
|-------|--------------|
| January | $25 |
| February | $50 |
| March | $65 |
| April | $40 |

---

## Guided Practice*

**MATHEMATICAL PRACTICES**

### Do you know HOW?

Use the chart to make a bar graph.

| Class | Tally | Number of People Signed Up |
|-------|-------|-----------------------------|
| Chess | IIII I | 6 |
| Guitar | IIII IIII | 10 |
| Painting | IIII II | 7 |
| Writing | IIII IIII | 9 |

1. Write a title. Choose the scale. What does each grid line represent?

2. Set up the graph with the scale, each class, and labels. Draw each bar.

### Do you UNDERSTAND?

In **3–5**, use the bar graph above.

© 3. **Communicate** In the bar graph above, explain why the bar for January ends between 20 and 30.

4. In which month did Greg save the most money?

© 5. **Use Structure** Suppose Greg saved $35 in May. Between which grid lines would the bar for May end?

---

## Independent Practice

In **6** and **7**, use the tally chart.

| Favorite Store for Clothes | | |
|-------|-------|-------|
| **Store** | **Tally** | **Number of Votes** |
| Deal Mart | IIII IIII IIII | 15 |
| Jane's | IIII IIII IIII IIII IIII IIII | 30 |
| Parker's | IIII IIII IIII IIII | 20 |
| Trends | IIII | 5 |

6. Make a bar graph to show the data.

© 7. **Generalize** Explain how to use the bar graph to find the store that received the most votes.

DIGITAL
eTools
**www.pearsonsuccessnet.com**

Write a title.

The title of this bar graph is Amount Greg Saved Each Month.

Choose the scale. Decide how many units each grid line will represent.

Each grid line will represent $10.

Set up the graph with the scale, each month listed in the table, and labels. Draw a bar for each month.

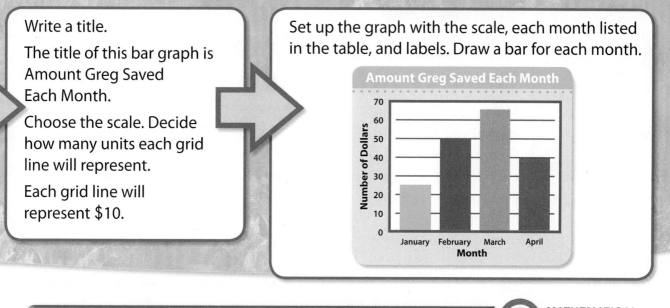

**Amount Greg Saved Each Month**

## Problem Solving

MATHEMATICAL
**PRACTICES**

For **8** and **9**, use the table at the right.

© **8. Model** Make a bar graph. Write a title. Choose the scale. Draw bars that go across.

| Favorite Kind of Movie | | | | |
|---|---|---|---|---|
| **Kind of Movie** | Adventure | Cartoon | Comedy | Science Fiction |
| **Number of Votes** | 16 | 8 | 10 | 7 |

© **9. Reason** Which two kinds of movies received about the same number of votes?

© **10. Use Tools** Each movie ticket costs $8. What is the total cost of tickets for a family of 6 people? Draw a picture to help solve the problem.

In **11** and **12**, suppose you are going to make a bar graph to show the data in the table.

© **11. Writing to Explain** What scale would you choose? Explain.

**12.** Which would be the longest bar?

| Speed of Birds | |
|---|---|
| **Kind of Bird** | **Flying Speed (miles per hour)** |
| Frigate Bird | 95 |
| Peregrine Falcon | 180 |
| Spin-Tailed Swift | 105 |

© **13. Use Structure** Luz made this graph to show how many friends wore each color of shoe. Which information does Luz need to complete the graph?

**A** How many friends wore black shoes

**B** The color of shoes with the longest bar

**C** The color of shoes worn by exactly 8 friends

**D** The color of shoes worn by exactly 7 friends

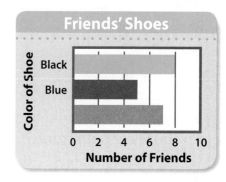

**Friends' Shoes**

**403**

**Lesson 16-6**

**Common Core**

3.MD.3 Draw a scaled picture graph and a scaled bar graph to represent a data set with several categories. Solve one- and two-step "how many more" and "how many less" problems using information presented in scaled bar graphs....

**Problem Solving**

# Use Tables and Graphs to Draw Conclusions

The tally chart shows data about the favorite hobbies of two Grade 3 classes. Compare the hobbies of the two classes.

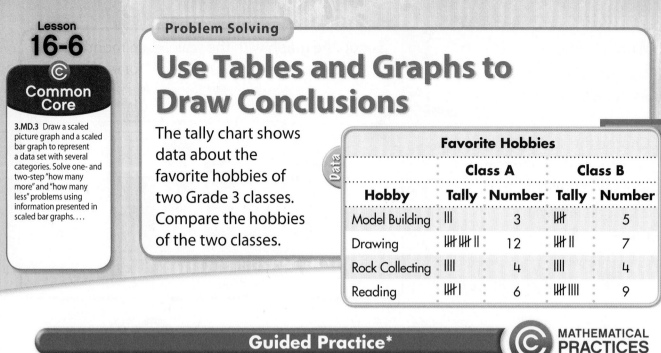

**Favorite Hobbies**

| Hobby | Class A Tally | Class A Number | Class B Tally | Class B Number |
|---|---|---|---|---|
| Model Building | IIII | 3 | 卌 | 5 |
| Drawing | 卌 卌 II | 12 | 卌 II | 7 |
| Rock Collecting | IIII | 4 | IIII | 4 |
| Reading | 卌 I | 6 | 卌 IIII | 9 |

---

## Guided Practice*

**MATHEMATICAL PRACTICES**

### Do you know HOW?

**Bicycle Club Miles**

| Member | Victor | Rosita | Gary | Hal |
|---|---|---|---|---|
| Number of Miles | 20 | 35 | 30 | 20 |

**1.** Which club member rode exactly 10 miles more than Hal?

**2.** Who rode the same distance as Hal?

### Do you UNDERSTAND?

**3. Communicate** How do the bars on a bar graph help you to compare data?

**4.** What is the favorite hobby of Class A above? of Class B?

**5. Write a Problem** Use the tally charts or graphs above or the table at the left to write a comparison problem. Then solve the problem.

---

## Independent Practice

**MATHEMATICAL PRACTICES**

For **6** and **7**, use the pictograph.

**T-Shirt Sales**

| | Store A | Store B |
|---|---|---|
| **Blue** | 👕 👕 ▮ | 👕 |
| **Red** | 👕 👕 | 👕 👕 ▮ |
| **Green** | ▮ | ▮ |

Each 👕 = 10 T-shirts. Each ▮ = 5 T-shirts.

**6.** What color was sold most often at each store? equally at both stores?

**7.** Where was blue sold more often?

### Applying Math Practices

- What am I asked to find?
- What else can I try?
- How are quantities related?
- How can I explain my work?
- How can I use math to model the problem?
- Can I use tools to help?
- Is my work precise?
- Why does this work?
- How can I generalize?

*For another example, see Set D on page 407.*

Make a bar graph for each class.

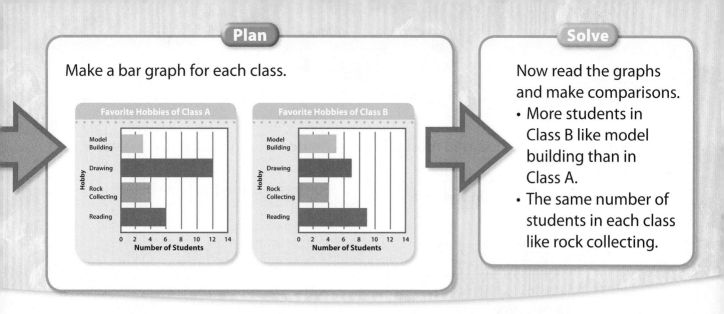

Now read the graphs and make comparisons.
- More students in Class B like model building than in Class A.
- The same number of students in each class like rock collecting.

For **8–10**, use the bar graph at the right.

**8.** How many people in all voted for their favorite type of exercise?

**9.** How many more people voted for gymnastics than for jogging?

© **10. Write a Problem** Write and solve a word problem different from Exercises 8 and 9.

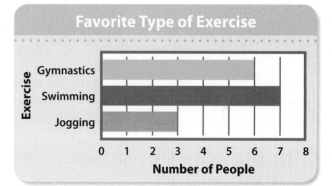

For **11–13**, use the tally chart.

© **11. Model** Make a graph to show the data. Choose a pictograph or a bar graph.

**12.** Who read exactly ten more books than Sandra?

**13.** Write the members in order from most to fewest books read.

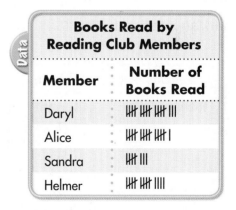

| Books Read by Reading Club Members | |
|---|---|
| **Member** | **Number of Books Read** |
| Daryl |卌 卌 卌 III |
| Alice | 卌 卌 卌 I |
| Sandra | 卌 III |
| Helmer | 卌 卌 IIII |

© **14. Reason** At the farmer's market, Matt gives 2 free apples for every 6 apples the customer buys. If Lucinda buys 24 apples, how many free apples will she get?

**A** 2 apples     **C** 6 apples

**B** 4 apples     **D** 8 apples

© **15. Writing to Explain** What kinds of comparisons can you make when you look at a bar graph or a pictograph?

**Set A,** pages 392–393

Which high temperature occurred most often in June?

**High Temperatures in June**

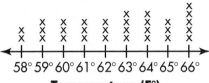

58° 59° 60° 61° 62° 63° 64° 65° 66°
**Temperature (F°)**

A high temperature of 66° occurred most often.

**Remember** that each result gets an X on a line plot.

For **1** and **2,** use the table below.

| Spin | 1 | 2 | 3 | 4 | 5 | 6 | 7 | 8 | 9 |
|---|---|---|---|---|---|---|---|---|---|
| Section | 3 | 2 | 2 | 2 | 1 | 2 | 1 | 2 | 2 |

**1.** Make a line plot of the data.

**2.** How many more spins landed on Section 2 than on Section 1?

**Set B,** pages 394–395

Steps to make a line plot:

- Draw a number line and choose a scale.

- The scale should show data values from the least to greatest.

- Write a title for the line plot.

- Mark an X for each length.

| Lengths of Lilly's Ribbons | |
|---|---|
| **Ribbon Colors** | **Length** |
| Red | $5\frac{1}{2}$ in. |
| Blue | 4 in. |
| White | $5\frac{1}{2}$ in. |
| Yellow | $4\frac{1}{4}$ in. |
| Pink | $4\frac{3}{4}$ in. |

Lengths of Lilly's Ribbons

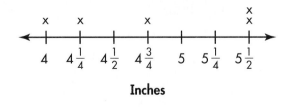

4    $4\frac{1}{4}$    $4\frac{1}{2}$    $4\frac{3}{4}$    5    $5\frac{1}{4}$    $5\frac{1}{2}$

Inches

**Remember** to mark an X for each result. Check your completed line plot against the data in the chart.

| Lengths of Carly's Strings | |
|---|---|
| **String Colors** | **Length** |
| Orange | 6 in. |
| Blue | $7\frac{3}{4}$ in. |
| Green | $7\frac{1}{2}$ in. |
| Yellow | $7\frac{1}{2}$ in. |
| Purple | 5 in. |

**1.** Draw a line plot to show the data.

**2.** How many strings does Carly have in all?

**3.** How long is the longest string?

**4.** How long is the shortest string?

**5.** Which length of string is the most common?

What is the favorite season of these students?

**Favorite Season**

| | | | | |
|---|---|---|---|---|
| Summer | Spring | Fall | Summer | Summer |
| Spring | Summer | Winter | Fall | Summer |

Make a tally chart and a pictograph.

Choose a title and label the columns. Make a tally mark for each answer. Count the tally marks. Record the number.

**Favorite Season**

| Season | Tally | Number |
|---|---|---|
| Fall | ‖ | 2 |
| Spring | ‖ | 2 |
| Summer | ||||| | 5 |
| Winter | | | 1 |

Choose a key for the pictograph. Each ● shows 2 votes; each ◖ shows 1 vote.

| Season | Votes |
|---|---|
| Fall | ● |
| Spring | ● |
| Summer | ● ● ◖ |
| Winter | ◖ |

**Remember** to make sure your tally marks and the symbols in the pictograph match the data.

For **1–3**, use the Team Name data.

Votes for Team Name

| | | | | |
|---|---|---|---|---|
| Aces | Fire | Aces | Fire | Aces |
| Aces | Fire | Fire | Aces | Stars |
| Fire | Stars | Fire | Fire | Fire |
| Aces | Aces | Aces | Fire | Stars |
| Fire | Fire | Fire | Aces | Fire |
| Stars | Fire | Stars | Fire | Aces |

1. Make a tally chart for the data.

2. How many more players voted for Fire than Stars for their team name?

3. Choose a key and make a pictograph to show the data.

How can you make a bar graph to draw conclusions about how much Don saved?

| Month | Amount | Month | Amount |
|---|---|---|---|
| January | $20 | March | $30 |
| February | $35 | April | $15 |

Choose 10 for the scale. Amounts with a 5 in the ones place will be halfway between 2 grid lines.

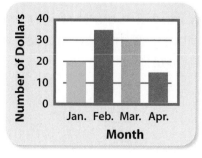

The longest bar in February shows the most.

The shortest bar in April shows the least.

**Remember** that you can compare the bars to draw conclusions.

1. Make a bar graph for the data below.

| | Pennies Saved | | |
|---|---|---|---|
| Day | Number | Day | Number |
| Mon. | 25 | Wed. | 15 |
| Tues. | 20 | Thurs. | 10 |

2. Suppose the bar for Friday is as long as the bar for Tuesday. What conclusion can you draw?

3. How many pennies were saved in all 4 days combined?

**Multiple Choice**

Use the pictograph for **1–3**.

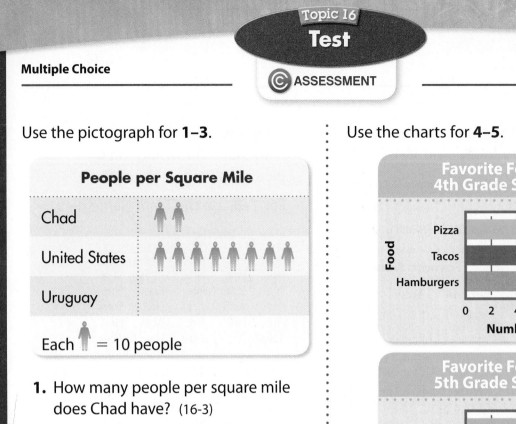

**People per Square Mile**

| | |
|---|---|
| Chad | |
| United States | |
| Uruguay | |

Each 🧍 = 10 people

**1.** How many people per square mile does Chad have? (16-3)

**A** 80

**B** 20

**C** 10

**D** 2

**2.** How many more people per square mile does the United States have than Chad? (16-3)

**A** 6

**B** 20

**C** 60

**D** 100

**3.** If Pedro knows Uruguay has 50 people for each square mile, how many symbols should he draw for Uruguay? (16-4)

**A** 5

**B** 10

**C** 25

**D** 50

Use the charts for **4–5**.

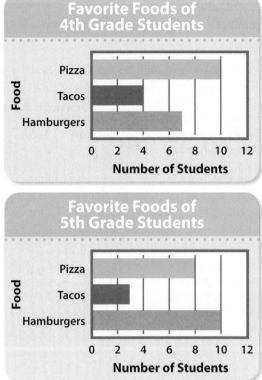

**4.** Which statement is true about the data in the graphs? (16-6)

**A** Pizza is the favorite in both grades.

**B** The same number of students in each grade like tacos.

**C** More students in Grade 4 than in Grade 5 like hamburgers.

**D** More students in Grade 4 than in Grade 5 like pizza.

**5.** How many more 5th grade students chose hamburgers than 4th grade students? (16-6)

**A** 2

**B** 3

**C** 5

**D** 6

Trudy took a survey and made the tally chart shown. Use the tally chart for **6**.

| First Initials | |
|---|---|
| **Initial** | **Tally** |
| J | II |
| S | III |
| T | IIII |

**6.** Which initial will have the tallest bar on a bar graph of Trudy's data? (16-5)

**7.** Jose spun a spinner 12 times. The line plot below shows his results.

**Spinner Results**

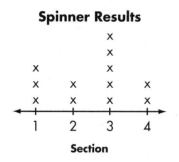

Section

What section of the spinner did Jose land on the most? (16-1)

**8.** Make a bar graph to show the data in the chart. (16-5)

| Favorite Type of Music | |
|---|---|
| **Type** | **Number of Votes** |
| Hip-Hop | 45 |
| Rock | 35 |
| Pop | 50 |
| Country | 30 |

Use the chart for **9–10**.

| Lengths of Tony's Strings | |
|---|---|
| **String Colors** | **Length** |
| Black String | $3\frac{1}{2}$ in. |
| Blue String | 4 in. |
| White String | $3\frac{1}{2}$ in. |
| Brown String | $3\frac{1}{4}$ in. |
| Green String | $4\frac{3}{4}$ in. |

**9.** Tony likes to collect colored string. Draw a line plot to show the lengths of his strings. (16-1)

**10.** What is the most common length of string that Tony has collected? (16-2)

Rick took a survey of the students in his grade. He asked them to vote for how many days they thought it would rain next week. The table shows the results of his survey. Use the table for **11** and **12**.

| Number of Days of Rain | Number of Student Votes |
|---|---|
| 0 | 15 |
| 1 | 30 |
| 2 | 25 |
| 3 or more | 10 |

**11.** Rick wants to make a pictograph to display the data. How many votes should each symbol in his pictograph stand for? (16-4)

**12.** How many students in all answered Rick's survey? (16-6)

Ask your classmates a question like the ones shown below. Then use your data to complete the following activities on a separate sheet of paper. This will help you organize your data and create charts. Afterwards you can compare the data in your charts.

| | | |
|---|---|---|
| Which of these fruits do you like the best— apple, banana, orange, or peach? | Which of these sports is your favorite— football, golf, swimming, or basketball? | Which of these subjects do you like the most at school-reading, math, science, or social studies? |

1.  Think of a question to ask your classmates. Write the question and 4 answer choices.

2.  Ask 20 classmates your question. Make a tally chart to record the answers your classmates give. Make columns in your tally chart for Answer Choice, Tally, and Number.

3.  Make a bar graph to show your survey results.

4.  Make a line plot to show your survey results.

5.  Write two statements that compare the data in your graphs.

6.  Roger made the pictograph below after asking 25 classmates to pick their favorite type of sandwich. The choices were peanut butter, turkey, cheese, or ham. Explain 3 mistakes Roger made when putting together his pictograph.

| Title goes HERE | |
|---|---|
| Peanut Butter | ☺ |
| Turkey | ☺☺☺ |
| | ☺ |
| Ham | ☺ |

Each ☺ = 5 votes

# Step Up to Grade 4

The following lessons provide a step up to, and a preview of Grade 4 Common Core.

## Lessons

Scott Foresman·Addison Wesley

enVisionMATH®
Common Core

Step-Up
Lesson
1

Common
Core

**4.NBT.5** Multiply a
whole number of up to
four digits by a one-digit
whole number . . . by using
equations, rectangular
arrays, and/or area models.

# Arrays and Multiplying by 10 and 100

## How can you multiply by 10 and 100?

$4 \times 5$ can be written as $5 + 5 + 5 + 5$.

Use this idea to multiply by 10 and 100.

How many photo buttons can Dara make if she buys 4 packs of 10 buttons?

10 buttons
in each pack

---

## Guided Practice

**MATHEMATICAL PRACTICES**

### Do you know HOW?

In 1 and 2, find each product.

**1.** $5 \times 10$

**2.** $1 \times 100$

### Do you UNDERSTAND?

**3. Model** Which product is greater: $4 \times 10$ or $4 \times 100$? Draw a picture to show how you know.

**4.** How many photo buttons could Dara make if she bought 7 packs of 100 buttons?

---

## Independent Practice

**Leveled Practice** For **5** through **8**, find each product.

**5.** $6 \times 10$

**6.** $3 \times 100$

**7.** $2 \times 10$

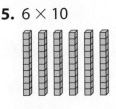

**8.** $4 \times 100$

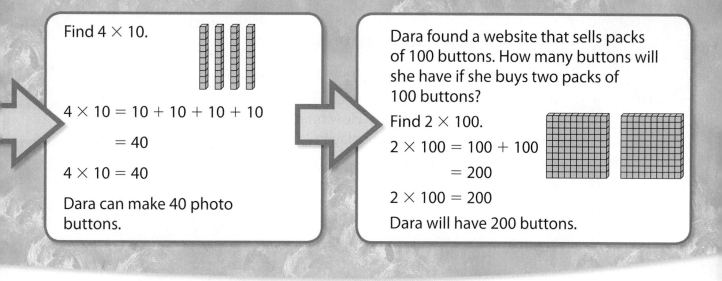

Find 4 × 10.

$4 \times 10 = 10 + 10 + 10 + 10$

$= 40$

$4 \times 10 = 40$

Dara can make 40 photo buttons.

Dara found a website that sells packs of 100 buttons. How many buttons will she have if she buys two packs of 100 buttons?

Find 2 × 100.

$2 \times 100 = 100 + 100$

$= 200$

$2 \times 100 = 200$

Dara will have 200 buttons.

For **9** through **12**, draw an array and find each product.

**9.** 8 × 10

**10.** 9 × 100

**11.** 8 × 100

**12.** 6 × 10

---

**Problem Solving**

© MATHEMATICAL PRACTICES

© **13. Reason** Give three whole number values for ▨ to solve the equation below.

▨ × 10 = ▨ 0

**14.** Kendra has earned $37 babysitting. She needs $75 to buy a skateboard. How much more money does Kendra need to earn?

© **15. Construct Arguments** Marni has 7 bags of balloons with 9 balloons in each bag. Kathleen has 6 bags of balloons with 10 balloons in each bag. Who has more balloons? Explain how you know.

**16.** Luis has 6 rolls of pennies. There are 50 pennies in each roll. How many pennies does Luis have?

**A**  30

**C**  65

**B**  56

**D**  300

© **17. Reason** The sabal palm is Florida's state tree. A sabal palm leaf can be up to 12 feet long and up to 6 feet wide. How many times as long can the leaf be as it is wide?

**18.** Ivan is counting the number of sabal palms in his neighborhood. There are 7 neighbors who have 10 palms each and one neighbor with 6 palms. How many total palms are in Ivan's neighborhood?

The sabal palm leaf can be up to 12 feet long.

Step-Up
Lesson
**2**

Common
Core

4.NBT.5 Multiply a
whole number of up to
four digits by a one-digit
whole number . ,.. by using
equations, rectangular
arrays, and/or area models.

# Breaking Apart Arrays

**Hands-On**
place-value blocks

## How can you use arrays to find products?

A display has 4 rows. Each row can hold 23 shampoo bottles. Each bottle is on sale for $6. How many shampoo bottles can the display hold?

**Choose an Operation** Multiply to find the total for an array.

4 rows

---

## Guided Practice

### Do you know HOW?

In **1** through **6**, use place-value blocks to build an array. Find the partial products and the product.

**1.** 3 × 21 =

**2.** 2 × 13 =

**3.** 6 × 25 =

**4.** 4 × 22 =

**5.** 2 × 29 =

**6.** 3 × 17 =

### Do you UNDERSTAND?

**7.** In the example above, what are the two number sentences that give the partial products?

**8.** In the example at the top, what would you pay to buy one row of these shampoo bottles?

---

## Independent Practice

**MATHEMATICAL PRACTICES**

ⓒ **Model** In **9** through **21**, use place-value blocks or draw a picture to show each array. Find the partial products and the product.

**Tip** *You can draw lines to show tens and Xs to show ones. This picture shows 2 × 28.*
_____ _____ X X X X X X X X
_____ _____ X X X X X X X X

**9.** 2 × 24 =     Find the partial products: 2 × 20 =     2 × 4 =
Add the partial products to find the product: 2 × 24 =

**10.** 2 × 33 =

**11.** 4 × 27 =

**12.** 5 × 23 =

**13.** 5 × 19 =

**14.** 7 × 17 =

**15.** 3 × 26 =

**16.** 5 × 25 =

**17.** 3 × 22 =

**18.** 3 × 14 =

**19.** 2 × 28 =

**20.** 4 × 23 =

**21.** 6 × 19 =

DIGITAL
Animated Glossary, eTools
www.pearsonsuccessnet.com

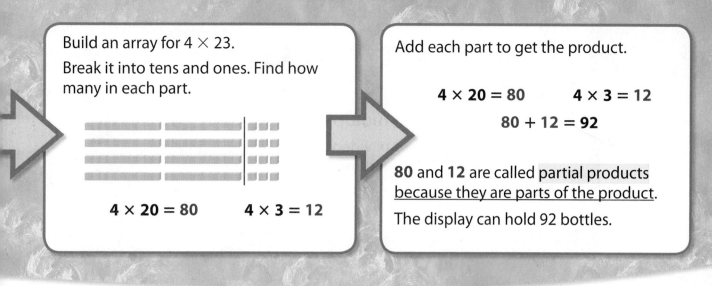

Build an array for 4 × 23.

Break it into tens and ones. Find how many in each part.

$4 \times 20 = 80$ $\qquad$ $4 \times 3 = 12$

Add each part to get the product.

$$4 \times 20 = 80 \qquad 4 \times 3 = 12$$
$$80 + 12 = 92$$

**80** and **12** are called partial products because they are parts of the product. The display can hold 92 bottles.

## Problem Solving

 **MATHEMATICAL PRACTICES**

© 22. **Use Structure** Look for patterns in the table. Copy and complete.

| x | | 2 | 3 | 4 | | 6 |
|---|---|---|---|---|---|---|
| y | 20 | 40 | ? | 80 | 100 | |

24. Paul's gymnastic scores for his first three events are shown in the table below. He needs a total of 32 points to qualify for the state meet.

  a   If his total score was 33 points, what was his score on the Horse routine?

  b   The total time (in seconds) for his routine on the Bars was 13 times the points he earned. What was the total time for the Bars routine?

| **Paul's Gymnastics Scores** | |
|---|---|
| Vault | 8 |
| Bars | 8 |
| Floor | 7 |
| Horse | |
| Total | |

Data

© 23. **Model** How many 1-foot by 1-foot tiles does it take to cover a rectangular floor that measures 7 tiles on one side and 25 tiles on the other side?

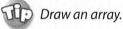 *Draw an array.*

25. Each cabin on the London Eye Ferris Wheel can hold up to 25 passengers. How many passengers can 6 cabins hold?

  **A** 150 passengers

  **B** 175 passengers

  **C** 200 passengers

  **D** 225 passengers

Each cabin can hold up to 25 people.

Step-Up
Lesson

**3**

Common
Core

4.NBT.5 Multiply a
whole number of up to
four digits by a one-digit
whole number . . . by using
equations, rectangular
arrays, and/or area models.

# Using an Expanded Algorithm

Hands-On
place-value blocks

## How can you record multiplication?

A store ordered 2 boxes of video games.
How many games did the store order?

**Choose an Operation** Multiply
to join equal groups.

Each box contains
16 video games.

16

16

---

**Another Example** **How do you record multiplication when the product has three digits?**

Gene played his new video game 23 times each day for 5 days.
How many times did he play his video game in 5 days?

**A** 18

**B** 28

**C** 115

**D** 145

**Choose an Operation** Since 5 equal groups of 23
are being joined, you will multiply. Find $5 \times 23$.

**What You Show**

**What You Write**

$$
\begin{array}{r}
23 \\
\times \quad 5 \\
\hline
15 \\
+ \ 100 \\
\hline
115
\end{array}
$$

Gene played his video game 115 times in 5 days.
The correct choice is **C**.

**Explain It**

**1.** Explain how the partial products, 15 and 100, were found in the work above.

**2. Reasonableness** How can an estimate help you eliminate choices above?

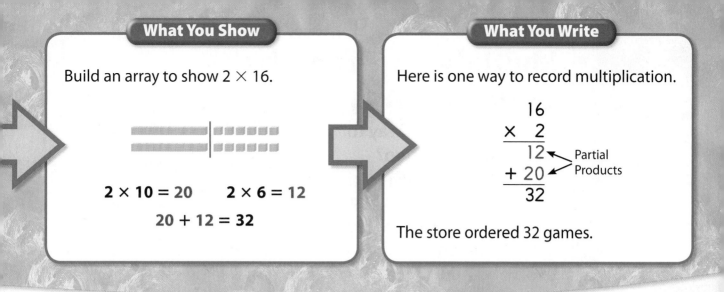

Build an array to show 2 × 16.

$2 \times 10 = 20$    $2 \times 6 = 12$

$20 + 12 = 32$

Here is one way to record multiplication.

$$\begin{array}{r} 16 \\ \times\ \ 2 \\ \hline 12 \\ +\ 20 \\ \hline 32 \end{array}$$

← Partial Products

The store ordered 32 games.

---

## Guided Practice

**MATHEMATICAL PRACTICES**

### Do you know HOW?

© **Model** In **1** and **2**, use place-value blocks or draw pictures to build an array. Copy and complete the calculation.

**1.** $2 \times 32 =$ ▨

$$\begin{array}{r} 32 \\ \times\ \ 2 \\ \hline \\ +\ \\ \hline \\ \end{array}$$

**2.** $3 \times 16 =$ ▨

$$\begin{array}{r} 16 \\ \times\ \ 3 \\ \hline \\ +\ \\ \hline \\ \end{array}$$

### Do you UNDERSTAND?

Use the array and the calculation shown for Problem 3.

$$\begin{array}{r} 14 \\ \times\ \ 3 \\ \hline 12 \\ +\ 30 \\ \hline 42 \end{array}$$

© **3. Reason** What calculation was used to give the partial product 12? 30? What is the product of $3 \times 14$?

---

## Independent Practice

**MATHEMATICAL PRACTICES**

**Leveled Practice** In **4** through **8**, copy and complete the calculation. Draw a picture to help.

**4.**
$$\begin{array}{r} 24 \\ \times\ \ 5 \\ \hline \\ +\ \\ \hline \\ \end{array}$$

**5.**
$$\begin{array}{r} 18 \\ \times\ \ 4 \\ \hline \\ +\ \\ \hline \\ \end{array}$$

**6.**
$$\begin{array}{r} 17 \\ \times\ \ 2 \\ \hline \\ +\ \\ \hline \\ \end{array}$$

**7.**
$$\begin{array}{r} 21 \\ \times\ \ 6 \\ \hline \\ +\ \\ \hline \\ \end{array}$$

**8.**
$$\begin{array}{r} 28 \\ \times\ \ 3 \\ \hline \\ +\ \\ \hline \\ \end{array}$$

**9.** Large tables have 8 chairs and small tables have 4 chairs. How many students can sit at 4 large tables and 6 small tables if each seat is filled?

© **10. Structure** The length of a side of a square is 12 inches. What is the perimeter of the square?

DIGITAL    eTools
www.pearsonsuccessnet.com

Step-Up
Lesson

4

Common
Core

4.NBT.5 Multiply a
whole number of up to
four digits by a one-digit
whole number ... by using
equations, rectangular
arrays, and/or area models.

# Multiplying 2-Digit by 1-Digit Numbers

## What is a common way to record multiplication?

How many T-shirts with the saying, *and your point is...* are in 3 boxes?

**Choose an Operation** Multiply to join equal groups.

| Saying on T-shirt | Number of T-shirts per Box |
|---|---|
| Trust Me | 30 T-shirts |
| and your point is... | 26 T-shirts |
| I'm the princess that's why 👑 | 24 T-shirts |
| Because I said so | 12 T-shirts |

---

**Another Example** **Does the common way to record multiplication work for larger products?**

Mrs. Stockton ordered 8 boxes of T-shirts with the saying, *I'm the princess that's why*. How many of the T-shirts did she order?

**Choose an Operation** Since you are joining 8 groups of 24, you will multiply. Find $8 \times 24$.

**Step 1**

Multiply the ones.
Regroup if necessary.

$$\begin{array}{r} \overset{3}{2}4 \\ \times \phantom{0}8 \\ \hline 2 \end{array}$$

$8 \times 4 = 32$ ones
*Regroup 32 ones as 3 tens 2 ones*

**Step 2**

Multiply the tens.
Add any extra tens.

$$\begin{array}{r} \overset{3}{2}4 \\ \times \phantom{0}8 \\ \hline 192 \end{array}$$

$8 \times 2$ tens $= 16$ tens
$16$ tens $+ 3$ tens $= 19$ tens
*or 1 hundred 9 tens*

Mrs. Stockton ordered 192 T-shirts.

**Explain It**

© **1. Reasonableness** How can you use estimation to decide if 192 is a reasonable answer?

**2.** In the example above, are you multiplying $8 \times 2$ or $8 \times 20$? Explain.

Remember, one way to multiply is to find partial products.

$$
\begin{array}{r}
26 \\
\times\ \ 3 \\
\hline
18 \\
+\ 60 \\
\hline
78
\end{array}
$$

← Partial Products

A shortcut for the partial products method is shown at the right.

Step 1

Multiply the ones. Regroup if necessary.

$$
\begin{array}{r}
{\scriptstyle 1} \\
26 \\
\times\ \ 3 \\
\hline
8
\end{array}
$$

Step 2

Multiply the tens. Add any extra tens.

$$
\begin{array}{r}
{\scriptstyle 1} \\
26 \\
\times\ \ 3 \\
\hline
78
\end{array}
$$

There are 78 T-shirts in 3 boxes.

## Guided Practice

MATHEMATICAL PRACTICES

### Do you know HOW?

Ⓒ **Reasonableness** Find each product. Estimate to check reasonableness.

1.  $\begin{array}{r} 17 \\ \times\ \ 5 \\ \hline \end{array}$

2.  $\begin{array}{r} 24 \\ \times\ \ 3 \\ \hline \end{array}$

**3.** $7 \times 34$

**4.** $4 \times 45$

### Do you UNDERSTAND?

Ⓒ **5. Communicate** Explain how you would estimate the answer in Exercise 3.

**6.** Carrie bought 8 boxes of T-shirts with the saying *Because I said so.* How many T-shirts did Carrie buy?

## Independent Practice

MATHEMATICAL PRACTICES

Ⓒ **Reasonableness** Find each product. Estimate to check reasonableness.

7.  $\begin{array}{r} 13 \\ \times\ \ 6 \\ \hline \end{array}$

8.  $\begin{array}{r} 16 \\ \times\ \ 7 \\ \hline \end{array}$

9.  $\begin{array}{r} 74 \\ \times\ \ 5 \\ \hline \end{array}$

10.  $\begin{array}{r} 39 \\ \times\ \ 8 \\ \hline \end{array}$

**11.** $4 \times 21$

**12.** $3 \times 52$

**13.** $2 \times 69$

**14.** $9 \times 42$

For **15** and **16**, use the table to the right.

**15.** What is the average length fingernails will grow in one year?

**16.** How much longer will hair grow than fingernails in one month? in 6 months?

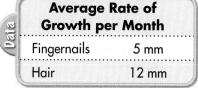

| Average Rate of Growth per Month | |
| --- | --- |
| Fingernails | 5 mm |
| Hair | 12 mm |

Step-Up
Lesson

**5**

© Common Core

4.NBT.6 Find whole-number quotients and remainders with up to four-digit dividends and one-digit divisors, using strategies based on place value, the properties of operations . . . by using equations, rectangular arrays, and/or area models.

# Using Models to Divide

## How can place value help you divide?

Hands-On
Place-value blocks

**57 student drawings**

Mrs. Lynch displayed 57 student drawings on 3 walls in her art classroom. If she divided the drawings equally, how many drawings are on each wall?

Estimate: $60 \div 3 = 20$

drawings on each wall

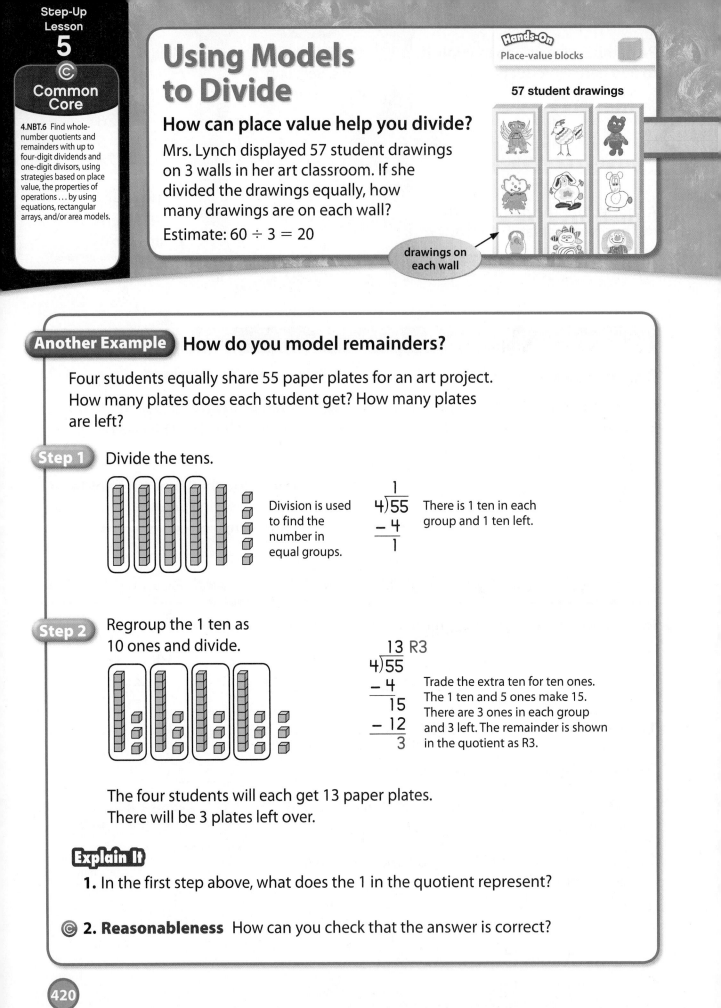

---

**Another Example** **How do you model remainders?**

Four students equally share 55 paper plates for an art project. How many plates does each student get? How many plates are left?

**Step 1** Divide the tens.

Division is used to find the number in equal groups.

$$\begin{array}{r} 1 \\ 4\overline{)55} \\ -4 \\ \hline 1 \end{array}$$

There is 1 ten in each group and 1 ten left.

**Step 2** Regroup the 1 ten as 10 ones and divide.

$$\begin{array}{r} 13 \text{ R3} \\ 4\overline{)55} \\ -4 \\ \hline 15 \\ -12 \\ \hline 3 \end{array}$$

Trade the extra ten for ten ones. The 1 ten and 5 ones make 15. There are 3 ones in each group and 3 left. The remainder is shown in the quotient as R3.

The four students will each get 13 paper plates. There will be 3 plates left over.

**Explain It**

**1.** In the first step above, what does the 1 in the quotient represent?

© **2. Reasonableness** How can you check that the answer is correct?

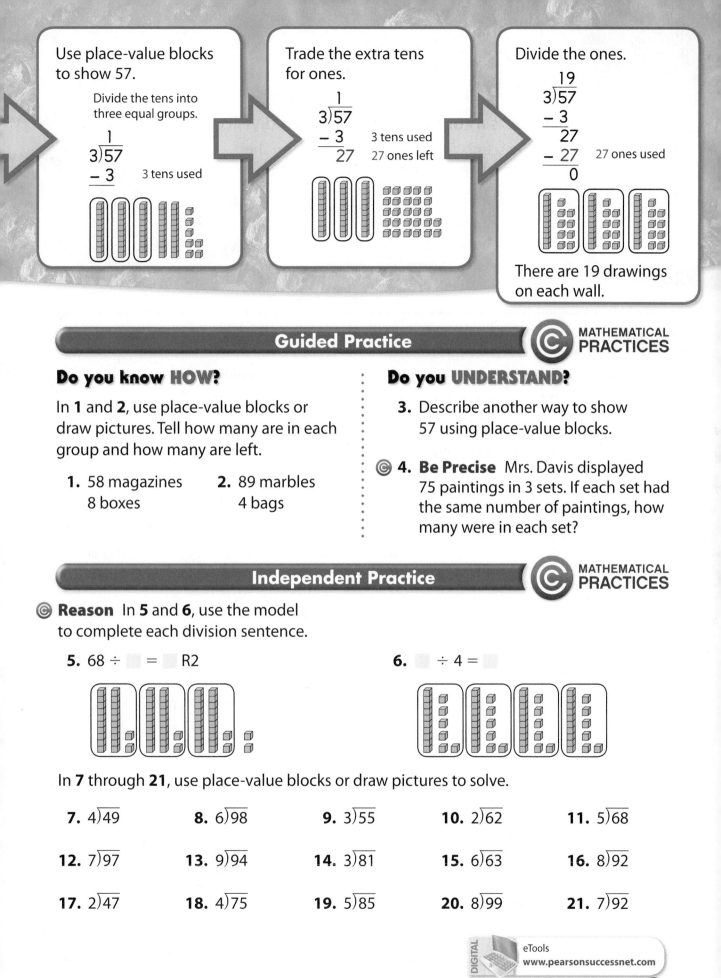

Use place-value blocks to show 57.

Divide the tens into three equal groups.

$$3\overline{)57}$$
$$-3$$  3 tens used

Trade the extra tens for ones.

$$\begin{array}{r} 1 \\ 3\overline{)57} \\ -3 \\ \hline 27 \end{array}$$  3 tens used
27 ones left

Divide the ones.

$$\begin{array}{r} 19 \\ 3\overline{)57} \\ -3 \\ \hline 27 \\ -27 \\ \hline 0 \end{array}$$  27 ones used

There are 19 drawings on each wall.

## Guided Practice

MATHEMATICAL PRACTICES

### Do you know HOW?

In **1** and **2**, use place-value blocks or draw pictures. Tell how many are in each group and how many are left.

**1.** 58 magazines
8 boxes

**2.** 89 marbles
4 bags

### Do you UNDERSTAND?

**3.** Describe another way to show 57 using place-value blocks.

© **4. Be Precise** Mrs. Davis displayed 75 paintings in 3 sets. If each set had the same number of paintings, how many were in each set?

## Independent Practice

MATHEMATICAL PRACTICES

© **Reason** In **5** and **6**, use the model to complete each division sentence.

**5.** $68 \div \square = \square$ R2

**6.** $\square \div 4 = \square$

In **7** through **21**, use place-value blocks or draw pictures to solve.

**7.** $4\overline{)49}$ **8.** $6\overline{)98}$ **9.** $3\overline{)55}$ **10.** $2\overline{)62}$ **11.** $5\overline{)68}$

**12.** $7\overline{)97}$ **13.** $9\overline{)94}$ **14.** $3\overline{)81}$ **15.** $6\overline{)63}$ **16.** $8\overline{)92}$

**17.** $2\overline{)47}$ **18.** $4\overline{)75}$ **19.** $5\overline{)85}$ **20.** $8\overline{)99}$ **21.** $7\overline{)92}$

DIGITAL

eTools
www.pearsonsuccessnet.com

Step-Up
Lesson

**6**

Common
Core

4.OA.3 Solve multistep
word problems posed with
whole numbers and having
whole-number answers
using the four operations,
including problems in
which remainders must
be interpreted.... Assess
the reasonableness of
answers....

# Dividing 2-Digit by 1-Digit Numbers

76 cans of
soup in all

## What is a common way to record division?

At the school food drive, Al needs to put the
same number of soup cans into four boxes.
How many soup cans will go in each box?

**Choose an Operation** Divide to find
the number in each group.

---

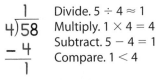 **How do you divide with a remainder?**

Al collects 58 cans of vegetables. He puts the same number
of cans in four boxes. How many cans of vegetables will go
in each box? How many cans will be left over?

**A**  14 cans, 2 cans left over      **C**  16 cans, 2 cans left over

**B**  15 cans, 2 cans left over      **D**  18 cans, 2 cans left over

### Step 1

Divide the tens.

Regroup the remaining
ten as 10 ones.

$$\begin{array}{r} 1 \\ 4\overline{)58} \\ -4 \\ \hline 1 \end{array}$$

Divide. $5 \div 4 \approx 1$
Multiply. $1 \times 4 = 4$
Subtract. $5 - 4 = 1$
Compare. $1 < 4$

### Step 2

Bring down the ones.

Divide the ones.

Multiply and subtract.

$$\begin{array}{r} 14\ R2 \\ 4\overline{)58} \\ -4\downarrow \\ \hline 18 \\ -16 \\ \hline 2 \end{array}$$

Divide. $18 \div 4 \approx 4$
Multiply. $4 \times 4 = 16$
Subtract. $18 - 16 = 2$
Compare. $2 < 4$

### Step 3

Check by multiplying and
adding: $14 \times 4 = 56$ and
$56 + 2 = 58$.

There will be 14 cans of
vegetables in each box
and 2 cans left.

The correct choice is **A**.

### Explain It

**1.** How are the steps *divide*, *multiply*, *subtract*, and *compare* used
in division?

© **2. Communicate** When you check division using multiplication, what do you do
with the remainder?

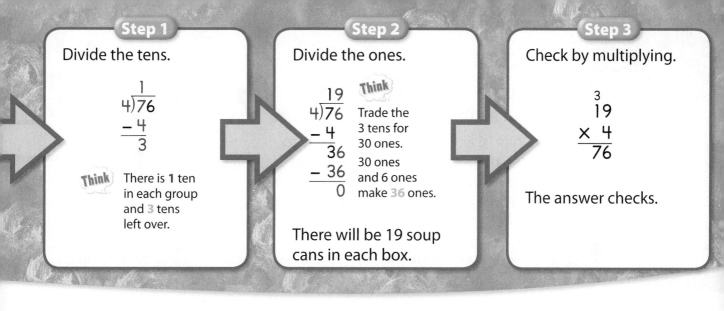

| Step 1 | Step 2 | Step 3 |
|---|---|---|
| Divide the tens. | Divide the ones. | Check by multiplying. |

**Step 1** Divide the tens.

$$\begin{array}{r} 1 \\ 4)\overline{76} \\ -4 \\ \hline 3 \end{array}$$

**Think** There is **1** ten in each group and **3** tens left over.

**Step 2** Divide the ones.

$$\begin{array}{r} 19 \\ 4)\overline{76} \\ -4 \\ \hline 36 \\ -36 \\ \hline 0 \end{array}$$

**Think** Trade the 3 tens for 30 ones.

30 ones and 6 ones make **36** ones.

There will be 19 soup cans in each box.

**Step 3** Check by multiplying.

$$\begin{array}{r} 3 \\ 19 \\ \times 4 \\ \hline 76 \end{array}$$

The answer checks.

## Guided Practice

  MATHEMATICAL
PRACTICES

### Do you know HOW?

In **1** and **2**, copy and complete each calculation.

**1.**
$$\begin{array}{r} 3 \\ 2)\overline{76} \\ - \blacksquare \\ \hline 6 \\ -1\blacksquare \\ \hline 0 \end{array}$$

**2.**
$$\begin{array}{r} 3\ R \\ 4)\overline{95} \\ -8 \\ \hline \blacksquare\blacksquare \\ -\blacksquare\blacksquare \\ \hline \blacksquare \end{array}$$

### Do you UNDERSTAND?

**©** **3. Construct Arguments** Explain how you would estimate to find the answer in Exercise 1.

**4.** Al collects 74 cans of fruit. He puts the same number of fruit cans in 5 boxes. Will he have any cans left over? If so, how many cans?

## Independent Practice

  MATHEMATICAL
PRACTICES

**Leveled Practice** In **5** through **8**, copy and complete each calculation.

**5.**
$$\begin{array}{r} \blacksquare\blacksquare \\ 7)\overline{91} \\ -7 \\ \hline \blacksquare 1 \\ -2\blacksquare \\ \hline 0 \end{array}$$

**6.**
$$\begin{array}{r} \blacksquare 8 \\ 3)\overline{84} \\ -\blacksquare \\ \hline 4\blacksquare \\ -2\blacksquare \\ \hline 0 \end{array}$$

**7.**
$$\begin{array}{r} \blacksquare\ R \\ 4)\overline{78} \\ -4 \\ \hline \blacksquare\blacksquare \\ -3\blacksquare \\ \hline 2 \end{array}$$

**8.**
$$\begin{array}{r} 1\ R \\ 6)\overline{93} \\ -\blacksquare \\ \hline \blacksquare\blacksquare \\ -\blacksquare\blacksquare \\ \hline \blacksquare \end{array}$$

**©** **Reasonableness** For **9** through **18**, find each quotient. Check your answers.

**9.** $4)\overline{75}$    **10.** $2)\overline{68}$    **11.** $6)\overline{80}$    **12.** $5)\overline{76}$    **13.** $3)\overline{93}$

**14.** $5)\overline{95}$    **15.** $3)\overline{79}$    **16.** $2)\overline{81}$    **17.** $4)\overline{88}$    **18.** $6)\overline{72}$

**©** **19. Writing to Explain** Why does 62 ÷ 5 have two digits in the quotient, while 62 ÷ 7 has only one digit in the quotient?

Step-Up
Lesson

**7**

**Common
Core**

4.OA.4 Find all factor pairs
for a whole number in the
range 1–100. Recognize
that a whole number is
a multiple of each of its
factors. . . .

# Factors

**Hands-On**
counters

## How can you use multiplication to find all the factors of a number?

Jean has 16 action figures. She wants to arrange them in equal sized groupings around her room. What are the ways that Jean can arrange the action figures? Jean needs to think of all the factors of 16.

16 action figures

---

## Guided Practice

**MATHEMATICAL
PRACTICES**

### Do you know HOW?

In **1** through **4**, write each number as a product of two factors in two ways.

**1.** 32          **2.** 48

**3.** 60          **4.** 72

In **5** through **8**, find all the factors of each number. Use counters to help.

**5.** 24          **6.** 30

**7.** 64          **8.** 80

### Do you UNDERSTAND?

© **9. Reason**  What factor besides 1 does every even number have?

© **10. Writing to Explain**  Is 6 a factor of 15?

**11.** Jean got 2 more action figures. What are all the different equal groupings she can make now?

**12.** Jean's brother has 31 action figures. What are all of the factors for 31?

---

## Independent Practice

In **13** through **32**, find all the factors of each number. Use counters to help.

**Tip**  *For each number, find each way you can arrange counters into arrays.*

**13.** 8          **14.** 38          **15.** 17          **16.** 13          **17.** 9

**18.** 25          **19.** 23          **20.** 44          **21.** 15          **22.** 50

**23.** 41          **24.** 48          **25.** 27          **26.** 21          **27.** 90

**28.** 34          **29.** 72          **30.** 35          **31.** 77          **32.** 19

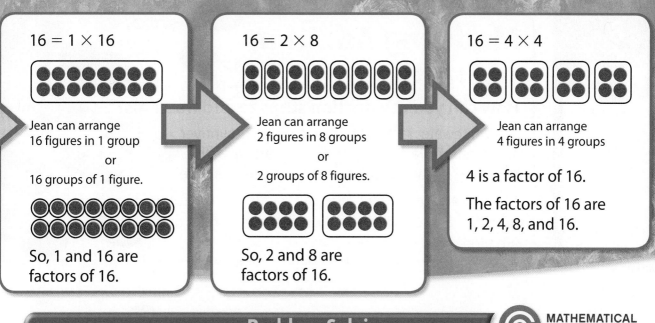

16 = 1 × 16

Jean can arrange
16 figures in 1 group

or

16 groups of 1 figure.

So, 1 and 16 are factors of 16.

16 = 2 × 8

Jean can arrange
2 figures in 8 groups

or

2 groups of 8 figures.

So, 2 and 8 are factors of 16.

16 = 4 × 4

Jean can arrange
4 figures in 4 groups

4 is a factor of 16.

The factors of 16 are
1, 2, 4, 8, and 16.

## Problem Solving

MATHEMATICAL
PRACTICES

**33.** Sue is making a model of a wind farm. She wants to put 24 turbines in her model. What are all the ways she can make arrays using 24 turbines?

4 is a factor of 24.

**34. Communicate** Amanda wants to include an array of 35 photos on her web site. Describe the arrays that she can make.

**35.** Which lists all the factors of 58?

A  1, 58        C  1, 2, 58

B  1, 2, 18, 58    D  1, 2, 29, 58

**36. Reason** Any number that has 6 as a factor also has 3 as a factor. Why is this?

**37. Reason** What factors do 16 and 24 have in common?

**38.** About 50 of the 1,500 possibly active volcanoes on Earth erupt every year. What are the factors of 50?

**39.** On a large wind farm, there are 4 rows of 15 wind turbines each and 6 rows of 11 wind turbines each. How many wind turbines are there on the wind farm in all?

**40.** The largest volcano on Earth is Mauna Loa, located in Hawaii. It is 30,080 feet tall from the sea floor to its highest point. If 13,680 feet of the volcano is above sea level, how many feet are below sea level?

**41.** A manatee is 10 feet long. If 1 foot equals 12 inches, how many inches long is the manatee?

A  12 inches      C  120 inches

B  24 inches      D  144 inches

Step-Up
Lesson

**8**

Common
Core

**4.NF.3.d** Solve word problems involving addition and subtraction of fractions referring to the same whole and having like denominators, ...

# Modeling Addition of Fractions

Hands-On
fraction strips

$\frac{1}{8}$

## How can you use fraction strips to add fractions?

Ten whitewater rafting teams are racing downriver. Two teams have red rafts and one team has a blue raft. What fraction of the rafts are either red or blue?

**Choose an Operation** Add the fraction of the total rafts that are red to the fraction of the total rafts that are blue.

---

## Guided Practice

MATHEMATICAL
**PRACTICES**

### Do you know HOW?

© **Reason** In **1** through **6**, use fraction strips to add fractions. Simplify, if possible.

**1.** $\frac{1}{4} + \frac{1}{4}$     **2.** $\frac{1}{5} + \frac{3}{5}$

**3.** $\frac{2}{5} + \frac{1}{5}$     **4.** $\frac{1}{4} + \frac{2}{4}$

**5.** $\frac{2}{6} + \frac{2}{6}$     **6.** $\frac{1}{6} + \frac{1}{6}$

### Do you UNDERSTAND?

© **7. Construct Arguments** In the problem above, what fraction of the rafts are yellow? What two fractions would you add to find the part of the rafts that are either red or yellow?

**8.** What two fractions are being added below? What is the sum?

---

## Independent Practice

In **9** through **23**, find each sum. Simplify, if possible. You may use fraction strips.

**9.** $\frac{1}{3} + \frac{1}{3}$

**10.** $\frac{7}{10} + \frac{1}{10}$

**11.** $\frac{2}{12} + \frac{4}{12}$

**12.** $\frac{1}{6} + \frac{1}{6} + \frac{2}{6}$

**13.** $\frac{3}{12} + \frac{3}{12}$

**14.** $\frac{5}{10} + \frac{2}{10}$

**15.** $\frac{6}{8} + \frac{2}{8}$

**16.** $\frac{2}{4} + \frac{2}{4}$

**17.** $\frac{4}{12} + \frac{3}{12}$

**18.** $\frac{1}{4} + \frac{2}{4}$

**19.** $\frac{3}{10} + \frac{5}{10}$

**20.** $\frac{1}{10} + \frac{2}{10} + \frac{1}{10}$

**21.** $\frac{3}{6} + \frac{2}{6}$

**22.** $\frac{1}{3} + \frac{2}{3}$

**23.** $\frac{1}{8} + \frac{4}{8} + \frac{1}{8}$

DIGITAL
eTools
**www.pearsonsuccessnet.com**

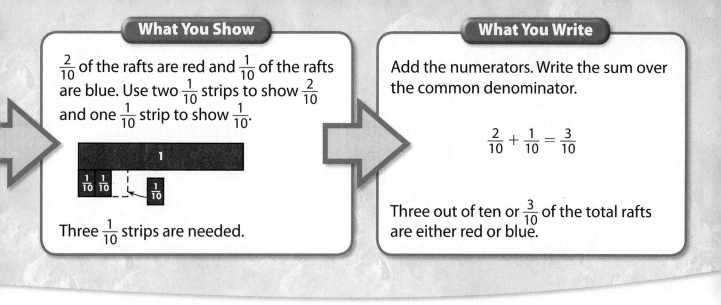

## What You Show

$\frac{2}{10}$ of the rafts are red and $\frac{1}{10}$ of the rafts are blue. Use two $\frac{1}{10}$ strips to show $\frac{2}{10}$ and one $\frac{1}{10}$ strip to show $\frac{1}{10}$.

Three $\frac{1}{10}$ strips are needed.

## What You Write

Add the numerators. Write the sum over the common denominator.

$$\frac{2}{10} + \frac{1}{10} = \frac{3}{10}$$

Three out of ten or $\frac{3}{10}$ of the total rafts are either red or blue.

---

## Problem Solving

**MATHEMATICAL PRACTICES**

**24. Model** A pizza is divided into 8 equal pieces. Draw a picture to show that $\frac{3}{8} + \frac{1}{8} = \frac{4}{8}$ or $\frac{1}{2}$.

**25.** Tomika has 2 cats. Fluffy weighs 9.316 pounds and Prince weighs 10.54 pounds. How much do the cats weigh together?

**26. Reason** Suppose two different fractions with the same denominators are both less than 1. Can their sum equal 1? Can their sum be greater than 1?

**27.** A chicken farm produces an average of 1,788 eggs per week. There are 12 eggs in a dozen. How many dozen eggs does the farm produce in an average week?

**28. Writing to Explain** Sophia walked $\frac{1}{4}$ of a mile to Sheila's house, and they both walked $\frac{2}{4}$ of a mile to the pool. How far did Sophia walk? Explain how you found your answer.

**29. Reason** Pencils come 20 to a package, 48 packages to a carton, and 12 cartons to a case. About how many pencils are in a case?

**30.** Find the missing value in the equation.

$$\frac{1}{10} + \frac{\phantom{0}}{10} + \frac{3}{10} = \frac{7}{10}$$

   **A** 2         **C** 4

   **B** 3         **D** 5

**31. Think About the Structure** Maribel had 9 stickers. She bought 3 more. Then she gave her sister 6 stickers.

What numerical expression shows how many stickers Maribel has now?

   **A** $(9 + 3) - 6$    **C** $9 - (3 + 6)$

   **B** $(9 \times 3) \div 6$    **D** $9 - (3 - 6)$

**32. Reason** When does the sum of two fractions equal 1?

Step-Up
Lesson

**9**

Common
Core

**4.NF.3.d** Solve word
problems involving
addition and subtraction
of fractions referring to the
same whole and having like
denominators, …

# Modeling Subtraction of Fractions

## How can you use fraction strips to subtract fractions?

A garden plot is divided into twelve equal sections.
If two sections are used to grow hot peppers,
what fraction is left to grow other crops?

**Choose an Operation** Take away a part
from the whole to find the difference.

---

## Guided Practice

**MATHEMATICAL PRACTICES**

### Do you know HOW?

For **1** through **6**, use fraction strips to
subtract. Simplify, if possible.

1. $\frac{3}{4} - \frac{2}{4}$

2. $\frac{5}{5} - \frac{3}{5}$

3. $\frac{6}{8} - \frac{3}{8}$

4. $\frac{8}{10} - \frac{2}{10}$

5. $\frac{11}{12} - \frac{8}{12}$

6. $\frac{4}{8} - \frac{2}{8}$

### Do you UNDERSTAND?

7. **Reason** In the problem above,
   what part of the garden is
   represented by each fraction strip?

8. **Communicate** In the example
   above, if 6 plots are used to grow
   hot peppers, what fraction is left to
   grow other crops? Explain.

---

## Independent Practice

In **9** through **26**, use fraction strips to subtract. Simplify, if possible.

9. $\frac{3}{3} - \frac{2}{3}$

10. $\frac{4}{5} - \frac{1}{5}$

11. $\frac{5}{10} - \frac{4}{10}$

12. $\frac{10}{12} - \frac{6}{12}$

13. $\frac{2}{2} - \frac{1}{2}$

14. $\frac{2}{4} - \frac{1}{4}$

15. $\frac{6}{6} - \frac{1}{6}$

16. $\frac{8}{8} - \frac{3}{8}$

17. $\frac{10}{12} - \frac{8}{12}$

18. $\frac{5}{6} - \frac{2}{6}$

19. $\frac{6}{8} - \frac{3}{8}$

20. $\frac{6}{10} - \frac{5}{10}$

21. $\frac{7}{10} - \frac{4}{10}$

22. $\frac{4}{5} - \frac{2}{5}$

23. $\frac{5}{6} - \frac{3}{6}$

24. $\frac{3}{5} - \frac{3}{5}$

25. $\frac{9}{10} - \frac{5}{10}$

26. $\frac{2}{3} - \frac{2}{3}$

eTools
**www.pearsonsuccessnet.com**

DIGITAL

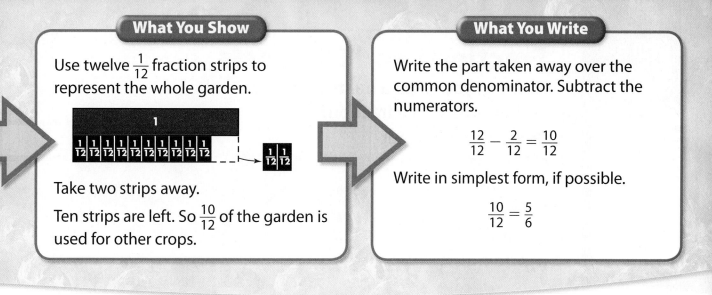

**What You Show**

Use twelve $\frac{1}{12}$ fraction strips to represent the whole garden.

Take two strips away.

Ten strips are left. So $\frac{10}{12}$ of the garden is used for other crops.

**What You Write**

Write the part taken away over the common denominator. Subtract the numerators.

$$\frac{12}{12} - \frac{2}{12} = \frac{10}{12}$$

Write in simplest form, if possible.

$$\frac{10}{12} = \frac{5}{6}$$

---

## Problem Solving

**MATHEMATICAL PRACTICES**

**27. Model** Draw a model of the garden plot according to the data table below. The plot is divided into 10 sections. What fraction of the plot will be flowers?

**Class Garden Plot**

| Crop | Number of Sections |
|------|--------------------|
| Strawberries | 1 |
| Hot Peppers | 2 |
| Corn | 2 |
| Tomatoes | 4 |
| Flowers | the rest |

**28. Reason** A quilt is divided into 8 equal panels. Seven panels are blue. Four blue panels are removed to be repaired. Which equation shows the blue part of the quilt that remains after four parts are removed?

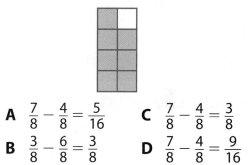

**A** $\frac{7}{8} - \frac{4}{8} = \frac{5}{16}$    **C** $\frac{7}{8} - \frac{4}{8} = \frac{3}{8}$

**B** $\frac{3}{8} - \frac{6}{8} = \frac{3}{8}$    **D** $\frac{7}{8} - \frac{4}{8} = \frac{9}{16}$

**29.** What fraction of the circle is the orange part? What fraction of the circle is not orange?

**30.** Marie had $\frac{4}{6}$ of a pound of almonds. She used $\frac{2}{6}$ of a pound to make a cake. How many pounds of almonds were left? Simplify, if possible.

**31.** **Science** To avoid predators, ghost crabs usually stay in burrows during the day and feed mostly at night. Suppose a ghost crab eats $\frac{2}{8}$ of its food before 10:00 P.M. By midnight, it has eaten $\frac{6}{8}$ of its food. How much of its food did it eat between 10:00 P.M. and midnight?

Step-Up
Lesson
**10**

© **Common Core**

**4.NF.6** Use decimal notation for fractions with denominators 10 or 100....

# Fractions and Decimals

## How can you write a fraction as a decimal and a decimal as a fraction?

On Kelsey Street, six out of 10 homes have swing sets in their backyards. Write $\frac{6}{10}$ as a decimal.

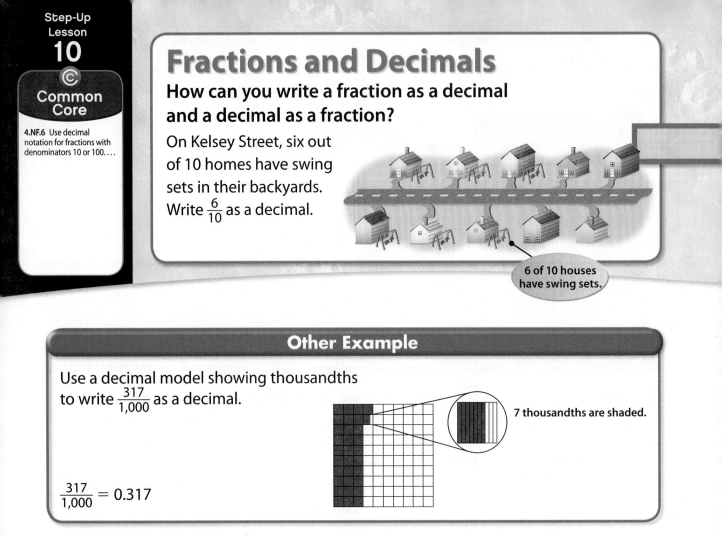

6 of 10 houses have swing sets.

---

### Other Example

Use a decimal model showing thousandths to write $\frac{317}{1,000}$ as a decimal.

7 thousandths are shaded.

$$\frac{317}{1,000} = 0.317$$

---

### Guided Practice

© **MATHEMATICAL PRACTICES**

#### Do you know HOW?

For **1** through **5**, write a decimal and a fraction for the part of each grid that is shaded.

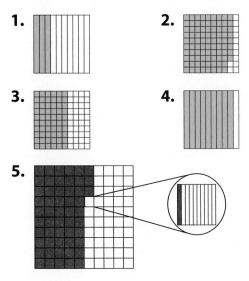

**1.**

**2.**

**3.**

**4.**

**5.**

#### Do you UNDERSTAND?

© **6. Writing to Explain** Why is the fraction $\frac{8}{10}$ not written 0.08?

© **7. Communicate** When the decimals 0.3 and 0.30 are each written as a fraction, are the fractions equivalent? Explain your answer.

© **8. Persevere** On Kelsey Street, what fraction of homes do NOT have swings? Write your answer as a fraction and a decimal.

**9.** Look back at Other Example. Write 0.317 in word form.

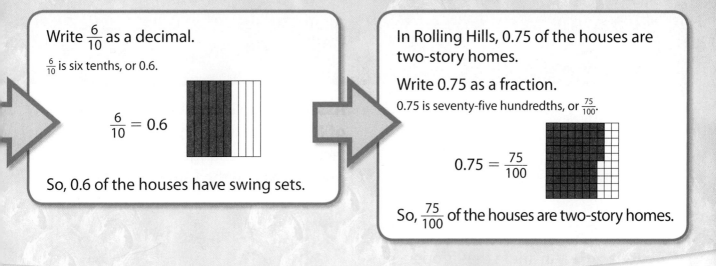

Write $\frac{6}{10}$ as a decimal.

$\frac{6}{10}$ is six tenths, or 0.6.

$$\frac{6}{10} = 0.6$$

So, 0.6 of the houses have swing sets.

In Rolling Hills, 0.75 of the houses are two-story homes.

Write 0.75 as a fraction.

0.75 is seventy-five hundredths, or $\frac{75}{100}$.

$$0.75 = \frac{75}{100}$$

So, $\frac{75}{100}$ of the houses are two-story homes.

## Independent Practice

For **10** through **24**, write an equivalent decimal or fraction.

**10.** $\frac{8}{10}$  **11.** $\frac{21}{100}$  **12.** 0.684  **13.** $\frac{81}{100}$  **14.** 0.934

**15.** $\frac{500}{1,000}$  **16.** 0.51  **17.** $\frac{9}{10}$  **18.** 0.32  **19.** $\frac{456}{1,000}$

**20.** 0.082  **21.** $\frac{37}{100}$  **22.** $\frac{206}{1,000}$  **23.** 0.852  **24.** 0.96

## Problem Solving

MATHEMATICAL PRACTICES

© **25. Estimation** About what fraction of the rectangle to the right is shaded green?

**26.** Social Studies The arena of the Colosseum in Rome was about $\frac{3}{20}$ of the entire Colosseum. Write this amount as a decimal.

**Tip** $\frac{1}{20} = \frac{5}{100}$

The arena is $\frac{3}{20}$ of the Colosseum.

**27.** Which fraction is the same as 0.65?

A $\frac{65}{1,000}$    C $\frac{65}{1}$

B $\frac{65}{100}$    D $\frac{65}{10}$

**28.** Science The table at the right shows the average monthly rainfall in inches for Vero Beach, Florida. For which month(s) shown is the rainfall greater than 3 inches?

| Average Rainfall in Inches | | | |
|---|---|---|---|
| Jan. | Feb. | March | April |
| 2.89 | 2.45 | 4.20 | 2.88 |

**A.M.** Time between midnight and noon.

**acute angle** An angle that is open less than a right angle.

**acute triangle** A triangle with three acute angles.

**addends** Numbers added together to give a sum.
*Example*: 2 + 7 = 9

Addend    Addend

**angle** A figure formed by two rays that have the same endpoint.

**area** The number of square units needed to cover a region.

**array** A way of displaying objects in rows and columns.

**Associative (Grouping) Property of Addition** The grouping of addends can be changed and the sum will be the same.

**Associative (Grouping) Property of Multiplication** The grouping of factors can be changed and the product will be the same.

**bar graph** A graph using bars to show data.

**benchmark fraction** A commonly used fraction such as $\frac{1}{4}, \frac{1}{3}, \frac{1}{2}, \frac{2}{3},$ and $\frac{3}{4}$.

C

**capacity** The volume of a container measured in liquid units.

**centimeter (cm)** A metric unit of length.

**Commutative (Order) Property of Addition** Numbers can be added in any order and the sum will be the same.

**Commutative (Order) Property of Multiplication** Numbers can be multiplied in any order and the product will be the same.

**compare** To decide if one number is greater than or less than another number.

**compatible numbers** Numbers that are easy to add, subtract, multiply or divide mentally.

**cup** A customary unit of capacity.

**data** Pieces of information.

**decagon** A polygon with ten sides.

**denominator** The number below the fraction bar in a fraction, the total number of equal parts in all.

**diagonal** A line segment other than a side that connects two vertices of a polygon.

Diagonal

**difference** The answer when subtracting two numbers.

**digits** The symbols 0, 1, 2, 3, 4, 5, 6, 7, 8, and 9 used to write numbers.

**Distributive Property** A multiplication fact can be broken apart into the sum of two other multiplication facts.
*Example*: $5 \times 4 = (2 \times 4) + (3 \times 4)$

**dividend** The number to be divided.
*Example*: $63 \div 9 = 7$
↑
Dividend

**division** An operation that tells how many equal groups there are or how many are in each group.

**divisor** The number by which another number is divided.
*Example*: $63 \div 9 = 7$
↑
Divisor

**eighth** One of 8 equal parts of a whole.

**elapsed time** Total amount of time that passes from the beginning time to the ending time.

**equation** A number sentence that uses = (is equal to).

**equilateral triangle** A triangle with all sides the same length.

**equivalent fractions** Fractions that name the same part of a whole, same part of a set, or same location on a number line.

**estimate** To give an approximate number or answer.

**expanded form** A number written as the sum of the values of its digits.
*Example:* 2,476 = 2,000 + 400 + 70 + 6

**fact family** A group of related facts using the same numbers.

**factors** Numbers that are multiplied together to give a product.
*Example:* 7 × 3 = 21

Factor    Factor

**fifth** One of 5 equal parts of a whole.

**foot (ft)** A customary unit of length. 1 foot equals 12 inches.

**fourth** One of 4 equal parts of a whole.

**fraction** A symbol, such as $\frac{2}{8}$, $\frac{5}{1}$, or $\frac{5}{5}$, used to name a part of a whole, a part of a set, or a location on a number line.

**gallon (gal)** A customary unit of capacity. 1 gallon equals 4 quarts.

**gram (g)** A metric unit of mass, the amount of matter in an object.

**half (plural, halves)** One of 2 equal parts of a whole.

**half hour** A unit of time equal to 30 minutes.

**hexagon** A polygon with 6 sides.

**hour** A unit of time equal to 60 minutes.

**hundredth** One of 100 equal parts of a whole, written as 0.01 or $\frac{1}{100}$.

**I**

**Identity (One) Property of Multiplication** The product of any number and 1 is that number.

**Identity (Zero) Property of Addition** The sum of any number and zero is that same number.

**inch (in.)** A customary unit of length.

**intersecting lines** Lines that cross at one point.

**isosceles triangle** A triangle with at least two sides the same length.

**K**

**key** Explanation of what each symbol represents in a pictograph.

**kilogram (kg)** A metric unit of mass, the amount of matter in an object. 1 kilogram equals 1,000 grams.

**kilometer (km)** A metric unit of length. 1 kilometer equals 1,000 meters.

**L**

**line** A straight path of points that is endless in both directions.

**line plot** A way to organize data on a line.

**line segment** A part of a line that has two endpoints.

**liter (L)** A metric unit of capacity. 1 liter equals 1,000 milliliters.

**M**

**mass** A measure of the amount of matter in an object.

**meter (m)** A metric unit of length. 1 meter equals 100 centimeters.

**mile (mi)** A customary unit of length. 1 mile equals 5,280 feet.

**milliliter (mL)** A metric unit of capacity. 1,000 milliliters equals 1 liter.

**millimeter (mm)** A metric unit of length. 1,000 millimeters equals 1 meter.

**minute** A unit of time equal to 60 seconds.

**mixed number** A number with a whole number part and a fraction part.
*Example:* $2\frac{3}{4}$

**multiple** The product of the number and any other whole number.
*Example:* 0, 4, 8, 12, and 16 are multiples of 4.

**multiplication** An operation that gives the total number when you put together equal groups.

**number line** A line that shows numbers in order using a scale.
Example:

number line 0 1 2 3 4

**numerator** The number above the fraction bar in a fraction.

**obtuse angle** An angle that is open more than a right angle.

**obtuse triangle** A triangle with one obtuse angle.

**octagon** A polygon with 8 sides.

**odd number** A whole number that has 1, 3, 5, 7, or 9 in the ones place; A number not divisible by 2.

**order** To arrange numbers from least to greatest or from greatest to least.

**ounce (oz)** A customary unit of weight.

**P.M.** Time between noon and midnight.

**parallel lines** Lines that never intersect.

**parallelogram** A quadrilateral in which opposite sides are parallel.

**partial products** Products found by breaking one factor in a multiplication problem into ones, tens, hundreds, and so on and then multiplying each of these by the other factor.

**pentagon** A polygon with 5 sides.

**perimeter** The distance around a figure.

**period** A group of three digits in a number, separated by a comma.

**perpendicular** Two lines, line segments, or rays that intersect to form right angles.

**pictograph** A graph using pictures or symbols to show data.

**pint (pt)** A customary unit of capacity. 1 pint equals 2 cups.

**place value** The value given to the place a digit has in a number. *Example:* In 3,946, the place value of the digit 9 is *hundreds*.

**point** An exact position often marked by a dot.

**polygon** A closed figure made up of straight line segments.

**pound (lb)** A customary unit of weight. 1 pound equals 16 ounces.

**product** The answer to a multiplication problem.

**pyramid** A solid figure whose base is a polygon and whose faces are triangles with a common point.

**Q**

**quadrilateral** A polygon with 4 sides.

**quart (qt)** A customary unit of capacity. 1 quart equals 2 pints.

**quarter hour** A unit of time equal to 15 minutes.

**quotient** The answer to a division problem.

**ray** A part of a line that has one endpoint and continues endlessly in one direction.

**rectangle** A quadrilateral with four right angles.

**regroup** To name a whole number in a different way.
*Example:* 28 = 1 ten 18 ones.

**remainder** The number that is left over after dividing.
*Example:* 31 ÷ 7 = 4R3

↑
Remainder

**rhombus** A quadrilateral with opposite sides parallel and all sides the same length.

**right angle** An angle that forms a square corner.

**right triangle** A triangle with one right angle.

**round** To replace a number with a number that tells about how much or how many to the nearest ten, hundred, thousand, and so on.
*Example:* 42 rounded to the nearest 10 is 40.

**scale** The numbers that show the units used on a graph.

**scalene triangle** A triangle with no sides the same length.

**second** A unit of time. 60 seconds equal 1 minute.

**side** A line segment forming part of a polygon.

**simplest form** A fraction with a numerator and denominator that cannot be divided by the same divisor, except 1.

**sixth** One of 6 equal parts of a whole.

**square** A quadrilateral with four right angles and all sides the same length.

**square unit** A square with sides 1 unit long, used to measure area.

**standard form** A way to write a number showing only its digits. *Example:* 3,845

**sum** The answer to an addition problem.

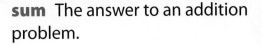

**tally mark** A mark used to record data on a tally chart.
*Example:* 𝍶 = 5

**tenth** One of 10 equal parts of a whole, written as 0.1 or $\frac{1}{10}$.

**third** One of 3 equal parts of a whole.

**ton (T)** A customary unit of weight. 1 ton = 2,000 pounds.

**trapezoid** A quadrilateral with only one pair of parallel sides.

**triangle** A polygon with 3 sides.

**twelfth** One of 12 equal parts of a whole.

**unit fraction** A fraction with a numerator of 1.
*Example:* $\frac{1}{2}$

**vertex of an angle** The end point of two rays that form an angle.

Vertex

**vertex of a polygon** The point where two sides of a polygon meet.

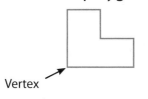

Vertex

**week** A unit of time equal to 7 days.

**weight** A measure of how heavy an object is.

**word form** A number written in words.
*Example:* 9,325 = nine thousand, three hundred twenty-five

**yard (yd)** A customary unit of length. 1 yard equals 3 feet or 36 inches.

**Zero Property of Multiplication** The product of any number and zero is zero.

## Illustrations

**142, 372** Kenneth Batelman; **171, 248, 250, 251, 252, 258, 260, 277, 291, 344, 345, 351, 361, 372** Rob Schuster.

## Photographs

Every effort has been made to secure permission and provide appropriate credit for photographic material. The publisher deeply regrets any omission and pledges to correct errors called to its attention in subsequent editions.

Unless otherwise acknowledged, all photographs are the property of Pearson Education, Inc.

Photo locators denoted as follows: Top (T), Center (C), Bottom (B), Left (L), Right (R), Background (Bkgd)

## Cover

Luciana Navarro Powell

**6** (TR) Eric Isselée/Fotolia; **8** (TR) ©Gregory Bergman/Alamy; **18** (R) ©Brad Perks Lightscapes/Alamy, (C) Comstock/Thinkstock, (BC) Getty Images, (BR) sculpies/Fotolia; **21** (CR) 2010/Photos to Go/Photolibrary, (L) Comstock/Thinkstock, (R) pandapaw/ Shutterstock, (CL) steve estvanik/Fotolia; **29** (L) NASA Image Exchange; **38** (C) Getty Images, (CL) IT Stock Free/Jupiter Images; **41** (TR) Jefery/Fotolia; **44** (R) Goodshoot/Thinkstock, (TR) Thinkstock; **46** (TR) ©Royalty-Free/Corbis; **63** (L) Getty Images, (L) Hemera Technologies/ Thinkstock; **74** (TR) ©imagebroker/Alamy, (TR) hotshotsworldwide/Fotolia; **75** (BR) ©John Luke/Index Open; **84** (BL) David R. Frazier Photolibrary, Inc./Alamy Images; **97** (CL) ©Jill Stephenson/Alamy; **115** (L) Dusty Cline/Fotolia; **141** (L) NASA/JPL-Caltech/M. Kelley (Univ. of Minnesota)/ NASA; **156** (TR) Comstock/Thinkstock; **157** (CR) Ian Scott/Fotolia, (BR) ©Mark William Penny/Shutterstock, (TR) Comstock Images/Thinkstock; **169** (CL) Thinkstock/ Getty Images, (L) vivalapenler/Fotolia; **183** (CR) Goran Bogicevic/Fotolia; **189** (CL) Goran Bogicevic/Fotolia; **192** (TR) Getty Images; **193** (BR) Goran Bogicevic/Fotolia; **212** (C) hotshotsworldwide/Fotolia, (TR) PB/ Fotolia; **219** (CL) Dream Maker Software, (Bkgrd) Photos to Go/Photolibrary; **227** (BL) Keith Levit Photography/Photos to Go/Photolibrary; **233** (BR) Photos to Go/Photolibrary; **243** (L) Getty Images/ Jupiterimages/Thinkstock; **277** (L) ©Uyen Le/Getty Images, (BL) Frances A. Miller/ Shutterstock; **289** (BR) ©Uyen Le/Getty Images; **301** (CL) NASA; **310** (TR) Getty Images; **325** (L) Jupiterimages/Thinkstock, (C) Photos to Go/Photolibrary; **329** (CR) Jupiterimages/Thinkstock; **339** (CL) Thinkstock; **369** 2010/Photos to Go/ Photolibrary; **371** Frogkick/Fotolia, (L) Getty Images; **374** (CL) ©Image Source Limited, (BL) Comstock Inc., (BC) Jupiter Images; **375** (CR) ©Simple Stock Shots; **376** (CL) ©photolibrary/Index Open, (BR) ©Simple Stock Shots; **377** (BR) Amur/Fotolia, (BR) Simple Stock Shots; **378** (BC) Getty Images, (BL) Jupiter Images, (C) Stockdisc; **380** (BC) ©D. Hurst/Alamy, (TR) ©Mark Duffy/Alamy, (CL, BR, BC) Getty Images, (BL) Jupiter Images; **384** (CR) MIXA/Getty Images, (TR) Stockdisc; **385** (CR) ©Lew Robertson/Corbis, 2010/Photos to Go/Photolibrary, Eric Isselée/ Fotolia, (TL) Getty Images, (CR) Index Open, (C) Jupiter Images; **389** (BL) Sir_Eagle/Fotolia; **412** (TR) Photos to Go/Photolibrary; **413** (BR) tsach/Fotolia; **415** (BR) SuperStock; **431** (CR) piotrwzk@go2.pl/Fotolia.

# Index